GD AXH-785

Fishes of Utah

Fishes of Utah

A Natural History

William F. Sigler
John W. Sigler

ILLUSTRATIONS
BY
Joseph R.
Tomelleri

FOREWORD
BY
Bruce
Schmidt

University of Utah Press
Salt Lake City

LIBRARY OF CONGRESS CATALOGING-IN-PUBLICATION DATA

Sigler, William F.
Fishes of Utah : a natural history / William F. Sigler,
John W. Sigler ; illustrations by Joseph R. Tomelleri ; foreword by
Bruce Schmidt.
p. cm.
Includes bibliographical references (p.) and index.
ISBN 0-87480-469-8 (alk. paper)
1. Fishes—Utah. 2. Fishing—Utah. I. Sigler, John W., 1946– .
II. Title.
QL628.U8S5 1996
597.09792—dc20 96-4349

Printed on acid-free
paper

5 4 3 2 1 2000 1999 1998 1997 1996

TO Robert Rush Miller, LONG-TIME FRIEND AND COLLEAGUE, AND WORLD-RENOWNED ICHTHYOLOGIST

Contents

List of Plates

List of Poems by Rodello Hunter

Foreword

Bruce Schmidt

As the second driest state in the United States, Utah contains a surprising number of fishes, both native and introduced. Utah's two major drainage areas, the Great Basin and the Green/Colorado River complex, are home to several unique native fishes. Although the total number of species is relatively low when compared with other major drainages, these fish evolved in unique and demanding environments. Over time, they developed a high degree of speciation as they adapted to their unusual environment. The Great Basin and Colorado River drainages likely have the highest percentage of endemism in any of the major U.S. drainages.

Utah waters are also home to approximately two dozen sport fishes, but surprisingly only four species are native. These include the Yellowstone, Bonneville, and Colorado River subspecies of cutthroat trout, mountain whitefish, Bear Lake whitefish, and Bonneville cisco. The remainder were all introduced over the years to create sportfishing opportunities. Those introductions now support most of Utah's extensive sportfishery, and in fact, there would be virtually no sportfishing if it were not for the ability to manage artificial habitats such as impoundments with introduced fishes.

The key to fish populations in Utah is clearly related to the quality and quantity of available habitat. Native species are most abundant where native aquatic habitats remain little changed from pioneer times. However, the majority of Utah's waters have been widely altered by damming or diversion to meet human needs or through pollution and degradation due to poor land management. In these highly altered environments or where inappropriate competitors or predators have been introduced the native fishes have suffered significant declines, and a number have been protected by the Endangered Species Act. The altered environments, however, have in many cases produced habitats that are ideal for nonnative sport fishes.

The great diversity of aquatic habitats, both natural and created, coupled with the diversity of fish species, both native and introduced, make Utah a stimulating and challenging state for the study and management of fishes. Preserving native species and preventing the extinction of those on the endangered species lists present major challenges for the management of water in this desert state. Equally challenging is the need to continue to provide quality fishing opportunity for the state's growing population. Accomplishing these goals without their impacting each other is a real measure of successful management.

Utah's introduced sport fishes include those from a number of different families, with significantly different potential as sport fish. They range in size from 50-lb lake trout and 40-lb striped bass to grayling and green sunfish that seldom reach a pound. They span tremendous elevational distances, from Sacramento perch in the desert southwest to the trout, whitefish, and grayling in the alpine mountains. In between, a variety of warmwater and coolwater species assure that all suitable habitats contain viable populations of sport fishes.

This book provides detailed information that will be of interest to students of the natural history of Utah's fishes and to anglers interested in learning more about the habits and distribution of their favorite quarry. The fishes of Utah play a variety of ecological roles; understanding how they interact should be of interest to all of us, those who manage the resource as well as those who wish to study and appreciate it.

A Personal Journey

Tom Wharton

The world seemed to be growing much too complicated. Bills were stacked high in the file. My boss wanted a dozen projects completed all at once. Our teenagers turned each small disagreement at home into a major fight. The house was a mess and both cars needed minor repairs.

There was only one thing to do.

Go fishing.

The world's problems seem so much smaller when I sit in an old wooden rental boat and troll for trout on a warm August morning at Strawberry Reservoir. The sounds of the motor and the gentle rocking of the waves all but put me to sleep as I stretch out in the bow of the boat and chuckle as my father tries to drive the boat and battle one of his legendary line tangles at the same time.

All seems peaceful when I strap a backpack on and head into the High Uintas for a three- or four-day fishing trip. Then the only problem is deciding which fly to use on some little lake or stream that may not have been fished all summer. The simple act of casting a fly and a bubble into the middle of a lake formed by ancient glaciers turns into a joyous occasion. What could be a better way to get away from it all than this?

Try to explain the enjoyment of sitting on Bear Lake in the middle of January when the temperature approaches zero and all you can do is stare into a hole in the ice as you use an ice rod to jig up and down for cisco, whitefish, and trout. This is sheer madness. But as the early-morning mist lifts and a sun low on the horizon casts a pale pink glow over the frosty morning, you, the angler, know the reason you're doing this. It's not to catch meat for the table. It's not to catch more fish than your buddy. It's about both relaxing and feeling alive at the same time.

Some of the fondest memories of my youth involve sitting in an old cabin at Moon Lake on the night before the opening of the fishing season and listening to my father and uncle tell fishing stories while playing cards well into the night. My younger brother and I would always try to judge when the game was going to break up so we could get to sleep first. That way, we'd at least get an hour or so of rest before the cabin would shake with the sound of snoring.

On one particular trip, it snowed all night and the men elected to stay in the warm cabin rather than brave the elements. I couldn't wait to fish. Fixing up my own outfit for the first time, I walked to where a stream flowed into Moon Lake. Delighted, I caught several trout before the men were even awake.

Fishing trips mean family vacations for most Utahns. Some of the only memories that remain of my two grandfathers were going to the Provo Boat Harbor on Utah Lake and watching them launch their old, somewhat leaky yellow rubber raft. We'd sit for hours in the hot sun without saying a thing or catching a fish. They assured me, though, that they occasionally caught a nice channel cat in the harbor. Much was learned on those early trips. One doesn't need to always catch fish to enjoy a fishing trip. And, when an angler owns a rubber raft, he ought to always bring along a patch kit.

When trying to teach my own daughter and sons the finer arts of Utah angling, we would head to the Charleston Bridge area of Deer Creek Reservoir, rent a boat, and fish for yellow perch in the channel. It didn't matter that the perch were only three to five inches in length. What was important was that the action was fast and furious much of the time. The kids would catch buckets of the little striped fish. We'd sit for hours filleting them and then have a gigantic perch fry with our friends who operate the boat camp. Sadly, the camp is gone and, for the most part, so are the perch. We've taken to traveling to Pineview Reservoir in Ogden Canyon where similar experiences can be enjoyed fishing for crappie, bluegill, bullhead, and perch.

On special occasions, the family would travel to Lake Powell when the striped bass "boiled" in surface feeding frenzies and we'd spend the day searching for boils and racing our boats from one to the other. We'd spend the night on a secluded beach using the driftwood to build a huge fire. One time, one of my twins landed a huge striped bass. As we greedily fished on, he watched the beautiful fish die in the bottom of the boat. That bothered him and resulted in a memorable conversation about life and death that evening as we lay in our sleeping bags and listened to the wind. Fishing trips foster such family togetherness. They seem to allow time for the most quiet child to express an opinion, or, even briefly, take the limelight.

Some fishing trips, though, aren't quite as calm and peaceful. I can remember the first time we rented a rubber raft and headed down the Green River below Flaming Gorge Dam. It was my first experience rowing a raft on a river, and though there were no dangerous rapids, the little ones scared us. Fishing, though important, became a secondary activity, but one that was a part of the entire adventure.

As an outdoor writer for the *Salt Lake Tribune* since 1976, I've been fortunate to spend time with Division of Wildlife Resources biologists learning not only how to catch fish but the complexities of keeping both riparian zones and reservoir systems healthy and productive. I've watched biologists pull gill nets full of huge lake trout out of the depths of Flaming Gorge Lake. I've seen them take the sperm and eggs from fish at the Perry Egan Hatchery near Bicknell which, if you ever travel to Capitol Reef National Park, is a fine spot to take the kids. Be prepared though, to give your children a little talk on the birds and the bees. I've seen biologists agonize over seeing too many chubs and suckers in a net and wonder what they'd do. I've watched as they've pulled a net out of Scofield Reservoir, seen no fish, and puzzled over what went wrong. I've stood near egg-taking stations at Bear Lake and Strawberry and watched biologists chest-deep in water give some species of fish a helping hand in the difficult task of reproducing.

Along the way, I've met many characters. Among the most memorable were a group of old gentlemen who sat around the same table—the Liar's Table they called it—at the Bowery Haven Resort at Fish Lake. They could remember their parents taking them to this place in horse-drawn covered wagons when the road was nothing more than a dirt path. They told of catching huge mackinaws using copper line and paddleboards, and they complained about the current management policies of "The Fish and Game" because the fish weren't quite as large as in the old days. Of course, fish never are these days.

Some parts of my personal Utah fishing journey involve touches of sadness. I've seen unthinking anglers ruin the perch fishing at Deer Creek by illegally dumping walleye into the reservoir because they thought they knew more than the biologists. The once great angling for striped bass at Lake Powell has been threatened because of the lack of a forage fish. Continued road building threatens two of Utah's greatest remaining trout rivers, the Provo and the Logan. County officials, acting in the name of flood control, ruined much of the Weber River by dredging it with bulldozers. The fantastic fishing for trophy brook trout on Boulder Mountain seems threatened by modern technology that allows mountain bikers and ATV riders to put too much pressure on the fabulous lake.

Sadly, increased fishing pressure often brings increased regulation. Utah's once simple angling regulations, which in the old days could be printed on the back of a license, now take nearly 100 pages. Before fishing, today's angler must read the rules carefully. Rules mandating slot limits, catch-and-release areas, fly fishing only, reduced or increased limits, and opening and closing days may seem confusing but, in modern society, are necessary to preserve what fishing survives.

What may not be necessary is all the fancy tackle my fellow anglers seem to need these days. Somehow, making it too easy to catch fish takes away from the fun. So do competitive tournaments, fishing tournaments, and the like. The world is too full of numbers, competition, and different sorts of gambling already. Why take such bad aspects of modern society and apply them to something as wonderfully simple as fishing?

No, life is too short for such nonsense. There are too many high mountain lakes, bubbling brooks, and little farm ponds full of bass to still find and explore. There are too many trips left with my father, my son, and my wife to worry about catching a limit of fish or trying to outdo my neighbor on the stream. I'd still like to cast a fly better than I do. It would be fun to have the time to spend several weeks in the Uintas fishing a new lake each morning. I've yet to catch a trophy lake trout at Flaming Gorge and bring in a 4-lb brown on a fly on the Green River.

One thing though, seems certain. As anglers, we must all work to preserve the resources. We must fight dams that adversely impact our trout streams. We can volunteer to plant willows along streams to help preserve damaged riparian zones, and we can demand that our political leaders clean up polluted waters so that we have a place to take our grandchildren fishing. We need to get involved in the fight for instream flows. Most important, we need to care about the state where we live.

For me, caring is easy. Fishing plays an important role in both how I make a living and how I spend my free time. When you've watched your daughter catch her first fish, taught your 15-year-old how to hook tiny cutthroats on a dry fly, and hiked into the Uintas with your wife, you know the value of Utah fishing and you'll work to do anything you can to preserve it.

Preface

We have attempted to make this book as broad as possible and still be manageable. Where we have included the original descriptions of fish species in the life history section, we hope to enlighten current students of fisheries and other interested individuals regarding what the original author saw and reported. Where we provide detailed management information, it is done to educate readers as to the current thinking of the Utah Division of Wildlife Resources fisheries managers.

The term "lake" refers to all standing waters, reservoirs, and ponds, regardless of size. The term "stream" refers to all flowing waters, from very small creeks to large rivers. The use of the term "fishermen," synonymous with "anglers," indicates no sexism. It is simply a device to cut down on verbiage.

The three temperature zones are defined as follows: coldwater 38° to 62°F; coolwater 48° to 72°F; and warmwater 58° to 82°F. These are not the only ranges in which fish can survive but are the optimum temperatures for fish to reproduce and grow.

Acknowledgments

This work could not have been completed without the assistance and input of numerous individuals. For the assistance provided we are truly appreciative. The work has been improved significantly by those who gave unselfishly of their time and talent. If the work is useful and scholarly, it is due in large part to the efforts of the peer reviewers and those who provided editorial assistance. While acknowledging the assistance and specified contributions of the following individuals, we retain full responsibility for any shortcomings or faults in the work.

Don Archer, former Chief of Fisheries Research, Utah Division of Wildlife Resources, Salt Lake City, Utah. Review of "Cypriniformes."

Ted Arnow, Geologist, U.S. Geologic Survey (retired), Salt Lake City, Utah. Review of "Geologic Aspects" and "The Great Salt Lake."

Genevieve Atwood, Director, Utah Geological and Mineral Survey (retired), Salt Lake City, Utah. Review of "Geologic Aspects" and "The Great Salt Lake."

Nancy Banks, Fisheries Research Librarian, Utah, Oregon, and Wisconsin. Investigative effort on fish life histories.

David H. Bennett, Professor, Fisheries and Wildlife Department, University of Idaho, Moscow. Review of "Cypriniformes" and "Perciformes."

Herb Boschung, Professor, Emeritus, Department of Biology, University of Alabama, Tuscaloosa, Alabama. Review of "Perciformes," "Cypriniformes," "Siluriformes."

Steven E. Clyde, Attorney, Clyde, Snow, and Swenson, P.C., Salt Lake City, Utah. Author: "Water and the Law."

Wally and Barbara Cooper, Portsmouth, New Hampshire (previously of Paris, France). Translation of fish life histories.

Glen Davis, Fishery Biologist (retired), Utah Division of Wildlife Resources, Salt Lake City, Utah. General information and assistance.

Donna and Oliver Falkenborg, Logan, Utah. Manuscript editors.

Wayne Gustaveson, Fishery Biologist, Utah Division of Wildlife Resources, Page, Arizona. Review of "Perciformes," "Cypriniformes," "Clupeiformes."

Don Hales, Dexter National Fish Hatchery, Dexter, New Mexico. Data on spawning requirements of Colorado River listed endemic fishes.

Michael Herbaugh, Alexandria, Virginia. Review of "Perciformes," sportsman's perspective.

Roy D. Hugie, President and Chief Wildlife Biologist, Pioneer Environmental Services, Inc. Logan, Utah. For support, both material and philosophical.

Rodello Hunter, author, poet, Salt Lake City, Utah.

John Irving, former Fisheries Biologist, EG&G, Idaho Falls, Idaho; now at Lockheed Idaho. Review of "Salmoniformes."

W. Carl Latta, Program Director, Michigan Department of Natural Resources, Institute for Fisheries Research, Ann Arbor, Michigan. Review of "Salmoniformes."

Jim Mayhew, Chief of Fisheries, Iowa Fish and Wildlife Division, Des Moines, Iowa. Review of "Cypriniformes," "Perciformes."

Robert R. Miller, Professor of Fisheries, Emeritus, University of Michigan. Review of "Salmoniformes."

Donal R. Myrick, President, Spectrum Sciences & Software, Inc., Fort Walton Beach, Florida. Encouragement, support, and understanding.

Sharon Ohlhorst, Department of Fisheries and Wildlife, Utah State University, Logan. Input and review of the endemic fishes information.

Sydney Peterson, secretarial and editorial assistance, Logan, Utah.

Albert Regenthal, Chief of Waterfowl, Utah Division of Wildlife Resources (retired), Salt Lake City, Utah. Review of "Fishing Utah."

Dudley Reiser, R2 Resource Consultants, Inc., Bellevue, Washington. Review of "Salmoniformes."

C. Richard Robins, Professor, Rosenstiel School of Marine and Atmospheric Sciences, University of Miami, Miami, Florida. Review of all fish life history nomenclature and taxonomic status.

Mark J. Rosenfeld, formerly Professor, Department of Geography and Curator, Utah Museum of Natural History, University of Utah, Salt Lake City. Author: "Biogeographic Considerations of Utah Fishes."

Bruce Schmidt, former Chief of Fisheries, Utah Division of Wildlife Resources, Salt Lake City, Utah. Author: "Management of Utah's Fishes—Agency Perspective for the Year 2000." Review of all game fish life history management sections.

W. B. Scott, Huntsman Marine Laboratory, St. Andrews, NB, Canada. Review of manuscript.

Betty J. Sigler, Canyon, Texas. Secretarial and editorial assistance on all chapters.

Elinor Jo Sigler, Paris, France. Translator, original species life history information and translations from French to English.

Margaret Sigler, Logan, Utah. Secretarial and editorial assistance on all chapters.

Gerald R. Smith, Curator of Fisheries, University of Michigan, Ann Arbor. Author: "An Illustrated Key to Utah Fishes, Native and Introduced."

Kent Summers, Fisheries Biologist, Utah Division of Wildlife Resources, Ogden, Utah. Information on Willard Bay Reservoir.

Frances Titchener, Assistant Professor, Language and Philosophy Department and History Department, Utah State University, Logan, Utah. Translations of original fish descriptions.

Richard A. Valdez, Senior Aquatic Biologist, Bio/West Inc., Logan, Utah. Review of "Cypriniformes."

Tom Wharton, Sports Writer, The *Salt Lake Tribune*, Salt Lake City, Utah. Author: "A Personal Journey."

Joe White, Deputy Director, Wyoming Game and Fish Department, Laramie, Wyoming. Information on Flaming Gorge Lake.

Larry Wilson, Director, Iowa Department of Natural Resources, Des Moines, Iowa. Review of "Cypriniformes," "Perciformes," and encouragement over the years.

About Fishing and Poetry

Sky and cliffs and water sheen
Could form the words to build a poem.
And strange as it may seem,
Most fly fishermen are poets—
That is, when they fish,
They feel like poets do when they write.
But if the fish aren't biting
Then the fisherman doesn't feel euphoric.
He feels like a poet with writer's block,
Especially, when he goes home and says, "No luck!"
To his wife who has made potatoes au gratin
To go with a big platter of pan-fried trout.
A poet can scratch a verse on a rock
And thus etch the wonders of the world.
But put a boat on the lake in front
    of the fisherman poet
And he thinks more of fishin' than poetry.
After all, you can't eat poems.
That's why most fishermen fish
And most poets starve to death!

Rodello Hunter

PART I

Natural History, Geology, Landforms, and Water Bodies

Midday Musin'

Folks have different ways of dividin' things up.
Good and bad, winter and summer, Republicans and Democrats.
A man classifies accordin' to his bent.
And if a feller is a fisherman or not,
    That's the way I see 'em.
I been fishin' since I was a lad, and I sure met a heap of nice guys.
A man who's trollin' or castin' ain't swearin' or cussin'. . . not very
    loud, anyhow.
He ain't lookin' for an easy mark or a loose vote, 'cept mebbe that
    fish.
It takes a real good man to be a good fisherman.
He's gotta be patient and quiet, careful and considerate.
He walks, he don't run through life.
He's gotta like himself pretty well to spend all day
With just the sun, and the water, and a skiff of a breeze,
    And his own conscience.
I bet my next catch that you'll find fewer crooks
And wise guys fishin' than most anywhere.
I think God must 'a been quite a fisherman, Himself.
He knew where to look when He wanted good men
He found 'em castin' their nets.
And He was probably fishin', restin' against the bole
Of a tree when He thought about buildin' the world.
Stands to reason.
'Cause He sure included plenty of good fishin' holes in His plan
And how else would we 'a got such pretty places to fish in?

Rodello Hunter

CHAPTER 1

Geologic Aspects

Utah is a land of contrasts. Its topographic features include mountain tops over 13,000 ft (3,962 m) high, above timberline, and lowland desert areas below 4,200 ft (1,280 m) in elevation (Greer et al. 1981). This variety of topography has had a profound effect on the settlement of the state and continues to influence the way Utahns obtain and utilize water resources (and hence water-related resources such as fish). We will discuss some of the major mountain ranges and related topographic features of Utah.

Three major geologic areas (Figure 1) dictate the presence and location of water in Utah and continue to affect Utah's present stream, lake, and impoundment configurations: Lake Bonneville, incorporating the Basin and Range Physiographic Province, and the Colorado River drainage, in the Colorado Plateau Physiographic Province, occupy the majority of the state. A third area, the Rocky Mountain Province, separates the two preceding areas. The Uinta Mountains and part of the Wasatch Range are included in this third physiographic area. Water in this latter area drains to one of the other two provinces (Minckley, Hendrickson, and Bond 1986).

Lake Bonneville's basin, generally referred to as the Great Basin, covered an area of 20,000 sq mi (51,800 sq km) in the Pleistocene and included drainage from Wyoming, Idaho, Nevada, and the northwestern half of Utah. Lake Bonneville (Figure 1.1) was bounded on the east by the Wasatch Mountain range and the western end of the Uinta Mountains, on the north by the Snake River Basin, on the south by the Colorado Plateau, and on the west by the Central and Lake Lahontan basins of Nevada (Sigler and Sigler 1987). The largest size reached by Lake Bonneville roughly matches the Basin and Range Province.

The Colorado Plateau Province is shared by Utah, Colorado, Wyoming, Arizona, and New Mexico. It is world famous for its scenic and geologic features and includes the only area in the United States where four states adjoin. It is bisected by the Colorado River and has thus been altered by the river and its tributaries (Figure 1.1). The Colorado River today is an important economic factor in the western states through which it and its tributaries drain. From a natural history standpoint, it is important because it supports five species of fish listed under the federal Endangered Species Act (Stokes 1986).

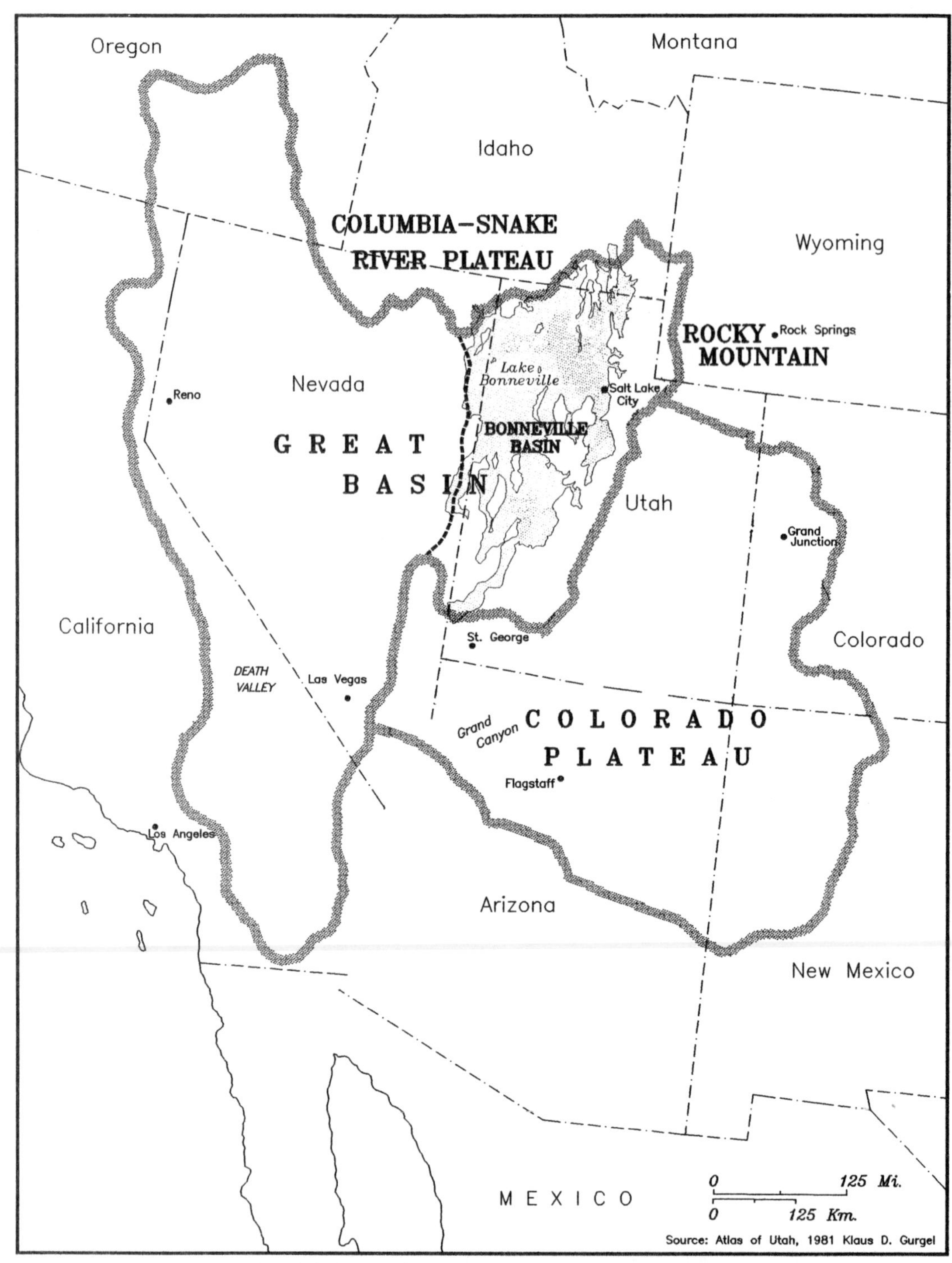

1. Utah's three major physiographic regions: Pleistocene Lake Bonneville, its drainage and remnants; drainage area of the Colorado River in Utah and surrounding states; major streams and reservoirs.

The Rocky Mountain physiographic region includes an area that roughly divides the Basin and Range Province from the Colorado Plateau Province, much like a backbone (Chronic 1990). The area includes the Uinta Mountains with their hundreds of lakes (600 of which support fish) and the highest point in Utah—Kings Peak at 13,528 ft (4,123 m)(Stokes 1986).

Formation of the Wasatch Range (Wasatch Front), perhaps as early as the Eocene (36.6 to 57.8 MYA [million years ago]) and the collapse of the Great Basin in the Oligocene (23.7 to 36.5 MYA) isolated the upper Colorado River and the Great Basin drainages. The Uinta Mountains developed into the origin of the Bear, Provo, Weber, and Duschesne rivers. The first three drain to the Great Basin, the fourth to the Colorado (Minckley, Hendrickson, and Bond 1986).

Separation of Utah into three physiographic regions facilitates discussion of mountains and other geologic features. However, the placement of rivers, streams, lakes, and reservoirs is less easily accomplished. The Bear River rises in the Uinta Mountains that are placed in either the Colorado Plateau or the Rocky Mountain physiographic group. However, it drains into the Great Basin sink of Great Salt Lake. In the discussion that follows, major rivers and streams, and subsequently reservoirs and lakes, have been assigned to one of two regions: Basin and Range (Great Basin) or Colorado Plateau (Colorado River drainage). Only a few Utah streams fall outside these qualifications.

Mountain Ranges and Formations

Basin and Range (Great Basin)

Wasatch Front

The term "Wasatch Front" describes a man-made social area, although its derivation is from the steeply rising mountains east of Provo, Salt Lake City, Ogden, and Brigham City. It is generally considered to include the area along the western edge of the Wasatch Mountains from Provo to Brigham City and include all of the cities in that area.

Wasatch Range

The Wasatch Range of mountains borders the Great Salt Lake on the east. Farmington Mountain, composed mainly of Precambrian crystalline rocks, is nearest the lake.

The Oquirrh Mountains border Great Salt Lake on the southeast and south. Limestone is the principal bedrock of these rugged mountains. Coos Peak is the highest point at 9,000 ft (2,743 m). The Oquirrh Formation is Pennsylvanian and Permian rock composed of limestone, shale, sandy limestone, quartzite, cherty limestone, and dolomite. This range is the site of the world-famous Bingham Canyon open-pit copper mine and the ghost towns of Mercur and Ophir (Stokes 1980).

The Stansbury Mountains border Great Salt Lake on the southwest and are not as high nor as rugged as the Oquirrhs. They are made up of rocks of the Cambrian, Ordovician, Silurian, Devonian, and Mississippian periods.

The Terrace and Hogup mountains bound most of the western shore of the northern part of the lake. They have elevations of over 6,500 ft (1,981 m). The bedrock exposures are mostly late Paleozoic strata.

The southeast part of the Raft River Mountains (which drain primarily to the Snake/Columbia drainage), Curlew Valley, Hansel Valley, and the Hansel Mountains border the northwest arm of the lake. The Rozel Hill and Promontory Mountains, form a west-facing bulge on the northern side of the Promontory Range. This range, 4 to 8 mi (6.4 to 12.9 km) wide and 30 mi (48 km) long, extends well into Great Salt Lake.

Sevier and Black Rock Deserts

The Sevier Desert is a Lake Bonneville remnant. Shoreline areas are represented here as elsewhere in the Bonneville Basin. Dunes have developed here (Little Sahara or Lynndyl sand dunes) with sand from Pleistocene delta deposits of the Sevier River (Chronic 1990). The igneous rocks of the Sevier Desert are mostly of late Cenozoic (0.9 to 1.3 MYA) origin.

The Black Rock Desert, between Scipio and Cove Fort in south central Utah, is an area of cinder cones and ancient lava flows. Some of the lava flows may have erupted into Lake Bonneville (Chronic 1990). There are hot springs, from volcanic geothermal areas, near Holden and elsewhere on the Black Rock Desert. Six separate volcanic centers are identified in the Black Rock Desert area (Stokes 1986).

Deep Creek Range

Later Precambrian rock is exposed in the Deep Creek Range of western Utah. Also present is Silurian rock, previously assigned to only one Utah range, the Laketown Dolomite. The Deep Creek Range is a potential producer of gold, copper, tungsten, and mercury. This area was previously glaciated, as can be seen in portions of the range that are deeply scarred. The highest point in this range is Ibapah Peak at 12,109 ft (3,691 m). Ibapah Peak is eroded from large granitic stock dated 18.1 MYA (Stokes 1986).

Great Salt Lake Desert

The western desert of Utah is part of the Great Basin. Geologically this area contains a number of areas, unique to the western United States, known as playas—intermittent water pool areas that have left large deposits of various salts. The Great Salt Lake Desert was inundated as part of Lake Bonneville in Pleistocene time. On the smooth surface of one of these "salt flats" can be found Utah's famous geologic feature, the Bonneville Speedway or Bonneville Salt Flats. The speedway, site of many land speed records over the last 30 years, is about 12 mi (19.2 km) long and 80 ft (24 m) wide (Chronic 1990).

Rocky Mountain Physiographic Region

Bear River Range

The Bear River Range, located in extreme northern Utah, lies to the east of the Wasatch Range and incorporates the area of Cache Valley, extending some 45 mi (72 km) into Idaho. Along with the Confusion Basin area of Millard County, the Bear River Range is world famous for outcrops of Cambrian sediments (Stokes 1986). Complete stratigraphic sections including Lower, Middle, and Upper Devonian sequences are found in this range. Glaciers left distinct and unmistakable erosive effects on many mountains and plateaus during the Pleistocene. Major glaciated areas are present in the Bear River Range (Stokes).

Uinta Mountains

Utah's Uinta Mountains are, in several ways, unique. Although they are similar to other ranges of the Rocky Mountains in being composed of a single, arched anticline with both edges broken (Chronic 1990), they are the only major east-west mountain range in North America. The mountains, along with the Uinta Basin, delineate the northern edge of the Colorado Plateau (and the Colorado Plateau physiographic region) in Utah. Formed during Cretaceous—early Tertiary—mountain building, the Uintas were buried by sediments, both mud and sand, that were washed off mountains to the east and north and subsequently reexposed when the soft sediments eroded off. Nearly in the center of the range is Kings Peak, highest point in Utah at 13,528 ft (4,123 m).

Wasatch Plateau

Located near the northern extremity of what has been termed "Utah's Backbone" (Chronic 1990), the Wasatch Plateau forms a portion of the Wasatch Range, longest of Utah's three major mountain groups. The plateau forms the eastern edge of the backbone, and with the Paunsaugunt, Aquarius, and Markagunt plateaus, is several thousand feet higher than the area to the east. It is composed of Cretaceous and Tertiary rock, much faulted, and arrayed with parallel north-south faults. Mt. Musinia rises above the rest of the Wasatch Plateau and is an upfaulted remnant of lake-deposited limestone.

Colorado Plateau Physiographic Region

San Rafael Swell

Forced up into a dome anticline 100 mi (161 km) from north to south and 40 mi (64 km) from east to west, the San Rafael Swell provides an excellent place to view rocks of the Triassic, Jurassic, and Cretaceous periods. On the west side of the swell, from top to bottom, the Navajo, Kayenta, and Wingate formations are visible. These are the major scenery-making layers of that part of the state (Chronic 1990). Largely inaccessible before the construction of Interstate 70, the eastern "reef" anticline area rises 800 to 2,000 ft (244 to 610 m). Coconino sandstone, the oldest rock exposed on the swell, and the Kaibab formation extend southward into Arizona where they are present in the uppermost walls of the Grand Canyon.

Henry Mountains

The Henry Mountains are a free-standing mountain range consisting of Tertiary intrusions that have pushed through Paleozoic, Triassic, and Jurassic rocks. Both Jurassic and Triassic rock in this area contain uranium. The Henry Mountains are classic laccolithic mountains described by G. K. Gilbert in 1877. The dominant peaks are Mt. Ellen (11,615 ft [3,540 m]), Mt. Pennell (11,371 ft [3,466 m]), Mt. Millers (10,650 ft [3,246 m]), Mt. Holmes (7,930 ft [2,417 m]), and Mt. Ellsworth (8,235 ft [2,510 m]). The Henry Mountains are the largest of the seven laccolithic mountain groups of the Colorado Plateau and form a chain about 40 mi (64 km) long in Wayne and Garfield counties (Stokes 1986; Chronic 1990).

La Sal Mountains

The La Sal Mountains, so named by Spanish explorers because of their white, snow-capped peaks (giving the appearance of salt), are composed of three separate groups of peaks. Each group represents a center of intrusive igneous rock that rose from great depths. Mt. Peale at 12,721 ft (3,877 m) is the highest peak in the range. This range formed in the Miocene when molten magma pushed up through sedimentary strata. The peaks of the range are igneous rock from the intrusions. The chief rock type in this range is diorite porphyry, with minor bodies of aegirine granite, orphyry, and soda rhyolite. Placer gold has been taken from several locations (Stokes 1986; Chronic 1990).

Book Cliff Mountains

The Book Cliff Mountains are composed of sandstone, shale, and coal of the Mesaverde group. This escarpment, approximately 200 mi (322 km) long, extends from Price, Utah, to Palisade, Colorado. The cliffs are formed of one, two, or three layers of ledge-forming sandstone. Although the exact origin of the name of this impressive range is lost in obscurity, one reasonable explanation is that the ledges of sandstone, cut with vertical fractures in many places, gives the appearance of books lying on their backs with the pages facing upward (Stokes 1986; Chronic 1990).

Navajo Mountain

Navajo Mountain, dominating the surrounding area with its 10,388-ft (3,168-m) top, is striking with its rounded rather than peaked appearance. Surface rock on Navajo Mountain is primarily Navajo Sandstone, that erodes into deep canyons. The lower foothills of the mountain contain Rainbow Bridge, now easily accessible from the waters of Lake Powell (Stokes 1986; Chronic 1990).

Snake River Drainage

The Goose Creek Mountains–Raft River Mountains of extreme northwestern Utah are tributary to both the Great Basin, on the southern flank, and the Snake River–Columbia River Basin, via the Raft River, on the north flank. The Raft River Mountains, like the Uintas, trend east-west and have a core of Precambrian metamorphic rocks. The highest point is 9,032 ft (2,754 m).

Rivers and Streams

Great Basin Drainages

Within the Great Basin of Utah there are several major river drainages and associated tributary networks, a number of which are impounded, providing important aquatic resources and fishing areas. A brief discussion of each is presented. Many were important historically and continue to contribute to Utah's aquatic resource base.

Sevier River

Sevier River, in west-central Utah, rises on the Markagunt and Paunsaugunt plateaus and drains north in the East Fork that contains Otter Creek Reservoir (52,500 acre-feet [af] or 64.8 ha/m), and the Main Fork that holds Piute Reservoir (71,800 af [88.6 ha/m]), and Sevier Bridge Reservoir (236,000 af [291 ha/m]). Near the town of Gunnison, it is joined by the San Pitch River. Downstream of Gunnison the river runs south and west and disappears into the desert sands about 140 mi (225 km) from its origin. Its historic terminus was Sevier Lake (a Lake Bonneville remnant) that had a surface area of 188 sq mi (487 sq km) in 1872 but is generally dry except in high precipitation years such as 1983–1987 (Houghton 1976; Bradley et al. 1980; Murphy 1981).

For water year 1986 (the 12 months ending Sept. 30, 1986) (USGS 1987) the Sevier River gauge at Lynndyl noted a drainage area of 5,966 sq mi (15,452 sq km), a total discharge of 501,200 af (618 ha/m) and a mean discharge of 569 cfs (cubic feet/second) or 16 cms (cubic meters/second). For the water year 1984 (USGS 1985) for the same gauge, there was a total discharge of 993,700 af (1,226 ha/m) and a mean discharge of 1,369 cfs (39 cms).

The Sevier River and its drainage area form a portion of the eastern boundary of Lake Bonneville and are part of the dividing line between the Basin and Range Physiographic Region and the Colorado Plateau region. Portions of the Sevier River contain brown trout, rainbow trout, and cutthroat trout. Other species of fishes include walleye, channel catfish, smallmouth bass, northern pike, and yellow perch.

Provo, Ogden, and Weber Rivers

Three major rivers in the metropolitan area of Utah are the Provo, Ogden, and Weber. All three originate on the west slope of the Rocky Mountains in the canyons of the Wasatch Front in northern Utah.

The Provo River, the shortest of the three, traverses only about 35 mi (56 km) from its headwaters to its terminus in Utah Lake near Provo. The Provo River and Utah Lake have both been extensively modified and diverted for irrigation since the mid-1850s. Deer Creek

Reservoir (149,700 af [184.7 ha/m]) is located in the upper reaches of the Provo (Murphy 1981). For water year 1984, total discharge was 352,600 af (435 ha/m) with a mean of 486 cfs (14 cms)(USGS 1985). For water year 1986, total discharge was 400,600 af (494.2 ha/m), with a mean discharge of 553 cfs (16 cms). The Provo has a drainage area of approximately 675 sq mi (1748 sq km)(USGS 1987). Portions of the Provo River contain rainbow trout, brown trout, cutthroat trout, and brook trout. It is stocked with catchable (8 in. [203 mm] or larger) rainbow trout. Portions of the river also contain mountain whitefish and walleye.

The Ogden River, noted in years past for its Class II fishing waters, originates in three separate forks east of Ogden in the Wasatch Front. Only 50 mi (81 km) from its headwaters, it joins the Weber River shortly before that stream empties into Great Salt Lake. Portions of the river contain rainbow trout, brown trout, cutthroat trout, and brook trout. It is stocked with catchable rainbow trout.

The Weber River has its headwaters on the northwestern flank of the Uinta Mountains. Its major tributary is the Ogden River. Other tributaries joining the river as it flows north and west are Beaver Creek, Chalk Creek, and Silver Creek before it flows past the town of Morgan. Below Morgan the river flows another 30 mi (48 km) before entering Great Salt Lake. The Weber River contributes approximately 25 percent of the total water flowing into the Great Salt Lake. Six mi (10 km) from its mouth, the Weber has a drainage area of 2,081 sq mi (5,390 sq km). In the 1984 water year (USGS 1985) discharge was 983,400 af (1,213 ha/m) and mean discharge was 1,355 cfs (38 cms). For the 1986 water year (USGS 1987) total discharge was 1,033,000 af (1,274 ha/m), with an average discharge of 1,427 cfs (40 cms). Portions of the river contain rainbow trout, brown trout, brook trout, and cutthroat trout. It is stocked with catchable rainbow trout. Mountain whitefish are also present.

Jordan River

The Jordan River originates at the north end of Utah Lake and flows only about 35 mi (56 km) north before terminating in Great Salt Lake. Prior to the coming of white people and extensive irrigation diversions and manipulation, it supported Bonneville cutthroat trout.

The Jordan River drains an area of approximately 3,450 sq mi (8,936 sq km). In the 1984 water year (USGS 1985) total discharge was 129,800 af (160 ha/m), with a mean discharge of 179 cfs (5 cms). In the 1986 water year, total discharge was 129,100 af (159.3 ha/m), with a mean discharge of 178 cfs (5 cms)(USGS 1987). Flow in the Jordan River is regulated by structures at Utah Lake for irrigation and flood control. Portions of the river contain brown trout, rainbow trout, channel catfish, sunfish, white and largemouth bass, walleye, carp, and suckers.

Bear River

Bear River, the longest and largest river in the Utah portion of the Great Basin, originates on the north slope of the Uintas as outflow from Amethyst and McPheters lakes. It flows northward into Wyoming, crossing the Utah-Wyoming border at least three times. It flows into Idaho, then turns west and south near Soda Springs, Idaho, and reenters Utah at the northern end of Cache Valley. The Cub, Logan, Little Bear, and Blacksmith Fork rivers are all tributary to Bear River within Cache Valley. The Bear flows out of Cache Valley into Box Elder County and empties into the north end of Great Salt Lake at Bear River Bay. Bear River, similar to its smaller and shorter southern relation, the Sevier, travels a great many miles (about 350 [563 km]) but terminates only a few miles (90 [145 km]) from its origin (Bradley et al. 1980).

Historically, the Bear River connected directly to Ancient Bear Lake in northeastern Utah–Southeastern Idaho and repeatedly changed its course during periods of the Pleistocene as a result of fault blocking and volcanic activity (Morrison 1965). It is not presently connected to Bear Lake naturally. Artificial channels connect it to Bear Lake through Dingle Swamp to provide irrigation and power storage for Utah and Idaho. The Bear River drained to the Portneuf River and into the Snake/Columbia 34,000 years ago (Minckley, Hendrickson, and Bond 1986) as did Lake Bonneville some 10,000 years ago. Waters from the Bear account for over 50 percent of the annual flow into Great Salt Lake. The Bear River near Corinne has a drainage area of 7,030 sq mi (18,208 sq km). In the water year 1984, total discharge from the Bear River was 3,666,000 af (45,231.9 ha/m), with a mean discharge of 5,050 cfs (143 cms)(USGS 1985). For the water year 1986 total discharge was 3,099,000 af (3,823 ha/m), with a mean discharge of 4,281 cfs (121 cms)(USGS 1987). Portions of the Bear River contain rainbow trout, cutthroat trout, and brook trout. Other species present include whitefish, carp, suckers, channel catfish, walleye, largemouth bass, yellow perch, green sunfish, black bullhead, and black crappie.

Logan River

The Logan River originates in southeastern Idaho and flows down the Logan Canyon, through the city of Logan, joining the Bear River west of Logan City. It is extensively diverted for irrigation, and flow regimes have been modified for hydropower production. Historically, the Logan River discharged into the Cache Valley arm of Lake Bonneville. Near the mouth of Logan Canyon, gravel deltas at the Provo level of Lake Bonneville can be seen.

Total area of the Logan River drainage is approximately 250 sq mi (648 sq km). For the water year 1987, total discharge was 329,500 af (406.5 ha/m). Mean discharge was approximately 455 cfs (13 cms), with a high of 1,870 cfs (53 cms).

Cub River

The Cub River arises in the mountains east of Preston, Idaho, and flows into Utah where it joins the Bear River just upstream of Cutler Reservoir. Average discharge of the Cub River is approximately 10,000 af (12.4 ha/m). Much of the stream is diverted for irrigation (USGS 1985).

Little Bear River

The Little Bear River rises as three streams in the mountains south of Logan and east of Brigham City. It is impounded at Porcupine Reservoir near Paradise, Utah, where kokanee can be found, and at Hyrum Reservoir, near Hyrum, Utah. Average discharge is 62 cfs (1.8 cms) and 44,990 af/year (55.5 ha/m).

Blacksmith Fork River

The Blacksmith Fork River rises in the mountains south and east of Logan, Utah, and drains an area of approximately 290 sq mi (751 sq km). Average discharge near Hyrum, Utah, is 134 cfs (4 cms) and 97,080 af (119.8 ha/m). The Blacksmith contains some of the best stream fishing in Utah. It contains brook trout, cutthroat trout, rainbow trout, and mountain whitefish. Much of the drainage is under special regulation for fishing.

Colorado River Drainages

Colorado River

The Colorado River is one of the great treasures of the West. At the Utah-Arizona border, it has a drainage area of approximately 111,700 sq mi (289,303 sq km). Although there are no dams on the main stem of the Colorado River in Utah, Glen Canyon Dam in Arizona backs water for over 180 mi (288 sq km) into Utah, flooding areas of the Colorado, San Juan, and Escalante rivers. Lake Powell is a combination fishery, producing both warmwater and coldwater fish species. Fishing, combined with sightseeing and other recreational activities, is a major industry throughout the reservoir. Prior to impoundment by Glen Canyon Dam, and other changes in the drainage, the Colorado River was home to four abundant endemic species of fishes. Much of their habitat has now been replaced with cold, fast waters that fluctuate in response to hydropower requirements, a situation that came under agency review in the early 1990s.

Green River

The Green River rises in southwestern Wyoming, travels through the Uinta Mountains and into Colorado before joining the Colorado River below Moab, Utah. The Green is joined by the White and Yampa before it joins the Colorado. In its course, it provides not only fishing but other recreational activities. At Flaming Gorge Dam, north of Vernal, Utah, the Green is impounded to produce a large reservoir.

Snake/Columbia River Drainages

Raft River

The Raft River, in extreme northwestern Utah, is the only river basin in Utah that drains into the Columbia River Basin. Just prior to its passage into Idaho, it has a drainage area of only a few hundred square miles.

Lakes and Reservoirs

Attempts to place lakes and reservoirs within one of the three physiographic regions of Utah are confounded by natural geologic barriers. Although the Uinta Mountains can be categorized as either Colorado Plateau, or Basin and Range (because the south portions of the mountains provide drainage to the Colorado River and the north portion provides drainage to the Great Basin through the Bear River), the mountain range itself can be considered to be part of any of the three provinces (Stokes 1986; Chronic 1990). We therefore discuss lakes and reservoirs under no area designation.

Bear Lake

Bear Lake is unique to Utah waters. It is a natural, clear, cold, oligotrophic body of water with a maximum depth of 210 ft (64 m) at a surface elevation of 5,923.65 ft (1,806 m). Among its unique features is the presence of four endemic fishes. Not presently connected naturally to the Bear River, the lake serves as a reservoir for irrigation and hydropower production downstream. Lake level, filling, and draining are controlled by a series of canals through Dingle Swamp and through pumps at Lifton Station on the north end of the lake. (See Chapter 2 for more details on the lake.)

Flaming Gorge Lake

Flaming Gorge Dam, in the northeastern corner of Utah, impounds water that backs into Wyoming. This reservoir is 91 mi (146 km) long. The dam is 502 ft (153 m) high. Flaming Gorge Lake has a storage capacity of approximately 3,750,000 af (4,626 ha/m)(Murphy 1981).

Lake Powell

When full, Lake Powell has a shoreline of 1,960 mi (3,154 km) and a length of 180 mi (290 km), with a storage capacity of over 27,000,000 af (33,308 ha/m). Lake Powell is an impressive asset for many uses (Murphy 1981). The water, some 560 ft (171 m) deep at the dam, provides sport fishing for coldwater as well as coolwater fishes and has produced some spectacular fishing since it first filled in 1980.

Utah Lake

Located near Provo, Utah Lake is now managed as a reservoir for irrigation. Past agricultural and land management practices in the watershed severely altered both the chemical content of the lake and its turbidity levels, resulting in changes in fish fauna. It is home to the June sucker, listed by the state as endangered and whose only habitat is the lake and portions of the surrounding watershed. The June sucker present today is a hybrid between the original June sucker and Utah sucker.

Sevier Lake

Sevier Lake, a true remnant of Pleistocene Lake Bonneville, is presently fed by waters from many plateaus along the western edge of the Wasatch Mountains. When first mapped in 1872, the Sevier Lake

Table 1.1 Drainages, number of lakes, number of fishable lakes, and representative fish species of the Uinta Mountains.

Drainage	*No. Lakes/Fishable*	*Representative Fish Species*
Ashley Creek	70+/27	BRKT, CTT, RBT
Bear River	38+/38	BRKT, CTT, AGRY
Beaver Creek	40+/12	BRKT, CTT, RBT
Blacks Fork	33+/22	BRKT, CTT, RBT
Burnt Fork	15+/11	CTT, BRKT
Dry Gulch	15/12	CTT, BRKT, RBT, GT
Duchesne	62/38	BRKT, CTT, RBT, GT
Henrys Fork	50+/19	CTT, BRKT
Lake Fork	90+/40	BRKT, CTT, RBT
Provo River	84+/55	BRKT, CTT, RBT, AGRY
Rock Creek	120+	AGRY, BRKT, CTT
Sheep Cr/Carter Cr	62+/34	BRKT, CTT, RBT, AGRY
Swift Creek	17	CTT, BRKT
Uinta River	93+/49	BRKT, CTT, RBT, GT
Weber River	59+/42	BRKT, CTT
Whiterocks River	70+/45	BRKT
Yellowstone River	50/25	BRKT, CTT

SOURCE: Material compiled from Utah Division of Wildlife Resources, 1981–1987, "Lakes of the High Uinta" series. Key to fish species abbreviations: BRKT = brook trout; CTT = cutthroat trout; RBT = rainbow trout; AGRY = Arctic grayling; GT = golden trout.

Playa had a water surface area of 188 sq mi (487 sq km). Except in times of extremely high precipitation and runoff, such as the 1983–1987 high-water years, Sevier Lake is dry (Houghton 1976).

Lakes of the Uinta Mountains

The Uinta Mountains are unique in many ways. They are the only major mountain range in North America that is oriented east-west. Several streams in both the Great Basin and Colorado Plateau have their headwaters within them. They have Utah's highest point (Kings Peak at 13,528 ft [4,123 m]) and several other peaks over 13,000 ft (3,962 m). There are hundreds of lakes in the area, over 600 of which contain fishable populations. A summarization of the drainages, numbers of streams, and representative fish species present is given in Table 1.1.

Huck Finn Summer

You weather fellers say it rained that year?
But you're way off! I guess I know.
'Twas next year the alfalfa rotted from the wet,
And the fields were muddy seas; nothing would grow.
Oh, summer just outdone herself. I wish
You could'a been there. Skies so blue
They ached your eyes. And I caught my first fish.
It was a whopper! Ask Jim, he was there, too.
We'd dangled lines for hours and never spoke.
The river teased our toes. And then she hit!
Lightnin'! You should'a seen it. My fish line broke,
And we got soaked anettin' it. We didn't care a bit.
Jim got thrashed for gittin' wet and skippin' church.
But my pa was a fisherman, and he was mighty proud.
Just rememberin', my old heart gives a lurch.
Ma stuffed and baked it, and it fed the Sunday crowd.
Now don't tell me it rained, I've not forgot.
Your book says that? Well, mebbe. Like as not,
You're right about the weather. It don't matter anyway.
'Twas a dandy summer, 'cause I caught that fish that day.

Rodello Hunter

CHAPTER 2 Utah's Aquatic Jewels: Great Salt Lake and Bear Lake

Two of Utah's unique waters, Great Salt Lake and Bear Lake, have played important roles in both social and natural history aspects of the state and its peoples. Each is discussed in this chapter.

Twelve Thousand Years Ago

If we could just turn the geological clock back 12,000 to 9,000 years ago, we might be able to see "Paleo Indians" hunting giant mammoths or some lesser big game animal around Great Salt Lake. These early hunters were adapted to killing large Pleistocene mammals, such as mammoth, camel, bighorn sheep, deer, bear, and musk-ox. Several archaeological sites on the west edge of the lake date back more than 10,000 years (Madsen 1980). Fossil deposits of late Pleistocene feature mammoth near Clarkston, Utah, musk-ox at Logan cemetery, horse on the Weber River, and bighorn sheep east of Bountiful. Bison and camel have also been reported as well as extinct species of cutthroat trout and grizzly bear (Nelson and Madsen 1980).

The next stage, based on subsistence adaption, was from 8,500 to 2,500 years ago; the emphasis was on the salt flat ecosystem. During this time the "Archaic people" lived in caves and rock shelters. The Formative Stage, the Sevier Culture, was from 1,000 to 500 years ago and was characterized by agriculture and settled villages. The Proto-Shoshoni culture was migratory hunting and gathering, 1,500 to 500 years ago (Madsen 1980).

Lake Bonneville

The predecessor of Great Salt Lake, Lake Bonneville, was a freshwater lake of the late Pleistocene covering much of what is now western Utah and extending into Nevada and Idaho. It began to form about 32,000 years ago. At its highest levels of elevation (5,200 ft [1,585 m]) it covered 20,800 sq mi (53,872 sq km), had a maximum depth of about 1,000 ft (305 m), and a shoreline of over 2,000 mi (3,218 km)(Gilbert 1890). This level occurred about 17,000 years ago. It was controlled by the Zenda Threshold, a natural barrier that is just north of Redrock Pass in southeastern Idaho. The overflow went into the Snake River (Currey, Atwood, and Mabey 1984).

The level of the great lake fell dramatically when the water breached the relatively unconsolidated sediments making up the rim of the threshold and cut them down to bedrock. The resultant "Bonneville Flood" in the Snake River was catastrophic (Gilbert 1890).

The Bear River, as we now know it, originally flowed into the Snake River. When a series of volcanic eruptions occurred, between 130,000 and 30,000 years ago, in the Soda Springs area of southeast Idaho, the river was diverted south into northern Utah. These events preceded the formation of Lake Bonneville, perhaps as long ago as 150,000 years. Lakes have existed in northwest Utah for about 15 million years (Genevieve Atwood, personal communication, 12 July 1989).

Although there were many levels of Lake Bonneville and its predecessors, today only four are well defined. These levels, with feet above sea level and years ago of presence (Currey, Atwood, and Mabey 1984) are:

- Stansbury, 5,090 ft (1,551 m), 16,000 to 14,500 years ago
- Provo, 4,740 ft (1,445 m), 14,500 to 13,500 years ago
- Stansbury, 4,500 ft (1,372 m), 23,000 to 20,000 years ago
- Gilbert, 4,250 ft (1,295 m), 11,000 to 10,000 years ago

The water was moderately saline at the Stansbury level.

When the waters broke through the sediments at Redrock Pass the level dropped 350 ft (107 m) to a level of 4,740 ft (1,445 m). This level formed the Provo Bench, which is the most prominent of the benches today. Three university campuses, Utah State University, the University of Utah, and Brigham Young University, are built on this level. When the Ice Age ended, the level receded to historic low levels. The Gilbert level was formed between 11,000 and 10,000 years ago when the lake again rose to 4,250 ft (1,295 m). Further drops in the water levels marked the end of Lake Bonneville and the beginning of Great Salt Lake.

The Great Salt Lake

The Great Salt Lake is coastal in character, according to Currey (1980), perhaps to a greater degree than any other nonmarine landscape in the Western Hemisphere. It is the fourth largest terminal lake, and the thirty-third largest lake in the world (Austin 1980; Arnow and Stephens 1990). The lake is about 50 mi (80 km) wide and 75 mi (121 km) long at elevation 4,200 ft (1,280 m). Its drainage basin is 35,000 sq mi (90,650 sq km). The annual average flow of water into Great Salt

Lake (1931–1976) was about 2.9 million af (357.8 ha/m). Surface water sources contribute about 66 percent, precipitation 31 percent, and ground water 3 percent. Evaporation averages 45 in./yr (114 cm/yr).

When the lake is at an elevation of 4,211.5 ft (1,284 m) it covers about 2,300 sq mi (5,957 sq km) and has a volume of 31.16 million af (384.4 ha/m); when it has a surface elevation of 4,191.35 ft (1,277 m)(the 1962 historic low) it covers 950 sq mi (2,461 sq km) and has a volume of 8.4 million af (103.7 ha/m) (Arnow 1980). At the approximate average level about which the lake has fluctuated during historic times (1847–1992) it covers about 1,700 sq mi (4,403 sq km) and has a maximum depth of 34 ft (10 m)(Arnow and Stephens 1990). At this level the volume of water is about 16 million af (197.4 ha/m). The highest level reached was 4,211.85 ft (1,284 m) on 3 June 1986. Surface levels change continually due largely to evaporation. Human activities have a lesser, but important, effect on lake levels.

In 1904 the Southern Pacific Transportation Company constructed a 20-mi (32-km) railway across Great Salt Lake from Promontory Point west to Lakeside. At each end the track was on a solid causeway, but there was a 12-mi (19-km) railroad trestle in the center. This railway considerably shortened the east-west rail route. Later, when the trestle began to deteriorate, it was replaced by a causeway completed in 1959. This structure effectively divided the lake into two separate entities, since the blocked-off north arm received very little fresh water (Newby 1980). The southern part of the lake was considerably higher and less saline than the northern part. This situation was true until August 1984 when the state breached a 300-ft-wide (91 m) stretch at the west end. Within a year the differences in water level had decreased to 0.5 ft (15 cm)(Arnow and Stephens 1990).

The concentration of salt in Great Salt Lake in 1980 was 25.5 percent as compared to 26.9 percent in the Dead Sea and 3.5 percent in most oceans. Until 1984 there was a marked difference in the color of the brine between the north and the south arm. In the north arm it was reddish pink and in the south arm it was blue green. This difference was altered somewhat by the breaching of the causeway and by dredging operations. Depth of visibility ranges from a few inches to about 3 ft (91 cm).

The major cations in the lake are sodium, magnesium, potassium, and calcium. The major anions are chloride and sulphate. The Bear, Weber, and Jordan river systems contribute over 90 percent of the flow into the lake. The Bear, for example, draining 7,030 sq mi (18,208 sq km), contributes 53 percent and discharges 940,000 af (11.6 ha/m) of water in an average year (Sturm 1980). The main factors that affect salt concentrations in the lake are: (1) the railroad causeway that virtually formed two lakes until 1984, (2) water inflow, (3) evaporation, (4) lake currents, and (5) mirabilite precipitation (Butts 1980). A typical yearly fluctuation in level is an increase from spring runoff, rain, and groundwater, and a decrease in spring or summer to fall when inflows decrease and temperatures increase. The density of the brine is not uniform throughout the lake due to a variety of factors. When the level of Great Salt Lake falls to 4,196.5 ft (1,279 m) the water becomes saturated with sodium chloride and sodium sulphate. This concentration is at about 27.6 percent. One of the most valuable resources of the lake is the natural brines that produce potassium, sodium chloride, and other products (Behrens 1980). There is also a brine shrimp industry.

Fish and Wildlife

There are three Merriam Life Zones in the Greater Salt Lake area: (1) the Lower Sonoran, the salt desert area, ranging from lake level to 5,500 ft (1,676 m); (2) the Upper Sonoran, pinyon-juniper belt ranging from 5,500 to 6,500 ft (1,676 to 1,981 m); and (3) the transition belt ranging from 6,500 to 7,372 ft (1,981 to 2,247 m)(Rawley 1980). The initial impression of the Great Salt Lake area is one of utter desolation, but this is far from true. The lake is surrounded by extensive marshes that are invaluable in many ways.

It has been said that marshes, from an energy standpoint, are the richest of all ecosystems. Great Salt Lake has no fish, but even considering the salt content this seemingly indisputable statement must be qualified. The size of the freshwater marshes around Great Salt Lake vary roughly inversely with the height of the lake. That is, the higher the lake level the smaller the marsh area not covered with salt water. These marshes at an average water level of 4,200 ft (1,280 m) or less support millions of waterfowl, shore birds, raptors, and other less abundant bird species. The marshes, both publicly and privately owned, are rich in food, cover, and nesting and rearing sites. The largest of the public areas is the federal Bear River Migratory Bird Refuge, with more than 64,000 acres (25,900 ha).

The water level of Great Salt Lake started rising rapidly in 1982 and continued until, in 1986, it had almost reached the 1873 presumed historic level of 4,211.85 ft (1,284 m). It was about the same level in 1987. The salt companies around Great Salt Lake were forced to raise substantially the dikes surrounding the drying ponds. Common carp and channel catfish were reported far out in the lake, but they were in the lighter, fresher surface area. And they could not tolerate the brine underneath. This phenomenon is not unusual. Freshwater fish have been reported far out in both Chesapeake Bay and the Gulf of Mexico. There was also a population of rainwater killifish near Stansbury Island that may or may not survive dropping water levels. The only multicellular animal organisms living in the brine are three species of brine shrimp and two species of brine fly. There are also bacteria, protozoans, and many species of algae.

There is an abundance of furbearers including muskrat, mink, and red fox. Rawley (1980) stated that among the vertebrates within the

Great Salt Lake area are 23 species or subspecies of fishes, 8 species or subspecies of amphibians, 2 species or subspecies of snakes, 257 species of birds, and 64 species of mammals.

Mountains

The Wasatch Range borders Great Salt Lake on the east. The section of range nearest the lake is Farmington Mountain, which is composed of mainly Precambrian crystalline rocks. The Oquirrh Mountains border the lake on the southeast and south. Limestone is the principal bedrock of these rugged mountains. Coos Peak is the highest point at 9,000 ft (2,743 m). The Oquirrh Formation is Pennsylvanian and Permian rock composed of limestone, shale, sandy limestone, quartzite, cherty limestone, and dolomite. This range is the site of the famous open-pit Bingham Canyon copper mine and the ghost towns of Mercur and Ophir (Stokes 1980).

The Stansbury Mountains bordering Great Salt Lake on the southwest are not as rugged or as high as the Oquirrhs. They are made up of rocks of the Cambrian, Ordovician, Silurian, Devonian, and Mississippian periods. Moving clockwise around the lake and across Skull Valley are the Southern and Northern Lakeside mountains that make up over one-third of the west shore. The highest peak in this area is Black Mountain at elevation 6,620 ft (2,018 m). The Terrace and Hogup mountains bound most of the western shore of the northern part of the lake. They have elevations of over 6,500 ft (1,981 m). The bedrock exposures are mostly late Paleozoic strata. The southeast part of the Raft River Mountains, Curlew Valley, and Hansel Valley and Hansel Mountains border the northwest arm of the lake. The Rozel Hills and Promontory Mountains complete the shore outline of the lake. The Rozel Hills form a west-facing bulge on the northern side of the Promontory Range. This range, 4–8 mi (6.4–13 km) wide and 30 mi (48 km) long (north-south axis) extends well into Great Salt Lake. Promontory rises about 6,200 ft (1,890 m)(Stokes 1980).

Islands

The number and size of islands in Great Salt Lake increase as the level of the lake falls and decrease as the water level rises. Those areas that are islands when the lake level reaches 4,212 ft (1,284 m) have been so designated; there are eight. During normally low water years Bird and Gunnison are the only islands that offer security to sensitive birds.

Antelope, the largest of the islands, is 15.5 mi (25 km) long and 4.5 mi (7 km) wide. It has an area of 23,175 acres (9,379 ha). Wildlife once included antelope that disappeared in the 1870s (and are now back), bison that were stocked in 1892, chukar partridge, coyote, mule deer, and other wildlife. Mormon pioneers used the island to hold and rear horses. Cattle and sheep were also stocked there (Morgan 1947). It is now a state park.

Fremont Island is 5.5 by 1.5 mi (8.9 by 2.4 km) and covers 2,945 acres (1,192 ha). Stansbury Island, usually a peninsula, is 11.5 by 4.5 mi (18.5 by 7.2 km) with an area of 22,314 acres (9,030 ha).

Circular Carrington Island is 2 mi (3.2 km) in diameter and has an area of 1,767 acres (715 ha). Gunnison Island, less than a mile long, has an area of 155 acres (63 ha). The highest point above average lake level is 85 ft (26 m). It is a prime nesting area for the white pelican. Other birds that nest on the islands include great blue heron, double-crested cormorant, California gull, and Caspian tern. Waterfowl and shore birds nest almost entirely on the freshwater marshes around the lake.

Discovery

The first authentic information regarding Great Salt Lake came from Francisco Atanasio Dominguez and Silvestre Velez de Escalante when they were trying to establish a route from New Mexico to California. These priests did not explore as far north as the lake but decided from what the natives told them that a large river drained from the north arm of the lake to the west. They labeled it the Buenaventura River. During the next half century many mapmakers used their imaginations in a big way. The lake was supposed to be connected to the Pacific Ocean by an underground channel. There was even an eyewitness who described it in detail. It is generally agreed that Jim Bridger was the first white man to see the lake, and he reported he had seen an arm of the Pacific Ocean (Miller 1980).

Highlights

The Great Salt Lake is a unique resource in a number of ways. Visitors from many countries come each year to wonder at and sometimes to swim in, or more specifically to float on, the water. As a remnant of ancient Lake Bonneville and many other earlier unnamed freshwater lakes, Great Salt Lake is of great geological interest. Real and potential multiple use includes recreation, mineral extraction, and wildlife management and development. The brine shrimp industry, although relatively small, is unusual. The United States Air Force has bombing ranges and other large complexes in the desert west of the lake. The racetrack on the Bonneville salt flats 8 mi (13 km) east of Wendover, Utah, has produced many world speed records by fossil-fueled machines. Ab Jenkins, later mayor of Salt Lake City, was the first to recognize (late 1920s) the value of the salt flats as a speedway and international testing ground. In the lake, 8-ft (2.4-m) waves weighing as much as 76 lb/cu ft (1218 kg/cu m) of water can be devastating, as sailboaters and builders of highways and railroads will attest. This capacity for violence makes the lake unique as well as dangerous. Antelope Island was of special value to early pioneers because horses could be raised on it. Gunnison Island has one of the largest white pelican rookeries in the United States. These are but a few examples of the many values of Great Salt Lake.

Bear Lake

Physical Description

Bear Lake is located at 42° North, 111° West and has approximately 110 sq mi (285 sq km) of surface at a maximum elevation of 5,923.65 ft (1,806 m) above sea level. A little more than 50 percent of the lake has a depth of more than 100 ft (31 m). Its surface drainage area is approximately 500 sq mi (1,295 sq km)(Sigler 1972). It is by far the largest natural body of fresh water in Utah, even given that the lake level is artificially controlled by pumping and dikes (Sigler).

Bear Lake presents a unique ecosystem. It is large, deep, and generally oligotrophic (unproductive). It also contains four endemic fishes, discussed below (Workman 1963; Workman and Sigler 1965).

Cultural Importance and Status

Bear Lake was first observed by white men in the winter of 1811–1812. Frequent visitors to the valley in this period were trappers, traders, and Native Americans, who met each year to rendezvous, trade, and socialize. Recognition of this era is provided by the Rendezvous State Park on the south shore of the lake. Farmers and ranchers established themselves in the 1860s but at low densities of approximately five people per square mile (2.6 sq km). Agriculture was the prime land use until the late 1960s and early 70s when recreation-based development significantly increased. Continuing into the 1990s, recreational summer homes have changed the landscape of the lake's watershed. Major developments along the lake's west and south shores have modified the stream riparian and lake littoral zones (Smart 1958; Workman 1963; Workman and Sigler 1965; Nyquist 1967; Sigler 1972).

Bear Lake is located within easy driving distance of the large metropolitan populace of the Wasatch Front of Utah and within smaller population centers in Utah, Idaho, and Wyoming. Human population in these areas is increasing every year. This increase, coupled with the availability of disposable income for recreational pursuits, has resulted in increased use of not only the lake itself but of the surrounding watershed for development of second homes, golf courses, and community infrastructure.

Water Quality[1]

Limnological information on Bear Lake has been collected sporadically since the mid-1920s. Early investigators found a lake high in magnesium and calcium and low in nitrogen and phosphorus. Upon completion of the Bear River diversion project in the late 1920s, the use of Bear Lake as an upper basin storage reservoir resulted in dramatic changes in the lake's macrochemistry. Calcium, which had been second in concentration to magnesium, became the dominant anion in the lake water.

[1] We thank Vince Lamarra of Ecosystems Research Institute, Logan, Utah, for input and review of the water quality data discussed here.

Table 2.1 Native and Endemic[1] Fishes of Bear Lake and Lake Bonneville Relicts from Deposits[2]

Species	*Authors*	*Common Name*
Catostomus ardens [2]	Jordan and Gilbert 1881	Utah sucker
Cottus extensus [1,2]	Bailey and Bond 1963	Bear Lake sculpin
Gila atraria [2]	(Girard 1856)	Utah chub
Prosopium abyssicola [1]	(Snyder 1919)	Bear Lake whitefish
Prosopium gemmifer [1,2]	(Snyder 1919)	Bonneville cisco
Prosopium spilonotus [1,2]	(Snyder 1919)	Bonneville whitefish
Rhinichthys osculus	(Girard 1956)	speckled dace
Richardsonius balteatus	(Richardson 1836)	redside shiner
Oncorhynchus clarki [2]	(Richardson 1836)	cutthroat trout

SOURCE: Adapted from G. R. Smith et al. 1968
Parentheses around authors' names indicate that the species has been transferred by subsequent taxonomic review to a genus different than the one in which the original authors placed it.

Accurate nutrient data has been collected intensively since 1971. Total and orthophosphate, nitrate, nitrite, and ammonia concentrations measured in the lake as well as in the major tributaries and the marsh located at the north end of the lake indicate that the nutrient loading to this oligotrophic lake ranges from upper oligotrophy to mesotrophy. The variations depend on the amount of water entering the lake from the Bear River, which contributes approximately 70 percent of the micronutrients nitrogen and phosphorus.

During wet years, total inorganic nitrogen concentrations have been observed to be as high as 500 μg/l with orthophosphate less than 10 μg/l. However, during hydrologic dry cycles, total inorganic nitrogen has dropped to less than 100 μg/l with orthophosphate concentrations in excess of 10 μg/l.

Biological responses to nutrient enrichment have occurred. Phytoplankton biomass as measured by chlorophyll *a* concentrations has exceeded 2.0 μg/l during periods of high nutrient loading and as low as 0.3 μg/l during low loadings.

Endemic Fishes[2]

Bear Lake's biogeography reflects the unique and varied ancestry of Utah fishes. The four Bear Lake endemics are probably holdovers from Pleistocene Lake Bonneville. An added element of interest is that Bear Lake has more endemic fish species than any other lake in North

[2]We thank Sharon Ohlhorst of the Department of Fisheries and Wildlife, Utah State University, Logan, Utah, for input and review of the endemic fishes information.

America (Smith and Todd 1984). Table 2.1 lists native and endemic Bear Lake fishes and those identified from Lake Bonneville deposits.

It is unclear exactly where and at what time these fishes arose as species, although it is clear that most species did occur in Lake Bonneville (Smith et al. 1968; Oviatt 1984). Identified remains could indicate speciation within the Bonneville Basin with entrance to Bear Lake after the Bear River diversion. Alternatively, the fish could have evolved in Bear Lake because Bear Lake Valley appears to have been a lake basin at least since the Pliocene, and there have been a number of lake stages (Peale 1879; Robertson 1978; Minckley et al. 1986). Between the time of blockage of flow of the Bear River northwest into the Snake River (approximately 34,000 years before present [YBP]), and the overflow of the Bear River through Oneida Narrows, Idaho, into Cache Valley, Utah (approximately 25,000 YBP) the Bear River flowed into Gentile Valley, forming Thatcher Lake (Bright 1967). Thus, Thatcher Lake could also have been the location for speciation events (Miller 1965). Several researchers consider *Prosopium williamsoni* to be the ancestor of the Bear Lake endemics (Norden 1970; Booke 1974). *P. williamsoni* was found in Pliocene Lake Idaho (Smith 1981b).

Most of the Bear Lake fish genera were in the Intermountain area during the Pliocene. *Rhinichthys* is the one genus for which fossil evidence is lacking (probably due to its small size). *R. osculus,* the speckled dace, is widespread in the Intermountain area and probably came from the Hudson Bay drainage via the Snake River (Smith 1981). *Onchorhynchus clarki,* the cutthroat trout, is also thought to have entered in this fashion. Although the Pliocene species then present differ from those currently found, the Pleistocene species are usually very similar to their recent counterparts (Smith 1978). *Richardsonius balteatus,* the redside shiner, probably arrived relatively late (approximately 12,000 YBP) from the Snake River during the Lake Bonneville overflow. This genus has been found in Pliocene Lake Idaho (Smith 1975, 1978) but not in Lake Bonneville (Smith et al. 1968). *Catostomus ardens,* the Utah sucker, and *Gila atraria,* the Utah chub are unique to the Bonneville Basin and the Upper Snake River drainages, although the genera have a long history in Utah and were present in Lake Bonneville.

Expert's Tip

It stumps me there's a man that don't like fishin'.
For I ain't found a better place to go.
And a man can ponder on equality
For, here, your catch depends on know-how
    Not on dough.
If you like an hour of peace, (Name me a
    family man that don't.)
And there's no place 'cept the grave
    where there is quiet,
Don't do it, Bud! A day of fishin's all you need.
Well, then, don't take my word for it—
    go and try it!

Rodello Hunter

CHAPTER 3

Mark J. Rosenfeld

Biogeographic Considerations of Utah Fishes

Biogeography draws on multiple disciplines (for example, anatomy, climatology, genetics, geomorphology, hydrology, molecular biology) to explain biological distributions (Koehn and Eanes 1978; Morain 1984; Kessler and Avise 1985; Felsenstein 1988; Mayden 1988). This chapter discusses aspects of Utah fish biogeography from historical and evolutionary perspectives: namely, where, when, and how these fishes originated and fell into their current distributions.

The fishes of Utah come from varied historical and geographic backgrounds. Fifty-nine percent of the species (39 of 66 recorded species) were brought here by humans. Some of these have been here long enough for many people to think of them as native fishes. Introductions started in the latter part of the nineteenth century with game fishes (Courtenay and Stauffer 1984). For example, most trouts (Salmonidae) come from elsewhere. The rainbow trout (*Oncorhynchus mykiss*) is the state fish, but a Pacific coast native. Brook trout (*Salvelinus fontinalis*) and lake trout (*S. namaycush*) are from northeastern North America, and brown trout (*Salmo trutta*) from Europe. Even though cutthroat trout (*O. clarki*) occurs naturally in Utah, stocks from more northern waters have been brought here (Allendorf and Leary 1988). (More details on the exotic fishes are given in the individual life history accounts in the second half of this book.) Before their arrival, climatic and geologic events during the preceding hundreds, thousands, and millions of years had fostered the evolution of unique native fishes (Hubbs and Miller 1948; Hubbs, Miller, and Hubbs 1974). Interactions with introduced species and other artificial situations have severely reduced their numbers (Schoenherr 1981; Ono, Williams, and Wagner 1983).

Native fishes live in variably sized habitats, from small desert springs to large lakes and rivers. Differences in habitat size and type are partly responsible for interpopulation variation at morphological and molecular levels (Smith 1981a; Rosenfeld 1990). Often, native fishes have patchy distributions, with populations separated by tens or hundreds of kilometers of dry land. Past connections among inhabited waters explain such disjunctions. Between some, there have been no strong connections for hundreds of thousands or millions of years (for example, Colorado River and Bonneville Basin) (Minckley,

Hendrickson, and Bond 1986). For species that ascend into headwaters, interbasin transfers have happened more recently via stream captures (for example, mountain whitefish [*Prosopium williamsoni*], and mountain sucker [*Catostomus platyrhynchus*]) (Smith 1978). Flow between other disjunct waters occurred up to 12,000 years ago or within the preceding few hundred years. Geographical isolation promotes the accrual of genetic differences through genetic drift, mutation, and natural selection (Bush 1975; White 1978). For the native fishes, this hydrologic history has contributed to differentiations at the species, subspecies, and lesser taxonomic levels (Smith 1981b).

Utah includes portions of several major drainages. Much of the state is in the Bonneville Basin, the largest and easternmost Great Basin drainage. Because no streams flow out of the Bonneville Basin, water can leave naturally only by evaporation. This region extends from Cache Valley, Utah-Idaho, in the north to Cedar City in the south and from the Wasatch Mountains in the east to Wendover, Utah-Nevada, the Great Salt Desert, and the Deep Creek Mountains in the west. Salt Lake City, Delta, Logan, Ogden, Provo, Richfield, and Tooele are in the Bonneville Basin. Bear Lake in northeastern Utah joins the Bonneville Basin via the Bear River.

Until the late Miocene, parts of the Bonneville Basin, upper Snake River, and Bear River had aquatic affinities with the Hudson Bay. Thus, several species stem from northeastern North American progenitors (Hubbs and Miller 1948; Miller 1958; Smith 1981b). These include certain minnows (Cyprinidae: redside shiner, *Richardsonius balteatus*, and longnose dace, *Rhinichthys cataractae*), suckers (Catostomidae: white sucker, *Catostomus catostomus*, Utah sucker, *C. ardens*, and mountain sucker, *C. platyrhynchus*), sculpins (Cottidae: mottled sculpin, *Cottus bairdi*, and the ancestor common to the Bear Lake sculpin, *C. extensus*, and Utah Lake sculpin, *C. echinatus*), and the Bear Lake whitefish (Salmonidae: *Prosopium* spp.).

Other drainages make up the rest of Utah. The Raft River carries water from northwestern Utah to the Snake River, Columbia River, and Pacific Ocean. Its fishes are mostly Bonneville Basin derivatives due to a late Pleistocene connection between the Bonneville Basin and Snake River, discussed more fully below. The Snake River cutthroat (*Oncorhynchus clarki bouveri*) or a natural cross between it and a Bonneville Basin form (the Bonneville cutthroat, *O. c. utah*) lives in the Raft River (Simpson and Wallace 1982; Allendorf and Leary 1988).

The Colorado Plateau extends over eastern Utah. This area is drained by the upper Colorado River and tributary Green River (Carlson and Carlson 1982). Of 16 fish species that originated in the Colorado River system (Minckley, Hendrickson, and Bond 1986), at least five reside in larger channels here (Tyus et al. 1982; Williams et al. 1985): the humpback chub (*Gila cypha*), bonytail chub (*G. elegans*), roundtail chub (*G. robusta*), Colorado squawfish (*Ptychocheilus lucius*), and razorback sucker (*Xyrauchen texanus*). Subspecies of cutthroat trout (the Colorado cutthroat, *O. c. pleuriticus*) and speckled dace (*Rhinichthys osculus yarrowi*) evolved in the upper Colorado River (Behnke and Benson 1980).

Southwest Utah, which includes St. George and Zion National Park, empties into the Virgin River. This channel joins the lower Colorado River downstream from the Grand Canyon, Arizona. Endemic species and subspecies include the Virgin roundtail chub (*Gila robusta seminuda*), Virgin River spinedace (*Lepidomeda mollispinis*) and woundfin (*Plagopterus argentissimus*) (Cross 1975; 1978). The Virgin roundtail chub may have originated as an ancient natural hybrid between the bonytail chub (*G. elegans*) and the Colorado roundtail chub (*G. r. robusta*) or their progenitors (Smith, Miller, and Sable 1979; Rosenfeld and Wilkinson 1989). Woundfin and spinedace are the descendants of a Pliocene lower Colorado River assemblage (Miller and Hubbs 1960; Minckley, Hendrickson, and Bond, 1986). The woundfin once lived throughout the lower Colorado River Basin, from the Virgin River to southeastern California and southern Arizona. Dams, agricultural diversions, and exotic fish introductions explain its decline (Ono et al. 1983). In contrast, the Virgin River spinedace reached its morphological distinctness here and differentiated from other forms (White River spinedace, *L. albivallis*, and Pahranagat spinedace, *L. altivelis*) in the tributary White River, Nevada, within the last 10,000 to 15,000 years (Miller and Hubbs 1960).

The Great Basin consists of 150+ more or less isolated drainages formed since the Miocene between the Rocky and Sierra Nevada Mountains (Smith 1978). Speciational consequences of this partitioning are exemplified with two minnow genera, squawfishes (*Ptychocheilus*) and chubs (*Gila*). Both groups likely originated within the region before the Miocene. The earliest known squawfish (*P. prelucius*) comes from upper Colorado River sediments, Miocene Lake Bidahochi in northern Arizona (Uyeno and Miller 1965; Baskin 1978). The oldest chub fossils come from deposits of like age in the Lahontan part of the Great Basin, Nevada (Smith 1981b).

During the Miocene, the area west of the Rocky Mountains was largely a plain sloping west to the Pacific Ocean (Minckley, Hendrickson, and Bond 1986). This topographic circumstance was conducive to broad continuous distributions, but later mountain-building activities or orogenesis led to segregated populations of squawfish and chub (McAllister et al. 1986; Minckley, Hendrickson, and Bond 1986). These isolations gave rise to three squawfishes over the western part of this region, in the Sacramento–San Joaquin, Columbia, and Umpqua river drainages (Mayden, Rainboth, and Buth 1991). A fourth one, the Colorado squawfish (*P. lucius*), evolved in the Colorado River drainage (Carney and Page 1990). It is restricted now mostly to waters in Utah (Tyus et al. 1982) due to human alteration of the river (Ono, Williams, and Waganer 1983). This fish, the largest North American minnow (150 cm [5 ft] long and weighing 45 kg [99 lb]) (Holden 1980), seems little changed morphologically from *P. prelucius*, its Miocene progenitor (G. R. Smith 1975; M. L. Smith 1981).

The chubs have differentiated into 19 described species, each within specific basins in the Great Basin and contiguous drainages (Uyeno 1960; Lee et al. 1980; Williams and Bond 1980). Isolation of the lineage giving rise to the Utah chub (*G. atraria*) came with segregation of the Bonneville Basin by the early Pleistocene (G. R. Smith 1981b; Minckley, Hendrickson, and Bond 1986). Hence, Utah chub fossils are found only there (Stokes, Smith, and Horn 1964; Smith, Stokes, and Horn 1968). The Utah chub occurs in disjunct springs, streams, and lakes within the Bonneville Basin and upper Snake River (that is, Snake River above Shoshone Falls, a 93-m [305-ft] vertical barrier to the upstream movement of fishes near Twin Falls, Idaho) (Simpson and Wallace 1982; McPhail and Lindsey 1986), due to late Pleistocene and Holocene hydrographic events.

As with the Utah chub, ranges fragmented since the late Pleistocene or Holocene characterize several Bonneville Basin species. For example, the Utah sucker (*Catostomus ardens*), mottled sculpin (*Cottus bairdi*), and a speckled dace subspecies (*Rhinichthys osculus carringtoni*) occur as disjunct populations in the Bonneville Basin and upper Snake River (La Rivers 1962; Simpson and Wallace 1982). The least chub (*Iotichthys phlegethontis*), the smallest North American minnow, is now only in the LeLand Harris Springs and Gandy Salt Marsh in Snake Valley, southwest Bonneville Basin (Crawford 1979). Museum records show that until recently it had a patchy basinwide presence, in the lower Bear River, Big Cottonwood Creek and other waters around Salt Lake City, the Provo River and Utah Lake, and Parowan Creek in the south.

The Bonneville Basin had no outflow to the Pacific Ocean until the late Pleistocene (McCoy 1987). Change to an open system began about 35,000 YBP (years before the present) when volcanism at Lava Hot Springs, Idaho, forced the Bear River south into the Bonneville Basin (Bright 1963). Until then, the Bear River had been a north-flowing tributary of the upper Snake River. Split apart from remaining Snake River populations was the ancestor to the unnamed Bear Lake cutthroat trout subspecies (Allendorf and Leary 1988). Thus, the Bonneville system has at least two cutthroat trout lineages (Behnke 1981). The subspecies in the Bonneville Basin proper, the Bonneville cutthroat trout (*O. c. utah*) (Hickman and Duff 1978), came from the Snake River much earlier in the Pleistocene (Smith 1978; Minckley, Hendrickson, and Bond 1986; Leary et al. 1987).

In the Bonneville Basin, the bluehead sucker (*Catostomus discobolus*) lives only in the Bear River but elsewhere inhabits the Portneuf, Green, and Colorado rivers (Simpson and Wallace 1982; Tyus et al. 1982). Bear River hydrologic history is paralleled by this distribution. The Bear River was first a Green River tributary; it flowed next to the upper Snake River (Minckley, Hendrickson, and Bond 1986), and then shifted into the Bonneville Basin. The Portneuf River had been the lower stretch of the Bear River before volcanic damming (Bright 1963). It enters the upper Snake River at Pocatello, Idaho. Divergence from the upper Snake River explains also why the Paiute sculpin (*Cottus beldingi*) is in the Bear River and otherwise in the Columbia River system (Wydoski and Whitney 1979).

The Bear River diversion doubled the amount of water entering the Bonneville Basin. This increase created Pluvial Lake Bonneville, 335 m (1,099 ft) deep with an area of 51,700 sq km (19,961 sq mi) (Currey, Atwood, and Mabey 1984). This lake is comparable in size to present-day Lake Michigan. By 15,300 YBP, Lake Bonneville filled to maximum capacity—the Bonneville level—and began spilling into the upper Snake River (Currey 1990). Water could then reach the Pacific Ocean via the Columbia River.

The Utah chub (*G. atraria*), leatherside chub (*G. copei*), and Utah sucker (*C. ardens*) live in the upper Snake River (Simpson and Wallace 1982). These and other Bonneville Basin fishes invaded through the overflow channel (Hubbs and Miller 1948). Glaciers blocked their access to headwaters in what is now Grand Teton National Park and Yellowstone National Park, Wyoming, until 13,000 YBP (Harrington 1985; Currey 1990). Upon entering the upper Snake River, Bonneville Basin species might have made up most of the fishes there. Volcanism or other catastrophic events possibly eliminated an earlier fauna after the formation of Shoshone Falls (Hubbs and Miller 1948; Malde 1965). This loss is evidenced by a lack of Columbia River fishes above this barrier (Simpson and Wallace 1982; McPhail and Lindsey 1986).

The Bonneville level lasted until the overflow threshold near Red Rock Pass, Idaho, collapsed 14,500 YBP (Currey 1990). This event caused a year-long flood of great intensity down the Snake and Columbia rivers (Malde 1968). As much as 25,000,000 cubic m (32,699,000 cubic yd) of water per second spilled from Lake Bonneville, about one-half the flow from all rivers into oceans today. Moderate spillover to the Snake River resumed when the new Provo-level threshold was reached. However, the 108-m (354-ft) drop in depth cut off some valleys from Lake Bonneville (Currey, Atwood, and Mabey 1984). Fishes in those regions are the oldest isolates stemming from this pluvial water body (for example, Utah chubs in Rush Valley, south of Tooele) (Rosenfeld 1990).

A shift to a drier climate (Madsen and Currey 1979; Benson et al.

1990) stopped flow to the upper Snake River and returned the Bonneville Basin to an insular state 14,200 YBP (Currey 1990). Upper Snake River and Bonneville Basin fishes have been separated since then. Tectonic faulting helped to isolate Bear Lake from the Bear River and the Bonneville Basin proper in the early Holocene (12,000 to 10,000 YBP) (Spencer et al. 1984). This disjunction lasted until completion of an artificial channel between the Bear River and Bear Lake in 1918 (McConnell, Clark, and Sigler 1957).

On average, the Great Salt Lake has blanketed 2,400 sq km (927 sq mi) at a maximum depth of 8.3 m (27 ft) (Currey, Atwood, and Mabey 1984). This size contrasts with the shrinkage of Lake Bonneville to a surface area of 300 sq km (116 sq mi) 12,000 to 11,000 YBP (Spencer et al. 1984). Desiccation polygons on the bottom of the Great Salt Lake are relicts of this extreme lowstand, and from the air, these can be seen off the west coast of Antelope Island.

From 10,900 to 10,300 YBP, water rose to the Gilbert level, more than 10 m (32.8 ft) above the historic mean shoreline of the Great Salt Lake (Currey 1990). During this period, fresh water coursed from marshy Lake Gunnison (now the Sevier Dry Lake, terminus of the Sevier River) near Delta, Utah, through the Great Salt Desert (via the Old River Bed) to the southern end of 17,000-sq-km (6,564-sq-mi) Lake Gilbert (Currey, Oviatt, and Plyer 1983).

A diluted Lake Gilbert probably contained fish (Rosenfeld 1990), but it receded to fishless Great Salt Lake levels around 10,000 YBP (Currey 1990). Since then, Bonneville Basin subdrainages (for example, Blue Creek Valley, Utah Valley, Skull Valley, Curlew Valley, Snake Valley, and Salt Lake Valley) have maintained, for the most part, their current separateness as have local fish populations within these regions (Currey, Atwood, and Mabey 1984).

Wetter circumstances than those of today existed in the Bonneville Basin 3,000 to 2,000 YBP (Currey 1990) and 400 to 200 YBP (that is, the Little Ice Age) (Grove 1988). Genetic similarities among Utah chub isolates in the Great Salt Desert or Rush Valley are due partly to channels that flowed then between inhabited water bodies (Rosenfeld 1990). The Great Salt Lake is too saline for native fishes (Smith 1978; Wurtsbaugh and Berry 1990). During these wetter periods, a general dilution and freshwater plumes or overflow channels (Wetzel 1983), in consort with moderate salt tolerance (Westenfelder et al. 1988), may have allowed the Utah chub to frequent the Great Salt Lake.

The Bonneville whitefish (*Prosopium spilonotus*), Bonneville cisco (*P. gemmifer*), Bear Lake whitefish (*P. abyssicola*), and maybe a fourth *Prosopium* species exist only in Bear Lake (White 1974; Sigler and Workman 1978). These fishes and the Bear Lake sculpin (*Cottus extensus*) make up the greatest number of species unique to a single North

American lake. The whitefishes could have speciated there since lakes have been in Bear Lake Valley over several millions of years (Minckley, Hendrickson, and Bond 1986). Bonneville whitefish and Bonneville cisco bones are in Lake Bonneville deposits from Salt Lake County (Stokes, Smith, and Horn 1964; Smith, Stokes, and Horn 1968) and the Great Salt Desert (Oviatt 1984). The remains could mean that these fishes evolved in the Bonneville Basin and entered Bear Lake via the Bear River after 35,000 YBP. Alternately, they could stem from Bear Lake dispersals to the Bonneville Basin after the Bear River diversion.

Late Pleistocene and Holocene isolation has led to morphological differences among fish populations (Hayes 1935; Hubbs, Miller, and Hubbs 1974; Smith 1978). Twelve thousand years of separation may have been enough to split a lake-adapted sculpin into forms considered separate species: the recently extinct Utah Lake sculpin (*Cottus echinatus*) and the Bear Lake sculpin (*C. extensus*) (Bailey and Bond 1963). More often, longer times—hundreds of thousands or millions of years—seem necessary for speciation (Smith 1981b).

An undescribed dace (*Rhinichthys* sp.) inhabits Snake Valley and the adjacent Fish Springs Flats, while speckled dace (*R. osculus*) live over the rest of the Bonneville Basin (Miller 1984; Minckley, Hendrickson, and Bond 1986). Although the morphological distinctness of the undescribed dace permits a species level discrimination (Miller 1984), it does not indicate genetic distance from speckled dace and, hence, when the two fishes became separated. Protein electrophoretic studies confirm an undescribed dace so distinct from speckled dace (fixed allelic differences and unique variants at some loci) (Rosenfeld, unpublished data) that they must have been apart much longer than the 10,000 or 12,000 years implied by some (Miller 1984).

The undescribed dace may be an older Bonneville Basin endemic now relegated to the Snake Valley region. Alternately, it may have evolved there. For example, the Little Valley lake cycle, 150,000 to 130,000 YBP, left a large silt deposit at the mouth of Snake Valley. This barrier prevented flows in or out for over 100,000 years (McCoy 1987). If the undescribed dace evolved in Snake Valley, it spread into Fish Springs Flats once Lake Bonneville flooded the region (Currey, Oviatt, and Plyer 1983). More extensive dispersals could have been prevented by competition with speckled dace and an aversion by dace to lakes (Hubbs, Miller, and Hubbs 1974).

The June sucker (*Chasmistes liorus*) is known only from Utah Lake, but it had been more widespread in Lake Bonneville (Smith, Stokes, and Horn 1968). Its ancestor may have come from the Snake River. *Chasmistes* was there during Miocene times (Smith 1975; Miller and Smith 1981). Members of this genus lived also in Pliocene Lake Idaho in what is now the Snake River of southwest Idaho, and the Bonneville Basin connected several times with the Snake River during the Miocene, Pliocene, and Pleistocene (Hubbs and Miller 1948; Smith 1975). Among living *Chasmistes*, the June sucker may be most closely related to the cui-ui, *C. cujus*, of Pyramid Lake in the Lahontan Basin, Nevada (Miller and Smith 1981). Maybe the June sucker originated from a lineage isolated by the separation of the Bonneville and Lahontan basins in Pliocene times (Minckley, Hendrickson, and Bond 1986). Miller and Smith thought that because of certain morphological differences the June sucker and cui-ui may not share the same immediate ancestor.

The June sucker hybridizes with the Utah sucker. This cross had occurred naturally at lower frequencies until drought in the late 1920s greatly reduced the volume of Utah Lake (Tanner 1936). Crosses during or since this lowstand have resulted in a morphological shift among June suckers in the direction of Utah sucker. This shift is reflected today with two scientific names, one for the earlier nonhybridized entities, *C. liorus liorus*, and another for the introgressed form seen today, *C. liorus mictus* (Miller and Smith 1981).

Do June suckers exist in the upper Snake River, albeit with Utah sucker genes as in the Utah Lake population? Recall that Lake Bonneville flowed into the upper Snake River for a long time. Dispersals by June sucker into the upper Snake River would have seemed a likely circumstance. In 1928, a *Chasmistes* × Utah sucker hybrid was caught in the upper Snake River at Jackson Lake, Wyoming (Miller and Smith 1981). Simon (1946) listed *Catostomus fecundus* as the most common sucker in Jackson Lake, Wyoming. This was the name given by Cope and Yarrow (1875) to suckers in Utah Lake found later to have genes from Utah and June suckers (Miller and Smith 1981). Today, a *Chasmistes* ancestry for Jackson Lake suckers seems a forgotten option. Without any morphological or molecular bases, fisheries workers there consider them now to be Utah suckers (Wyoming Game and Fish Department, personal communication). In any case, Miller and Smith described a new species, *C. murei*, from the specimen caught in the 1920s. They felt that *C. murei* was an upper Snake River relict stemming from before the early Pleistocene, when the Snake River was still a drainage independent of the Columbia River (Wheeler and Cook 1954). This assessment is not conclusive and an alternate hypothesis seems reasonable. Miller and Smith assessed only morphology. The molecular genetics of *C. murei* remain uninvestigated. Within species, varied morphologies exist due to biotic and abiotic differences among habitats (Barlow 1961; Hubbs, Miller, and Hubbs 1974; Smith 1981a). Could these variations explain differences between Utah Lake *C. liorus* and the upper Snake River specimen? Also, the morphological consequences of hybridization are difficult to predict or assess, but they can entail traits beyond the limits of the parental species (Leary et al. 1983). The type specimen of *C. murei* is of hybrid origin, and the effects of a mixed genome remain unexplored.

CHAPTER 4

Keys to Native and Introduced Fishes

Gerald R. Smith

Dichotomous keys are artificial classifications used to separate and identify living organisms. In this chapter, fishes are identified or "keyed" using a system of dichotomous statements, that is, at each step the reader has two choices. Characteristics to be used in the key are selected not for their biological or phylogenetic relationships but for clarity in making the choices. If, for instance, you start with the first pair of statements in the key below, the choices are:

1a. Belly scales form a hard, sharp, sawtooth keel (Fig. 00); more than 60 gill rakers on the first arch . . . . **Clupeidae**, HERRINGS

or

1b. Belly scales mostly rounded, without a sawtooth keel (Fig. 00); fewer than 50 gill rakers on first arch 2

If the specimen being keyed has hard, sharp, belly scales forming a sawtooth keel or has more than 60 gill rakers on the first arch, it is a herring of the family Clupeidae. If it does not meet either of these specifications, the reader progresses to couplet 1b, which then progresses to couplet 2a and 2b, which again present alternative choices. In this fashion, an undetermined specimen can be identified to family, to genus, and finally to species.

Key to Families of Utah Fishes

1a) Belly scales form a hard, sharp, sawtooth keel (Fig. 4.1.a); more than 60 gill rakers on first gill arch . . . . **Clupeidae**, HERRINGS
1b) Belly mostly rounded, without a sawtooth keel (Fig. 4.1.b); fewer than 50 gill rakers on first gill arch (Fig 4.8.g) 2

2a) Adipose fin present (Fig. 4.1.b) 3
2b) Adipose fin absent (Fig. 4.1.d) 4

3a) Large, serrated pectoral spines present; 4 pairs of barbels on snout and around mouth; no scales (Fig. 4.1.c)
. . . . **Ictaluridae**, CATFISHES

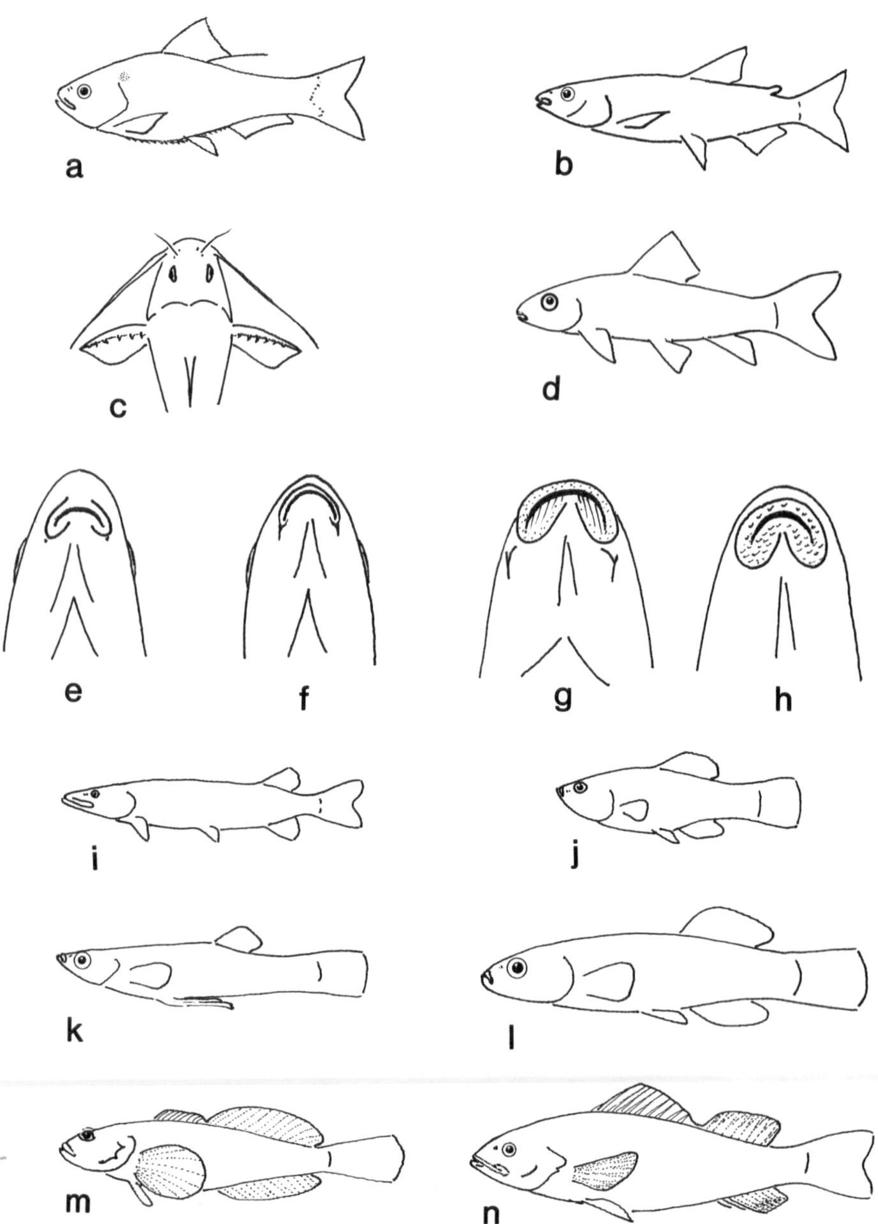

4.1. a. Clupeidae, sawtooth belly, elongate last dorsal ray, no adipose fin; b. Salmonidae, adipose fin present, no pectoral spines or barbels; c. Ictaluridae, pectoral spines and barbels present; d. Cypriniformes, no pectoral spines or lengthy barbels, dorsal fin mostly ahead of anal fin, no second dorsal fin, no scales on cheeks; e-f. Cyprinidae, no jaw teeth, lips thin with no visible sensory structures; g-h. Catostomidae, no jaw teeth, lips fleshy with visible sensory structures; i. Esocidae, pointed caudal fin lobes, large mouth; j. Cyprinodontiformes, rounded caudal lobes, small mouth; k. Poeciliidae, concave snout profile, modified anal fin in males; l. Fundulidae, rounded snout, anal fin not modified; m. Cottidae, first dorsal spines flexible, fin rays (except caudal) unbranched; n. Percoidei, dorsal spines sharp, fin rays branched.

3b) Large pectoral spines and barbels absent, scales present (Fig. 4.1.b) ..... **Salmonidae**, WHITEFISH, GRAYLING, TROUT, AND SALMON

4a) Jaws with no teeth (Fig. 4.1.e–h); dorsal fin positioned mostly ahead of anal fin and above pelvic fins (Fig. 4.1.d); second dorsal fin absent (Fig. 4.1.d); head and cheeks with no scales
.... **Order Cypriniformes** 5
4b) Jaws with teeth; soft-rayed dorsal fin mostly over anal fin, less above pelvic fins (Fig. 4.1.i–n); head and cheeks with scales 6

5a) Lips fleshy, with visible sensory papillae or ridges; mouth ventral or subterminal (Fig. 4.1.g–h); 18 principal caudal rays; more than 17 pharyngeal teeth on each arch.......... **Catostomidae**, SUCKERS
5b) Lips thin, without visible sensory structures, mouth usually terminal or subterminal (Fig. 4.1.e–f); 19 principal caudal rays; fewer than 10 pharyngeal teeth on each arch..... **Cyprinidae**, MINNOWS

6a) Dorsal fin single and small (Fig. 4.1.i–l); pelvic fins on abdomen as close or closer to anal fin than to pectoral fin (Fig. 7.1.i–l); pelvic, dorsal, and anal fins without spines 7
6b) Dorsal fin large with two parts (Fig. 4.1.m–n); pelvic fin under pectoral fin (Fig. 4.1.m–n); pelvic with 1 spine; dorsal and anal spines present (flexible in sculpins) 9

7a) Caudal fin large with two pointed lobes (Fig. 4.1.i); mouth much larger than eye diameter (Fig. 4.1.i); bladelike teeth in jaws and roof of mouth; adult length longer than 12 cm
.... **Esocidae** (NORTHERN PIKE)
7b) Caudal fin not forked, mouth and teeth small (Fig. 4.1.j–l), body length less than 12 cm .... **Order Cyprinodontiformes** 8

8a) Profile of upper snout convex in side view (Fig. 4.1.l); mouth rounded as seen from above; gill rakers fewer than 10; anal fins broadly rounded in both sexes (Fig. 4.1.l); egg layers
.... **Fundulidae**, TOPMINNOWS
8b) Snout concave or flat above (Fig. 4.1.k); mouth square as seen from above; gill rakers more than 12; anal fin in males slender and pointed (Fig. 4.1.k); not egg layers
.... **Poeciliidae**, LIVEBEARERS (WESTERN MOSQUITOFISH)

9a) First dorsal fin with soft spines; head wider than deep; pectoral fin large; eyes dorsal; dorsal, anal, and pectoral fin rays unbranched (Fig. 4.1.m) .... **Cottidae**, SCULPINS

9b) Dorsal spines hard and sharp; head not usually wider than deep; eyes lateral; most fin rays deeply branched (Fig. 4.1.n) . . . . **Suborder Percoidei** 10

10a) Two dorsal fins connected (Fig. 4.2.a), the last spine of the spiny dorsal fin reaches and overlaps the first spine of the second dorsal fin (Fig. 4.2.a); usually a conspicuous pigment spot on opercular flap (Fig. 4.2.a) . . . . **Centrarchidae**, SUNFISH
10b) Two dorsal fins clearly divided (Fig. 4.2.b), the last spine of the spiny dorsal does not overlap the first spine of the second dorsal fin (Fig. 4.2.b); no conspicuous pigment spot over opercular spine (Fig. 4.2.b) 11

11a) Anal spines 3 (Fig. 4.2.c); partial gill with about 20 distinct filaments on inside surface of gill cover (Fig. 4.2.d) . . . . **Moronidae**, TEMPERATE BASSES
11b) Anal spines 2 (Fig. 4.2.b); partial gill on inside of gill cover with rudimentary filaments (Fig. 4.2.d) . . . . **Percidae**, PERCH and WALLEYE

Key to Herrings (Clupeidae) in Utah

1a) Upper and lower jaws about equal; tail not yellow; scales small, 55 or more lateral series; anal fin rays 29–35 . . . . GIZZARD SHAD (*Dorosoma cepedianum*)
1b) Lower jaw longer than upper; tail yellow; scales large, 50 or fewer lateral series; anal fin rays 20–25 . . . . THREADFIN SHAD (*Dorosoma petenense*)

Key to Catfishes (Ictaluridae) in Utah

1a) Caudal fin distinctly forked, with pointed lobes (Fig. 4.3.a) . . . . CHANNEL CATFISH (*Ictalurus punctatus*)
1b) Caudal fin square or slightly rounded at posterior margin, not forked (Fig. 4.3.b) . . . . BULLHEADS (*Ameiurus*) 2

2a) Chin barbels white (Fig. 4.3.c); total number of anal fin rays more than 23 . . . . YELLOW BULLHEAD (*Ameiurus natalis*)
2b) Chin barbels dark (Fig. 4.3.d); total number of anal fin rays fewer than 22 . . . . BLACK BULLHEAD (*Ameiurus melas*)

Key to Suckers (Catostomidae) in Utah

1a) Left and right lobes of lower lips separated by a broad notch (Fig. 4.4.c) 2

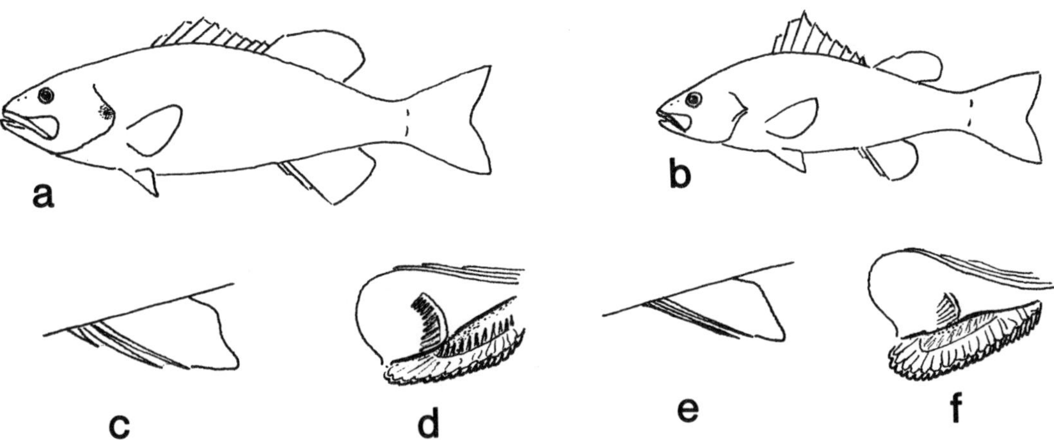

4.2. a. Centrarchidae, dorsal fins connected, pigment on opercular flap; b. Percidae and Moronidae, dorsal fins separated, no spot on opercular flap; c. Moronidae, 3 anal rays; d. Moronidae, numerous well-developed pseudobranchs on inside of gill cover (lifted right opercle shown); e. Percidae, 2 anal spines; f. Percidae, inside of gill cover with rudimentary pseudobranchs.

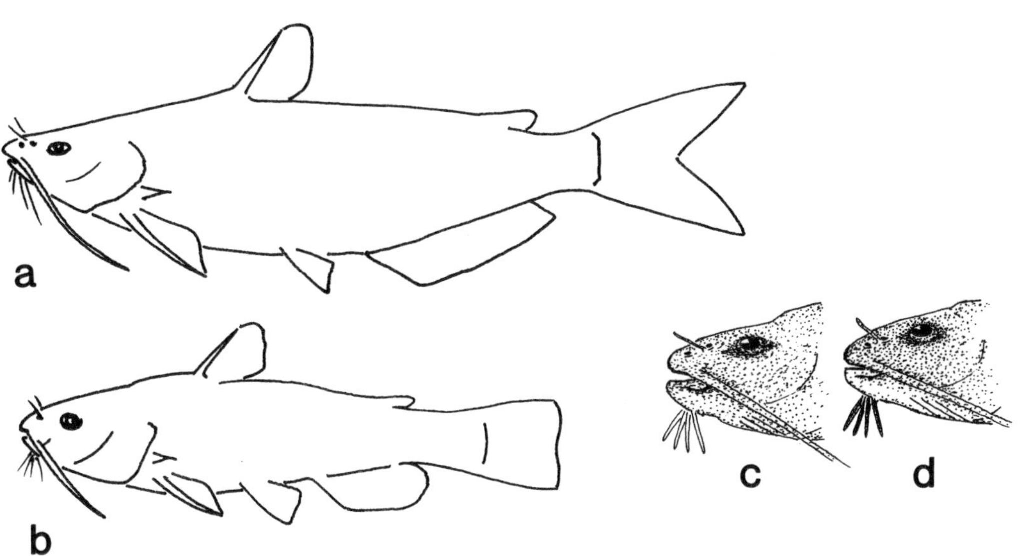

4.3. a. *Ictalurus punctatus*, forked caudal fin with pointed lobes; b. *Ameiurus*, unforked caudal fin with rounded lobes; c. *Ameiurus natalis*, pale chin barbels; d. *Ameiurus melas* black chin barbels.

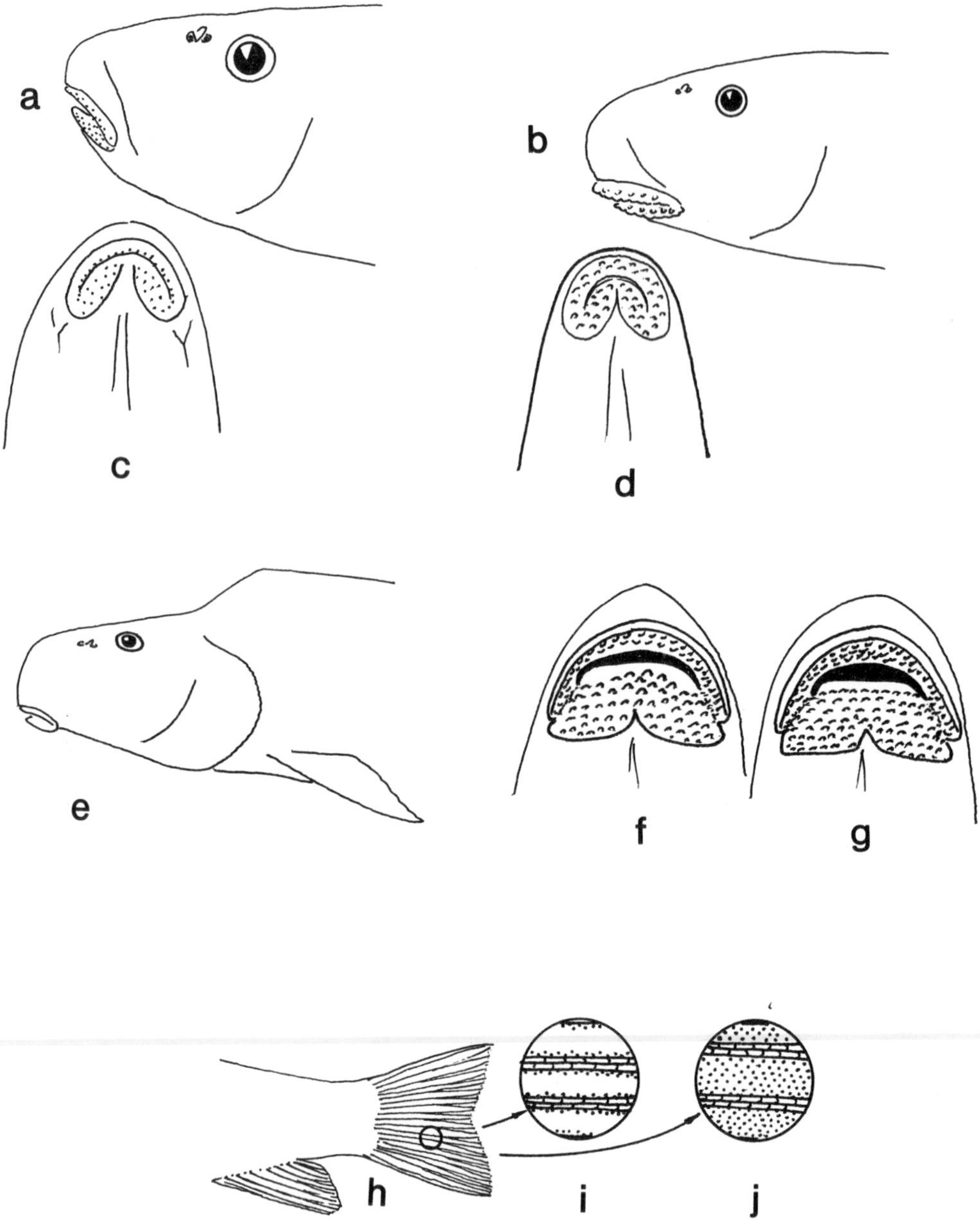

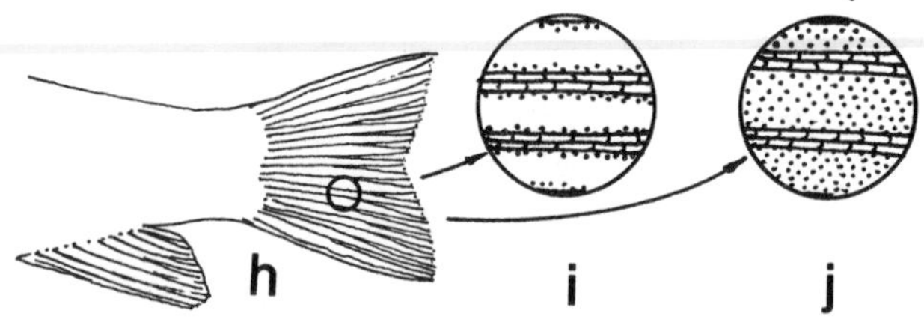

4.4. a. *Chasmistes liorus*, subterminal mouth; b. *Catostomus*, ventral mouth; c. *Chasmistes liorus*, gap between lower lip lobes (also in *Xyrauchen*), rudimentary sensory papillae, d. *Catostomus*, connected lower lip lobes, well-developed sensory papillae; e. *Xyrauchen texanus*, nuchal keel, long face, ventral mouth; f. *Catostomus platyrhynchus*, notched lip corners, rosette of papillae on anterior edge of lower lip; g. *Catostomus clarki* and *discobolus*, notched lip corners, lower lip papillae in straight line at leading edge; h, *Catostomus*, deep caudal peduncle; i. *Catostomus platyrhynchus*, spotless caudal fin membranes; j. *Catostomus discobolus* and *clarki*, pigmented caudal fin membranes.

1b) Lobes of lower lips connected, not separated by a notch (Fig. 4.4.d) 3

2a) Mouth ventral (Fig. 4.4.e); lips papillose (Fig. 4.4.b), nuchal keel present Fig. 4.4.e) . . . . . RAZORBACK SUCKER (*Xyrauchen texanus*)
2b) Mouth subterminal; lips with weak papillae (Fig. 4.4.a,c); no nuchal keel (Fig. 4.4.a) . . . . JUNE SUCKER (*Chasmistes liorus*)

3a) Lips rounded at outer corners, with no notch; jaws without cartilaginous scraping edges (Fig. 4.4.d) 4
3b) Lips notched at the outer corners; jaws with cartilaginous scraping edges (Fig. 4.4.f,g) 6

4a) Scales large, fewer than 74 in lateral line; lower lip not enlarged (Fig. 4.4.d) 5
4b) Scales smaller, more than 80 in lateral line; lower lip lobes elongate . . . . FLANNELMOUTH SUCKER (*Catostomus latipinnis*)

5a) Dorsal rays usually 12 or 13; gill rakers on first arch more than 31 . . . . UTAH SUCKER (*Catostomus ardens*)
5b) Dorsal rays usually 11; gill rakers on first arch fewer than 32 (Fig. 4.8.h). . . . . WHITE SUCKER (*Catostomus commersonni*)

6a) Dorsal rays usually 10; anterior papillae on lower lip arranged in a central rosette pattern, with flat area on either side (Fig. 4.4.f); caudal fin membranes unpigmented between rays (Fig. 4.4.i) . . . . MOUNTAIN SUCKER (*Catostomus platyrhynchus*)
6b) Dorsal rays usually 11; anterior papillae in a broad line behind cartilaginous jaw edge (Fig. 4.4.i); caudal fin with abundant pigment cells on membranes between rays (Fig 4.4.j) 7

7a) Predorsal scales small, 43 or more rows between head and dorsal fin origin; caudal peduncle slender (Fig. 4.6.e.f) in Colorado drainage, thicker in Weber and Bear drainages; color often bluish or greenish above . . . . . . BLUEHEAD SUCKER (*Catostomus discobulus*)
7b) Predorsal scales larger, usually 42 or fewer rows between head and dorsal fin origin; caudal peduncle deeper (Fig. 4.4.h); color tan above . . . . DESERT SUCKER (*Catostomus clarki*)

Key to Minnows (Cyprinidae) in Utah

1a) Dorsal fin with more than 14 rays (Fig. 4.5.a); dorsal and anal fins each with one large serrated spine (Fig. 4.5.a) . . . . (CARP and GOLDFISH) 2

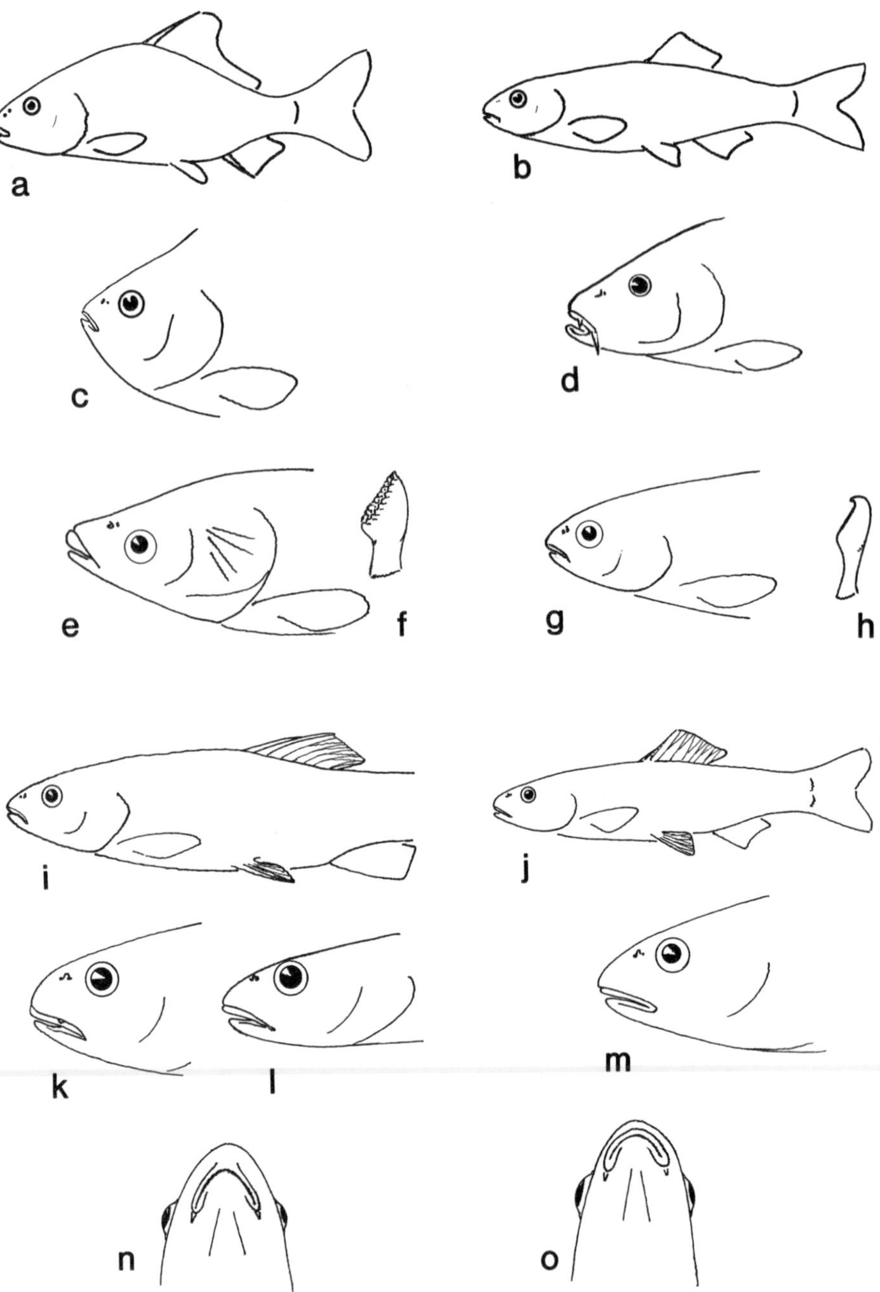

4.5. a. carp and goldfish, long dorsal fin with spine; b. American minnows, short dorsal fin, usually without spines; c. goldfish, no barbels; d. carp, with barbels; e. grass carp, low eyes, thick lip; f. grass carp, pharyngeal teeth with ridges; g. American minnows, high eyes, usually thin lips; h. American minnows, pharyngeal teeth without ridges; i. spinedace, dorsal and pelvic spines; j. non-spiny minnows; k. *Semotilus atromaculatus*, barbel above maxilla, mouth large; l. dace, barbel at end of maxilla, mouth small; m. minnow, no barbels; n. *Rhinichthys cataractae*, no groove between long snout and upper lip; *Rhinichthys osculus*, groove between snout and upper lip.

1b) Dorsal fin with fewer than 12 rays (Fig. 4.5.b); dorsal (usually) and anal fins without spines (Fig. 4.5.b), dorsal spines, if present, double and not serrated (4.4.i). 3

2a) Mouth without barbels (Fig. 4.5.c); more than 35 gill rakers on first arch (Fig. 4.8.g); pharyngeal teeth 4–4 (Fig. 4.6.l), not molariform . . . . GOLDFISH (*Carassius auratus*)
2b) Mouth with 2 barbels on each side of upper jaw (Fig. 4.5.d); fewer than 30 gill rakers on first arch (Fig. 4.6.h); pharyngeal teeth in more than one row on each side, molariform
. . . . CARP (*Cyprinus carpio*)

3a) Position of anal fin relatively close to caudal fin (Fig. 4.4.h), distance from anal fin origin to caudal base is 1/3 distance from anal fin origin to snout; head wide and flattened between eyes; eyes nearly centered on side of head (Fig. 4.5.e); upper lip thickened anteriorly (Fig. 4.5.e); pharyngeal teeth with strong ridges (Fig. 4.5.f)
. . . . GRASS CARP (*Ctenopharyngodon idella*)
3b) Anal fin origin closer to center of body (Fig. 4.5.b), distance from anal origin to caudal base less than or equal to 1/2 the distance from the anal origin to snout; head rounded; eyes in upper part of head (Fig. 4.5.g); pharyngeal teeth lacking strong ridges (Fig. 4.5.h)
. . . . 4

4a) Front of dorsal fin with 2 smooth spines (Fig. 4.5.i); pelvic fins with 1 smooth spine and internal margin broadly attached to body (Fig. 4.5.i). . . . . SPINEDACE 5
4b) Dorsal fin with segmented rays but no spines (Fig. 4.5.j); pelvic fins with branched and segmented rays, connected to body only at the fin base (Fig. 4.5.j) 6

5a) Body wholly silver colored; no scales; barbel at posterior end of upper jaw (Fig. 4.5.l); anal rays 10
. . . . WOUNDFIN (*Plagopterus argentissimus*)
5b) Body countershaded, colorful on back and sides and pale below; 80–90 scale rows; no barbel at posterior end of upper jaw (Fig. 4.5.m); anal rays 8 or 9
. . . . VIRGIN RIVER SPINEDACE (*Lepidomeda mollispinis*)

6a) Barbel at the posterior end of the maxilla (upper jaw, Fig. 4.5.l) or a barbel-like flap of skin in groove above the maxilla (Fig. 4.5.k); scales small, 50–80 lateral rows 7
6b) No barbel or barbel-like flap of skin near the end of the upper jaw (Fig. 4.5.m); scales large or small 9

7a) Barbel-like flap of skin in groove above maxilla (Fig. 4.5.k); mouth large, reaching to below pupil (Fig. 4.5.k)
. . . . CREEK CHUB (*Semotilus atromaculatus*)
7b) Barbel at end of maxilla (Fig. 4.5.l); mouth small, not reaching to below pupil (Fig. 4.5.l,n,o). . . . . DACE 8

8a) Snout elongated beyond mouth and connected to center of upper lip by a broad bridge of skin (Fig. 4.5.n)
. . . . LONGNOSE DACE (*Rhinichthys cataractae*)
8b) Snout projecting slightly ahead of mouth and separated from center of upper lip by a groove (Fig. 4.5.o)
. . . . SPECKLED DACE (*Rhinichthys osculus*)

9a) Scales small, more than 52 lateral rows, standard length usually more than 12 cm as adults (except in the redside shiner and leatherside chub) 10
9b) Scales large, fewer than 50 lateral rows (Fig. 4.8.i); standard length usually smaller than 12 cm as adults (except golden shiner, which may get larger, but is unique in having a keeled abdomen)
. . . . 17

10a) Scales larger, number of lateral rows 52–70. 11
10b) Scales smaller, number of lateral rows more than 70. 12

11a) Anal rays usually 8; dorsal origin directly above pelvic origin (Fig. 4.6.a) . . . . UTAH CHUB (*Gila atraria*)
11b) Anal rays 10–13; dorsal origin more posterior than pelvic origin (Fig. 4.6.b). . . . . REDSIDE SHINER (*Richardsonius balteatus*)

12a) Scales 70–80; adult size less than 15 cm; fins small, longest caudal rays slightly less than distance between dorsal and pelvic origins
. . . . LEATHERSIDE CHUB (*Gila copei*)
12b) More than 80 scales in lateral line; adult size more than 30 cm; fins large, longest caudal rays longer than distance between dorsal and pelvic origins 13

13a) Body slender, less than 1/4 standard length (Fig. 4.6.c); jaws long, upper jaw length equal to or greater than 1/2 body depth (Fig. 4.6.c); adult size over 45 cm
. . . . COLORADO SQUAWFISH (*Ptychocheilus lucius*)
13b) Body deeper, more than 1/4 standard length (Fig. 4.6.d–f); jaws shorter, upper jaw length less than 1/2 body depth (Fig. 4.6.d–f); adult size less than 45 cm
. . . . COLORADO RIVER CHUBS, 14

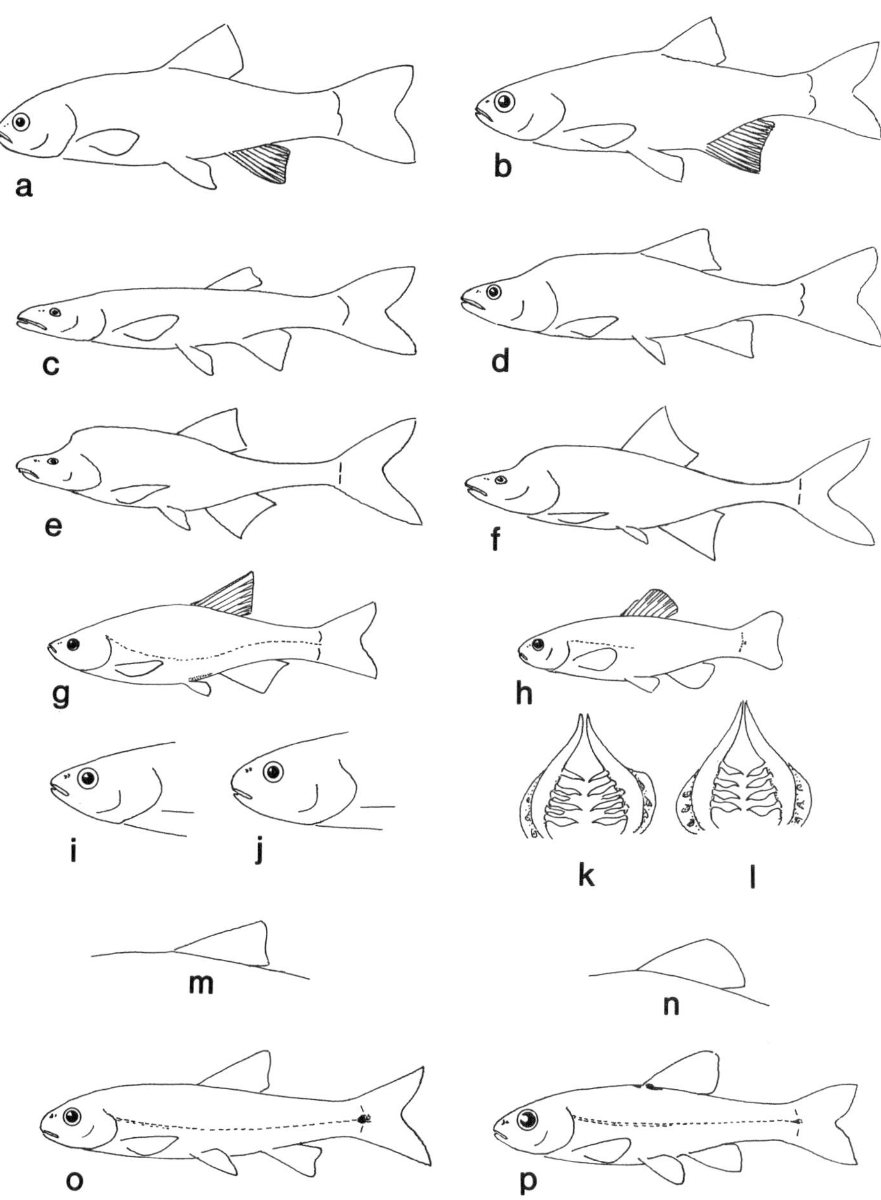

4.6. a. *Gila atraria*, dorsal fin origin above pelvic origin; b. *Richardsonius balteatus*, dorsal fin origin behind pelvic origin, anal fin large; c. *Ptychocheilus lucius*, slender body, large mouth; d. *Gila robusta robusta*, no steep hump, short caudal peduncle; e. *Gila cypha*, abrupt hump, snout overhangs upper lip; f. *Gila elegans*, steep but not abrupt hump; g. *Notemigonus crysoleucas*, belly keel, decurved lateral line, small upturned mouth; h. *Pimephales promelas*, first dorsal ray short and separate from next, lateral line incomplete; i. sharp snout, terminal mouth; j. blunt snout, subterminal mouth; k. pharyngeal teeth, dorsal view, formula 2,4-4,2; l. pharyngeal teeth, dorsal view, formula 4-4; m. *Notropis atherinoides*, first dorsal ray overlaps last dorsal ray when fin is depressed; n. *Cyprinella lutrensis*, first dorsal ray does not overlap last dorsal rays when depressed; o. *Notropis hudsonius*, round caudal spot; p. *Notropis stramineus*, wedge-shaped caudal spot, === on lateral line scales, broken spot at dorsal origin.

14a) Dorsal and anal rays usually 9; moderate deepening of body at the back of the head (Fig. 4.6.d); distance from anal origin to caudal base less than distance from anal origin to opercle (Fig. 4.6.d) . . 15
14b) Dorsal usually 9 or 10; anal rays usually 10 or 11; steep hump deepens the body at the back of the head in adults (Fig. 4.6.e,f); distance from anal origin to caudal base longer than distance from anal origin to opercle (Fig. 4.6.e,f); caudal peduncle extremely slender in adults (Fig. 4.6.e,f) 16

15a) Gill rakers 12–15 (Green and Colorado rivers)
. . . . COLORADO RIVER ROUNDTAIL CHUB (*Gila robusta robusta*)
15b) Gill rakers 15–19 (Virgin River) (as in Fig. 4.8.h)
. . . . . VIRGIN RIVER ROUNDTAIL CHUB (*Gila robusta seminuda*)

16a) Nuchal hump abrupt (Fig. 4.6.e); anal rays usually 10; snout overhangs upper lip (Fig. 4.6.e); young with eye diameter less than 2/3 caudal peduncle depth . . . . HUMPBACK CHUB (*Gila cypha*)
16b) Nuchal hump angled (Fig. 4.6.f); anal rays 10 or 11; snout does not overhang upper lip (Fig. 4.6.f); young with eye diameter greater than 2/3 caudal peduncle depth . . . BONYTAIL (*Gila elegans*)

17a) Lateral line absent; color pattern speckled
. . . . LEAST CHUB (*Iotichthys phlegethontis*)
17b) Lateral line present; pattern barred, striped, or plain 18

18a) Keel on belly behind pelvic fins (Fig. 4.6.g); lateral line strongly decurved (Fig. 4.6.g); pharyngeal teeth 5 in a single row on each arch; adult color golden, mouth small and angled upward (Fig. 4.6.g) . . . . GOLDEN SHINER (*Notemigonus crysoleucas*)
18b) Belly rounded behind pelvic fins; 4 pharyngeal teeth in main row; (Fig. 4.6.k or l); silver, brassy, or colorful; mouth variable . . 19

19a) Dorsal fin with a short anterior ray separated from first long ray by a membrane (Fig. 4.6.h); lateral line incomplete (Fig. 4.6.h); base of caudal peduncle with a black line slightly off vertical; predorsal scales small and crowded;
. . . . FATHEAD MINNOW (*Pimephales promelas*)
19b) Dorsal fin with the first principle (long) ray closely attached to the shorter ray ahead of it (Fig. 4.6.g); lateral line complete (Fig. 4.6.o); base of caudal not marked by oblique line; predorsal scales not smaller or more crowded than other scales 20

20a) Peritoneum black; intestine more than twice as long as body and much coiled on right side; color brassy; pharyngeal process flattened horizontally . . . . BRASSY MINNOW (*Hybognathus hankinsoni*)

20b) Peritoneum silvery; intestine less than twice body length; pharyngeal process vertical or rodlike; body silvery, straw-colored, emerald, or red 21

21a) Snout sharp, mouth terminal (Fig. 4.6.i). 22
21b) Snout blunt, mouth slightly ventral (Fig. 4.6.j) 23

22a) First dorsal rays extend to or beyond last rays when fin is depressed (Fig. 4.6.m); anal rays 10 or 11; pharyngeal teeth 2,4–4,2 (Fig. 4.6.k); lateral scales 35–38; body slender; color silver and emerald . . . . EMERALD SHINER (*Notropis atherinoides*)
22b) First dorsal rays do not extend to end of last rays when fin is depressed (Fig. 4.6.n); anal rays usually 9, sometimes 8 or 10; pharyngeal teeth 4–4 (Fig. 4.6.l); lateral scales 33–36; body deeper; not silver, breeding males red and blue
. . . . RED SHINER (*Cyprinella lutrensis*)

23a) Base of caudal fin with a large, rounded, black spot (Fig. 4.6.o); lateral scales 36–40, with faint dashes on lateral line scales
. . . . SPOTTAIL SHINER (*Notropis hudsonius*)
23b) Base of caudal fin with a small black wedge (Fig. 4.6.p); lateral scales 32–35, with black "equal signs" on anterior lateral line scales
. . . . SAND SHINER (*Notropis stramineus*)

Key to Species of Salmon, Trout, and Whitefish (Salmonidae) in Utah

1a) Teeth prominent on jaw bones (Fig. 4.7.a); scales small, more than 100 in lateral line (TROUT, SALMON, GRAYLING) 5
1b) Teeth absent or minute on jaw bones (Fig. 4.7.b); scales large, fewer than 95 lateral series (WHITEFISHES) 2

2a) Dorsal and anal fin rays usually 12 or 13; mouth moderate (Fig. 4.7.c). . . . . MOUNTAIN WHITEFISH (*Prosopium williamsoni*)
2b) Dorsal rays usually 10–12, anal rays usually 9–11 (BEAR LAKE WHITEFISHES) 3

3a) Gill rakers 18–23; snout blunt (Fig. 4.7.e,f) 4
3b) Gill rakers 37–45; snout elongate (Fig. 4.7.d)
. . . . BONNEVILLE CISCO (*Prosopium gemmifer*)

4a) Mouth size moderate; maxilla reaches to end of lacrimal (Fig. 4.7.e); lateral line scales 76–86; "Roman nosed" (Fig. 4.7.e); size large, reaching 40 cm
. . . . BONNEVILLE WHITEFISH (*Prosopium spilonotus*)

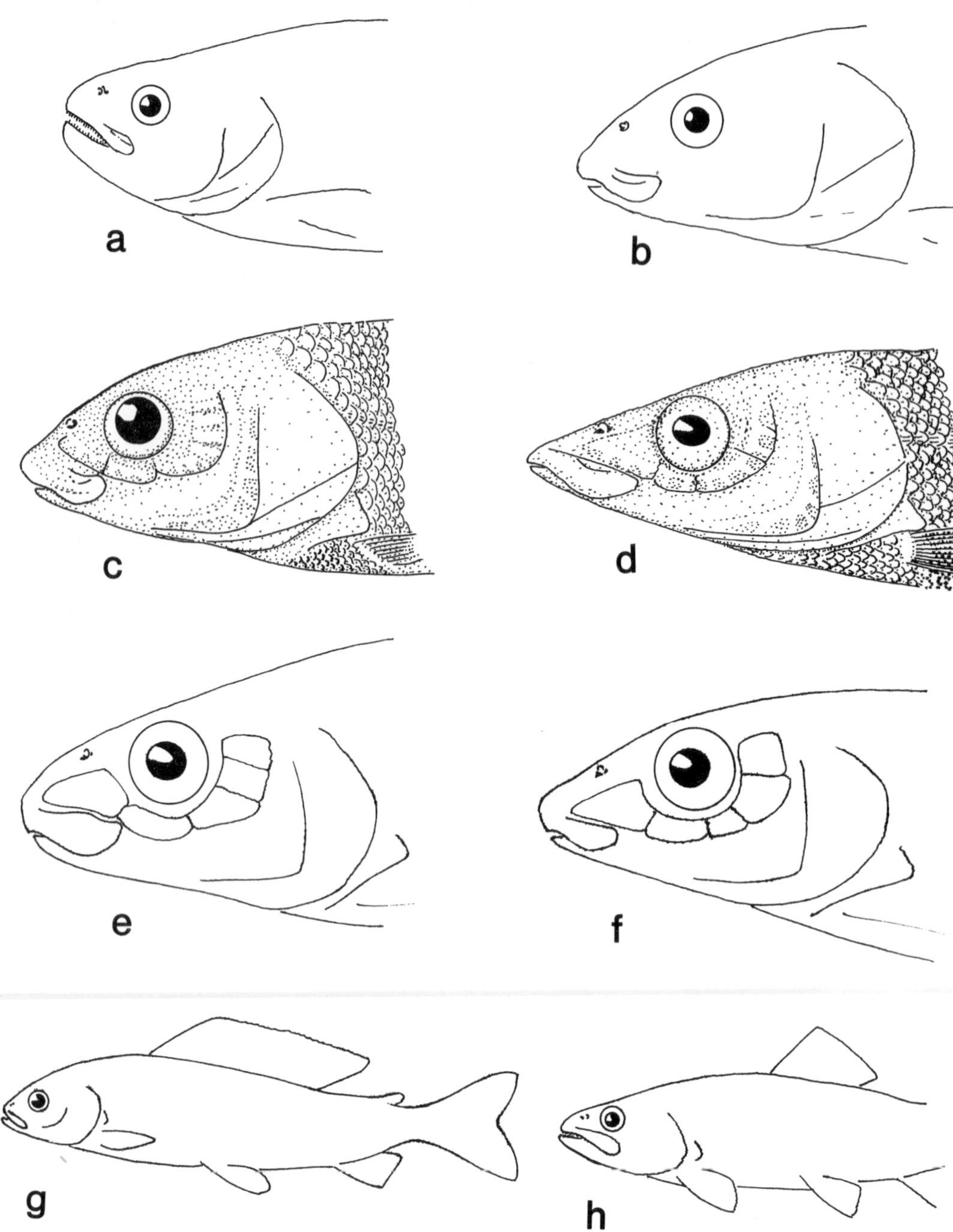

4.7. a. Salmoninae and Thymallinae, large terminal mouth with prominent jaw teeth; b. Coregoninae, small mouth without prominent jaw teeth; c. *Prosopium williamsoni*, moderate mouth size; d. *Prosopium gemmifer*, jaws elongate; e. *Prosopium spilonotum*, mouth size moderate, "Roman nose;" f. *Prosopium abyssicola*, mouth small, "peak nose;" g. *Thymallus arcticus*, large dorsal fin; h. Salmoninae, mouth large, small dorsal fin.

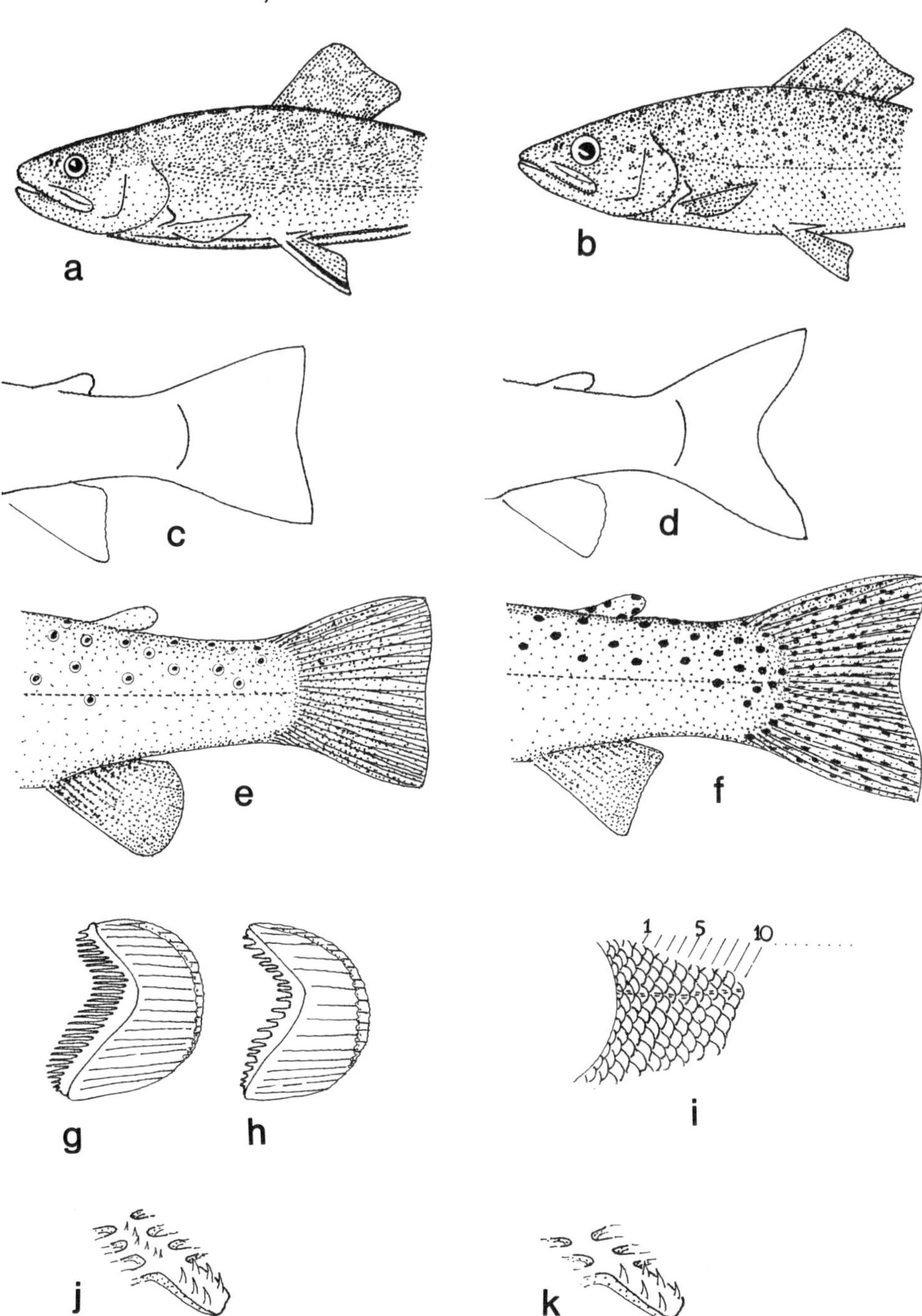

4.8. a. *Salvelinus*, light spots on dark background; b. *Oncorhynchus* dark spots on light background; c. *Salvelinus fontinalis* square caudal fin; d. *Salvelinus namaycush*, forked caudal fin; e. *Salmo trutta*, black and red spots with halos; no spots on caudal; f. *Oncorhynchus*, black spots on body and fins; g. *Oncorhynchus nerka kennerlyi*, more than 30 gill rakers; h. *Oncorhynchus clarki*, *aguabonita*, and *mykiss*, fewer than 22 gill rakers; i. how to count lateral scale series from opercle back to base of caudal fin; j. *Oncorhynchus clarki*, basibranchial teeth behind tongue teeth; k. *Oncorhynchus mykiss* and *aguabonita*, no basibranchial teeth behind tongue teeth.

4b) Mouth small; maxilla reaches halfway to end of lacrimal (Fig. 4.7.f); lateral scales 67–78, "peak nosed" (Fig. 4.7.f); size small, reaching to 25 cm
. . . . BEAR LAKE WHITEFISH (*Prosopium abyssicola*)

5a) Dorsal fin long (Fig. 4.7.g), with more than 17 rays; mouth size moderate (Fig. 4.7.g); teeth small; scales large, fewer than 100 in lateral line . . . . ARCTIC GRAYLING (*Thymallus arcticus*)
5b) Dorsal fin short (Fig. 4.7.h), with fewer than 14 rays; mouth large (Fig. 4.7.h); teeth large
. . . . (CHARS, TROUTS, AND SALMON) 6

6a) Spots on back lighter than background (Fig. 4.8.a)
. . . . (CHARS) 7
6b) Spots on back darker than background (Fig. 4.8.b)
. . . . (TROUTS, SALMONS) 8

7a) Caudal fin not deeply forked (Fig. 4.8.c); lower fins with black stripe behind light leading edge (Fig. 4.8.a); gill rakers 9–12
. . . . BROOK TROUT (*Salvelinus fontinalis*)
7b) Caudal fin deeply forked (Fig. 4.8.d); lower fins with pattern faint or absent, without black stripe; gill rakers 12–14
. . . . LAKE TROUT (*Salvelinus namaycush*)

8a) No spots on caudal fin (Fig. 4.8.e); background color tan to yellow, with black and red spots in halos (Fig. 4.8.e); young with orange on adipose fin . . . . BROWN TROUT (*Salmo trutta*)
8b) Spots present on caudal fin (Fig. 4.8.f); color silver, bluish above and with reddish or yellowish wash but not red spots; spots black on sides and back, never reddish and never with halos; young with olive adipose fin. PACIFIC TROUTS and SALMON

9a) Anal rays 13–15; gill rakers on first gill arch 31–44 (Fig. 4.8.g)
. . . . KOKANEE (*Oncorhynchus nerka kennerlyi*)
9b) Anal rays 8–12; gill rakers on first gill arch 14–22 (Fig. 4.8.h)
. . . . (PACIFIC TROUT) 10

10a) Scales small, usually 150–200 lateral rows (Fig. 4.8.i); red cutthroat mark present under each lower jawbone; sides usually with yellow or gold pigment, sometimes red-orange; parr marks present in adults; large dusky parr spot behind eye; basibranchial teeth present or absent 11
10b) Scales larger, usually 120–140 lateral rows; no cutthroat mark under lower jaw; sides greenish, rose, and silver; parr marks in young

only; spots behind eye, if present, small like other head spots; basibranchial teeth lost (Fig. 4.8.k)
. . . . RAINBOW TROUT *Oncorhynchus mykiss*

11a) Basibranchial teeth present on back of tongue (Fig. 4.8.j); red cutthroat mark present; tips of anal, dorsal, and pelvic fins plain
. . . . CUTTHROAT TROUT (*Oncorhynchus clarki*)
11b) Basibranchial teeth usually absent (Fig. 4.8.k); weak orange line under lower jaw; anal and dorsal fins rounded with cream to orange tips . . . . GOLDEN TROUT (*Oncorhynchus aguabonita*)

Key to Killifishes (Fundulidae) in Utah

1a) Snout much longer than eye diameter; color pattern of about 13 vertical bars; scales small, more than 50 lateral series
. . . . PLAINS KILLIFISH (*Fundulus zebrinus*)
1b) Snout usually shorter than eye diameter; color pattern cross-hatched over scale edges; scales large, fewer than 35 lateral series
. . . . RAINWATER KILLIFISH (*Lucania parva*)

Key to Sunfish and Bass (Centrarchidae) in Utah

1a) Anal spines 5–8, usually 6 (Fig. 4.9.a) 2
1b) Anal spines 3 (Fig. 4.9.b). 4

2a) Dorsal spines usually 11–13 (Fig. 4.9.a)
. . . . SACRAMENTO PERCH (*Archoplites interruptus*)
2b) Dorsal spines usually 6–8 (Fig. 4.9.c,d). 3

3a) Dorsal spines usually 7; distance from eye to first dorsal fin less than length of dorsal fin; color pattern black calico (Fig. 4.9.c)
. . . . BLACK CRAPPIE (*Pomoxis nigromaculatus*)
3b) Dorsal spines usually 6; distance from eye to first dorsal spine greater than length of dorsal fin; color pale with uneven vertical bands (Fig. 4.9.d) . . . . WHITE CRAPPIE (*Pomoxis annularis*)

4a) Jaws large, upper jaw extending to below center of pupil or beyond (Fig. 4.9.e,f); notch separating spiny and soft dorsal fins (Fig. 4.9.e,f); juveniles with multicolored caudal fin
. . . . BASS (*Micropterus*) 5
4b) Jaws small, upper jaw extending to below front of pupil or shorter (Fig. 4.9.g,h); spiny and soft dorsal fins broadly joined as one fin (Fig. 4.9.g,h); juveniles with plain caudal fin
. . . . SUNFISH (*Lepomis*) 6

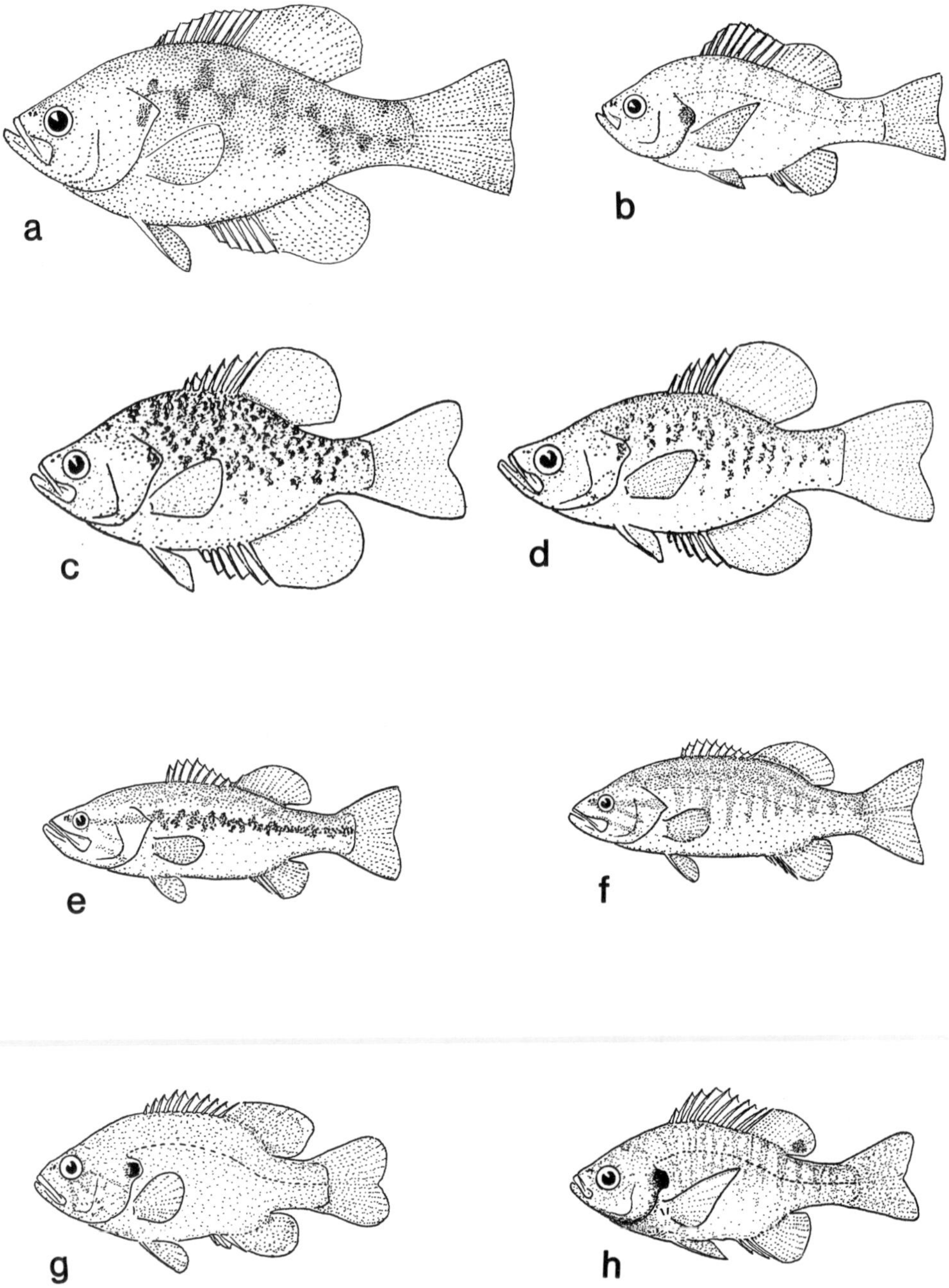

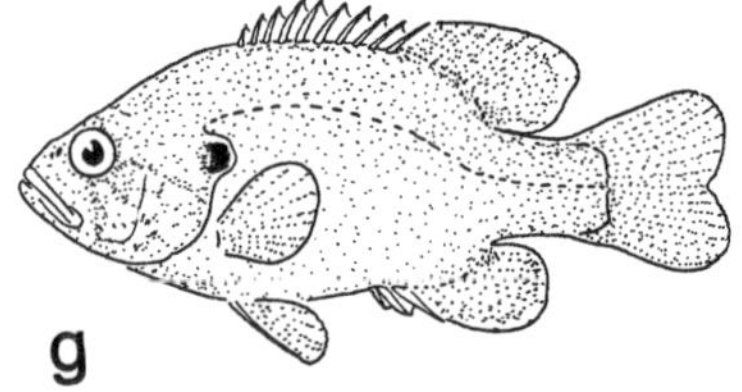

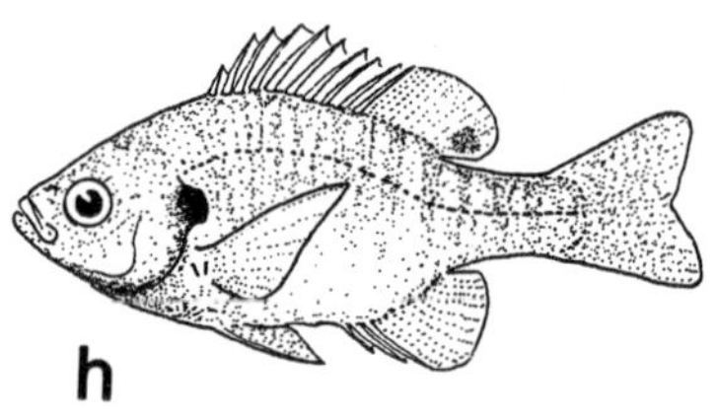

4.9. a. *Archoplites interruptus*, 6 anal spines and more than 10 dorsal spines; b. sunfish, 3 anal spines; c. *Pomoxis nigromaculatus*, 7 dorsal spines and long dorsal fin; d. *Pomoxis annularis*, 6 dorsal spines and short dorsal fin; e. *Micropterus salmoides*, large mouth, short dorsal spines, dark lateral stripe; f. *Micropterus dolomieui*, smaller mouth, longer dorsal spines, no dark lateral stripe; g. *Lepomis cyanellus*, large mouth, short dorsal spines, short pectoral fin; h. *Lepomis macrochirus*, small mouth, long dorsal spines, long pectoral fin.

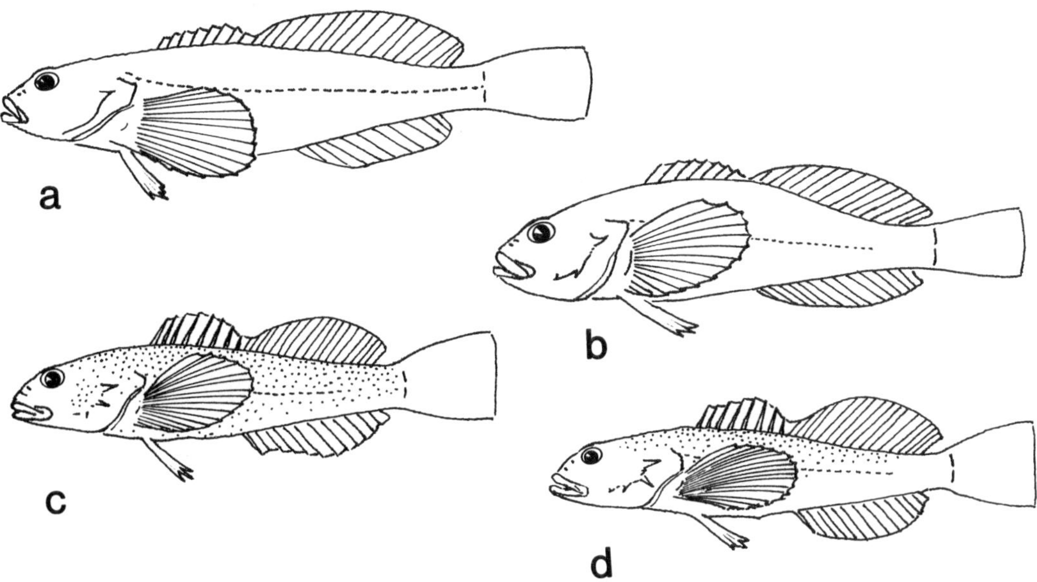

4.10. a. *Cottus beldingi*, single preopercular spine and complete lateral line; b. *Cottus bairdi*, four preopercular spines (often under skin) and incomplete lateral line; c. *Cottus echinatus*), prickles over most of body, including breast and belly; d. (*Cottus extensus*), prickles not extending to breast or belly.

5a) Jaw large, upper jaw extending to back of eye or beyond (Fig. 4.9.e); shortest spine at dorsal notch less than half the length of the longest spine (Fig. 4.9.f); lateral scales 58–69; bases of anal and soft dorsal fins not covered by small scales
. . . . LARGEMOUTH BASS (*Micropterus salmoides*)

5b) Jaw moderate, upper jaw extending to below middle of pupil (Fig. 4.9.f); shortest spine at dorsal notch more than half the length of the longest spine (Fig. 4.9.f); lateral scales 68–81; small scales extending onto bases of anal and soft dorsal fins
. . . . SMALLMOUTH BASS (*Micropterus dolomieui*)

6a) Upper jaw at least as long as longest dorsal spine (Fig. 4.9.g); pectoral fin short and rounded (Fig. 4.9.g), not reaching eye when bent forward . . . . GREEN SUNFISH (*Lepomis cyanellus*)

6b) Upper jaw much shorter than longest dorsal spine (Fig. 4.9.h); pectoral fin long and pointed (Fig. 4.9.h), reaching beyond eye if bent forward . . . . BLUEGILL SUNFISH (*Lepomis macrochirus*)

Key to Perches (Percidae) in Utah

1a) Mouth large, reaching to below eye or beyond; posterior edge of preopercle serrated . . . . PERCH and WALLEYE 2

1b) Mouth small, not reaching to below eye; preopercle margin smooth . . . . LOGPERCH (*Percina caprodes*)

2a) Dorsal rays 12–15; anal rays 6–8; scales large, 51–61 in lateral line; jaws with small teeth, no canines; pattern of vertical bars; caudal fin plain. . . . . YELLOW PERCH (*Perca flavescens*)
2b) Dorsal rays 18–22; anal rays 11–14; scales small, 83–104 in lateral line; jaws with large canines in addition to small teeth; lower lobe of caudal fin with cream-colored tip . . . . WALLEYE (*Stizostedion vitreum*)

Key to Temperate Basses (Percichthyidae) in Utah

1a) Body deeper than 1/3 standard length; two connected patches of teeth on back of tongue; fewer than 57 scales in lateral line; dorsal rays 14–15 . . . . WHITE BASS (*Roccus chrysops*)
1b) Body slenderer than 1/3 standard length; left and right tooth patches separated on back of tongue; more than 58 scales in lateral line; dorsal rays 11–14. . . . . STRIPED BASS (*Roccus saxatilis*)

Key to Sculpins (Cottidae) in Utah

1a) Preopercle (cheekbone) with single spine (Fig. 4.10.a); palatine teeth absent or almost so; lateral line complete or nearly complete to base of caudal fin (Fig. 4.10.a) . PAIUTE SCULPIN (*Cottus beldingi*)
1b) Preopercle (cheekbone) with 3 or 4 spines (Fig. 4.10.b,c,d); palatine teeth well developed and numerous in one patch on each side of roof of mouth; lateral line incomplete (Fig. 4.10.b,c,d) . . . 2

2a) Preopercle with upper spine angled upward and backward and next lower spine below angled downward and forward (Fig. 4.10.b); pectoral rays usually 13–15; anal rays 11–14 (Fig. 4.10.b) . . . . MOTTLED SCULPIN (*Cottus bairdi*)
2b) Preopercle with upper spine angled backward and next lower spine below angled downward and backward (Fig. 4.10.c,d); pectoral rays 15–18; anal rays 13–16 (Fig. 4.10.c,d) 3

3a) Prickles broadly distributed over body, including breast and belly (Fig. 4.10.c) . . . . UTAH LAKE SCULPIN (*Cottus echinatus*)
3b) Prickles restricted to dorsal part of body, never present on breast or belly (Fig. 4.10.d) . . . . . BEAR LAKE SCULPIN (*Cottus extensus*)

Hybrid Fishes

In addition to the species described in Part II are hybrid fishes. Fishery managers use hybrid fishes to make use of otherwise unused habitat niches. Also, hybrid fish rarely breed, a management plus under certain conditions. If they do not breed, there is uninterrupted growth throughout life and often over a longer life span, producing larger fish.

The hybrids currently being stocked in Utah waters are tiger muskellunge (female muskellunge × male northern pike), splake (female lake trout × male brook trout), and wiper (female striped bass × male white bass). A mutant albino rainbow trout is also stocked in limited numbers.

Successful crosses of female brown trout and male lake trout have yielded "brake trout." None has been stocked in Utah waters.

Plate 20
Plate 35
Plate 41

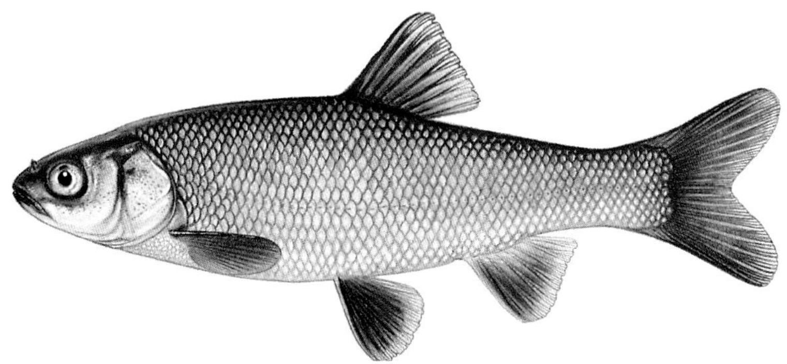

1. Utah chub, p. 74
Gila atraria

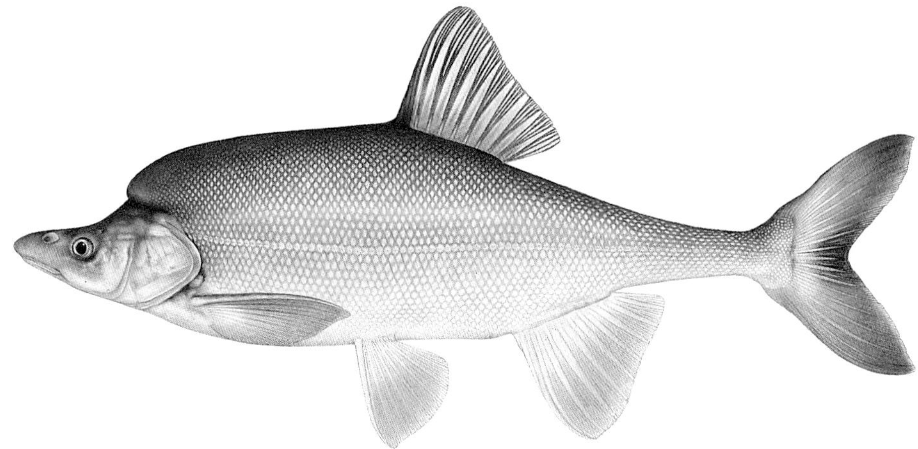

2. Humpback chub, p. 79
Gila cypha

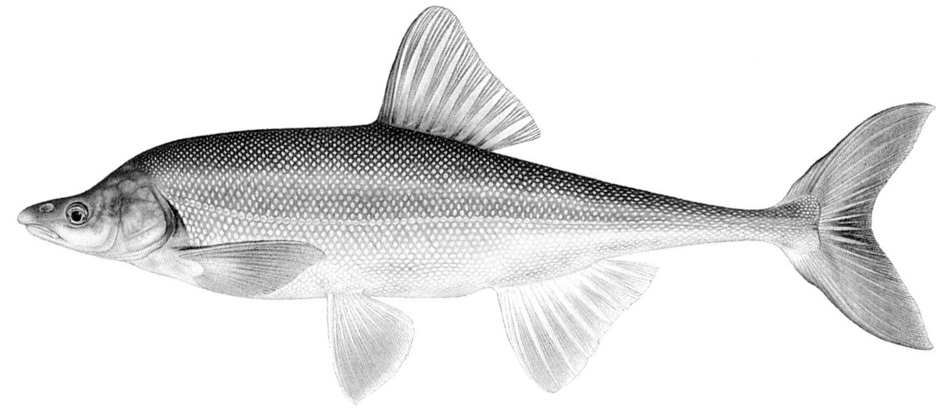

3. Bonytail chub, p. 84
Gila elegans

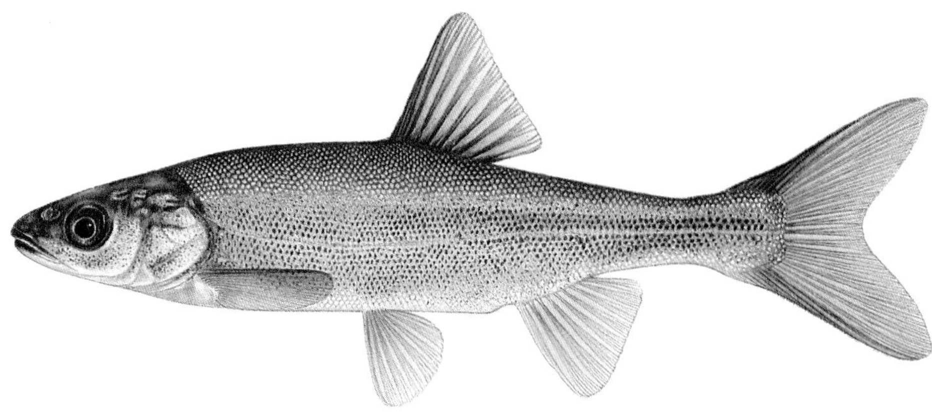

4. Roundtail chub, p. 86
Gila robusta

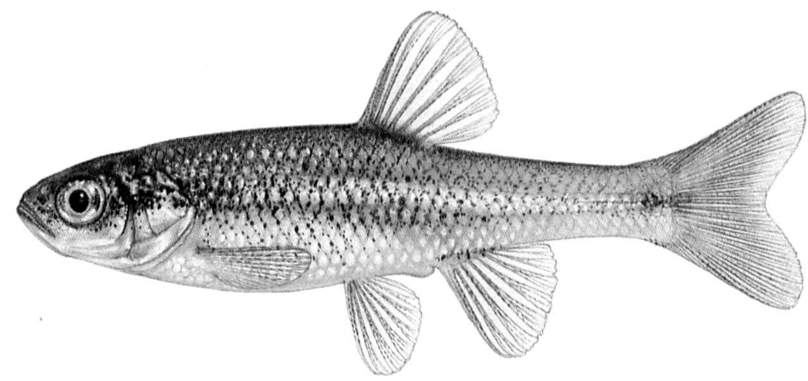

5. Least chub, p. 90
Iotichthys phlegethontis

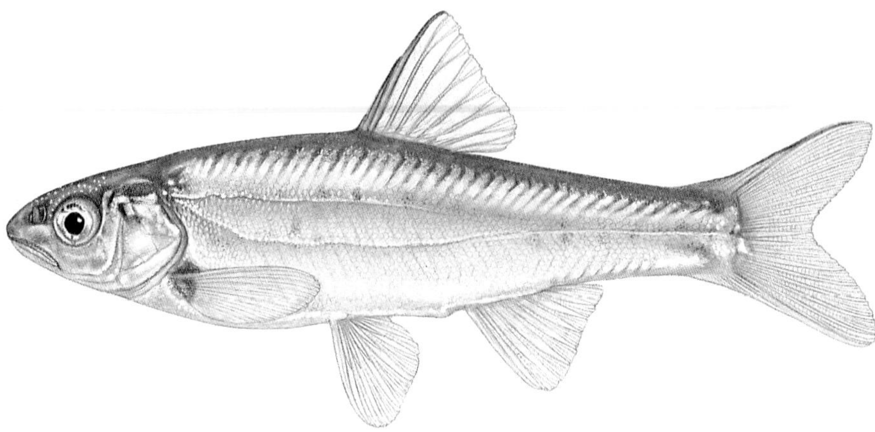

6. Virgin spinedace, p. 93
Lepidomeda mollispinis

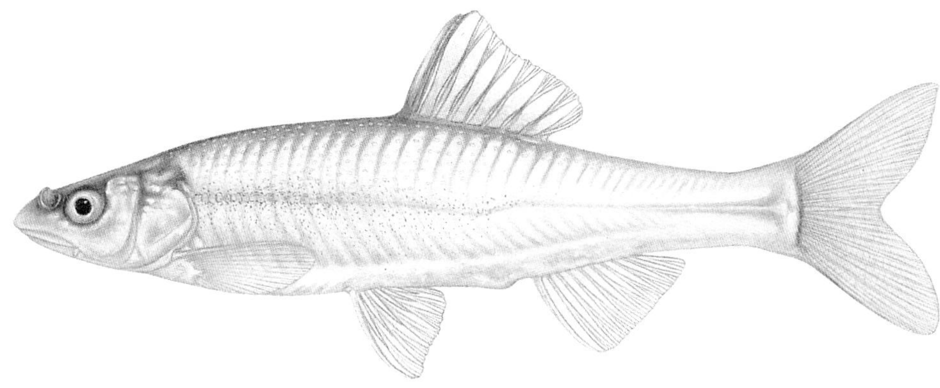

7. Woundfin, p. 107
Plagopterus argentissimus

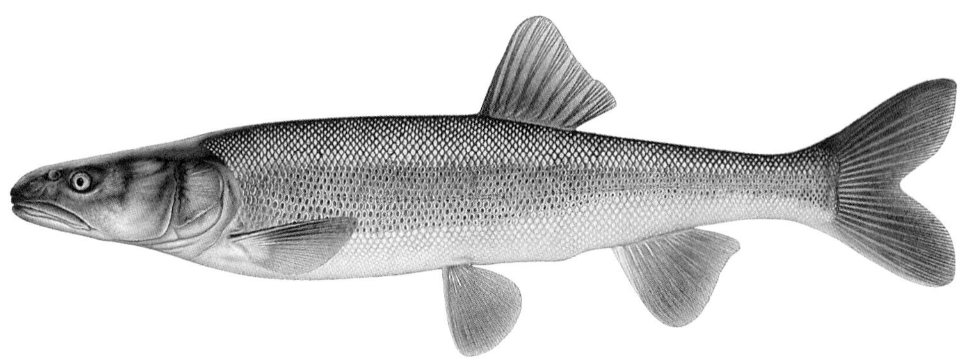

8. Colorado squawfish, p. 109
Ptychocheilus lucius

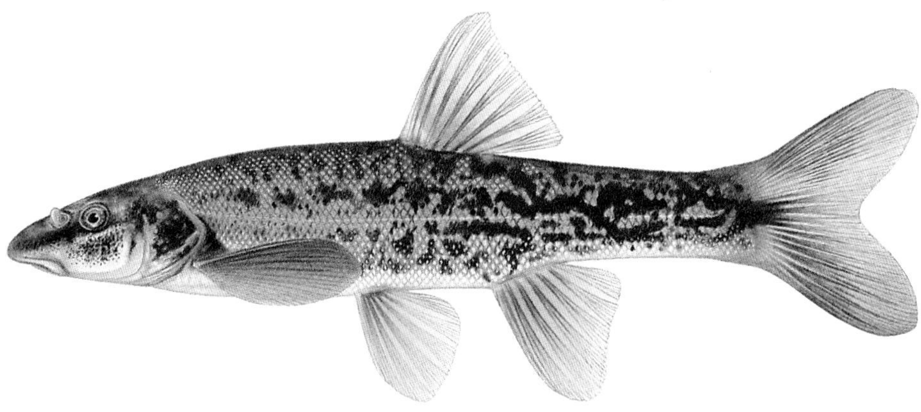

9. Longnose dace, p. 114
Rhinichthys cataractae

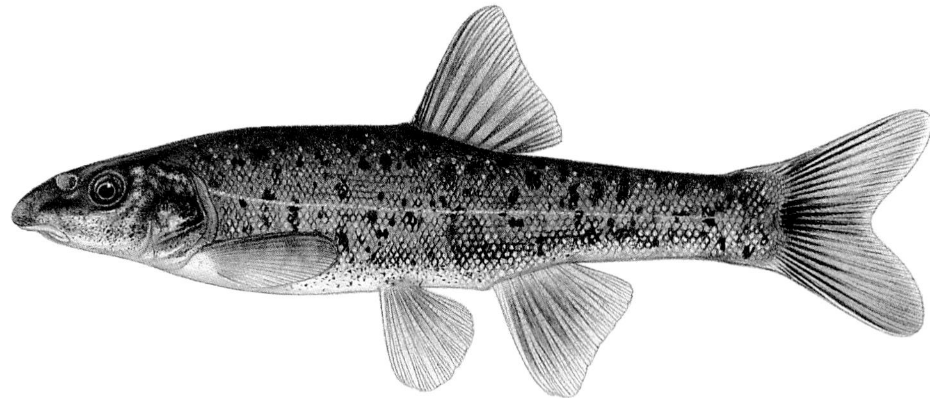

10. Speckled dace, p. 117
Rhinichthys osculus

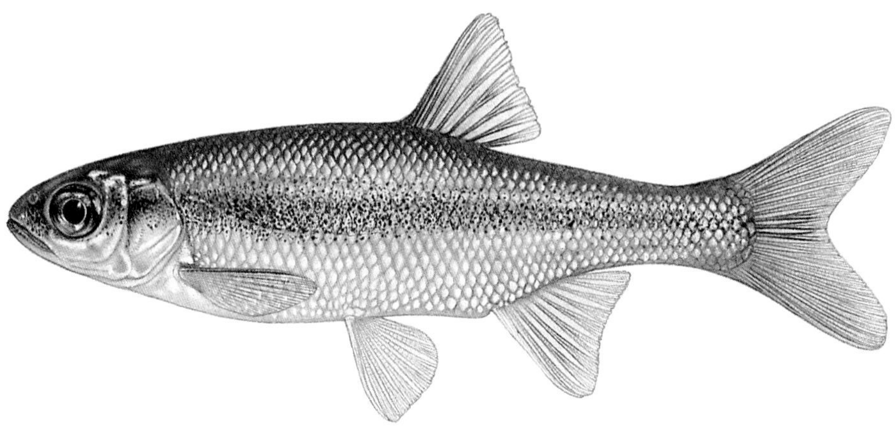

11. Redside shiner, p. 119
Richardsonius balteatus

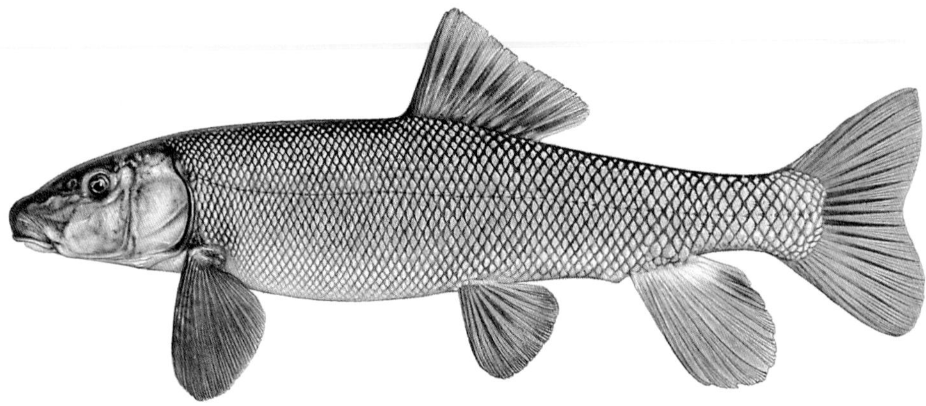

12. Utah sucker, p. 125
Catostomus ardens

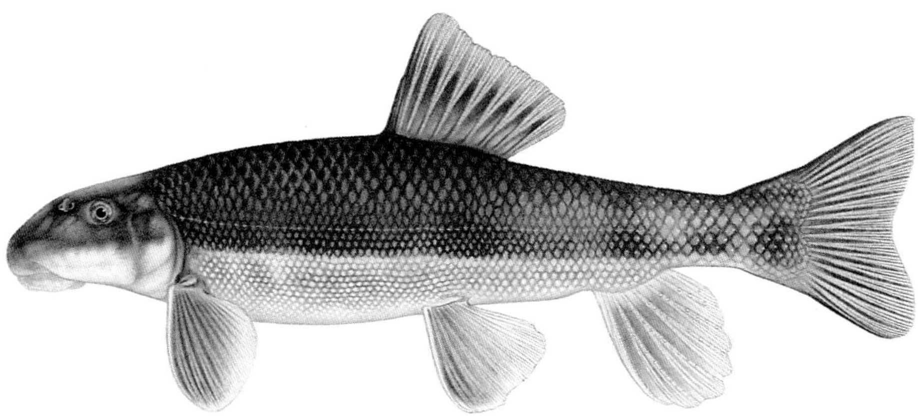

13. Desert sucker, p. 129
Catostomus clarki

14. Bluehead sucker, p. 133
Catostomus discobolus

15. Flannelmouth sucker, p. 136
Catostomus latipinnis

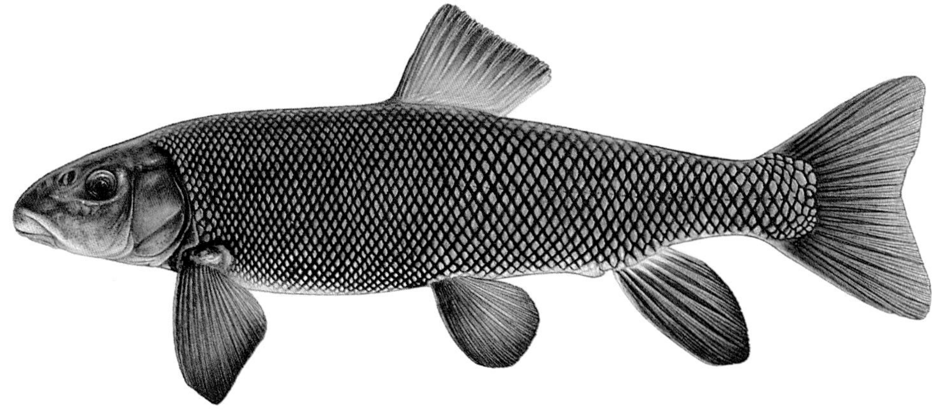

16. June sucker, p. 142
Chasmistes liorus mictus

17. Razorback sucker, p. 145
Xyrauchen texanus

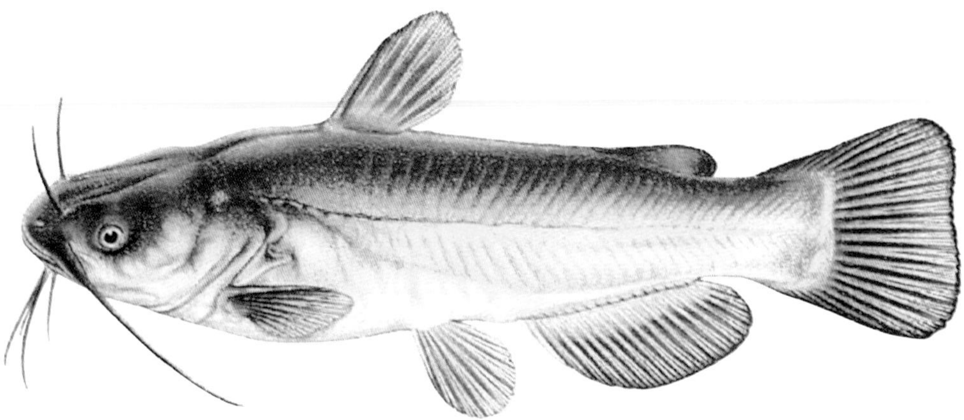

18. Black bullhead, p. 151
Ameiurus melas

19. Channel catfish, p. 156
Ictalurus punctatus

20. Tiger muskie, p. 55
Esox lucius x Esox masquinongy

21. Golden trout, p. 166
Oncorhynchus aguabonita

22. Yellowstone cutthroat, p. 169
Oncorhynchus clarki bouvieri

23. Colorado River cutthroat, p. 169
Oncorhynchus clarki pleuriticus

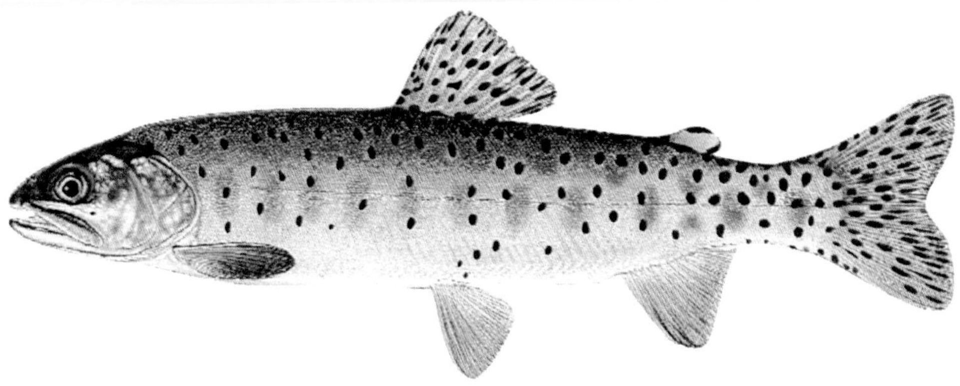

24. Bonneville cutthroat, p. 169
Oncorhynchus clarki utah

25. Rainbow trout, p. 177
Oncorhynchus mykiss

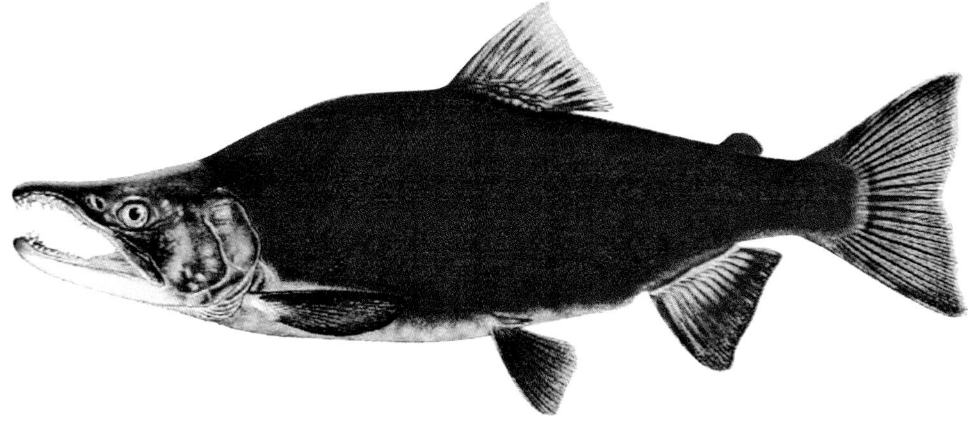

26. Sockeye salmon (kokanee), breeding male, p. 186
Oncorhynchus nerka

27. Sockeye (kokanee) salmon, female, p. 186
Oncorhynchus nerka

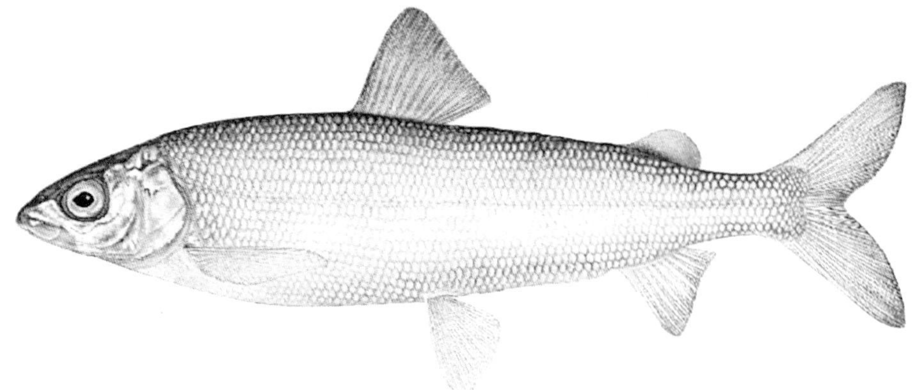

28. Bear Lake whitefish, p. 191
Prosopium abyssicola

29. Bonneville cisco, p. 194
Prosopium gemmifer

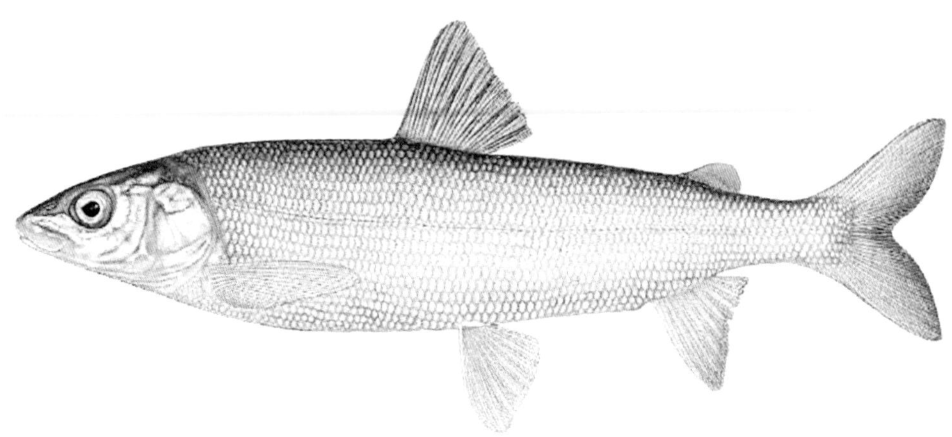

30. Bonneville whitefish, p. 198
Prosopium spilonotus

31. Mountain whitefish, p. 201
Prosopium williamsoni

32. Brown trout, p. 204
Salmo trutta

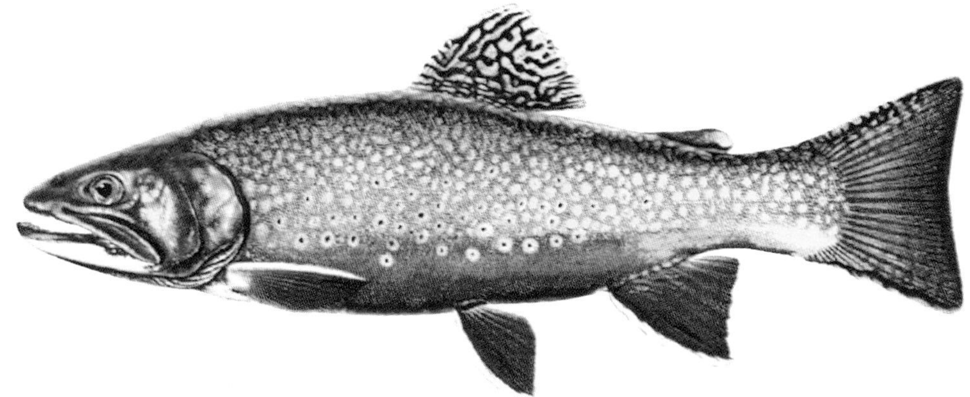

33. Brook trout, p. 208
Salvelinus fontinalis

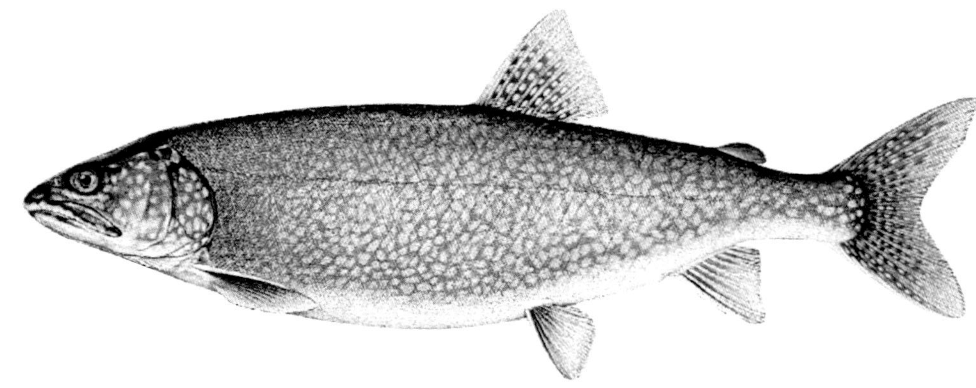

34. Lake trout, p. 213
Salvelinus namaycush

35. Splake, p. 55
Salvelinus namaycush x Salvelinus fontinalis

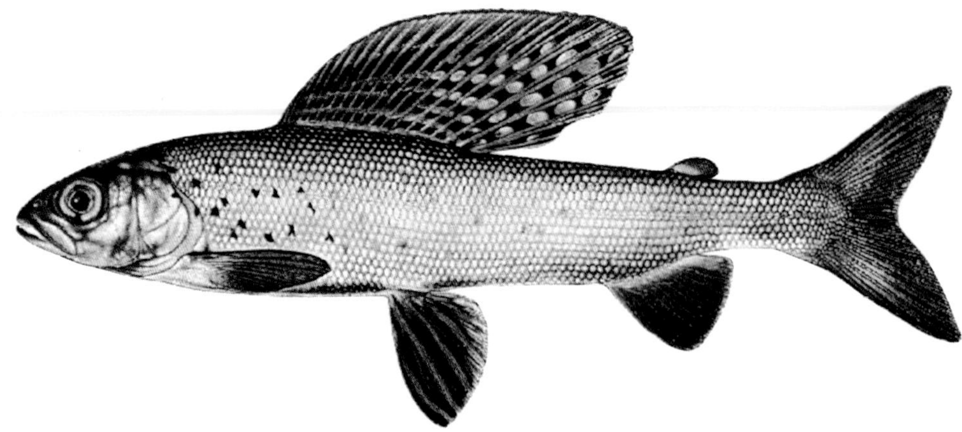

36. Arctic grayling, p. 218
Thymallus arcticus

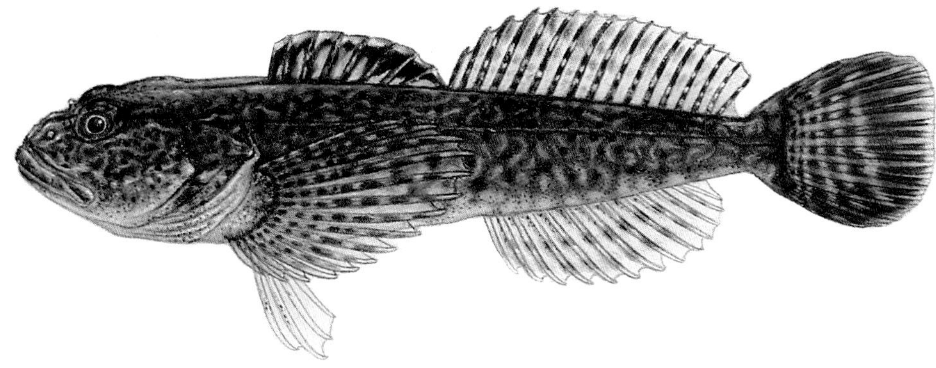

37. Mottled sculpin, p. 230
Cottus bairdi

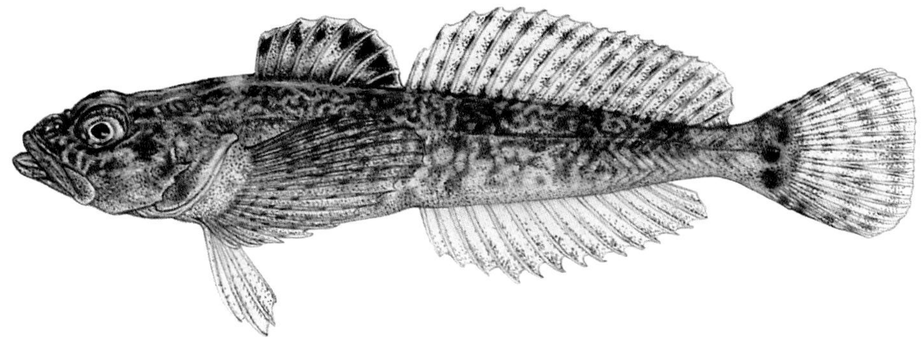

38. Bear Lake sculpin, p. 235
Cottus extensus

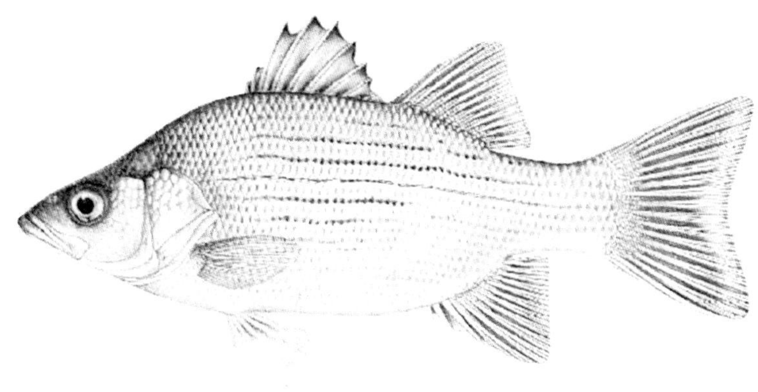

39. White bass, p. 239
Morone chrysops

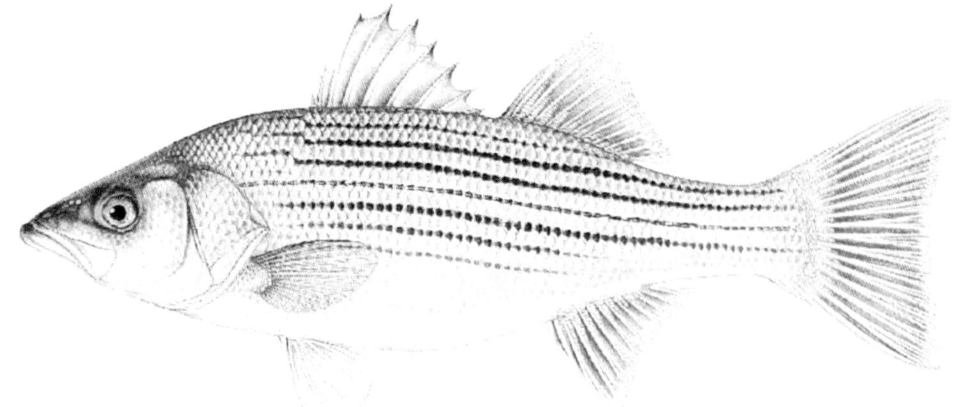

40. Striped bass, p. 244
Morone saxatilis

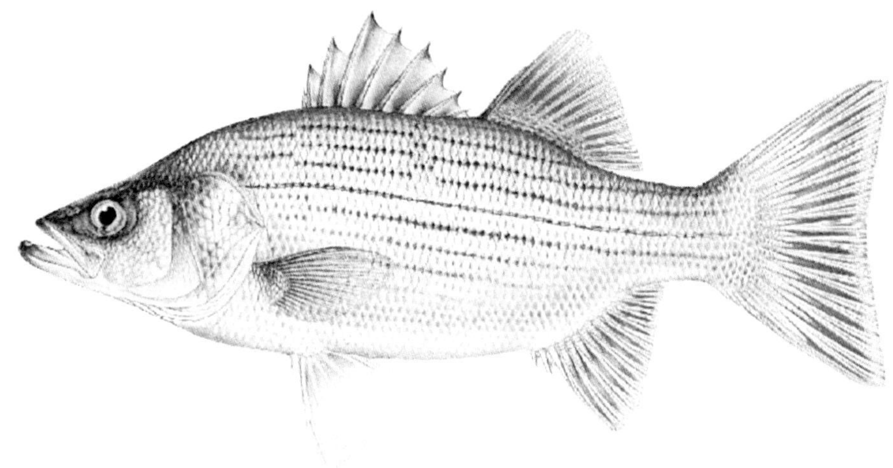

41. Wiper, p. 55
Morone saxatilis x Morone chrysops

42. Green sunfish, p. 252
Lepomis cyanellus

43. Bluegill, p. 255
Lepomis macrochirus

44. Smallmouth bass, p. 259
Micropterus dolomieu

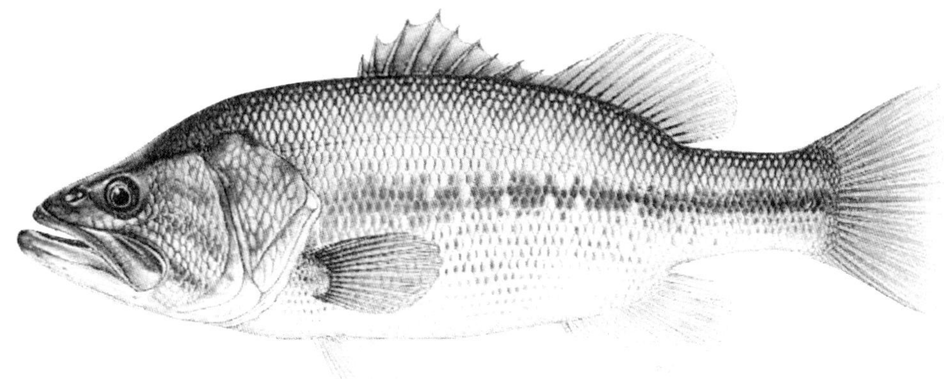

45. Largemouth bass, p. 264
Micropterus salmoides

46. Black crappie, p. 276
Pomoxis nigromaculatus

47. Yellow perch, p. 280
Perca flavescens

48. Walleye, p. 285
Stizostedion vitreum

PART II

Species Life Histories, Descriptions, and Management

CHAPTER 5

Clupeiformes

This order includes the herrings and closely related allies. These lower bony fishes have soft rays and cycloid, usually deciduous scales. The gas bladder extends forward in two branches that enter the skull and terminate in small bulbae. These silvery fishes have compressed keel-like bellies, often with scutes. They originated in the upper Jurassic Period (Bond 1979).

Herrings (Family Clupeidae)

Herrings are primarily marine except in Antarctic waters, but many are anadromous and a few landlocked. They are small to medium-sized, silvery, pelagic fishes that are at times extremely abundant and schooling. The head is naked; there is no lateral line, the skeleton is osseous, vertebra number 40 to 56. Pseudobranchiae are present, the mouth is terminal, pyloric caeca are numerous, the cycloid scales are deciduous. There are about 190 species, 2 in Utah (Scott and Crossman 1973; Forbes and Richardson 1920).

---

gizzard shad, *Dorosoma cepedianum* (Lesueur)

Etymology: *Dorosoma* = Greek meaning lance body, *cepedianum,* name for Count Citoyen Lacépède

Nomenclature: *Megalops cepediana* Lesueur 1818, *Dorosoma cepedianum* Jordan 1878a

IMPORTANCE

Gizzard shad are very prolific, producing an abundance of young that are forage for game fishes. In the negative, adults grow rapidly to a size too large for most predators. They may then become competitors with young game fishes. It is always a trade-off. In Missouri, in large reservoirs, Pflieger (1975) thought the positive aspects outweigh the negative. Heavy mortality may create a temporary nuisance.

DESCRIPTION

Original

Body subelliptical; tail narrow; snout short, round, semigelatinous; dorsal-fin pointed, in some lunated, in others slightly rounded, higher than long at its base; anal-fin long, its anterior part largest; opercula large, rounded, with a slight depression on their posterior part.

The body of this species differs from the foregoing in its form; it is short and deep, its length being more than five times that of the head, and its depth about a head and three-quarters; the back is greatly elevated, almost sharp, having a line, unfurnished with scales, which extends from the nape as far as the base of the dorsal-fin, abdomen hanging very low, or very much arcuated, carinated, and armed with twenty-nine spines; head short; mouth very small; intermaxillaries large; maxillaries very narrow, not passing beyond the eyes; mandibles large, forming an angle within the mouth; teeth none; the extremity of the pectorals passing beyond the anterior part of the base of the ventrals, which are situated somewhat before the dorsal-fin; caudal-fin of considerable extent, but not so forked as in the foregoing species; length of specimens examined from eight to twelve inches; colour of the back a grayish blue, pale silver on the sides, head of a burnt terra de sienna, mixed with golden; throat and abdomen white; extremity of the ventrals black, the remainder of the fins tinted with gray-blue, yellow and green, blackish at their extremities; eyes small, irises brownish yellow, pupil black; scales very narrow, and crowded.

B. 7.-D. 15-P. 18-V.8.-A.33-C.19 5/5 rays.

Contemporary

Coloration on the back and upper sides is primarily silvery blue, grading into silver and white on the lower sides and belly. There is a shoulder on the young that disappears in about one year. The body is oblong, deep, and strongly compressed laterally. There are about 190 gill rakers on the lower limb of the first arch. Scales are cycloid, numbering 52 to 70 in the lateral series. The dorsal fin usually has 10 to 12 rays, the last ray is greatly prolonged in adults. The snout is rounded, overhanging the ventral mouth with its short lower jaw. The maxillary reaches beyond the anterior margin of the eye. No teeth are present on the jaws or tongue, except during the larval stage. The caudal fin is deeply forked (Miller 1963).

RANGE

Native habitat for this species is the Great Lakes and St. Lawrence River to eastern South Dakota and central New Mexico; then south across New Mexico to the Gulf of Mexico, and throughout Mississippi and the Great Lakes drainage to about 40° north latitude on the Atlantic coast (Lee et al. 1980). Gravid adults were stocked in Willard Reservoir in spring 1990, and were shortly reproducing.

Size and Longevity

Gizzard shad are fast growing but relatively short lived. An Oklahoma population grew each year for 5 years as follows: in inches, 4.3, 11.3, 14.3, 16.2, and 17.3; in mm, 109, 287, 363, 411, 439 (Carlander 1953). A few may live 10 years, but 4 to 6 is the usual life span (Pflieger 1975). Becker (1983) reported one measuring 19 in. (438 mm) and weighing 3 lb, 4 oz (1.47 kg) caught in Lake Michigan. Miller (1963) reported fish 4 to 19 in. (102 to 483 mm). Individuals 10 to 13 in. (254 to 330 mm) long weigh about 1 lb (0.45 kg). The heaviest specimen weighed 3 lb, 7 oz (1.6 kg).

Food and Feeding

Newly hatched young are long and cylindrical with a terminal mouth and teeth in both jaws. They start feeding on zooplankton the fifth day after hatching and do so until they are about 1 in. (25.4 mm) long when they change shape, lose their teeth, and become filter feeders (Smith 1979; Miller 1963). At this time the gizzard, from which the common name derives, becomes evident. In adults, this is a short, thick-walled, muscular structure, much like that of a fowl. Adults feed on free-floating plankton and small invertebrates including insects. Throughout their life, gizzard shad feed on zooplankton or on phytoplankton, whichever is most abundant; they also ingest sand (Becker 1983). Gizzard shad that are feeding travel in large, more or less constantly moving schools, often near the surface. They frequently leap clear of the water or skip along the surface on their sides. They also graze over logs or other bottom objects (Pflieger 1975).

Limiting Factors

Lethal temperature for shad is 98° to 99°F (36.6° to 37.2°C); however, they may be stressed at a much lower level, about 93°F (33.8°C). Their northern range is limited by cold temperatures, although they are caught for bait in unfrozen areas of the Chippewa River, Wisconsin (Becker 1983).

Breeding Habits

Most gizzard shad mature at age 2, or rarely 1 or 3, when water temperatures reach 50°F (10°C) and may continue to spawn until the temperature is 70°F (21°C). A 2-year-old female may produce 378,990 adhesive eggs, 0.03 in. (0.8 mm) in diameter. Eggs hatch in 72 hours at 77°F (25.6°C) or 36 hours at 80°F (26.6°C). Spawning occurs in shallow, fresh waters over sand bars, stones, plants, or debris. Egg production is highest in age 2 females, but they probably spawn every year for the rest of their lives (Becker 1983; Smith 1979; Pflieger 1975).

HABITAT

Gizzard shad live in cool to warm (48° to 82°F [8.8 to 27.7°C]), medium to large rivers, swamps, reservoirs, bays, and sloughs. They prosper in either silty or clear water, but avoid fast-flowing streams. They are an open-water species, often at or near the surface. One study lists the preferred temperature at 73° to 75°F (22.8° to 23.8°C) and satisfactory growth at 93°F (33.9°C). Another found that shad selected 72° to 84°F (22.2° to 28.8°C) water. They thrive in waters with a large plankton population (Miller 1963).

MANAGEMENT

With minor exceptions, gizzard shad are valuable to humans only as forage fish. Because they are essentially available for forage for only the first year of life (10 to 11 in. [254 to 279 mm]), it is important that there be an adequate number of predators to keep adult shad populations in check. Probably three or four species of predators are the minimum required for this control. Devries and Stein (1990), after a literature review, concluded that no generalities could be reached regarding the positive and negative aspects of either gizzard shad or threadfin shad.

---

threadfin shad, *Dorosoma petenense* (Günther)

Etymology: *Dorosoma* = Greek meaning lance body *petenense* = named for the type localities, Lake Peten in Yucatán

Nomenclature: *Meletta petenensis* Günther 1867, *Dorosoma petenense* Berry, Huishy, and Moody 1956

IMPORTANCE

Threadfin shad are valuable as forage in areas where they do not compete for food with small game fishes. They are prolific, small, and vulnerable to predation. Their value in Lake Powell is less than formerly, due to depressed numbers.

DESCRIPTION

Original

D. 14—15. A. 20—23. L. lat. 40. Distinguished from *M. thrissa* by its larger head, the length of which is two-sevenths of the total (without caudal). Lake Peten.

Contemporary

Threadfin shad have large pseudobranchiae, about 350 short gill rakers at 5.2 in. (131 mm) standard length, and a compressed, short, deep body. Coloration is bluish black above with silvery sides and belly. Heads of breeding males and the upper part of the paired fins are bright yellow. They have only 40 to 45 vertebrae, a small anal fin and a long, pointed snout. The thick-walled stomach is gizzardlike; the gut has many pyloric caecae. The dorsal fin normally has 12 rays, and the last ray is long and threadlike; the anal fin has 24 rays; both fins are soft. Scales in the lateral series number 41 to 48 (Miller 1963; La Rivers 1962).

Range

This species is native from the Ohio River of Kentucky, and southern Indiana, west and south to the states of Oklahoma, Texas, and Florida. It is also present along the Gulf of Mexico to Belize (Lee et al. 1980).

A landlocked form was introduced into Lake Mead, from Kentucky Lake, Tennessee, in 1953. In 1954, stock from California was added. By 1956 they inhabited the main stem of the Colorado River from Lake Mead to Mexico. They were stocked in Lake Powell, Utah, in 1968. They have also been established elsewhere in the United States (Minckley 1973; La Rivers 1962).

Size and Longevity

Threadfin shad in Colorado River waters are fast growing, but short lived. They may reach an age of 2 years, or less often, 3. They reach a size of about 2 in. (51 mm) the first year, and 3 or 4 in. (76–101mm) the second. In another habitat where ample food is present, they grow larger and faster (Johnson 1970; Miller 1963).

Food and Feeding

Threadfin shad often inhabit open water near the surface. They are plankton feeders (Miller 1963). Gerdes and McConnell (1963) found that, by volume, shad relied heavily on animals, primarily copepods. Shad were found to swim back and forth through concentrations of food, mouth open for 2 to 3 seconds at a time. Attempts to engulf individual items were also made. These authors suggested, based on the 50 percent of amorphous and unidentified materials eaten by the fish, that threadfin feed on the bottom. Sand is ingested, which may aid digestion in the gizzardlike stomach. Organic debris may provide nutrition in the form of attached bacteria. Diets vary considerably between populations, indicating omnivory. If there is a food preference, it is for zooplankton. Winter feeding is greatly reduced.

Limiting Factors

W. A. Gustaveson (personal communication, 1991) suggested that the great depth of Lake Powell, which provides a constant temperature (46°F [7.8°C]), is a sanctuary for these fish. He has detected no winter kill in his tenure at Lake Powell (1975 to 1995). Miller (1963) reported that there is a high mortality at 45°F (7.22°C) with few surviving at 40°F (4.4°C). When the population was high there probably was intraspecific competition for food. They may also have competed with young game fishes. Predation by striped bass and other game fishes is high.

Breeding Habits

Some threadfin shad may spawn in the fall of their first year (Miller 1963). Most do not. They spawn at 68° to 70°F (20° to 21.1°C), from dawn to sunrise. Breeding schools travel along shore near the surface. Males may live to 3 years, females 4 years (Pflieger 1975). They may spawn both spring and fall. In small Arizona impoundments, young of the year were ripe in November (Gerdes and McConnell 1963). Eggs produced per female are from 700 to 8,000. At spawning time, females, generally larger than the males, move along shore and deposit small adhesive eggs on grass, debris, or floating objects. Eggs hatch in 4 to 5 days at 68° to 70°F (20° to 21.1°C) (Minckley 1973; Johnson 1971).

Habitat

Lake-inhabiting threadfin spend much of the daytime in the upper 5 ft (1.5 m) of open water. Young tend to be in deeper water than adults. On dark nights schools may disperse over shallow as well as deep water. When there are moonlight nights behavior tends to be more like it is in the daytime. Cooler temperatures result in radical changes. The schools are less organized and deeper. They may be inshore or seek warm springs. In streams they are present in moderate currents, tending to congregate below riffles and dams. They do, however, avoid swift, turbulent streams (Pflieger 1975; Johnson 1970).

Management

The abundance of predators, primarily striped bass, in Lake Powell, has greatly reduced the population of threadfin. Temperatures are not a concern for this species in Lake Powell. Temperature sanctuaries exist both summer and winter that allow brood stock to survive. Restocking has not been considered.

CHAPTER 6 Cypriniformes

Worldwide the order Cypriniformes consists of about 2,000 species, most of which are important ecologically and economically. Its members are widespread; it is the dominant freshwater fish group in many parts of the world but is not native to Australia. Of the 25 or so families of Cypriniformes, 15 are limited to Central or South America, 3 to Africa, and none to North America. North America shares the cyprinids and catostomids with Africa and Europe. In the United States and Canada, the minnows (Cyprinidae) and suckers (Catostomidae) are predominant; there is also one characin and one loach. In South America the characins are widespread and somewhat similar ecologically to minnows in North America.

The order includes such diverse species as freshwater flying fishes of South America, which actually flap their pectoral fins in flight, and the electric eel, which can produce as much as 650 volts in specialized organs. Some members of the order are naked, although most have scales. Most have pharyngeal teeth; a lesser number have jaw teeth. The third and fourth vertebrae are not fused to each other; there are subopercular bones. All members of the order are physostomous. Many have spinous, enlarged, and hardened rays at the front of the dorsal and anal fins.

Along with the catfishes this order has a Weberian apparatus, made up of the first four or five vertebrae. These modified vertebrae form the attachment points for a series of small ossicles. The most posterior pair remain in contact with the gas bladder, and the anterior pair is in contact with the membranous labyrinth (Robins et al. 1991; Bond 1979).

Carps and Minnows (Family Cyprinidae)

This large and widely distributed family of over 1,500 species inhabits fresh waters of North America, Eurasia, and Africa. North America has 235 species, mostly native east of the Continental Divide. These fishes occupy almost all conceivable niches, and they range in weight from less than an ounce (28 grams) to nearly 300 lb (136 kg). Most species, however, are small. Many are important as food, both wild and cultivated, forage, pets, and in research (Sigler and Sigler 1987).

All members of this family have toothless jaws; rather, they have strong pharyngeal teeth that break up food. Cycloid scales and abdominal pelvic fins are distinctive family traits. Fins are soft without true spines; however, in a few species, the posterior surface of the first ray of the dorsal and sometimes the anal fin (as in the common carp) is hardened into a spinelike structure resembling a true spine. Cyprinids have no adipose fin. A Weberian apparatus, a series of small bones which connect the gas bladder to the inner ear, is an unusual structure common to this family and probably gives them an acute sense of hearing (Simpson and Wallace 1978; Bond 1979). Fifteen genera contain 12 native species, 6 subspecies, and 10 introduced species in Utah.

---

goldfish, *Carassius auratus* (Linnaeus)

Etymology: *Carassius* = vernacular name for Curican carp, *C. carassius*, *auratus* = gilded, referring to the coloration

Nomenclature: *Cyprinus auratus* Linnaeus 1758, *Carassius auratus* Günther 1868

IMPORTANCE

These highly regarded aquarium and research fish are invariably a negative factor in the wild. They compete with more desirable fishes and may disturb habitat. Goldfish have been cultivated for centuries, and there is extensive literature covering every phase of their life history. In some cases they can be considered as indicators of really low water quality or pollution. In earlier years, the city of Chicago, Illinois, dumped raw sewage in the Illinois River. In some of the upper reaches of the river, only goldfish and common carp survived.

DESCRIPTION

Original

C. pinna ani gemina, caudæ transversa trifurca. *Sn. svec. p.* 125. *t.* 2.

ACT. Stockh. 1740. *p.* 403. *t.* 1. *f.* 1-8 idem. D. 2/18. P. 16. V. 9. A. 8. 8. C. 37.

Gron. mus. 1. *n.* 15. idem. D. 8. P. 11. V. 7. A.—C. 20. *mus.* 2. *n.* 150. C. pinna ani simplici, cauda trifurca. D. 18. P. 11. V. 8. A. 8. C. 44.

Edw. av. t. 209.

Pet. gaz. t. 78. *f.* 7.

Habitat in Chinæ, Japoniæ *fluviis.*

Piscis colitur in vasis murrhinis ob aureum fulgorem, tum multum pinnis varians. Radius secundis *ani osfice serratus.* * * * * *Pinna caudæ bifida.*

Translation
Carp with twin anal fins, and a three-pronged fan-shaped tail. It lives in the rivers of China and Japan. The fish is kept in murrhine vases to promote a brilliant gold color, being then much varied in its fins. A posterior serrated spur near the anus. Paired caudal fins.

Contemporary
Goldfish have a short head, oblique mouth, and are without jaw teeth. They have a moderately compressed, robust body with large scales. Coloration is highly variable in the wild, and at times they revert to color much like common carp. The dorsal fin has an anterior serrated spine and 18 to 20 rays. There is no chin barbel, a characteristic that helps distinguish them from common carp.

RANGE

Goldfish, native to China, have been introduced in all inhabited parts of the world (Brown 1971). Goldfish were introduced in the U.S.A. at least as early as 1889. They, like many exotics, have been stocked by well-meaning people. There are a few small populations in Utah streams. Large numbers of goldfish are found in livestock watering tanks in the southern deserts of Utah.

SIZE AND LONGEVITY

Goldfish are medium to small fish in the wild, averaging 6 to 10 in. (152 to 254 mm) long. In some populations they reach 12 to 14 in. (305 to 356 mm). Six years of age is the average longevity.

LIMITING FACTORS

Competition with and predation by other fishes are probably the worst enemies of wild goldfish. Because goldfish can and do live and reproduce in badly polluted waters in some areas, they often thrive where no other fishes live.

FOOD AND FEEDING

Food is largely algae and aquatic invertebrates.

BREEDING HABITS

Goldfish spawn more or less continuously for several weeks, starting when water temperatures reach 63° to 68°F (17.2° to 20°C). Eggs are adhesive and stick to plants and debris. Spawning areas are shallow and weedy.

HABITAT

Prime wild goldfish habitat ranges from small, sluggish streams and ponds to the backwaters of large rivers and lakes. They live largely where they have been put, moving little within a stream course.

MANAGEMENT

Distribution of goldfish should be discouraged and wild populations exterminated where feasible because of their negative impact on native species, including endemics, with which they compete for space and food.

red shiner, *Cyprinella lutrensis* (Baird and Girard)

Etymology: *Cyprinella* = from diminutive form of *Cyprinus*, "little carp"; *lutrensis*, from the Latin *lutra*, for otter (the species was first known from Otter Creek, Oklahoma)

Nomenclature: *Leuciscus lutrensis* Baird and Girard 1853, *Notropis lutrensis* Forbes 1884, *Cyprinella lutrensis* Mayden 1989

IMPORTANCE

In their native range, red shiner have value as both forage and bait. In Utah they are primarily a nuisance, outcompeting native fishes for food and space and providing little benefit in return. Adaptability to new habitat may make them useful in instances where a forage fish is needed.

DESCRIPTION

Original

Leuciscus lutrensis Baird and Girard 1853.

Baird and Girard 1853:391. TYPE LOCALITY: Otter Cr., trib. to N. k. of Red R., either Kiowa or Tillman Co., Oklahoma. (Locality erroneously given in original description as being in Arkansas.) SYNTYPE: USNM 104 (1, 44.8), R. B. Marcy and G. B. McClellan, 1852.

REMARKS.—Girard (1858:272–273) listed five original syntypes (USNM 104). He also listed 10 specimens (USNM 107) from Gypsum Creek, a tributary of the Canadian River, but these were not collected till late August 1853 (Whipple 1854:18–19; 1856; appendix D), and thus almost certainly could not have been examined by Baird and Girard when preparing the original description. *Leuciscus bubalinus*, which was originally described in the same paper as *Leuciscus lutrensis*, was found by Hubbs and Ortenburger (1929a:34) to be identical with that species. As first revisers they selected the name *lutrensis* over *bubalinus*. Contreras (1975) reviewed species in Mexico and the Rio Grande basin. Counts for extant syntype: teeth 4–4; anal rays 9. Original description date 5 September 1853.

= *Notropis lutrensis lutrensis* (Baird and Girard)

3. LEUCISCUS LUTRENSIS, B. and G.—Body elongated, fusiform, compressed, largest specimen examined, two inches and three-eighths; head forming a little less than the fourth of the entire length. Eyes proportionally large. Anterior margin of the dorsal fin at an equal distance from the snout and base of caudal. Caudal forked. Anal fin entirely behind the dorsal. Insertion of ventrals in advance of the dorsal; their tip not reaching the anterior

margin of the anal. Tip of pectorals almost contiguous to the base of the ventrals. Scales large. Lateral line forming a very open curve convex towards the abdomen, and nearer to it than to the back.

D I 8. A I 9. C 2. I. 9. 8. I l. V 8. P 11.

Ground color bluish brown; back blue; dorsal fin yellowish brown; caudal, pectorals and ventrals, reddish.

Specimens of this species were caught in the Otter Creek, Oklahoma.

Contemporary

Coloration is olive green above, with silvery sides and a white belly. Scales are edged in pigment. Breeding males are distinguished by pale blue sides and a purple crescent behind the head. The top of the head is red, the sides of the body rosy. Both sexes have breeding tubercles. Pharyngeal teeth are 0, 4–4, 1, or 1, 4–4, 1. Gill rakers are short, narrow, and round tipped, the eye is small. The lateral line is decurved and complete. Scales in the lateral series are 32 to 36 (Becker 1983).

Range

Red shiner originally occurred in the Mississippi and Gulf drainages from South Dakota and Illinois through northern Mexico. In Utah they are common to abundant in the Colorado River system, where they make up 80 to 85 percent of the species composition in backwaters. They also invaded the Virgin River drainage in Utah in 1984, where they are now numerous. They are less abundant elsewhere in the state, including Taylor Hollow (Lee et al. 1980; Tyus et al. 1982; Valdez 1990).

Size and Longevity

Red shiner rarely reach lengths of over 3 in. (76 mm), achieving 1.5 to 1.9 in. (38 to 48 mm) the first year, and almost 3.0 in. (76 mm) the second year. Three years is generally the maximum life span.

Food and Feeding

An omnivorous sight feeder, red shiner eat algae, insects, and other small invertebrates. Terrestrial insects in the diet indicate surface feeding, but they also feed on bottom-dwelling aquatic larvae and nymphs. Midwater prey include copepods, rotifers, and protozoans (Becker 1983).

Limiting Factors

Shortage of food or space limits numbers of red shiner (Becker 1983). Because these fish are short lived, two years with no reproduction would eliminate most populations. Red shiner are rare in ponds and artificial lakes.

Breeding Habits

May to August is the spawning period, when water temperatures range from 60° to 85°F (15.6° to 29.4°C). Average temperature for spawning is 73°F (22.8°C). One- and two-year-old fish spawn in summer, but older fish breed earlier. Eggs number from 500 to over 1,000 per female; they are demersal and sink to the bottom or adhere to substrate after fertilization. Eggs are laid over sand, gravel, or mud bottom. The long spawning period indicates intermittent or multiple spawning (Smith 1979; Becker 1983).

HABITAT

Red shiner tolerate high levels of salinity and turbidity. They have been taken from water at temperatures higher than 103°F (39.4°C), but they also prosper in the cool to cold waters of the upper Colorado River Basin, preferring streams of moderate flow with sand to gravel or mud bottoms. They adapt to new environments readily. Clear water is not actively sought. They prosper in the backwaters and shorelines of the cool, fast waters of the Colorado River and in the warm, slow waters of the Virgin River, where they survive intermittent flows and extremes in habitat. In brief, their adaptability to extremes is unusual (Smith 1979; Becker 1983; Valdez 1990).

MANAGEMENT

This exotic species needs no protection to prosper and extend its range in Utah. Competition and predation by the red shiner on Colorado River endemic cyprinids may be contributing to the endangerment of the native fishes.

---

common carp,
Cyprinus carpio
Linnaeus

Etymology: *Cyprinus* = ancient name for carp, may be derived from Cyprus, abode of the goddess Venus, alluding to its fecundity; *carpio* = Latinization of the name carp
Nomenclature: *Cyprinus carpio* Linnaeus 1758

IMPORTANCE

In quite a number of places in North America, some in Utah, carp are sought for sport and food. Their great abundance makes them a good source of high-protein food. They produce a quality smoked product. Carp have been used to feed poultry, furbearers, and trout. Carp, when hooked, put up a substantial fight. However, common carp, as game and food fish, are viewed with mixed emotions in North America. In Utah they have a few supporters. From about 1876 until 1910 they were praised as a delicacy and stocked by state and federal fish agencies and private landowners. Attitudes changed abruptly. For one thing, the culinary qualities of wild North American carp do not match those of Asian and European carp. They often pick up a muddy flavor in early to late spring and retain it until winter. This taste is caused by soil-inhabiting bacteria ingested by carp, through aquatic invertebrates. Common carp also compete for food with native fishes, and large schools of carp can destroy fish and waterfowl habitat. Young carp furnish forage for fishes and birds.

DESCRIPTION

Original

C. pinna ani radiis 9, cirris 4, pinnæ dorsalis radio secundo postice serrato. D. 2/24. P. 16. V. 9. A. 9. C. 19

Art. gen. 4. *syn.* 3. *spec.* 25. Cyprinus cirris 4. ossiculo tertio pinnarum dorsi anique uncinulis armato. D. 24. P. 16. V. 9. A. 9. C. 19.

Sn. svec. 317. idem.

Gron. mus. 1. *n.* 19. idem. D. 23. P. 17. V. 8. A. 8. C.—

Habitat in Europa.

Nobilis piscis sæpius in piscinis educatus, circa a. 1600 *primum in Anglian introductus.*

Translation

Carp with 9 rays on the anal fin, 4 tufts, a second posterior serrated ray on the dorsal fin; with "bony armor" of barbs around the dorsal and anal fins. It lives in Europe. A well-known fish very often kept in fish ponds; first introduced into England ca. 1600.

Contemporary

Carp are deep-bodied fish with triangular heads. Adults are usually olive green to gold on the back and yellow on the belly with a reddish hue on the lower half of the caudal and anal fins, generally stronger in larger fish. Young, above a size of about 5 in. (12.5 cm), have the same body form as the adult. Two sets of barbels bracket the mouth, one shorter than the other. A stout, serrated spinelike ray occurs on the anterior surface of the first ray of the dorsal fin, which has 17 to 21 rays. A similar spine-like ray occurs on the anal fin. The laterally compressed body has large scales numbering 35 to 38 in the lateral series. Carp may be full and uniformly scaled, or partially and irregularly scaled, to near naked. Local names, such as mirror and leather carp, apply to almost scaleless carp.

RANGE

Common carp were introduced in Utah around 1888 and in other western states at approximately the same time. Initially they were accepted, due primarily to the efforts of federal and local fish biologists. They were subsequently rejected when it became apparent that they were a detriment to native species and habitat.

Common carp are native to Asia where they have been extensively cultivated for human consumption for hundreds of years. They were brought into Germany and other European countries from the Orient several hundred years ago. From about 1876 to 1910 they were stocked in the United States, initially from Europe (Hessel 1878), then later from both European and established local stock. Today they range over most of the warm and cool waters of the contiguous 48 states. They also survive in a few cold waters such as Bear Lake, Utah-Idaho.

Size and Longevity

Carp are relatively long lived, with high growth rates under favorable (warm) conditions. They reach ages of 20 years or more, and weights of over 80 lb (36.3 kg), although these are undoubtedly exceptions. Waters near Pretoria, South Africa, have produced the world's largest carp, weighing 82 lb, 8 oz (37.4 kg). Iowa produced a North American record carp, weighing 59.5 lb (26.9 kg) in 1955. Utah produced a 35-lb (15.9-kg) carp, taken from the Bear River Migratory Bird Refuge.

Length at the end of each year of carp age 1 to 8 from the Ogden Bay Bird Refuge, near Ogden, is: in inches, 6.8, 13.9, 20.4, 25.0, 27.2, 28.2, 28.5, and 28.4; in mm: 173, 353, 518, 635, 691, 717, 724, 721. A measurable increase in the rate of growth of carp in the Ogden Bay Bird Refuge occurred immediately after a heavy reduction in population numbers. Carp in nearby Bear River Migratory Bird Refuge, at the mouth of the Bear River near Brigham City, grew at a slightly slower rate. No fish older than 8 years was taken from either Ogden Bay or the Bear River Refuge. In cold, inhospitable waters such as Bear Lake, it takes carp 13 years to grow to a length of 26.7 in. (678 mm) (Sigler 1958).

Food and Feeding

Insects, primarily midge larvae and pupae, make up as much as 98 percent of the carp diet in Bear River Migratory Bird Refuge. In general, carp feed primarily on aquatic invertebrates, mostly insects. Algae is eaten if the more desirable invertebrates are lacking. In Bear Lake, where aquatic invertebrates are much less abundant, carp feed more on algae. Carp in the Bear River Migratory Bird Refuge were observed sucking midge larvae from vascular plants. On a few occasions, large adult carp in the Bear River Refuge fed on their young—possibly those that had been killed or immobilized by hot water. This situation is probably unusual (Sigler 1958a).

Carp are characteristically omnivorous and opportunistic with respect to feeding. One school of carp was observed feeding on fly larvae as they emerged from an animal carcass partly submerged in a riverbed. Carp feed on seeds, including elm and wild rice, as well as on vascular aquatic plants and terrestrial insects.

Limiting Factors

Young carp may be preyed upon heavily by fishes, birds, and occasionally mammals. In the Bear River Migratory Bird Refuge, the white pelican feeds extensively on primarily young or yearling carp. Rapid drops in water levels, just after spawning, may destroy eggs and young. In the Bear River Migratory Bird Refuge during the hottest part of the summer, young carp sometimes move into the very shallow, hot water and die. Carp are killed by pollution or siltation, but their tolerance is high. When spawning, carp lose much of their natural wariness and become quite vulnerable to bow-and-arrow fishermen and seiners. A rare disaster killed large numbers of carp in the Ogden Bay Bird Refuge when high winds and high water caused the saline waters of Great Salt Lake to sweep over an Ogden Bay Bird Refuge dike into the area inhabited by carp (Sigler and Sigler 1987). The historically high waters of Great Salt Lake in the years 1983 to 1987 are suspected of having killed all fishes in the Bear River Migratory Bird Refuge.

Breeding Habits

Carp are spring spawners, initiating spawning activities when water temperatures reach 58° to 67°F (14.4° to 19.4°C); the optimum is 62°F (16.7°C). To spawn, carp move into warm, shallow, weedy areas, and spawn day or night, but the preference may be twilight. Spawning often takes place in water so shallow that the backs of the carp are exposed. Much disturbance is created by spawning carp that swim rapidly about, come to the surface, and splash. In Spirit Lake, Iowa, the noise created by spawning carp moving large boulders could be heard for 0.5 mi (0.8 km). Carp build no nest and provide no care for eggs or young. Eggs are slightly adhesive and stick to debris, plants, or bottom substrate. A given population may spawn for a period from early May to late August. Females lay from 500 to 600 eggs at one time; one large female was estimated to have more than 100,000 eggs. Carp first spawn at age 2 to 4 years. In some areas carp hybridize with goldfish (Cooper 1987).

Habitat

Carp are adaptable. They occupy a wide range of habitats from large, deep, and sometimes cold lakes, rivers, and reservoirs, to small, warm, farm ponds. Waterfowl refuges in Utah and elsewhere in the West are ideal carp habitat. These areas provide an abundance of food; the water warms rapidly in spring in the shallow areas and there are deep canals to retreat to in winter or when the shallow water becomes too warm. Large numbers of carp congregate in upper Lake Powell during spring runoff from the Colorado River.

Carp are exceptionally wary, except when spawning, disappearing into cover or deep water at the slightest sign of danger. Small carp are seldom seen, indicating an additional level of wariness. In a flooded cornfield along the Illinois River, Illinois, carp cruised leisurely down the rows of corn, until there was a 2 to 3 in. (5.1 to 7.6 cm) drop in water level, then they went scurrying back through a break in the dike at the edge of the field and back to the safety of the river. Unmolested populations of carp in small artesian-fed ponds in northern Utah have standing populations of from 1,000 to 2,000 lb (450 to 900 kg) per surface acre (4,047 sq m). Carp generally do not form well-defined schools. However, in the Bear River Migratory Bird Refuge, they form schools of several thousands, when both spawning and feeding.

MANAGEMENT

Common carp preservation is rarely a problem. Efforts to eliminate or reduce carp populations are expensive and have been only partially successful. A substantial increase in utilization of carp flesh and offal is probably the only way to promote reduction of carp numbers to acceptable levels. Large-scale reductions are currently not economically feasible over much of the nonnative range of carp in North America but can be promoted by resource agencies where possibilities exist. A pilot processing plant would be a good starting place in an effort to reduce carp numbers.

Common carp also adversely impact fish ponds and bird refuges through the creation of high turbidity levels. This in effect destroys or greatly reduces macrophyte populations and production.

Utah chub, *Gila atraria* (Girard)
Plate I

Etymology: *Gila,* named for the Gila River, Arizona, probably a misnomer; *atraria,* from *ater* and *arius*, one who is black (perhaps in reference to the coloration of this species in the waters of the type location)
Nomenclature: *Siboma atraria* Girard 1856, *Gila atraria* Miller 1945b

IMPORTANCE

Utah chub are a serious competitor of game fishes, particularly outside the chub's native range. This is especially true for trout in delicate or disrupted habitats. The chub's adverse impact is primarily because of their great abundance, wide distribution, small to moderate size, and general feeding habits. Utah chub have become so abundant in some areas that special eradication programs have been initiated (that is, the massive treatment program on Strawberry Reservoir in 1990). In most treatment efforts, populations have been reduced but not eliminated. This one was apparently 100 percent successful.

A note of ecological significance is that those waters in which the species has become a nuisance are either not within its native range or, if so, are in areas where the habitat has been greatly modified by humans. This fact should serve as a warning for anglers not to attempt additional introductions. Utah chub are easily taken on hook and line and are often a nuisance to trout fishermen. Utah chub are not socially acceptable game fish in Utah. On a positive note, they provide important forage for game fishes in some areas (that is, they are the major forage species for record brown trout and lake trout in Flaming Gorge Lake on the Green River). Their abundance and ease of capture make them attractive to youngsters.

Description

Original

> The general aspect is elongated, the body being subfusiform, and the head small and conical, constituting a little less than the fourth of the total length. The ground color is yellowish; the center of the scales of the upper regions being black, the back and upper half of the flanks appear as if marked with alternate lines of black and yellow.
>
> Specimens of this species were likewise collected by Lt. E. G. Beckwith.

Contemporary

Coloration is highly variable and changes with age and habitat; the back and upper sides vary from metallic or olive green, to blue on the back, to dark olive brown or almost blackish; the sides are silver, brassy, or golden. Coloration of the belly is whitish or silvery in most, black in some. In breeding season, male Utah chub are more golden than females and may have a narrow golden stripe along the upper side, brighter than in females. Fins are sometimes dull olive, yellow, or golden, and the dorsal fin may have a blue sheen. Breeding males have a trace of yellow or orange in the axil of the pectoral fins, around the mouth, and along the preopercle.

Utah chub have rather robust bodies. The origin of the dorsal fin lies directly over the origin of the pelvic fins. There are nine rays in the dorsal fin. Lateral series scales number 45 to 65; gill rakers vary from 8 to 16 and are most numerous in populations that inhabit lakes.

Range

Ancient Lake Bonneville's historic drainage area defines most of the native range of Utah chub in Utah. They are also native to the Snake River drainage above Shoshone Falls and the lower Wood River system, Idaho. Their range is restricted in the Henry's Fork of the Snake River to the area below Mesa Falls (Lee et al. 1980).

Utah chub have had their range extended in Utah via the bait bucket of well-meaning fishermen. They have been illegally stocked into a number of lakes, including Fish Lake, and many reservoirs and streams in the Colorado River drainage.

Size and Longevity

Bear Lake has produced an 11-year-old chub that was 22 in. (559 mm) long and weighed 3 lb (1.36 kg). Elsewhere, Utah chub rarely reach a size of more than 16 in. (406 mm) and 2 lb (0.9 kg). In general, size is in the 10- to 12-in. (254- to 305-mm) range; more commonly they reach 5 to 8 in. (127 to 203 mm). Normal life span is 5 to 8 years, with a few living 11 years (Carbine 1936; Neuhold 1957). Lengths of Utah chub age 1 to 7 in Hebgen Lake, Montana, were: in inches, 1.6, 3.5, 6.1, 8.2, 9.7, 10.9, and 12.4; in mm, 41, 89, 155, 208, 246, 277, 315 (Graham 1961). Utah chub age 1 to 7 in Panguitch Lake achieved lengths as follows: in inches, 1.3, 2.3, 3.6, 4.9, 5.7, 6.3, and 6.8; in mm, 33, 58, 91, 125, 145, 160, 173 (Neuhold 1957).

Limiting Factors

Utah chub are well able to sustain themselves even under adverse conditions. They are preyed upon by fishes and to some extent by birds and mammals. Fluctuating water levels during the spawning season may kill eggs and young.

Food and Feeding

In Fish Lake, Utah chub regularly eat about the same food as small trout (Sigler 1953). They are omnivorous, readily eating plant material, insects, snails, crustaceans, and occasionally fishes. As they increase in size they are able to feed on a large variety of foods. In desert springs, they have been observed eating green algae and feeding on their own eggs.

Breeding Habits

Spawning occurs in late spring and summer, with peak activity between June 5 and 15 in Scofield Reservoir and between late June and early July in Hebgen Lake, Montana. Spawning was first noted in Scofield Reservoir on May 15, and the last mature fish was taken August 15 (Olson 1959). At Utah Lake, mature fish were taken in April (Carbine 1936). The water temperature during spawning in Scofield Reservoir varies from 52° to 62°F (11.1° to 16.7°C) and from 54° to 68°F (12.2° to 20°C) in Hebgen Lake (Olson 1959; Graham 1961).

Generally, spawning occurs in water less than 2 ft (0.61 m) deep. A female is attended by two to six males; the yellowish eggs are deposited at random; no care of eggs or young is provided. When held in the laboratory, at a constant temperature of 64.8°F (18.2°C), eggs hatched within 9 days; at 67.3°F (19.6°C), they hatched within 6 days (Sigler and Sigler 1987). Lake populations have spawning migrations. In late spring fish move from deep to shallow water.

In 22 females ranging in total length from 5.2 to 15.2 in. (132 to 386 mm) the number of eggs varied from 10,470 to 38,123, with an average of 25,282. These fish ranged from 2 to 7 years old (Olson 1959). Seven females, ranging in length from 8.8 to 13.8 in. (224 to 351 mm), averaged 40,750 eggs in Hebgen Lake (Graham 1961). Male chubs in Scofield Reservoir mature at age 2 and females at age 3; in Hebgen Lake males mature at age 3 and females at age 4.

Habitat

Utah chub occur in Utah in a wide range of habitats and thrive over a broad range of water temperatures. They prosper in streams with slow or fast currents, near bottoms that range from clay, mud, sand, gravel, peat, to rubble, or marl. Often chub stay near the surface in waters whose depths range between 1.5 and 4 ft (0.46 and 1.22 m), but in Bear Lake they are in water 100 ft (30.5 m) deep or more (McConnell et al. 1957). They are equally at home in cool waters ranging from 60° to 68°F (15.6° to 20°C) or warm waters 81° to 88°F (27.2° to 31.1°C). They prosper in such diverse habitats as irrigation ditches, reservoirs, ponds, sloughs, creeks, large rivers, and large lakes. Typically, they are associated with dense vegetation. Chub are present in springs and in spring-fed ditches on the desert floor, which are often alkaline or salty (for example, Snake Valley).

Utah chub are extremely rare in the main stem and tributaries of the Colorado River. In 10 years of sampling the Colorado, Green, Gunnison, Delores, Yampa, lower Duchesne, and White rivers, Valdez observed only one Utah chub. The single specimen was captured at the confluence of the Green and Colorado rivers in Canyonlands National Park (Valdez and Williams 1993). Utah chub thrive under a wide range of chemical and physical conditions and readily adapt to conditions not encountered in their natural range.

MANAGEMENT

Utah chub have been greatly reduced in numbers in their native Bonneville Basin, particularly in Utah Lake where they once coexisted in balance with predaceous Bonneville cutthroat trout. The lake was called "the greatest sucker pond in the world" by Jordan (Jordan and Gilbert 1881). Utah chub are prospering and are a nuisance outside their native range, but, ironically, are threatened in some locations within their native habitat. Eradication efforts for populations that are a nuisance are expensive and in many areas not feasible.

---

leatherside chub, *Gila copei* (Jordan and Gilbert)

Etymology: *Gila,* named for the Gila River, Arizona, probably a misnomer; *copei,* named for Edward Drinker Cope

Nomenclature: *Squalius copei* Jordan and Gilbert 1881, *Gila copei* Uyeno 1960

IMPORTANCE

Leatherside chub provide forage for game fishes. They are of interest ecologically.

DESCRIPTION

Original

(*Hybopsis egregius* Cope, Ann. Rept. U.S. Geol. Surv. Terr. 1870, 438; Cope and Yarrow, Wheeler's Expl. W. 100th Mer. v. 662, 1877; not *Tigoma egregia* Girard.)

> Numerous specimens of this species were obtained at Evanston, Wyo., of boys fishing with hook and line in tributaries of Bear River. It has not been observed in Utah Lake. As the original types of *Tigoma egregia*, examined by us, have 66 scales only in the lateral line, the species called *Tigoma egregia* by Professor Cope is distinct from it, and may receive the above specific name.

Contemporary
In both sexes, coloration of the body is bluish above and silvery below. Orange to red coloration may occur on the axils of the paired fins of both sexes, the base of the anal fin, and the lower lobe of the caudal fin. Males also have a golden-red speck at the upper end of the gill opening and between the eyes and the upper jaw. The skin has a leathery texture, from which the fish derive their common name. Pharyngeal teeth of the leatherside chub are in two rows and typically number 2, 4–4, 2. The dorsal fin originates behind the insertion of the pelvic fins. Scales number 75 to 85 in the lateral series and are very small. The body is trim and gradually tapering. Both dorsal and anal fins are rounded, each with eight rays, a characteristic distinguishing leatherside chub from most other minnows (Sigler and Miller 1963).

Range

Leatherside chub are native to the eastern and southern parts of the Bonneville Basin; that is, the rivers draining into Great Salt Lake (Bear, Logan, and Weber), into Utah Lake (Provo River), and into the Sevier River system (Beaver and Sevier rivers and their tributaries). They were introduced into Strawberry Reservoir and the Price River, but a 1990 rotenone treatment project removed them from the former.

Size and Longevity

Leatherside chub have a life span of not longer than 5 years. The average length is 3 to 5 in. (76 to 127 mm), with an maximum length of about 6 in. (152 mm).

Limiting Factors

Habitat degradation, particularly within their native range, is detrimental to the leatherside chub. They are preyed on by a number of fishes and birds.

Food and Feeding

Neither food nor feeding habits have been documented for leatherside chub. Their ecological occurrence suggests that they probably feed on small drift organisms, algae, and aquatic insects.

Breeding Habits

Leatherside chub spawn from June to August in waters ranging in temperatures from 60° to 68°F (15.6 to 20°C). No protection is provided for eggs or young.

HABITAT

Leatherside chub typically seek and occupy cool to cold creeks and rivers, preferred temperatures are from 50° to 74°F (10° to 23.3°C), usually 60° to 68°F (15.6° to 20°C). Adults are in pools or riffles; young are in brush areas or quiet water near shore. Acceptable waters range from slightly turbid to muddy with typical bottom types of gravel, sand, rubble, stones, boulders, and silt. Preferred vegetation, which may be dense, consists of algae and pondweeds, but is more frequently sparse and sometimes absent. Leatherside chub frequent waters 2 to 3 ft deep or less with moderate currents (Sigler and Miller 1963).

MANAGEMENT

Rapid fluctuations in water levels and poor water quality adversely affect leatherside chub. During rapid water level fluctuations, they are more vulnerable to predation by fishes and birds. Leatherside chub are greatly reduced and threatened in much of their native habitat.

---

humpback chub,
Gila cypha Miller
Plate 2

Etymology: *Gila*, named for the Gila River, Arizona, probably a misnomer; *cypha* = hump-backed
Nomenclature: *Gila cypha* Miller 1945a

IMPORTANCE

Humpback chub are too scarce to have value as food or forage. They are part of a unique fish fauna that has adapted to the fastest waters of the Colorado River. Humpback chub are listed as an endangered species under the federal Endangered Species Act of 1973, as amended. As native fish, adapted to extraordinary habitat, they have intrinsic value.

DESCRIPTION

Original

Diagnosis.—A strongly compressed *Gila* with the sides of the body slightly convex and with a prominent abrupt hump over the occiput; body almost entirely devoid of scales (except for about 80 in lateral line) which have basal radii; fins expansive, falcate; snout fleshy; mouth inferior; eye very small.

Holotype.—The holotype (U.S.N.M. no. 131839) is a specimen about 305 mm in standard length. . . . The following description is of the holotype, in rays: Dorsal iii, 9, the first full-length ray unbranched and preceded by 3 graduated, rudimentary rays, the first one very small; anal iii, 11, the first full-length ray unbranched and preceded by 3 graduated, rudimentary rays; pectoral rays 18 in each fin; pelvic rays 9 in each fin; principal caudal rays 20, 18 branched plus a full-length unbranched ray above and below.

Scales in lateral line about 80, embedded and only slightly imbricated anteriorly and becoming more embedded and less imbricated posteriorly until those on the caudal peduncle are scarcely evident. . . . Scales above the lateral line deeply embedded and, for the most part, completely isolated from one another, not evident above the level of the base of the nuchal hump. Scales below the lateral line similar to those above, not evident below the base of the pectoral fin except in the region behind the pectoral fin. Back, breast, and belly completely devoid of scales. Dorsal and ventral surfaces of caudal peduncle completely smooth and scaleless, about 3 or 4 irregular rows of embedded scales above and below the lateral line anteriorly which taper off to only 1 or 2 such rows above and below the lateral line posteriorly. . . .

Dental formula 2, 5–4, 1?, 3 teeth (1 in main row, 2 in lesser row) missing on the left arch and 1 tooth (in main row) missing from the right arch, with the definite possibility that there is also 1 tooth missing from the lesser row of this arch (if so, the formula would be 2, 5–4, 2 as usual in *Gila*. The teeth in the main row are thick, especially toward the base, bluntly pointed, with a weak grinding surface on the first 2. . . .

In coloration the holotype of *Gila cypha* (originally preserved in formalin, in which it remained for some time) is brownish-pinkish brown on the sides and belly and yellowish-brown along the back. On close examination, most of the head, back and sides above the level of the lateral line are densely covered with dark puncticulations, those extend below the lateral line in the region above and behind the pectoral base and near the base of the caudal fin. The same pigmentation occurs near the base of the first pectoral ray (left fin particularly), and also near the bases of the interradial membranes of the dorsal and caudal fins.

Contemporary

Humpback chub coloration includes a light olive gray back and silver sides fading to a white belly. The nuchal hump of adults is distinctive, becoming increasingly more pronounced as fish size increases. The body is extremely streamlined and deep in adults, with a thin but not long caudal peduncle. A long fleshy snout dominates the inferior mouth of adults; the eyes are small. Dorsal fin rays are usually nine, anal fin rays are usually 10 or more, and teeth are normally 2, 5–4, 2 (Holden and Stalnaker 1970; Minckley 1973; Holden 1978).

Range

Originally, humpback chub ranged through the whitewater canyons of the Colorado River and some of its tributaries from the Green River south on the Colorado River to what now is Lake Mead. The following notes were made by W. F. Sigler.

> Anecdotal Information.... "The senior author and crew collected fish in Hideout Canyon, now under the waters of Flaming Gorge Lake, in August 1950. The take was large, including 20 humpback chub, numerous bonytail, roundtail chub, flannelmouth, sucker, razorback sucker, two Colorado squawfish, and eight or ten intergeneric hybrids (*Catostomus* × *Xyrauchen*). Most of the Gila spp. ranged in length from 10 to 14 in. The main channel current was too fast for collecting gear. However, the current inshore, off an island about 50 ft from shore and 160 ft long, was much slower. We used both a haul seine and a 110 volt, 2,000 watt alternating current generator. The fish, excluding channel catfish, were in good shape. Black flecks, presumably from some petroleum product upstream, were present throughout the collection.

Many of the populations have been extirpated by reservoir inundation of habitat and alteration of flow and temperature regimes. Presently, there are six populations, all in whitewater canyons: Westwater Canyon, Cataract Canyon, Desolation–Grey Canyon, Yampa Canyon, Black Rocks Canyon, and the Little Colorado River of Grand Canyon (Valdez and Clemmer 1982). Only the first three populations noted are in Utah.

Size and Longevity

Humpback chub reach a maximum length of about 16 in. (406 mm) occasionally longer. Most probably live 7 or 8 years. Kaeding and Zimmerman (1983) reported 1-year-olds were about 4 in. (102 mm) long, and 3-year-olds about 10 to 12 in. (254 to 305 mm) long. Annulus formation is in May. Not all fish form an annulus the first year. Those taken in Hideout Canyon in 1950 averaged 12 in. (305 mm) long. Valdez (1990) furnished additional information on growth rates for this species.

Food and Feeding

Humpback chub feed mainly on invertebrates, and occasionally on fishes. Kaeding and Zimmerman (1983) reported that humpback chub feed heavily on midge and blackfly larvae but show less preference for *Gammarus*. Humpback chub feed from bottom to surface, and, like many fish, take floating insects.

Capture of some fish in the interfaces between the eddies and adjacent runs suggests that the humpback chub use these areas for feeding on drift and other organisms. Karp and Tyus (1990) found that some fed on hymenopterans (bees, ants, wasps) and plant debris, and others fed on hymenopterans and terrestrial insects.

Limiting Factors

Degraded and lost habitat are the two main factors contributing to decimation of humpback chub. Degradation and loss of habitat by dam building causes lowered flows, different stream temperature regime, creation of large impoundments with cold, clear water releases from impoundments, and channel damage. Also, humpback chub were not able to compete with introduced exotic species for food and space. Exotics transmit diseases against which humpback chub have no immunity. Humpback chub in the Little Colorado and Colorado rivers were infected with 13 species of bacteria, including *Aeromonas hydrophila,* 6 protozoans, the fungus *Saprolegnia*, and the parasitic copepod *Lernia cyprinacea*. The degree of infection depended on the pathogen, size of fish, time of year, and water temperature (Valdez and Clemmer 1982; Kaeding and Zimmerman 1983).

Breeding Habits

Humpback chub spawn in April, May, and June (Valdez and Clemmer 1982) when water temperatures reach 66° to 70°F (18.9° to 21.1°C). They are then 8 to 12 in. (203 to 305 mm) long and 3 to 4 years old. In the hatchery, fish mature as early as 2 to 3 years of age (Hamman 1982b). Males may mature a year earlier than females. Many stretches of the main stem of the Colorado River are too cold and fast and do not provide shallow, slow backwater areas in which chubs can breed. Spawning occurs over cobble/boulder substrate and young rear along shallow shorelines or backwaters. Breeding fish are distinguished by tubercles on the head and paired fins.

Hamman (1982b) at the Willow Beach National Fish Hatchery, Arizona, has done the only culture work on humpback chub. In 1981 he used 30 fish taken from the Black Rock and Little Colorado rivers. The unweighted average size of the males was 14 in. (356 mm) and 12.3 oz (349 g); of the females 15.3 in. (389 mm) and 19.3 oz (547 g). Ages were unknown. Females produced an average of 2,386 eggs per pound of body weight. The highest hatching rate for eggs was 84 percent in water 66° to 68°F (18.9° to 20°C), the hatching time was from 115 to 160 hrs. However, the highest survival rate for swimup fry was 99 percent at 70° to 72°F (21.1° to 22.2°C). Swimup fry are individual fish with some yolk sac remaining and which have recently emerged from the gravel or spawning area. Substrate for natural spawning in confinement was 11 to 16 in. (279 to 406 mm) in boulders, overlain with cobble 1.5 to 3.9 in. (3.8 cm to 10 cm); the water was from 3.9 to 30 in. (10 cm to 76 cm) deep (Kaeding et al. 1990).

A sample of 133 humpback chub included 39 breeding adults and 29 juveniles, indicating that a reproducing population exists in Yampa Canyon. Ripe humpback chub were collected during declining spring flows and in increasing river temperatures after the highest runoff. This event occurred in May and June in low water years but extended into July in high water years (Kaeding and Zimmerman 1983). No humpback chub in breeding condition were captured during pre- or post-runoff periods. Karp and Tyus's (1990) data suggest that females may be ripe for a limited time only. Ripe humpback chub were captured at temperatures of 67° to 68°F (19.4° to 20°C). These temperatures are in reasonably good agreement with other studies, although they are slightly higher than ones noted by Valdez and Clemmer (1982).

HABITAT

Humpback chub are adapted to the fast, turbulent, muddy waters of the historic Colorado River and its tributaries. The young seek turbid, slow, shallow shoreline areas. Clear water forces them into deeper, less hospitable habitat. Humpback chub prefer levels of 1,000 to 2,500 ppm total dissolved solids (TDS) and avoid levels greater than 5,100 ppm (Pimentel and Bulkley 1983). Before the introduction of exotics, their associates were the *Gila* complex, Colorado squawfish, and flannelmouth and razorback suckers. Miller (1945a) pointed out that some interesting concepts can be perceived by reviewing Colorado River gauging station data. At the station 240 mi (386 km) below Grand Canyon, the rate of flow varied between 1,800 and 174,000 cfs (51 and 4,928 cms) over the period 1917 to 1926; water level flucuation was about 25 ft (7.6 m), potentially providing the basis for an explanation of population declines following impoundment and reduction of variation in flows by closure of Glen Canyon Dam.

Humpback chub move relatively little from the turbulent deep water habitat of the Black Rocks area according to Archer et al. (1985). This fact suggests that the habitat requirements of adult humpback chub, including those essentials necessary for spawning, are met within the Black Rocks River reach. Moreover, these authors wrote that this observation suggests that humpback chub populations might be limited by the scarcity of turbulent deep-water habitats.

Humpback chub were rare from upper Yampa Canyon to Upper Whirlpool Canyon. They were most prevalent in, and presumably selected, eddy habitats rather than steep reaches. Humpback chub were most abundant in Yampa Canyon but were not captured in Split Mountain Canyon or in Ladore Canyon (Valdez et al. 1991a; Karp and Tyus 1990).

MANAGEMENT

Further degradation of their habitat should be prevented as the first step in humpback chub protection. No additional potentially competitive exotic fishes should be planted near viable chub populations. The natural hydrograph of the Colorado River (that is, below Glen Canyon Dam) should be restored as near to pre-dam level as possible. Subpopulations should be identified, and hatchery fish from these populations maintained to preserve genetic diversity. The Yampa River in Dinosaur National Monument supports all native fishes known to have occurred there, so perhaps this area should be considered as a refugium for the humpback chub and other native fishes (Valdez et al. 1990).

bonytail,
Gila elegans
Baird and Girard
Plate 3

Etymology: *Gila,* named for the Gila River, Arizona, probably a misnomer; *elegans* = elegant
Nomenclature: *Gila elegans* Baird and Girard 1853b

IMPORTANCE

Bonytail are part of a unique fish fauna that evolved in a harsh and unusual environment. Their highly specialized adaption to this habitat is perhaps best demonstrated by the fact that when that environment changed, they decreased from being a common species in main river channels of the Colorado River system to the rarest. They were listed as an endangered species by the U.S. Fish and Wildlife Service on April 23, 1980. As a native species, adapted to extraordinary habitat, they have intrinsic value.

DESCRIPTION

Original

> Closely allied to the *Gila robusta*. Its body, however, is more slender, and its tail proportionally more elongated. The caudal fin is more deeply emarginate and more developed, as indeed are all the fins. The head is very much depressed and flattened on the snout. Eyes elliptical. The scales are proportionally more elongated than in the *Gila robusta* and are broader anteriorly than posteriorly; the lateral line has about ninety of them. The number of rays in the fins affords also a distinctive mark between *Gila robusta* and *Gila elegans*. The ventrals have no rudiment of spiny ray. Color light brown. in rays: D III. 9. C 9. I. 9.9 I 10. A III. 10. V 9. P. 16.

Contemporary

Adult coloration includes an olive and dark gray back, fading to silver sides, and a white belly. Males are slightly more colorful and have more breeding tubercles than do females, a more or less typical pattern for cyprinids. The long caudal peduncle of adults is the most distinctive feature of bonytail. The body is very streamlined, the skull is concave. The adult has a predorsal hump that is much smaller than that of the humpback chub and is partially scaled. The mouth is typically terminal; both dorsal and anal fins usually have 10 rays. Teeth are 2, 5–4, 2 (Minckley 1973).

RANGE

The main stem of the Colorado River and some of its tributaries, as far north as southern Wyoming (Green River) and south into Mexico, is the original range of bonytail (Valdez and Williams 1991). The largest tributary populations originally were probably in the Green and Gila rivers. They were very abundant in Hideout Canyon, now under the waters of Flaming Gorge Lake, in August 1950. (See author note under humpback chub, "Range" section). Since 1980 fewer than 10 specimens have been captured in the upper Colorado River system, including Desolation and Cataract canyons, the lower Yampa River, and the Colorado River near the Colorado-Utah state line. Large adults have been reported in Mohave and Havasu lakes. Very little reproduction has been documented; however, it should be pointed out that techniques for separating the young of the *Gila* complex need further refinement (Holden 1978; Valdez and Clemmer 1982; Valdez 1985).

Size and Longevity

Bonytail rarely grow to lengths of over 24 in. (610 mm); most are 10 to 15 in. (254 to 381 mm). In 1950, those in Hideout Canyon, ranged in length from 10 to 14 in. (254 to 356 mm). (See author note under humpback chub, "Range" section). Vanicek and Kramer (1969) give the following lengths for bonytails at the end of each year of life for years 1 through 7: in inches, 2.2, 3.9, 6.2, 10.2, 12.7, 14.0, and 14.7; in mm, 56, 99, 158, 260, 323, 356, 373. The largest bonytail collected by them was 7 years old, 15.3 in. (389 mm) long, and weighed 14.9 oz (422 g). The length-weight regression is $\text{Log}_{10}\ W = -4.7899 + 2.680\ \text{Log}_{10}\ L$, where L equals total body length in mm, and W equals weight in grams. Bonytail probably live as long as 20 years. Growth rates for bonytail are also presented by Valdez (1990).

Food and Feeding

Bonytail over 8 in. (203 mm) long feed on terrestrial and aquatic insects, plant debris, filamentous algae, and plankton. They also eat fishes. Small fish (bonytail and roundtail not separated) feed on chironomid (midge) larvae and mayfly nymphs (Vanicek and Kramer 1969).

Limiting Factors

Loss or severe degradation of riverine habitat are primary reasons bonytail are rare and endangered. Other destructive factors compound the effects of degraded habitat. Such habitat causes stress, which, in turn, makes a species less competitive, more likely to hybridize, and more susceptible to disease and parasites (for example, *Lernaea cyprinacea*).

Breeding Habits

Bonytail spawn in the spring, generally at water temperatures between 64° and 70°F (17.8° to 21.1°C), over gravel bars. The fertilized eggs are strewn at random and adhere to rocks or settle in crevices; no care is given eggs or young. One female is attended by several males. Bonytail are readily cultured where they may also spawn in ponds. Maturity in hatcheries is at age 2; it is probably a year later in the wild.

Hamman (1985) spawned a hatchery population of 24 females. Average weight was 4.5 oz (127.6 g). Females averaged 4,677 eggs per female. However, in earlier work Hamman (1982a) found that 6 females with a median weight of 43.3 oz (1,227.6 g) and length of 20.7 in. (52 cm) had a mean fecundity of 25,090. These eggs hatched in 99 to 174 hrs at 68° to 70°F (20° to 21.1°C), with a survival rate of 90 percent. In contrast, eggs hatched at 53° to 55°F (11.7° to 12.8°C) had a survival rate of 4 percent. Survival of swimup fry at 68° to 70°F (10° to 21.1°C) was 98 percent, and at 53° to 55°F (11.7° to 12.8°C) was 25 percent.

HABITAT

Bonytail have long been considered a main stem river fish, but reportedly live much of the time in backwaters and eddies rather than fight the strong current (Karp and Tyus 1990). (See author note under humpback chub, "Range" section.) Bonytail are able to survive in lakes and ponds, including Lakes Mohave and Havasu, whereas humpback chub perished with the filling of the reservoirs. The TDS preference level of bonytail is 4,100 to 4,700 ppm (mg/l). They avoid less than 560 and more than 6,600 ppm TDS (Pimentel and Bulkley 1983).

MANAGEMENT

Protection of some of the most acceptable segments of the original habitat should be the number one priority of any restoration program or plan. Identification of these areas should be followed closely by a detailed management plan. Any recovery plan should include the continued production of bonytail in at least two hatcheries and the establishment of populations in two to several refuges. The U.S. Fish and Wildlife Service issued a revised bonytail recovery plan in 1991.

---

roundtail chub,
Gila robusta
Baird and Girard
Plate 4

Etymology: *Gila,* named for the Gila River, Arizona, probably a misnomer; *robusta* = robust, stout

Nomenclature: *Gila robusta* Baird and Girard 1853b, *Gila robusta seminuda* Cope and Yarrow 1874 (Virgin roundtail chub), *Gila robusta robusta* Miller 1945c (Colorado roundtail chub)

IMPORTANCE

Roundtail chub were sometimes used for bait. They provide forage for carnivorous fishes. For people interested in catching, but not necessarily eating, a fish, fishing for them can be fun. Intramuscular bones reduce their table value and desirability. They are protected in Utah.

DESCRIPTION

Original

Body very much swollen anteriorly, and tapering very suddenly from the dorsal fin to the insertion of the caudal. Head very much depressed above, sloping very rapidly from the nape to the snout and forming 1 fourth of the entire length. Eyes proportionally small and subcircular. Mouth tolerably large; the posterior branch of the maxillary does not reach the vertical line of the pupil. Dorsal fin situated on the middle of the back, and a little higher than long. Caudal crescentic. Anal situated behind the dorsal. Insertion of ventrals in advance of the anterior margin of the dorsal. The posterior tip of the pectorals does not reach the insertion of the ventrals. All the soft rays are bifurcated. Lateral line composed of about ninety scales. Color greyish brown above, lighter beneath. Formula of the fins: D I. 9. C 8. I. 8. 9. I. 7. A I. 9. V I. 9. P. 15.

Contemporary

Although roundtail lack the strong nuchal hump of humpback chub and bonytail, they are stoutly built. Generally they are dusky to green on the back and upper sides, but sometimes metallic blue, and silvery or white below. Dorsal and anal fin rays vary from 8 to 11, but are usually 9 or 10. A flat head appears curved in profile; the eye is small. Lateral series scales number 75 to 95. The teeth are 2, 5–4, 2 (La Rivers 1962; Sigler and Miller 1963).

RANGE

Roundtail chub and certain subspecies range throughout most Colorado River Basin main stem and tributary rivers from Fontanelle Reservoir in Wyoming south through southeastern Nevada and Arizona. They are common to abundant in the upper Colorado River subbasin (Sigler and Miller 1963; Tyus et al. 1982). The Colorado roundtail chub is widespread in the upper and lower Colorado River Basin. The Virgin roundtail chub occurs in the Virgin River drainage (Lee et al. 1980).

SIZE AND LONGEVITY

Roundtail chub may reach a length of 17 in. (432 mm) and a weight of 1.4 lb (0.64 kg). In acceptable habitat, most are 10 to 14 in. (254 to 356 mm); in marginal habitat they may be no longer than 8 to 10 in. (203 to 254 mm). (See author note under humpback chub, "Range" section). Average life span is probably 8 to 10 years, although occasionally one will live longer (Sigler and Miller 1963). In the Green River their total lengths for the first 7 years were as follows: in inches, 2.1, 3.9, 6.1, 8.6, 10.5, 12.3, and 13.4; in mm, 53, 99, 155, 218, 267, 312, 340 (Vanicek and Kramer 1969). The length-weight regression is $\text{Log}_{10} W = -5.2462 + 3.086 \times \text{Log}_{10} L$, where W equals weight in grams and L equals total length in millimeters.

Food and Feeding

Roundtail chub are generally carnivorous and opportunistic, feeding on insects, crustaceans, and snails, but may feed on filamentous algae (Sigler and Miller 1963). Virgin roundtail chub in the Virgin River largely consume *Spirogyra*, benthic and drift animals, and plant material (Greger and Deacon 1988). Tyus and Minckley (1988) reported that roundtail chub fed heavily on Mormon crickets in Dinosaur National Monument in 1986 and 1987. Mormon crickets are long-horned, flightless mountain grasshoppers that readily swim streams; many are swept downstream in the process. Young roundtail chub feed on midge larvae and mayfly nymphs (Vanicek and Kramer 1969). As roundtail grow larger, a greater diversity of food items is included in the diet, among them aquatic insects and terrestrials such as beetles and ants.

Limiting Factors

Drastic reductions in habitat quality since historic times and competition with exotics have reduced roundtail chub. More diseases and parasites that fare better when the fish are stressed are now present. Vanicek and Kramer (1969) found that 73 percent of fish over 8 in. (20 cm) had tapeworm (*Proteocephalus* sp.).

Breeding Habits

Roundtail chub breed in June to early July, when temperatures reach 65°F (18.3°C). One female is accompanied by three to five males. Roundtail mature at age 5 at 10 to 12 in. (254 to 305 mm) in length. The eggs, 0.03 in. (0.7 mm), pasty white and adhesive, stick to rocks or other substrate or drop into crevices; no care of eggs or young is provided. One 12-in. (305-mm) female had about 10,000 eggs. Spawning is generally over gravel in water up to 30 ft (9.1 m) deep (Sigler and Miller 1963; Constanz 1981; Kaeding et al. 1990).

Habitat

Roundtail chub live in big rivers. Habitat in Utah includes the Colorado River and its tributaries. Roundtail chub occur in Fontanelle Reservoir, Wyoming and Flaming Gorge Lake, Utah-Wyoming. Young are typically in quiet water near shore or in backwaters. Bottom types selected by roundtail chub range from silt to sand and gravel to rocks. Murky rather than clear water is sought, and they generally do not frequent vegetation (Sigler and Miller 1963; Tyus et al. 1982; Valdez et al. 1991a). Adults live in eddies and pools, adjacent to, but not in, strong current (Vanicek and Kramer 1969).

Management

Roundtail chub apparently need no special protection. However, they are declining throughout much of their native range, in particular the Green River subbasin. Surveys and studies are required to accurately identify population trends and document current distribution. Preservation of the habitat in which they occur should protect them. They are protected in Utah because they are quite rare in part of their native range and the endangered *Gila* complex may be confused with them.

brassy minnow, *Hybognathus hankinsoni* Hubbs

Etymology: *Hybognathus* = Greek for swollen jaw, *hankinsoni* named for T. L. Hankinson

Nomenclature: *Hybognathus hankinsoni* Hubbs in Jordan 1929

IMPORTANCE

Brassy minnow are currently of such rare occurrence in Utah as to preclude determination of importance. Brassy minnow are, however, easily confused with fathead minnow and may be more abundant than suspected.

DESCRIPTION

Original

Head blunter; color darker; fins more rounded than in *nuchalis*, and scales with many weak, instead of a few strong, radii. S. Ont. and Great Lakes region, W. to N. Dak., Colo., and Mo. (Diagnosis by Hubbs.) (To T. L. Hankinson.)

Contemporary

Coloration is brassy above, fading to silvery white on the lower sides and belly. Scales on the upper dark area of the sides have dark margins. The body is elongate and slightly compressed laterally. The long, blunt snout has a slightly overhanging upper jaw. Pharyngeal teeth are 4–4. Both dorsal and anal fins usually have 8 rays, pectoral fin rays are usually 13, pelvics 8. There are 35 to 38 scales in the lateral series.

RANGE

Native range of the brassy minnow is from eastern Colorado, Wyoming, and Montana north into Alberta and Saskatchewan, east to Quebec, south as far as northern Illinois (Smith 1979). In Utah they have been taken in the Colorado River near Moab. Occurrence has been reported in the Gunnison River, Colorado, just upstream from Utah.

SIZE AND LONGEVITY

A Sand Creek, Wyoming, population of brassy minnow had total lengths each year for 3 years: in inches, 2.2, 2.8, and 3.2; in mm, 56, 71, 81. The growth of a Wisconsin population was almost identical. Few fish reached age 3 (Copes 1975).

FOOD AND FEEDING

Diet of brassy minnow varies considerably, probably indicating availability and omnivory. Brassy minnow feed on algae, drift organisms, and other small invertebrates. On one occasion a school of brassy minnow moved into very shallow water and fed on mosquito larvae until all were gone (Copes 1975).

LIMITING FACTORS

Brassy minnow numbers in Utah are too low to determine what may limit them.

BREEDING HABITS

Brassy minnow breed in the spring when water temperatures reach 60° to 80°F (15.6° to 26.6°C). Spawning occurs principally from 1100 to 1700 hrs over vegetation in flooded marshes. They mature at age 2, although some breed at age 1. The spawning season is short, perhaps no more than 10 days. Both sexes are about the same size. One female may produce 1,000 to 2,500 eggs (Copes 1975).

HABITAT

Brassy minnow are bog area fish, living in slow-moving streams. Sometimes they are in stained waters, often over mud or debris-strewn bottoms, and near vegetation. They tolerate a wide range of temperatures from near freezing to 84°F (28.9°C) and may frequent the coldwater habitat of trout or the warmwater of sunfishes. They are strongly schooling fish and avoid strong currents; young generally school inshore near shallow vegetated areas (Copes 1975).

MANAGEMENT

No particular programs or plans to alter the numbers or populations of brassy minnow in the state are recommended.

---

least chub, *Iotichthys phlegethontis*(Cope)
Plate 5

Etymology: *Iotichthys,* from the Greek iota and *ichthys* (small fish), *phlegethontis* = color resembling a river of fire, burning
Nomenclature: *Clinostomus phlegethontis* Cope 1874, *Iotichthys phlegethontis* Jordan, Evermann, and Clark 1930

IMPORTANCE

Least chub are natural predators of mosquito larvae. Least chub should be preserved because they are an interesting and unusual element of the native fauna. They are listed as a candidate species under the federal Endangered Species Act.

DESCRIPTION

Original

Teeth 1.5–4.2; body, deep, short; scales larger than in any other species of the genus, viz.: eleven longitudinal and thirty-seven transverse series. There is no lateral line, which may be due to the immature state of the only specimen at my disposal. The depth enters the length without the caudal fin 3.5 times, while the length of the head is counted in the same four times. The orbit is large, entering the head 2.75 times, and .2 greater than interorbital width; in older fishes the orbit will be found as usual relatively smaller. The lips are even, and the mouth quite oblique, the end of

> the maxillary reaching the line of the orbit. Radii, D. I. 7; A. I. 8; the ventrals originate in front of the line of the dorsal, and extend to the vent, and are not nearly reached by the pectorals. Length without caudal fin, .034; ditto to basis of dorsal, .0186; length of head, .008; width ditto at pterotica, .0038. A broad plumbeous band on the side, below which the color is golden, above it probably translucent in life, with a dusky median dorsal line. Discovered in Bear River, Utah, with the *Myloleucus parovanus*, by Dr. Yarrow.

Contemporary

Least chub are the smallest cyprinids in Utah. They have a very oblique mouth, large scales (34 to 38) along the side. No lateral line is present but rarely one or two pored scales are present. These characteristics readily distinguish least chub from other minnows. Female least chub and young are pale olive on the back, silvery on the sides with white fins. The eyes of females are silvery, with only a little gold, rather than definitely golden, as in the males. Males are olive green above, steel blue on the sides with a golden stripe behind the upper end of the opercle. The brightest males have golden sides that become reddish dark gold, in a band that runs from the bright red pectoral fin axis to above and in front of the anal fin. Single fins are lemon amber. Paired fins may be bright golden amber. Pharyngeal teeth are in two rows, 2, 5–4, 2. The dorsal fin lies behind the insertion of the pelvic fins and has eight, or rarely, nine rays. The anal rays number eight (Sigler and Miller 1963).

Range

Originally, least chub occurred in the Bonneville Basin, in streams near Salt Lake City, and in freshwater ponds and swamps around Great Salt Lake. They were also present in Utah Lake, Beaver River, Parowan Creek, Clear Creek, and Provo River. The first specimens to be taken from Millard County, western Utah, were from springs in Snake Valley in 1942, by C. L., L. C., and E. L. Hubbs. Least chub were first collected in LeLand Harris Spring, Juab County, Utah, by R. R. Miller in 1970. Their range may now be limited to Snake Valley, western Utah (Sigler and Workman 1975; Crist 1990). Stockings of this species in the late 1980s have not been evaluated.

Size and Longevity

Least chub are short lived and slow growing. In three separate studies totaling 112 fish from the LeLand Harris Spring area, Juab County, the total length for fish age 1 to 4, at the end of each year, was: in inches, 0.7, 1.3, 2.0, and 3.0; in mm, 18, 33, 51, 76. Only two fish reached 4 years of age. In another study of 207 fish from the same general area, the total length at the end of each year for fish aged 1, 2, and 3 years was: in inches, 1.0, 1.4, and 1.6; in mm, 25, 36, 41. Only 6 percent (12) of these fish reached age 3. A least chub 1.3 in. (33 mm) long weighs 0.02 oz (0.57 g) (Sigler and Workman 1975; Workman et al. 1976; Crawford 1979).

Limiting Factors

Least chub face predation by introduced species, such as game fishes, and by Utah chub and bullfrogs. Trampling and organic pollution by livestock in the vicinity of LeLand Harris Spring is a problem for fish in this area. Fish-eating ducks, great blue herons, and gulls also prey on the least chub (Osmundson 1985). In the LeLand Harris Spring area least chub are able to survive cold weather. Habitat degradation, inability to compete with exotics, and predation by exotic fishes probably caused elimination of least chub over much of their original range.

Food and Feeding

Least chub commonly eat algae, diatomaceous material, mosquito larvae, and midge adults, larvae, and pupae. Copepods, ostracods, and other small invertebrates are also eaten. One was observed swimming up to a clump of algae, grabbing a mouthful, and thrashing about until the algae was freed then swallowed.

Breeding Habits

Least chub spawn in the spring when water temperatures reach 60°F (15.6°C), usually from April to July. Initiation of least chub spawning is a function of both temperature and sunlight. Least chub held indoors in aquaria at a constant photoperiod and temperature did not show a tendency to spawn until they were exposed to sunlight (Crawford 1979). Both males and females mature at age 1 when they are slightly over 1 in. (25 mm) long. Spawning occurs around vegetation, primarily algae. The number of eggs produced per female ranges from less than 300 to over 2,700. Mature eggs range in diameter from 0.03 to 0.05 in. (0.76 to 1.3 mm) and are adhesive and heavy; they sink until they strike some object to adhere to. They hatch in about 2 days at 72°F (22.2°C). Females spawn intermittently throughout the late spring and early summer (Crawford 1979). Newly hatched least chub live on their yolk sac for 3 to 4 days, then begin feeding.

Baugh (1980) reported on hatchery-reared least chub. The fish were taken from the Logan Fisheries Experiment Station raceways in May. In October, spawning substrate was added to the artificial habitat, and in late October, eggs were present. Free-swimming fry were noted on October 31 and November 2. Conditions at the time of spawning were: temperature—approximately 70°F (21.1°C); photoperiod—14 hours of daylight; pH—7.6; and total alkalinity—84.1 ppm (mg/l).

Habitat

Originally, least chub habitat included slow rivers, clear creeks, springs, ponds, and swamps, which at times were quite alkaline. The LeLand Harris Spring area, where the chub is present today, is moderately heavily vegetated with algae, chara, duck weed, and watercress with bulrushes, cattails, and sedges around the edges. Other associated plants include rabbitfoot grass, muskgrass, water parsnip, wire rush, and motherwort. Common components of bank cover are *Juncus* spp., *Eleocharis* spp., and *Carex* spp. *Lemna* spp. and filamentous green algae are the only two plants growing on the surface of spring ponds (Osmundson 1985). The pH of the water in LeLand Harris Spring in 1975 was 8.0, oxygen 4.5 ppm (mg/l), total hardness 120 ppm (mg/l), calcium hardness 63 ppm (mg/l), and alkalinity 150 ppm (mg/l). The bottom material in LeLand Harris Spring least chub habitat is hard to very soft clay, mud, soft mud, and some peat. Water temperatures in 1975 ranged from 55° to 75°F (12.8° to 23.9°C), except in some shallow areas. In winter some areas freeze lightly. The area varies in depth from a few inches to 10 or more ft (3.05 m). Some of the area is covered by a floating bog with openings only 3 to 4 ft (0.9 to 1.22 m) across.

MANAGEMENT

Primarily, least chub need protection from predators and habitat degradation. It is not practical to protect them from birds, mammals, or amphibians, but there are areas where all other fishes could be removed. Probably the most serious hazard would be a lowering of the water table. The Bureau of Land Management controls most of the property surrounding least chub habitat in western Utah (for example, LeLand Harris Spring). This area is managed for least chub under their designated "sensitive species" status. No physical modification or other potentially adverse actions can occur without agency review.

Virgin spinedace, *Lepidomeda mollispinus* Miller and Hubbs
Plate 6

Etymology: *Lepidomeda,* from the Latin for scaled, and *Meda*, another species of spinedace; *mollispinus,* from the Latin for smooth spine
Nomenclature: *Lepidomeda mollispinus* Miller and Hubbs 1960

IMPORTANCE

When abundant, Virgin spinedace were used as bait fish, and they provided forage. This member of a unique group of spiny-rayed minnows, native only to the Colorado River system, has declined so greatly in range and numbers that they are endangered. They are protected by the states of Arizona, Nevada, and Utah.

DESCRIPTION

Original

Diagnosis.—This subspecies is most closely related to *L. m. pratensus*, from which it differs in having the dorsal fin less elevated and more rounded, the pelvic fin shorter, and the mouth smaller and less oblique.

Types.—The holotype, UMMZ 141673, an adult 88 mm. long, was seined by C. L., L. C., and E. L. Hubbs from Santa Clara River, 3 mi. SE of Shivwitz and 4.5 mi. NW of Santa Clara, Washington Co., Utah, on July 29, 1942. Secured with the holotype were 103 paratopotypes, 23–80 mm long, UMMZ 141674. An additional 604 specimens were examined from localities in Arizona, Nevada, and Utah [data from this table omitted]. (Table I showing vertebral variation in the Plagopterini omitted).

Life colors were noted in the field as follows: body silvery with a more or less brassy sheen and with sooty specklings on sides; axils of paired fins and basal band on anal fin orange-red to translucent orange-pink; a little spot of golden red at upper end of gill-slit. Younger fish look whitish in the water and some adults have the sides blackish, especially conspicuous in the water.

The nuptial tubercles, best developed on males in a collection of June 17, but evident also in July specimens, are distinctive. Those on the head are almost wholly confined to the dorsal surface, extending onto the sides only in a definite patch across the upper part of the opercle. They are irregularly scattered over the dorsal surface, from near the occipital edge forward to the upper part of the snout and outward to the orbital margins. They are of moderate size, and their spiny tips are weakly curved forward. Tubercles occur on the scales over the entire body, but become obsolescent on the midsides and belly. Those near the margin of the head, between the lateral lines, are considerably strengthened. Here the partly fused tubercles form a single straightish transverse (or vertical) series, with the points essentially erect. On the caudal peduncle the points are smaller and form a more curved series on each scale. On the breast the tubercles are somewhat strengthened, and usually single on each scale. The scales in a band just behind the shoulder girdle, above the pectoral fin, have the soft tissue considerably swollen, and are weakly tuberculate. On the first pectoral ray there is a single file of tubercles, and on the outer part of several succeeding rays a file branched once near the base. Each tubercle has one to several weakly antroverse spiny points. Weak tubercles line pelvic and anal rays. Despite our large collections none of the other species seems to be represented by nuptial males.

This subspecies often attains a total length of nearly 4 in. The largest specimen we have seen is the holotype, about 4.25 in long (88 mm. in standard length). It is the only specimen among 718 that is longer than 80 mm.

Habitat.—This subspecies is common in the Virgin River and its tributaries in Utah, Arizona, and Nevada, in moderate to swift current, chiefly in pools. Where the collections were made the bottom was usually sand and gravel, often with stones and occasionally with boulders and some mud. Green algae and sparse pondweed were often associated, and depth of capture varied from 1 to 3 ft. The water was either clear, or, as in the Virgin River, very milky; with bottom visibility from about 3 in to 3 ft.

Contemporary

Coloration is silvery with a brassy sheen, with sooty blotches on the sides. Scales number 77 to 91 in the lateral series, the terminal mouth is without a barbel, and the head and belly are rounded. Two anterior spiny rays occur in the dorsal fin, the second longer and stronger than the first. The dorsal has 8 rays and the anal fin 8 to 10, but usually 9. Pharyngeal teeth are 2, 5–4, 2. In breeding condition, males have a basal band on the anal fin, and the bases of the paired fins are orange to pinkish red. There may also be a spot of gold to red at the upper end of the gill slit (Valdez et al. 1991b; Minckley 1973; Sigler and Miller 1963; Miller and Hubbs 1960).

RANGE

Historically, Virgin spinedace ranged through the Virgin River drainage of Arizona, Nevada, and Utah. Today there are small populations in portions of nine tributaries: lower Beaver Dam Creek, the North Fork and the East Fork of the Virgin River in Zion National Park, Santa Clara River, Ash Creek, LaVerkin Creek, and North Creek. They are also present in the upper Virgin River above Quail Creek Diversion (Valdez et al. 1991b; Cross 1975; Sigler and Miller 1963). Valdez et al. 1991b estimated that the original range has been reduced from 172 mi (275 km) to 66 mi (105 km).

SIZE AND LONGEVITY

Occasionally, this subspecies reaches a length of 5 in. (127 mm) but most older ones are less than 4 in. (102 mm), with a life span of 3 years. They reach lengths for each year as follows: in inches, 2.6, 3.1, and 3.3; in mm, 66, 78, 84. Population age composition for this group is generally age 1, 90 percent; age 2, 5 percent, and age 3, 2 percent (Cross 1975; Rinne 1971; Sigler and Miller 1963).

FOOD AND FEEDING

Both omnivorous and opportunistic, spinedace are not much different from many other fishes in a fluctuating, unstable environment. Primarily they feed on aquatic insect larvae and nymphs, but will readily turn to terrestrial insects that fall into the water. Rinne (1971) reported that they rise to the surface to feed on floating material consisting mainly of Diptera (flies), Coleoptera (beetles), plant material, and organic debris (Cross 1975, Minckley 1973).

LIMITING FACTORS

With its extremes of flow, turbidity, salinity, and temperature, the Virgin River is a harsh environment for native fishes. Overgrazing has impacted much of the watershed, and the river has been extensively diverted. It is not uncommon to find portions of the river essentially dry, with only isolated pools, crowded with many fishes. Only flushing from rain or irrigation return flow rescues fishes trapped under these extreme conditions (Hickman 1984).

BREEDING HABITS

Older females, age 3, spawn earlier in the spring than females age 1 or 2, starting in late May. Young females complete spawning in late June or early July. There is some evidence 3-year-olds spawn twice in 1 year. The two younger age groups initiate spawning later and for a shorter period. Because relatively few fish live as long as 2 years, the burden of perpetuating the species falls on the 1-year-olds. Temperatures ranging from 55° to 63°F (12.8° to 17.2°C) during spawning, and high stream flows are most conducive to successful reproduction. Adverse high temperatures or unseasonably low flows are the two negative factors in reproduction (Cross 1975; Minckley 1973).

HABITAT

Virgin spinedace live in relatively clear water about 3 ft (0.9 m) deep and near cover such as overhanging banks and shrubs or boulders. They prefer to be near vegetation and over sand and gravel bottoms. Summer temperatures may reach 85°F (29.4°C) or higher. They prefer slow water, with flows of not much more than 1 cfs (0.03 cms). They are absent in areas of habitually torrential floods. They seem to have adjusted to some degree to the degradation of habitat in the last 75 years, but probably will not survive much more environmental insult (Cross 1975; Sigler and Miller 1963).

MANAGEMENT

Spinedace should be protected through the establishment of areas set aside for their prime use. A flow regime as nearly natural as possible should be developed and maintained. No additional exotic fishes should be introduced into the system. Habitat degradation problems involve four areas: dewatering, impoundment and accompanying changes in flow and temperature regimes, unstable bank conditions associated with grazing livestock, and introduction of exotics. Each problem area should be addressed.

---

golden shiner, *Notemigonus crysoleucas* (Mitchill)

Etymology: *Notemigonus* = back; half; angle, keel-like back; *crysoleucas*, from *chrysos* (gold) and *leucas* (white)
Nomenclature: *Cyprinus crysoleucas* Mitchill 1814b, *Notemigonus crysoleucas* O'Donnell 1935

IMPORTANCE

Forage is the primary value of golden shiner in Utah. They have been introduced extensively in the United States to provide forage and bait and are probably the most widely cultivated bait minnow. When they markedly outnumber other species at a site, golden shiner are a good indicator of pollution (Smith 1979) or habitat modification (degradation).

DESCRIPTION

Original

> Lives in fresh ponds; head small and smooth; rather depressed on the upper side; mouth small, even, and toothless; eyes large in proportion to the head; body deep in proportion to its length. Colour blackish, with shining white scales; eyes and gill-covers golden, with a tinge of the same along the belly; lateral line bends downward, to correspond with the curve of the abdomen: pectoral and ventral fins, especially the latter, yellowish brown; tail forked; belly whitish, with ruddy rays. Rays, B. 3: P. 17: V. 9: A. 14: D. 9: C. 19.

Contemporary

Coloration is green to olive on the back with a faint dark stripe along the midline. Sides are golden or silver, the belly silvery or white. They are deep bodied and slab sided. There is a fleshy, scaleless keel along the belly, from the anus to the base of the pelvic. The mouth is a bit upturned and small, the eye forward of the jaw. Young from clear waters sometimes have a dusky midstripe. They have a sickle-shaped outer margin on the anal fin and a strong downwardly curved lateral line. There is no barbel. Dorsal rays number eight, anal fin rays 11 to 15. There are 45 to 54 scales in the lateral series (Pflieger 1975). Fins have no marks.

RANGE

Originally, golden shiners ranged in eastern North America from the Maritime Provinces south to Florida, west to the Dakotas and Texas, and north to Quebec (Lee et al. 1980). Golden shiners were introduced in Utah Lake in the mid-1950s.

SIZE AND LONGEVITY

One of the larger of the many small cyprinids, they may reach lengths over 7 in. (17.8 cm). Becker (1983) noted Wisconsin golden shiners age 1 to 7 have yearly lengths of: in inches, 1.1, 2.3, 3.3, 5.0, 6.1, 6.8, and 7.3; in mm, 28, 58, 84, 127, 155, 173, 185. Females grow larger and more rapidly than males. Moyle (1976) reported a length of 3 in. (76 mm) in 1 year and 5.5 in. (140 mm) in 2 years. At higher elevations they grow much slower (Carlander 1969). Maximum age is 9 years.

LIMITING FACTORS

Golden shiner are preyed upon heavily by fishes, including their own species. Their decline in western and northern Illinois is due to extensive draining of marshes, flood plains, and swales (Smith 1979). They have great tolerance to adversity, persisting in badly polluted, highly turbid, high-temperature streams.

Food and Feeding

Cladocerans, particularly *Daphnia* but including other zooplankton, are important food for golden shiners of all ages. Small flying insects are of secondary importance. In Clear Lake, California, most of the diet is zooplankton. Occasionally they take small fishes, mollusks, and aquatic insect larvae. According to Becker (1983) they feed by sight. When animal food is in short supply, filamentous algae is eaten.

Breeding Habits

Spawning of golden shiner may occur as early as March in extreme cases, or it may occur as late as August, generally early in the morning. Maturity is age 1 or 2 for both sexes. In California, spawning begins at 68°F (20°C). In Missouri, golden shiners spawn from late April to early June, beginning when water temperatures rise to 70°F (21.1°C) and stopping when temperatures exceed 80°F (26.7°C). Spawning may be resumed in mid- or late summer if water temperature is reduced (80°F [26.7°C] or less) by cold rain (Pflieger 1975). This agrees with Wisconsin studies (Becker 1983). No nest is prepared, and no protection given to eggs or young. Adhesive eggs are scattered over debris, filamentous algae, or higher plants and may be distributed over the nests of largemouth bass or green sunfish. Eggs hatch in 4 to 5 days at 75° to 80°F (23.9° to 26.7°C). Young form schools near the surface in shallow waters.

Habitat

Quiet waters with little or no current are the preferred habitat of golden shiner. This preference includes sloughs, ponds, lakes, or quiet pools of low gradient streams. They prosper in clear water with dense mats of vegetation but tolerate high turbidity and pollution and oxygen as low as 1.4 ppm (mg/l)(Becker 1983).

Management

In Utah Lake, golden shiner are barely maintaining population levels. They may be a problem in high mountain lakes where they can compete with trout. Eradication programs are common in California (Moyle, personal communication, 1983).

---

emerald shiner,
Notropis atherinoides
Rafinesque

Etymology: *Notropis* = Greek for keeled back; *atherinoides* = like *atherina*, that is, it has a resemblance to the silver sides
Nomenclature: *Notropis atherinoides* Rafinesque 1818a

IMPORTANCE

The emerald shiner is valuable as both a bait and a forage fish where it is abundant. It once constituted a substantial bait fishery around Lake Michigan (Becker 1983).

DESCRIPTION

Original

Head silvery, brown above: body pale, fulvous transparent, with a broad silver band; lateral line in the band: fins whitish, dorsal, and anal, with eleven rays, the first very short, tail slightly forked.

History: This new fish was discovered in Lake Erie by Gov. DeWitt Clinton who had the kindness to present me with many specimens; they are now deposited in the Lyceum of Natural History. I have ascertained that they belonged to a new genus, next to *Atherina*, and the specific name which I have adopted implies such an affinity. Those fishes come on the shores of Lake Erie and even in the river of Niagara, in the spring, in great shoals; but they are so small that they are scarcely noticed, and escape through the common nets; their usual size being from one to two inches and very thin and slender: they are called *Minny* or *Minnew*, together with twenty different other species of fish, and often considered as the young of other fishes. They live in the depth of the lake at other seasons, and are probably common over the great lakes. Their eyes are exceedingly large, occupying nearly the whole foreside of the head, the lips are very thin and membranaceous, the nostrils large, the gill cover is nearly round, and split above to the eyes; they have small thin broad scales, the rays of the fins are scarcely articulated simple and brittle: the pectoral fins have about fifteen rays, and the caudal fin about twenty-four.

Contemporary

The emerald shiner is a slender, moderate-sized minnow with no barbels, and 10 or more anal fin rays. The body is moderately compressed and slab sided. The caudal is moderately forked, the lobes somewhat pointed. The dorsal surface is dusky and has blue or green iridescence. A midlateral stripe posteriorly that disappears anteriorly. Sides silvery, belly silvery white (Becker 1983; Smith 1985).

RANGE

Widely distributed from Galveston Bay, Texas, east to Mobile Bay, Alabama. North through Mississippi and St. Lawrence rivers drainage through southern Canada to Great Slave Lake and Mackenzie River, Northwest Territory. Then south through Alberta, Montana, North Dakota, and South Dakota (Lee et al. 1980). In Utah it is present in Willard Reservoir.

SIZE AND LONGEVITY

Becker (1983) reported yearly growth of: in inches, 2.0, 3.2, and 3.6; in mm, 51, 81, and 91. In Lake Erie emerald shiner grew as follows: in inches,

2.4, 3.6, and 4.0; in mm, 61, 91, 102 (Flittner 1964). The largest emerald shiner was collected in Lake Michigan, it was 4.9 in. (125 mm) long.

FOOD AND FEEDING

Young emerald shiner feed on rotifers, copepods, cladocerans, green algae, blue-green algae, diatoms, and protozoans. Adults eat insects, mostly terrestrial, entomostracans, fishes, fish eggs, mayflies, caddis flies, and chironomids (midges) (Becker 1983).

LIMITING FACTORS

The emerald shiner is heavily preyed upon by fishes and birds. It is also seined for bait. It almost disappeared from Lake Michigan in the early 1960s when the alewife populations increased and presumably competed with it for food (Becker 1983). In the second and third year males have a higher mortality rate than females. Spawning mortality is high.

BREEDING HABITS

Emerald shiner breed at 75°F (23.9°C), and eggs hatch in about 24 hrs. Spawning is over gravel preferably; sand, boulders, and rubble are also used. A female may spawn more than once in a summer. The time span of spawning for a population may be two and one-half months. Fertilized nonadhesive eggs sink to the bottom; there is no paternal care of eggs or young. Maturity is at age 1. A 3-in. (76-mm) long female may have 2,000 to 3,000 eggs (Becker 1983; Flittner 1964).

HABITAT

This minnow is a pelagic (open-water) species, preferring lakes or large rivers. In summer months schools stay offshore and near the surface. In autumn they move inshore, and winter in deep water. In spring they frequent surface waters at night and deep waters during the day (Scott and Crossman 1973).

MANAGEMENT

No management technique is obvious for emerald shiner in Willard Reservoir.

---

spottail shiner, *Notropis hudsonius* (Clinton)

Etymology: *Notropis* = Greek for keeled back. Rafinesque evidently gave the name to the generic type specimen with a shriveled appearance; *hudsonius,* named for the Hudson River

Nomenclature: *Clupea hudsonia* Clinton 1824, *Notropis hudsonius* Forbes 1884

IMPORTANCE

Although spottail shiner are important forage fish over much of their native range, their importance in Utah has not been established.

DESCRIPTION

Original

With a broad satin stripe extending from the gill covers to the tail, and a dark rounded spot at the base of the tail.

Frequent at Albany, and other places on the Hudson River. Cabinet of the Lyceum.

Head rather small; *mouth* moderate; *lower jaw* shorter, and shuts into the upper; *rostrum* obtuse; *nostrils* double, nearly approximated, and nearer the eyes than to the rostrum; *eyes* moderately large, the pupils black, and the iris silvery; *teeth* none; *gill-covers* silvery, with a narrow membrane on the edges, and furnished at their superior part with a minute flat spine; *gill openings* ample; *body* 4 times the length of the head, cylindrical; *back* slightly arched, dark brown; *lateral line* straight, nearly obsolete; *pectorals* low, pointed; dorsal above the ventrals, trapezoidal, nearly straight on its margin; *caudal* furcated, lobes equal, with accessory rays; *scales* radiate, and very deciduous; *air bladder* divided into 2 cylindrical portions placed lengthwise, and connected by a small tube.

Length—Three to six in. Br. 4. P. 11. D. 8. V. 8. A. 8. C. 20 3/3.

Contemporary

Overall coloration is silver with some yellow or gold but the back is a pale green or olive, the sides silver, the belly near white. Fins are clear except for the distinctive black spot at the base of the caudal. Spottail shiner have stout and laterally compressed bodies with large, triangular heads and large eyes. The rounded snout overhangs the mouth. A single dorsal fin with 8 rays originates over the forward edge of the pelvics. The caudal is forked. The anal fin has 8 or, occasionally, 9 rays. Pharyngeal teeth are variable, but generally are 2, 4–4, 2. The pelvic fins are small with 7 or, rarely, 8 rays and the pectoral fins are of moderate size with 12 to 17 rays. Scales are cycloid, numbering 36 to 41 in the lateral series, which is complete (Becker 1983; Smith 1979).

RANGE

Spottail shiner have been stocked in Willard Reservoir. They are one of the most widely ranging native North American fishes. Spottail shiner occur naturally from Georgia north through Canada and the upper Mississippi River Basin (Lee et al. 1980).

SIZE AND LONGEVITY

Spottail shiner do not typically reach lengths over 5 in. (127 mm). Females are larger than males. They are relatively fast growing but are short lived. Total length of Wisconsin spottail shiners age 1 to 5 is: in inches, 2.5, 3.8, 4.3, 4.7, and 4.9; in mm, 64, 97, 109, 119, 125 (Becker 1983; Trautman 1981).

LIMITING FACTORS

Trematodes, cestodes, nematodes, and protozoans may all parasitize spottail shiner. A variety of piscivorous fish and birds prey upon them.

Food and Feeding

Filamentous algae as well as a variety of organisms, including aquatic insect larvae (especially chironomids and mayflies), crustaceans, aquatic insects, and their own eggs are consumed by spottail shiner (Smith 1979). With increased size, they tend to shift from small invertebrates to insects (Becker 1983).

Breeding Habits

Spottail shiner spawn at age 1 in spring and early summer. Spawning occurs in closely packed groups, with no evidence of nesting or care for eggs or young. Generally they spawn over gravelly riffles in 3 to 15 ft (0.9 to 4.6 m) of water or along the sandy shoals of lakeshores. Ripe females contain 100 to 4,600 yellowish eggs (Becker 1983; Smith 1979).

Habitat

Large lakes and rivers are the preferred habitat of spottail shiner, but smaller lakes and streams are also used. Large schools occur near shorelines with sparse to moderate vegetation in Lake Michigan. Generally they occur in moderately shallow water or shoal areas, but reports of occurrences at depths to 150 ft (46 m) exist (Becker 1983; Smith 1979).

Management

Spottail shiner will survive in Willard Reservoir if they are able to reproduce yearly and avoid excessive predation.

---

sand shiner, *Notropis stramineus* (Cope)

Etymology: *Notropis* = Greek for keeled back. Rafinesque evidently gave the name to the generic type specimen with a shriveled appearance; *stramineus* = Latin for made of straw, probably referring to the color

Nomenclature: *Hybopsis stramineus* Cope 1865, *Notropis stramineus* Forbes 1884

Importance

Sand shiner are important as forage for game fishes in their native range and are used as bait and as a bioassay animal. In Utah they provide some forage. Negative impacts are undetermined.

Description

Original

Hybognathus stramineus.

This genus embraces the described *argyritis, evansi, nuchalis, nitidus, regius,* and probably *gardoneus* (C. V.), to which are added here three others.

In the present species, the dorsal is situated nearer the end of the muzzle than to the base of the caudal, and its height is much less than half the distance from the base of its first ray to the same point; the head enters the length to the caudal a little over four times, being relatively longer than in the species described by Agassiz and Girard, while the eye, entering the length of the head but three times, is relatively larger. The depth enters the length 4 3/4 times. Scales 5/4 36; in *evansi* (brought by Hammond from the Upper Platte) 5/4 40. Ventral fins do not extend to the vent. The dorsal outline rises gently to the base of the dorsal; the profile descends abruptly at the end of the muzzle, which is prolonged in front of the orbit about three-fourths the longest diameter of the latter. Superior border of operculum usually shorter than the posterior. Pharyngeal teeth 4–4.

The general form is stout, and the head broad; caudal not deeply forked. in rays—D. I. 8. C. 19. A. 7. V. 8. P. short, 13. Length about three inches. Color brownish straw color; sides and below silvery, the former most brightly. No dorsal line; a faint line on posterior part of lateral line, and a small spot at base of tail.

Many specimens from Grosse Isle, Detroit River.

Hybognathus stramineus Cope 1865

Cope 1865a:283. TYPE LOCALITY: Detroit R., Grosse Isle, Michigan. LECTOTYPE: ANSP 4131 (51.0), Prof. Manly Miles. Fowler (1910: [pl. 15], fig. 5) designated lectotype by illustrating "type" (ANSP 4131); calculated length 53.3 mm SL. LECTOPARATYPES: ANSP 4132-4136 (5), paratopotypes.

REMARKS.—This species was often erroneously called *N. blennius* in the early literature; Fowler (1910:274–276) first demonstrated, and Hubbs (1926:42–43) subsequently confirmed, that *blennius* is a distinct species. The form *stramineus* was regarded either as a subspecies (Jordan 1885b:811; Hubbs 1926: 37,43) or a junior synonym of *N. deliciosus* until Suttkus (1958) showed that the lectotype of *Moniana deliciosa* earlier designated by Clark Hubbs (1954a) represents the species now called *N. texanus* (Girard). It should be noted that none of the extant syntypes of *M. deliciosa* are *N. stramineus*, although some specimens of this species may have been present in the original series. Bailey and Allum (1962:65) showed the subspecific separation of *deliciosus* and *stramineus* proposed by Hubbs (1926:37,43) to be invalid, but at the same time they demonstrated (1962:64–68) the subspecific distinctness of *stramineus* and *missuriensis*. *N. stramineus* and *N. volucellus* also were variously regarded as subspecies (Jordan 1885b:811), synonyms, or as distinct species in the early literature; Hubbs and Greene (1928:375) were the first to demonstrate conclusively their specific distinctness. *Alburnus lineolatus* Agassiz 1863 likely is a senior synonym of *N. stramineus*, but inasmuch as no unquestioned types appear to be extant, this cannot be proved conclusively. One of the two extant syntypes of *Cyprinella ludibunda* Girard 1857 represents *N. stramineus*; the other syntype is *N. volucellus* (Cope 1865). Original description date 13 February 1865.

= *Notropis stramineus stramineus* (Cope)

Contemporary

Coloration is olive yellow on the back, silvery on the sides, and the belly is white. A diamond-shaped design on the back and sides is the result of scales edged in pigment and is very distinctive. A middorsal stripe expands into a wedge-shaped blotch in front of the dorsal fin origin but does not encircle the base of the dorsal fin. The body is terete. Scales in the lateral series are 34 to 38 and the lateral line is complete. Pharyngeal teeth are 4–4, the mouth is small, the eyes large. There are 7 anal rays and 8 dorsal rays. A slightly oblique terminal mouth is accompanied by a blunt snout. Gill rakers are short, conical, and widely spaced (Becker 1983; Smith 1979).

RANGE

Native range of the sand shiner includes the Gulf slope drainage, Trinity River to Rio Grande drainages, northwest of the Mississippi River (excluding Louisiana and Arkansas) into the upper Mississippi Valley, including the Missouri River, the lower Red River of the north drainage (Canada), and lower Great Lakes east into the upper Ohio Basin, and from there into the Tennessee River drainage. In Utah they are rare in the Yampa and Green rivers but common in the Colorado River above Cataract Canyon (Valdez et al. 1990; Tyus et al. 1982; Lee et al. 1980).

SIZE AND LONGEVITY

Most sand shiner die at age 2; a few live to be 3 years old. Length at the end of each year for 3 years may be: in inches, 1.5, 2.2, and 2.8; in mm, 38, 56, 71. One 3.1-in. (79-mm) fish weighed 0.17 oz (4.8 g) (Becker 1983).

FOOD AND FEEDING

Sand shiner feed at all levels in the water column and are omnivorous, feeding on algae and invertebrates. They feed on microflora and aquatic insect larvae and nymphs on the bottom, miscellaneous invertebrates at midwater, and terrestrial insects at the surface (Becker 1983; Smith 1979).

LIMITING FACTORS

Cold, turbid streams with clay or silt bottoms, or a shortage of food and space, all negatively affect sand shiner. They do not do well in low gradient streams or in areas of heavy pollution or siltation (Smith 1979).

BREEDING HABITS

Sand shiner breed at age 1, 2, and 3. Larger, but numerically fewer, 3-year-olds produce the most eggs. A female may produce 200 to 1,100

0.03 in. (0.8 mm) eggs. Spawning occurs throughout the summer on an intermittent basis, generally near vegetation. Temperatures for spawning are 81° to 99°F (27.2° to 37.2°C). Eggs are adhesive and stick to plants, debris, or substrate, but no care is given eggs or young (Becker 1983; Trautman 1981; Smith 1979).

HABITAT

Sand shiner are adaptable to small streams and to rivers as large as the Mississippi. They prosper in clear lakes and reservoirs where there is a sand or gravel bottom. Apparently they also thrive in large, fast, medium-size streams, with gravel bottoms. They tolerate little turbidity (Trautman 1981; Smith 1979).

MANAGEMENT

Unless currently unknown benefits are identified for this species, this adaptable exotic should have no special protection in Utah.

---

fathead minnow, *Pimephales promelas* Rafinesque

Etymology: *Pimephales* = Greek for fathead, *promelas* = Greek for before and black referring to the blackish forespot
Nomenclature: *Pimephales promelas* Rafinesque 1820

IMPORTANCE

In their preferred habitat, fathead minnow are often the predominant species. They are one of the most commonly used bait minnows in North America (Tomelleri and Eberle 1990). In their native range they are propagated in hatchery ponds as bait and as food for smallmouth bass and other game fishes. As forage fish fathead minnow provide an important link in the food web, converting algae, organic detritus, and planktonic organisms to food for other fishes (Sigler and Miller 1963).

DESCRIPTION

Original

Body more or less short and deep; head short, blunt, almost globular in adult; V. reaching beyond front of A.; scales before D. about 27; lateral line wanting or more or less imperfect. Olivaceous; a black bar across middle of D. (faint in young); a dark shade along caudal peduncle; adult dusky, the head jet-black, with large tubercles on snout. Head 4; depth 4. D. I, 7. A.7. Scales 7–47–4. L. 2 1/2. Maine and Montana to Mexico; abundant in sluggish brooks; very variable. S. W. specimens (subspecies *confertus* Girard) have the lateral line almost complete, the mouth a little oblique, and the nuptial tubercles lacking on chin.

Contemporary
Overall coloration of fathead minnow is generally dark. They may be olive green or brown above and white below with brassy or silver sides. Breeding males are quite dark. Nuptial tubercles on breeding males are light in color, and the spongy pad on the back is slate blue or gray. The dorsal fin has 8 rays and the anal 7. Pelvic fins are small, having 8 rays and originating below the origin of the dorsal. Pectoral fins usually have 15 to 16 rays. The body is short, thick, and laterally compressed. The head is triangular, the mouth small and nearly terminal. There are 41 to 54 cycloid scales in the lateral series. The lateral line is almost complete. They may be distinguished from brassy minnow by the presence of few radii on the lateral scales as opposed to 4–20 radii on the lateral scales of brassy minnow (Sigler and Miller 1963).

RANGE

They occur naturally through most of central North America from Louisiana and Chihuahua, Mexico, north to Great Slave Lake, Canada, and from New Brunswick to Alberta, Canada (Lee et al. 1980). They were stocked in Utah Lake in 1969 where they are considered rare (Heckmann et al. 1981a). They were common to abundant in the Colorado River drainage in Utah in 1980 (Tyus et al. 1982)

SIZE AND LONGEVITY

Fathead minnow are short lived, rarely reaching more than 2 years of age. Adult lengths range from 2.0 to 3.5 in. (51 to 89 mm). Typical of fish in which the male guards the eggs and sometimes the young, males grow both faster and larger than females (Sigler and Miller 1963).

LIMITING FACTORS

As is the case with many small minnows, they are parasitized by invertebrates and preyed on by fishes and birds.

FOOD AND FEEDING

Fathead minnow eat algae, organic detritus, aquatic insect larvae, and zooplankton.

BREEDING HABITS

Spawning begins in the spring when water temperatures near 64°F (17.7°C) and may continue for months. Fathead minnow mature at age 1 year or less. Males select spawning sites and construct nests on the underside of a log, board, or lily pad, in water 2 to 3 ft (0.6 to 0.9 m) deep. Once the adhesive eggs are deposited and fertilized, males drive off the females. Females may produce up to 12,000 eggs, which hatch in 4 to 6 days in 77°F (25°C) water (Sigler and Miller 1963; Scott and Crossman 1973). Males guard the nest, driving off potential predators. While guarding the eggs, males aerate and clean them by rubbing them with their dorsal fins and the spongy pad on their backs (Tomelleri and Eberle 1990).

HABITAT

Preferred habitat of fathead minnow includes sluggish streams, lakes, bogs, and ponds.

MANAGEMENT

Predation on limited populations may endanger them. In these instances, restocking may be the only option. Fathead minnow may be of benefit as forage fish in Utah lakes. In the Colorado River Basin, they threaten many native species with their presence, especially where they are present in large numbers in backwaters.

---

woundfin, *Plagopterus argentissimus* Cope
Plate 7

Etymology: *Plagopterus* = wound fin, *argentissimus* = most silvery
Nomenclature: *Plagopterus argentissimus* Cope 1874

IMPORTANCE

Woundfin are one of six species composing a unique group of New World minnows, those that are spiny-rayed. Their dorsal fin has a pair of smooth spines, the pelvic fins have spinelike modifications. All other North American minnows lack true spines (Sigler and Miller 1963). Woundfin are confined to the Colorado River system and were listed as endangered in 1973 under the federal Endangered Species Act of 1973, as amended.

DESCRIPTION

Original

This is a small fish of slender proportions, with a rather broad head, with slightly depressed muzzle, overhanging by a little, a horizontal mouth of moderate size. The caudal peduncle is of medium depth, and the caudal fin is deeply forked. The eye is somewhat oval, and enters the length of the side of the head 4.2 times, and the interorbital width 1.5 times. The greatest depth (near the ventral fin) enters the total length nearly 6 times, or 5 and 3 quarters, exclusive of the caudal fin. The latter measurement is 4 times the length of the head. The origin of the dorsal is entirely behind the proper basis of the ventral; its first spine is curved and longer than the second, and its basis is intermediate between the base of the caudal and the end of the muzzle. The dorsal rays behind the spine have the basal 2-thirds to 1-half thickened and completely ossified, the articulated portions issuing from the apices of the spines.

Radial formula, D. II. 7; C. 19; A. I 10-9; V. 2. V; P. 16. The first or osseous ray of the anal is rudimental; the fifth spinous ray of the ventral is bound by nearly its entire length to the abdomen by a membrane. The pectoral rays from the second to the sixth exhibit a basal osseous spinous portion, which is not nearly so marked as in the ventrals. The pectorals reach the basis of the latter.

The lateral line is complete and is slightly deflexed opposite the dorsal fin. The lips are thin, and the end of the maxillary bone extends to the line of the front of the orbit.

Total length m 0.071; ditto to middle of basis of caudal fin .0565; ditto to anterior basis of anal fin .004; ditto to basis ventral .021; ditto of head .0145; of muzzle .004; width at posterior nares .006; at middle of pterotic .0078. Color, pure silver for a considerable width above the lateral line. Dorsal region somewhat dusky from minute chromatophorae. Numerous specimens from the San Luis Valley, Western Colorado.

Contemporary

Woundfin derive their common name from the first dorsal spine, which is stronger than the second and almost as long. The spine is sharply pointed at the tip and can inflict a wound. Color is burnished silver with blue reflections on the side. Breeding males may have a pinkish color. They are naked (no scales). The body is thick anteriorly, thinning posteriorly. A well-developed barbel hangs from the upper lip. They have a slightly decurved and complete lateral line. The mouth is inferior but nearly horizontal. The dorsal has 8 or 9 rays, the anal usually 10. Teeth are 1, 5–4, 1 (La Rivers 1962; Sigler and Miller 1963; Minckley 1973).

Range

Historically, woundfin ranged through the Virgin and Gila river basins. Today, alterations in habitat have confined them to the Virgin River below LaVerkin where it is threatened by red shiners, Asian tapeworm, and extensive water developments (Johnson and Jensen 1991).

Size and Longevity

Adults may range up to 3.5 in. (89 mm) in total length, but many are no more than 2.0 in. (51 mm). Young are 0.7 to 1.4 in. (17 to 36 mm) in June and reach 2.0 in. (51 mm) in August. Young fish are a significant part of the population; most woundfin probably live less than 2 years, and a few, under ideal conditions, 3 years (Deacon 1977; Sigler and Miller 1963; La Rivers 1962).

Food and Feeding

To survive in a historically harsh and presently degraded habitat, woundfin are omnivorous and opportunistic. They feed on aquatic insect larvae, filamentous algae and, to a lessor extent, terrestrial insects and amphipods. Violent flow increases feeding; low temperatures and low water levels inhibit feeding.

Limiting Factors

Woundfin are better adapted for hazardous conditions than most fishes of the Virgin River. However, extremes, particularly for young fish, may be fatal. Temperatures above 86° to 90°F (30° to 32.2°C) are harmful, and few or none survive over 95°F (35°C). As in most fishes, spawning and larval stages are the most sensitive periods. Exotics have brought disease, and they compete for food and space and prey on young. Extremes of water flow and degraded quality contributed to loss of range. This species is in jeopardy due to extreme stress caused by alterations in its ecosystem (Cross 1975; Deacon 1977).

BREEDING HABITS

Woundfin exhibit spawning behavior in April when temperatures are about 58°F (14.4°C). Most spawning occurs in April and May. Upper limits of temperature for spawning and larval rearing is about 86°F (30°C). Population segments in the lower reaches of the river spawn earlier than those in the upper reaches.

Flows of less than 60 cfs (1.7 cms) and more than 200 cfs (5.7 cms) are extreme, and deleterious; those of 80 to 100 cfs (2.3 to 2.8 cms) are more nearly optimum. Beyond mid-July, flows may drop to 60 cfs (1.7 cms). Females congregate in pools, then move into flowing water where males wait to spawn. Areas used for spawning may be less than 2 ft (0.61 m) wide and no more than an inch (2.54 cm) deep. Eggs are strewn randomly, and no care is provided eggs or young (Cross 1975; Deacon 1977).

HABITAT

Adult woundfin select areas of relatively strong current, often over areas of shifting sand bottom where flows are 2 to 3 cfs (0.06 to 1.09 cms). The young stay in slow, shallow areas, often near shore or cover, and over sand, gravel, or mud bottoms. Temperatures below 88°F (31.1°C) allow fish to prosper, but temperatures more than 95°F (35°C) are highly stressful or fatal. They tolerate higher salinities than most fishes in their native habitat. Areas sought are often silty or murky (Deacon 1977; Sigler and Miller 1963).

MANAGEMENT

Woundfin are threatened with extinction in the Virgin River, primarily as a result of habitat dewatering. Habitat degradation in areas important to this species should not be allowed to progress further, and no additional species should be stocked into critical habitat. Current hatchery programs to maintain the gene pool should continue. Stocking in habitable areas of their former range should continue, and two or three refuges should be established.

Colorado squawfish, *Ptychocheilus lucius* Girard
Plate 8

Etymology: *Ptychocheilus* = folded lip, in reference to the folding of the mouth skin behind the jaws; *lucius* = pike
Nomenclature: *Ptychocheilus lucius* Girard 1856a

IMPORTANCE

Colorado squawfish were once an important food fish for native Americans and settlers. They provided human and animal food and fertilizer and were caught both by hook and line and nets. Young provided forage for larger, carnivorous squawfish. Currently no direct economic value per se is attached to the Colorado squawfish because of reduced numbers, although consideration is being given for a limited sportfishery in Colorado. They are unique fish adapted to a specialized environment and as such deserve protection. They were originally listed as endangered on March 11, 1967, and are currently protected by the federal Endangered Species Act of 1973, as amended. There are three other living member of this genus. None is endangered.

Description

Original

> A very characteristic species. The body is compressed, but the head is flattened or depressed and very much developed, constituting nearly the fourth of the entire length. The dorsal and ventrals are situated quite posteriorly. The scales are below the medium size, and the lateral line is bent downwards upon the abdomen.
>
> The pharyngeal bones are very slender; the inferior limb is almost exiguous and proportionally as long as in *P. grandis*. There are, however, but 4 teeth upon the main row, instead of 5, as in the case of *P. grandis*. Color bluish grey above; silvery golden beneath. Collected in the Rio Colorado, by A. Schott, under Major W. H. Emory, Commissioner U.S. and Mex. Boundary.

Contemporary

Coloration is bright olive green, darkest above, the lower sides are somewhat yellowish, the abdomen white. Young have a dark, wedge-shaped spot on the caudal. They have a pikelike elongate body, terminating anteriorly in a cone-shaped head; the mouth is nearly horizontal. They may be most easily separated taxonomically from the roundtail chub by the fact that the upper jaw reaches to about the middle of the pupil, the eye is small, and also by the narrow elongate lower limb of the pharyngeal arch. The dorsal fin, originating behind the insertion of the pelvic fins, almost always has 9 rays, as does the anal fin. The lateral series has 80 to 95 scales. Pharyngeal teeth in 2 rows number 2, 5–4, 2, are fragile, elongate, and hooked at the tips (Sigler and Miller 1963).

Range

Native only to the Colorado River and its tributaries from Wyoming to Mexico, current range is restricted to the upper Colorado River drainage; populations occur in the Green River from Echo Park downstream, in the Colorado River at Palisades Dam, in the Gunnison, White, and San Juan rivers, and in the Yampa River at Maybell Dam. Colorado squawfish may be increasing in the Green and Yampa rivers but declining in the Colorado River (Hamill 1993). They have only sparingly been transplanted outside their native range; 10,000,000 have been placed in the Verde and Salt rivers (Richard A.

Valdez, personal communication 1991). Degradation of habitat is the primary reason for their current decimated population status.

Size and Longevity

Colorado squawfish have been reported to reach lengths of 6 ft (1.83 m) and weights over 100 lb (45.4 kg) (Sigler and Miller 1963). However, these length and weight estimates were based on skeletal remains. These are reported to be the largest minnows in North America and the only major predatory fish of the Colorado River (Johnson and Jensen 1991). Reports from "old-timers" persist that fish weighing from 80 to 100 lb (36.3 to 45.4 kg) and lengths over 6 ft (1.83 m) were once common (the *Salt Lake Tribune* [Utah], 11 Jan. 1994). During the mid-1960s, fish taken from the upper Green River had total lengths for the first 11 years of age as follows: in inches, 1.7, 3.7, 6.4, 9.4, 12.6, 15.4, 17.9, 19.6, 21.1, 22.4, and 23.6; in mm, 43, 94, 163, 239, 320, 391, 455, 498, 536, 569, 599. Vanicek and Kramer (1969) reported a length to weight relationship of $\text{Log}_{10} W = 5.418 + 3.126 \times \text{Log}_{10} L$ (where W is weight in grams and L is total length in mm). Seethaler's (1978) research confirms Vanicek's and Kramer's results. Hawkins (1991) measured the length to weight relationship for Colorado squawfish from the upper Colorado River Basin and separates fish into Colorado River, Green River, White River, and Yampa River populations. His relationships approximate previously reported values. Richard Valdez (personal communication, 1991) found that current maximum size is 13.4 in. (340 mm) and 10 oz (284 g), reflecting reduced and abused habitat. Valdez (1990) furnished additional growth rates for this species.

Food and Feeding

Early piscivory, at lengths of 3 to 8 in. (76 to 203 mm), is a reflection of this voracious minnow's ability to achieve historically reported sizes (Holden and Wick 1982). Vanicek and Kramer (1969) stated that fish up to 2 in. (51 mm) in length eat cladocerans, copepods, and chironomid larvae. When the fish reach 4 in. (102 mm), they rely more on insects. As they grow larger they consume more vertebrates, primarily fishes. An interesting comparison between the food habits of squawfish and northern pike, another ever-hungry predator, can be made. Both turn to fishes for food at an early age and subsequently rarely eat anything else.

Limiting Factors

Flaming Gorge Lake, the area which was once prime squawfish habitat, provides an example of habitat loss. Before creation of the impoundment, the Green River was a warm, turbulent, turbid river with violent fluctuations in flow, both annually and over the years. Native warmwater fishes, mainly suckers and minnows, were dominant. Many backwater areas with eddies and pools existed, and the river was moderately rich in nutrients as well as sand and silt. Since impoundment, this area is a cold, deep, stratified lake that stores nutrients as well as sand and silt. Below the dam flows a cold, clear stream regulated only by human demands.

Prior to impoundment, water temperatures in July were about 72°F (22.2°C), following impoundment, stream temperatures were typically 35° to 50°F (1.67° to 10°C). It is no longer squawfish habitat. This scenario has been repeated many times before in the lower Colorado River Basin. Spawning and spawning migration routes have been cut off and feeding habitat has been drastically reduced or destroyed. Cold water adversely affects young squawfish. For example, 14-day-old Colorado squawfish larvae, when conditioned at 71.6°F (22°C), had significant mortality when shocked at 59°F (15°C) water for 5 minutes; 40-day-old fish, however, were not affected. Shocks in 50° and 59°F (10° and 15°C) water for 5 minutes caused behavioral changes in 14-day-old fish that could result in mortality in the wild (Berry 1986).

Total dissolved solids (TDS) are typically lowered below dams in rivers that carry high TDS loads. These lowered TDS levels adversely affect young squawfish by reducing cover. Pimentel and Bulkley (1983) found juvenile (age 0–1) squawfish preferred TDS levels of 560 to 1,150 ppm (mg/l) but avoided levels greater than 4,400.

Having been subjected to catastrophic habitat alterations and insults, squawfish were ill prepared to cope with a flood of exotic species. Exotics competed for food and space and carried a variety of exotic diseases. This large game minnow may be faced with near extinction in much of its former range.

Breeding Habits

Male squawfish mature at lengths of about 17 in. (432 mm) and 6 years of age, females 1 year later. They spawn in spring water temperatures of 58° to 70°F (14.4° to 21.1°C) (Tyus et al. 1987; Seethaler 1978). Work at the U.S. Fish and Wildlife Service Willow Beach National Fish Hatchery (WBNH), Arizona, and the Dexter National Fish Hatchery (DNH), New Mexico, has provided comprehensive breeding data on Colorado squawfish, bonytail chub, humpback chub, and razorback sucker. Hatchery-reared male squawfish at WBNH mature at age 5, when they are 12 to 15 in. (305 to 381 mm) long and weigh 7.8 to 12 oz (221 to 340 g). Females mature at age 6, when they are 16.7 to 17.4 in. (340 to 424 mm) long and weigh 23.8 to 29.3 oz (675 to 831 g). Optimum spawning temperature is 70° to 72°F (21.1° to 22.2°C). Eggs hatch in 90 to 121 hrs at temperatures of 68° to 75°F (20° to 23.9°C). Egg diameters range from 0.06 to 0.08 in. (1.5 to 2.0 mm). Spawning of these fish was not induced (Hamman 1981). Although a population of squawfish may spawn over a period of 4 or 5 weeks or even more, once an individual female becomes ripe she must spawn within a period of 1 or 2 weeks to produce the most viable eggs.

Wild brood stock at DNH produced an average of 25,310 eggs per lb (55,799/kg) of body weight (Jensen 1983). However, Don Hales (personal communication, 30 January 1990) looking at Dexter National Fish Hatchery data sheets, pointed out that a regression correlation between the weights and the number of eggs per pound of fish shows little relationship between weight of spawners and number of eggs produced.

In natural reproduction, adhesive eggs are strewn at random over the bottom, and no care is given either eggs or young. They generally spawn in riffle areas (Tyus 1990). One suspected spawning site in the Yampa River consisted of cobble with large interstitial spaces devoid of organics, silts, or clays (Lamarra et al. 1985). Squawfish reportedly travel many miles to reach a preferred spawning site. Probably most long runs have now been cut off by dams and diversions.

In contrast to Colorado squawfish breeding in the Green River system, adults in the Colorado River make a relatively short spawning run. Most movements are less than 40 mi (64.4 km). Archer et al. (1985) hypothesized that long-distance movements to spawning areas in the Colorado River are unnecessary because suitable spawning areas occur in shorter reaches of the river. The onset of breeding of the squawfish occurs when seasonal temperatures reach about 68°F (20°C) and as seasonal runoffs recede.

Valdez and Williams (1991) confirmed the presence of adult Colorado squawfish in Cataract Canyon but failed to document any evidence of spawning, although they believed that the deep pools and cobble habitat present should have been adequate. They also found a larval fish less than 1 in. (25.4 mm) long. Cataract Canyon has a summer flow ranging from about 5,000 cfs (142 cms) to about 70,000 cfs (1,982 cms), with a record of 120,000 cfs (3,398 cms). It is inhabited by 28 species of fishes representing 10 families and includes 20 nonnative and 8 native species.

HABITAT

Colorado squawfish evolved into their present form in the Colorado River drainage, which extends from Wyoming to the Gulf of California in northwest Mexico. This evolution required a period of thousands of years. Before humans changed the river and the squawfish habitat, the warm river and its tributaries fluctuated widely in flow, turbidity, and temperature. Temperatures ranged from the high 90s°F (mid 30s°C) at the southern extreme to the low 70s°F (low 20s°C) in the north. (See author note under humpback chub, "Range" section.) Although deep, fast channels were scoured, backwater pools afforded food and protection for young. Historically, Colorado squawfish probably preferred TDS levels of 560 to 1,150 ppm (mg/l) and avoided levels over 4,400 ppm (Pimentel and Bulkley 1983). Today, only remnants of the original habitat remain as moderately disturbed from Lake Powell, on the Colorado, upstream to the junction of the Green and Yampa rivers.

Colorado squawfish in the Green River overwinter in specific regions, generally less than 3 mi (4.8 km) long. These fish may remain for days in an area no longer than 109 yds (100 m) within slow waters, eddies, or backwaters. The squawfish moves periodically to one of the several favorite spots or microhabitats characterized by greater than average depth and low current velocity. The position of each fish is often associated with underwater structures such as sand ridges, jetties, and other obstructions (Valdez and Masslich 1991).

The Colorado squawfish has been extirpated from about 75 percent of its historic range. It is most common in the Green River Basin of Colorado and Utah in habitats that have been least affected by manmade alterations. Rick and Hawkins (1991) indicated that several squawfish have demonstrated a fidelity to specific fall and winter habitats and river reaches for one or more years.

MANAGEMENT

Recovery plans have been prepared by the Colorado River Fishes Recovery Team for this endangered fish as of fall 1991. Remnants of the original habitat are useable by Colorado squawfish, especially sections of the Colorado River from the Yampa River downstream to the San Juan River and through Lake Powell. The most desirable of these areas should be protected from further diversion, damming, or pollution with certain exceptions. Maintenance of the gene pool in hatchery facilities should be continued.

A limited number of Colorado squawfish that were hatchery-reared have been introduced and recaptured in the river. Some of these adult hatchery-reared squawfish stocked near Potash, Utah, in 1980 were recaptured in aggregations with adult wild fish. This situation suggests, according to Archer et al. (1985), that the hatchery-reared Colorado squawfish are probably augmenting wild populations. A major factor in the conservation of the squawfish is the proper hydrologic regimen. Studies have shown that water management, not water quality alone, is one of the most important features for recovery of the squawfish (Tyus 1991).

---

longnose dace,
Rhinichthys cataractae
(Valenciennes)
Plate 9

Etymology: *Rhinichthys* = Greek for snouted fish; *cataractae* = Latinized form of cataract, as the type specimen was from Niagara Falls

Nomenclature: *Gobio cataractae* (Valenciennes 1842, in Cuvier and Valenciennes 1842); *Rhinichthys cataractae* Jordan 1878a

IMPORTANCE

In both stream and lake ecosystems, longnose dace provide forage for game fishes and other piscivorous species.

DESCRIPTION

Original

Les eaux douces de l'Amérique septentrionale nourrissent cette espèce de goujon.

Elle a le corps alongé et arrondi, semblable à une loche. La hauteur, moitié de la longueur de la tête, est comprise huit fois dans celle du corps entier. L'oeil est assez grand et sur le haut de la joue; le museau est obtus; la bouche en dessous, à lèvres épaisses, mais sans voile comme les catastomes, et à chaque angle de la bouche est un petit barbillon, si court qu'on ne le voit qu'avec le plus grand soin.

La dorsale, sur le milieu de la longueur, est petite; la caudale est échancrée et a ses lobes arrondis; l'anale est arrondie et plus large que la dorsale; les ventrales sont petites, mais les pectorales sont larges.

D.3/6; A. 2/6; C. 19. etc.

Les écailles sont petites; j'en trouve soixante-dix rangées entre l'ouïe et la caudale: elles sont lisses, sans stries, et à la loupe on aperçoit un fin sablé noir qui les colore. Le dos est en effet plus coloré en gris foncé, qui devient plombé, pour passer au blanc argenté du ventre. La pectorale, la dorsale et la caudale sont grises, la ventrale et l'anale sont blanches.

Ce poisson est long de cinq pouces. Nous le devons à M. Milbert, qui l'a rapporté du saut de Niagara.

Translation

This species of gudgeon is found in the rivers of North America.

The body is long and rounded, similar to a loach. The depth, half the length of the head, goes eight times into that of the entire body. The eye is quite large and high on the cheek; the snout is obtuse; the mouth is inferior, with thick lips, but without a membrane like that of the catostomes, and at each angle of the mouth is a little barbel, so short that it can only be seen upon careful examination.

The dorsal, in the middle of the body, is small; the caudal fin is serrated and has rounded lobes; the anal is rounded and wider than the dorsal; the ventrals are small, but the pectorals are wide. D.3/6; A.2/6; C. 19, etc.

The scales are small; I found 70 rows of them between the gill cover and the caudal: they are smooth, without striations, and examination under a magnifying glass shows a fine sandy black color. In comparison, the back is a more intensely colored dark gray, becoming lead gray, and then silver white on the stomach. The pectoral, dorsal and caudal are gray, the ventral and anal are white.

This fish is 5 in. long. We owe it to Mr. Milbert, who brought it back from Niagara Falls.

Contemporary
Coloration of the back varies from olive green to brown, changing to cream or silvery white on the belly. In lakes, due to either water chemistry differences or other environmental factors, the back may be grayish. Scattered, darkened scales along the sides may produce a mottled appearance. Young have a lateral stripe. Breeding males may be orange red on the mouth, cheeks, the posterior axis of the paired fins, and the base of the anal fin. Females are duller colored than males. Longnose dace are nearly round in cross section with a broad, triangular head. The caudal fin is shallowly forked. The dorsal and pelvic fin have 8 rays, the short pectorals 13. There are 61 to 72 cycloid scales in the lateral series. The lateral line is complete and straight (Scott and Crossman 1973; Sigler and Miller 1963). Longnose dace can be distinguished from speckled dace by a flap of skin bridging the upper jaw to the lip.

The name "dace" originated in England as a modification of the word "darce" referring to the quick movements characteristic of minnows (Tomelleri and Eberle 1990). The term now applies to several species.

Range

Longnose dace are widely distributed naturally from the Atlantic to the Pacific. In eastern North America, they occur south to Virginia, west to the Mississippi River drainage basin, and as far south as Iowa. They occur from Labrador south along the Rocky Mountains into New Mexico, Texas, and northern Mexico (Lee et al. 1980). In Utah, they are present in Bear Lake, Great Salt Lake, and Utah Lake drainages and in the Bear, Blacksmith Fork, Ogden, Weber, Jordan, and Provo rivers.

Size and Longevity

Longnose dace are relatively slow growing and short lived. Fish reach an average length of 5 in. (127 mm) and live 5 years (Wydoski and Whitney 1979). In Utah populations, they may attain lengths over 4.5 in. (114 mm) but most individuals are between 2.5 and 3.5 in. (64 to 89 mm) long (Sigler and Miller 1963).

Limiting Factors

Longnose dace are preyed upon by other fishes. They may be parasitized by trematodes and nematodes.

Food and Feeding

Adults feed benthically (on the bottom), young on drift organisms. Aquatic insect larvae are the main food, although other aquatic invertebrates and algae may be eaten.

Breeding Habits

Spawning occurs in riffles over sand or gravelly bottoms in the spring when temperatures reach about 53°F (11.7°C). Although no nest is built, territories are established and defended by one parent, which also guards the eggs. Guardianship of eggs and young may be an incidental by-product of male territoriality (Tomelleri and Eberle 1990). From 200 to 1,200 transparent, adhesive eggs are laid. They hatch in 7 to 10 days at 60°F (15.6°C). Yolk sac absorbance occurs in about 7 days, then, when the posterior lobe of the swim bladder is inflated, young rise to the surface. Young stay in the pelagic stage about 4 months. Young live in the midwater column, unlike adults, which are primarily associated with the bottom in quiet water near shore (Scott and Crossman 1973; Sigler and Miller 1963).

Habitat

As body form indicates, adult longnose dace are adapted to swift waters. In lakes they live near shore over rocky, gravelly bottoms, moving into deeper water in hot weather. Water temperature preference is 53° to 70°F (11.7° to 21.1°C) (Trautman 1981; Scott and Crossman 1973; Sigler and Miller 1963).

Management

Longnose dace require habitat protection and acceptable water quality.

---

speckled dace, *Rhinichthys osculus* (Girard)

Plate 10

Etymology: *Rhinichthys* = Greek for snouted fish, *osculus* = small mouthed

Nomenclature: *Argyreus osculus* Girard 1856b; *Rhinichthys osculus* Wales 1946; *Rhinichthys osculus adobe* (Jordan and Evermann 1891) (Sevier River speckled dace); *Rhinichthys osculus carringtoni* (Cope 1871a) (Bonneville speckled dace)

Importance

Utah populations of speckled dace are moderately important as forage fish.

Description

Original

Has more the facies of *A. atronasus* than any other of its congeners, both by the outline of its body and head, and the shape and position of the mouth. The head is comparatively small, forming the fifth of the length, with the exception of the lobes of the caudal. The eye is rather large and subcircular, its diameter entering about 4 times in the length of the side of the head. The dorsal and anal fins are well developed, the former being convex superiorly, and the latter subconvex exteriorly. The posterior margin of the caudal is crescentric. The posterior extremity of the ventrals extend as far as the vent, which is not the case in the 2 species described above. D 8+2; A 7+2; C 5, 1, 9, 8, 1, 6; V 8; P 14.

The anterior 2 rays of both the dorsal and anal fins are mere rudiments, as already stated. The color is reddish brown above; olivaceous on the sides, with numerous dark blotches and dots. Beneath uniform yellowish white or silvery white.

Many specimens, the largest of which measuring less than 3 in, were collected by John H. Clark, under Col. J. D. Graham, U.S.A. in the Babocomori, a tributary stream of the Rio San Pedro, itself flowing into the Rio Gila.

Contemporary

Coloration and body shape of speckled dace are extremely variable. Individuals are generally gray or gray brown with dark flecks, usually above the midline. Lower sides and belly are yellow or cream colored. A faint, darker lateral band originates under the dorsal fin and extends to the caudal peduncle. There is a spot on the base of the caudal. Elongate and laterally compressed describe the body of speckled dace. The mouth is inferior and small, commonly with a small barbel present at the corners; the snout is pointed, and the head triangular. The dorsal fin may have 8, sometimes 6, 7, or 9 rays. The caudal fin is forked with rounded lobes. Origin of the anal fin is under the posterior base of the dorsal fin; it generally has 6 or 7 rays. Paired fins are relatively small and rounded, the pelvics with 8 or 9 rays, the pectorals with 13 or 14 rays. Lateral series scales number 60 to 80; scales are cycloid (Sigler and Miller 1963).

Range

Speckled dace are present in western North America from the Columbia River to the Colorado River drainage (Lee et al. 1980). They occur in major streams and some desert springs in Utah and are common in southeastern streams.

Subspecies distinctions between Sevier River speckled dace and Bonneville speckled dace can be partially justified on the basis of the original descriptions. The Sevier River speckled dace was described by Jordan and Evermann in 1891 based on specimens collected from the Sevier River, in Juab County, Utah. The Bonneville speckled dace was described by Cope in 1871 based on specimens from the Weber River at Echo, Utah, and was referred to as a "Snake River Basin and Great Basin" species by Jordan, Evermann, and Clark (1930).

Size and Longevity

Speckled dace are small and short lived. Three years and 4 in. (102 mm) are probably maximums for age and length.

Limiting Factors

Fishes and birds prey on speckled dace. A variety of organisms parasitize them. Their survival on the subspecies level is insured by their abundance and wide distribution.

Food and Feeding

As bottom dwellers, speckled dace feed primarily on benthic insects, freshwater shrimp, plant material, and zooplankton. Algae may compose 21 percent of the food by volume (Wydoski and Whitney 1979). Young feed on midwater plankton. Occasionally they feed on eggs and larvae of other fishes.

Breeding Habits

Speckled dace mature during their second summer. They spawn throughout the summer, but peak activity occurs in June or early July, when temperatures reach 65°F (18.3°C). Males gather in spawning areas and clean detritus from small areas over rocks or gravel. When females enter the substrate, they are surrounded by males. Eggs are adhesive and are deposited underneath rocks or other substrate. Larval fish remain in the gravel for some time and then congregate in the warm shallows of streams near cover (Moyle 1976; Sigler and Miller 1963).

Habitat

These fish occupy a wide variety of habitats, from swift, cold riffles of mountain streams to quiet, warm backwaters. They may be the sole species in intermittent streams and desert springs. Large schools are maintained except during spawning. Active at night more than in daylight hours, they spend days among rocks in shallow water.

Management

Protection of water quality, spawning, and nursery grounds is required.

---

redside shiner, *Richardsonius balteatus* (Richardson)

Plate 11

Etymology: *Richardsonius*—this species was originally named by the prominent English zoologist Sir John Richardson, who described many species from the United States. Girard honored him when he changed the generic name in 1856; *balteatus* = girdled, possibly referring to the brilliant red streaks that occur on males during breeding

Nomenclature: *Cyprinus (Abramis) balteatus* Richardson 1836, *Richardsonius balteatus* Girard 1856b; *Richardsonius balteatus balteatus* (Richardson, 1836) (Columbia redside shiner); *Richardsonius balteatus hydroflox* Cope 1871b (Bonneville redside shiner)

Importance

Their small size make redside shiner important as forage fish throughout their life cycle. They may eat the same foods as small game fish, thereby detracting from their value as forage. They may also prey on game fish young and eggs.

DESCRIPTION

Original

This pretty little bream, which is an inhabitant of the Columbia, was sent to me by Dr. Gairdner.

Colour.—"Back of head and body mountain-green, with iridescent tints of yellow and blue. Belly silvery-white.

A bright gold-yellow band behind the eye on the margin of the preoperculum, and a broad scarlet-red stripe beneath the lateral line, extending from the gill-opening to the anal. Fins of an uniform greenish-grey colour without brilliancy." (Gairdner.)

Form much compressed, the depth of the body being equal to 1-fourth of the distance between the tip of the snout and the caudal fork, while its thickness is only equal to a tenth of the same distance. The profile curves moderately from the snout to the dorsal, just before which the depth of the body is greatest, but it continues to be considerable at the insertion of the anal, the belly running as it were into an acute edge at that place; the short piece of the tail behind the anal is narrow. The *head* forming exactly 1-fourth of the length of fish, excluding the caudal, has a conical profile when the mouth is shut, the apex being formed by the tip of the lower jaw, which projects a very little beyond the commissure of the mouth. The top of the head is comparatively broad and rounded, its thickness at the nape being equal to that of any part of the body, and the snout, when viewed from above, appearing obtuse. *Eyes* large, much nearer to the snout than to the gill-opening. *Nostrils* near the eyes. *Mouth* toothless, small, its commissure descending obliquely and not reaching farther back than the nostrils: the lower jaw, when depressed, projects considerably beyond the upper 1. GILL-COVERS—Bony *operculum* quadrangular, its slightly-convex under edge being equal to the anterior 1, and fully 1-third longer than the upper or posterior 1: the latter is widely emarginated, or cut with a concave curve. The *suboperculum*, 1-third of the height of the operculum, is rounded off posteriorly in the segment of a circle, forming an obtuse tip to the gill-cover: both these bones are edged with membrane. *Preoperculum* narrow.

SCALES thin and sub-orbicular, their transverse diameter being rather greater than their longitudinal 1. A few crenatures may be obscurely seen on their basal edges with a lens, and very faint lines proceeding from them towards the center.

There are about fifty-seven scales on the lateral line, and the greatest diameter of 1 taken from the anterior part of the sides measures a line and a half. A linear inch includes sixteen or seventeen of them *in situ*. The *lateral line* is curved convexly downwards, just before the ventrals, rising so as to run straight through the tail. It is formed by a short tube on each scale. INS.—Br. 3–3; P. 17; D. 11; V. 9; A. 19 to 22; C. 19 7/7.

The *ventrals* are attached a little anterior to the middle, between the tip of the snout and base of the caudal, or opposite to the eighth ray of the dorsal; their tips reach to the anal. The anal and dorsal are high anteriorly, and become considerably lower posteriorly, with a slight concave sweep; the articulations of the first ray of each are obsolete.

The *air-bladder* is divided by a contraction into 2 portions, of which the lower 1 is largest. There are forty vertebrae in the spine. [Table of dimensions omitted.]

Contemporary

Coloration of redside shiner is vivid. Lying just below a dark band running from behind the head to the base of the caudal, adults have a prominent orange, red, or pink stripe on each side. A red stripe, from the shoulder girdle to above the anal fin, is especially bright in breeding males and tends to be broadened and intensified toward the front and rear. This stripe is present in females in a more somber shade, especially during the breeding season. During part of the year, the red stripe is absent. The side above the dark band may be bright golden. Upper parts are bluish to metallic green and the sides are silvery. Below the red stripe, sides may be pale golden. Axils of the pectoral fins may be golden to red (Sigler and Miller 1963).

Head length goes 4.0 to 4.5 times into total body length. The mouth is terminal and somewhat oblique. Moderate-sized cycloid scales number 50 to 60 in the lateral series, the lateral line itself is weakly decurved. Pharyngeal teeth are 2, 5–4, 2. The large sickle-shaped anal fin has 9 to 13 rays. The dorsal fin with 8 to 10 rays originates behind the insertion of the pelvic fins. The caudal fin is strongly forked (Sigler and Miller 1963; La Rivers 1962). Two subspecies are recognized and can generally be separated on the basis of anal fin ray counts. The Columbia redside shiner, described by Richardson in 1836, was based on specimens from the Columbia River. The Bonneville redside shiner, described by Cope in 1871, was based on specimens taken from Utah Lake, Utah.

RANGE

Native distribution of redside shiner is mostly west of the Rocky Mountains, from Washington, south through Oregon and the Columbia drainage. In Utah they occur naturally in waters of the Bonneville Basin but have been transplanted into several areas of the Colorado River drainage.

SIZE AND LONGEVITY

Maximum size of redside shiner is 7 in. (178 mm), but most are less than 5 in. (127 mm). Maximum life span is 5 years.

Limiting Factors Redside shiner are preyed upon by fishes and birds. As they are cannibalistic on their own eggs, they may be their own worst predator (Sigler and Miller 1963; La Rivers 1962).

Food and Feeding Omnivorous adults feed on aquatic and terrestrial insects, snails, and zooplankton. They may feed upon fish eggs and fry, including their own. Fry feed on zooplankton and algae (Wydoski and Whitney 1979; Sigler and Miller 1963).

Breeding Habits Breeding occurs in shallow waters, usually in the second year of life. The adults spawn in groups of 2 to 15, from April to July. Females deposit only a few eggs at one time, which adhere to rocks or detritus. Egg production varies from 829 to 3,602 for females 3.3 to 4.1 in. (84 to 104 mm) in length. Spawning activities are initiated in water as cool as 50°F (10°C), over fine gravel, rocky riffles, or in upwelling springs. They may also spawn over submerged plants along lakeshores (Wydoski and Whitney 1979; Sigler and Miller 1963).

Habitat Redside shiner occupy a wide variety of habitats. They occur in ponds, lakes, streams, and irrigation ditches where summer temperatures range from 44° to 75°F (7° to 24°C). Vegetated areas in shallow water are preferred by schools. In many lakes, daily and seasonal movement patterns have been documented. They remain in shallow water during daylight hours, moving into deeper water at dark. In spring they move inshore and remain until July when they retreat to deeper water, returning to shallow water again in September and October (Wydoski and Whitney 1979; Sigler and Miller 1963).

Management Species preservation for redside shiner requires only maintenance of acceptable water quality and habitat.

---

creek chub, *Semotilus atromaculatus* (Mitchill)

Etymology: *Semotilus,* from the Greek *sema* for banner, referring to the dorsal, and *tilus* for spotted, a word evidently improperly applied by Rafinesque; *atromaculatus* = Latin for black spot

Nomenclature: *Cyprinus atromaculatus* Mitchill 1818, *Semotilus atromaculatus* Large 1903

Importance Throughout their native range, creek chub provide abundant forage and bait. Utah populations currently have too few numbers to assess their importance.

DESCRIPTION

Original

Mud-fish.—So called because he is prone to conceal himself in the muddy bottoms of the fresh brooks in which he lives. Is about 6 in long; rather large in the girth and toward the head, though tapering at the tail.

The lateral line is curved downward. A dark or blackish stripe horizontally from the middle of the tail through the eye to the nose; back, sides, belly, and fins irregularly marked by black dots, consisting of a soft or viscous matter, capable of being detached by the point of a knife without lacerating the skin; back furcated into a groove between the head and dorsal fin; colour of the back brown; of the sides, except the before mentioned stripe, yellowish or brassy; belly white; fins carnation or ruddy; mouth of a middling gape; lips distinct; jaws toothless; tongue plain; nostrils large. Found in the Wall-kill.

Rays br. 3, p. 13, d. 7. v. 7, a. 7, c. 21.

Contemporary

Coloration is dark olive to slate gray on the back, the sides are silvery, the belly white. Young have a dark lateral stripe that diffuses and eventually disappears as they mature. A dark spot is present on the base of the caudal fin. The body is terete and stout with a large head and a very large terminal mouth. There are 49 to 66 scales in the lateral series. Pharyngeal teeth are generally 2, 5–4, 2 (Becker 1983; Smith 1979).

RANGE

Native creek chub range extends from Montana and northern New Mexico east to the Atlantic Coast (Lee et al. 1980). A population may have invaded the Colorado River in Utah from Colorado, although individuals have only rarely been captured in the Green and Colorado rivers in Utah.

SIZE AND LONGEVITY

Median size of four populations at the end of each of 5 years of age was: in inches, 2.3, 4.0, 5.0, 6.3, and 7.2; in mm, 58, 102, 127, 160, 183. The largest known creek chub, 12.9 in. (328 mm), caught by hook and line in Pembina River, North Dakota, was taken in 1964. Normal length is about 6 in. (152 mm) (Tomelleri and Eberle 1990). The age of an 11.4-in. (290-mm) fish was estimated at 8 years but few live longer than 6 years (Copes 1978).

FOOD AND FEEDING

Largely carnivorous, creek chub feed on plants at times. Principal food items are terrestrial and aquatic invertebrates; the chub turn to piscivory as they grow larger. They feed mostly by sight and from surface to bottom in small streams.

Limiting Factors Limiting factors for Utah populations cannot be determined due to the restricted occurrence of this species.

Breeding Habits Differing from most minnows in their breeding habits, male creek chub build nests, covering them after eggs are laid, and guard them. Creek chub spawn over gravel bottoms in shallow waters. Males build nests by fanning out a shallow depression with their tails and moving small stones with their mouths. When a female has deposited eggs in the spawning pit, the male enlarges the pit downstream (Tomelleri and Eberle 1990). Males, generally larger than females, develop breeding tubercles and a bit of orange color during the spawning period. The tubercles account for the common name horned chub in some parts of the range. Spawning commences when spring water temperatures reach about 55°F (12.8°C). Females mature at age 1 or 2, males at age 2 or 3. A large female may produce 2,000 to 3,000 eggs (Becker 1983).

Habitat Low-gradient streams with mud or clay substrate are preferred habitat. Large numbers of creek chub in a habitat may indicate excessive habitat modification, such as pollution or siltation (Smith 1979). They are tolerant of high levels of turbidity. Creek chub are the most widespread minnow of the genus (Tomelleri and Eberle 1990). They inhabit lakes only infrequently and then stay near shore. Creek chub demonstrate a wide tolerance to a range of environmental conditions including quite warm water. They have been collected only rarely in the Colorado River, presumably in quiet backwaters.

Management There is probably little or nothing that can or should be done to preserve Utah populations of creek chub. It is also doubtful that they are a valuable addition to the natural fauna.

Suckers (Family Catostomidae)

Suckers, thought to have their origin in Asia, make up a distinct element of the North America fish fauna and include approximately one hundred species distributed from the Arctic to the tropics (Simpson and Wallace 1978). One species, *Myxocyprinus asiaticus*, represents the sole survivor of this family in China. Only *Catostomus catostomus* occurs in the Old World (Siberia) (Sigler and Miller 1963). They probably invaded there from North America during the Pleistocene epoch 2 million years ago (Bond 1979).

Suckers have soft fin rays, toothless jaws, and cycloid scales. The 10 or more pharyngeal teeth are in a row on two pharyngeal arches. The mouth is typically sucking, as the family name implies, and in most species is protrusible with papillose lips. However, the shortnose suckers, *Chasmistes* ssp., have terminal and rather oblique mouths, with thin lips and almost no papillae. Suckers are very closely related to minnows, and larvae of the two families may be misidentified. Suckers typically run upstream in the spring to spawn, but some spawn along lakeshores. Many adults use the mouth as a suction device, picking up detritus, plants, and animals, especially aquatic insects. Larvae have terminal mouths and feed at the surface. Several species have substantial commercial value.

In the United States and Canada there are 59 species of suckers in 11 genera (Robins et al. 1991). In Utah 8 species and 3 genera occur, of which 7 species are native.

Utah sucker, *Catostomus ardens* Jordan and Gilbert

Plate 12

Etymology: *Catostomus* = inferior mouth, or mouth below; *ardens* = burning, probably referring to the bright red colors of breeding males

Nomenclature: *Catostomus ardens* Jordan and Gilbert 1881

Importance

Early pioneers used Utah sucker heavily as food, particularly the populations in Utah and Bear lakes. The fish were eaten fresh, canned, smoked, or brined (salted). They are used some today, but not often fresh. Utah suckers are important as forage and, in the recent past, accounted for the greatest total weight of any species in Bear Lake, numerically ranking third (McConnell et al. 1957). They are no longer the most abundant fish in Utah Lake.

Trappers' diaries from excursions into Utah during the 1830s to 1850s tell of hundreds of Indians, during Indian and trapper rendezvous, dropping whatever they were doing and catching thousands of fish on the east side of Bear Lake. This catch could only have taken place during a spawning run of suckers, which were easy to catch (Sigler and Sigler 1987).

Description

Original

A large, thick-lipped species, allied to *C. macrochilus*, & c.

Body rather elongate, subfusiform, little compressed, the back broad and somewhat elevated. Head conical, broad and convex above, the front regularly sloping from the nape to the snout. Mouth entirely inferior, the mandible quite horizontal, the premaxillaries scarcely raised above the level of the base of the mandible. Upper lip very wide, full, pendant, with about 8 rows of coarse, irregular papillae, of which the second and third rows from the inside are much larger than the others; upper lip continuous with the lower at the angle of the mouth, the lower lip cut to the base in the middle by a deep, abrupt incision.

Front of eye midway in head. Eye very small, 7 in head, 3 1/2 in the convex interorbital space. Isthmus broad, half broader than the eye. Fontanelle large, as in the other species noticed in this paper. Scales crowded anteriorly, 9–65–9. Breast with evident imbedded scales. Dorsal fin inserted a little behind the middle of the body, long and low, its anterior rays but 3-fourths the length of the base of the fin, 1 1/2 the length of the last rays; the free edge of the fin straight. Caudal fin short and broad, about equally forked, its upper lobe 2-thirds the length of the head. Pectorals short and broad, their length 3-fourths that of the head. Ventrals short, not quite reaching vent. Anal very high, reaching caudal. Dorsal rays 13; anal 7. Length of head 3 2/3 in body to base of caudal; greatest depth 4 1/2. Teeth essentially as in the others.

Color blackish above, blotched with darker, the whole back and sides obscurely spotted; belly white; a narrow, bright, rosy, lateral band on the anterior part of the body, overlying the blackish; fins mostly dusky mottled; top and sides of head rendered dusky by the presence of many dark specks.

This species is described from a large adult male nearly 18 inches in length, besides which we have a single young specimen.

There is another specimen in the collection, a large male fish 18 in long, which agrees entirely with the type of *C. ardens*, with the following exceptions: The lower lip is wider, with less conspicuous, coarse, irregular papillae, in 8 to 10 rows; the upper lip with 2 rows of large papillae and several series of small ones. The caudal fin is much larger, the upper lobe 3-fourths the length of the head, the lower broader than the upper; the pectoral fin is very long, but little shorter than the head; and the ventrals reach the vent. The dorsal has 12 rays, and is long and low, as in *C. ardens*. The scales on the breast are almost obsolete. The isthmus shows a structure very different from that of any other Catostomoid fish known. The gill membranes are partly free posteriorly, their free margins forming a broad fold across the narrow isthmus, as in the genus *Cottus*. This structure appears normal, and is not the result of injury. If it be permanent, this form should probably constitute a distinct genus; if not, it may not be separable as a species from *Catostomus ardens*. Meanwhile we abstain from giving a new name until more specimens can be obtained to settle the question. Indiana State University, December 4, 1880.

Contemporary

Coloration of Utah sucker is bronze or gray above, whitish below, with dark fins. During breeding season, males have a bright rosy lateral stripe. Utah suckers have a long and somewhat compressed body; the back is broad and slightly elevated. The short, conical head is broad and the mouth is inferior, with weak lips, which are without a lateral notch. The caudal fin is short, broad, and weakly forked. The eye is small. Large cycloid scales number 60 to 70 in the lateral series. Dorsal fin rays number 11 to 13.

RANGE

Utah suckers are native throughout the historic Lake Bonneville Basin, Utah, Idaho, Wyoming, and Nevada. Populations also occur in the Snake River drainage above Shoshone Falls (Lee et al. 1980). Since at least the early 1980s they have been present in the Colorado River drainage (Tyus et al. 1982).

SIZE AND LONGEVITY

Utah suckers are relatively fast growing and medium lived fish, most surviving 10 to 12 years. A sample of the Bear Lake population of 144 Utah suckers had a median size of 10.5 in. (267 mm). Yearly length of Utah suckers age 1 to 10 in Bear Lake is: in inches, 1.5, 5.1, 8.4, 10.3, 13.1, 14.6, 16.5, 17.6, 19.0, and 22.0; in mm, 38, 130, 213, 262, 333, 371, 420, 447, 483, 559. In Blackfoot Reservoir, Idaho, 8-lb (3.63-kg) and larger fish have been taken regularly by commercial seiners. Weights of 12 lb (5.4 kg) may be achieved. In some areas they attain lengths of 25.5 in. (648 mm) and weights of more than 5 lb (2.3 kg). Spawning adults in cold Bear Lake, where growth is slow, weigh between 2 and 3 lb (0.9 and 1.36 kg).

FOOD AND FEEDING

Utah suckers are frequently observed feeding on filamentous and other algae attached to fixed objects. In areas where food selections are minimal, both young and adult feed on about the same items, except for differences based on size. They feed on both plants and animals. Adults take most food items from the bottom in deep lakes, feeding far and wide throughout the year. Bear Lake adults feed at all depths, whereas larvae feed at the surface. Young may remain near shore in shallow water or in the tributary streams where they were hatched.

LIMITING FACTORS

A 1955 study examined over 200 Utah suckers from Bear Lake. Almost all were parasitized by *Ligula intestinalis*, a body-cavity tapeworm. The larva is a plerocercoid, free in the body cavity. No other Bear Lake fishes examined were highly parasitized. Tapeworms up to 3 or 4 ft (0.9 or 1.22 m) were found in fish as small as 7 or 8 in. (178 or 203 mm). One hundred Utah suckers from Bear Lake were examined in a 1983 study; none was parasitized and no explanation for this change has developed. Utah suckers are preyed upon by fishes, birds, mammals, and humans. Postspawning mortality of stream spawners is often high. Mortality of spawners on the east shore of Bear Lake has not been evaluated. However, travel to the spawning site is obviously less tiring than upstream migrations, presuming better condition of these fish. Adults caught in July are often in poor condition, indicating spawning stress is a factor, although the level is undefined.

Breeding Habits

Utah suckers spawn in spring, moving out of lakes or large rivers into small streams when water temperatures reach about 60°F (15.56°C). Individual females are usually attended by two or more males. When a female is ready to spawn, two males approach, one on either side, and as all three fish quiver rapidly, eggs and milt are ejected. Gravel and sand on the bottom are then stirred by violent tail movement of the males. There is no nest and no care of eggs or young. Maturity is at 2 or 3 years of age.

Bear Lake populations of Utah suckers, and likely other lake populations as well, have discrete lake-spawning segments. These fish congregate and move inshore, both day and night, but more often just at dusk, where spawning activities become frenzied. Spawning starts in Bear Lake on June 12, on the average. In mid-June 1976, at 2:30 A.M., one continuous school was observed on the east side of Bear Lake. It was more than 3 mi (4.8 km) long and about 6 ft (1.83 m) wide, extending from water 6 in. (15 cm) deep out to water 24 in. (61 cm) deep. These fish were almost without fear, continuing to spawn even when a person walked near them or shined a light on them. On 13 June 1983, around midday in the same area, spawning schools of 400 to 500 were very wary.

In St. Charles Creek, Idaho, a tributary to Bear Lake, Utah suckers start spawning runs in early to mid-June. Two distinct runs exist: one consists of small, darker, immature fish and the other large, faded, and somewhat battered spawners.

Habitat

Utah suckers are, above all, an adaptable species. They prosper over a wide range of habitats from large, deep, cold lakes to shallow warm lakes and to small warm streams (above 80°F [26.7°C]). They occur over a variety of current conditions, either fast or slow. Waters selected may be turbid to clear, bottom types varying from mud to clay to sand and gravel. They prosper in Bear Lake in deep water, feeding near the bottom where the temperatures are often 42° to 46°F (5.6° to 7.8°C). Adults often feed in water more than 100 ft (31 m) deep. Young are more likely to be in tributary streams or near shore. Adults range widely over all portions of the lake.

Before the drought of the early 1930s, Utah suckers occurred in warm, shallow Utah Lake in numbers that were astounding. Commercial catches of hundreds of thousands probably did not depress the population for more than a short time. They are presently greatly reduced in numbers. Ecologically, the contrasts between Bear Lake and Utah Lake are extreme, but suckers prosper in both.

MANAGEMENT

Utah suckers adapt to a wide range of environmental conditions, and probably need no special protection.

---

desert sucker,
Catostomus clarki
Baird and Girard
Plate 13

Etymology: *Catostomus* = inferior mouth, or mouth below; *clarki*, after John H. Clark
Nomenclature: *Catostomus clarki* Baird and Girard 1854

IMPORTANCE

Desert sucker provide prey for other fishes and are used to some extent as a bait fish.

DESCRIPTION

Original

A rather small and short species, in shape subfusiform and compressed. The dorsal line is gently arched. Head small, subconical, truncated anteriorly, forming a little less than the sixth of the total length of the fish. The eyes are subcircular, of medium size, their diameter being contained about 4 times in the length of side of head. The mouth is larger than in *C. congestus*, and surrounded with more developed lips. The upper margin of the dorsal fin is slightly concave, its anterior margin as high as long. The caudal is subcrescentric posteriorly, with rounded lobes. The insertion of the anal is narrow, its height is twice and a half the width. The insertion of ventrals is under the posterior third of the dorsal. The pectorals are elongated and of medium development. D II. 11+1; A II. 7; C 5. I. 8. 8. I. 4; V 10; P 17.

The scales are rather large; about twenty rows across a line from the base of ventrals to anterior margin of dorsal. Sixty-eight to seventy scales in the lateral line, which extends to caudal fin.

Colors in alcohol: greyish brown above, with scattered darker nebulous spots; sides greyish; belly whitish; fins unicolor, vertical ones greyish; horizontal ones yellowish.

Rio Santa Cruz, Gila.—John H. Clark.

Contemporary

Coloration of desert sucker is light tan to darkish green above and silvery to yellowish below. Caudal fin pigment is dispersed over rays and membranes. Lateral series scales range from 61 to 104, usually 80 to 100 in the Virgin River population. Dorsal fin rays number 8 to 12, usually 10 to 11, pelvic rays 8 to 12, usually 9 or 10. The caudal peduncle is 6.9–11.2 percent, usually 8.5–10 percent of the standard length. A distinct notch appears at each corner of the mouth, and the edge of the jaw inside the lower lip has a hard, cartilaginous ridge or sheath. The upper lip is curved, and there is a small flap of skin at the base of each pelvic fin. Lateral axillary processes behind the pelvic fins are poorly developed or absent (Minckley 1973; La Rivers 1962).

RANGE

Desert sucker are native throughout Colorado River basin streams, including the main-stem Colorado, downstream from the Grand Canyon in south central and southern Arizona, and western New Mexico. Utah populations are limited to the Virgin River.

SIZE AND LONGEVITY

Maximum size for adult desert sucker is about 13 in. (330 mm) and life expectancy is 8 to 10 years.

FOOD AND FEEDING

Desert sucker, principally herbivores, feed on encrusted diatoms and other algae. They feed by scraping epilithic algae from stones or other surfaces using their cartilage-sheathed jaws. Small invertebrates living in the algal mats are also ingested. Desert sucker exhibit an interesting habit when feeding: They have been observed pulling themselves along the stream bottom with their expanded suctionlike mouth scraping the tops and sides of stones (Minckley 1973). In some areas they may feed heavily on midges and mayflies.

LIMITING FACTORS

Other fishes and some birds prey on desert sucker. They are parasitized by nematodes. Occasionally they are used as bait. Utah populations suffer from extreme changes in stream flow and from desiccation of habitat. When stressed, they may hybridize with other suckers such as the bluehead.

BREEDING HABITS

Desert sucker spawn in late winter to early spring on riffles. Spawning habits are similar to other western suckers. Maturity is at age 3. Young congregate along the bank in quiet waters in tremendous numbers, then progressively move into the mainstream as they increase in size (Minckley 1973).

HABITAT

Desert sucker are stream fish, tending to live more in rapid waters than in pools. At the very least they move to swift areas to feed and spawn, remaining in pools during daylight hours. Waters inhabited may be muddy or turbid and water temperatures vary seasonally and fluctuate from 45° to 85°F (7.2° to 29.4°C) from spring to September; however, they may invade trout waters. Adults may live in water as deep as 6 to 8 ft (1.83 to 2.44 m), but are frequently found at depths of 3 to 4 ft (0.9 to 1.22 m). Shallow water, 6 to 18 in. (15.2 to 45.7 cm) deep, is used by larvae and juveniles.

MANAGEMENT

Rapid and drastic changes in habitat conditions in the Virgin River adversely impact desert sucker populations. These populations are also adversely affected by exotic fishes, diseases, and parasites carried by exotics as well as direct and indirect competition. Desert sucker needs less competition from exotics and a more stable water flow in the Virgin River and its tributaries.

---

white sucker, *Catostomus commersoni* (Lacépède)

Etymology: *Catostomus* = inferior mouth, or mouth below; *commersoni* = named for Philibert Commerson, an early French naturalist

Nomenclature: *Cyprinus commersonii* Lacépède 1803, *Catostomus commersoni* Jordan 1878b

IMPORTANCE

White sucker are important throughout their native range as both food and sport fish. They, especially the young, are important as forage, as bait, in fish culture, and commercially. Utah populations provide limited value as forage.

DESCRIPTION

Original

Onze rayons à la dorsale; sept à la nageoire de l'anus; neuf à chaque ventrale; huit ou neuf à chaque pectorale; la nageoire du dos et celle de l'anus quadrilatères; l'anale étroite; l'angle de l'extrémité de cette dernière nageoire très-aigu; le caudale en croissant; la ligne latérale droite; la mâchoire supérieure un peu plus avancée que celle d'en-bas; les écailles arrondies et très-petites. La Cépède, *Histoire Naturelle des Poissons*, 5:503.

Translation

Eleven rays in the dorsal; 7 in the anal; 9 in each ventral; 8 or 9 in each pectoral; the dorsal and anal fins quadrilateral; the anal narrow; the angle of the extremity of this last fin very sharp; the caudal crescent-shaped; the lateral line straight; the upper jaw slightly longer than the lower one; the scales rounded and very small.

Contemporary

Coloration is bronze to slate to olive above and white underneath. A distinctive pattern of black blotches is present. Small scales number 55 to 85 in the lateral series. Adults of this terete sucker have a large papillose mouth, a bilobed lower lip, and a rounded snout projecting just beyond the tip of the lower lip. Young, for the first 10 to 15 days following hatching, have a terminal mouth. The mouth migrates to the inferior position as they grow. Pharyngeal teeth number 56 per arch in adults. Pelvic fin rays number 10 to 11, and the slightly convex to straight dorsal fin has 10 to 13 rays, and anal fin rays number 7 (Becker 1983; Smith 1979).

Range

A substantial part of North America, from Labrador and the Mackenzie River on the north, south to British Columbia, then as far south as northern Georgia, and into New Mexico and much of Colorado is the native range of white sucker. Along the Atlantic Coast, native populations occur north to Nova Scotia and Cape Breton Island. Excluded from the native range are the states of Washington, Oregon, California, Nevada, Utah, Idaho, and Arizona (Lee et al. 1980). In Utah they have been introduced in limited numbers in the Weber River system (principally Willard Reservoir), and scattered populations exist throughout the upper Colorado River drainage (Tyus et al. 1982).

Size and Longevity

White sucker in Lakes Winnebago and Michigan (Green Bay) achieved lengths about as follows for 8 years: in inches, 6.4, 12.6, 15.4, 16.5, 17.1, 18.1, 18.6, and 18.7; in mm, 162, 320, 391, 419, 434, 460, 472, 474. Those from Pensaukee River, a tributary to Green Bay, achieved total lengths as follows for 10 years: in inches, 7.0, 11.6, 14.4, 15.8, 16.6, 16.7, 17.2, 17.4, 17.5, and 17.9; in mm, 178, 295, 366, 401, 422, 424, 437, 442, 445, 455 (Becker 1983). Occasionally they reach sizes over 2 ft (610 mm) and 5 lb (2.3 kg). Twelve years is maximum life expectancy, although occasionally individuals may live to 15 years. The world record for hook and line weighed 7 lb, 4 oz (3.3 kg) and was caught from Big Round Lake, Wisconsin (Tomelleri and Eberle 1990).

Food and Feeding

Surface feeding on crustaceans, bloodworms, protozoans, and diatoms reflects feeding habits of larval white sucker with their near terminal mouths and short intestines. Upon reaching about 1 in. (25.4 mm) in length, the mouth begins to migrate ventrally and the gut lengthens. They become bottom feeders when migration of the mouth parts is complete. Adults are omnivorous, feeding on aquatic invertebrates, mostly insects, and some plant material. Some noninsect invertebrates include mollusks, rotifers, crustaceans, and entomostracans (Tomelleri and Eberle 1990; Becker 1983).

Limiting Factors

White sucker stocked in Utah appear to be establishing and expanding their range. Where they occur as natives, they are widespread over a large range of habitats. Near lethal factors such as low pH (for example, 3 to 4), temperatures approaching 90°F (32.2°C), and crowding under adverse conditions, increase stress, thereby increasing susceptibility to disease and parasites.

Breeding Habits

White sucker breed primarily in streams, starting upstream runs soon after the ice goes out, when water temperatures are 40° to 45°F (4.4° to 7.2°C). Best hatching results are at temperatures of 55° to 65°F (12.8° to 18.3°C). Sand or gravel bottoms and medium- to slow-flowing water are preferred. In streams, spawning begins at dusk, lasting to near midnight. Males precede females to spawning grounds. One female is attended by two or more males. Each female spawns briefly, 1 or 2 seconds, then the trio moves on to repeat the act. Females may change male partners after one or more spawning acts. Eggs are covered by the actions of the trio of spawners. No territory is established, although males jockey for position, no redd is prepared, and no care is given eggs or young. The demersal, adhesive eggs sink and attach to plants, debris, or substrate. Large females may produce up to 50,000 eggs, although the average is much less. Spawning lasts 2 to 3 weeks depending on temperature patterns and age composition of mature fish. Under certain conditions they may spawn in lakes (Tomelleri and Eberle 1990; Becker 1983; W. F. Sigler, personal observation). White sucker hybridize with native flannelmouth and bluehead suckers in the Colorado River Basin, and thereby pose a threat to native species' genetic integrity.

Habitat

Preferred habit is clean, cool water, of near neutral pH, with sandy to gravel substrates in medium-size streams. A wide range of habitats from lakes or large rivers to turbid streams, with high or low temperature and low pH, is acceptable. White sucker distribution over a widespread natural range in North America, and ready adaption outside their native range, attest to their versatility.

Management

White sucker have adapted readily to Utah conditions. Their adaptability and relatively low economic value here indicate that no special protection requirements exist.

---

bluehead sucker,
Catostomus discobolus
Cope
Plate 14

Etymology: *Catostomus* = inferior mouth, or mouth below; *discobolus* = a thrower of the discus in ancient Greece; here disco = disk and bolos = lump or morsel, probably in reference to the pendentlike upper lip
Nomenclature: *Catostomus discobolus* Cope 1872b

Importance

Throughout the upper tributaries of the Colorado, Green, and Bear rivers, the native bluehead sucker is an abundant forage fish. They compete little with trout populations. Where game fishes and sucker habitat overlap, the suckers may sustain a portion of the predation, reducing pressure on young game fishes. Bluehead sucker are particularly valuable in converting algae into fish food (Sigler and Miller 1963).

Description

Original

Remarkable for its very large lips, especially the upper. In general it is allied to the *C. griscum*, being of the same cylindric form. The upper lip is pendent, and somewhat expanded all round. Its margin extends outside of that of the lower lip, where it joins it, thus forming an entering right angle with it. The commissural margins of both are wide and abruptly separated from the tuberculated portions. Tubercles subequal; those of the lower jaw projecting in a convex enlargement, concentric with the lower commissure; behind deeply incised. Muzzle projecting a little beyond upper lip; head wide, flat above; eye superior, small, entering length of head 5.5 times; 3 times in muzzle. Pharyngeal bones expanded below; teeth delicate laminar, with acute inner cusp. Length of head, entering total to end of caudal scales, 4 and a half times; ventral fins originating opposite posterior third of dorsal, barely reaching vent; pectorals well separated; isthmus very wide. Radii, D. 11; A. 8; V. 9. Scales in 38–40, longitudinal series between dorsal and ventral fins; color, olive brown above, black on head, passing into light yellow below, gradually on the body, abruptly on the head.

	M
Total length	0.153
Length to orbit	0.016
Length to opercular border	0.029
Length to dorsal fin	0.065
Length to ventral fin	0.095
Length to anal	0.097
Width of frontal bones	0.014
Length of ventral fins	0.022

Two specimens, 1 certainly, the other probably, from the Green River, Wyoming. This striking species was discovered by Cam. Carrington.

This species may be compared with *C. plebeius*, Girard, and *C. generosus*, Girard. In the first the eye is larger and more median, the scales are subequal, and there are only 8 ventral rays. In the second the eye is also larger. In neither is the great development of the lip seen.

Contemporary

Coloration of bluehead sucker is a blue head, bluish gray to olivaceous back, and white upper sides and belly. Breeding males have yellow or orange lower fins and an interrupted red or rosy band on the side. Brassy reflections occur on the sides and green reflections around the opercle. A heavy snout overhangs a large mouth and the head is short and broad. The eye is moderate. A large upper lip forms a fleshy hood over the mouth opening, and the lower lip is shallowly notched at the midline. Both jaws have well-developed cartilaginous scraping edges (Sigler and Miller 1963). Bluehead sucker vary in body form according to size and swiftness of streams inhabited. For instance, the caudal peduncle may be elongate, small and compressed, or relatively deep. The dorsal fin may have 11 or 12 rays, expansive and strongly falcate, or it may be smaller with 9 or 10 rays, less expanded and only slightly concave. Moderate to small scales range from 75 to 118 in the lateral series.

RANGE

Common and widely distributed in the Green River, upper Colorado River, and upper Bear River drainages southwest to the Bill Williams River Basin, Arizona, bluehead sucker are not abundant in the Weber River and they are scarce in western Arizona. They are also present in the Snake River above Shoshone Falls (Sigler and Miller 1963; Tyus et al. 1982).

SIZE AND LONGEVITY

Most adult bluehead suckers are between 6 and 10 in. (152 to 254 mm), although occasionally some reach a length of 18 in. (457 mm). These are the largest of the mountain (subgenus *Pantosteus*) suckers. Life expectancy is probably 6 to 8 years.

FOOD AND FEEDING

Bluehead sucker feed effectively on algae-covered rocks and other fixed objects, using the cartilaginous scraping edges of their jaws. Aquatic insects and other invertebrates living in algal communities are included. They feed in riffles where strong current exists or in deep rocky pools. They may feed lying on their side, or even upside down, around boulders or other objects (Maddux and Kepner 1988). Both young and adult eat the same food.

LIMITING FACTORS

Bluehead sucker are decimated primarily by predation from fishes, birds, and mammals. Hybridization with other species of the genus *Catostomus,* such as flannelmouth and white sucker, dilute their genetic structure.

BREEDING HABITS

Spawning occurs in the spring and early summer at lower elevations and warmer waters, and mid- to late summer in higher, colder waters. Spawning is initiated at about 60°F (15.6°C). Length at first spawning is probably 5 to 7 in. (127 to 179 mm). Most mature at 2 years of age, but a few mature at age 1 or as late as 3. Nervous and cautious, they flee at the sight of a shadow or the sound of a crunch of gravel (Baxter and Simon 1970; Sigler and Miller 1963). When spawning, however, they lose their wariness. They compress themselves to the bottom when disturbed. They spawn in shallow water, so they can often be captured by hand during spawning.

HABITAT

Bluehead sucker are mainstream, mountain fish. Preference is for large, cool streams of 68°F (20°C) or less, but they prosper in warm, small creeks, tolerating waters as warm as 82°F (27.8°C). Often bluehead sucker outnumber larger species of *Catostomus* (Baxter and Simon 1970; Sigler and Miller 1963). Flannelmouth and bluehead sucker larvae are the most common species caught by drift nets in the upper Colorado River Basin (Valdez et al. 1985).

MANAGEMENT

Generally, bluehead sucker are too small to be taken for human food. They do not prosper in impoundments. Their optimum requirement is medium-size, cool to cold mountain streams.

---

flannelmouth sucker
Catostomus latipinnis Baird and Girard
Plate 15

Etymology: *Catostomus* = inferior mouth, or mouth below; *latipinnis* = broad fin
Nomenclature: *Catostomus latipinnis* Baird and Girard 1853b

IMPORTANCE

Flannelmouth sucker were used by Native Americans and early settlers as food. They provide forage and some bait today. Interestingly, these fish, originally adapted to historic Colorado River conditions, have adapted to today's changed habitat in the Colorado River Basin better than several other native fishes.

DESCRIPTION

Original

General shape subfusiform; head proportionally small, contained 5 times and a half in the total length. Eyes small, situated near the upper surface of the head; the mouth is small, the lips large and fleshy. All the fins are very much developed and constitute a very prominent feature. The upper margin of the dorsal is slightly concave; the posterior margin of the caudal, crescent shaped; the anal, ventrals and pectorals are posteriorly rounded or subconical. D I. 14. A II. 8. C 5. I. 8. 8. I. 6. V 10. P 18.

The scales are of medium size, considerably smaller on the back than on the sides and belly. The lateral line runs through the middle of the sides from head to tail.

> The upper part of the body is reddish brown; the upper part of tail and sides, greenish brown: the belly, yellowish orange; the caudal is olive; the anal, ventrals, and pectorals show traces of deep orange, especially on their outer margin. Rio San Pedro, of the Rio Gila.

Contemporary

Flannelmouth sucker have lower lips with large, fleshy lobes, hence the common name. Coloration of adults on the back and upper sides is greenish or bluish grey, the scales outline the dusky color. Lower sides are deep yellow to orange red; the ventral surface is pale, except the head, which is pink. Young are much lighter in color with silvery sides. The dorsal fin is large and falcate with 10 to 14, usually 12 or 13, rays. Lateral series scales number 90 to 116 (Sigler and Miller 1963).

RANGE

Historically, the range of flannelmouth sucker is the Colorado River Basin, from as far north as the present-day Fontanelle Reservoir on the Green River in Wyoming, south to Mexico. Presently their range is much the same, although numbers are much reduced or absent in many parts of the lower Colorado River Basin. In the upper basin, numbers are less than they were originally, but they are still common to abundant in most historic locations (Tyus 1987).

SIZE AND LONGEVITY

Recent studies of flannelmouth sucker indicate that large individuals reach lengths of 21 in. (533 mm), weights of about 3.6 lb (1.6 kg), and live an average of 10 years. Adults over 30 in. (762 mm) have been reported. Upper Colorado River system populations achieve lengths about as follows for fish age 1 to 8 years: in inches, 2.5, 5.0, 9.8, 13.9, 16.6, 18.1, 18.9, and 19.3; in mm, 64, 127, 249, 353, 422, 460, 480, 490. The length-weight relationship is $\text{Log}_{10} W = -5.21 + 3.09 \times \text{Log}_{10} L$, where W = weight in grams and L = total length in mm (McAda 1977; Minckley 1973; Sigler and Miller 1963).

FOOD AND FEEDING

Flannelmouth sucker feed extensively on algae and other plants. In the Salt River, they feed on bottom invertebrates (Marsh and Langhorst 1988; Minckley 1973). The larval stage feeds in the water column. Adults do not appear to be especially selective of food items.

LIMITING FACTORS

Flannelmouth sucker have not suffered adversity from environmental degradation to the same degree in the Colorado River system as have several other native fishes, but they have been impacted. Numbers are drastically reduced in the lower basin and somewhat reduced in the upper basin. Larvae and young are preyed upon heavily by predators.

Both spawning and rearing sites have been adversely impacted, as have feeding sites (McAda 1977; Minckley 1973; Sigler and Miller 1963).

Breeding Habits

Flannelmouth sucker, like most suckers, run upstream in the spring to spawn. Unlike some suckers, their migration to spawning grounds is not long. Males mature earlier in the spring as well as in life and remain fertile longer than females. Males begin to ripen in the spring not long after the ice goes out at about 43° or 44°F (6.1° or 6.7°C), the females later, probably at 50°F (10°C). Maturity is at age 4 or 5 years. A population continues to spawn for 3 to 5 weeks, individual females much less. Fecundity ranges from 9,000 to 23,000 eggs per female (McAda and Wydoski 1980). Spawning occurs over gravel bars where the adhesive, demersal eggs are fertilized and sink to the bottom, attaching to substrate, or drift between crevices. No care is given eggs or young.

Habitat

Flannelmouth sucker are big-river fish, easily navigating the swift waters of the Colorado River. Young are found in shallow riffles and eddies while adults abound in deep riffles and runs. Flannelmouth and bluehead sucker larvae are the most common species caught by drift nets in the upper Colorado River Basin (Valdez et al. 1985). Pools inhabited may be 6 to 150 ft (1.8 to 45.7 m) wide with little or no vegetation and are generally murky; depths are 3 to 20 ft (0.9 to 6.1 m). The bottom is gravel, rocks, sand, or mud. Young live in quiet, shallow areas, generally close to shore. Tributaries, rather than the main stem of the river, may be frequented (Sigler and Miller 1963). They do not prosper in impoundments, or natural lakes. (See author note under humpback chub, "Range" section.) (Marsh and Minckley 1989; Minckley 1973.)

Management

Numbers of flannelmouth sucker have declined drastically in the lower Colorado River Basin in recent years. Despite this, they are not in danger of extinction. Because changes in the historic habitat are essentially irreversible (dams, water temperature regimes, and so on), no further negative changes in the upper basin would appear to be the best management practice. Commercial harvesting should be prohibited, except where study has shown that long-term welfare of the species will not be adversely impacted.

---

mountain sucker, *Catostomus platyrhynchus* (Cope)

Etymology: *Catostomus* = inferior mouth, or mouth below; *platyrhynchus* = flat snout

Nomenclature: *Minomus delphinus* Cope 1874, *Catostomus platyrhynchus* Smith 1966

IMPORTANCE

Their small size renders mountain sucker readily available as forage. They inhabit the same waters as trout and supply a source of food that may be locally important. They are also used as bait in some locales.

DESCRIPTION

Original

The subequal size of the scales of this species would refer it indifferently to the true group Catostomus of Girard, or his group *Minomus*, which he did not distinguish clearly. The preceding species would enter his *Acomus*, which is, however, only an undefined group of species, to which, by the way, the type of *Catostomus*, *C. teres* belongs.

This species is especially distinguished from those heretofore described by the shortening of the caudal part of the vertebral column, and the consequent posterior position of the dorsal fin. Add to this a short, wide head, and thick body, and its physiognomy is expressed.

The dorsal outline is arched, the head flat above, but elevated behind, and much depressed on the muzzle. The muzzle is wide and does not project beyond the upper lip, which is appressed to its lower face and bears 4 rows of warts; its smooth commissural part is narrow. On the lower lip the tubercles advance nearly to the commissure; this lip is deeply emarginate posteriorly; the eye enters the length of the head 5 times, 2 and 1-half times measuring the muzzle, and twice the interorbital region. Head 4 and 2-thirds times in length to end of caudal basal scales.

Scales in thirty longitudinal series, between dorsal and ventral fins; ventrals remarkably short, extending little more than half way to vent, originating under posterior third of dorsal. Pectorals well separated. Radii, D. 11; A. 8, V. 10. Isthmus wide.

Color above blackish, with a strong inferior marginal shade on the lower part of the sides, and lighter tint above; a brown spot just above axilla, is cut off from it by a band of the yellow color which covers the belly and head below.

	M
Total length	.149
Length to orbit	.013
Length to opercular border	.0295
Length to dorsal fin	.069
Length to ventral fin	.074
Length of ventral fin	.015
Length to anal fin	.097
Interorbital width	.0115

The only species concerning which any doubt can arise in the nomenclature of this one is the *C. bernardini* of Girard. That

> writer states that the latter possesses 15 D. radii; this, with the ascription of a slender form and other peculiarities, will always separate them.
>
> Three specimens in Professor Hayden's collection without locality. This should be probably a tributary of Green River.

Contemporary

Coloration of the mountain sucker is dark greenish above with black speckling and white on the lower sides and belly. A slight separation exists between the light underparts and the dark lateral stripe and also between that mark and the reddish stripe above it. Dorsal and caudal fins may both be greenish; lower lobe of the caudal may be amber. Paired lower fins are yellowish. Males in spawning condition have a deep orange to reddish lateral stripe on each side above a greenish black stripe that runs from the tip of the snout to just below the middle of the caudal fin base. Well-developed tubercles occur over much of the body of males in spawning condition. Breeding females also have tubercles on the head, back, and sides but are much more somberly colored than males. Young are mottled on the back and side.

A distinct notch is present on each side of the mouth where upper and lower lips meet, the upper lip is smooth and curved upward, and the lower lip has a shallow, median incision. The edges of the jaws, inside the lower lips, have cartilaginous sheaths used for scraping algae from rocks. An opening beneath the skin in the roof of the skull, the fontenella, is typically open rather than closed (grown over by bone) as in other species. Gill rakers on the internal row of the first arch are 31 to 51, on the external row 24 to 37. There are usually 80 to 85 scales along the lateral series. The dorsal fin rays number 9 to 11, and pelvic fin rays are typically 9 or 10. Mountain sucker commonly have well-developed axillary processes behind the pelvic fins (Sigler and Miller 1963).

Range

Mountain sucker are native to the ancient Lake Bonneville Basin, the Snake River system above Shoshone Falls, Idaho, the Lahontan Basin of Nevada, and in British Columbia, Wyoming, Nevada, and Montana east to the Black Hills of South Dakota. They occur commonly in the Duchesne River drainage, where they were introduced, and are rare elsewhere in the Colorado River drainage. They have also been introduced in the Price River (Tyus et al. 1982; Sigler and Miller 1963).

Size and Longevity

Mountain sucker are small, slow growing, and not long lived. Total length for some Montana populations, age 1 to 5, is: in inches, 1.2, 2.2, 4.0, 5.0, 6.0; in mm, 31, 56, 102, 127, 152; for age 8, 8 in. (203 mm) (Brown 1971). The oldest mountain sucker Brown recorded for Montana was 9 years old. Hauser (1969) reported males 7 years old and females as old as 9 and almost 10 in. (254 mm) long in Montana. In his study, fish grew somewhat faster than reported by Brown. Tomelleri and Eberle (1990) measured a maximum length of 12 in. (305 mm) and normal size range of 6 to 8 in.(152 to 203 mm).

Food and Feeding

Periphyton on rocks and other substrate are a staple for mountain sucker. These fish also benefit from invertebrates living in the periphyton community. In Montana (Brown 1971) diatoms were the most abundant food item taken. Invertebrates were a more important food item for small fish than larger ones in Montana (Hauser 1969). Scraping ridges of the jaws and the very long intestine are indications of their plant diet. Adults especially may feed on higher plants. Baxter and Simon (1970) reported this species' habit of turning upside down to feed on algal growth attached to undersides of large boulders.

Limiting actors

Fishes, birds, and mammals prey on mountain sucker. Water temperatures in the mid- to high 70s°F (mid 20s°C) are harmful. Persistent water diversions may adversely affect habitat. Occasional hybridization with the Tahoe sucker may dilute genetic structure.

Breeding Habits

Sexual maturity in males is reached in 2 to 3 years, when they are 5 to 6 in. (127 to 152 mm) long, and females in 4 to 5 years, at 5 to 7 in. (127 to 178 mm). Females produce between 900 and 4,000 eggs. Spawning occurs in spring when water temperatures exceed 50°F (10°C). Spawning may be terminated when temperatures reach the high 60s°F (high 20s°C). Fry first appear in Montana waters in mid-June, so the incubation period is probably short (Brown 1971). Mountain sucker in the headwaters of the Sevier River were in spawning condition at the end of July 1942 (Sigler and Miller 1963).

Habitat

As is implied by their name, mountain sucker prefer habitat that includes riffles and clear, cold waters of creeks and rivers. They seek habitats including areas of gravel, rubble, sand, or boulders. However, they do occur in turbid streams with mud, sand, or clay bottoms and in large lakes. Although a mountain fish (occurring at elevations up to 9,200 ft [2,804 m]), they also live near sea level. Adults and subadults need moderate to swift currents in water from 1 to 3 ft (0.3 to 0.9 m) deep, but young occupy shallower, quieter waters. Aquatic vegetation sought includes algae, *Chara*, and pondweeds. Preferred summer water temperatures are between 55° and 70°F (12.8° and 21.1°C), although temperatures in the low 80s°F (high 20s°C) are tolerated. In northern Utah there are abundant populations in Blacksmith Fork River, but they are absent, for unknown reasons, from nearby and similar Logan River (Sigler and Miller 1963; Smith 1966).

MANAGEMENT

Mountain sucker prosper in locales that include an abundance of periphyton and relatively cool water. Prevention of habitat degradation is their principal protection requirement.

June sucker, *Chasmistes liorus mictus* Miller and Smith
Plate 16

Etymology: *Chasmistes* = one who yawns, possibly referring to the large near-terminal mouth of this sucker; *liorus* = Latin meaning smooth margin, in reference to the lack of papillae on the lips; *mictus* = Latinized from the Greek work *miktos*, meaning mixed or blended, in reference to its hybrid origin

Nomenclature: *Chasmistes liorus liorus* Jordan 1878b, *Chasmistes liorus mictus* Miller and Smith 1981

IMPORTANCE

June sucker are Utah Lake endemics. In the mid-1800s they provided an important food item for pioneers. Due to the early 1930s droughts and overharvest by commercial fishing, the subspecies *liorus* was believed to have been extirpated (Tanner 1936). Presently they are listed as endangered.

DESCRIPTION

Original—Chasmistes liorus mictus

Holotype.—UMMZ 203995, adult male, 1.7 kg, about 395 mm SL (515 mm TL) from Utah Lake at Goshen, Utah, collected in 1978 by personnel of the Utah Division of Wildlife Resources.

Paratypes.—All material is from Utah Lake: UMMZ 138986(7), 299–358 mm, about 9 km S of Provo River mouth. Madsen, 13 Feb. 1942; UMMZ 141458(1), 309 mm, Municipal Park, Provo, C. L. and E. L. Hubbs, and W. W. Tanner, 18 June 1942; UMMZ 141478(6), 285–330 mm, rock crusher, Provo, C. L. Hubbs family, and W. W. Tanner, 19 June 1942; UMMZ 180680 (2 skeletons, 3 ads.), 334–395 mm, near Bird Island, B. Arnold, 21 March 1959; UMMZ 203994(3), 407–463 mm Provo Bay Channel, Utah Div. Wildlife Res., 25 Aug. 1978; UMMZ 203997(3), 400–430 mm, same coll., summer 1978; and UMMZ 207720(7), 354–475 mm, S. of Lincoln Pt., B. Loy, 1967.

Resembling *Chasmistes l. liorus* in gill-raker structure, but more variable, and with fewer gill rakers (37 to 47), better developed lip papillae, a less oblique mouth and shorter mandible, a shorter, slenderer head, smaller eye, smaller scales (60–70 in lateral line), a more anterior dorsal fin, and a somewhat longer caudal peduncle. Mouth and lips variable but readily distinguished from those of *Catostomus ardens* by the sparse papillae and subterminal position.

Original—Chasmistes liorus liorus

Holotype. USNM 75832, female (probably) 282 mm SL (recataloged in 1914; probably originally was USNM 20932, now catalogued as *Osmerus eperlanus*), designated by Jordan (1878b:151) as "Type *Chasmistes*." This specimen, examined by RRM in 1946, has in its jar the original, much-yellowed parchment "Wheeler Survey" label, bearing original number 455, Henshaw and Yarrow, Utah Lake, Nov. 25, 1872. This is not the fish drawn by Denton (Jordan and Evermann 1900:Fig 85), which is USNM 27361, spec. no. 3.

Other specimens examined are listed at the end of this paper. Proportional measurements of 3 adults are given in Table 1. or those measurements that distinguish this subspecies from *C. l. mictus*, described below, 5 additional specimens were available (Table 2).

Diagnosis. A *Chasmistes* with large scales, 55 to 64 in lateral line, 9 to 11 above and 8 to 10 below lateral line, 29 to 35 before dorsal fin, 52 to 61 around body, and 19 or 20 around caudal peduncle; gill rakers in first row of first arch 45 to 53 (Table 3). [Tables of Diagnostic Characters omitted.]

Contemporary

Coloration is blackish or brown above, fading to a flat white on the belly. Breeding males have a red lateral stripe, females are bluish gray at all times. As opposed to "typical" western suckers, June sucker have a large ventro-terminal mouth in a large head, which is wide and rounded. Adults have weakly developed lip papillae, with widely separated lower lobes. The body is robust. Scales are medium sized, numbering 60 to 70 in the lateral series. There are 10 to 12 rays in the dorsal fin and seven rays in the anal fin.

RANGE

June sucker occur nowhere but Utah Lake, and its major tributary, the Provo River. There is no evidence to indicate the historic form occurred elsewhere in Utah. There are two other species of *Chasmistes*; neither is present in Utah.

SIZE AND LONGEVITY

Species of *Chasmistes* are typically slow growing and long lived. The June sucker is probably no exception. Lengths to approximately 2 ft (610 mm) and weights to 6 lb (2.7 kg) have been reported historically. Age and growth data for June sucker are not available.

FOOD AND FEEDING

Midwater feeding habits can be assumed from the near terminal mouth of the June sucker. Principal food is zooplankton, aquatic insects, and algae (Radant and Hickman 1983).

Limiting Factors

Adult, and conceivably immature, forms were decimated between 1847 and the mid-1920s by commercial fishing. Additional impacts upon the population and their habitat during that same time period, and continuing to the present, include irrigation diversions and dewatering of the main stem of the Provo River which adversely affects spawning success. An estimated 1,500 tons (1,524,000 kg) of spawning suckers (all species) were killed in a 2-mi (3.2-km) stretch of the Provo River in one instance in the late 1800s as a result of irrigation dewatering of the river (Carter 1969). Current hazards include dewatering of spawning habitat and predation of young by other fishes.

Breeding Habits

Principally, June sucker spawn in one section of the Provo River below the Tanner Race diversion, a permanent upstream barrier. Ripe females were captured in the Provo River on June 22 (Shirley 1983). Peak spawning activity is over a brief period of time between June 1 and June 29. Spawning activity is greatest during midday from approximately 11 A.M. to 2 P.M.

June sucker have been observed resting in the deeper pools of the lower Provo River and moving into shallow riffles to spawn. Spawning activity is typical for a river spawning sucker: Movement is in small groups of three to six individuals, generally a female accompanied by several males. Periodically, in a few seconds of intense activity, females release eggs and males fertilize them. Spawning activity subsides for a few moments and is then repeated. Water depths at spawning sites range from 1 to 2.5 ft (0.3 to 0.8 m), with a mean depth of 1.7 ft (0.52 m). Substrate in spawning areas is a mixture of coarse gravel and cobble-sized stones. June sucker do not spawn in sand, silt, or calm backwater areas. Bottom water velocities reported for a spawning site in the Provo River in 1982 was 0.6 ft/sec (0.18 m/sec). During spawning, mean daily water temperatures range from 53° to 55°F (11.7° to 12.8°C) (Shirley 1983). Eggs of June sucker are pale yellow and demersal, with a mean diameter of 0.02 in. (0.5 mm). At a mean temperature of 70°F (21.1°C), they hatch in 4 days. Newly hatched larvae, averaging 0.3 in. (7.6 mm) in length, remain on the bottom and enter the water column approximately 10 days after hatching. Larval and juvenile June sucker remain near the mouth of the Provo River, the only significant inflow to Utah Lake, during June and July. Areas frequented are shallow, calm backwaters with depths of 3 to 8 in. (76 to 203 mm). Larvae form large schools of several hundred to several thousand. They begin to range into swifter, deeper water after metamorphosis (Shirley 1983).

Habitat

Except during spawning, adult June sucker remain in Utah Lake (93,000 acres [37,636 ha], 12 to 14 ft [3.66 to 4.27 m]) deep. Historically, June sucker probably inhabited the entire lake and throughout the water column. Current populations, especially young, are much reduced and inhabit more restricted areas.

MANAGEMENT

Utah Lake is a unique Utah geologic feature. It has played a significant role in the history of the state and currently has the potential to provide additional recreational sportfishing as well as other recreational uses. June sucker are a Utah Lake endemic; they require habitat protection to increase population numbers. Preservation and protection of the limited spawning habitat in the Provo River is essential.

---

razorback sucker, *Xyrauchen texanus* (Abbott)
Plate 17

Etymology: *Xyrauchen* = razor nape; *texanus* = the original locality data (listing Texas) were in error since the species does not range into Texas. The Colorado River was mistaken for a river in Texas.
Nomenclature: *Catostomus texanus* Abbott 1861, *Xyrauchen texanus* Snyder 1915

IMPORTANCE

All of the Colorado River fishes are unique. This statement is true first because 74 percent of the native species are endemic, and second because several species have specially adapted forms for the historically turbulent, fast waters of the river (Miller 1958). Razorback sucker were once abundant enough to be harvested commercially. Today they are rare. Their endemic status and unique life history requirements justify significant efforts to prevent species loss. They are protected as endangered by the states of Arizona, California, Colorado, Nevada, and Utah, and are a proposed species under the federal Endangered Species Act of 1973 (as amended).

DESCRIPTION

Original

Head somewhat compressed, large, constituting somewhat more than 1-fourth of the total length. Eye small, longitudinally oval; its longitudinal diameter constituting 1-twelfth of the length of the side of the head. Mouth large, with labial papillae moderately developed. Body moderately compressed; a dorsal gibbosity extends from the occiput, attaining its greatest height an inch from the occiput, and disappearing at the anterior insertion of the dorsal fin; it is carinated throughout its whole extent. Dorsal fin 1-third longer than high; its base enter five and a-half times in the total length; its anterior margin equidistant between the base of the caudal and the extremity of the snout. The insertion of the ventrals is opposite the center of the dorsal fin, and much nearer the base of the caudal than the extremity of the snout. The posterior extremity of the anal fin extends beyond the rudimentary rays of the caudal. The scales are of medium size, with a subcentric nucleus near the anterior margins of their free portions, from which radiate numerous striae, and around which are numerous well defined ridges. The lateral line is nearly straight throughout its course. The numbers of the fin rays are D, 15. P, 16. V, 10. A, 7. C, 18 5/5.

Color. Upper surface of the head, back, and sides, a dull slate color; belly white (not silvery). Throat yellow.

Total length, 14 in.

Habitat. Colorado and New rivers.

I am indebted to Dr. John L. LeConte, for a note containing a description of this fish, noticing many peculiarities which the specimen (a stuffed one) does not now exhibit.

Contemporary

Adults are easily identified by the large, keel-like bony ridge (hump) on the back, which is not present in young. Coloration is olive to dark brown above, sides are pink to reddish brown. The ventral area is yellow to yellow orange. Fins are particularly colorful, the dorsal fin is olive, the anal orange yellow and the caudal fin yellowish olive. There are 68 to 87 scales in the lateral series. The number of rays in the large dorsal fin range from 13 to 16, but are generally 14 to 15. In fish over 5 in. (127 mm) long the gill rakers number from 44 to 50. Breeding adults acquire spawning tubercles, which are present most heavily on the fins and caudal peduncle (Minckley 1973; Sigler and Miller 1963). Snyder and Muth (1990) published information on separation of razorback and other Colorado River endemics.

Range

Razorback sucker are native to the Colorado River system from lower Wyoming south to Mexico, and also the Gila River Basin, Arizona and New Mexico. In the lower basin they are now rare downstream from Lake Mohave, although there are a few as far south as Senator Wash Reservoir. In the upper basin there are small numbers in the vicinity of Grand Junction on the Colorado River, and below Split Mountain on the Green River. They are scarce to absent from there south to Lake Powell (Marsh and Minckley 1989; Osmundson and Kaeding 1989). The population in the upper Green River has declined 50 percent since 1989. There are older individuals now and limited recruitment (Modde and Wick 1993).

Size and Longevity

Lengths to 3 ft (0.9 m) have been reported historically for razorback sucker. Weights of 16 lb (7.26 kg) were also reported. La Rivers (1962) listed 2 ft (0.6 m) and 10 lb (4.5 kg). They are the largest native sucker of the western United States. Razorback sucker from the Upper Colorado River (McAda and Wydoski 1980) ages 4 to 8 had total lengths as follows: in inches, 19.3, 20.5, 20.4, 21.6, and 23.3; in mm, 490, 521, 518, 549, 592 (sexes combined, lengths unweighted). Difficulty in determining age is reported. The length-weight relationship of razorbacks from the Walker Wildlife Area, Colorado River, is $\mathrm{Log}_{10}\,W = -5.36 + 3.16 \times \mathrm{Log}_{10}\,L$, where *W* equals weight in grams, and *L* equals total length in mm. McAda's data (1977) from the same area are in close agreement. Razorback sucker growth rate may be as much as 9.8 in. (249 mm) in 6 months (Marsh and Minckley 1989). Some probably live to be 12 years old.

FOOD AND FEEDING

Razorback sucker feed on algae, fly larvae and other aquatic insects, planktonic crustaceans, and probably whatever midwater invertebrates are available. Adults may feed on fish larvae. Larval razorbacks apparently select *Bosmina* spp. Adults feeding in about 20 ft (6 m) of water move in an up-and-down pattern with mouths projecting forward. The pectoral fins are held stiffly, and there is lateral movement of the head. In a lotic environment, feeding is on midwater drift and near the bottom. In lentic habitats, it is mostly midwater (Marsh and Langhorst 1988; Minckley 1973).

LIMITING FACTORS

Razorback sucker habitat has been degraded significantly; only small segments of historic range resemble original habitat. The greatest impact is from main-stem dams, which have adversely altered spring runoff temperatures and flow regimes. Stress levels associated with this significant loss of habitat have negatively affected every phase of species life history. These fish are attacked by such parasites as *Ichthyophthirius* spp., *Lernea cyprinacea*, *Myosoma* spp., and pathogenic bacteria including *Aeromonas* spp. and *Pseudomonas* spp. (Roselund 1975). Young are preyed upon so heavily by other fishes, mainly exotics, that few survive beyond the larval stage. The best, but unnatural, standing water habitats are Lake Mohave and numerous gravel pits. Razorbacks may also choose irrigation canals, where hazards are high, rather than riverine waters (Marsh and Minckley 1989). Ability to compete and prosper is lessened considerably in this alien environment.

BREEDING HABITS

Prior to destruction of habitat by humans, razorbacks made long upriver spawning migrations into tributaries and quiet water areas, producing hundreds of millions of young. Today only a few areas, most of which have been drastically altered, are useable. Although larvae are produced in these places, few or no juveniles have been captured. Reported current spawning sites include the Yampa River; Colorado River near Grand Junction, Colorado; Colorado River below Hoover and Davis dams; Lake Mohave; Senator Wash Reservoir; Split Mountain on the Green River; and man-made backwater areas such as gravel pits and canals.

Spawning is initiated in late winter or early spring when water temperatures reach about 54°F (12.2°C). Optimum temperature is 64°F (17.8°C). Neither sex prepares a redd, but repeated spawning acts on one site may create depressions. Eggs are transparent and adhesive and attach to the substrate, or fall between crevices. There is no care of eggs or young. Those depressions below Hoover Dam covering 2.7 sq ft (0.25 sq m) were in water 4 to 6.5 ft (1.2 to 1.98 m) deep, with a velocity, 4 in. (10 cm) from the substrate, of 0.5 ft/sec (1.3 cm/sec) (Mueller 1989). Females appear to deposit relatively few eggs at one time; however, the spawning act is repeated many times. In lentic waters razorback sucker may spawn in depths ranging from 1 to 20 ft (0.3 to 6.1 m). Osmundson and Kaeding (1989) reported even flooded pastures have been used for spawning. Fecundity of Green River razorback populations averages 46,740 eggs for a 20-in. (508-mm) fish weighing 2.9 lb (1.32 kg) (Sigler and Miller 1963; Minckley 1973; McAda and Wydoski 1980; Tyus 1987; Lanigan and Tyus 1989).

Two-year-old male razorbacks at the Dexter National Fish Hatchery were mature. They averaged 15.6 in. (396 mm) long and weighed 2.9 lb (1.32 kg). Females matured at age 2 or 3; they were 16.2 in. (411 mm) long and weighed 1.9 lb (862 g). Females became gravid at a water temperature of 50°F (10°C) and were ready to spawn at 55°F (12.8°C). A period of 5 to 6 weeks was required for all females to complete spawning. Optimum incubation temperature was 70°F (21.1°C). Incubation time ranged from 96 to 144 hours. The average fecundity was 124,522 eggs (Hamman 1981). A regression correlation between the weights of spawning females and the number of eggs per pound of fish indicates there is little relationship. This observation was on hatchery razorbacks but may well apply to wild populations (D. Hales, personal communication, 30 January 1990; Jensen 1983).

Habitat

Historically, habitat of razorback sucker included cool waters of the upper Colorado River and its tributaries to as far south as the very warm waters of upper Mexico. This once swift, turbid river system has been greatly altered, and with it the habitat of razorback sucker. Agricultural and industrial interests have built dams, diversions, canals, and drainage ditches that have changed much of the river basin into an environment alien, and often hostile, to razorbacks. Small numbers of them inhabit the upper river basin, and somewhat larger numbers the lower basin. (See author note under humpback chub, "Range" section.) Most are in impoundments (for example, Lake Mohave), gravel pits, irrigation canals, and other human-altered areas.

There are some below Hoover and Davis dams. Although present in some of the swift waters of the main stream, they more often live in slower water areas.

MANAGEMENT

Habitat assessment followed by preservation of required areas is essential for the survival of the razorback sucker. Areas identified as critical to any life history stage should be protected from further degradation or planting of exotic fishes. Hatcheries should produce fish for stocking, preferably no smaller than 5 in. (127 mm) and from brood stock determined to be representative of the stock naturally occurring in the area to be stocked. A minimum of two refuges should be established where all other fishes have been removed. These refuges should serve as research tools for further study of this unique endemic.

CHAPTER 7

Siluriformes

This order of catfishes is distributed worldwide in generally warm, fresh, and salt water. Over half of the approximately 2,000 species are in South America. There are about 30 families. Some Old World species may reach weights close to 300 lb (136 kg). None has true scales; some are covered with bony plates, many are naked. The order is widely diversified. For example, there are electric catfishes, and some have poison glands associated with the pectoral fin spine. Some have breathing apparatus that allows them to live out of water part of the time. One is parasitic on other fishes and, rarely, on humans.

This order, as in the Cypriniformes, has a Weberian apparatus; that is, the second, third, fourth, and in some the fifth vertebrae are fused to one another. The modified vertebrae form the attachment points for a series of small ossicles; the anterior pair is in contact with the membranous labyrinth, the posterior pair can remain in contact with the gas bladder. The premaxillary bone bears teeth. The dorsal and pectoral spines are different in origin from those of spiny-rayed fishes. Siluriformes have barbels around the mouth and generally an adipose fin (Bond 1979).

Bullhead Catfishes (Family Ictaluridae)

Bullhead catfishes are easily recognized by four pairs of barbels around the mouth. The longest pair extends past the head; there are two pairs that are flattened, wide barbels under the chin; and the outer pair is twice as long as the inner pair; the fourth pair, located just behind the posterior opening of the paired nostrils, is short. They have large heads, the body is naked (scaleless), and both the soft dorsal fin and pectoral fins are preceded by a sharp spine. They have a small adipose fin.

These somewhat nocturnal fishes are native to the warm waters of North America east of the Rockies, except in Mexico (Bond 1979). The family has 5 genera and 39 species in the United States and Canada (Robins et al. 1991). There are 2 genera and 3 species in Utah. Catfishes guard their nests and young for varying periods of time. The bullheads, having somewhat square tails, are easily separated from the channel catfish, which have forked tails.

black bullhead, *Ameiurus melas* (Rafinesque) Plate 18

Etymology: *Ameiurus* = not (a fish without), curtailed, the caudal fin not notched; *melas* = black

Nomenclature: *Silurus melas* Rafinesque 1820b, *Silurus xanthocephalus* Rafinesque 1820b, *Ameiurus* Rafinesque 1820 corrected spelling, *Ameiurus melas* Jordan and Evermann 1896–1900, *Ictalurus melas* Taylor 1954, *Ameiurus melas* Bailey and Robins 1988 and Lundberg 1989

IMPORTANCE

Black bullhead are ideal prey for youngsters and people who prefer minimum effort in their sportfishing. Black bullhead strike slowly and without subtlety. They provide many hours of fishing pleasure in some areas where otherwise few fishing opportunities exist. The negative aspect is that they often produce very large numbers of fish too small to be of interest to anyone.

DESCRIPTION

Original

Black cat-fish. Body blackish, jaws and barbs unequal, the lateral barbs shorter than the head, lateral line straight, eyes rounded, spinous rays short and smooth, anal fin with twenty rays, tail semi-truncate.

A small species from 3 to 10 in long, throat and belly hardly pale, iris black slightly elliptical. D. 1 and 6. P. 1 and 7. Abd. 8. An. 20. C. 24.

Contemporary

Adults are blackish, dark olive in some waters, or dark brown on the back. The belly is greenish white, or, again depending on the water, bright yellow. It is more brightly colored during the breeding season (Smith 1979).

The black bullhead has a distinct pale vertical bar at the base of the caudal fin. The membrane of the anal fin is darker than the rays, which are usually 17 to 20. The chin barbels are darker than the chin (Smith 1979).

RANGE

The northern edge of original range of the black bullhead is from southern Ontario, western New York, including the Great Lakes, and the St. Lawrence River. They occur as far west as North Dakota then south to New Mexico, the Gulf of Mexico, and northern Mexico (Lee et al. 1980). They are now common in most of the lower 48 states.

They are common in many warm waters of Utah and abundant in Utah Lake.

Size and Longevity

A few black bullhead reach a size of 14 in. (356 mm) and about 2 lb (0.9 kg). Average weight is less than half this. The world all-tackle hook-and-line record is 8 lb, 15 oz (4.06 kg) (Fishing Hall of Fame 1993). The Utah record is 2 lb, 7 oz (1.13 kg). Young average 2 to 4 in. (51 to 102 mm), but an abundance of food may occasionally produce much larger fish in one year. When reproduction is high and food is in short supply, there may be very little growth. Very few black bullhead live beyond 6 years.

Food and Feeding

Black bullhead are opportunistic, omnivorous scavengers. They feed on or near the bottom on plant material, snails, fishes, frogs, crayfish, and waste or detrital material. Abundant crustaceans may make up 75 percent of their food. Adults have a tendency to be nocturnal when feeding. Young are more apt to feed at twilight.

In an Iowa study, Harlan and Speaker (1956) determined that black bullhead feed on midge and mayfly larvae, small crayfish, worms, and small mollusks. Aquatic vegetation, fishes, mollusks, snails, leaches, oligochaetes, and aquatic insects are identified as food items by La Rivers (1962).

Limiting Factors

Many fishes and even frogs feed on black bullhead eggs and young. Predators even attack and decimate young when they are schooled and guarded. This action usually causes schools to break up.

Adult fighting is severe during breeding season. Many are scarred; some die from fight-sustained injuries. In certain areas there is a tendency to produce dominant year classes; this is followed by years of paucity of young. Lethal temperature is in the mid-90s°F (about 35°C).

Breeding Habits

Black bullhead spawn from May to July when temperatures reach 66° to 72°F (18.9° to 22.2°C). Nests are located in protected areas such as submerged logs, abandoned muskrat dens, stumps, rooted vegetation, and rock crevices. Eggs are yellowish and adhesive and are laid in a single gelatinous mass. A female may produce from 2,000 to 6,000 eggs, which hatch in less than a week at 72° to 75°F (22.2° to 23.9°C). Either the male or female or both may guard the eggs and provide aeration. The female may soon leave the vigil (Sigler and Miller 1963). Young school when they leave the nest and form a jet-black, compact ball that may be 18 in. (0.45 m) in diameter. The school does not travel fast or far. Individuals appear to be swimming at random or in circles rather than forward. The school is guarded by one or both parents until young are 1 to 2 in. (25 to 51 mm) long. Schooling continues for 2 to 3 weeks or may last as long as most of the summer.

Habitat

Black bullhead are warmwater fish, preferring small ponds, quarries, small reservoirs, shallow lakes, intermittent creeks, and muddy backwaters. Common associates are minnows and sunfishes but in Utah Lake the other dominant fishes are white bass, common carp, walleye, and channel catfish.

They are able to survive in less than 2 ppm (mg/l) of oxygen. Best temperatures are the low 70s°F (21°C) but the fish can survive in waters as warm as the high 80°sF (26.7°C). Greatest population numbers occur where the water is turbid, the bottom silty, and current is weak or absent.

MANAGEMENT

Black bullhead may not be able to compete for food in large reservoirs, but in ponds or small, shallow lakes, they may become the single most abundant species present. Under certain conditions, they may produce large numbers of fish too small to be of interest to anglers. Only when a large percent of these fish are eliminated, such as by some natural disaster, will the remainder grow to acceptable size for anglers.

---

yellow bullhead,
Ameiurus natalis
(Lesueur)

Etymology: *Ameiurus* = not (a fish without), curtailed, the caudal fin not notched; *natalis* = having large nates or buttocks

Nomenclature: *Pimelodus natalis* Lesueur 1819, *Ameiurus natalis* Günther 1864, *Ictalurus natalis* Taylor 1954, *Ameiurus natalis* Bailey and Robins 1988 and Lundberg 1989

IMPORTANCE

Yellow bullhead have a restricted range in Utah. This factor limits their importance as sport fish. In some areas, however, yellow bullhead are the most important catfish in the creel.

DESCRIPTION

Original

Caract. spéc. Corps égal, nageoires teintes de rouge foncé, couleur olivâtre et unie sur le dos, jaune sous le ventre.

Ce Pimelode a le corps égal depuis la dorsale jusqu'à la queue, et peut être compris entre deux parallèles. Il est aussi haut à la base de la nageoire adipeuse et à la fin de l'anale, que depuis la base de la première dorsale, en descendant derrière les pectorales; tandis que dans les autres espèces, la partie voisine de la queue est toujours la moins élevée, la forme des nageoires diffère peu de celle des précédens; celle de la queue est tronquée en ligne droite; l' anale est longue, arrondie; leur couleur est d'un rouge foncé, mêlé d'un peu de jaune; le dessus de la tête est d'une teinte olivâtre foncée, qui est plus claire sur le dos, passe au jaune sur les côtés et devient d'un jaune clair sur l'abdomen. La ligne latérale est droite et plus apparente dans cette espèce que dans les autres.

La tête est large et un peu orbiculaire; les dents ont la même distribution que dans les autres espèces. Il en est ainsi des barbillons qui sont au nombre de huit. Ceux de la machoire inférieure sont inégaux; les deux du centre se trouvent les plus courts.

Cette espèce ne parvient pas à une taille remarquable; elle n'excède guère huit pouces de France.

J'indique ici sous le nom de Pimelodon *livrée* une petite espèce qui s'éloigne des autres par la forme de sa deuxième nageoire dorsale, qui est longue, trés-basse et réunie avec celle de la queue, dont elle est séparée par une légère échancrure. La queue est ronde, large, réunie par une légère membrane à l'anale. Celle-ci est grande, arrondie; la première dorsale est petite; le premier rayon osseux, sans dentelure; celui des pectorales est court, osseux et dentelé dans sa partie antérieure. Ces dentelures sont tournées vers le bas et assez espacées entre elles. La première dorsale, l' anale, la caudale, et les pectorales sont bordées d' une bande très-noire.

La couleur générale est d'une teinte pâle et roussâtre; elle s'étend sur la tête, les narines, les barbillons, etc., qui d'ailleurs ne diffèrent en rien de ceux des autres Pimelodes. La peau de ce poisson est unie, avec de petites pustules sur le dos; la ligne latérale est sensible.

Rayons: B. 8; D. 8; P. 12; V. 9; A. 20; C. 50. Tous ces rayons sont sous-divisés.

Translation

Species characteristics. Equal body, fins colored dark red, uniform olive color on the back, yellow belly.

This pimelode has an equal body from the dorsal to the tail and can be included between two parallel lines. It is as high at the base of the adipose fin and at the end of the anal, as from the base of the first dorsal, descending behind the pectorals, whereas in other species the part adjacent to the tail is always the least elevated; the form of the fins differs little from that of preceding pimelodes; that of the tail is truncated in a straight line; the anal is long, rounded; their color is dark red, mixed with a little yellow; the upper part of the head is a deep olive hue, which is lighter on the back, passing to yellow on the sides and becoming pale yellow on the abdomen. The lateral line is straight and more apparent in this species than in the others.

The head is large and a little orbicular; the teeth have the same distribution as in the other species. The same is true for the barbels of which there are 8. Those of the lower jaws are unequal; the two center ones are the shortest.

This species doesn't attain a remarkable size; it hardly exceeds 8 French inches.

I indicate here under the name of *Pimelodon livrée* a small species that differs from the others by the form of its second dorsal fin, which is long, very deep, and reunited with that of the tail, from which it is separated by a slight dip. The tail is round, wide, joined by a light membrane to the anal. This fin is big, rounded; the first dorsal is small; the first ray bony, without notches; that of the pectorals is short, bony, and notched in its anterior part. These notches are turned down with space between them. The first dorsal, the anal, the caudal, and the pectorals are bordered by a deep-black band.

The general color is a pale reddish brown; it extends over the head, the nostrils, the barbels, etc., that moreover differ not at all from those of other pimelodes. The skin of this fish is smooth, with some little pustules on the back; the lateral line is noticeable.

Rays: B. 8; D.8; P. 12; V. 9: A. 20; C. 50. All of these rays are subdivided.

Contemporary

Coloration of the dorsal area of the yellow bullhead is yellow, olive, or brown, the sides are lighter, the belly yellow to white. Immaculate white or yellow chin barbels and a long rounded caudal fin are their most distinctive features. They have 24 to 27 anal fin rays including rudimentaries, and a vague dark stripe running through the middle of the anal fin. The dorsal fin has 6 soft rays and the pelvics 8 rays. These characteristics help distinguish it from the black bullhead. There is a finely serrated posterior edge on the pectoral spines. Young are distinctive because of the long anal fin and immaculate chin barbels (Smith 1979).

Range

Originally, the range of the yellow bullhead was the eastern and central United States; from the East Coast and the Great Lakes west to the Dakotas, south to Mexico, Texas, and Florida (Lee et al. 1980). In Utah, they are in upper Lake Powell near the inflows of both the Colorado and San Juan rivers (Wayne Gustaveson, personal communication, March 1990). The range has been extended by a few plantings but they have not been planted as extensively as have some of the other catfishes.

Size and Longevity

Yellow bullhead generally live 6 or 7 years. In general, they grow faster and larger than the black bullhead.

In Wisconsin, they grow in length as follows for the first 6 years: in inches, 5.7, 7.8, 8.6, 9.3, 10.7, and 11.4; in mm, 145, 198, 218, 236, 272, 290 (Becker 1983). The world all-tackle hook-and-line record is 4 lb, 8 oz (2.4 kg) (Fishing Hall of Fame 1993).

Food and Feeding

Black bullhead feed on invertebrates, small fishes, and carrion. Invertebrates include crayfish, amphipods, cladocerans, insect larvae, snails, and copepods. They also eat algae.

Limiting Factors

Yellow bullhead do not adapt well to lakes or ponds but thrive in small to large streams.

Breeding Habits

Yellow bullhead spawn in water from 18 in. to 4 ft (0.46 to 1.22 m) deep in May or June. Nests are located in protected areas such as submerged logs, abandoned muskrat dens, stumps, rooted vegetation, and rock crevices. Females lay from 650 to 7,000 eggs, which hatch in 5 to 10 days. Eggs are yellowish, adhesive, and are laid in a single gelatinous mass. Fry are guarded by the parents until late July or August. They reach 3 to 6 in. (76 to 152 mm) in size the first year and mature the third year.

Habitat

Yellow bullhead are typically stream fish; black bullhead prefer ponds, sloughs, and backwaters; and brown bullhead are present principally in lakes. Yellow bullhead are the most abundant catfish in Illinois because they are a small-stream species and such streams are many (Smith 1979).

In Ohio, the most fish are in shallow portions of large bays, lakes, ponds, and streams where there is a low gradient, clear water, and aquatic vegetation. Yellow bullhead prosper in such diverse bottom types as gravel, sand, peat, and muck (Trautman 1981).

Management

Habitat destruction and competition from other catfishes reduce populations of yellow bullhead. They should be stocked only where competition from these species is absent.

---

channel catfish, *Ictalurus punctatus* (Rafinesque)

Plate 19

Etymology: *Ictalurus* = fish cat; *punctatus* = spotted, mainly in fish 12 in. or less

Nomenclature: *Silurus punctatus* Rafinesque 1818b, *Ictalurus punctatus* Eigenmann 1895

Importance

Channel catfish are one of the more important warmwater fishes in the United States. They are sought by anglers of all ages (Sigler and Miller 1963). Channel catfish are popular in Utah, providing a fishery in waters that will not support trout. From a management viewpoint, catfishes have the additional benefit of feeding on organic debris, plants, and other bottom material avoided by most other game fishes.

Fee fishing in ponds for channel catfish has not been developed in Utah as extensively as elsewhere in the United States. This situation may be due to the preference for trout and the availability of public waters. The commercial production of channel catfish exceeds that of any other fish in the United States.

Fee fishing and aquaculture for channel catfish has tremendous potential. These fish tolerate brackish water, allowing them to be reared in waters not suited for salmonids; because of their omnivorous nature, channel catfish adapt well to commercial food rations in captivity, thereby making them a relatively easy species to culture.

Description

Original

Body whitish gilt shades and many brown unequal dots on the sides, 8 barbels, 4 underneath, 2 lateral long and black, dorsal fin 7 rays, 1 spiny, pectoral fins 6 rays, 1 spiny, anal 27 rays, lateral line a little curved beneath at the base, tail forked unequal, upper lobe longer.

Contemporary

Channel catfish are distinguished from other Utah catfishes by their long anal fin and deeply forked tail. The upper caudal lobe may be slightly longer than the lower lobe; both are pointed. The body is pale bluish olive above and bluish white below. They may have spots but generally lose them when older, especially the males. Males, at breeding time, become more brightly colored; they have wider heads, thickened lips, and fatty pads around the eyes.

Both the dorsal and pectoral fins have strong, sharp spines. The dorsal fin has 6 to 7 soft rays; anal fin 24 to 27 rays, pelvic fins 8 rays, pectorals have 4 to 5 rays; the adipose is soft and fatty. The mouth is short, wide, subterminal, and horizontal. The chin and snout barbels are lightly pigmented.

Range

Native range of the channel catfish extends from the St. Lawrence River in Quebec, Canada, south on the western side of the Appalachian Mountains, to southern Georgia and central Florida, west through the Gulf states to eastern Texas and northern Mexico, and then northwest through New Mexico to Montana. They have been widely introduced throughout the eastern and western United States (Scott and Crossman 1973). Channel catfish were successfully introduced into Utah in 1888. They are now widely distributed in warmwater lakes, reservoirs, and streams including the Colorado and Bear rivers, and Utah Lake.

Size and Longevity

Channel catfish occasionally reach a large size, but most are 2 to 4 lb (0.91 to 1.81 kg). A few live 15 years; a 30-in. (762-mm) fish weighs 15 lb

(6.8 kg). The world all-tackle hook-and-line record is 58 lb (26.3 kg) (IGFA 1993). The Utah record is 32 lb, 5 oz (14.7 kg). Optimum growth is achieved when water temperatures are in the mid- to high 80s°F (high 20s° to low 30s°C).

Sigler and Miller (1963) reported that young catfish at the mouth of the Bear River, just inside the Bear River Migratory Bird Refuge, are 6 to 7 in. (152 to 178 mm) when they are 1 year old. Utah Lake channel catfish age 1 to 12 measured as follows: in inches, 3.1, 6.9, 9.4, 12.1, 14.5, 16.7, 17.9, 18.9, 19.7, 20.6, 21.2, and 21.6; in mm, 78, 175, 239, 307, 368, 424, 455, 480, 500, 523, 539, 549 (Lawler 1960). Purkett (1958) found that channel catfish in the Salt River, Missouri, grew somewhat slower and did not live as long as those in Utah. Mississippi River fish age 1 to 12 grew as follows: in inches, 2.9, 6.3, 9.0, 11.7, 14.2, 16.6, 19.2, 21.1, 24.0, 25.9, 26.6, and 27.9; in mm, 74, 160, 229, 297, 361, 422, 488, 536, 609, 658, 676, 709 (Appleget and Smith 1951).

Food and Feeding

Adult channel catfish are omnivorous; the young feed on insects, other arthropods, and other invertebrates. Organic debris and plants, foods consistently avoided by other game fishes, were reported as principal foods of channel catfish by La Rivers (1962). In the Des Moines River, Iowa, when elm tree seeds are abundant, channel catfish feed on nothing else (Harlan and Speaker 1956).

In Utah they eat clams, crayfish, earthworms, snails, fishes, plant material, and seeds (Sigler and Miller 1963). They may feed both in daylight and darkness but mostly from twilight to midnight. Bottom feeding is characteristic, but they occasionally feed at the surface. This habit is especially true of the young. During daylight hours, in clear water, channel catfish apparently rely more on sight than smell, a somewhat unique trait for a catfish. Feeding commences in the spring when temperature reaches about 50°F (10°C) and stops when it reaches 94°F (34.4°C). There is some evidence that channel catfish commence feeding at temperatures as low as 38°F (3.3°C), mainly on carrion, which is principally fish that died during the winter. They do not feed in winter.

Clady (1981) stated that channel catfish in early spring (52° to 54°F [11.1 to 12.2°C]) grow more rapidly in waters stocked with golden shiners and *Tilapia* sp. than they do when stocked alone. Cannamela et al. (1979) indicated that the presence of other catfishes may affect both food selection and the amount of feeding by channel catfish. In two western Kentucky impoundments, young catfish relied heavily on zooplankton and aquatic insects (Cannamela et al. 1979). Other food items that were seasonally important included trichopterans (caddisflies), bryozoans, and fishes. Fishes are the most important food of channel catfish measuring 6 to 12 in. (152 to 305 mm). Large channel catfish (> 20 in. or 508 mm) are almost exclusively predatory on fishes.

LIMITING FACTORS

Channel catfish are relatively easy to catch, so heavy fishing pressures can reduce a population substantially. The young are quite vulnerable unless there is heavy cover or high turbidity. The minimum acceptable oxygen content for three temperatures is: 77°F (25°C)—.95 ppm (mg/l); 86°F (30°C)—1.05 ppm; and at 95°F (35°C)—1.08 ppm (Becker 1983).

BREEDING HABITS

Channel catfish are cautious spawners. They seek murky water or some other cover. They spawn in spring or early summer at water temperatures between 71° and 75°F (21.7° and 23.9°C) and may continue spawning until temperatures reach 80°F (26.6°C). Semidark nests are built by the males in holes, undercut logs, milk cans, banks, or boulder areas. Female spawning is 4 to 6 hours, only once a year, but the males may spawn several times (Scott and Crossman 1973). A female may lay as many as 34,500 eggs (about 4,000/lb [1820/kg] of female), which are approximately 0.12 to 0.16 in. (3 to 4 mm) in diameter before water hardening. Males guard and aerate nests after the eggs have been deposited and fertilized; the young hatch in 7 days at 80°F (26.7°C).

The young have a yolk sac for approximately 2 to 5 days, then begin to feed. The male remains with the young for a month or more after hatching. Either parent may devour the eggs if they are disturbed too often during incubation. Age of maturity varies more than for most catfishes—average age at maturity is 3 to 5 years.

HABITAT

Channel catfish, with a streamlined body and deeply forked tail, are obviously adapted for living in moderately swift streams, more so than other North American catfishes. But they also prosper in lakes and impoundments. In streams, adults spend the day in shelter, such as logs or undercut banks, moving into riffle areas to feed at dusk. Storms that wash in food may cause channel catfish to start feeding at any time. Young tend to stay and feed in the riffles more than the adults.

Channel catfish seek clear-water lakes and streams with a variety of bottom types, except during spawning. They also prosper in rather turbid water. Moderate populations live in the Colorado and Green rivers of Utah; they are abundant in the lower Bear River and Utah Lake. They also do well in farm ponds. Some populations move upstream in the spring and downstream in the fall.

MANAGEMENT

In ideal habitat, stocking channel catfish is rarely necessary. In borderline areas, it often is, preferably with fish at least 7 to 8 in. (178 to 203 mm) long, particularly in small lakes and ponds. In clear-water ponds or lakes with little or no vegetation, brush piles offer the young protection and increase zooplankton. In clear-water lakes with minimum spawning sites, artificial devices may be useful. Legal limits on numbers are necessary in most areas. The use of minimum size limits is questionable because most fish are caught on worms or meat or fish products. Mortality of hooked and released fish is high.

CHAPTER 8 Salmoniformes

The species in the order Salmoniformes constitute the majority of species of coldwater, recreational sport fishes in North America. Salmoniformes are soft-rayed and mostly physostomous (having a connection between the gas bladder and the esophagus), but not all species have a gas bladder. This order is characteristic of the bony fishes, although many primitive structures are present. An adipose fin is present in the majority of the species including all members of the salmon family. The order originated in the Cretaceous, possibly as long ago as 135 million years (Bond 1979).

The suborder Salmonoidei includes the salmons, trouts, and their relatives, represented by one family, Salmonidae, with 5 genera and 12 species in Utah (all but one species of trout have been introduced). The suborder Esocoidei includes the pikes, mudminnows, and the Alaska blackfish. In Utah this group is represented by one introduced family, Esocidae (pikes), and one species, the northern pike (Sigler and Sigler 1987).

Pikes (Family Esocidae)

The ducklike bill and the long teeth make Esocidae easily recognizable. The dorsal fin is short and far back, and the tail is forked (Smith 1979). Only one genus, *Esox*, exists in this Holarctic family. Five species are present in North America and one in the former Union of Soviet Socialist Republics (USSR). Teeth on the jaws, a primary characteristic of the family, are large and prominent. *Esox* has large patches of cardiform (comblike) teeth on the vomer and palatines (bone in roof of mouth) and tongue. The pectoral fins are low, the pelvic fins abdominal. The native range of the pikes includes much of the northern hemisphere. Only one species occurs in Utah.

northern pike, *Esox lucius* Linnaeus

Etymology: *Esox,* an old name for the pike in Europe; *lucius,* supposedly the Latin name for this species
Nomenclature: *Esox lucius* Linnaeus 1758

IMPORTANCE

Northern pike are not very important as a game fish in Utah because of their limited range and relatively sparse populations. However, their large size and fighting ability makes them locally popular. Their palatability is generally, but not always, favorably regarded. They are highly piscivorous so pike are a useful management tool. In some waters inhabited largely by nongame fishes, this trait can be successfully exploited.

DESCRIPTION

Original

E. rostro depresso subæquali.

Art. gen. 10. *syn.* 26. *spec.* 53. *sn. svec.* 304. Esox rostro plagioplateo. D.21.P.15.V.11.A.18.C.19.

Gron. mus. I. *n.* 28. idem. D.18.P.11.V.9.A.15.C.

Habitat in Europa.

Voracissimus exhaurit pascinas; *ab Anatibus feritur.*

Translation

Esox, a pikelike fish of the Rhine with a flattened, drooping snout. Pike with a broad predatory snout. It lives in Europe. A most vicious fish, it can empty the fishpond; it preys upon ducks.

Contemporary

The body of adult northern pike appears to be flecked with gold. This look is caused by tiny gold spots on the tip of the exposed edge of most body scales. Adults are distinctive because of a pattern of light-colored marks on a green or brown background. Young have discrete, black over brown, spots on the dorsal, anal, and caudal fins. Dark color markings on the back and sides are lacking (Smith 1979). The flanks have a light background and have seven to nine irregular, longitudinal rows of yellow to whitish, bead-shaped spots, some as large as the eye diameter in pike over 15 in long. Juveniles have a pattern of long, wavy, white-to-yellow vertical bars extending up almost to the lateral line; in adults, these break into rows of spots. This distinctive juvenile coloration at one time caused them to be confused with other (adult) species. The sides of the head are vermiculated with bright golden marks (Scott and Crossman 1973). Cheeks are fully scaled, a characteristic separating pike from other members of the genus. Only the upper half of the opercle is scaled. The teardroplike mark below the eye is weak.

RANGE

In Utah the range of the northern pike includes Redmond Lake, Yuba and Sevier Bridge reservoirs, the San Juan River, and Lake Powell. In

1981 they invaded the Green River from the Yampa (Tyus and Beard 1990). In the northern hemisphere, northern pike have circumpolar distribution. In North America, their native range is from Alaska south to Missouri and west to Nebraska. They occur east of the Rocky Mountains and west of the Appalachians. They are native in Lake Champlain and the Hudson River and south to the Connecticut River, New Hampshire, and central Massachusetts. They are also native in the United Kingdom, Ireland, Europe, northern Italy, around the Dead and Caspian seas, northeast into Siberia, in Lakes Balkhash and Baikal, and east to the Chukchi Peninsula (Lee et al. 1980). Northern pike have not been stocked as extensively in the United States as some other species of game fishes.

Size and Longevity

Northern pike are both fast growing and long lived. They live 12 or more years in the southern part of the range. Slow-growing Arctic populations may be as old as 26 years. Young fish grow rapidly in length. They are about 0.33 in. (8.3 mm) long when hatched and reach 6 to 12 in. (152 to 305 mm) at the end of the first year. In an unusual case in a Missouri River backwater area, with a large number of gizzard shad, young pike reached 20 in. (508 mm) the first summer. This rapid growth rate indicates the potential for achieving large size in a short time when there is abundant food. Populations of large individuals can in some cases be produced for a sport fishery. The average yearly length of northern pike age 1 to 6 years in Montana is: in inches, 10, 15, 18, 21, 24, 30; in mm, 254, 381, 457, 533, 609, 762; and for 10-year-olds, 40 in. (1,016 mm) (Brown 1971). Growth in length is rapid during the first 3 or 4 years, but slows after sexual maturity, when weight increases relatively more rapidly. The female grows much larger than the male. In Lake Athabasca, Canada, one study group grew each year for 24 years as follows: in inches, 4.2, 6.5, 9.3, 12.2, 14.7, 17.3, 20.0, 22.3, 24.5, 26.5, 28.6, 30.6, 31.4, 34.0, 35.2, 36.7, 38.3, 40.0, 40.9, 43.6, 44.1, 45.1, 47.2, and 48.4; in mm, 107, 165, 236, 309, 373, 439, 508, 566, 622, 673, 724, 777, 798, 864, 894, 932, 973, 1,016, 1,039, 1,107, 1,120, 1,143, 1,199, 1,229 (Miller and Kennedy 1948). The largest one weighed 31.25 lb (14.2 kg).

Northern pike in Utah generally do not exceed 10 lb (4 kg). The record pike for Utah, caught in Sevier Bridge Reservoir, weighed 22 lb, 1 oz (9.9 kg). The world record for pike, 55 lb, 1 oz (24.9 kg) was caught in Lake of Grefeern, West Germany (IGFA 1993).

Food and Feeding

Young northern pike up to 2 in. (51 mm) long feed heavily on large zooplankton and immature insects starting as soon as they have absorbed the yolk sac. Small fish enter the pike's diet soon after, and by the time young are 2.5 in. (64 mm) long, they prefer fish. Northern pike are visual predators and as such are active primarily during daylight hours (Inskip 1982). Adult pike are omnivorous carnivores that eat virtually anything they can catch and swallow, but are primarily piscivorous. Adults may feed heavily on frogs and crayfish and are not hesitant to take such animals as mice, muskrats, and ducklings.

Limiting Factors

Northern pike typically spawn in very shallow water in weedy areas. This habit subjects the young, and occasionally the adults, to the hazards of being trapped by rapidly dropping water levels (as a result of either natural or human-caused events). Dropping water levels not immediately followed by a migration of young into deeper, safer waters leave young trapped in shallow waters and easy prey to fishes, aquatic insects, birds, and mammals. Eggs are eaten by some of these predators. Rapid temperature changes also negatively affect eggs and young.

When spawning, northern pike lose their normal wariness and are more susceptible to predation by humans, bears, eagles, and ospreys. In other seasons, adults are secretive and even belligerent; in most places they have only humans to fear. They are vulnerable to overfishing because they strike lures readily and inhabit inshore areas.

Breeding Habits

Mature northern pike move into shallow, weedy areas, and commence spawning almost immediately after ice-off in the spring, generally when temperatures range from 40° to 52°F (4.4° to 11.1°C). In southern Canada and the northern United States, females mature at age 3 to 4 and males at 2 to 3 years. In the more northerly part of their range, a female may not mature until 6 years of age and males 5 (Scott and Crossman 1973).

The spawning act is repeated many times during a 3- to 5-day period. After spawning is complete, adults move out of the area. The young begin feeding early and leave the area in 4 to 6 weeks.

Pike usually spawn in heavily vegetated floodplains of rivers, marshes, and bays. One female, and the normally smaller male, swims through the vegetation in water perhaps only a few inches deep. The spawning act is usually followed by a thrust of the tail, which both moves the female out and scatters the eggs. Northern pike build no nests; their adhesive eggs, diameter 0.12 in. (3.1 mm), stick to vegetation or debris. Females are highly prolific: Estimates of number of eggs range from 10,000 to 18,000 per lb of female (4,536 to 8,165 per kg). Both number of eggs produced and mortality are high. Scott and Crossman (1973) quoted a 99.8-percent mortality from egg to young when the fish leave the spawning grounds. This percentage is in agreement with mortality estimates of some other fishes with high fecundity that provide no care for egg or young. Eggs hatch in 4 to 14 days.

Habitat

Northern pike prefer cool water (48° to 72°F [8.88 to 22.2°C]). They occur in a wide range of habitats including large, relatively cold, deep lakes to small, warm farm ponds. Slow, meandering, heavily vegetated river habitat is preferred to fast, shallow water. The fish are generally inshore in lakes, unless water temperatures are high. These areas have an abundance of vegetation that provides both cover and food. The fish are more active in summer than winter, although they provide an under-ice sportfishery. They occur in lakes with alkalinities as high as 1,000 ppm (mg/l) and pH as high as 9.5.

MANAGEMENT

Habitat, and subsequently management, of northern pike is strongly related to stable water levels in spawning areas until adults and young have emigrated. Catch regulations should be adapted to population status. Slot limits may be used when there is a disparity in age-size classes. Stocking may be needed in heavily fished areas, particularly if fishing occurs both summer and winter. Management considerations should not overlook the fact that at times the northern pike is both a competitor with, and a predator on, more locally desirable species of game fishes.

Trouts (Family Salmonidae)

A preponderance of North American coldwater game fishes are included in this family: salmon, trout, char, whitefish, and grayling. Salmonids are widespread and numerous in the northern hemisphere. Most species inhabit largely fresh water and all spawn there. Several trouts have anadromous populations. Anadromous fishes migrate to sea when young to attain their growth, then return to natal streams to spawn. Brown trout, arctic char, Dolly Varden, brook trout, Atlantic salmon, rainbow, and cutthroat all have sea-run races.

All five species of Pacific salmon (*Oncorhynchus* spp.) in North America are anadromous. They spawn only once, but other species are repeat spawners (Sigler and Sigler 1987). Pacific salmon may also be landlocked, which means most or all of the species have the ability to reproduce without migrating to the sea. Valuable for sport, Pacific salmon are also harvested commercially.

This family of sport fishes is economically the most important family of coldwater fishes in North America. Salmonids are reared in state, federal, and private hatcheries, and other aquaculture operations and as sea-run species that have been allowed to migrate to the sea and return to their original rearing areas. Sizes of fish in this family vary widely: chinook salmon may weigh over 125 lb (57 kg), the Bonneville cisco about 2.5 oz (71 g). Extensive hatchery rearing has increased the incidence of disease in reared fish and sometimes in the wild.

Salmonids are characterized by a lateral line that is well developed, an adipose fin, and a small fleshy appendage (auxiliary process) at the base of the pelvic fins. Scales are cycloid and generally small (Simpson and Wallace 1978).

A more poetic presentation is provided by the following discourse on one genus by Jordan and Evermann (1904):

> There is no other group of fishes which offers so many difficulties to the ichthyologist, with regard to the distinction of the species, as well as to certain points in their life history, as this genus. The colouration, is first of all, subject to great variation, and consequently this character but rarely assists in distinguishing a species, there being not 1 which would show in all stages the same kind of colouration. The water has a marked influence on colours: trout with intense ocellated spots are generally found in clear, rapid rivers and in Alpine pools; in the large lakes, with pebbly bottom, the fish are bright silvery, and the ocellated spots are mixed with or replaced by x-shaped black spots; in dark lakes, or lakes with peaty bottom, they often assume an almost uniform blackish colouration.

Salmonids occur in a wide range of habitats, in both streams and lakes in Utah. Species inhabit high mountain lakes (for example, the Uintas), small streams (for example, the Little Bear River and Otter Creek), and large rivers (Bear, Logan, Green, and Colorado rivers). Where water temperatures are cool throughout the year they may occur in a drainage from headwaters to the valleys (for example, the Logan River in northern Utah). They inhabit streams of both high and low gradient over a wide range of water quality. Temperature preferences range from trout that tolerate temperatures of almost 80°F (26.7°C) to the arctic grayling, which prefer water in the low 40s°F (4.4°C).

The American Fisheries Society (Robins et al. 1991) lists 39 species and 7 genera of salmonids in the United States and Canada. There are 12 species and 4 subspecies within 5 genera in Utah. Of the 12 species, 3 are endemic to Bear Lake, 2 more are native to Utah, and 7 are introduced (historic ranges do not include Utah).

---

golden trout, *Oncorhynchus aguabonita* (Jordan)
Plate 21

Etymology: *Oncorhynchus* = hooked snout, referring to the condition of the migrating adults in Pacific salmon; *aguabonita* = Latin for beautiful water, "the name of a cascade on Volcano Creek, near which this trout abounds" (Jordan and Evermann 1896)

Nomenclature: *Salmo mykiss aqua-bonita* Jordan 1893a, *Oncorhynchus aquabonita* Smith and Stearley 1989

IMPORTANCE

Golden trout attract anglers primarily because they are relatively scarce and brilliantly colored. They are the official state fish of California, and an important sport fish in Wyoming. Some people claim the golden trout's fighting ability is equal to that of the rainbow trout. Often they are easier to catch. In Utah they do not have high sport-fish value because of their rarity. Few people catch or even see this species.

DESCRIPTION

Original

Head, 3 3/4 in length; depth 4 1/2. D 2,12; A. 1,10. Scales, 130 to 200 rows; 121 to 124 pores. Length 7 in.

Body formed about the same as usual in *Salmo mykiss* and its varieties. Head rather long, bluntish at tip; mouth moderate, the maxillary extending a little beyond the eye, 1 4/5 in head. Hyoid teeth not evident; opercle moderate. Its greatest length 4 1/3 in head; its posterior margin moderately convex. Eye 4 2/3 in head; snout, 4 1/2 ; gill-rakers not very short, x + 11 or 12 in number.

Scales extremely small, smaller than as in any other species of *Salmo*. Fins moderate; the anal high, the caudal moderately emarginate; pectoral, 1 4/7 in head; ventral, 2; caudal 1 2/5.

Olive above; sides and belly light golden; about twelve dark crossbars on middle of sides; these the usual parr-marks; middle of sides along lateral line with a deep scarlet lateral stripe, broadest under the dorsal where it is about as wide as eye; thence narrowing to either end, and not reaching either head or caudal; middle line of belly with a broad scarlet band, extending from chin to anal fin, equally bright all the way; a fainter shade along lower side from anal fin to tip of caudal; no crimson dash at throat between branches of lower jaw; the whole region uniform bright orange; opercle largely orange. Dark spots chiefly posterior, as in *spilurus* and *pleuriticus*, large and well marked, some as large as pupil on tail and posterior part of body; smaller and well marked on dorsal; a few small ones scattered along forward to the head in 2 specimens; none on body before adipose fin in the other.

Upper anterior angle of dorsal abruptly yellowish white; this color edged by a dark oblique streak, made by coalescent spots; the rest of the fin light olive with 4 or 5 rows of small black spots; pectorals light orange; ventrals deep orange, with a faint blackish tip; the anterior edge of the fin conspicuously and abruptly whitish, as in *Salvelinus fontinalis*; anal dusky orange, the tips of the last rays blackish, the outer anterior corner abruptly white, the white stripe wider than the pupil, and separated from the color of the fin by a dusky shade.

Caudal olive, tinged with orange on its lower edge, and profusely spotted with black. Inside of mouth pink, of gill cavity light orange.

Contemporary
Coloration of the belly and cheeks of the golden trout is bright red to orange, the lower sides are bright gold, making this species the most brilliantly colored trout in Utah. The midlateral band is red orange, the back is deep olive green. Ten parr marks are usually present in both adults and young. Absence of the cutthroat mark and the lack of basibranchial teeth distinguish them from their close relative, the cutthroat. The dorsal, anal, and pelvic fins have white tips offset by a black bar. Lateral-series scales number from 175 to 210; scales above the lateral line, 34 to 45; pelvic rays, 8 to 10; gill rakers, 17 to 21; pyloric caeca, 25 to 40 (Schreck and Behnke 1971). Jordan and Evermann (1904) call them the most beautiful of all of the many beautiful western trout.

Range

In Utah they are present in Corn and Atwood creeks and Echo Lake. The golden trout is native above 6,900 ft (2,103 m) in the upper Kern River Basin, Tulare and Kern counties, California (Lee et al. 1980).

Size and Longevity

Average yearly length for fish age 1 to 5, is: in inches, 1.5, 5.5, 8.4, 9.9, and 10.4; in mm, 38, 140, 213, 251, 264 (Carlander 1969). Although a 10- to 12-in. (254- to 305-mm) golden trout is average, fish as large as 24 in. (610 mm) are taken. Golden trout are short lived and slow growing. The world record all-tackle hook-and-line golden trout, caught in Cooke Lake, Wyoming, weighed 11 lb (5 kg) (IGFA 1993). The largest Utah specimen, from Atwood Creek, weighed 13.5 oz (383 g).

Food and Feeding

Insects are the primary diet of golden trout. The trout prefer caddisfly larvae and midges, but other available insects are also eaten. In lakes they feed primarily on copepod and cladoceran zooplankton.

Limiting Factors

Golden trout are one of the easiest of all trouts to catch; perhaps their best defense is the remote areas they inhabit. When they interbreed with rainbow trout, golden trout lose their genetic identity. The same may be true when they hybridize with cutthroat trout. Three-way hybrids (rainbow, cutthroat, golden) are common in upper Wind River drainage, Wyoming (R. Behnke, personal communication, 1983). Introduced lake populations tend to migrate into streams where they are poor competitors. Behnke (1992) wrote that he knows of no example where introduced California golden trout were able to coexist with brown trout or brook trout, or where preexisting golden trout avoided hybridization with introduced rainbow or cutthroat trout.

Breeding Habits

Spawning is initiated from late May to August, depending on the altitude, and when water temperatures reach 45° to 50°F (7.2° to 10°C).

The fish mature in the third or fourth year, and females produce 300 to 2,300 eggs. Golden trout require gravel riffles for successful stream spawning. Although spawning activity has been observed in lakes, it may not be successful in producing progeny.

HABITAT

Golden trout do best in swift streams and lakes in altitudes ranging from 6,000 to 11,500 ft (1,829 to 3,505 m). They are a true wilderness animal (Sigler and Sigler 1987).

MANAGEMENT

Heavy angling pressure may decimate local populations. In addition, the golden trout needs protection from other fishes, especially salmonids. Their range may best be extended by stocking them in fishless, remote lakes and streams.

Golden trout have been stocked occasionally and are present in one or two areas in the Uintas. Consideration has been given toward identifying a few lakes with habitat suitable for them. This habitat would have acceptable spawning gravel in high mountain lake outlets. These fish have high landowner acceptability in the Uintas, and some landowners would like to have this highly colorful species stocked every year. However, stocking is difficult because few eggs are available from other states and the parent stocks do not meet Utah disease certification standards. The Division of Wildlife Resources (DWR) will continue to look for suitable egg sources and will consider stocking these fish when a suitable source of eggs becomes available.

---

cutthroat trout,
Oncorhynchus clarki
(Richardson)
Plate 22
Plate 23
Plate 24

Etymology: *Oncorhynchus* = hooked snout, referring to the condition of the migrating adults in Pacific salmon; *clarki* and previously *lewisi* = the respective leaders of the Lewis and Clark expeditions to western America in 1804–1806

Nomenclature: *Salmo clarkii* Richardson 1836; *Fario stellatus* Girard 1857; *Fario clarkii* Girard 1857; *Salmo purpuratus* Günther 1867 and others; *Oncorhynchus clarki* Smith and Stearley 1989; Yellowstone cutthroat trout, *O. c. bouvieri* (Bendire 1882); Lahontan cutthroat trout, *O. c. henshawi* (Gill and Jordan, in Jordan 1878c); Colorado cutthroat trout, *O. c. pleuriticus* (Cope 1872a); Bonneville cutthroat trout, *O. c. utah* (Suckley 1874).

IMPORTANCE

Elitists and average anglers alike pursue cutthroat, making them one of the more popular sport fish in Utah. Both their sporting and table qualities rate high. Today they are not as abundant over their native range as the rainbow trout, although Behnke (1992) reported 13 extant subspecies. Over the years they have been stocked in other areas in limited numbers.

Lahontan cutthroat trout in Pyramid Lake are economically and ethnically important to the Pyramid Lake Paiute Indian Tribe in Nevada. In Pyramid Lake they have adapted to highly saline waters containing 5,000 to 5,500 ppm (mg/l) TDS (total dissolved solids). This subspecies is listed by the U.S. Fish and Wildlife Service as threatened. Within Utah, occurrence of the Lahontan subspecies is restricted to one or two small streams in the Deep Creek Mountains in extreme western Utah. They are not native.

Western Utah was once covered, over a period of many thousands of years, by at least three distinct levels of ancient freshwater Lake Bonneville. Native cutthroat trout probably gained access to the Bonneville Basin when the Bear River changed course from the Snake River drainage to the Bonneville Basin (with its terminus in Great Salt Lake), as much as 30,000 years ago (Broecker and Kaufman 1965). After the Bear River became tributary to Lake Bonneville, the lake reached its maximum size (20,000 sq mi [51,800 sq km]) some 16,000 to 18,000 years before the present (Broecker and Kaufman).

Bonneville cutthroat, native to the Bear River, are adapted to a highly variable and severe stream environment. They are dominant in the Thomas Fork and Smith Fork drainages, near Cokeville, Wyoming, where streams are turbid and carry a heavy silt load (Duff 1988). The environment is marginal for trout, but cutthroat prosper and dominate brown trout.

Another group of Bonneville cutthroat is native to the Snake Valley region in extreme western Utah. Snake Valley was an arm of Lake Bonneville when it was at maximum elevation, but after a slight decline in lake level Snake Valley became isolated. The Snake Valley Bonneville cutthroat lives in small, clear streams, isolated from other populations (island concept). The third group constitutes the balance of the Bonneville cutthroat that range in other areas of the Bonneville Basin. The Bonneville cutthroat trout is currently listed by the U.S. Fish and Wildlife Service as threatened (Behnke 1981).

The Colorado cutthroat trout is native to the upper Colorado River Basin above Grand Canyon. It evolved in isolation from other trout. This evolution left it vulnerable to hybridization with rainbow trout and to replacement by brown trout and brook trout. Pure populations of Colorado cutthroat are gone from much of its original range. Today it is present in isolated headwater streams (Behnke 1992; Martinez 1988).

Compared to other subspecies, the Yellowstone cutthroat is doing quite well. Cutthroat trout subspecies life histories in general are discussed by Trotter (1987).

DESCRIPTION

Original

COLOUR.—Back generally brownish purple-red, passing on the sides into ashy-grey, and into reddish-white on the belly. Large patches of dark purplish-red on the back. Dorsal and base of the caudal ash-grey, end of caudal pansy-purple. Back, dorsal, and caudal studded with small semilunar spots. A large patch of arterial-red on the opercle and margin of the preopercle. Pectorals, ventrals, and anal greyish-white, tinged with rose-red.

TEETH.—Both jaws armed with strong hooked teeth, a single row on each palate-bone, a double row on the anterior half of the vomer and on the tongue. Dorsal profile nearly straight. Ventrals opposite to the middle of the first dorsal. Fissure of mouth oblique. Extremity of caudal nearly even. FINS.—Br. 11; P.12; V. 8; A.13; D. 11–0.

Contemporary

Classically, a red or orange slash mark, present in adults but sometimes lacking in young, runs along both sides of the lower jaw and is the basis for the common name. Steel-gray color predominates on the back and sides of cutthroat trout, which are frequently covered with spots. These spots are larger and more regular in shape and size but more restricted in distribution than on brown or rainbow trout. Color and spotting are variable between watersheds, subspecies, and even local populations. Young have 9 or 10 oval parr marks along the lateral line (La Rivers 1962; Simpson and Wallace 1978). The dorsal fin has 8 to 11 rays and the anal fin has 10 or 11. The caudal is slightly forked. The body, although elongate and typically troutlike, is rounded and slightly compressed; scales are cycloid and small to medium; 125 to 190 in the lateral series (Behnke 1981). The head is conical, moderate to short, eyes moderate, and snout rounded. The mouth is rather large and terminal. The jaw, vomer, and tongue have sharp teeth. There is a median basibranchial plate, typically with teeth, between the lower end of the gill arches. There are 16 to 28 gill rakers, fewer on the upper than the lower limb (Behnke).

RANGE

Cutthroat are the only trout native to Utah. They are present in many of Utah's high coldwater streams and lakes. There are representative populations in Bear Lake, Bear River, Moon Lake, Logan River, Blacksmith Fork River, and elsewhere.

Cutthroat trout are more widely distributed than any other species of trout in western North America. Their most westerly range is from southeastern Alaska south to the Eel River in northern California. In western North America they are native to all major river drainages east to central Colorado. They are present on both sides of the Continental Divide and occur over a wide range of salinities, having populations in fresh, brackish, and salt water. Original population numbers have been reduced by many factors, but they have also increased because of extensive stocking (Lee et al. 1980). The present range of cutthroat is little if any greater than the original. The original range of the Yellowstone cutthroat trout extends into the Raft River, northwestern Utah.

Size and Longevity

Growth is slowest in cold, high mountain lakes or streams (some above the timberline) where there is a short growing season and food is limited. Platts (1958) reported that the yearly length for cutthroat ages 1 to 7 in Strawberry Reservoir was: in inches, 4.0, 7.3, 10.6, 13.4, 16.0, 19.3, and 22.3; in mm, 102, 185, 269, 340, 406, 490, 566. The Pyramid Lake, Nevada, Lahontan cutthroat trout are fast growing and short lived (Sigler et al. 1983). A total of 562 Lahontans ranged in size from 7.5 in. (191 mm) and 2.9 oz (82 g) to 31 in. (787 mm) and 13.5 lb (6.1 kg). A total of 676 fish, ages 1 to 7, reached the following yearly total lengths: in inches, 9.1, 12.3, 15.2, 18.2, 20.6, 23.7, and 25.5; in mm, 231, 312, 386, 462, 523, 610, 648. Cutthroat trout from 2 high Uinta lakes, ages 1 to 4, had lengths as follows: in inches, 5.0, 7.3, 7.9, and 8.7; in mm, 127, 185, 201, 221 (Sigler and Low 1950). Nielson and Lentsch (1988) reported that a 9-year-old cutthroat from Bear Lake was 19.7 in. (500 mm) long. Adults grow at the rate of about 2 in. (51 mm) a year. Stream cutthroat grow slower than ones living in lakes. The Yellowstone cutthroat grows at about the same rate as other subspecies, a few reaching the age of 8 or 9 years.

The world record hook-and-line cutthroat trout was a Lahontan weighing 41 lb (18.6 kg) caught in Pyramid Lake, Nevada, in 1925 (Fishing Hall of Fame 1993). The largest cutthroat caught in Utah was landed in 1930 and weighed 26 lb, 12 oz (12.1 kg).

Food and Feeding

Adult cutthroat trout are omnivorous. They prefer fishes but feed readily on invertebrates. When Bear Lake cutthroat are 10 in. (254 mm) long they are 20 percent piscivorous. At 22 in. (559 mm) they are 95 percent piscivorous. Fishes most preyed upon are sculpins, Bonneville cisco, and whitefishes, the latter in winter. Cutthroat trout also feed on whitefish eggs. Stocked yearling cutthroat feed on terrestrial insects (Nielson and Lentsch 1988). Jacobson and Wurtsbaugh (1989) divided Bear Lake cutthroat into three groups for food analyses: 10 in. (254 mm), 10 to 14 in. (254 to 356 mm), and over 14 in. (356 mm). Large ones feed mainly on Bonneville cisco in winter and newly stocked cutthroat in spring. Intermediate-sized ones eat sculpins in winter and insects during summer and fall. The smallest group eat terrestrial insects, chironomid larvae, and emerging adult insects.

Young cutthroat, spawned in the wild, start feeding 14 to 23 days after hatching. In the high Uinta Mountain lakes in northeastern

Utah, where the growing season is about 5 weeks and lake productivity is very low, cutthroat trout subsist primarily on terrestrial insects, including swarming migrants (Sigler and Low 1950). Small cutthroat trout (8 to 10 in. [254 to 302 mm]) in Pyramid Lake, Nevada, feed on insects and zooplankton. They start feeding on fish at lengths of 12 to 13 in. (305 to 330 mm) and eat an ever-increasing percentage of fish as they grow older (Sigler et al. 1983). Stream-dwelling cutthroat trout in California defend feeding territories and feed mostly on drift, including terrestrial insects (Moyle 1976).

Limiting Factors

Habitat loss may be the single most important limiting factor. Habitat loss is caused by reduced flows, degradation of water quality, or changes in stream morphology. One can appreciate the dramatic decline of native cutthroat trout in Utah by comparing the trout population of today with that of 100 years ago. According to Behnke (1992), it is astonishing how rapidly native cutthroat can disappear. In some streams, low water and inadequate overwintering habitat may be the most serious hazard. Boulders, log jams, and debris are all important habitat components in these situations (Hickman and Raleigh 1982). Cutthroat trout are readily taken by hook-and-line fishing, often establishing it as the number one mortality factor (assuming acceptable habitat). Disease devastates cutthroat populations more often since the advent of fish hatcheries. In some populations females may spawn only once or possibly twice, and postspawning mortality is high in both sexes. Other populations have many repeat spawners. Loss of habitat is a hazard more often facing stream-dwellers than lake inhabitants. In degraded habitat or outside their native range, cutthroat trout often do not compete well with introduced fishes such as rainbow trout, brown trout, or brook trout. In some streams, cutthroat trout hybridize with rainbow trout, and the hybrid then becomes the dominant species. Or the rainbow trout may be more aggressive than either cutthroat trout or cutthroat-rainbow hybrids and displace both. Mass hybridization follows when rainbow trout are introduced into interior waters inhabited only by cutthroat trout.

In prime cutthroat trout habitat, and within their native range, genetically pure cutthroat compete very well. For example, when rainbow trout were introduced into Yellowstone Lake, Yellowstone National Park, Wyoming, the rainbow trout did not prosper. In Bear Lake, Utah-Idaho, the cutthroat trout fares better than the rainbow trout. In Thomas Fork and Smith Fork drainages, Wyoming, Bonneville cutthroat trout are dominant over brown trout (Behnke 1981).

Breeding Habits

Cutthroat trout generally spawn in the clear, cold, shallow riffles of small streams soon after the ice is off in the spring. Spawning initiation is influenced by water temperature, runoff, ice melt, elevation, and latitude (Hickman and Raleigh 1982). Lake-dwelling cutthroat migrate up inflow streams to spawn. Male cutthroat trout in some populations mature at ages 2 or 3, females mature a year later (Hickman and Raleigh 1982). The oldest male in a Pyramid Lake study (Sigler et al. 1983) was 7 years; the oldest female was 6 years. A few hatchery-reared male Lahontans mature at age 1. Because of the relatively high post-spawning mortality, in some populations many fish spawn only once.

Nielson and Lentsch (1988) stated that cutthroat trout in Bear Lake may start maturing at age 5 but some may not spawn until they are more than 10 years old. Mature fish average 22 in. (559 mm) total length and weigh 4.4 lb (2 kg). Males and females are about the same size. They typically enter the spawning streams (Swan and St. Charles creeks) on sunny afternoons. The average age of fish in the 1987 spawning run was 6.8 years (range 4 to 11); over 92 percent of the run was age 6 or older. Repeat spawners account for less than 4 percent of the run.

Distances migrated to spawn are generally short, but in some populations much longer distances are covered. Lahontan cutthroat trout, before the construction of Derby Dam between Reno and Pyramid Lake in 1905, migrated from Pyramid Lake up the Truckee River and into Lake Tahoe to spawn in its tributaries, a distance of 120 stream mi (193 km) between lakes (Sigler et al. 1983).

The female cutthroat fans out a nest (redd) with her tail in a gravel bed then deposits her eggs. Egg numbers per female range from a few hundred to well over 8,000. The male fertilizes the eggs then stands guard against other males. Immediately after the eggs are fertilized, the female moves upstream and covers them. A typical redd is 30 in. (0.76 m) long by 18 in. (0.46 m) wide, and in 7 to 24 in. (17.8 to 61 cm) of water. The eggs may be covered with 5 to 7 in. (12.7 to 17.8 cm) of coarse gravel (Wydoski and Whitney 1979). Eggs usually hatch within 28 to 40 days but may take longer. Optimal incubation temperature for embryos is approximately 50°F (10°C) (Hickman and Raleigh 1982).

When temperatures are greater than 40°F (4.4°C) (daily maximum), males move into spawning areas. First spawning takes place when daily maximum is 42° to 45°F (5.5° to 7.2°C), peaking at 44° to 48°F (6.7° to 8.9°C). The upper safe range for gravid females and embryos is considered to be 57°F (13.9°C).

Yellowstone cutthroat were stocked in several western states from about 1905 until 1955. Marion Madsen, chief of fisheries for the Utah Fish and Game Department, went to Yellowstone National Park in the late 1940s and early 1950s to help take eggs. His pay was in fish eggs, which were hatched and stocked in many state waters including Logan River. Earliest cutthroat trout propagation in the United States was in either Utah or California; in Utah it predates 1972.

HABITAT

Stream habitat most advantageous to cutthroat trout is characterized by clear, cold, relatively silt-free water with rocky substrate in which riffle:pool ratios are approximately 1:1. Cover is an essential factor (Hickman and Raleigh 1982). Streams occupied by cutthroat trout range in elevation from sea level to altitudes of over 10,000 ft (3,048 m) (for example, high Uinta Mountains). Cutthroat have wide adaptability, inhabiting many cold waters and some cool ones, ranging from large alkaline lakes (for example, 5,000 ppm, (mg/l) TDS), to small, clear mountain lakes (less than 100 ppm, (mg/l) TDS), to major rivers, to small tributaries (Moyle 1976; Sigler et al. 1983).

In large lakes, cutthroat trout prefer areas near cover such as rubble and deep water. In high-elevation streams cutthroat choose habitat near rocky areas, riffles, or deep pools, and near such cover as overhanging logs, shrubs, or banks. Fry do best in stream areas with about 40 to 50 percent pool areas. Cutthroat trout are rarely present in waters where maximum temperatures consistently exceed approximately 72°F (22.2°C)(Hickman and Raleigh 1982).

Some thriving populations of cutthroat in the Uinta Mountains live in waters with a pH of 7.0, total dissolved solids of 40 ppm (mg/l), and a very sparse benthic fauna. Some of these small lakes are fed by glaciers (permanent snowbanks) (Sigler and Low 1950).

For thousands of years, cutthroat trout evolved in Yellowstone Lake with only one other fish—the longnose dace. Such narrow evolutionary programming with respect to other fishes and the highly stable and oligotrophic environment of Yellowstone Lake makes the Yellowstone cutthroat trout ill adapted to successfully coexist with other fishes or to thrive in an unstable environment (Behnke 1992).

MANAGEMENT

Competition from other trouts, especially in marginal habitat, should be reduced or removed. Other trouts should not be stocked with an established population of cutthroat trout unless they will not compete or interbreed with them. Different subspecies, races, or strains of cutthroat should be separated in hatcheries. Genetic strains should be stocked back into habitat where they have evolved and adapted. Good cover is necessary for acceptable cutthroat trout habitat. In some areas, this may require in-stream structures and bank protection. Maintenance or upgrading of cutthroat trout habitat is probably the most urgent present need, admittedly often a difficult or impossible task.

Angling restrictions should be compatible with the size and age composition of the population and expected fishing pressure. Where the number of spawning fish each year is a limiting factor, restrictions on the number of mature fish taken should be severe. In many cases the number of smaller fish allowed may be more liberal, and slot limits (for example, 12 to 18 in. [305 to 457 mm]) may be used to protect larger fish.

Recent research (Busack and Gall 1981) indicates that introgressive hybridization (assimilation of genes from one species into another) occurs and is a cause of decline in some native western trout populations. Hybridization situations should be avoided where possible. In areas where egg taking and restocking are standard procedures and when more eggs are produced than are needed, sterilization of a segment of the reared fish (for example, 10 to 30 percent) will produce larger, faster-growing, longer-lived fish and ones with no spawning mortality.

Statement of Utah Division of Wildlife Resources

The subspecies of cutthroat trout most often encountered is the Yellowstone. Attempts in the late 1800s to culture trout to make up for the already evident human impact on native fish stocks proved to be difficult due to the wild nature of the native cutthroat found in Utah. When rainbow trout from California and cutthroat trout from Yellowstone became available, culture attempts with the Bonneville and Colorado cutthroat were dropped.

The Yellowstone cutthroat were valuable in the colder waters of Utah and were particularly successful in the High Lakes program in the Uinta Mountains. This fish became a highlight of the fishery at Strawberry Reservoir, which for decades provided the brood stock for the statewide culture program. These fish are now referred to as the Strawberry strain. These cutthroat are capable in a few instances of reproducing in marginal tributaries above reservoirs; therefore, a number of waters have angling restrictions to protect the spawners. Yellowstone cutthroat appear to be more insectivorous than the rainbow and are fairly adaptable in high-quality water. They are stocked in reservoirs to provide an element of diversity in the fishery and as the primary species in higher elevation streams and lakes.

Recent successes in expanding populations of the native subspecies of cutthroat trout are leading to increased experimentation for sport management. Bear Lake cutthroat are Bonneville cutthroat trout and appear well adapted to lake environments. These fish have several traits that are noticeably different from the Yellowstone cutthroat. They mature much later than the Yellowstone, usually at 5 or 6 years, and have shown a stronger propensity to switch to a fish diet and become an aggressive predator. The Bear Lake Bonneville cutthroat attain weights approaching 20 lb (9.1 kg), and recent experimentation in more fertile reservoirs suggests that even larger sizes can be attained. Because they become piscivorous at an early age, experiments are under way to determine whether these fish can control nongame fish such as Utah chub in reservoirs. The Utah chub and Bonneville cutthroat are coadapted native species, and there is some hope that the Bear Lake cutthroat may be able to help maintain balance in fisheries with Utah chub present. This concept is a key element of the new management plan for Strawberry Reservoir. Now that Utah chub and Utah suckers have been eliminated, the Bear Lake Bonneville cutthroat will be the primary sport fish.

The Bonneville cutthroat have a few negative traits that need to be considered in management. The fish appear to be highly vulnerable to angling and may need special regulations to protect them long enough to survive to spawning age. There also is a larger demand for this subspecies than can be provided by existing wild and captive brood stocks. Activities over the next few years will be directed at establishing viable self-sustaining populations of Bear Lake Bonneville cutthroat in a number of waters, particularly Strawberry Reservoir, with the intent of developing new egg sources for these fish.

Management trials using other subpopulations of cutthroat subspecies are not quite as far along as for Bear Lake. Brood populations have been established for Bonneville cutthroat in Manning Meadow Reservoir and Red Butte Reservoir and sites are being selected for Colorado River subspecies cutthroat in the Uinta Basin. Once adequate egg sources are available for the native subspecies, investigations will begin into the characteristics of the various strains in a variety of sport management situations. If these fish perform in sportfisheries as well as expected, it is likely that the use of the Strawberry (Yellowstone) cutthroat will be phased out and the Bonneville strains substituted into management programs. Depending on the characteristics of these fish, there may also be opportunities to utilize more native cutthroat in waters presently managed for rainbow. How far that trend progresses, however, will depend on anglers' acceptance of these fish as a replacement for rainbow.

rainbow trout,
Oncorhynchus mykiss (Walbaum), *Salmo gairdneri* (Richardson)
Plate 25

Etymology: *Oncorhynchus* = hooked snout, referring to the condition of the migrating adults in Pacific salmon; *mykiss* = the vernacular name of the Asian form, previously recognized as a separate species

Nomenclature: *Salmo mykiss* Walbaum 1792; *Salmo Gairdneri* Richardson 1836 (by Richardson for Doctor Meredith Gairdner of the Hudson's Bay Company Columbia River expeditions); *Salmo iridea* Gibbons 1855; *Oncorhynchus Kamloops* Jordan 1893b; and others; *Oncorhynchus mykiss* Smith and Stearley 1989. We have retained the more familiar *Salmo gairdneri* and incorporate the now correct *Oncorhynchus mykiss* Walbaum nomenclature.

IMPORTANCE

Throughout the Western States, when the majority of rank-and-file fishermen think trout, they think rainbow. Solely on the basis of the rainbows' contribution to the sportfishery and associated values, they are the most important trout in the United States as well as one of the two or three most important game fish in Utah. This species is continuously stocked in substantial numbers in almost all habitable trout waters in Utah and some that are borderline. It is a hard fighter, leaps repeatedly when hooked, and is highly palatable whether smoked, eaten fresh, or canned. As a result of all of these positive attributes, the total catch (and catch rate) is high. In 1962 the gates were closed on the Flaming Gorge Dam, and the lake began to fill. Fifty-six million rainbow trout were planted between 1962 and 1983 (Schneidervin and Hubert 1987). What followed for several years was one of the most fabulous trout fisheries in the world.

Wide acceptance of massive stocking of rainbow is based on the rationale that they are an easy and economical trout to raise. Most hatchery strains are semidomesticated. This factor is not important from the hatcheryman's or manager's view. Commercial trout producers in the United States ship more rainbow trout than any other coldwater species. One area in south-central Idaho, Thousand Springs, produces millions of pounds of rainbow trout each year.

Steelhead are a sea-run form of rainbow. Kamloops are another form of rainbow trout, which grow to a large size in big lakes. Kamloops have been stocked in Bear Lake, but not in recent years, and were never successfully established. With the exception of an unnamed redband trout (*Oncorhynchus* sp.) in the Oregon Desert basins and the rainbow trout in Eagle Lake, California, all western inland stocks of rainbow are nonnative.

DESCRIPTION

Original (*Salmo gairdneri*)

The specific name which I have given to this salmon is intended as a tribute to the merits of a young though able naturalist ... (Dr. Meridith Gairdner).

COLOUR.—Back of head and body bluish-grey; sides ash-grey. Belly white. The only traces of variegated markings are a few faint spots at the root of the caudal.

FORM.—Profile of dorsal line nearly straight, tail terminating in a slightly semilunar outline. Ventrals correspond to commencement of dorsal and adipose to end of anal.

TEETH.—Vomer armed with a double row for two-thirds of its anterior portion. Palate-bones also armed with strong teeth.

Original (*Salmo mykiss*)

Salmo, *Mykiss. Pennant, artt. zool. introd.* 126. D. 12. P. 14. V. 10. A. 12.

Corpus bipedale, macrolepitodum. Rostrum obtusum. Dentes

numerosi. Dorsum obscurum, nigro maculatum; abdomen album; tænia lata, ruberrima in utroque latere adeft. Sapore alios antecellit. Habitat in Kamschatka.

(h) Salmo, *Eriox*, maculis cinereis; caudæ extremo æquali. L.S. N. 509. Br 12. D. 14. P 14. V. 10. A. 12.

The Grey Pennant. br. zool. III. 298.

Caput latius, quam Salaris. Dentium 4 series in maxillis. Linguæ octo dentes. Dorsum et latera super lineam lateralem obscure cinerea, maculis purpureis conspersa. Abdomen argenteum. Caudæ pinna æqualis.

Translation (*Salmo mykiss*)

Salmon. *Mykiss*. Pennant. artificial. zoological introduced 126. D. 12. P. 14. V. 10. A. 12.

Body [is] two feet long, iridescent. Blunt snout. Numerous teeth. Dark back, spotted with black; white abdomen; there is a wide band, very red, on either side. It surpasses others in taste. It lives in Kamschatka.

(h) Salmon, *Eriox*, with ash-colored spots; symmetrical tail-tip. L.S.N. 509. Br. 12. D. 14. P. 14. V. 10 A. 12.

The Grey. Pennant br. zool. III. 298.

Wider head than the Salt-water. Four rows of teeth in the jaw bones. Eight teeth on the tongue. Back and sides above the dim lateral line [are] ash-colored, sprinkled with purplish spots. Silvery abdomen. Symmetrical caudal fin.

Contemporary

Rainbow trout vary greatly in color, as the common name indicates. Color and color patterns depend on habitat, size, and sexual condition. Stream residents and migrant spawners are darker and have more intense colors than lake residents or nonspawners. Lake residents tend to be silvery. Cutthroat trout in Bear Lake, Utah-Idaho, tend to have a bluish nose and be without spots. Rainbow, stocked in Bear Lake until about 1980, lose their spots and follow this pattern. The magnesium content in Bear Lake has historically been much higher than the calcium, the reverse of most lakes. Fisheries researchers have speculated that this may have caused the somewhat atypical color patterns of both rainbow trout and cutthroat trout.

A mature rainbow is dark green to bluish on the back with lighter and silvery sides. The reddish horizontal band typifies the species. The belly may be white to silvery. Irregular black spots are generally present on the head, back, and sides. This pattern varies considerably between populations and habitat. The dorsal, adipose, and caudal fins are spotted. Young rainbow trout have silvery sides, are blue to olive on the back, and have a white belly. The back has five to ten irregular marks. There are also five to ten oval parr marks spaced on the sides and straddling the lateral line.

Rainbow trout have 120 to 160 cycloid scales in the lateral series. The body is elongate, compressed, and deep. The head is short, eyes are moderate, the mouth terminal, the snout rounded, and the teeth on the jaws and tongue small and sharp but poorly developed on the vomer and absent from the basibranchial plate. Both the dorsal and anal fins have 11 to 12 rays and the caudal fin is moderately forked (Robert Behnke, personal communication, 1983; Simpson and Wallace 1978). Although there are no nuptial tubercles during the breeding season, minor changes in the shape of the head and mouth occur among males.

Range

Utah's Division of Wildlife Resources stocks hatchery-reared rainbow heavily in almost every cold- or coolwater drainage in Utah. There are few large populations of natural lake-dwelling rainbow in the state. Fish Lake and Lake Powell have sizeable populations. Bear Lake has a small and dwindling population. Flaming Gorge Lake (stocked heavily in the 1960s and 1970s) at one time had one of the densest populations in the United States. This species has been introduced into South America, Japan, New Zealand, Australia, Tasmania, Africa, southern Asia, Europe, and Hawaii (Lee et al. 1980). Rainbow trout (including all forms) are native to western North America, mainly west of the Rocky Mountains in the north and the Sierra Nevada in the south. They are native from Rio del Presidio, Durango, Mexico, north to the Kuskokwim River, Alaska (Behnke 1979). In Canada they range from British Columbia and the Avalon Peninsula of Newfoundland, across the southern portions of the provinces from Nova Scotia to Ontario, north through central Manitoba and central Saskatchewan, to northern Alberta and the Yukon Territory (Scott and Crossman 1973). They have been introduced throughout the United States and now occur in habitats from sea level to over 12,000 ft (3,658 m) (Raleigh et al. 1984).

Size and Longevity

Rainbow trout from the Uinta high mountain lakes live only 4 to 5 years (Sigler and Low 1950). In the Logan River, approximately 3 percent of the stocked rainbow trout live through the first winter. Fish stocked in lakes have a somewhat higher overwintering survival rate, provided ice cover, freezing, and low oxygen are not factors. However, the mortality rate for rainbow trout stocked in Bear Lake, when they were less than 8 to 9 in. (203 to 229 mm) long was extremely high the first 18 months (McConnell, Clark, and Sigler 1957). Rainbow trout in Fish Lake, at ages 1 through 6, grow as follows in total length: in inches, 6.4, 10.2, 13.1, 16.4, 20.6, 24.3; in mm, 163, 259, 333, 417, 523, 617 (Sigler 1953). Rainbow trout in Fish Lake and Bear Lake grow faster after they become piscivorous. Flaming Gorge Lake produced the Utah record rainbow trout, which weighed 26 lb, 2 oz (11.9 kg).

The world record rainbow, weighing 42 lb, 2 oz (19.1 kg), was from Belle Island, Alaska (IGFA 1993). With the exception of Kamloops, nonmigratory rainbow trout average 2.5 to 4 lb (1.1 to 1.8 kg) and are considered large at 5 to 8 lb (2.3 to 3.6 kg). Rainbow trout markedly larger than 2 to 4 lb (0.9 to 1.8 kg) in size are often piscivorous and fast growing. Simpson and Wallace (1978) reported a Kamloops taken from Idaho's Pend Oreille Lake in 1947 that weighed 37 lb (16.8 kg). Steelhead weighing 28 lb (12.7 kg) have been taken from the Columbia River (Don Chapman, personal communication, 1983). Rainbow trout in habitats with temperatures of 68° to 70°F (20° to 21.1°C) grow faster but can survive only when there is cooler, well-oxygenated water into which they can retreat as the surface waters warm to over 70°F (21.1°C). Benefits of fast growth at high temperatures may be offset by greater levels of disease.

After absorbing the yolk sac, fry 0.4 to 0.6 in. (10 to 15 mm) long emerge from the gravel. By the end of the first summer they may be 4 in. (10 cm) long and weigh 0.4 oz (11.2 g). Scott and Crossman (1973) reported the following total lengths for fish ages 1 to 7 from a British Columbia lake: in inches, 2.6, 4.7, 11.4, 17.1, 20.3, 23.2, and 28.0; in mm, 66, 119, 290, 434, 516, 589, 711. Stream fish often grow slower than lake fish, probably because of less food.

Simpson and Wallace (1978) believed the life span of rainbow trout is fairly short, few living beyond 5 years of age. An 11-year-old rainbow, from Eagle Lake, California, an alkaline former arm of ancient Lake Lahontan, has been reported (Moyle 1976; Busack et al. 1980). Life expectancy may be as low as 3 or 4 years in stream and lake populations, but for most inland populations it would appear to be 6 to 8 years (Scott and Crossman 1973).

Food and Feeding

Generally, young rainbow trout feed on various invertebrates, including zooplankton, crustaceans, and insects; some older fish continue to feed on these organisms but others shift to fishes. Rainbow, more than most trout, feed on invertebrates, algae, and to some extent, vascular plants. Larger rainbow feed on invertebrates until they reach a weight of about 2 lb (0.9 kg); then they tend toward fishes. Stream-dwelling rainbow trout are bottom drift feeders, but they also rise to the surface and feed. Feeding rates are considerably reduced in winter, primarily due to a paucity of drift organisms and the fact that trout metabolism (as with all cold-blooded animals) is reduced by cold water.

Rainbow trout in lakes have a stronger tendency to feed on fish than do stream rainbow, although these fish do not normally become an important element in their diet until the trout reach 12 to 16 in. (305 to 406 mm) in length. In some high-altitude, low-productivity mountain lakes, rainbow feed heavily on terrestrial insects, especially ants.

Zooplankton populations in Flaming Gorge Lake were not adequate for young rainbow trout in 1983 or 1984; most of the daphnids were too small for them to eat. Rainbow competed ineffectively with kokanee, Utah chub, and white sucker. There was both dietary and spatial overlap and only moderate diet specification in these four fishes (Schneidervin and Hubert 1987).

In the 1950s and early 1960s rainbow trout stocked in Bear Lake usually reached a size of 2 to 3.5 lb (0.9 to 1.59 kg). Later, Kamloops were stocked, and many reached a weight of 8 to 9 lb (3.63 to 4.08 kg). One explanation for this is that Kamloops learned more readily to feed on fishes than previously stocked rainbow. Rainbow trout in Fish Lake, after reaching a size of about 1.5 lb (0.68 kg) feed heavily on Utah chub and grow rapidly (Sigler 1953).

Limiting Factors

Predation by other trout, by diving birds, and several mammals all normally limit rainbow populations. Rapid water quality changes, particularly in lakes, detrimentally affect rainbow trout. They do well in waters with pH from 7 to 8 but can survive in waters ranging from 5.8 to 9.6 pH. Fishing, the number one mortality factor for rainbow trout, is a result of the ease of capture and zeal with which they are pursued. The embryos and young of the normally spring-spawning rainbow trout face the multiple hazards of turbid fast water, scouring, siltation, and oxygen depletion. Emerging fry can be negatively affected by either quantity or quality of water or both. During high water, fry may be pushed downstream into less desirable habitat. According to Wydoski and Whitney (1979) although 95 percent of rainbow trout eggs are fertilized in natural spawnings, only 65 to 85 percent survive beyond the embryonic stage. Don Chapman (personal communication, 1981) believes embryo survival is no more than 30 percent.

Lack of deep pool overwintering habitat may be a major limiting factor for some stream populations. Beaver Creek in northern Utah is sometimes covered with 3 or more feet (0.9 m) of snow before the surface freezes. At times the water warms and thaws the snow along both banks, causing a large mass of snow to drop into and temporarily clog the stream. Fish that do not escape to deep pools or undercut banks suffocate.

Temperatures of 60°F (15.6°C) are ideal for growth of rainbow trout (Leitritz and Lewis 1980). Female rainbow produce lower numbers of viable eggs when water temperatures exceed 56°F (13.3°C) (preferably 54°F [12.2°C]) for 6 months before initiation of spawning. Adverse lower limit temperatures (42°F or lower [5.6°C or lower]) also negatively affect embryo development (Leitritz and Lewis). Water temperatures in the high 70s°F (24° to 26°C), except when oxygen is at saturation levels and activity is minimal, may cause stress that can predispose individuals to disease, or, in some cases, death (Black 1953). Leitritz and Lewis thought yearlings and adults can withstand temperatures up to 78°F (25.6°C) for a short time. Rainbow trout will survive for short periods at temperatures up to 82°F (27.8°C) if acclimated to the upper temperature, and the water is oxygen saturated (Moyle 1976). The rigors of spawning induce stress that can cause up to 100 percent postspawning mortality (Simpson and Wallace 1978; Wydoski and Whitney 1979).

Mortality is highest when rainbow are stocked in relatively small numbers in a stream with a wild trout population. New introductions are sometimes unable to establish themselves where there is a dominant hierarchy. Stocked fish may also carry diseases that affect them but not the wild populations. When large numbers of rainbow trout are stocked in streams sheer numbers may disrupt the established hierarchies. This is not a factor in lake stocking.

During the high water years of 1983 to 1987, Great Salt Lake flooded Bear River Bay and the Bear River Migratory Waterfowl Refuge with salt water, killing plants and fish alike. This situation forced birds that eat fish to Mantua and possibly Minersville reservoirs where they preyed on all species of fish, including rainbow, exerting atypical mortalities on all populations.

Breeding Habits

Rainbow trout normally spawn in the spring. However, there are hatchery strains that spawn every month of the year. The average age for first spawners is 2 to 3 years; some hatchery rainbow spawn at age 1 and some wild fish do not spawn for the first time until they are age 5.

Rainbow and cutthroat trout that spawn in the same area and at the same time may hybridize. The rainbow is a stream spawner and, unlike the chars, is rarely able to spawn in lakes. Spawning in some drainages may occur in intermittent tributary streams (Raleigh et al. 1984). There are cases where populations have spawned on gravel bars near the lake outlet. In Lake Rotoma, New Zealand, they spawn successfully along the shore in the presence of suitable gravel (Penlington 1983). A high percentage of some hatchery strains of rainbow do not spawn in the wild.

In the early spring rainbow trout seek out stream gravel bars when water temperatures reach about 50°F (10°C). Ideal gravel size for incubation ranges from 0.1 to 4.0 in. (0.25 to 10 cm) (Raleigh et al. 1984). The female digs a redd by turning on her side and beating her tail against the substrate. In this way she cleans the gravel and at the same time excavates a pit that for a large female may be 2 to 4 ft (0.6 to 1.22 m) long and up to 1.5 ft (0.45 m) deep. Nest building takes place both day and night. The spawning female rests near the bottom, over the nest, then the male moves alongside her. As both bodies are pressed together the eggs and milt are released in 4 to 5 seconds. The dominant male courts the digging female and attempts to drive other males away, although more than one male may succeed in spawning with her. After laying eggs in one redd she covers them with gravel. Scott and Crossman (1973) suggested that females may dig and spawn in several redds with one or more males. Chapman doubted this; he thought that defense of an individual redd is a key adaptive mechanism and that multiple redds are maladaptive (Don Chapman, personal communication, 1983). Numbers of eggs laid per female is related to adult size and is highly variable. Raleigh et al. (1984) reported ranges from 500 to 3,161 eggs for stream-residing females and 935 to 4,578 for lake-residing females. Embryos emerge in 4 to 7 weeks. Alevins take 3 to 7 days to absorb the yolk then become free swimming. At a constant water temperature of 50°F (10°C), eggs hatch in 31 days (Leitritz and Lewis 1980).

Rainbow trout may spawn as often as 5 successive years in a row. However, some researchers believe that survival rates for repeat spawners are very low, probably less than 10 percent (Scott and Crossman 1973). According to Behnke (1992), the overwhelming majority of rainbow trout hatchery broodstock worldwide are various mixtures of steelhead and coastal rainbow trout. The common belief is that all hatchery stocks are derived from the McCloud River of California.

Habitat

Rainbow trout are highly adaptive, occupying a wide range of aquatic habitats. They are at home in large, deep lakes or in small farm ponds. They prosper in large rivers and in small streams. There are strains of rainbow trout that appear to be habitat specific, but basic knowledge in this area is minimal. In Bear Lake, in the 1950s, most stocked rainbow were littoral zone fish, but another group, presumably Kamloops, was rarely found inshore (Sigler and Sigler 1987).

Optimum temperature for growth is about 60°F (15.5°C). Rainbow can tolerate high temperatures for short periods if there is plenty of oxygen. They can tolerate and adapt to pH levels ranging from 5.8 to 9.6, but most strains thrive best at levels of 7.0 to 8.4.

Stream-dwelling rainbow trout are more aggressive than lake inhabitants. They establish and defend feeding territories. Deep pools are important to stream-dwelling rainbow as a refuge during the winter (Raleigh et al. 1984). Territoriality is evidently not present in lake populations. Schools move about randomly in search of food. They do not migrate great distances.

Management

There are relatively few self-sustaining populations of wild rainbow trout in Utah. The hatchery program supplies a high percentage of caught rainbow. Where, when, how, and at what size rainbow are stocked are governed by several to many factors. Size and species of resident predators and competitors determine in part the size and number of rainbow stocked. Physical factors such as hatchery overcrowding or breakdown may override biological factors. Triploid (sterile) rainbow trout grow faster, become larger, and live longer. For these reasons there are places where they are a valuable supplement to genetically normal trout.

Budget constraints generally dictate how many rainbow will be stocked each year. Fish stocked in small, high mountain streams may not survive the winter and should be stocked in spring and early summer and put where they are easiest to catch. Rainbow stocked in lakes survive the winter better and are stocked with the expectation of successful overwintering. The strong and weak links in the food chain may dictate the size stocked. Fish-eating birds may make heavy inroads in lake stocks, causing managers to rethink stocking times or even places. Bag limits may be governed more by the cost of a fish in the creel than by biological considerations. The rainbow trout fishery may well be the heart of the coldwater trout program. It is certainly the difference in many cases between happy and unhappy anglers.

Statement of Utah Division of Wildlife Resources

Since most of Utah's aquatic resources are near or in the mountains, much of it located above 6,000 ft (1,829 m) elevation, sportfishery management has been dominated by trout. For the majority of waters that means rainbow trout, initially brought to Utah in the late 1800s. Rainbow trout possess a variety of traits that make them ideal for management in both artificial environments and natural waters. They are highly adaptable, both to a hatchery environment and to a variety of conditions in the wild. Adaptability to hatchery culture is important because most rainbow trout populations in Utah are not self-sustaining. Rainbow have proven much more adaptable to the culture environment than cutthroat trout and have gained a high degree of approval among Utah's anglers. Their catchability and adaptability to various conditions have clearly made them Utah's number one sport fish, even to the extent that they were selected as Utah's official state fish.

Rainbow trout have clearly been the most successful species for managing Utah's coldwater irrigation reservoirs. They are adapted to feeding on zooplankton, so they are able to utilize the open water areas in fluctuating reservoirs where vegetation and associated insects are lacking. To provide the basic fisheries in the majority of Utah's reservoirs, the DWR stocks approximately 5 1/4 million rainbow trout annually, from fingerling and advanced fingerling to catchable sizes.

The rainbow's weaknesses for fisheries management include low ability to compete with other species for plankton. Reservoirs that are taken over by other planktivores such as white sucker, Utah sucker, or Utah chub are not able to sustain viable rainbow fisheries regardless of the number stocked. As a result, these artificial environments are managed largely to produce an agricultural crop. That is, competing species are removed, and the rainbow trout are then managed as close as possible to a monoculture. This procedure has been an effective and efficient means of producing quality fishing and provides the backbone of fishing opportunity. The Utah chub and Utah sucker, native to the Great Basin, are rare exceptions among the native species in Utah in that they have been able to adapt to the highly modified artificial environments created by humans. Neither species is in any danger from periodic treatments that remove them from specific reservoirs. Treatments to remove nongame fish are conducted only to reduce abundant species and are not practiced where rare native species are impacted.

Some strains of rainbow trout are not well adapted for feeding on other fish and therefore seldom control competing species. Wild strains, however, have shown an ability to switch to a fish diet and to survive in the face of predators or competitors. Experiments were undertaken at Flaming Gorge Lake comparing three strains of wild rainbows; two of them have shown promise. These strains are Eagle Lake rainbow from Eagle Lake, California, and the Duncan River Kamloops from the Kootenai Lake system of British Columbia. These two strains seem to be responsible for the resurgence of rainbow trout fishing at Flaming Gorge Lake in recent years.

An albino strain of rainbow trout was developed several decades ago at the Fisheries Experiment Station, Logan, Utah, and has proven to be valuable in managing intensive yield fisheries subjected to heavy fishing pressure. In a number of Utah's most heavily fished waters, approximately 20 percent of the catchable rainbow trout stocked are albinos. These yellowish, highly visible fish are more easily seen by anglers than naturally colored rainbows. This conspicuousness alerts anglers to the presence of fish, even if the fish are not biting on a particular day. The anglers seem to appreciate knowing that the fish have been stocked in a body of water and frequently continue to fish even when fishing is slow. A number of people have even developed a particular desire to fish specifically for albino trout. The fish behave very much like their nonalbino relatives, but are noticeably less hardy and seldom survive over winter.

---

sockeye salmon (kokanee),
Oncorhynchus nerka
(Walbaum)
Plate 26
Plate 27

Etymology: *Oncorhynchus* = hooked snout referring to the condition of the migrating adults in Pacific salmon; *nerka*, from the Russian name for the anadromous form

Nomenclature: *Salmo nerka* Walbaum 1792, *Oncorhynchus nerka* Jordan and Copeland 1878

IMPORTANCE

Kokanee may be noncompetitive with other game fishes and provide forage for them. Or this landlocked sockeye salmon may at times be both a valuable sport and forage fish and a competitor with trout. They are an excellent table fish and are reasonably sporting, considering their small size (Sigler and Miller 1963). In Porcupine Reservoir in northern Utah they provide good fishing and viewing at spawning time by the local Audubon Society and other interested groups. The Flaming Gorge Lake population is self-sustaining.

The kokanee fishery of Pend Oreille Lake in northern Idaho was at one time unique among kokanee fisheries. During the 1950s and 1960s, a hand-line fishery was catching fish at the average rate of four fish/hour, with maximum catches as high as 20 fish/hour. In the mid-1960s, a decline in the catch rate was predicted and had become fact by the early 1970s. The uniqueness of the fishery was based on the exclusive use of hand lines and high catch rates for both sport and commercial fishing (Simpson and Wallace 1978).

DESCRIPTION

Original

Salmo, *Nerka*. Ruffis *Krasnaya ryba*, i.e., piscis ruber. *Pennant arct. zool. introd*. 125. D. 11. P. 16. V. 10. A. 15.

Salmoni Salari forma similis, sed minor. Pondus 16 libras non superat. Quando flumina intrat colore argenteo splendet, dorso & pinnis cærulescentibus: Dentes tunc sunt parvi & maxillæj rectae. Postea, dum in aqua dulci moratur, dentes cresunt & maxillæ præsertim in maribus incurvantur. E mari adscendit æstate flumina Kamtschatkæ. Caro intense purpurea.

Narka. Krascheninnikow deser. Kamtschatkae, *c*. 9. p 181.

Caput per parvum. Rostrum breve acutum. Lingua subcærulea. Corpus parum compressum longitudine circiter 21 unciarum & latitudine 4 unc. macrolepidotum. Dorsum subcæruleum nigro maculatum; abdomen & latera alba. Cauda bifurca. Caro ruberrima.

Translation

SALMON, Nerka. In Russian *Krasnaya ryba*, i.e., red fish.

Similar in shape to the salt-water salmon, but smaller. Weight does not exceed 16 lb. When it enters rivers, it shines with a silvery color, its back and fins being blue; at that time its teeth are small and its jaws straight. Later, as long as it stays in fresh water, its teeth grow and its jaws are curved, especially in the sea. From the sea during summer, its ascends the Kamschatkan rivers. Deep purple flesh.

"Narka." Krascheninnikow desc. Kamschatkae, c. 9. p. 181. Small head. Short sharp beak. Tongue tinged with blue. Body insufficiently compressed, ca 21" in length and 4" in width, with large scales. Back tinged with blue and spotted with black; belly and sides white. Forked (bifurcal) tail. Very red flesh.

Contemporary

Kokanee have no definitive spotting pattern. Anal fin rays may number 14 to 16 but never less than 13. This characteristic helps separate kokanee from rainbow, cutthroat, and brown trout, which have less than 13 anal rays. Kokanee have a dark blue back with silvery sides. As the spawning season approaches, both male and female kokanee turn a deep red (shades from gold to orange to red are prevalent) and the lower jaw of the male develops a characteristic hook common to the Pacific salmon. The tail is deeply forked, which also distinguishes them from rainbow, cutthroat, and brown trout. Another separating characteristic is the number of branchiostegals (small bones on the underside of the head), which is 13 to 19 for kokanee and 10 to 12 for other trout.

Range

Kokanee were first stocked in various waters in Utah in 1922 (Popov and Low 1950). They are present in Flaming Gorge Lake and Porcupine and East Canyon reservoirs.

Kokanee probably occur over much of the worldwide range of sockeye. North American distribution of sockeye extends from the Klamath River, California, to Point Hope, Alaska. In Asia the distribution of sockeye is from northern Hokkaido, Japan, to the Anadyr River (Lee et al. 1980). Kokanee are native in Alaska, the Yukon Territory, British Columbia, and, in the lower 48 states of Washington, Oregon, and Idaho (Nelson 1968). Original populations of kokanee probably developed from sockeye runs along the west coast of United States and Canada and from fish that were trapped or stocked where they could not return to sea. Introductions have been made in the western states of Nevada, California, Montana, Colorado, North Dakota, and Wyoming (Scott and Crossman 1973).

Size and Longevity

Most Utah populations of kokanee produce mature fish that average 12 to 14 in. (305 to 356 mm). Those in Flaming Gorge Lake reach 15 to 17 in. (381 to 432 mm) (Bradford and Hubert 1988). Record fish may weigh more than 6 lb (2.7 kg) but the range in most areas is 1 to 2 lb (0.45 to 0.91 kg). The Utah record kokanee, weighing 5 lb, 5 oz (2.5 kg) was caught in Flaming Gorge Lake. The current record for kokanee is 9 lb, 6 oz (4.3 kg) (Fishing Hall of Fame 1993); the record for the sockeye form is a 15 lb, 3 oz (6.99 kg) fish from the Kenai River, Alaska (IGFA 1993).

Kokanee may live as long as 7 years but more often only 3 to 5 years. They die after spawning. Janssen (1983) reported no fish over 34 months old in Porcupine Reservoir, Utah.

Food and Feeding

Kokanee eat mainly zooplankton, feeding from sundown to dark (Sigler and Miller 1963). They travel in large schools, sometimes near the surface but usually in deeper waters. Emerging insects, especially midges, are eaten occasionally, and newly emerged fry in streams may live on aquatic insects. Food changes little as fish grow larger. Kokanee do not feed after beginning their spawning run, although they may strike a lure.

LIMITING FACTORS

Blocked access to spawning grounds is the most severe limiting factor for kokanee. Depletion of their food, primarily large zooplankton, causes stunting. Kokanee mortality may occur unless they avoid the hypolimnion when it is depleted of oxygen. They thrive best in well-oxygenated water at 50° to 60°F (10° to 15.6°C); deviations from this requirement may have an adverse effect on rate of growth and general welfare. In Flaming Gorge Lake they compete heavily with several other species (Schneidervin and Hubert 1987). Competition with *Mysis* in Lake Tahoe is one potential explanation of decreased growth in that population (Cooper and Goldman 1980).

BREEDING HABITS

Kokanee spawn in the fall from late August to January as temperatures fall from 46° to 39°F (7.8° to 3.9°C). As spawning time approaches, mature fish, usually in their third or fourth year (the range may be from 2 to 7), cease to feed and seek one of the lake's tributary streams for spawning. In Idaho there are two recognized stocks: one spawns from August to October, the other from late October to January (B. Riemen, personal communication 1984). Females may die before releasing all or any of their eggs. Cordone et al. (1971) noted particularly low spawning success in the Lake Tahoe population. Only 11 percent and 28 percent of the dead females examined in 1967 and 1968 were spawned out, and 30 and 46 percent, respectively, had died without spawning.

Like other members of this genus, kokanee normally migrate to the stream in which they hatched, or were stocked as fry, to complete their reproductive cycle (Foerster 1968). However, Simpson and Wallace (1978) documented notable exceptions to this popular belief. They noted that the majority of a population will inexplicably desert their natal streams and spawn elsewhere and then, just as suddenly, the population, or a segment of it, will return to the original spawning site. The genetic and survival implications of straying are not well understood. Foerster reported that late spawners may dig up and destroy earlier redds. Incubation time is from 80 to 140 days.

Kokanee generally spawn in gravel bars of streams and will spawn along lakeshores only when unsuitable or insufficient spawning areas are available in streams (Foerster 1968). When kokanee spawn along the lakeshore the depth is generally less than 30 ft (9.1 m). Stream spawning occurs in much shallower water. In Kamchatka Peninsula populations, this habit is generally important where there are springs.

Females build the redd and defend the area against other females while the male defends the area from other males. Generally, each female lays from 200 to 1,800 eggs, depending upon her size and age. The female occasionally defends the area after spawning, although she will die shortly thereafter. Spawners in northern climates may produce more but smaller eggs than those of more southerly distribution (Fleming and Gross 1990).

Habitat

High, cold mountain lakes are the best habitat for kokanee. At temperatures between 50° and 60°F (10° and 15.6°C), they inhabit surface waters. As the surface water warms, they move down from the warmer surface water, very often into the thermocline. In winter they tend to be at all depths (Foerster 1968).

Management

Kokanee are generally stocked either as forage for trout or to produce a fishery, and in either case are stocked at a small size. Costs associated with sustaining a fishery, even where natural reproduction does not occur, are less than for stocking catchable-size trout (Wydoski and Whitney 1979). In small lakes, they may actually depress growth and population size of other trout by competing with them for zooplankton. Although angling for them has become a popular sport in recent years, particularly at Porcupine Reservoir and Flaming Gorge Lake, kokanee in Utah are generally underexploited. This underexploitation is related to the rather specialized techniques and gear required to catch them during much of the season. Low fishing mortality and a small plankton population may lead to stunted kokanee populations. On the other hand, overfishing can produce the same result (Foerster 1968). Unless there is an adequate zooplankton population and moderate fishing pressure, it may be unwise to stock kokanee in deep, cold lakes.

The presence of direct competitors, such as *Mysis*, for large zooplankton may alter the growth rate of kokanee, reducing numbers of large fish (Cooper and Goldman 1980). Detailed study of the kokanee population and the prey base is needed before *Mysis* is stocked in any water body where a kokanee fishery is maintained.

Statement of Utah Division of Wildlife Resources

Kokanee salmon were stocked in a number of reservoirs throughout Utah in the early 1960s for only a couple of years before the brood stock developed disease problems and was destroyed. Those early stockings established self-sustaining populations only in three waters; Porcupine Reservoir, Flaming Gorge Lake, and East Canyon Reservoir. Those populations existed without active management for several decades and provided only scarce fishing opportunity for people interested in a bit of diversity. Expansion of the kokanee population in

Flaming Gorge and recent studies into their ecology have increased interest in this landlocked salmon. Kokanee are widely known in other states as highly prized game fish with excellent table qualities and may face a much larger role in Utah in the future.

Experience at Flaming Gorge has shown that the kokanee are able to expand and prosper in the face of severe competition for plankton. Their ability to efficiently utilize small size plankton gives them a significant advantage over trout species and nongame fish competitors. As a result, kokanee may be useful in waters where a fishery is desirable, but it is not possible to chemically remove competitors. Kokanee have a large role in plans for managing Strawberry Reservoir now that competitors have been removed. Kokanee are being stocked to utilize small plankton resources and outcompete any reinvading chubs and suckers that may gain reentry to the reservoir.

Although highly prized as game fish, kokanee have several negative attributes, which have to be managed. They can outcompete rainbow trout and have a potential to take over some waters where abundant spawning habitat is available. In those situations kokanee need to be balanced with an effective predator, which can help thin the numbers of small kokanee and keep the population in check. This plan has been attempted in Porcupine Reservoir by introducing hybrid splake and in Strawberry Reservoir where the Bear Lake Bonneville cutthroat trout should prey on young kokanee. Kokanee are a pelagic species, which can produce an excellent fishery from boats, but kokanee are seldom vulnerable to shore anglers.

Kokanee likely face expanded use in management in the future to provide diversity in the pelagic fishery and also in waters that are subject to overabundant chub populations and have adequate spawning tributaries. At present, kokanee eggs are available in Utah only from Sheep Creek on Flaming Gorge Lake and the East Fork of the Little Bear River above Porcupine Reservoir. All eggs from these sources are being used to establish a population at Strawberry Reservoir. Once established there, however, eggs should become available for experimental use in a number of waters throughout Utah.

Bear Lake whitefish,
Prosopium abyssicola
(Snyder)
Plate 28

Etymology: *Prosopium* = a small mask, from the large preorbitals; *abyssicola,* for their presence in the deep lake they inhabit

Nomenclature, *Coregonus abyssicola* Snyder 1919, *Prosopium abyssicola* Jordan, Evermann, and Clark 1930

Importance

Bear Lake is the only lake in North America (Great Lakes as a unit excluded) with four endemic fishes: Bear Lake whitefish, Bonneville cisco, Bonneville whitefish, and Bear Lake sculpin. All four originated between 10,000 and 35,000 years ago. Bear Lake whitefish provide limited forage for lake trout and cutthroat trout. They are rarely taken by hook and line.

Description

Original

Small examples of this species (8 to 10 in long) closely resemble those of *C. spilonotus* except that the latter are spotted. With increasing age the spots of *C. spilonotus* grow indistinct and finally disappear, while the maxillary and snout elongate, and the body becomes deeper. Consequently when the lack of spots fails to distinguish *C. abyssicola*, it may be easily separated from *C. spilonotus* by its much shorter maxillary.

Local fishermen usually distinguish between spotted examples of *C. spilonotus* and this species, both of which they call herring, but they do not seem to suspect that the spotted fishes will grow to become the immaculate adults of *C. spilonotus*.

Mr. Stock reports that this species is taken in sufficient numbers to ship to near-by points.

It spawns from the latter part of January to early in March at a depth of about 100 ft.

Examples seen alive in August were moss-green above, silvery on the sides, and white beneath. These bleached in alcohol leaving very little dark pigment, while specimens taken during the breeding season are considerably darker, indicating that they are then much more highly colored.

Spawning fishes measure from 200 to 310 millimeters in length. The males are darker than the females, and the scales from the middle of the back to near the ventral surface bear mucous nodules. The females are smooth in most cases, an occasional one having small nodules on 2 or 3 rows of scales above and below the lateral line.

Type No. 83500, United States National Museum. Locality, Bear Lake near Fish Haven, Idaho. Length 310 millimeters. J. P. Stock collector.

Head 4.6 in length to base of caudal; depth 4.5; depth caudal peduncle 2.8 in head; snout 3.7; eye 5.2; interorbital width 3.4; maxillary 4.1; scales lateral series 78; between occiput and dorsal 30; above lateral line 8; below lateral line 7; dorsal 10; anal 11.

The body is relatively slender, head short, snout short and rounded, maxillary just reaching a perpendicular through anterior margin of orbit, the latter being very angular anteriorly, and extending well forward of the iris. Gill rakers 7 + 11, short, thick, and pointed. Fins large, the pectorals and ventrals bluntly pointed; dorsal with a straight edge; adipose much larger than maxillary; caudal deeply cleft, and lobes pointed.

Color dusky above, silvery on the sides and below; no spots; scales on sides and below outlined with fine blackish dots; fins dusky, the caudal dark edged. Sex male. Each scale from the back to the level of the pectoral fin with a round, pearly mucous nodule.

In a series of specimens the scales in the lateral series number from 69 to 78; between occiput and dorsal fin 25 to 30; above lateral line 8 or 9; dorsal rays 10 to 11. [Table, Measurements of Ten Examples of *Coregonus abyssicola*, omitted.]

As indicated by the scales, the rate of growth appears to be as follows: 5 years old—180 mm; 7 years old—210–240 mm; 8 years old—250 mm; 9 years old—265 mm; 10 years old—300 mm; and 13 years old—310 mm.

The gill rakers number 6 to 8 + 13 to 15 on the first arch; the caeca 73 to 78; branchiostegals 7 to 8.

Contemporary

Bear Lake whitefish and Bonneville whitefish are not easily distinguished. Bear Lake whitefish have larger scales than those of Bonneville whitefish and have a "Roman nose." Bonneville whitefish are spotted until they are about 10 in. long; Bear Lake whitefish do not have notable spots during any phase of their life history. They have an average of 10 dorsal rays and 11 anal rays. Scales in the lateral series are usually 69 to 78 and scales around the body are 39 to 43. As the common name implies, they are whitish in color through all of their life (Sigler and Sigler 1987).

RANGE

Bear Lake whitefish are found only in Bear Lake, Utah-Idaho.

SIZE AND LONGEVITY

Bear Lake whitefish seldom exceed 10 in. (254 mm) in length. The largest individual taken during a 5-year study on Bear Lake was just short of 11 in. (279 mm). This individual was judged to be 11 years old. Snyder (1919) recorded a 12-in. (305-mm) fish that was 13 years old. Whitefish ages 1 to 8 caught between 1952 and 1954 were the following year-end sizes: in inches, 1.3, 3.0, 4.4, 5.2, 5.9, 6.5, 7.0, and 7.5; in mm, 33, 76, 112, 132, 150, 165, 178, 191 (Sigler 1958).

FOOD AND FEEDING

Bear Lake whitefish feed heavily on several groups of small invertebrates: ostracods, copepods, midge larvae, and aquatic oligochaetes. They may occasionally eat fishes and aquatic insects other than midges. Feeding habits suggest complete dependence on the soft marl bottom, which is primarily deep-water habitat in Bear Lake (Sigler and Sigler 1987). Adult whitefish feed heavily on ostracods and chironomid (midge) larvae, the young on zooplankton (Wurtsbaugh, Hawkins, and Moreno 1989).

LIMITING FACTORS

Bear Lake whitefish appear to be affected only by predation and senility.

BREEDING HABITS

Bear Lake whitefish spawn in water ranging in depths from 50 to 100 ft (15.2 to 30.5 m) from late December to early February. Ripe females have been recovered in March, when water temperatures range from 36° to 39°F (2.2° to 3.9°C). They probably spawn first at age 3 or 4 and produce an average of 800 to 1,000 eggs.

HABITAT

Bear Lake is a cold, infertile (oligotrophic) lake. It is approximately 8 mi (12.9 km) wide by 20 mi (32.2 km) long in a north-south direction, with a maximum surface elevation (by law) of 5,923.85 ft (1,805.6 m). Approximately one-third of Bear Lake's volume is in Utah, the balance in Idaho. Slightly more than 50 percent of the lake has a depth of more than 100 ft (30.5 m) (Sigler 1972). Bear Lake whitefish are deep-water fish that live near the bottom, rarely frequenting inshore areas either summer or winter, except to spawn.

MANAGEMENT

Deterioration of water quality from increased lake productivity or the presence of toxic materials would detrimentally impact this species. However, the lake appears to be less fertile than it was 75 to 80 years ago, and the only potentially toxic material would appear to be small amounts of fertilizer or pesticides draining off agricultural lands or lakeshore residences.

Bonneville cisco,
Prosopium gemmifer
(Snyder)
Plate 29

Etymology: *Prosopium* = masked, from the large preorbitals; *gemmifer* = set with gems.
Nomenclature: *Leucichthys gemmifer* Snyder 1919, *Prosopium gemmifer* Bailey et al. 1960

IMPORTANCE

Bonneville cisco are fished for by dip net about 16 days each year. During this time they provide thousands of recreational fishing days and food for fishermen. Historically, they supplied a limited local commercial fishery before that activity was barred. They are an important forage fish for cutthroat trout and lake trout (Sigler 1962). Numerically they are the most abundant species in Bear Lake.

DESCRIPTION

Original

Leucichthys gemmifer, new species. Bonneville cisco.

The Bonneville cisco is taken during the winter in large numbers. It is caught in gill nets set through the ice. It may also be taken in the summer, when it is not so numerously represented on the bottom. Large schools may then be seen near the surface. It is at no time found near shore. Although of small size, it is an excellent food fish. It is largely used by the local fishermen as bait, and when so employed it seems to be selected in preference to other fish by both the larger whitefish and the trout.

This species, locally known as "peak-nose" because of its pointed snout, measures about 7 1/2 in when mature. It is pale moss-green above, with silvery sides which have a pearly iridescence. The under parts are white. The tip of the snout is pale pink, and a few scales on the base of the caudal are strongly tinged with purple.

Spawning occurs in deep water during the latter half of January. Examples of both males and females collected at that time by Mr. Stock have conspicuous pearly nodules on all the scales from head to tail except those of the ventral surface. These nodules are conical in shape, sharply pointed, and larger in the region of the lateral line. No trace of the nodules appears in summer specimens, when the mucous coating of the scales is rather thin, and the surface is bright and smooth. Similar nuptial ornaments have not been reported as occurring on the other species of the genus.

An examination of a few stomachs revealed nothing.

Forty specimens show a range in size from 162 to 180 millimeters in total length, and, unless the scale markings are wrongly interpreted, the ages of these examples are 4 and 5 years.

The species differs from others of the genus in the possession of a slender head with a long, sharply pointed snout, and a narrow maxillary which is entirely in front of the eye. The cisco does not resemble any other whitefish of the basin, and it will not be confused with any of them by the casual observer.

Type No. 83498, United States National Museum. Locality, Bear Lake, near Fish Haven, Idaho. Length 173 millimeters. Collectors, J. O. Snyder and C. L. Hubbs.

Head 4.4 in length to base of caudal; depth 5.6; depth caudal peduncle 3.8 in head; snout 3.2; eye 4.5; interorbital area 4.5; maxillary 3.4; scales lateral series 71; between occiput and dorsal 29; above lateral line 8; below lateral line 7; dorsal rays 11; anal rays 12.

Body elongate and slender, the head pointed; eye large; maxillary entirely in front of eye; no teeth; gill rakers long and slender, 14 to 27 on first arch; caeca 85; fins short, caudal lobe pointed, adipose small. Color dusky above, silvery on the sides, no spots. [Table, Measurements of Ten Examples of *Leucichthys gemmifer*, omitted.]

The color soon fades after death. An alcoholic specimen is brown to a point 2 scales above the lateral line, from where it is silvery to the midventral surface. Along the back the scales are dusky. The snout is black on the upper anterior half. The fins are without color.

The intestinal canal is short and straight. There are 84 to 86 caeca just beyond the pyloris, the posterior 10 or 12 extending in a single row along the intestine. The gill rakers are longest near the center of the arch, about one-half the length of the maxillary. They number 14 to 16 + 27 or 28. Branchiostegals 8. The air bladder is large, thin, and single lobed, extending the whole length of the visceral cavity. The peritoneum is somewhat silvery in places, but is without dark pigment. No teeth are found.

Contemporary

Their overall appearance is that of a herring, pale moss green above, with silver sides that have a pearly iridescence. They are a brassy color with tubercles during the breeding season. The long, sharply pointed snout, with a projecting lower jaw and a thin body, are dominant characteristics of the Bonneville cisco. The eye is large, the maxillary is entirely in front of the eye, they have no teeth, and the gill rakers are longest near the center of the arch.

RANGE

Native only to Bear Lake, the Bonneville cisco has been stocked in Lake Tahoe, Nevada-California; Twin Lakes, Colorado; high mountain lakes in South Dakota; and Flaming Gorge Lake, Utah-Wyoming. No survival has been documented in any of these areas. Fossils of the Bonneville cisco were discovered in the Stansbury level of prehistoric Lake Bonneville, which was of much greater area but not a part of Bear Lake.

SIZE AND LONGEVITY

Bonneville cisco are small fish, rarely attaining lengths over 8.5 in. (216 mm) or weights over 2.5 oz (71 g). They normally do not live longer than 7 years, although a few have been aged at 11 years. Sexual divergence is not demonstrated in size; male and female Bonneville cisco grow at about the same rate in both length and weight. Typically the Bonneville cisco yearly length for fish age 1 to 8 is: in inches, 2.9, 4.6, 5.8, 6.4, 6.9, 7.2, 7.6, 8.1; in mm, 74, 117, 147, 162, 175, 183, 193, 206. They grow slightly, if any, per year after their eighth year (Sigler and Workman 1978).

Food and Feeding

Zooplankton is the principal diet of Bonneville cisco. One copepod, *Epischura*, is the predominant food and is important all year. These fish do, however, feed heavily on cladocerans, principally *Bosmina*, in winter. They feed more on chironomid larvae in winter and early spring than other times of the year. Bonneville cisco feed year around (Sigler and Sigler 1987; Wurtsbaugh, Hawkins, and Moreno 1989).

Limiting Factors

Fishing pressure and predation have the primary impacts on Bonneville cisco, and it is doubtful that fishing is a serious factor. Disease and parasites are minor factors of mortality. Some fish are infested with stomach nematodes.

Breeding Habits

Bonneville cisco predictably start to spawn on January 15, plus or minus 5 days, and continue for 12 days plus or minus 4 days (Sigler and Workman 1978). Both sexes mature at 3 years of age. The female produces from 2,000 to 3,600 eggs. Each year, hundreds of thousands of Bonneville cisco move out of the depths inshore to spawn in water ranging in depth from a few inches to 40 ft (12.2 m). Males move inshore ahead of females and remain there throughout the spawning season. Females move inshore when they are ripe and go back out to deep water after they have spawned. During the breeding season large schools of cisco move inshore, then swim parallel to it at distances of from 3 to 8 ft (0.9 to 2.4 m). The distance from shore depends upon the turbulence of water, the presence of fishermen, and whether or not there is ice cover, which occurs 4 years out of 5. During spawning, a female is typically attended by three to five males. When the group stops to spawn, it is particularly vulnerable to dip netting. Bonneville cisco spawn at temperatures ranging from 33° to 42°F (0.5° to 5.6°C). Nuptial arrays consist of tubercles that project significantly above the scales and of bright colors, primarily brassy yellow. Although the tubercles are confined primarily to the male, an occasional female has a few small ones (Sigler and Workman 1978).

Habitat

Bonneville cisco prefer temperatures less than 58°F (14.4°C). At temperatures lower than this they are widely scattered through the lake. As the water warms in the spring and early summer, they descend into the deeper, colder water. After Bear Lake is stratified, or formed into three temperature layers, the greatest concentration of Bonneville cisco is in the metalimnion, the middle layer of rapidly changing temperature. Although the cisco is generally at depths of 50 to 100 ft (15.2 to 30.4 m) during the summer, they may leave this area of cool water and move into the warm surface waters to feed. This movement of Bonneville cisco occurs near twilight when they move inshore, then swim parallel to shore. Movement is generally from early evening twilight to dark (Sigler and Sigler 1987).

MANAGEMENT

Bonneville cisco, taken almost entirely with dip nets while on the spawning ground, are vulnerable for only 12 to 16 days a year. The catch rate by dip netting is three to five males for each female. The males move inshore earlier than the females and remain there throughout the season, whereas the females move in, spawn, and then return to deep water. This situation presents an interesting management possibility. If fishing pressure is depressing the numbers markedly, the summer (mixed) population should show a predominance of females, indicating overfishing. However, the sex ratio and depression of the population presents an enigma. The fishing success over the past few years has shown a marked decline, yet the summer sex ratio in the lake remains at 1:1. Other management requirements are maintenance of the present water quality, including oxygen saturation through and below the metalimnion, and the exclusion of pollutants.

Bonneville whitefish,
Prosopium spilonotus
(Snyder)
Plate 30

Etymology: *Prosopium* = masked, from the large preorbitals; *spilonotus* = spot + back
Nomenclature: *Coregonus spilonotus* Snyder 1919; *Prosopium spilonotus* Jordan, Evermann, and Clark 1930

IMPORTANCE

Bonneville whitefish are taken by hook and line in limited numbers. They provide forage for large cutthroat and lake trout. Perhaps their unique value, from a natural history standpoint, is that they are one of four Bear Lake endemics.

DESCRIPTION

Original

Coregonus spilonotus, new species. Bonneville whitefish.

Gill nets set at a depth of about a hundred ft in Bear Lake in August caught numbers of a spotted whitefish which measured from 155 to 200 millimeters in length. They were pale moss-green above, silvery on the sides, and white beneath. Spots, dusky in color, round, and somewhat larger than the pupil, extend from the occiput to the base of the caudal. These fishes differ from *C. williamsoni* in that the spots are smaller and more numerous, the scales are larger, and the heads longer. They were from 4 to 5 years old, and the condition of the ovaries seems to indicate that they were mature individuals. At the same time and at the same depth large whitefish colored like the above, except that they were without spots, were taken on baited hooks. Besides being plain in color, these fish were much larger, 400 to 500 millimeters long;

the heads were longer, the body deeper, the maxillary larger, and they were distinguished also by their general appearance. They were from 7 to 10 years old, and mature.

Locally these 2 forms are regarded as distinct, but a considerable series of specimens collected by Mr. Stock supplies examples intermediate in size and age, and seems to demonstrate without much doubt that they belong to the same species. The question need not be considered as settled, however, until more complete data have been obtained.

This species appears to inhabit the deep water. It is to be found there as late as the month of August, and it is in the same region in January and February, when it feeds upon the eggs of other whitefish. In December, however, it migrates shoreward and spawns in shallow water. It does not enter the rivers.

Type No. 83499, United States National Museum. Locality, Bear Lake, near Fish Haven, Idaho. Length 425 millimeters. Collectors, J. O. Snyder and C. L. Hubbs.

Head 3.8 in length to base of caudal; depth 3.6; depth caudal peduncle 3.5 in head; snout 2.9; eye 4.8; interorbital area 3; maxillary 3.2; scales lateral series 80; between occiput and dorsal 34; above lateral line 11; below lateral line 9; dorsal rays 11; anal 11.

Body deep and rather heavy, the head very large, with a long snout and broad maxillary. Gill rakers short, thick, and pointed, 6 + 13 on first arch. Fins rounded; caudal small; adipose about equal in size to maxillary. Color dusky above, silvery on the sides, white below; no spots.

The spots disappear with age, the head grows relatively larger, the maxillary longer, and the body deeper. The lateral series of scales numbers from 74 to 81; series above lateral line 9 to 11; between occiput and dorsal fin 30 to 37. The dorsal has 10 to 12 rays; anal 9 to 11.

[Table, Measurements of *Coregonus spilonotus*, omitted.]

The gill rakers numbered 6 to 8 + 12 to 14. The air bladder is large and extends the entire length of the abdominal cavity. The peritoneum is immaculate. There are 135 to 140 pyloric caeca, the posterior ones extending in a single series along the digestive tract. There are 8 branchiostegals.

The growth appears to be about as follows: 4 years old, 155 to 180 mm; 5 years old, 200 mm; 6 years old, 255 to 260 mm; 7 years old, 280 to 437 mm; 8 to 10 years old, 420 to 470 mm.

Old examples are fat and weigh 2 1/2 lb or more. Nothing was learned of the food of the species except that the stomachs of specimens caught during the months of January and February were stuffed with whitefish eggs. These were taken on the spawning grounds of *L. gemmifer* and *C. abyssicola*.

Contemporary
As the common name states, Bonneville whitefish are whitish in color. They have spots on the sides and upper back until they reach about 10 in. (254 mm) in length. They do not have the "Roman nose" of the Bear Lake whitefish. The dorsal rays number 10 to 12 and the anal rays 9 to 11. The mouth is small and slightly inferior (upper jaw longer), partly explaining perhaps the reason for its poor catchability on hook and line. The caudal fin is deeply forked. Scales along the lateral series total 74 to 94; gill rakers 19 to 26 (Sigler and Sigler 1987).

RANGE

Bonneville whitefish are found only in Bear Lake, Utah-Idaho.

SIZE AND LONGEVITY

Bonneville whitefish, age 1 to 8, have yearly lengths in inches of: 3.2, 5.7, 7.5, 9.2, 10.7, 12.7, 14.6, 16.4; in mm, 81, 145, 191, 234, 272, 323, 371, 417. Occasionally 18- to 22-in. (457- to 559-mm) specimens are caught. Average life span is 6 to 8 years (McConnell, Clark, and Sigler 1957). The Utah (and world) hook-and-line record is 5 lb, 6 oz (2.47 kg) (IGFA 1993), but most fish caught weigh less than 2 lb (0.9 kg).

FOOD AND FEEDING

Diet of Bonneville whitefish in Bear Lake is largely chironomid larvae and pupae. Other aquatic and terrestrial insects and worms make up the balance of the diet. They occasionally take fish. Bonneville whitefish diet indicate that they are wide ranging and feed part of the time in shallow water, more so in winter than summer. Adults feed heavily on ostracods and chironomid larvae; the young eat zooplankton. They feed heavily on the eggs of other whitefishes (Snyder 1919; Wurtsbaugh, Hawkins, and Moreno 1989).

LIMITING FACTORS

No single factor accounts for a significant reduction in numbers. Relatively few Bonneville whitefish are caught by hook and line. An unknown number, probably also insignificant, fall prey to other fishes and to birds. The balance of this relatively abundant fish die from disease, a minor factor, or advanced age.

BREEDING HABITS

Spawning takes place along shore and over rocky, shallow areas or sandy points from mid-February to early March, although Snyder (1919) reported that they spawn in December. Both sexes mature in their third or fourth year at 8 to 10 in. (203 to 254 mm) in length. When a female stops to spawn, 5 or 6 males attend her. One 9-in. (229-mm) female contained 1,200 eggs (Sigler 1958). After the spawning act, which lasts from 5 to 15 seconds, the spawners resume travel with the school. Temperature preference for spawning appears to be 45°F (7.2°C).

HABITAT

Bonneville whitefish frequent the 40- to 100-ft (12.2- to 30.5-m) layer of water most of the time, but they may be much deeper. Adults are in the shallow water more often than the young. They inhabit shallow water both summer and winter, and more often than either the Bonneville cisco or the Bear Lake whitefish.

MANAGEMENT

Bonneville whitefish receive relatively little attention from anglers. However, some persistent anglers using red and white spoons bounced along the bottom have had a high success rate. The fish are eaten either smoked, canned, or fresh. The best time to fish is just at daybreak. These fish are underutilized and inadequately appreciated. It follows that fishing pressure has had slight effect on the population. As with other Bear Lake coldwater fishes, the primary requisite for their continued welfare is maintenance of an optimum water quality.

---

mountain whitefish, *Prosopium williamsoni* (Girard)
Plate 31

Etymology: *Prosopium* = masked, from the large preorbitals; *williamsoni,* after Lt. R. S. Williamson of the United States Pacific Railroad Explorations

Nomenclature: *Coregonus williamsoni*, Girard 1856; *Prosopium oregonium*, Dymond 1943; *Prosopium williamsoni* (Dymond 1947)

IMPORTANCE

Sportfishermen regard the mountain whitefish with mixed emotions. One school of thought holds that they are a good food and sport fish, another feels they are a negative and detractive factor. As a result of the second, and prevailing attitude, and the fairly high reproductive potential of the mountain whitefish, they are more abundant in many waters than would be preferred by many fishermen and fishery managers. Angling for whitefish is more popular in winter, when they feed more actively than trout and can provide a substantial fishery.

DESCRIPTION

Original

A most important (I was going to say unexpected) discovery of a white fish was made by the party on the R. R. Survey of California and Oregon, commanded by Lt. R. S. Williamson. And since it is different from its hitherto known congener, we will call it *Coregonus williamsoni* as commemorative of that Survey. Its head is rather small, being contained about 5 times in the total length, which measures eleven in. The mouth is very small and the posterior extremity of the maxillary does not extend as far back as the anterior rim of the orbit.

The scales are large, eighteen rows of them may be counted between the anterior margin of the dorsal and the insertion of the ventrals; 9 above the lateral line, and 8 below it. The lateral line, itself, is perfectly straight, the caudal fin forked as usual. The pec-

> torals are rather small. I have alluded to the color in saying it was a white fish; add to it a bluish grey hue along the back. It was collected by Dr. Newberry in the Des Chutes River, a tributary of the Columbia.

Contemporary
Mountain whitefish are light brown on the back and fins and silvery to white on the belly and sides. Young generally have several parr marks on each side, providing a distinguishing pattern. Both the dorsal and anal fins have 9 to 12 rays. The lateral series cycloid scales number 75 to 94, although 80 to 90 is the usual range. Depth of the body is approximately 0.2 the length. The snout and lower jaw are short and blunt, and there is a flap between the nostrils. Holt (1955) found it difficult to distinguish mountain whitefish from Bonneville whitefish.

RANGE

In Utah, mountain whitefish are present in many cool and cold waters, such as the Bear River drainage and the Sevier, Escalante, Weber, and Logan rivers. They are widely distributed over the western United States, occurring from the Lahontan Basin in Nevada to Wyoming, Montana, and Idaho. They are widespread in British Columbia, Canada, from the Fraser and Columbia river systems and extending northward to the Peace and Liard systems (Lee et al. 1980). Most existing populations are semi-isolated from others.

SIZE AND LONGEVITY

Logan River anglers report mountain whitefish weighing up to 4 lb (1.8 kg), but most weigh under 2 lb (0.9 kg), with a few slightly over 3 lb (1.4 kg). The yearly average length for whitefish age 1 to 9 in Logan River, Utah, is: in inches, 4.6, 8.1, 10.2, 11.6, 12.8, 14.1, 15.4, 16.4, 17.4; in mm, 117, 206, 259, 295, 325, 358, 391, 417, 442 (Sigler 1951). A fish weighing 4 lb, 6 oz (2 kg) was taken from the Provo River, Utah. Mean lengths within a population vary considerably. Fish from British Columbia and Alberta are reported by Scott and Crossman (1973) to attain the following total lengths for ages 1 through 9: in inches, 2.6–5.3, 4.2–8.8, 6.4–11.7, 7.7–12.9, 8.7–13.0, 11.2–14.1, 12.8–15.4, 13.8–16.4, 14.8–17.4; in mm, 66–135, 106–224, 163–297, 196–328, 221–330, 285–358, 325–391, 351–417, 376–442. In Canada, California, and part of the Rocky Mountains, mountain whitefish did not grow as long or as fast as those from the Logan River, but lived longer. McHugh (1941) found that slow-growing populations tend to live longer and eventually reach the same size as fast-growing ones. The world record hook-and-line for mountain whitefish is 5 lb, 2 oz (2.3 kg) for a fish from the Columbia River, Washington (Fishing Hall of Fame 1993). Average age reached by mountain whitefish is 8 or 9, although some live over 10 years. McHugh (1941) reported much older fish in some populations.

Food and Feeding

Food of mountain whitefish in Logan River, Utah, in order of importance, by volume, is caddisfly larvae, true fly (Diptera) larvae, and mayfly and stonefly nymphs. Terrestrial insects are also consumed. Interestingly, mountain whitefish have a trait of feeding more actively in winter than in summer (Sigler 1951). Twilight or night are the most frequent feeding times for mountain whitefish. They often feed on the bottom, but occasionally surface to feed on drift or terrestrial insects. Simpson and Wallace (1978) noted that whitefish in Idaho commonly feed on whitefish eggs during spawning season. In the Columbia River they feed on hatchery salmon fry as the latter drift out of the tributaries, and they may eat salmon eggs, probably ones that would not have hatched (Sigler and Miller 1963). McHugh (1940) observed that fish 2 years and older have a more varied diet than younger ones.

Limiting Factors

Current levels of commercial and sportfishing have not substantially reduced mountain whitefish populations in many places. Local fishing pressure may reduce populations where they are avidly sought by anglers. Small mountain whitefish are preyed on by trout. But even when they are with a numerically large population of trout, the trout rarely make inroads into the whitefish population. Inhat (1981) stated that adults during the prespawning period in October seek temperatures high enough to be lethal to embryos.

Breeding Habits

Mountain whitefish begin spawning in mid-to-late October to early December, depending on latitude and at a falling temperature of about 42°F (5.6°C) (Brown 1972). In northern Idaho they spawn during late October and early November when water temperatures range between 40° and 45°F (4.4° and 7.2°C) (Simpson and Wallace 1978). They mature at age 3 or 4 or occasionally 2. Spawning for a population lasts approximately 2 weeks. The eggs hatch in about 5 months at temperatures above 35°F (1.67°C) or 36 days at 52°F (11.1°C).

Distances moved to spawn are not great. Stream whitefish move upstream to riffles to spawn. Lake dwellers move to the nearest stream. They travel a short distance and spawn 6,900 to 9,400 eggs per lb (3,130 to 4,264 per kg) of female. Whitefish do not build redds (nests). Although mountain whitefish prefer the riffle areas of streams for spawning, they may spawn in shallow water along gravel shores of lakes if there is aeration generally by springs or undertow. Spawning takes place where there is adequate current to clear silt from the eggs. The adhesive eggs stick to stream bottom gravels.

Habitat

In the Logan River, whitefish prosper in waters with a mean temperature of 48° to 51°F (8.9° to 10.6°C), with a near-saturation of oxygen and a pH of 8.1 to 8.4. They apparently prefer streams rather than lakes. They do, however, occur in some mountain lakes (for example,

Lake Tahoe). They live anywhere in the Logan River (except the valley, although they were there in earlier times) where pools are at least 16 ft (4.9 m) wide and 3 ft (0.9 m) deep at the season of least flow. They do not live in the river above elevations of 7,300 ft (2,225 m) (Sigler 1951).

MANAGEMENT

Anglers prefer trout because they are generally easier to hook, they put up a more spectacular fight, there is more prestige in catching them, and they have better table qualities. However, pickled, canned, or smoked whitefish compete well with trout for taste. Long-held prejudices are hard to change, and when both trout and whitefish are available the latter loses out. Mountain whitefish appear to be prospering throughout their range. Number reductions are probably not attainable through management options. Attempts at population reductions are not generally successful. A mountain whitefish experimental commercial fishery, designed to improve trout fishing in eastern Idaho, did not notably reduce the population.

---

brown trout,
Salmo trutta
Linnaeus
Plate 32

Etymology: *Salmo* = Latin name for the salmon of the Atlantic, from *salio*, to leap; *trutta* = Latin name for trout
Nomenclature: *Salmo trutta* Linnaeus 1758

IMPORTANCE

Some of the finest wild trout fishing in North America is provided by established populations of brown trout. They are probably the second most important trout in Utah, when viewed as contributors to sportfishing. At a time when hatchery rearing costs are rising and more people are fishing, a wild trout that can reproduce and hold its own against both the hazards of its environment and elevated fishing pressure is unusual. They are also prized as table fish. They are generally more able to adapt to a degraded habitat than either brook or cutthroat trout. The brown trout is more difficult to catch than most trout—a gratuity for the exceptional fisherman and a problem for those with less experience. Brown trout are aggressive, more so than most trout and they readily feed on other fishes (Sigler and Sigler 1987). It is necessary to stock brown trout annually in Flaming Gorge Lake to sustain an adequate population, although there is some reproduction (Joe White, personal communication, 1989).

DESCRIPTION

Original

Salmo Trutta Linnaei 1758

S. ocellis nigris iridibus brunneis, pinna pectorali punctis 6. *Sn. svec.* 308. B.—D.12.P.13.V.10.A.9.C.20.

Art. gen. 12. *syn.* 14. Salmo latus, maculis rubris nigrisque, cauda æquali.

Gron. mus. 2. *n.* 164. Salmo latus, cauda subrecta maxillis æqualibus, maculis nigris annulo albido. D. 14. P. 12. V. 12. A. 10. C.—*Habitat in fluviis* Europæ.

Translation
A salmon with small black eyes, brown scales, with 6 small spots on the pectoral fin. B.—D. 12. P. 13. V. 10. A. 9. C. 20.

A broad salmon, with red and black spots, and a balanced tail. A broad salmon, with a drooping tail and level jaws, with black spots and a whitish ring. Dorsal rays 14, pectoral rays 12, ventral rays 12, anal rays 10, caudal rays.—Lives in European waters.

Contemporary
The dorsal fin of the brown trout has 9 to 14 major rays; the anal fin 10 to 12 major rays; pelvic fins 9 or 10 (almost always 9) and the pectoral fins 12 to 14 rays. The tail fin is truncate (square) in adults but slightly forked in young. Cycloid scales number 115 to 135 in the lateral series (Sigler and Miller 1963). Basibranchial teeth are absent. There are 14 to 21 gill rakers on each arch and 9 to 11 branchiostegal rays.

Coloration of brown trout is olive to greenish brown on the back with lower portions of the body often yellowish, fading beneath to gray or white. Males, particularly during the spawning season, tend to have yellow coloring. Notable large, dark spots appear on the back and sides, but not on the head or caudal fin. More or less ocellated reddish spots with pale borders are profligate over the upper body. The front edge of the pelvic fins and the anal fin is often outlined with a yellow margin. In young brown trout, the adipose is orange and has no dark spots or margin outlines (La Rivers 1962).

RANGE

Brown trout were introduced into Utah Lake prior to 1900 and were being stocked regularly by 1910 (Heckman, Thompson, and White 1981a). They have now been stocked and have self-sustaining populations in many of Utah's cool (48° to 72°F [8.9 to 22.2°C]) lakes and streams. Few have been stocked in high Uinta waters.

The native range of brown trout includes Europe and western Asia. Being partially anadromous in these locations, they are also present in the British Isles and Iceland. Brown trout were first introduced into North America in 1883 in New York and Michigan. In 1884 they were introduced into Newfoundland and in 1890 into Quebec. Subsequent introductions were made over much of Canada and the United States (Lee et al. 1980). They have been stocked in South America, Africa, India, Australia, and New Zealand.

Size and Longevity

In 1937 a brown trout weighing 37 lb, 12 oz (17.1 kg) was taken from the lower impoundment of the Logan River; it is not a hook-and-line record because it was not landed legally. In one week on the Logan River, one fisherman caught two brown trout, one weighing 14 lb, 4 oz (6.5 kg) and the second weighing 14 lb, 14 oz (6.8 kg) from the same general area. Other large fish captured in the Logan River included an 18-lb (8.2-kg) and a 23-lb (10.4-kg) fish. In recent years, Flaming Gorge Lake has produced more trophy brown trout than any other water in Utah. The all-tackle world record is a fish weighing 40 lb, 4 oz (18.3 kg) (Fishing Hall of Fame 1993). The Utah record is 33 lb, 10 oz (15.2 kg), a brown trout taken from Flaming Gorge Lake.

Brown trout are fast growing, moderately long lived (> 13 years) fish. They grow best at temperatures between 65° and 72°F (18.3° and 22.2°C) (Brynildson, Hacker, and Klick 1963). In some populations, males grow faster than females, in others the opposite is true. Generally both sexes grow at about the same rate. In one Utah stream study, brown trout ages 1 to 6 had a yearly length of: in inches, 3.5, 6, 10, 14, 16, and 18; in mm, 89, 152, 254, 356, 406, 457. In the Logan River, at the end of each year 1 through 8 they had a total length as follows: in inches, 4.0, 6.9, 9.7, 12.1, 15.6, 18.3, 25.5, 27.7; in mm, 102, 175, 246, 307, 396, 465, 648, 704 (Sigler 1952).

Food and Feeding

Brown trout are carnivorous, feeding on aquatic and terrestrial insects as well as mollusks, frogs, and rodents. Larger fish feed more on fish, crayfish, and large organisms. Both lake and stream populations of young brown trout feed on zooplankton and insects. Other invertebrates eaten include aquatic earthworms, snails, shrimp, freshwater clams, midge larvae, and crayfish. At an age younger than most trout, they begin a more strictly fish diet. Brown trout, except the young, feed more actively at twilight and early hours of the night than during midday. Their secretive habits make their presence less known than other trout in many streams (Brynildson, Hacker, and Klick 1963). A typical feeding progression for stream-dwelling brown trout, as they grow older, is from drift organisms and zooplankton to aquatic and terrestrial insects, to small fish, and then to large fish. Brown trout less than 2 lb (0.9 kg) live largely on such insects as mayflies, caddisflies, stoneflies, and midge larvae and pupae.

Limiting Factors

Low water temperatures restrict distribution of the brown trout. They do not frequent the cold, high reaches of mountain streams. They are also restricted from waters that warm to the high 70s°F (25° to 26°C). Optimum temperature is from 48° to 72°F (8.9° to 22.2°C). Unlike the rainbow trout, brown trout do not prosper in very small bodies of water.

Major causes of mortality among brown trout populations are

fishing and habitat destruction, especially stream channelization (straightening by use of heavy equipment, generally for flood control), and flash floods. Brown trout are preyed upon to some extent by birds, mammals, and fishes. They require at least 5 ppm (mg/l) oxygen when temperatures reach 68°F (20°C) or above. Waters above 81°F (27.2°C) are generally lethal. In a Wisconsin stream, survival from egg to legal-size fish was about 2 percent (Brynildson, Hacker, and Klick 1963). Streams that lack adequate spawning gravels or aeration limit production.

On one occasion in an extensive riffle area in the Logan River dredging was done just after large numbers of brown trout had spawned. Another time farther downstream, the river was straightened and deepened (channelized) by removing bank cover and bottom substrate and depositing it on the bank. In both cases, required habitat was destroyed, resulting in reduced brown trout numbers.

Breeding Habits

Brown trout initiate spawning in the fall with the onset of a decreasing temperature of between 50° and 45°F (10° and 7.2°C). This may be from late October to December. The age of maturity is 2 to 3 years; males often mature 1 year earlier than females. Some mature as early as age 1 or as late as 8 years (Raleigh, Zuckerman, and Nelson 1986). Spawning takes place during the daytime.

To initiate spawning, brown trout move out of deep pools or lakes upstream to the nearest acceptable riffle area. A female selects the redd site and digs the redd with her tail. This activity attracts a dominant male who defends the female and redd from other males. The male does not help with the construction of the redd, although he may court the female as she digs. After the redd is complete, the female drops over the nest, the male swims alongside, and eggs and sperm are deposited. The female then moves upstream and covers the eggs. Brown trout redds range in width from less than 12 in. to more than 40 in. (less than 0.3 m to more than 1.02 m). Size range of preferred gravel is from 1/3 to 3 in. (0.8 to 7.6 cm) but larger gravels may be used (Reiser and Wesche 1977). Water depths at redd sites are from 11 to 24 in. (0.2 to 0.6 m). Mean water velocities over redds are 18 to 30 in./sec (46 to 76 cm/sec) (Raleigh, Zuckerman, and Nelson 1986). The largest females breed first. A female lays from 200 to more than 6,000 eggs, which hatch in 41 days at a constant water temperature of 50°F (10°C) (Leitritz and Lewis 1980). Females at higher altitudes tend to produce more but smaller eggs. Fish in productive streams produce more eggs than in unproductive ones.

Brown trout are reared in hatcheries in limited numbers. That is because most hatchery personnel believe that they are more difficult to raise than rainbow trout and that wild populations tend to be more self-sustaining than rainbow.

HABITAT

Brown trout are more of a big-water fish than most trout. They inhabit all areas of large lakes and streams; in medium-size streams they frequent deep pools. They do not seek small streams, and they do not prosper in small ponds. The upper limiting and near lethal temperature for brown trout is 81°F (27.2°C). Temperatures above 32°F (0°C) to below 80°F (26.7°C) can be tolerated for a limited time only. Canopy cover is important in streams. Riparian trees and brush assist in holding temperatures down (Raleigh, Zuckerman, and Nelson 1986). Adult brown trout in streams inhabit glide or rubble areas or the bottom of deep pools; the young are in shallow pools, close to shore in either shallow water or riffles. They can tolerate high turbidities for short periods of time. At twilight, adults move to the surface or into riffle areas to feed.

In the Logan River, they do not generally move upstream above an altitude of 5,500 ft (1,676 m), although when a few were inadvertently stocked at 6,200 ft (1,890 m) they appeared to prosper.

MANAGEMENT

Established brood stock in outstanding habitat will generally produce a sustained population of brown trout. In Flaming Gorge Lake they produce a trophy fishery. However, although they are somewhat difficult to catch, frustrating neophytes and experts alike, they can be overfished by above-average persistent anglers. Brown trout should not be stocked where there are existing or proposed rainbow or cutthroat trout populations, or in small waters such as spring-fed ponds. Unfortunately, in many cases, this has already occurred, leaving the fishery manager with a dilemma.

---

brook trout,
Salvelinus fontinalis
(Mitchill)
Plate 33

Etymology: *Salvelinus,* an old name for char; *fontinalis* = living in springs
Nomenclature: *Salmo fontinalis* Mitchill 1814, *Salvelinus fontinalis* Jordan and Copeland 1878

IMPORTANCE

Brook trout are not a very important component in Utah's trout fishery. However, their popularity, in part, is based on their occurrence where other trout are scarce. They have the ability to reproduce and sustain a fishable population in high, cold lakes and small streams. Small- to medium-size fish in a population are readily caught on both live baits and artificial lures; large ones are exceptionally wary. Most state fishery agencies raise only fixed numbers, although the species is easy to culture. In the early 1900s they were the most frequently stocked trout in many states. They are one of the few trouts that perpetuates themselves in lakes without tributaries, but they tend to overpopulate these lakes unless heavily fished. This situation results in large numbers of small trout.

DESCRIPTION

Original

Common Trout. (*Salmo fontinalis.*)

With yellow and red spots on both sides of the lateral line, concave tail, and sides of the belly orange red. Back mottled pale and brown. Sides dark brown, with yellow and red spots; the yellow larger than the red, and surrounding them. The latter appear like scarlet dots. Lateral line straight. The yellow spots and red dots both above and below that line. Sides of the belly orange red. Lowest part of the abdomen whitish, with a smutty tinge. First rays of the pectoral, ventral, and anal fins white, the second black, the rest purplish red. Dorsal fin mottled of yellowish and black.

Tail rather concave, but not amounting to a fork; and of a reddish purple, with blackish spots above and below. Eyes large and pale. Mouth wide. Teeth sharp. Tongue distinct. Skin scaleless.

Is reckoned a most dainty fish. They travel away to Hempstead and Islip, for the pleasure of catching and eating him. He is bought at the extravagant price of a quarter of a dollar for a single fish not more than ten or twelve in long. He lives in running waters only, and not in stagnant ponds; and, therefore, the lively streams, descending north and south from their sources on Long Island, exactly suit the constitution of this fish. The heaviest Long Island trout that I have heard of, weighed 4 lb and a half.

Rays, Br. 10. P. 12. V. 7. D. 13 and O. A. 11. C. 23.

I copy the following article from the news-paper:

"Mr. Robbins, of the Philadelphia theatre, visiting Long-Island (New-York State) in the summer of 1814; during his stay in that place, he caught *one hundred and ninety fresh-water trout*.

"The largest fish caught at Patchoque, weighed two pounds and eight ounces, and the largest at Fireplace, three pounds.

"Dr. Post, of New York, caught one hundred fifty trout, weighing one hundred and five pounds, in the month of April, 1814, in the waters of Long Island.

"Mr. Purvis, of New York, caught a trout weighing four pounds eight ounces, measuring twenty-four inches in length. A drawing of this fish remains at Fireplace, near where it was caught."

Contemporary

Brook trout exhibit a wide range of colors. They may be olive to blue gray on the back to white on the belly. Red spots, with or without bluish rings around them, are present on the sides, but they are not numerous. Characteristic wavy marks on the back are the most distinguishing feature. This, along with the notable white and then black stripe along the fore edge of each of the lower fins, aids in separating brook trout from any other trout (Sigler and Miller 1963). The caudal fin has variable black lines, sometimes two or three, parallel to the trailing edge of the fin. The colors become more intense as spawning time approaches, the lower flanks and belly of males becoming orange red with black pigment on either side of the belly.

The fins are soft-rayed, the dorsal fin has 10 rays and the anal fin 9. The caudal fin is square or only lightly forked. Scales are small and cycloid and arranged in about 230 rows in the lateral series (Scott and Crossman 1973). Brook trout have a streamlined, somewhat compressed body, which is about five times as long as it is deep. The head is large, but not long; the mouth is terminal and reaches behind the eye. There are well-developed teeth on the maxillary, premaxillary, and the head of the vomer.

Range

Brook trout were first stocked in Utah in streams near Salt Lake City in 1875 (Popov and Low 1950). They are now present in such diverse locations as Antimony Lakes, reaches of the Bear River, and in mountain lakes. Brook trout are one of the most widely transplanted species of trout in the world. They have been planted in South America, the Falkland Islands, New Zealand, Asia, and Europe. They are native in northeastern North America, from the north Atlantic seaboard south to Cape Cod, in the Appalachian Mountains southward to Georgia, west of the upper Mississippi and Great Lakes region to Minnesota and north to Hudson Bay (Lee et al. 1980).

Size and Longevity

More so than in most fish, growth is highly variable. Abundant food and moderate temperatures result in rapid growth. In cold, high, infertile waters they may reach a size no greater than 8 in. (203 mm). Temperatures for optimum growth are 55° to 60°F (12.8° to 15.6°C). Females may live longer than males.

Most brook trout are neither fast growing nor long lived. Yearly total length for fish ages 1 through 6, in stream populations is: in inches, 2.4, 5.0, 7.1, 9.2, 10.8, and 12.9; in mm, 61, 127, 180, 234, 274, 328. Two ecologically distinct forms have been identified: a small, short-lived one of 3 to 4 years and 8 to 10 in. (203 to 254 mm) living in small, cold streams and lakes (Reimers 1979) and the larger form, which lives 8 to 10 years and reaches weights of 9 to 14 lb (4.1 to 6.4 kg) and frequents large lakes, streams, and estuaries (Raleigh 1982). Scott and Crossman (1973) observed that a number of brook trout weighing 5 to 6 lb (2.3 to 2.7 kg) are caught each year in Canada. They also pointed out that in the 1968–1970 Ontario Federation of Anglers' and Hunters' Big Fish Contest, there were many brook trout in the 6-lb (2.7-kg) class.

The world record brook trout, weighing 14 lb, 8 oz (6.6 kg) was caught in Ontario, Canada (Fishing Hall of Fame 1993). The Utah record brook trout, caught in Boulder Mountain Lake, weighed 7 lb, 8 oz (3.4 kg).

Food and Feeding

It may be fairly stated that brook trout will eat almost anything. They are carnivorous, voracious feeders. They eat insects throughout their life when other foods are not readily available. Young in streams feed primarily on drifting invertebrates; in lakes they feed on plankton (Grant and Noakes 1988). A 1-in. (25.4-mm) fish may live on entomostracans, 2-in. (50.8-mm) fish appear to prefer midges, and 4-in. (102-mm) ones look for mayfly nymphs and caddisfly larvae. For larger fish the dominant food is aquatic insects, including caddisfly larvae, pupae, and adults; stonefly nymphs; midge larvae; and mayfly nymphs or other larger organisms. Terrestrial worms, mollusks, crustaceans, and fishes are also taken (Sigler and Miller 1963). Brook trout on rare occasions may take frogs, salamanders, snakes, and small mammals such as field mice and shrews. However, even large brook trout are not especially piscivorous (Scott and Crossman 1973).

Limiting Factors

In some areas the most serious predators of brook trout are fish-eating birds, such as kingfishers and mergansers. Brook trout living in beaver ponds may at times be displaced through the destruction or abandonment of the dam. In small ponds and streams they are vulnerable to mink and other fish-loving mammals.

Brook trout generally do not live as many years as most trout and have, except very large ones, an above-average vulnerability to fishing. At times there is cannibalism on eggs and young. In some high mountain lakes they may live only 3 years because spawning in the fall so depletes their energy that they cannot survive the winter. Lethal temperatures are around 80°F (26.7°C). From embryo to the first fall season, there may be a 2 to 5 percent survival rate.

Breeding Habits

Spawning behavior may be initiated as early as late summer in the northern part of the brook trout's range and as late as early winter in the southern portion. Most reach sexual maturity in 2 or 3 years, although some males may mature at age 1 and a few females at age 4. They initiate spawning activities as water temperatures decline past 50°F (10°C). They spawn over gravel beds in the headwaters of streams, and in gravel areas of lakes, assuming there is a spring upwelling and a moderate current (Raleigh 1982). Spawning is also successful in spring-fed ponds.

A female chooses a spawning site and digs the redd by turning on her side, moving gravel by rapid movements of her tail. Usually this behavior is initiated when there are males nearby. More than one male is attracted to one female. The dominant male defends the redd.

According to Moyle (1976) redds often are located in territories already defended by males. In this case the female chases away other females, although on occasion the male may help. The dominant male constantly courts the digging female by swimming alongside, nudging her, and quivering. When the redd is complete, the female settles to the bottom and is joined by the male. Eggs and sperm are released together. The female covers the eggs with gravel using her tail in a sweeping fashion. This new digging activity simultaneously covers the newly spawned eggs and builds another redd. Optimum substrate/gravel size reported by Reiser and Wesche (1977) ranges from 0.13 to 2.0 in. (3 to 51 mm). Only 15 to 60 eggs are laid at one time, and because brook trout females contain from 50 to 2,700 eggs, each female has to dig several redds. The average number of eggs per lb of female is 1,500 to 1,800 (680 to 817/kg).

Eggs of fall- and winter-spawning fish overwinter at low temperatures. Development takes 35 days at 55°F (12.8°C) but it takes 68 days at 45°F (7.2°C) (Leitritz and Lewis 1980). Optimum egg incubation temperatures are in the 40° to 53°F (4.4° to 11.7°C) range (Raleigh 1982).

Habitat

Brook trout are coldwater fish (38° to 62°F [3.3° to 16.7°C]) that seek water temperatures of 50° to 58°F (10° to 14.4°C), reaching greatest abundance in cool, clear headwater streams and spring-fed streams or lakes. However, there is also a sea-run form. Warmer waters cause stress or occasional mortality. Only the golden trout and the Arctic grayling consistently seek colder water temperatures than the brook trout (Sigler and Sigler 1987). In streams, both adult and young brook trout are territorial and defend their territories against all fish, including other brook trout. In lakes they are not generally territorial but may school when alarmed or when in close proximity to exceptional habitat, such as a spring. Large brook trout are loners in either streams or lakes.

Management

Although small brook trout are easy to catch, stunted and underexploited populations occur frequently in some areas. Fishing regulations can generally be quite liberal. Large fish are difficult to catch. Brook trout prosper in cold, well-oxygenated, clear, high mountain waters. Where overpopulation occurs, the species may be its own worst enemy. Limited or no stocking and liberal regulations for small-sized fish may in part be the solution. Without heavy fishing pressure to reduce numbers, management is difficult.

Statement of Utah Division of Wildlife Resources

The brook trout native to the northeastern United States has been used in high mountain lakes and streams in Utah for many decades. They have proven to be prolific when they find suitable spawning habitat and are well suited to higher elevations. These colorful fish are relatively easy to catch and enjoy a great deal of support from Utah anglers.

Because the brook trout can frequently become overabundant and stunted in waters where they have adequate reproductive habitat, it is Utah's policy to limit the stocking of brood trout to waters that are more likely to establish natural populations. This manner of stocking high mountain lakes on a cycle of 3 to 5 years maintains populations of low enough density to ensure that quality-size fish are present.

Because brook trout can establish in a number of stream types, they have had some negative effect on remaining populations of cutthroat trout at higher elevations. There is no stocking of brook trout in waters that have remnants of native cutthroats. Where brook trout are presently established in waters targeted for reintroduction of native trout, it will ultimately become necessary to remove them. This action may be feasible only on certain smaller drainages and the management of brook trout will remain a significant consideration in plans to expand populations of cutthroat. We expect brook trout to maintain their high degree of support by anglers, and they will remain a part of the management plan at higher elevations.

lake trout, *Salvelinus namaycush* (Walbaum)
Plate 34

Etymology: *Salvelinus,* an old name for char; *namaycush,* a historic Indian name

Nomenclature: *Salmo Namaycush* Walbaum 1792; *Cristivomer namaycush* Jordan 1878c; *Salvelinus namaycush* Shapovalov, Dill, and Cordone 1959

IMPORTANCE

As a result of their large size and consequent trophy value, lake trout are highly prized as sport fish. Catch per unit of effort may be small but once hooked they are not vigorous fighters. Commercially, they are important in the Great Lakes area and parts of Canada, where there are conflicts between sport and commercial interests. Lake trout were fished commercially around the turn of the century in Utah Lake, but the venture was short lived because the stocked fish did not prosper in this shallow, cool- to warmwater, polluted lake. Lake trout are popular with trophy fishermen in such waters as Bear Lake, Fish Lake, and Flaming Gorge Lake, where they produce a world-class fishery. Small ones are tasty both fresh and smoked; large ones may be too oily to be eaten fresh.

DESCRIPTION

Original

Salmo, Namaycush Pennant. arct. zool. introd. 191.

Caput, dorsum, pinna dorsalis obscure cærulea. Latera subfusca, maculis albis & rubicundulis notata. Abdomen argenteum. Caro alba egregii saporis. Habitat in freto Hudsonis.

Translation
Salmon. Head, back, and dorsal fin dark blue. Somewhat brown sides, marked with white and somewhat ruddy spots. Silver abdomen. White flesh of excellent taste. It lives in the Hudson Strait.

Contemporary
Lake trout have a background color of gray overlaid with light spots that vary in intensity with age and environment. This background color covers the back, sides, and fins and serves to highlight the lighter gray spots and vermiculations (worm-tracklike lines). Generally no intense white edging appears on the lower fins, but an occasional narrow band is present (Sigler and Miller 1963). Trout in large lakes are sometimes so silvery that the spots are difficult to see. Spotting is usually more intense on small fish. Lake trout have no red spots but orange or orange red colors are sometimes present on pectoral, pelvic, anal, and even caudal fins. Seven to 12 distinctive parr marks are present on young lake trout (Scott and Crossman 1973).

The dorsal fin has 8 to 10 major rays, the anal fin 8 to 10, and the pelvic fins 8 to 11. Vomerine teeth are confined to the head of that troughlike bone. The caudal fin is deeply forked, pyloric caeca number 95 to 170. The deeply imbedded cycloid scales in the lateral series number 175 to 228 (Sigler and Miller 1963). The stocky head is broad dorsally and its length is from 21 to 28 percent of total body length. The eye is relatively small in adults, occupying 12 to 20 percent of head length. The mouth is large and terminal. Teeth are developed on both jaws, and those in the vomer are confined to the head of the bone, as in brook trout. Gill rakers number 16 to 26, and branchiostegal rays total 10 to 14.

RANGE

In Utah they are present in Fish Lake, Bear Lake, and Flaming Gorge Lake. All are introduced populations. Lake trout occur naturally over a large area of northern North America, their range extending on the north from Alaska to Labrador, and on the south from the Frazier and Columbia rivers and across Canada (including all the Great Lakes) to the northern tier of New England states. In Canada they occur in southwestern Nova Scotia, New Brunswick, and east to northern Quebec. They are present in Ontario, but not in the Hudson and James Bay lowlands. Lake trout are present through northern Manitoba and Saskatchewan, in the southwestern portion of Alberta and northern British Columbia and are widely distributed in the Yukon and Northwest Territories and many Arctic islands (Lee et al. 1980). Even in their normal range, distribution shows a peculiar clustering in certain regions and complete absence from others that appear to be equally suitable.

Size and Longevity

In Fish Lake the yearly total length for fish ages 1 to 9 is: in inches, 7.5, 11.4, 14.6, 17.1, 19.1, 20.9, 22.8, 24.5, 25.8; in mm, 191, 290, 371, 434, 485, 531, 579, 622, 655 (Bulkley 1960). For 1- to 6-year-old Montana lake trout the yearly total length is: in inches, 3, 6, 9, 14, 20, 25; in mm, 76, 152, 229, 356, 508, 635; for a 9-year-old fish, the length is 30 in. (762 mm) (Brown 1971). Lake trout are slow-growing and long-lived fish, but the age of very few trophy-size fish has been determined. It is probable that these large fish dominate their age class and turn to eating fish early in life. This diet, more than age, accounts for the large size. It is possible that some of them never spawned, a factor that would encourage large size (Scott and Crossman 1973).

The world record all-tackle hook-and-line fish weighed 66 lb, 8 oz (30.2 kg) (Fishing Hall of Fame 1993). The Utah record lake trout, caught in 1988 in Flaming Gorge Lake, weighed 51 lb, 8 oz (23.4 kg). The largest lake trout reported in North America was caught in a gill net in Lake Athabasca, Saskatchewan. It weighed 102 lb (46.3 kg) and was 49.5 in. (1,257 mm) long. According to Scott and Crossman (1973), it was 20 to 25 years old. They attribute the rapid growth to the fact that it had never matured sexually. Most lake trout growth takes place from June to September, although growth continues slowly in winter.

Food and Feeding

Fish eaten by lake trout in Bear Lake are sculpin, the three whitefishes, Utah sucker, and a few Utah chub. The lake trout diet in Fish Lake is predominantly Utah chub. In Flaming Gorge Lake they feed heavily on Utah chub and kokanee. In most lakes they have a tendency to move inshore in the spring and feed until the waters warm to above 50°F (10°C).

Small insects, crustaceans, and other zooplankton are the primary diet of young lake trout. Those trout larger than 2 lb (0.9 kg) may feed almost entirely on fish. In Lake Tahoe, lake trout shorter than 5 in. (127 mm) feed on zooplankton and midge larvae and pupae, then graduate to Paiute sculpins. Larger fish eat fish and crayfish. The fish taken are Tahoe suckers, tui chubs, mountain whitefish, and a few kokanee (Moyle 1976).

Limiting Factors

Lake trout are a coldwater fish (38° to 62°F [3.3° to 16.7°C]) and cannot tolerate temperatures over 71°F (21.7°C); their preference is 55°F (12.8°C) or lower. Their salinity tolerance is also low for a salmonid: 11,000 to 13,000 ppm (mg/l). Many species of fish, both game and nongame, prey on small lake trout. Fishes also feed on their eggs. In Utah, sportfishing is the primary cause for most population declines. In Bear Lake and in Fish Lake there are relatively few good spawning areas. This lack has the net effect of low or zero reproduction some years. The Flaming Gorge Lake population is self-sustaining.

BREEDING HABITS

Lake trout initiate spawning activity on a dropping fall temperature of 55° to 50°F (12.8° to 10°C). Mature fish move inshore at dusk and initiate spawning in shallow to relatively deep water over gravel, rubble, or large rocks. Spawning depths generally range from 10 to 40 ft (3.1 to 12.2 m) although 150 to 180 ft (45.7 to 54.8 m) have been reported. Most lake trout mature at 5 to 8 years of age, but a few fall out both sides of this range. It is not known how many times a female spawns in a lifetime. The eggs range in diameter from 0.20 to 0.40 in. (5 to 10 mm). A female produces about 750 eggs for each lb of weight (340/kg) (Sigler and Miller 1963; Sigler and Sigler 1987). They do not build redds or guard the eggs or young. The only protection afforded the eggs is gained from the crevices into which they fall. Eggs hatch in about 50 days at 50°F (10°C).

HABITAT

Except in the northern part of their range, lake trout generally live only in deep, cold, stratified lakes; an exception is Green River, Wyoming, above Flaming Gorge Lake. Populations in lakes spend much of their time living near the bottom of the hypolimnion. In most lakes the general fertility is low, resulting in a relatively sparse growth of aquatic plants and small animals. An adequate amount of oxygen in the hypolimnion and metalimnion is necessary. In Lake Tahoe they have been reported at depths of 1,400 ft (427 m). In the spring they move into shallow water to feed and in the fall to spawn. Lake trout in Canada occur only in relatively deep lakes throughout the southern part of their range, but in the northern half, especially in the Northwest Territories, they also occur in shallow lakes and rivers. They often occur in surface waters immediately after ice breakup. As the surface water warms with the advance of spring, lake trout return to the cooler waters (Scott and Crossman 1973). In Flaming Gorge Lake, they live near the bottom for most of the year. They are mostly solitary except during the spawning season.

MANAGEMENT

Optimum habitat includes clear, cold, unpolluted waters. Stocking is a prime requisite for sustaining many lake trout populations. Where there is both summer and winter fishing, monitoring numbers of trophy fish present and caught may be required. Management options for the Flaming Gorge Lake population, which receives the greatest fishing pressure of any in Utah, include: (1) yearly creel limit of fish over a given size; (2) closed season either in time or place or both; (3) certain tackle restrictions or banishment; (4) slot limits protecting a particular size range; or (5) any combination of the above. Management practices have long included the use of hatcheries for artificial propagation. Young fish are reared to fingerling or yearling stages before they are released.

In Lake Tahoe *Mysis* may affect the numbers of large lake trout caught because the trout feed on *Mysis* rather than fish, thus potentially decreasing growth rates. Management options in ecosystems containing lake trout should be carefully reviewed prior to introduction of *Mysis*.

Statement of Utah Division of Wildlife Resources

Lake trout fisheries presently occur in only three lakes in Utah: Flaming Gorge Lake, Bear Lake, and Fish Lake. Although lake trout have been stocked in a number of other lakes, including some smaller lakes at high elevations, no other viable population exists. It is unlikely that attempts will be made to further expand the range of the lake trout.

Lake trout are presently established and self-sustaining in Flaming Gorge Lake and partially so in Fish Lake, but are completely supported by stocking in Bear Lake, where there is no evidence of reproduction. Stocking occurs in Fish Lake on an alternate year basis.

Lake trout's primary attributes include its large size. All three populations routinely produce trophy-sized fish above 20 lb (9 kg), with fish over 50 lb (23 kg) recorded at Flaming Gorge. These populations exist at the very southern edge of North American lake trout range. Warm average temperatures, particularly in the surface waters, lead to fast growth rates and large size in a relatively short time. Lake trout are highly popular as a trophy fish, popular to the point that there has been some concern over low population levels. A slot limit was experimentally imposed in Flaming Gorge Lake in 1989 to reduce pressure on intermediate-size fish.

One concern over lake trout is their voracious predatory nature and their ability to decimate forage bases. Idaho, for example, has documented a number of cases where reproducing lake trout populations have nearly eliminated kokanee. Recent declines in populations of nongame fish in Flaming Gorge Lake are of particular concern. These declines may be the result of lake trout and/or smallmouth bass predation, but regardless of the cause, the major decline in forage base would undoubtedly negatively impact the trophy lake trout fishery. Studies are under way to determine whether the forage fish production in the upper, more productive end of the reservoir will be sufficient to maintain the quality lake trout fishery or whether management must be undertaken to reduce lake trout recruitment.

Lake trout in Bear Lake are stocked and managed only as an element of diversity in a cutthroat fishery and because the 50-year history has shown no negative impact. The lake trout are popular with a specific clientele at Bear Lake and traditionally the largest fish coming out of Bear Lake are lake trout. Studies are under way there, however, to see how far the fish size of the native Bear Lake Bonneville cutthroat population can be increased. Concern exists whether the forage base in Bear Lake is able to sustain both an expanded cutthroat population and a large lake trout population. Because the native cutthroat is the primary focus on Bear Lake, it is conceivable that stocking lake trout should be reduced. The fact that forage fish in Bear Lake are all endemic whitefishes or sculpin makes this concern a high priority.

The lake trout population at Fish Lake has persisted for many decades and it is not certain at this time that the extensive stocking over the years has actually contributed to the fishery. Present evidence suggests that a significant amount of natural recruitment is taking place and stocking may not be necessary. A number of changes in the fishery at Fish Lake are taking place and investigations are under way.

Arctic grayling, *Thymallus arcticus* (Pallas)
Plate 36

Etymology: *Thymallus* = thymelike, an old name for grayling, because of its odor; *arcticus* = of the arctic
Nomenclature: *Salmo arcticus* Pallas 1776, *Thymallus Pallasii* Dall 1870, *Thymallus arcticus* (Pallas) Scott 1958, Walters 1955

IMPORTANCE

Arctic grayling are valued as a sport fish for their prestige and beauty; most people have never seen a grayling. In some remote areas of Alaska they make a substantial contribution to subsistence fishing (Wynne-Edwards 1952; Morrow 1980). They are not very important as a sport fish in Utah because of limited distribution and remoteness of populations.

DESCRIPTION

Original

Salmo (Truttac.) *arcticus*

Longitudo digitalis; *forma* Thymalli iunioris. *Caput* vix compressum, fronte plana, rugis tribus longitudinalibus porcata. *Rostrum* rotundatum, simulum, maxillis subaequalibus. *Irides* argenteae. *Corpus* microlepidotum, argentatum, punctis lineolisue fuscis, per quatuor utrinque series digestis. *Radii* membranae branch. 9. pinn. pectoralium 16. ani 10. dorsalis 18. *Cauda* bifurca. In rivulis saxosis iugi arctici frequentissima species.

Translation

Arctic Salmon.

Length: a finger's. Shape: of a young Thymallus.

Head: somewhat narrow with a smooth front, marked with three longitudinal wrinkles.

Snout: rounded-off, blunt, with underslung jaws. Silver scales. Body: small scales, silver, with dark spots or lines, distributed along four rows on either side. Rays of the gill membranes, 9; of the pectoral fins, 16; of the anal fins, 10; of the dorsal fin, 18. Tail: 2 pronged. Species found most frequently in the rocky rivers of arctic mountain summits.

Contemporary

Silvery to light purple colors on the sides and bluish white on the belly are the distinctive colors of grayling. They are relatively slender and are most easily distinguished by their characteristic long, high, brilliantly colored (bright purple), sail-like dorsal fin. The upper margin of the dorsal has gray and rose bands and is green with pink or red spots. The pectoral fins are blue and intermixed with pink at the tip. A black slash, similar to the red slash of a cutthroat trout, runs along its chin. The grayling dorsal fin has 17 to 25 rays and its pelvic fins have 10 or 11 rays. They have an adipose fin. The cycloid scales number between 77 and 103 in the lateral series and are large pored. The head is average; the mouth small with sparse teeth on the jaws, prevomer, and palatines. The caudal fin is well forked (Scott and Crossman 1973).

RANGE

In Utah, Arctic grayling are present in Blind, Navajo, Lockawaxen, Caroly, Round, Sand, and Blue lakes. They are also in Red Creek, Big Ells, and Labaron reservoirs. This species is native across eastern Siberia and over much of North America to Hudson Bay and south to Michigan, Montana, and British Columbia. Originally four isolated stocks in America were considered separate species. Walters (1955) considered *Thymallus arcticus* to be the only valid species.

SIZE AND LONGEVITY

Grayling are slow growing and moderate to short lived. Most live less than 6 years, but a few live as long as 10 (Brown 1971). Yearly length for grayling ages 1 to 6 in Yellowstone National Park is: in inches, 3.5, 8, 11, 13, 14.5, and 15.5; in mm, 89, 203, 279, 330, 368, 394 (Varley and Schullery 1983). In Red Rock Creek, Montana, fish ages 1 to 6 grow as follows: in inches, 6.1, 11.1, 13.5, 14.7, 15.6, 16.0; in mm, 155, 282, 343, 373, 396, 406 (Nelson 1954). The average size is about 1 lb (0.45 kg) although fish in many populations are smaller. The average length of various age classes in the Lobdell Lake, California, population, sampled in 1980, was: young-of-year fish, 3.4 in. (86 mm); 1-year-old fish, 12 in. (305 mm); and 3-year-old fish, 14.6 in. (371 mm) (Reiber 1983).

The world all-tackle, hook-and-line record grayling caught in the Katseyedie River, NWT, Canada, weighed 5 lb, 15 oz (2.7 kg)(Fishing Hall of Fame 1993). The Utah record grayling, caught in the Uinta primitive area, weighed 1 lb, 1/2 oz (0.47 kg).

Food and Feeding

Much of the diet of stream-dwelling grayling is drift insect larvae, pupae, and adults. They also feed on cladocerans and terrestrial insects. Grayling are primarily surface to mid-depth drift feeders; they do not feed on the bottom except in the fall when drift is reduced. They occasionally eat fishes (Morrow 1980). Fry begin searching for food when they are about one week old. The yolk sac food supply of grayling is utilized more rapidly than that of trout, explaining why they begin feeding earlier in life than do trout. Brown (1971) stated that aquatic insects and crustaceans form the bulk of the diet and that grayling are extremely voracious, feeding without caution. Their lack of caution when feeding was observed in Red Rock National Wildlife Refuge, Montana.

Limiting Factors

Grayling suffer readily from habitat degradation. The stream form is listed as threatened. They do not compete well with other fish. A marked decline in the grayling population in Upper Granite Lake, Washington, was noted after cutthroat trout were planted. Grayling, being easy to catch, may be overfished. The amount of adequate spawning space limits population size because the aggressive territoriality of the male limits the number of spawners at any one area (Eschmeyer and Scott 1983). They are easy prey for birds as they appear to be fearless.

Breeding Habits

Spawning in Alaska takes place from mid-May to June at 37° to 50°F (2.8° to 10°C) following ice breakup (Morrow 1980). Further south, spawning may commence in March. In Alaska, grayling begin to congregate at the mouths of clearwater tributaries and start upstream in channels cut through the ice by surface runoff. As soon as the stream is open, fish move upstream to the spawning grounds. This movement may be a 100-mi-long (161-km) migration (Morrow 1980). At Grebe Lake in Yellowstone National Park, grayling generally begin spawning the day after the ice goes off; spawning migration is only a short distance. During spawning activity, they tend to be oblivious to and ignore danger (Varley and Schullery 1983).

Grayling usually reach sexual maturity in 2, 3, or rarely 4 years. A 1-lb (0.4-kg) female produces about 5,000 to 7,000 eggs, a 2-lb (0.9-kg) one may have as many as 12,000 (Brown 1971). A male establishes a territory and defends it against other males by threat posturing. He may erect his dorsal fin, open his mouth, and assume a rigid posture. Persistent intruders are driven off. Rarely are females attacked. The male courts the female with dorsal fin display. He next drifts beside her and pulls his dorsal fin over her back. Both fish arch their bodies and vibrate. The female releases eggs and the male releases milt at the same time. The adhesive eggs stick to particles of sand or gravel. In 52°F (11.1°C) water the eggs hatch in 17 days (Varley and Schullery

1983). No redd is constructed (Morrow 1980) nor are eggs or young guarded. The orange-colored eggs are about 0.09 in. (2.2 mm) in diameter before water hardening. Young have been described as "two eyeballs on a thread."

The grayling run, of shorter duration than that of trout, is complete in 2 or 3 days to a week. In Yellowstone National Park, grayling fry begin their migration from the stream to the lake between 7 and 10 P.M. (Varley and Schullery 1983). In Lobdell Lake, California, grayling have been observed spawning in the lake inlet stream (Reiber 1983).

Grayling show no particular preference for substrate when spawning, although sandy gravel with overhead cover seems to be used most often, possibly due to its abundance.

Habitat

Grayling prefer water temperatures from 46° to 50°F (7.8° to 10°C) for spawning, but live in warmer waters at other times. They prefer clear, very cold streams with stretches of bottom that have abundant plant life. There appears to be an exception to this. A number of grayling released from the Utah Division of Wildlife Fisheries Experiment Station hatchery at Logan migrated down a ditch to the Logan River, then several miles upstream, where the river is cool to warm and turbid.

Grayling may live in lakes but are more of a stream fish. Lakes that have as much as 50 percent of the bottom covered by vegetation generally have successful populations. They form large schools. In streams grayling stay in the open, often in plain sight even when approached. In the fall, grayling leave the tributaries and overwinter in lakes or deep stream pools.

Management

Grayling require an unusual amount of protection where fishing pressure is heavy. They have been reported as difficult to raise, and relatively few attempts have been made to carry them to maturity. However, in hatcheries, grayling are more docile during spawning than trout, they are not afraid of people, and the eggs can be taken easily (Ron Goede, personal communication, 1986). Stocking should be in waters where there is minimum or no competition from other fishes. Additional stream cover (artificial or natural) may provide visual isolation for territorial males and thereby increase spawning (Sigler and Sigler 1987). Although they are not well known, or often seen, grayling are highly regarded and, in some locations, provide an additional sportfishery.

CHAPTER 9 Atheriniformes

Species of this order have two dorsal fins; the first has weak but true spines. When present, the pelvic fins are small. Scales may be either cycloid or ctenoid. When present, the lateral line is poorly developed. The members of this order range in size from moderate-size marine fishes to small, freshwater, livebearers (Bond 1979). In Utah there are three species, in three genera, representing two families.

Killifishes (Family Cyprinodontidae)

Killifishes resemble minnows in having soft-rayed fins, abdominal pelvic fins, and cycloid scales, but minnows and killifishes are not closely related. Killifishes have a rounded or squared caudal fin, toothed jaws, and scales on the head; these characteristics distinguish them from minnows.

In general, cyprinodontoids live no longer than a year, with a few individuals surviving to two or more years of age. This limit is especially true in captivity. A short life span has both positive and negative aspects with respect to management. Most species can be bred quickly and easily under artificial conditions, and large populations build rapidly. Short life spans make these fishes subject to relatively short-lived perturbations, which may prove disastrous (Minckley, Meffe, and Soltz 1991).

Killifishes are small and highly colorful, 2 to 4 in. (51 to 102 mm) long. The top of the head is flattened, with the mouth opening near or along its upper surface; these adaptations aid feeding at the surface. Killifishes are aggressive, usually with strong sexual dimorphism.

This family is present in cool and tropical regions over most of the world, including Africa, Spain, the Mediterranean area, southern Asia, and the East Indies. None occur in Australia. Various species inhabit salt, brackish, mineralized, and fresh waters. They occur in desolate regions such as Death Valley, California-Nevada, and around the Dead Sea. Some have adapted to temporary ponds, laying eggs that survive in bottom soil after pond water is gone and the adults are dead. These eggs hatch when seasonal rains restore water to the ponds. One of the most remarkable species in this family is the Devil's Hole pupfish. The native population occupies the smallest known range of any vertebrate, approximately 23 sq yd (19 sq m), in Devil's Hole, Death Valley National Monument, California-Nevada (Sigler and Miller 1963; Moyle 1976). Part of the population has recently been transplanted elsewhere.

In the United States and Canada there are 10 genera and 48 species (Robins et al. 1991). In Utah there are 2 species in 2 genera.

---

plains killifish,
Fundulus zebrinus
Jordan and Gilbert

Etymology: *Fundulus* = bottom, with respect to its habitat; *zebrinus* = striped

Nomenclature: *Fundulus zebrinus* Jordan and Gilbert 1883

IMPORTANCE

Plains killifish are not native to Utah. Their effect on native species has not been well documented but is probably negative. They provide limited forage for game fishes.

DESCRIPTION

Original

Body elongate, compressed, subfusiform, the back slightly arched. Head subpyramidal, very much depressed. Eye fore in head. Fins moderate; higher in the males than in the females. Scales smaller than in *F. similis* and more closely imbricated. Olivaceous above, with a blackish spot upon each scale; sides yellowish, with narrow transverse black bands or bars, about 16 in number, more conspicuous in the males than in the females, and extending from the back to the belly; interspaces wider than the dark bars. Fins plain. Sexes similar. Head 3 3/4. D 13. A. 14. L. 3 in. Rio Grande in New Mexico. (Girard) added. Males without sharp markings; scales rough in spring. Females nearly plain.

Contemporary

A dozen or more vertical bars on the sides give rise to one of the common names, "zebra killifish." The bars are narrower on the female than the male. During breeding, males have red to orange color on the sides and lower fins (Sigler and Miller 1963). The body is compressed and slender, the head large. The mouth is almost superior. There are 52 to 70 scales in a series from the head to the base of the caudal fin; there is no lateral line. There are 14 to 16 dorsal and 14 anal fin rays.

RANGE

Plains killifish are native to the Pecos, Brazos, and Colorado rivers of New Mexico and Texas, parts of Wyoming, Montana, and Missouri. In Utah, they occur in Juab County, near Mona Reservoir (Sigler and

Miller 1963; Lee et al. 1980; Randy Radant, personal communication, 1984).

Size and Longevity Plains killifish ordinarily reach lengths of 3 in. (76 mm) or less, although a few may be 6 in. (152 mm). Most adults are between 1.5 and 2 in. (38 and 51 mm) and live 3 years or less.

Food and Feeding Plains killifish are omnivorous. Their superior mouth enables them to feed at the surface. Food is largely surface insects and floating matter although they may feed on the bottom if other food is scarce (Sigler and Miller 1963). Diatoms and other plant material are eaten when invertebrates are scarce (Lee et al. 1980).

Limiting Factors Plains killifish are eaten by predatory fishes and birds. Some populations are parasitized. Rapid or extreme fluctuations of temperature or water levels are detrimental.

Breeding Habits Plains killifish spawn in the summer over sand or gravel in shallow waters. No care is provided eggs or young. Males are not territorial but are aggressive during spawning. A male courts a receptive female by swimming a zig-zag course ahead of her. When a female is attracted, the male moves laterally and spawning occurs (Sigler and Miller 1963; Minckley 1973; Lee et al. 1980).

Habitat Plains killifish generally live in small, shallow, open streams with moderate to slow currents, and in reservoirs, lakes, and springs. Tolerance to alkalinity and salinity is high (Sigler and Miller 1963).

Management Until a positive benefit has been demonstrated for the plains killifish, no extension of range should be contemplated.

---

rainwater killifish, *Lucania parva* (Baird and Girard)

Etymology: *Lucania,* the meaning is obscure, coined by Charles Girard; *parva* = small

Nomenclature: *Cyprinodon parvus* Baird and Girard 1855, *Lucania parva* Greeley 1939, Hubbs and Miller 1965

Importance Rainwater killifish may be important in mosquito control in certain areas. They are kept as pets.

DESCRIPTION

Original

Form elongated, resembling a diminutive *Leuciscus*; head constituting less than a fourth of the total length; eye quite large and circular, being contained three times in the length of the side of the head; caudal posteriorly rounded.—D. 10; A. 10; C. 5. I. 7.6. I.4; V. 6; P. 15. Scales quite large, deeper than long, and disposed in eight longitudinal series upon the line of greatest depth of the body; seven series may be observed upon the peduncle of the tail.

This species was found in the small ponds of the salt meadows, generally in the grass; and owing to their diminutive size the males were not often taken, and, in fact neither sex was found in anything like the abundance of most other species. The colors during life were very plain, being without any of the peculiar patterns of other species. I observed it, sparingly, in many localities in Long Island, especially at Greenport. It has a close resemblance to the females of *Heterandria*.

Contemporary

Rainwater killifish are often confused with the mosquitofish, but the mosquitofish is of chunkier build, without distinctive markings, and the dorsal fin originates well in advance of the anal fin. The dorsal fin of the rainwater killifish has 10 to 12 rays, rarely 9. The anal fin has 9 or 10 rays, 8 or 11 are possible. There are 26 to 28 scales in the lateral series. The upper and lower jaws both have an outer row of well-developed teeth, the inner row may be absent or have only one or two strong teeth in the upper jaw (Sigler and Miller 1963).

Coloration of the back and sides of the rainwater killifish is dark olive to greenish yellow and paler below. Underlying black pigments outline the scales, producing a rhomboidal pattern. Anterior sides of the scales have a bluish silver reflection. There is a dark streak along the midline in advance of the dorsal fin. Breeding males are deep yellow with black markings on the dorsal, anal, and caudal fins; the anal, and pelvic fins are sometimes orange to red and the pectorals yellow.

RANGE

Rainwater killifish have a wide range on the Atlantic slope of North America, from Massachusetts to Tampico, Mexico, and the Rio Grande and Pecos rivers, Texas, and New Mexico (Lee et al. 1980). In Utah they are in Timpie Springs near Timpie, Tooele County, and in Blue Lake on the Utah-Nevada border. They were incidentally introduced into Blue Lake with largemouth bass from the vicinity of Dexter, New Mexico (Sigler and Miller 1963; Hubbs and Miller 1965).

SIZE AND LONGEVITY

Rainwater killifish reach a maximum size of about 2 in. (51 mm); females are larger than males. They live no more than two or, rarely, three years.

Limiting Factors They are limited by predation, chiefly by game fishes, and abrupt changes of habitat.

Food and Feeding Rainwater killifish eat mosquito larvae, copepods, crustaceans, and aquatic insects. Young, when only about 0.5 in. (13 mm) long, feed almost exclusively on mosquito larvae, and larger fish feed to a great extent on crustaceans.

Breeding Habits Sexual maturity is attained at three to five months when the female is about 1 in. (25 mm) long. Spawning takes place in late spring and summer. Females spawn more than once each year. Once breeding begins, males establish a territory near vegetation beds. At this time, they develop a cross-hatched pattern on their sides. They display vigorously to other males holding nearby territories. When a female approaches, the male circles her rapidly. If she is receptive to spawning, she stops and he moves quickly beneath her. In this position they swim to the surface near plants and spawn. Eggs are fertilized upon release. They hatch in about six days at 75°F (23.9°C). Larvae settle to the bottom and begin feeding actively in about a week, after the yolk sac is absorbed. Eggs are about 0.04 in. (1.0 mm) in diameter. As many as 104 have been reported for one female (Sigler and Miller 1963; Foster 1967).

Habitat Rainwater killifish occur in quiet water, especially small pools that are adequately supplied with plants. They may become abundant in their native range. They often inhabit brackish water (Sigler and Miller 1963; Moyle 1976).

Management In their present range in Utah they compete to some extent with young game fishes. They eat mosquito larvae. The overall impact on the environment is probably neutral.

Livebearers (Family Poeciliidae)

Livebearers resemble killifishes in size and general appearance, but bear live young (that is, are viviparous). They are easily distinguished from killifishes by their small, posteriorly placed dorsal fin, and by the presence of embryos rather than eggs in gravid females. Males have a highly specialized anal fin, the gonopodium. It is a rodlike organ used for internal fertilization, that is, guiding spermatozoa into the female. All other fishes living in Utah are oviparous, that is, females produce eggs that are fertilized after leaving the body.

Livebearers are best known for the popular pet species, such as the guppy. The family is present only in North and South America. It ranges from the upper Mississippi valley to Argentina. The greatest number of species occur in Mexico and Central America.

In addition to their value as pet fish, the group is well known for eating mosquitoes. Some species have been used in studying genetics and the production and mode of inheritance of cancer (Sigler and Miller 1963). Twenty species in six genera occur in North America (Robins et al. 1991). Only one species occurs in Utah.

---

mosquitofish,
Gambusia affinis
(Baird and Girard)

Etymology: *Gambusia,* from gambusina, a Cuban word relating to the fact that to fish for gambusia is to fish for nothing; *affinis* = showy, brilliant

Nomenclature: *Heterandria affinis* Baird and Girard 1853a, *Gambusia affinis* Large 1903

IMPORTANCE

Mosquitofish may be used to some extent as a bait and forage fish. *Gambusia* have been stocked throughout the world for mosquito control, particularly in areas where there is malaria. They were used during the building of the Panama Canal for that purpose. They are used extensively in organized mosquito abatement districts and in ornamental pools and small ponds. They are not effective for mosquito control where freshwater marshes are extensive.

DESCRIPTION

Original

Body elongated, subfusiform and compressed. Head forming about one-fifth of the entire length. Body yellowish brown above, orange beneath. Fins unicolor, except the caudal which has 2 narrow bands of black.

D 6. A 8. C 3. I. 7. 6. I. 2. V 5.P 15.

Rio Medina and Rio Salado.

Contemporary

A rounded caudal fin, large scales on the head and body, superior mouth, a posteriorly located dorsal fin originating behind the origin of the anal fin and a modification of the male anal into a spikelike reproductive organ, all serve to identify the mosquitofish. The dorsal fin usually has 6 rays, sometimes 7. There are about 30 scales in the lateral series. A true lateral line is lacking.

Coloration is olive or dull silvery, darkest on the head and back and lightest on the belly. Scales are outlined by dark pigment. There are usually several rows of black spots across the caudal fin that are more prominent in females than males. There may be a wedge-shaped bar below the eye and a very narrow dark line running along the mid-side from the head to the base of the caudal fin. Pregnant females are potbellied and have a black spot just above the anus (Sigler and Miller 1963).

Range

Mosquitofish are native to parts of the United States from southern Illinois and southern Indiana to Alabama and the Rio Grande River, Texas (Lee et al. 1980). In Utah they are established in warm springs and littoral zones of ponds in the Bonneville Basin.

Size and Longevity

Female mosquitofish are larger than males because they continue to grow throughout their life. Males do not grow after reaching maturity, usually at 4 to 6 weeks of age. Males are not more than 1.75 in. (45 mm) long, but large females may be 2.5 in. (64 mm) or more. Newborn young are little more than 0.33 in. (8 mm) and are able to fend for themselves at birth. Most fish die the same year they reach maturity, although a few live 15 months or more.

Food and Feeding

In addition to mosquito larvae, the preferred food, mosquitofish feed chiefly on other small invertebrates, such as crustaceans and insects. They turn to diatoms and algae when other food is absent. They also feed on small fishes. They live and feed at or near the surface, rarely invading deep water (Harrington and Harrington 1961; Sigler and Miller 1963). Diet is about the same throughout life except that larger fish eat larger items.

Limiting Factors

Mosquitofish cannot tolerate sustained water temperatures much below 40°F (4.4°C), although in northern Utah they live in ponds that frequently form a thin layer of ice in winter. Presumably they are able to find warmer water in springs or adjust to colder water. They are heavily preyed upon by fishes and birds. Meffe (1992) reported on the plasticity of life history characters in eastern mosquitofish when exposed to thermal stress. Both maturation and size can be affected by stress.

Breeding Habits

Mosquitofish reach maturity at a length of 1 in. (25 mm) and an age of 6 weeks. The gestation period is 3 to 4 weeks. Therefore, 3 to 4 generations a year are possible in warm water. The potential for a rapid increase in a mosquitofish population is very high. A large female may give birth to as many as 315 young, the number usually increasing with the size of the fish (Krumholtz 1948), but the number may decrease in older females.

Courtship and copulation are constant among mosquitofish for most of the summer. The male swims in front of the female, orienting his body at a 90 angle to hers, partially folds his dorsal and anal fins over her, bends his body into an S, then quickly swims around behind the female and attempts to insert his gonopodium into the female's genital opening (Sigler and Sigler 1987). Receptive females are quickly surrounded by males. A female that has previously been bred tends to be nonreceptive but will breed again as little as 30 minutes after giving birth (Itzkowitz 1971). In the wild many attempts at copulation fail because the female is nonreceptive.

HABITAT

This warmwater (58° to 82°F [14.4° to 27.7°C]) species inhabits lakes, rivers, creeks, ponds, springs, and ditches, anywhere there is quiet, shallow water and dense vegetation. In a spring-fed pond in southeastern Idaho, an artesian well had a temperature of 120°F (48.9°C) in the center of the pond and 108°F (42.2°C) in a band about 4 ft (1.2 m) wide around the edge. Mosquitofish were living and prospering in the 108°F water. When they were caught and tossed out into the center of the pool they died instantly. However, it has been demonstrated that mosquitofish can be acclimated to fairly severe climates. They are not inhibited by low oxygen levels since they skim along just at the surface, using the very thin layer of surface water oxygen. A population of mosquitofish was observed in a dump in Logan. The puddle in which the mosquitofish were evidently reproducing was 3.5 ft (1.1 m) across, 10 to 12 in. (25 to 31 cm) deep, and partially covered by a discarded door.

MANAGEMENT

Mosquitofish need little protection in heavily vegetated, warm water with an abundance of food, but they cannot survive heavy predation in open water. It is doubtful that they should be protected in Utah waters.

CHAPTER 10 Scorpaeniformes

This order contains 20 families with 269 genera and about 1,160 species. The arrangement of families and family boundaries in this order, and, indeed, the classification and placement of the order itself, is very provisional and subject to much debate and discussion (Nelson 1984).

Sculpins (Family Cottidae)

Sculpins are distinguished by large flattened heads, fanlike pectoral fins, and an absence of true scales. The ctenii or hooks, remnants of ctenoid scales, remain in some species as patches of prickles. They have two dorsal fins, the first composed of feeble dorsal spines. The anal fin lacks spines, but the thoracicly placed pelvic fins have one imbedded spine and three or four soft rays. The body tapers from the head to a relatively narrow caudal peduncle. The skull is low, generally broad, and composed of thin bones. The preopercular bone is often variously armed with spines; the eyes are in a dorsal position, high on the head and prominent. The jaws are strong with well-developed teeth. There are five to seven branchiostegal rays. Most members of this large and diverse family are bottom-dwelling marine fishes, but sculpins of the genus *Cottus* have invaded fresh water and there are numerous species, especially in the northwestern United States. Fresh water sculpins are small, generally 7 in. (178 mm) or less, but some marine species reach a length of 24 in. (610 mm) or more. They have existed from the Oligocene epoch to the Recent. There are 111 species in 36 genera in North America (Robins et al. 1991). Only 1 genus and 3 species occur in Utah.

---

mottled sculpin,
Cottus bairdi Girard
Plate 37

Etymology: *Cottus,* an old European name for the European sculpin *C. gobio; bairdi,* for the first U.S. Fish Commissioner, S. F. Baird
Nomenclature: *Cottus bairdi* Girard 1850

IMPORTANCE

Mottled sculpin provide food for trout and other coldwater fishes. Their presence is considered an indicator of quality trout waters.

DESCRIPTION

Original

Radii, D. VII–18; A. 13; V. 1–4; first ray of anal below third of second dorsal. Skin prickly above the lateral line, smooth below it posteriorly; body compressed, profile rising rather steeply to the basis of first dorsal fin. Eye 4.5 times in head, 7.5 times in interorbital space. Muzzle contracted, maxillary bone reaching to below middle of pupil. Two spines of preoperculum. On an inferior anterior angle of operculum [sic]. Lateral line discontinued on the last fourth of caudal peduncle. Head one-third length without caudal fin.

Below yellow; dorsal line with a series of black spots; sides with large, dark clouds.

Contemporary

A broad, flattened head, expansive pectoral fins, and scaleless body readily distinguish this bottom-dwelling sculpin from its contemporaries. The first dorsal fin has slender spines. It is joined at the base to the second dorsal. The dorsal spines and the single spine in each pelvic fin are so feeble compared with other spiny-rayed fishes that they pass unnoticed (Sigler and Miller 1963).

The first dorsal fin is bordered with red, brown, or cream color in adults, especially in breeding males. Females rarely show much color, and none exists in young and half-grown fish. The body is olive to slate, barred and spotted. The lower sides may have some green gold color. The caudal fin is more or less randomly speckled, the anal fin darkly speckled and the pectoral fins banded.

RANGE

The native range of the mottled sculpin is discontinuous over a wide area, through North America from the Tennessee River system of Georgia and Alabama to Labrador on the north to west of the Great Lakes Basin. They inhabit parts of the Missouri River and the Columbia River system in southern Canada and the Bonneville system of the Great Basin (Sigler and Miller 1963; Lee et al. 1980). They are present in most coldwater streams throughout Utah.

SIZE AND LONGEVITY

Mottled sculpin may live 5 years and reach a length of 6 in. (152 mm). Adults in the Logan River are between 3 and 4 in. (76 to 102 mm) long.

FOOD AND FEEDING

Food of the mottled sculpin in the Logan River is largely aquatic insects, with plant material and fishes a minor part of the diet. Fish eaten are generally small sculpin. Only three trout eggs had been eaten by 275 sculpin in a Logan River study (Zarbock 1952). In Montana, bottom-dwelling aquatic insects made up almost 100 percent of the diet (Bailey 1952). Larval sculpins use the lateral line to sense food and may also use it to avoid predation.

Limiting Factors

Mottled sculpin require clear, well-oxygenated water. They are preyed upon by fishes, mostly trout, and are parasitized by protozoans, trematodes, cestodes, nematodes, acanthocephalans, mollusks, and crustaceans. Heckmann et al. (1987) reported that seven genera of protozoans and one genus of nematodes parasitize them in Utah.

Breeding Habits

Spawning can occur in either rapid- or slow-moving water during late winter and early spring, generally February to May. As spawning time approaches, the male's head becomes dark colored. He selects a spawning site under a rock or other cover. After suitable courtship, the female enters the nest, deposits her salmon-colored adhesive eggs in a mass on the ceiling of the nest while upside down. She then departs or is driven off by the male. More than one female usually deposits eggs in one nest. The male fertilizes the eggs and guards against predation. He also fans them with his pectoral fins, presumably to keep the eggs supplied with oxygen. At 52° to 55°F (11.1° to 12.8°C) eggs hatch in 9 days. Adult males are larger than females and ripen earlier. An average of 629 eggs per female was observed in Logan River sculpin (Zarbock 1952). Maturity is at age 2 or 3 for both sexes (Sigler and Miller 1963).

Habitat

Preferred summer temperatures for the mottled sculpin vary from 55° to 65°F (12.8° to 18.3°C); for a limited time they can tolerate water over 70°F (21.1°C). They live near vegetation, under stones, and part of the time in moderately swift riffles (Sigler and Miller 1963).

Mottled sculpin seek clear, cool mountain streams with moderate to rapid current. Bottom types typically include coarse gravel, small loose rocks or rubble, but some individuals live over sand, clay, or mud bottoms, and around lake margins.

Management

Mottled sculpin need clear, cold, well-oxygenated water and an abundance of cover. If all cover is removed, predation is heavy.

Paiute sculpin, *Cottus beldingi* Eigenmann and Eigenmann

Etymology: *Cottus*, an old European name for the European sculpin *C. gobio; beldingi,* named after L. Belding
Nomenclature: *Cottus beldingi* Eigenmann and Eigenmann 1891

Importance

Paiute sculpin serve as forage fish within their limited range in Utah.

Description

Original

In October, 1889, Mr. L. Belding obtained three specimens of a species of *Cottus* in Lake Tahoe, California. During June 1890, we obtained a much larger number at the same place. A series of these was sent to the British Museum. The rest are in the collections of the California Academy of Sciences, No. 504. Mr. Belding's specimens are also in the collection of the Academy, No. 702. We also obtained a number from Donner Lake, California, No. 505, California Academy of Sciences.

These specimens represent a variety or species distinct from the Alaskan *Cottus minutus* with which it is most closely related. Head 2 3/4–4; depth 4–5; D.VI.–VIII. 15 1/2–18; A. 11–13; V. I. 4.

Head rather short and broad, the profile convex, more steep from eye forward; eye large, orbit 4–5 in head; interorbital concave, 2 in orbit; mouth large; maxillary reaching at least to below the pupil, about two in the head. Preopercle with a simple, backward-directed spine, very slightly curved upwards. Teeth on jaws and vomer, none on palatines. Skin smooth. Pectorals reaching vent, or further in young; ventrals 1 1/3–2 in head. Distance of anal from caudal 1 1/3 in its distance from snout. Anus nearer insertion of caudal than to end of snout.

Mottled with black and white. About six blackish cross bars on back; the first across head just behind eyes, next at origin of dorsal. First dorsal tinged with rust, the second less so. All the fins except the ventrals spotted with dark. The ground color varies greatly with the bottom over which these fishes live.

Contemporary

The head of the Paiute sculpin is typical of the genus—moderately robust with the preopercle having a single spine. The large mouth has much reduced or absent palatine teeth. The lateral line may be incomplete. There are no prickles on the body. The dorsal fin has 15 to 18 rays, the anal fin 11 to 13, the caudal is rounded; fins are flecked with black (Simpson and Wallace 1978). The body of the Paiute sculpin is heavily mottled with 5 to 7 crossbars on the back and may also have lateral banding. Color is brown to nearly black on the back and upper sides but somewhat paler below.

Range

Paiute sculpin are the only native sculpin found in the Lahontan system of California and Nevada, including Lake Tahoe and tributaries. They are also native in portions of the Columbia River drainage in Oregon and Washington, the Bear River of the Bonneville system in

Utah, Wyoming, and Idaho, and the upper Colorado system in Colorado (Lee et al. 1980).

Size and Longevity

A short life and slow growth rate are characteristic of Paiute sculpin. Fish from Lake Tahoe and Sagehen Creek, California, grow at about the same rate. Their yearly length for fish age 1 to 4 years is: in inches, 2.1, 2.7, 3.3, and 3.7; in mm, 53.3, 69, 84, 94. The largest sculpin recorded from Lake Tahoe is 5 in. (127 mm). Sculpin of this size are rare and generally males (Miller 1951; Ebert and Summerfelt 1969).

Food and Feeding

As with most fish, the diet of the Paiute sculpin varies with availability. They feed year round but reduce feeding in winter water temperatures. There is little or no evidence of Paiute sculpin preying on trout eggs.

Ambushing bottom dwellers is a principal feeding mechanism of the Paiute sculpin. When a prey organism moves within range of a largely concealed sculpin, it lunges out and engulfs the prey. Sculpins forage at night. In Sagehen Creek, California, 63 percent of the sculpin's diet by volume is aquatic insect larvae, especially mayflies, stoneflies, and caddisflies. The remainder of the diet consists of miscellaneous bottom organisms such as snails, water mites, aquatic beetles, and algae. In Lake Tahoe 65 percent of the Paiute sculpin diet is bottom organisms, mainly midge larvae. Snails are the most commonly taken food at depths of 100 to 200 ft (30 to 61 m), and oligochaetes are the most abundant food for sculpin feeding in still deeper water (Miller 1951; Ebert and Summerfelt 1969).

Limiting Factors

Degraded habitat that adversely affects reproduction limits Paiute sculpin populations. Some populations suffer from excessive predation.

Breeding Habits

Paiute sculpin in Lake Tahoe, California-Nevada, spawn in the spring in shallow, wind-swept shore waters near the mouths of streams. Females lay eggs in clusters on the underside of rocks that are tended and defended by a male. They select crevices under rocks that are located on gravel bottoms. Some spawning in deep water in lakes may take place. In streams most spawning sites are located in riffles. The number of eggs in each nest is usually 100 to 200, indicating that multiple spawning is not common. Maturity is generally at age 2. After the half-inch (12.7 mm) fry are hatched, they drop into the gravel and remain there for 1 or 2 weeks until the yolk sac is absorbed (Miller 1951; Ebert and Summerfelt 1969).

Habitat

Bottoms of rubble and gravel are the preferred habitats of Paiute sculpin, although it is not unusual to find them living on other substrates. The typical stream habitat is rocky riffles with clear, cold water.

They are associated with trout. The Paiute sculpin spends daylight hours in hiding and comparative inactivity. There is no evidence of territoriality or schooling. There are two pronounced times of drift of young sculpin, one immediately following yolk sac absorption, and the other in slightly larger individuals about two weeks later. Young move off the bottom into the currents and drift downstream, presumably populating new areas (Miller 1951).

MANAGEMENT

Paiute sculpin need a stable, unpolluted habitat, including spawning areas.

Bear Lake sculpin, *Cottus extensus* Bailey and Bond
Plate 38

Etymology: *Cottus,* an old European name for the European sculpin *C. gobio; extensus,* referring to the slender form of this species
Nomenclature: *Cottus extensus* Bailey and Bond 1963

IMPORTANCE

Numerically, Bear Lake sculpin are the second most abundant fish in Bear Lake, second only to Bonneville cisco. They are important as a forage fish for large predators such as cutthroat trout and lake trout.

DESCRIPTION

Original

A species of the *bairdi* species group with exposed palatine teeth in a band of moderate length and two to four rows wide; preopercle with three sharp spines and an obtusely pointed or blunt knob, the principal spine almost straight and directed backward and slightly upward, the one below directed downward and backward. Fin rays: Dorsal (VI) VII or VIII, 16–19; anal 13–15 (16); pectoral 15–17 (18); pelvic I,4 (occasionally I,3). Body very slender, greatest depth 15.4 to 21.1 percent of standard length and depth of caudal peduncle (6.1) 6.5 to 7.5 (8.1) percent of standard length; head rather short (27.4) 29 to 32 (33.3) percent of standard length; lateral line straight, incomplete, typically terminates below dorsal soft ray 13 to 18, with 22 to 31 pores; no median chin pore; postmaxillary pore present; prickles well developed on dorsum and side, often as far back as caudal peduncle; breast and belly naked; body almost uniform tan or brownish above, lighter below, a few large blotches sometimes visible on side, dorsal saddles obsolete; standard length to 109 mm (total length 130 mm).

Distinguishable from *echinatus* by the naked breast and belly, smaller head, and more slender body. Separable from *bairdi* by the more slender body, smaller head, plain coloration, the more general distribution of prickles, the backward projection of the second preopercular spine, and the more numerous vertebrae, pectoral rays and anal rays.

Additional Characters. Counts and measurements of the holotype are given in Table One [omitted]. The mouth is large, nearly horizontal; the maxilla extends to below middle of pupil; the lower lip hides the upper as viewed from below; the exposed part of the maxilla is slender. The interorbital space is narrow and slightly concave; the head is broadest just behind the preopercle, tapering forward to the rounded snout. The eyes are placed in the anterior half of head, and there is a median concavity posterior to the orbits. The top of the head is rough. Palatine teeth are consistently well developed and exposed.

Preoperculomandibular pores number 11–11; infraorbital pores variable, from 8–9 to 10–10. The dorsal fins are usually narrowly separated but are often slightly conjoined, rather broadly so in the holotype. Depressed pectoral fin reaching at least to origin of anal; pelvic reaching more than two-thirds way from origin to anus, sometimes reaching anus in juveniles. Caudal vertebrae, counted from dissected specimens, are 22 in one, 23 in five. Total vertebrae, counted from skiagraphs are 33 in four, 34 in 23. Pyloric caeca three in eight specimens, four in one.

The pigmentation is almost uniform, the overall tone light to medium brown with underparts light. In adults there is usually no concentration of melanophores to form dorsal or lateral blotches, although one to three small, diffuse blotches may be present at the caudal base. In small juveniles, from four to six faintly defined dorsal saddles may be discerned, and there may be one or two series of diffuse lateral spots, those on the ventrolateral surface being most evident since they contrast with the lighter background. The melanophores of the upper parts are more or less gradually on the ventrolateral surface and the lower surface is devoid of pigment except that the lower jaw is uniformly dusky and the rest of the lower surface of the head may be dusted with melanophores. The base of the first dorsal is dusky and there are some melanophores along the rays; usually there are no pronounced dark markings, but loose aggregations of melanophores form diffuse anterior and posterior blotches in breeding males. The soft dorsal and pectoral fins have clumps of melanophores that are aligned to form vague, weak bands. The caudal sometimes has similar faint cross bands, and it has several dusky spots on the simple and procurrent rays, both above and below. The pelvic and anal are clear, with only a few scattered melanophores.

Contemporary
Coloration of the Bear Lake sculpin is tan or brown above, light below, sometimes with a few large splotches visible on the sides. The body, although somewhat more slim, has the general shape of other sculpins. The lateral line is straight and incomplete; it terminates below the dorsal fin. This sculpin has no true scales, but has prickles, remnants of ctenoid scales, which are well developed on the upper part of the body and sides. The short head is 29 to 32 percent of the standard length.

The preopercle has three spines, the principal one directed backward and slightly upward. The middle spine is directed downward and backward. The dorsal fin is in two parts: the first short and spiny, the second with 16 to 19 rays. The anal fin has 13 rays, the pectorals 16. The caudal fin is rounded (Bailey and Bond 1963).

RANGE

The Bear Lake sculpin is native (endemic) to Bear Lake. They have been planted in Flaming Gorge Lake on the Green River. Their fate there is unknown.

SIZE AND LONGEVITY

A sample of 120 Bear Lake sculpin taken in gill nets averaged 3 in. (76 mm) in length. They probably live 4 to 5 years and grow at about the same rate as the Paiute sculpin.

FOOD AND FEEDING

Bear Lake sculpin eat primarily the dominant bottom-dwelling zooplankton and midge larvae. In one study, 330 sculpin stomachs contained 59 percent ostracods by weight and 39 percent adult cyclopoid copepods by weight. Although juvenile fish had a pronounced daily vertical migration, moving into the water column at dusk and returning to the bottom at dawn, they did not feed while in the water column. Sculpin fed only when they were on the bottom, and stomach fullness peaked just prior to the dusk ascent. Movement into the warmer midcolumn water is evidently an adaptation to assist and speed digestion (Wurtsbaugh and Nevermann 1988).

LIMITING FACTORS

Water quality changes (degradation) in Bear Lake, or a drop in water levels so that the best spawning and daytime cover habitat are exposed adversely, impact the Bear Lake sculpin. They are preyed on heavily by cutthroat trout and lake trout.

BREEDING HABITS

Temperature for initiation of spawning for Bear Lake sculpin is 40°F (4.4°C). Spawning takes place in late winter to early spring, April to May, and near shore. They lay their eggs on the underside of rocks. Spawning behavior is similar to the Paiute and mottled sculpins. When water levels drop to where there is no rocky cover, spawning success is probably minimal. After spawning they migrate to deeper water.

HABITAT

Bear Lake sculpin move into shallower water in late winter to spring to spawn, and some live there year-round. Others live in water from 50 to 175 ft (15 to 53 m) deep. This is an area of few plants (*Chara*) and no cover other than the soft marl bottom. In deep water they partially bury themselves in the soft marl for cover (Workman 1963; Dalton et al. 1965). Wurtsbaugh and Nevermann (1988) found that Bear Lake sculpin spend the daylight hours on or near the bottom, ascend into the warmer water column at dusk, and return to the bottom at dawn.

MANAGEMENT

Suitable water quality and water levels high enough to cover the rocks and rubble for spawning are the principal needs for these sculpin. They can survive in the deep-water marl bottom, but without some type of inshore cover, it is doubtful they can spawn with any degree of success.

CHAPTER 11

Perciformes

This largest of all orders of fishes has at least 135 families and more than 6,000 species (Robins et al. 1991). In Utah there are 7 genera and 12 species in 3 families. These perchlike fishes vary widely in shape, size, and habitat. They are typical spiny-rayed, bony fishes. The elongate skull is heavily ossified with strong jaws and generally well-developed teeth. There are usually 2 dorsal fins: the first spiny, the second soft. The caudal fin has no more than 17 rays. The pectoral fins are high, the soft-rayed anal is preceded by 2 or 3 spines; the pelvics are thoracic or jugular. Their swim bladder is physoclistic, and they typically have ctenoid scales. Usually marine, they have representatives in fresh waters of all continents except Australia. They date to the upper Cretaceous (Scott and Crossman 1973; Bond 1979).

Temperate Basses (Family Percichthyidae)

Temperate basses have spines in the dorsal, anal, and pelvic fins; the latter lie beneath the pectoral fins and have a single sharp spine followed by five soft rays. The scales are ctenoid. They have branchiostegal rays. There is a stout spine on the opercle. These are laterally compressed, deep-bodied fishes with well-developed jaws armed with numerous teeth. Eight species in four genera represent this family. Two introduced species (one genera) are present in Utah.

---

white bass,
Morone chrysops
(Rafinesque)
Plate 39

Etymology: *Morone,* an unexplained fish name; *Roccus*, an earlier name means rock; *chrysops* = golden eye, although it may not be conspicuous

Nomenclature: *Perca chrysops* Rafinesque 1820a, *Roccus chrysops* Nelson 1876, *Lepibema chrysops* Hubbs 1926, *Morone chrysops* Whitehead and Wheeler 1967

IMPORTANCE

White bass are fast growing. They thrive in both deep impoundments and shallow lakes. When they are in large schools, anglers find it relatively easy to catch more than one, provided they quickly retrieve the catch and then cast into the school before it moves beyond range. The fish fight strongly when hooked and have good table qualities. In areas where there is an abundance of small fishes, white bass may be able to convert them to a large poundage of sport fish. Medium to large white bass are popular with fishermen of all ages (Sigler and Miller 1963). Stunted populations are unacceptable to most anglers.

DESCRIPTION

Original

2nd Species. GOLDEN-EYE PERCH. *Perca chrysops*. Percho oeuil-d'or.

Upper jaw longer, 1 spine on the opercle, body oblong, breadth one fourth length, silvery with 5 longitudinal brownish stripes on each side, head brown above: lateral line diagonal and straight; first dorsal fin with eight rays, the second has 14, whereof one is spiny, tail forked, roseate, tip brown, base scaly.

Vulgar names Rock fish, Rock bass, Rock perch, Gold eyes, Striped bass, & c. It is commonly mistaken for the Rock fish or Striped bass of the Atlantic Ocean, the *Perca Mitchelli* of Dr. Mitchell (Trans. of the Philos. Society of New York, Vol. 1. page 413, tab. 3. fig. 4), to which it is certainly greatly similar; but it differs from it, by the single spine of the opercule, the shape of the lateral line, the less number of stripes, the scaly tail & c. It is not very common in the Ohio, and is hardly ever seen at Pittsburgh, being more common in the lower parts of the river, where it frequents the falls, ripples, and rocky shores. Its usual size is about one foot. It is very good to eat. It bites at the hook. The mouth is large with very small teeth, the 3 pieces of the gill cover are slightly serrate and crenulate. The eyes are large black with a large golden iris. The lateral line begins at the corner of the opercule and does not follow the curve of the back, the stripes are parallel with it and only 2 of them reach the tail. The branchial membrane has 6 rays; the spine of the opercule is not terminal. The dorsal fins are rufous and quite separate, the 2 first rays of the first are shorter, the second is brown posteriorly and diagonally, its base is scaly and such is also the base of the anal fins, which has similar colours, and 15 rays, whereof 3 are spiny. Pectoral fins with 16 rays. Thoracic fins incarnate with 6 rays, whereof one is spiny.

It will appear that this fish differs so widely from the foregoing, as to be hardly reducible to the same genus, but its great similarity with the *Perca Mitchelli* has compelled me to retain it in this genus, notwithstanding many peculiar characters. I shall however venture to propose a new subgenus or section in the genus *Perca* for this fish, to which the *P. Mitchelli*, may perhaps be found to belong. It may be called *Lepibema* and distinguished by the scaly bases of the caudal, anal, and second dorsal fins, this last with some spiny rays, and all the 3 parts of the gill cover with more or less serrulate, besides the small teeth.

Contemporary
White bass have a silvery color overall. Coloration on the back is gray or dark green, with silvery sides and white belly. They have five to seven often discontinuous, but generally unbroken, longitudinal stripes on each side. The yellow tint of the eye may be difficult to see in many individuals. Gill rakers are usually stiff and armed with teeth (Pflieger 1975). Psuedobranchiae are large and conspicuous. There are 11 to 12 anal fin rays. Scales are ctenoid; the mouth is moderately large with conical teeth in bands on the jaws; the lower jaw extends beyond the upper jaw. The dorsal fins are definitely separated.

RANGE

The original range of the white bass is from Minnesota, Wisconsin, and Michigan south in the Mississippi drainage to the gulf states of Alabama, Mississippi, and part of Texas. Originally one of the greatest concentrations was in the Great Lakes, primarily Lake Erie (Lee et al. 1980). They have been introduced widely in the United States. Some of the densest populations today are in impoundments in Texas, Oklahoma, and other south-central states. In Utah, the most concentrated population is in Utah Lake, where the white bass literally dominates all other fishes. It is present in the Jordan, Provo, Spanish Fork, and Sevier rivers, Benjamin Creek, Gunnison Bend, and other reservoirs.

SIZE AND LONGEVITY

White bass are fast-growing and relatively short lived fish in the southern portion of their range; in the northern portion, they grow slower and live longer. In northern Iowa, the yearly size for fish age 1 to 8 is: in inches, 5.2, 9.7, 12.8, 14.6, 15.3, 15.8, 16.0, 16.6; in mm, 132, 246, 325, 371, 389, 401, 406, 422. In northern Iowa, 7- and 8-year-old fish are not uncommon (Sigler 1949). They weigh 0.5 lb (0.2 kg) when 10 in. (254 mm) long, 1 lb (0.45 kg) when 13 in. (330 mm) long, and 2 lb (0.9 kg) when 16 in. (406 mm) long. Generally females weigh slightly more than males at the same length, and they grow somewhat faster. In Spirit Lake, Iowa, the growing season starts in late May and continues to the middle of October. A high percentage of the growth occurs from June to late July or early August, when juvenile yellow perch are most abundant. When the population of small perch has been reduced, by as much as 90 to 95 percent, the rate of growth of white bass drops sharply (Sigler 1949). In Oneida Lake, New York, bass live as long as 9 years and reach a length of 17.4 in. (442 mm).

The world record all-tackle, hook-and-line white bass weighed 6 lb, 13 oz (3.1 kg) (IGFA 1993). The Utah record is 4 lb, 1 oz (1.8 kg) from Utah Lake.

Food and Feeding

White bass are carnivores. Juvenile fish feed on small crustaceans, insect larvae, and small fishes. The preferred food of adult white bass is fishes; insects and crustaceans are second choice. However, they switch easily to invertebrates when fishes are scarce. Vertebrate animals other than fishes are rarely taken. In Spirit Lake, Iowa, most of the insects taken belong to two orders: the true flies (Diptera) and the mayflies (Ephemeroptera). Crustaceans eaten are mostly small individuals. *Leptodora kindti* (a cladoceran) is the most commonly taken invertebrate. This species is so abundant that at times it gives the water a milky appearance (Sigler 1949).

Schools of large white bass, while feeding, often swim with the tip of the dorsal fin out of water. When these schools feed in open water, they may drive small fishes to the surface, where the little fishes can be seen skipping along the surface trying to escape the white bass. Schools at other times swim parallel to shore until they detect small fishes between themselves and shore. They then turn toward shore and drive some of the small fishes into shallow water or sometimes out onto the beach. Large feeding schools are so effective that few small fishes escape. As an indication of how they behave when feeding, on occasion schools were decoyed close inshore by throwing gravel into the water just short of the school and then as they turned and moved shoreward, more gravel was splashed shoreward of them until some of them were so close to shore their backs were partly out of water (Sigler 1949). Adults in lakes often feed close to shore areas where waves are lashing the beach, but the young feed in the quiet waters on the lee side.

Limiting Factors

Eggs and fry of white bass are fed on by minnows, suckers, and other fishes. In Spirit Lake, Iowa, the juveniles are preyed on by largemouth bass, northern pike, and walleye. Neither eggs nor young are provided care. In the southernmost part of their range, life is so short (5 or 6 years) that old age may be considered a limiting factor.

Breeding Habits

Male white bass move into the spawning area much earlier than females. Males have been observed performing the spawning ritual with each other. A seine haul early in the spawning season usually nets only males.

In northern Iowa, most white bass mature in their second year of life, a few in the third year, none the first year. They spawn in the spring when water temperatures reach approximately 62°F (range, 58° to 66°F) (16°C, range 14.4° to 18.9°C). Preferred spawning sites are over sandy to rocky shoal areas in lakes, in the vicinity of running water, or in streams. In Spirit Lake, Iowa, they spawn at the inlet in water 3 to 4 ft (0.9 to 1.22 m) deep or in deeper water away from the inlet. They spawn in daylight with little or no fear of humans. White bass spawn in large schools, with no tendency to establish territories. They are definitely big-water fish, a fact demonstrated by their lack of reproduction in small ponds. An absolute figure has not been established but it is has been suggested that lakes of less than 300 to 500 acres (121–202 ha) may be too small for white bass reproduction (Sigler and Miller 1963).

A female may produce from 240,000 to 933,000 adhesive eggs, each measuring about 0.03 in. (0.76 mm). Eggs are distributed at random over the bottom. No parental care is given eggs or young. Eggs hatch in 45 hours at 62°F (16.7°C).

HABITAT

Large streams, lakes, and impoundments are habitats where white bass prosper. An example of this is the large population in Lake Erie and the almost explosive population in Lake Texoma, Texas-Oklahoma, shortly after it was formed. It is generally believed that shallow lakes are less acceptable than deeper ones. However, Utah Lake has a very large population of stunted white bass and much of the lake is only 7 to 12 ft (2.1 to 3.7 m) deep. In Spirit Lake, Iowa, just before twilight, large schools of white bass move inshore and swim parallel to shore for several miles, often at a distance of no more than 50 ft (15 m) from shore (personal observation, senior author). Even when anglers cause them to move out, they often move right back and continue downshore.

The very large Utah Lake population of white bass, which matures at a length of 7 to 8 in. (178 to 203 mm), averages only 8 to 10 in. (203 to 254 mm), with few individuals reaching a weight of 2 or more lb (0.9 kg). Many of these fish are probably 6 to 8 years old. In 1956, 189 white bass were stocked in Utah Lake. In 1958 they were least abundant of any fish in gill net catches and, in 1978, the most abundant of any fish (Heckman, Thompson, and White 1981). They are now so voracious and so abundant there that they appear to dominate all other fishes in the lake through their feeding habits and sheer numbers.

Following years of low numbers, dominant year classes were produced in Spirit Lake, Iowa. This increase is not an unusual phenomenon for species on the periphery or outside their native range (Paul Errington, personal communication, 1946). In Utah Lake, on the other hand, white bass apparently dominate the lake by spawning successfully most years.

MANAGEMENT

Once a population of white bass becomes established and reproduces successfully, it needs little protection from fishermen. Large threadfin shad populations that have developed in many western reservoirs may at times be controlled by white bass. But there is some evidence that in Nacimiento Reservoir, California, threadfin shad may control the white bass population by outcompeting the bass for food (Moyle 1976).

In Utah Lake, white bass have become so abundant that they severely depleted the food supply and adversely affected growth of several species, themselves included. Resultant numbers are high but the fish remain small. This case indicates that white bass should be stocked only where heavy fishing pressure is assured.

---

striped bass,
Morone saxatilis
(Walbaum)
Plate 40

Etymology: *Morone,* an unexplained fish name; *Roccus*, an earlier name, means rock; *saxatilis* = growing among rocks
Nomenclature: *Perca saxatilis* Walbaum 1792, *Morone saxatilis* Whitehead and Wheeler 1967

IMPORTANCE

Marine striped bass are important both as sport fish and commercially. For the Plymouth, Massachusetts, colonists in 1623, they were a main item of food. Early settlers were amazed at their abundance and quality (Pearson 1938). In recent years, numbers have decreased drastically. The land-locked form has been stocked in many large waters, notably Tennessee Valley Authority (TVA) and Colorado River impoundments. In Utah they provide an important fishery in Lake Powell.

DESCRIPTION

Original

Perca saxatilis, argentea, lineis 7 fuscis longitudinalibus insignita; pinnis dorsi distinctis; cauda subbifurca. W.

Perca *Rockfish*, vel *Stricked Baff*. *Schoepfii* in *Schriften* N. Fr. VIII, 160. Dr. 7. D 8/8, 1/13. P. 15. V. 1/6. A. 2/14. C. 18.

Caput subplanum, declive. Iris argentea. Maxilla supera parum brevior infera et protractilis. Dentes parvi, fetosi, duabus interdum 3 seriebus dispositi. Opercula squamosa; anterius subtiliter denticulatum; posterius diacanthum. Corpus compressum; argenteum, ad dorsum subviride, in abdomine album. Lineæ 7 fuscæ a capite ad caudam paralelæ. In earum media latiore linea lateralis recta punctata existit. Squamæ ciliatæ. P.C. plus minusve bifurca. Longitudo fere pedalis.

Translation

Silver Rock Perch, marked with seven brown longitudinal lines; distinct dorsal fins; drooping two-pronged tail.

Rockfish Perch, or Striped Bass. N. Fr. VIII. 160. Br. 7. D. 8/8., 1/13/ P. 15. V. 1/6. A 3/14.

Sloping, somewhat level head. Silver scales. Upper jaw somewhat shorter than the lower protractilis and not as long.

Small teeth, bristles, sometimes arranged in two rows. Scaly gillplate, small anterior teeth; posterior bristles. Compressed body; silver greenish on the back, white on the abdomen. Seven brown parallel lines from the head to the tail. There is between those lines a wider lateral line of horizontally marked scales. Tail more or less two-pronged. Length scarcely 1 ft.

Contemporary
Coloration is bluish black to dark grey, or olive green above, the sides are silvery, the belly white. The dorsal, caudal, and pectoral fins are dusky. The pelvic fins are white. Striped bass have 7 to 9 unbroken stripes on each side, 2 or 3 of which extend to the base of the tail. These stripes are really spots on the scales. Fish less than 4 in. (101.6 mm) long have 8 to 10 dark vertical bars; as the lateral stripes darken, these disappear. The body is somewhat streamlined, with little arch to the back. The head is almost as long as the body is deep. The mouth is oblique and the lower jaw longer than the upper. The dorsal fins are clearly separated, the second dorsal is falcate. The caudal is forked. The anal fin spines are graduated; the pectoral fins are shorter than the pelvics. There are 65 scales in the lateral series (Minckley 1973; Smith 1985).

RANGE

Originally, striped bass occurred on the east coast of North America, from the St. Lawrence River, Canada, to the Tchefuncta River, Louisiana. In 1879 and 1882, a total of 435 small fish were transplanted from New Jersey into San Francisco Bay. From these relatively few fish, the range was extended 850 mi (1,360 km) along the West Coast from the Columbia River to San Diego (Pearson 1938). They have been stocked and established in 279 large inland waters, including Lake Powell, and 15 to 20 streams at various locations (Stevens 1984).

SIZE AND LONGEVITY

Nichols (1966), using scales, aged Chesapeake Bay striped bass to 14 years, and speculated that they may live much longer. He offers no validation of his method. Females age 1 to 14 weighed as follows: in lb/oz, 1/0, 1/13, 2/0, 3/10, 6/7, 9/15, 14/3, 18/0, 23/15, 28/2, 31/4, 37/8, 41/4, 49/6; in mm, 0.4, 0.8, 0.91, 1.6, 2.9, 4.5, 6.4, 8.2, 10.9, 12.8, 14.2, 17, 18.8, 22.4 kg. These fish had the following lengths for ages 1 through 14: in inches, 4, 12, 16, 19, 22, 26, 29, 32, 35, 36, 37, 41, 40, 46; in mm, 102, 305, 406, 482, 559, 660, 737, 813, 889, 914, 940, 1041, 1016, 1168. Males, after the first year, grew slower and did not live as long as females; the oldest was 11 years and weighed 25 lb, 5 oz. (11.75 kg). Pearson (1938), on the other hand, found that on the West Coast, fish of both sexes grew at the same rate the first year, then until the fourth year males grew faster; beyond that point, females grew faster. He reported that males rarely lived longer than 10 years, and females no longer than 16; otherwise, the growth of females was about the same as Chesapeake Bay females. The all-tackle hook-and-line record is 67 lb, 8 oz (30.62 kg) (IGFA 1993). The Utah record is 48 lb, 11 oz (22.1 kg).

Food and Feeding

Striped bass are carnivorous. Small fish feed on small crustaceans, insect larvae, and small fishes. The preferred food is fishes; insects and crustaceans are second choice. Invertebrates are taken when fishes are scarce. Vertebrate animals other than fishes are rarely taken.

Limiting Factors

Striped bass were first stocked in Lake Powell in 1974, threadfin shad in 1968. By 1987, the food base for the bass was composed almost entirely of threadfin shad and had been reduced to the point that the average size of stripers taken was dropping rapidly. The inadequate food base limits striper size but apparently does not reduce numbers. In the absence of shad, striped bass subsisted on plankton and their mean size decreased.

Breeding Habits

Striped bass have been stocked in some 435 reservoirs and are established in 279 of them in 36 states (Stevens 1984). However, most reservoirs are continually restocked because there is inadequate natural reproduction to produce an acceptable fishery. Striped bass spawn in the spring in temperatures between the low 50s°F and 70°F (10° and 21.1°C). Optimum appears to be 65°F (18.3°C). Spawning migrations from marine waters to fresh water may be as long as 100 mi (160 km), but in land-locked environments, it is much shorter. In most areas, striped bass seek rocky shoreline areas, where the spawning act is accompanied by much splashing and racing about. One female is attended by several males. This type of spawning behavior is typical of many fishes. They seek rapids or areas of strong current, which are necessary to keep the semibuoyant eggs afloat. Eggs hatch in about 48 hours at 65°F (18.3°C) and 36 hours at 71°F (21.7°C). Fifteen minutes after fertilization and water absorption, eggs are about 0.072 in. (1.8 mm) in diameter; eggs water-hardened for 12 hours are 0.13 in. (3.3 mm). Newly hatched fish live in open water until they are about 0.5 in. (12.7 mm) long, then move inshore and form schools for the balance of the first year.

A 3-lb (1.4-kg) female may produce as many as 14,000 eggs, a 50-lb (22.7-kg) one 3,220,000. Thirty-five percent of the females may be ripe at age 4, 100 percent at age 7. All males are ripe at age 5, some at age 3 (Pearson 1938; Nichols 1966). In Lake Powell, where males are ripe at age 2 and some females at age 3 (all are ripe by age 4), there is no need for stocking. Unique to this population is the ability to reproduce not in the river just above the lake, but in the reservoir (Gustaveson et al. 1984).

HABITAT

Striped bass are highly adaptable to a wide range of environmental conditions. On the East Coast, they range from the cold waters of the St. Lawrence River south to the warm tributaries of the Gulf of Mexico (Van Dan Argle and Evans 1990). On the West Coast, they range from the Columbia River south to San Diego, California. They prosper in fresh, brackish, or salt water. An example indicates the extent of their adaptability: fish stocked in San Francisco Bay in 1879 and 1882 were producing a fishery in 1889.

Sixty-one percent of the reservoirs stocked in the United States since 1941 are producing an acceptable striped bass fishery. There are also stream populations. In reservoir fish, breeding habitat and growth area are much different. They spawn in turbulent, turbid streams, and adults in the lentic waters are pelagic and live at all depths. Young remain in the stream for some time, probably up to a year, but when they enter the impoundment, they seek quiet backwater, the shallow water areas near shore.

MANAGEMENT

In the marine environment, overfishing, loss and degradation of habitat, and other less easily defined factors have reduced populations of striped bass. In Lake Powell, the food base, largely threadfin shad, is not sufficient to produce many trophy-size fish. The number of stripers is large, but the size is rarely more then 8 to 10 lb (3.6 to 4.5 kg). Rainbow smelt have been suggested as an acceptable addition to the food base but to date political, more than biological, considerations have the plan on hold.

Striped bass were introduced into Lake Powell in 1974 as part of a long-range plan to utilize the extensive pelagic areas in this reservoir, which were largely underutilized by sport fish already there. The introduction was immediately successful and within five years it was documented that the striped bass had adapted to spawning within the lake proper rather than requiring a tributary to spawn. Although spawning in the Colorado River was expected as a likely occurrence, the extensive in-lake spawning produced much greater than expected recruitment to the reservoir, ultimately leading to the near collapse of the single forage species, the threadfin shad. The initial fishery following introduction had been directed toward producing a limited catch of large trophy-sized striped bass, so regulations were changed to emphasize massive harvest of small striped bass in an attempt to control the population.

The present fishery is below desirable levels. Without adequate threadfin shad in past years, striped bass are selected against and most die of starvation. The fishery is dominated by small stripers feeding primarily on zooplankton and existing in poor conditions. These fish generally have medium desirability to anglers and as a result very little control is placed on them through angling pressure. The fishery does show some signs of cycling, however, in that in some years when striped bass conditions are so poor that reproduction is affected, a failed year class allows a short resurgence of shad population. The remaining stripers then are able to utilize shad for a short time and gain acceptable condition and become desirable once again to anglers. Studies are under way, however, to determine how fast the increased condition of striped bass results in an increase to the spawning success of striped bass and subsequent removal of threadfin shad.

Long-term management of the striped bass remains in doubt. A proposal has been developed to introduce a coldwater pelagic forage fish that would live in the deeper levels of Lake Powell and provide additional forage for the striped bass while also luring them away from the littoral threadfin shad. Under this scenario, larger piscivorous striped bass populations would be enhanced, but the young-of-the-year striped bass would face substantial competition for zooplankton from the smelt and shad together, resulting in much more survival of striped bass and overall reduction in the total biomass of the population. There is significant concern that the native Colorado River fishes downstream would be detrimentally affected by the addition of any new species in the system even though the rainbow smelt was selected specifically because they require very cold water and are obligate lake-dwellers.

Sunfishes (Family Centrarchidae)

Sunfishes are a North American family containing 9 genera and 34 species. They have been widely stocked. There are 4 genera with 7 species in Utah. Centrarchids are important in recreational fishing. They are prolific spawners and, with rare exceptions, protect the nest and young (Pflieger 1975). The habits and life histories of members of this family are similar, differing only in detail. Populations of sunfishes in situations where there are few predators often become stunted. They may produce numerous small, mature fish unless they are fished heavily. A bass-bluegill combination is often stocked in ponds or reservoirs to produce a high-yield fishery. This technique appears to be more successful in southern and midwestern states than elsewhere. In small ponds, anglers may be requested to not release bluegills regardless of size.

Sunfishes are native to North America east of the Mississippi River to the Atlantic coast. Prior to the Miocene Epoch, sunfishes occupied waters over much of what is now the United States. Changing geology and geography and increasing dryness eliminated all species west of the Rocky Mountains except the Sacramento perch (Miller 1958). Sunfish populations are established in most suitable warmwater habitats throughout Utah.

Mouth size in sunfishes ranges from small to large; the mouth has bands of villiform teeth on the jaws, vomer, palatines, and tongue of most species. The eyes are large. Sunfishes are small to moderate-sized, with spiny-rayed fins and laterally compressed bodies. The dorsal fin has a spinous portion of 6 to 13 spines and a soft-rayed portion, joined lightly or heavily. The pectoral fins are high on the body; the pelvic fins have 1 spine and 5 rays and are thoracic. The anal fin, with 3 spines preceding the soft rays, may be as long as the soft dorsal fin. The caudal fin is emarginate to slightly forked.

Sacramento perch, *Archoplites interruptus* (Girard)

Etymology: *Archoplites* = anus, armature in reference to the shiny anal fin; *interruptus* = broken or irregular, regarding the transverse bands

Nomenclature: *Centrarchus interruptus* Girard 1854, *Archoplites interruptus* Jordan and Copeland 1878

IMPORTANCE

Sacramento perch are the only members of the sunfish family native west of the Rockies. They are not native to Utah. Sacramento perch have retained the high number of fin spines and centrarchid body shape that is more characteristic of fossil sunfishes (Moyle 1976). In simple fish communities where they are numerically dominant, where there is not heavy competition with other fishes, and where habitat is adequate and food abundant, they grow rapidly and achieve a large size. They are scarce in Utah and contribute little to sportfishing.

DESCRIPTION

Original

General form rather elongated, very much compressed. Nuchal region swollen; oculo-cephalic region subconcave. Snout tapering; lower jaw longest. Posterior extremity of upper maxillary reaching a vertical line drawn back of the pupil. Head forming a little less than the third of total length. Eyes large and circular; their diameter being comprised four times in the length of side of the head. Scales on cheeks rather small; a little larger on the opercle than on the cheek. D XIII. 11. A. VII. 10. C. 5. 1. 8. 7. 1. 4. VI. 5. P 13.

The origin of the spiny dorsal is situated opposite the base of the pectorals, and the origin of the anal, opposite the space between the eleventh and twelfth dorsal spines. The tip of rays, as well as the base of anal, extends a little farther back than the dorsal. The base of ventrals falls upon the same vertical line as that which would intersect the base of pectorals. Scales of medium size; minutely serrated.

Greyish brown above, silver grey beneath. Irregular transverse bands of dark brown or black, interrupted along the lateral line, the portion of the band above it is somewhat alternating with the portion beneath it. A large black spot may be seen at the upper angle of opercle. Specimens from Sacramento River, Calif.

Contemporary

Sacramento perch are blackish on the back, mottled black brown and white on the sides and white to silvery underneath. They have 6 to 7 irregular, dark vertical bars on each side and black spots on the opercle. The sides have a metallic sheen of green to purple (La Rivers 1962).

Sacramento perch are deep bodied; their body length is between 2.75 and 3.00 times body depth. The mouth is large and oblique; the broad and long maxillary reaches back to about the middle of the eye. They have 38 to 48 scales in the lateral series, 25 to 30 long gill rakers, and teeth on the jaws, vomer, tongue, and palatines. There are 2 patches of lingual teeth, and the pharyngeal teeth are pointed.

This species has more spines (11–12) in the dorsal fin than any other sunfish. The spiny portion of the dorsal is continuous with the soft, 10-rayed posterior portion. The prominent anal fin has 6 to 7 spines and 10 rays. The caudal fin is weakly emarginate.

RANGE

The original range of this species is the Sacramento–San Joaquin drainage, San Francisco Bay tributaries, the Russian River, the Paharo-Salinus drainage, and Clear Lake in California (Lee et al. 1980). They were introduced in western Utah in Garrison Reservoir and in Cutler Reservoir on the lower Bear River.

SIZE AND LONGEVITY

A maximum length of 24 in. (610 mm) has been documented for Sacramento perch by Jordan and Evermann (1896–1900). La Rivers (1962) reported that a fish weighing nearly 8 lb (3.62 kg) was taken from Walker Lake, Nevada. One weighing 4 lb, 9 oz (2.1 kg) was caught in Pyramid Lake, Nevada (IGFA 1993). Overcrowding, competition, diet, and sex affect growth rate. Vigg and Kucera (1981) observed that females live longer and grow faster than males.

Sacramento perch generally grow more rapidly than most other centrarchids with a similar diet. In Pyramid Lake, Nevada, lengths for fish ages 1 to 5, at the end of each year, was: in inches, 6.8, 9.0, 10.8, 12.1, 12.7; in mm, 172, 229, 274, 307, 322 (Vigg and Kucera 1981). In a composite of 5 California lake studies, the yearly length for fish ages 1 to 6 was: in inches, 3.4, 5.7, 7.0, 7.9, 8.6, and 9.9; in mm, 86, 145, 179, 210, 218, 252. The world hook-and-line record is 4 lb, 9 oz (2.1 kg) (Fishing Hall of Fame 1993). The Utah record is 4 lb, 5 oz (1.96 kg).

Food and Feeding

Sacramento perch are rather languid and sluggish, spending most of their time close to the bottom. They stalk prey slowly and feed with a sudden rush by "inhaling" with a rapid expansion of the buccal cavity and then closing their mouths. Feeding occurs either day or night but peaks of activity occur at dusk and dawn (Moyle 1976). La Rivers (1962) observed them taking bait such as worms, minnows, spinners, and wet flies at all times of the year. There is some indication that they do not feed during spawning.

Sacramento perch are opportunistic feeders. Selected prey size depends on body size of the predator. Young feed on small, bottom-dwelling crustaceans or ones associated with aquatic plants. Large fish take aquatic insect larvae and pupae, especially midges. In big bodies of water, where prey species are abundant, fishes are the most important food of Sacramento perch over 3.5 in. (89 mm) (Vigg and Kucera 1981). In smaller waters lacking fishes for prey, aquatic insects are important in the diet.

Limiting Factors

The most likely causes of decline of a particular population of Sacramento perch are interspecific competition (primarily with other centrarchids) as well as the lack of acceptable spawning sites. In the perch's native range these factors, along with habitat destruction and egg predation, have contributed to its decline. It is not a highly competitive fish. Lack of wetlands for spawning and nursery areas reduce numbers.

Breeding Habits

Water temperatures of 70° to 84°F (21.1° to 28.9°C) are required for Sacramento perch to spawn, according to Murphy (1948), but in Pyramid Lake, Nevada, spawning is initiated at 68°F (20°C) some years (Vigg and Kucera 1981). These perch mature at age 2 or 3 years. Spawning starts in late March and ends in early August. However, late May and early June are peak times.

During spawning, perch congregate in water 8 to 20 in. (20 to 51 cm) deep where there are heavy growths of macrophytes or filamentous algae, or debris. Rock piles, boulders, and submerged sticks or logs may also be used as sites for egg deposition. Males vigorously defend a territory even though there is no nest. Following a brief courtship, the male allows the female to enter his territory and spawning is initiated. Males may guard the nest until the larval fish are able to swim (La Rivers 1962); however, some observers have noted that both parents abandon the nest shortly after spawning (Murphy 1948).

Spawning takes place from about 9 A.M. to 4 P.M., ceasing abruptly in late afternoon. The fecundity of females is higher than most centrarchids but still size related. In Pyramid Lake, Nevada, females averaged 84,203 eggs (Vigg and Kucera 1981). Young remain in schools among aquatic plants near the spawning area.

HABITAT

Sacramento perch originally inhabited sloughs, sluggish rivers, and lakes of the Central Valley, California. Historic water-quality fluctuations in which they evolved allow them to tolerate high turbidities, temperatures, salinities, and alkalinities (Moyle 1976). They are bottom dwellers in both their native and transplanted range. Beds of rooted and emergent aquatic vegetation for spawning beds and nursery areas are important. They are not active, but remain near cover or the bottom. At times they may be heavily infested with internal and external parasites.

MANAGEMENT

Preservation of habitat and low numbers of predators will help preserve this species. Other centrarchids should not be stocked with Sacramento perch. The latter may become overpopulated and stunted if numbers are not controlled by harvest or predation. They are harder to catch than most other centrarchids, so liberal catch regulations are in order. If adequate spawning habitat is not present, artificial areas can be provided.

---

green sunfish, *Lepomis cyanellus* Rafinesque
Plate 42

Etymology: *Lepomis* = scaled operculum; *cyanellus* = blue
Nomenclature: *Lepomis cyanellus* Rafinesque 1819

IMPORTANCE

Green sunfish are rarely important as game. In Canada, only youngsters seek them. They are the most common sunfish in smaller streams and lakes in the eastern United States. In many states, including Utah, they are regarded as a nuisance or worse because of their abundance and their ability to outcompete the young of more desirable game species (La Rivers 1962; Scott and Crossman 1973).

DESCRIPTION

Original

Lepomis. (Thoracique.) Corps arrondi, ovale ou oblong, très-comprimé. Tête et opercules écailleux, ceux-ci mutiques, le postérieur flexueux, membraneux, quelquefois auriculé. Bouche petite, mâchoires à petites dents, lèvre supérieure à peine extensible. Une nageoire dorsale, nageoire thoracique à 6 rayons dont 1 épineux, sans appendices. Anus au milieu.

L. cyanellus Corps oblong, tout couvert de points bleus, joues à lignes flexueuses bleus, opercule sans auricule, tache oblongue, queue bilobée.

Translation
Lepomis. (Thoracic) Rounded body, oval or oblong, very compact. Scaly head and opercules, the latter not pointed, with flexible membranes, sometimes auriculated. Small mouth, jaws with small teeth, upper lip barely extensible. The dorsal fin and a thoracic fin with six rays including the spiny one, without appendices. Anus in center.

L. cyanellus. Oblong body, completely covered with blue specks, jaws with sinuous blue lines, opercule without auricle, oblong spot [on the opercule], two-lobed tail.

Contemporary
Green sunfish have short, laterally compressed, and robust bodies. The head is large, there is a depression over the eyes, the opercular flap is stiff, long and black in the center, with a pale red, pink, or yellow margin. They have a large, terminal mouth and jaws of equal length. There are fine teeth on the palatines, vomer, and both jaws, but not the tongue. The gill rakers in the center of the arch are long and thin. There are 14 gill rakers on the lower limb and 4 or 5 on the upper limb. Branchiostegal rays are usually 6, sometimes 7.

The body is generally brown to olive with an emerald sheen and is darker on the dorsal surfaces and upper sides. The sides are light yellowish green, the upper sides have 7 to 12 dark but vague vertical bars. The belly is yellow to white and the breast is not conspicuously colored. The head has emerald spots and at times, wavy, radiating emerald lines. In spawning males, the dorsal, caudal, and anal fins are dusky to olive; the membranes are darker and edged with a white, yellow, or orange border. Young do not have the emerald coloring, dark bars or fin spots (Scott and Crossman 1973; Simpson and Wallace 1978).

Green sunfish have two dorsal fins, broadly joined, and appearing as one. The first has 9 to 10 spines; the second is soft with 10 to 12 rays and, in breeding males, a rounded or slightly pointed edge. The stubby, moderately high pectorals are broad, with an average of 13 rays. There are 40 to 50 ctenoid scales in the lateral series. The peritoneum is white or silvery, the intestine long and differentiated. The slightly forked caudal fin is broad with rounded tips. There are 3 sharp spines on the anal fin and 9 to 10 soft rays. The anal fin is round to slightly pointed in breeding males. Pelvic fins are thoracic and rather long with 1 spine and 5 rays. Green sunfish have 6 to 8 pyloric caeca (Sigler and Miller 1963; Scott and Crossman 1973).

RANGE

The native range of the green sunfish is restricted to fresh waters of east-central North America. Green sunfish range from southwestern New York, west of the Appalachian Mountains, south to Georgia, Alabama (west of the Escambia River), west and south to Texas and northeastern Mexico, then north from New Mexico to Wyoming and eastern North Dakota, finally east below the Red River system (except the Hudson Bay drainage of western Ontario) to Michigan and Ontario (Lee et al. 1980).

Green sunfish have been stocked in the panhandle of Florida, the western states, and in Germany. The green sunfish has been introduced extensively in the lower elevation, warm waters of Utah.

Size and Longevity

Growth of most green sunfish is slow, the ultimate size small. Stunting occurs in many populations. Lengths at the end of each year for Michigan green sunfish ages 1 to 8 are approximately: in inches, 1.0, 2.0, 3.0, 4.1, 4.9, 6.0, 6.3, 7.3: in mm, 25.4, 50.8, 76.2, 104, 125, 152, 160, 185 (Hubbs and Cooper 1935). They may rarely reach a length over 11 in. (275 mm) in California waters (Moyle 1976). In Ohio the largest fish was 10.8 in. (270 mm) long and weighed 14.5 oz (406 g) (Trautman 1981). In a northern Utah artesian-fed pond, the length of green sunfish at the end of each year, for fish ages 1 to 6, is: in inches, 2.0, 3.0, 4.0, 4.8, 5.4, 6.4; in mm, 50.8, 76.2, 102, 122, 137, 163. Out of the 351 fish examined only 4 were more than 6 in. (152 mm) long.

Green sunfish may rarely reach an age of 10 or 11 years. The world record all-tackle, hook-and-line fish weighed 2 lb, 2 oz (0.96 kg) (Fishing Hall of Fame 1993). The largest green sunfish caught in Utah weighed 12.5 oz (0.3 kg).

Food and Feeding

Green sunfish in northern Utah ponds commonly feed on insects in early winter, crustaceans and fishes in midwinter, and freshwater shrimp in late winter (Sigler and Miller 1963). In general, they feed on insects, mollusks, and small fish. They are able to eat large, hard-bodied organisms and fairly large fish. They prey readily on large, active invertebrates. As they increase in size, they depend more on crayfish, fish, and large aquatic and terrestrial insects.

Limiting Factors

Predation by other warmwater species, parasites, and stunting affect local populations of green sunfish. They freely hybridize with at least five other species of the genus *Lepomis*.

Breeding Habits

Green sunfish start spawning in spring in water from 2 to 8 ft (0.61 to 2.44 m) deep at temperatures about 66°F (18.9°C). They may spawn every 8 to 10 days until the water reaches 82°F (27.7°C), generally in August. Spawning by a pair takes place over a 1- to 2-day period. Males construct a 6- to 15-in. (15- to 38-cm) oval nest near rocks, logs, clumps of grass, or other debris. They establish and vigorously defend territories. Precocious males have been observed trying to defend selected areas. A female enters the nest with a male and they spawn. Eggs are yellow, adhesive, and hatch at median temperatures (74°F [23.3°C]) within 3 to 5 days. Males guard the nest and fan the embryos until hatching, then guard the young for varying periods of time (Sprugel 1955; Sigler and Miller 1963).

Even though there is considerable fighting among males, there may be as many as 25 nests in a 50-sq-ft (4.6-sq-m) area. However, once the eggs are laid and boundaries accepted, there are few additional disputes. Maturity is at age 2 or 3, when the fish is usually 3 to 4 in. (76 to 102 mm) long; although, in stunted populations, individuals may be smaller (Sigler and Miller 1963).

In aquarium studies, males established and guarded areas so precisely that their territories could be defined when researchers marked the sides of the aquaria. Attacking males met intruders head on, sometimes grasping them by the jaw.

HABITAT

Green sunfish inhabit small, warm streams, ponds, and shallow areas of lake, generally at low elevations (4,500 ft [1,372 m] or less in Utah). They are not abundant in ecosystems with more than three or four other fishes. They may be locally abundant in shallow or weedy areas of reservoirs that are not frequented by other species. Green sunfish occur with other species in turbid or muddy streams but are evidently able to take over physically disrupted areas only when native species have been depleted (Sigler and Miller 1963).

A suitable ecological description of a green sunfish is that it is a miniature largemouth bass. It frequents the same areas and eats the same food as a young largemouth bass. Adult green sunfish are as aggressive as adult largemouth. They prosper in ponds inhabited with largemouth, bluegill, and black bullheads. Although they prefer moderately warm water, they prosper in water in the high 80s°F (30° to 32°C) or in the borderline trout waters of the middle to high 60s°F (18° to 21°C).

MANAGEMENT

As with other centrarchids, a suitable habitat, with weedy areas for spawning and nursery areas, is necessary. Green sunfish suffer predation from other warmwater fishes. As they do not qualify as a valuable game fish, their welfare is not a fisheries concern, unless they are in an area fished heavily by youngsters. They may adversely affect native species if stocked over them.

---

bluegill,
Lepomis macrochirus
Rafinesque
Plate 43

Etymology: *Lepomis* = scaled operculum; *macrochirus* = large hand, referring to the pectoral fin
Nomenclature: *Lepomis macrochirus* Rafinesque 1819

IMPORTANCE

Bluegill are one of the most important pan fish in the United States. They can be taken with a light fly rod on wet or dry flies, very small lures, or worms, all rather easily. A large bluegill on light tackle provides fun for youngsters and adults alike. They are one of the best known of the smaller sunfishes. Many people enjoy just watching this active, colorful, little fish. In palatability they are ranked equivalent to most warmwater fish (Sigler and Miller 1963). They are also an important forage fish for piscivores, especially largemouth bass. Bluegill are often stocked with largemouth bass or other fish eaters in ponds (Pflieger 1975). Bluegill offer a moderate fishery in Utah, with a few locations in the central part of the state providing the majority of good to excellent fishing. The most famous place for bluegill fishing has been Pelican Lake near Vernal. They do well in a wide variety of environmental conditions, thriving in many waters that will not support other sport fishes.

DESCRIPTION

Original

Corps ovale, points bruns, point d'auricle, tache oblongue toute noire, pectorales très-longues atteignant l'anale, queue fourchue.

Translation

Oval body, brown specks, no auricle, completely black oblong spot [on the opercule], very long pectorals running all the way to the anal, forked tail.

CONTEMPORARY

The body of the bluegill is slab-sided, short, and deep; the greatest depth is at the third dorsal spine. The head is deep and narrow; the mouth is rather small, terminal, and slightly oblique. The lower jaw is longer than the upper. Brushlike teeth occur on the jaws and vomer.

Ctenoid scales number 38 to 44 in the lateral series. The pectoral fins, placed fairly low on the body, are long and pointed. The pelvic fins are thoracic. The anal fin has 3 spines. The spinous dorsal, with the soft portion attached, has 10 spines (Sigler and Miller 1963; Simpson and Wallace 1978).

Highly colorful, bluegill become even more so in the breeding season. Spawning males may have copper-colored heads. The breast of the male is red, the opercles are often blue with a black spot on the posterior margin of the ear flap. This characteristic separates them from other sunfishes. They have a black spot at the back of the soft-rayed portion of the dorsal fin. Young are silvery, adults are yellowish olive to dark olive green above with a bluish luster; sides are bluish and the breast and belly yellowish. They have 5 to 10 dusky, vertical bars on the sides, which are best developed in small fish (Sigler and Miller 1963; Simpson and Wallace 1978).

RANGE

The original range of bluegill includes the fresh waters of eastern and central North America. They occur from Virginia to Florida, west to Texas and northern Mexico. From the St. Lawrence River west of the Appalachian Mountains south to the region of the Chattahoochee River in Georgia. The western edge of the range is eastern New Mexico to eastern Minnesota and western Ontario (Lee et al. 1980).

In Utah they are present from Cache Valley to Lake Powell. The largest concentrations of bluegill are in central Utah.

SIZE AND LONGEVITY

Utah bluegill generally grow slowly and rarely reach lengths of over 7 or 8 in. (178 to 203 mm) (Sigler and Miller 1963). The exception to this was in Pelican Lake in east central Utah, where large bluegill were the rule. This is no longer true. From 1976 to 1978, lengths were as follows for fish ages 1 to 9: in inches, 2.2, 4.4, 6.5, 7.6, 8.3, 9.0, 9.6, 10.0, and 10.2; in mm, 55.9, 112, 165, 193, 211, 229, 244, 254, 259 (Burdick 1979). In 1983, a 2 lb, 3 oz (0.9 kg) bluegill was caught there. The world all-tackle record fish is 4 lb, 12 oz (2.2 kg) (Fishing Hall of Fame 1993).

A newly hatched bluegill is approximately 0.25 in. (6.3 mm) long. By the end of its first year, it has reached a length of 1.5 to 2 in. (38 to 50.8 mm) and may grow about 1 in. (25 mm) each year thereafter. They live to 9 or more years. Bluegill grow best in areas where water temperatures range from 59° to 77°F (15° to 25°C). Pflieger (1975) gave the yearly size for fish ages 1 to 5 years as: in inches, 1.5, 3.1, 4.4, 5.4, 6.2; in mm, 38, 79, 112, 137, 157 in Missouri streams; and for fish ages 1 to 4 years in new reservoirs: in inches, 2.8, 4.2, 5.6, and 6.6; in mm, 71, 107, 142, 168. Bennett et al. (1983) reported mean total lengths as: in inches, 1.4, 2.8, 4.8, 5.9, 6.9, 7.6, 8.3; in mm, 35.6, 71, 122, 150, 175, 193, 211 for fish ages 1 through 7 in lower Snake River reservoirs.

FOOD AND FEEDING

Bluegill feed day and night but less at night. Peak feeding occurs in early morning, midafternoon, and/or late evening and just after dark. Throughout their life, bluegill feed on small animals, but the size of food item taken increases with increasing fish size. Small mouth size limits the size of their prey. Adults will feed anywhere, in shallow waters, deep waters, and bottom to the surface, but generally in the vicinity of vegetation.

Adults prefer insects, small fishes, frogs, crayfish, and snails. When animal material is not available, they turn to plants. Young, feeding in shallow water, eat zooplankton, primarily cladocerans and copepods. Feeding is primarily by sight. Bluegill can hover at any depth by using their paired fins. When prey is located, they dart forward to capture it. When mayflies and other aquatic insects are emerging, the fish feed largely at the surface (Sigler and Miller 1963; Pflieger 1975). Feeding is drastically reduced when temperatures drop below 50°F (10°C).

Limiting Factors

Temperatures in the high 80s°F (30° to 31°C) are reported as near lethal, but Snow, Ensign, and Klingbiel (1960) thought that bluegill can tolerate temperatures to 95°F (35°C). Vegetation destruction by common carp or other causes has previously been observed to reduce population numbers. But research in Iowa indicated that even with a 90 percent reduction in macrophytes, population density of bluegill remains the same. Large fish are the result (James Mayhew, personal communication, 1991). Low oxygen levels (0.60 ppm [mg/l]) in winter are lethal. Bluegill are host to a number of parasites, including several flukes, tapeworms, round worms, spinyheaded worms, "fish lice," and snail larvae (Snow, Ensign, and Klingbiel 1960).

Stunting may reduce numbers of desirable-sized fish but not total numbers. Spawning decreases in overcrowded populations. Natural mortality from all causes is generally higher than angling mortality.

Breeding Habits

Bluegill are prolific; females, depending on size, lay from 500 to 50,000 eggs. Several females often spawn in the same nest guarded by one male. One nest contained 61,000 eggs, and a group of Michigan nests had an average of 18,000 eggs (Sigler and Miller 1963). In Pelican Lake, two-year-old females had an estimated 11,102 eggs, and 5-year-olds 46,281 (Burdick 1979).

Spawning begins in May when water temperatures approach 67° to 68°F (19.4° to 20°C) and ends in August. Some biologists believe that temperatures of 80°F (26.6°C) are required for continuous spawning. Mature fish may rarely be only 1 or 2 years old but usually are 2 to 3 (Sigler and Miller 1963). Males construct nests, generally on a sand or gravel bar in water 12 to 40 in. (31 to 102 cm) deep. Males create a depression 8 to 12 in. (20 to 31 cm) or more in diameter, and 2 to 6 in. (5 to 15 cm) deep. This process is accomplished by the male fanning his fins. Although nests are generally constructed on gravel or sand, mud and debris may be used. Males build nests in close proximity to one another and defend their territory, but they are more tolerant of each other than most sunfishes (Breder and Rosen 1966). Prespawning females stay in schools in the general area of the nests. When a female is ready to spawn, she approaches a nest area and is in turn approached by a male, generally the largest in the vicinity. The male attracts the female to his nest and the two spawn. Courtship movements are accompanied by distinctive grunting sounds (Gerald 1971). Eggs are adhesive and attach to debris on the bottom of the nest; they hatch in 2 to 3 days in 68°F (20°C) water. Males guard their nest and to some extent the fry. Fry soon move from the nests to aquatic plant beds or other cover. They may be pelagic for a period of 1 month or more (Sigler and Miller 1963).

Habitat

Bluegill are true warmwater fish, prospering in rich, weedy, shallow, clear water. During hot midday weather (85° to 90°F [29.4° to 32.2°C]), they may retreat to deeper waters or to the shade of trees or docks. They move into shallower water in early morning and evening to feed, although they may feed all day. Bluegill prefer to be close to cover such as beds of aquatic vegetation. They tend to spend most of their lives in rather restricted areas, even in large lakes. Bluegill are gregarious, forming large schools that travel together.

They do well in creeks, ponds, lakes, and reservoirs where the bottom is sand or gravel, where there is abundant vegetation, and summer water temperatures reach 70° to 80°F (21.1° to 26.6°C). The latter temperature, although not required for successful spawning, evidently promotes higher success. Young spend their time in shallow water. Neither adults nor young can tolerate low oxygen levels.

MANAGEMENT

Bluegill need acceptable spawning habitat, but from a fisheries management standpoint, predators are necessary in early life stages. An established population is difficult to overfish and liberal harvest regulations are advisable, although there are exceptions. Rarely is a minimum size limit dictated. Creel limits of 20 to 25 may be in order, not to limit total harvest but to more equally distribute the take among varying levels of talents of the fishing public. It may be necessary to reduce large numbers of carp in prime bluegill habitat. Where there are few predators, a local eradication program may be necessary to reduce numbers. In areas of scarce cover, brush piles or other submerged cover may be beneficial.

---

smallmouth bass, *Micropterus dolomieu* Lacépède
Plate 44

Etymology: *Micropterus* = small fin (apparently the type specimen for this genus was deformed); *dolomieu,* after M. Dolomieu
Nomenclature: *Micropterus dolomieu* Lacépède 1802

IMPORTANCE

The attraction of the smallmouth bass for anglers is legendary. Techniques for capture and the thrill of capturing this species, along with many "sea stories" are the subject of an untold number of popular books and articles.

Smallmouth bass are one of the more sought-after game fishes in North America. The magnitude, antiquity, and intensity of interest in this fish is reflected in the fact that angling results were mentioned in Fothergill's 1816–1836 "account of the natural history of eastern Canada" (Scott and Crossman 1973). They do not rate close to the largemouth bass in importance in Utah, principally because of their limited range and numbers. But smallmouth are increasing in numbers and popularity in Utah and have a bright future as a sport fish. They may impact native species when stocked in certain waters.

Description

Original

Dix rayons aiguillonnés et sept rayons articulés à la première nageoire du dos; quatre rayons à la seconde; deux rayons aiguillonnés et onze rayons articulés à la nageoire de l'anus; la caudale en croissant; un ou deux aiguillons à la seconde pièce de chaque opercule.

Je désire que le nom de ce poisson, qu'aucun naturaliste n'a encore décrit, rappelle ma tendre amitié et ma profonde estime pour l'illustre Dolomieu, dont la victoire vient de briser les fers. En écrivant mon Discours sur la durée des espèces, j'ai exprimé la vive douleur que m'inspiroit son affreuse captivité, et l' admiration pour sa constance héroïque, que l'Europe mêloit à ses voeux pour lui. Qu'il m'est doux de ne pas terminer l'immense tableau que je tâche d'esquisser, sans avoir senti le bonheur de le serrer de nouveau dans mes bras!

Les microptères ressemblent beaucoup aux sciènes: mais la petitesse très-remarquable de leur seconde nageoire dorsale les en sépare; et c'est cette petitesse que désigne le nom générique que je leur ai donné.

La collection du Muséum national d'histoire naturelle renferme un bel individu de l'espèce que nous décrivons dans cet article. Cette espèce, qui est encore la seule inscrite dans le nouveau genre des microptères, que nous avons cru devoir établir, a les deux mâchoires, le palais et la langue, garnis d'un très-grand nombre de rangées de dents petites, crochues et serrées; la langue est d'ailleurs très-libre dans ses mouvemens; et la mâchoire inférieure plus avancée que celle d'en-haut. La membrane branchiale disparoit entièrement sous l'opercule, qui présente deux pièces dont la première est arrondie dans son contour, et la seconde anguleuse. Cet opercule est couvert de plusieurs écailles; celles du dos sont assez grandes et arrondies. La hauteur du corps proprement dit excède de beaucoup celle de l'origine de la queue. La ligne latérale se plie d'abord vers le bas, et se relève ensuite pour suivre la courbure du dos. Les nageoires pectorales et celle de l'anus sont très-arrondies; la première du dos ne commence qu'à une assez grande distance de la queue. Elle cesse d'être attachée au dos de l'animal, à l'endroit où elle parvient au-dessus de l'anale; mais elle se prolonge en bande pointue et flottante jusqu'au-dessus de la seconde nageoire dorsale, qui est très-basse et très-petite, ainsi que nous venons de le dire, et que l'on croiroit au premier coup d'oeil entièrement adipeuse.*

---

*5 rayons à la membrane branchiale.

16 rayons à chaque pectorale.
1 rayon aiguillonné et 5 rayons articulés à chaque thoracine.
17 rayons à la nageoire de la queue.

Translation
The Micropter Dolomieu
(Small-Mouth Bass)

Ten spiny rays and seven articulated rays on the first dorsal fin; four rays on the second; two spiny rays and eleven articulated rays on the anal fin; the caudal fin is crescent shaped; one or two spiny rays on the second part of each opercule.

I would like the name of this fish, that no naturalist has previously described, to recall my friendship and deep esteem for the illustrious Dolomieu, whose victory has just liberated us. In writing my discourse on how long species last, I expressed the anguish that his horrid captivity inspired in me and my admiration for his heroic constance, that Europe joins to its best wishes for him. It is very agreeable to me not to finish the immense description that I am attempting to undertake without first having felt the joy of holding him once again in my arms.

The micropters look very much like sciaenas, but what distinguishes them from that fish is the particularly small size of their second dorsal fin; and it is this small size that the genus name I have given them indicates.

The collection of the National Museum of Natural History has an excellent example of the species described in this article. This species, which is as yet the only one in the new genus of micropters that we have felt it appropriate to create, has both jaws, the palate and the tongue covered with a very large number of rows of small teeth, hooked and close together; the tongue is very free moving; and the lower jaw juts further forward than the top one. The branchial membrane is entirely hidden under the opercles which have 2 parts, the first rounded on the edge, and the second angular. This opercle is covered by several scales; the back scales are quite large and rounded. The depth of the body itself is much greater than the body at the beginning of the tail. The lateral line drops downward and then swings up to follow the curvature of the back. The pectorals and the anal fin are very rounded; the first dorsal does not begin until quite far from the tail. It is no longer attached to the animal's back when it reaches a point above the anal fin; but it is prolonged as a pointed and floating strip until a point just above the second dorsal fin which is very low and very small, as we have already noted, and that one would think at first glance to be entirely adipose.*

---

*5 rays in the branchial membrane.
16 rays in each pectoral.

1 spiny ray and 5 articulated rays at each thoracic fin.
17 rays in the tail fin.

Contemporary
The body of the smallmouth bass is moderately compressed and is more elongate than other sunfishes except the largemouth bass. The head is large and deep with a shallow depression over the eyes. The snout is long and bluntly pointed, the lower jaw slightly longer than the upper jaw. Fine, brushlike teeth cover the jaws, palatine, and vomer. The maxillary normally does not extend beyond the middle of the eye.

Smallmouth bass vary in color with habitat but are normally dark olive to brown on the back with the sides lighter and yellowish and the belly yellowish. Most scales have golden flecks. There are 8 to 15 (average 9) dark vertical bars on the sides, a characteristic distinguishing them from the largemouth bass (Simpson and Wallace 1978). In clear or stained waters they are darker than in turbid waters. The head has dark bars radiating from its red or orange eyes.

The spinous dorsal fin has 10 spines, is low, and strongly joined to the soft dorsal. The thoracic pelvic fins have 1 spine and 5 rays. The pectoral fins are broad, short, and rounded. The anal fin has 3 graduated spines and 13 to 15 soft rays. There are 68 to 76 ctenoid scales in the lateral series. Young fish look much like adults except they have prominent vertical bars or rows of spots. The caudal fin has an orange and then black band at the base and white to yellow tips (La Rivers 1962; Scott and Crossman 1973; Simpson and Wallace 1978).

Range

Smallmouth bass were restricted to fresh waters of central and eastern North America in their native distribution. Their original range was limited to the Great Lakes–St. Lawrence system and the Ohio, Tennessee, and upper Mississippi river systems (MacCrimmon and Robbins 1975; Stroud and Clepper 1975; Lee et al. 1980; Edwards, Gebhart, and Maughan 1983). Their range has been expanded by stocking so that they now occur in suitable habitats over much of the United States. They have been successfully introduced in England, Europe, Russia, and Africa.

In Utah, smallmouth bass have been stocked and are prospering in Flaming Gorge and Powell lakes, the Uinta and Sevier rivers, and Starvation Reservoir. Other plantings may also have succeeded.

Size and Longevity

Smallmouth bass are the second largest member of the sunfish family. Young at hatching are approximately 0.25 in.(6 mm) long, and after the yolk sac is absorbed, 0.33 in. (8.4 mm) long. In a Lake Michigan–Green Bay study, the length at the end of each year for fish ages 1 to 13 was: in inches, 3.1, 6.3, 9.2, 10.4, 11.9, 13.1, 15.0, 15.9, 16.3, 17.5, 17.8,

18.5, and 19.9; in mm, 79, 160, 234, 264, 302, 333, 381, 404, 414, 445, 452, 470, 505 (Becker 1983). In the Clearwater River, Idaho, bass 1 to 9 years old grew as follows: in inches, 3.3, 5.6, 7.9, 9.5, 10.6, 11.6, 12.4, 12.8, and 13.3; in mm, 84, 142, 201, 241, 269, 295, 315, 325, 338 (Carlander 1977). Few live longer than 15 years. The world record all-tackle, hook-and-line fish weighed 11 lb, 15 oz (5.4 kg)(Fishing Hall of Fame 1993). The Utah record is 6 lb, 12 oz (3.1 kg).

Food and Feeding

Smallmouth fry begin feeding even before the yolk sac is absorbed, largely on such microcrustaceans as *Daphnia* and small midge larvae. Early in their lives, they start feeding on fish. They feed throughout the day. At 1.5 inches (38 mm) in length, the young feed on fish and insects; at 3 inches (76 mm) they start feeding on small crayfish (Becker 1983). Crayfish, fish, and insects, in that order, are dominant food of adults in Little Goose Reservoir on the lower Snake River (Bennett et al. 1983). They take a variety of food from the surface to the bottom. In some areas, crayfish make up 60 to 90 percent of the diet, fishes 10 to 30 percent and aquatic and terrestrial insects up to 10 percent. Smallmouth feed on frogs, tadpoles, and fish eggs. Dead food is usually but not always rejected.

Limiting Factors

Smallmouth bass do not prosper in warm, turbid streams with very low flows or in turbid, shallow lakes or reservoirs. Fluctuating water levels or high winds, just after spawning, may destroy nests or cause desertion. Predation on eggs and fry, angling, and the bass tapeworm all reduce reproduction and fry survival. These problems may result in a weak year class. Smallmouth bass are sensitive to domestic, industrial, and thermal pollution. In the northern part of their range, smallmouth bass are limited by the availability of young-of-the-year overwintering habitat (Shuter et al. 1980).

Breeding Habits

Smallmouth bass usually spawn over a period of 6 to 10 days or longer in late spring and early summer when water temperatures reach 61° to 65°F (16.1° to 18.3°C). Females mature at 4 to 6 years, males 1 year earlier (Scott and Crossman 1973). Males build a nest 1 to 6 ft (0.3 to 1.8 m) in diameter in 2 to 20 ft (0.6 to 6.1 m) of water over sand, gravel, or rocky bottoms of lakes and rivers. Nests are close to cover such as logs or brush. A male may return to the same nest or close by year after year. A ripe female convinces the nest-defending male of her intent to spawn by returning to the nest area and by other behavioral events such as changing colors. There is considerable prespawning activity, displaying, rubbing, and nipping. The male and female come to rest on the bottom, and eggs are deposited and fertilized in about 5 seconds. The act may be repeated for 2 hours. A female produces approximately 7,000 eggs/lb (3,175/kg) of female. The embryos are light amber to pale yellow in color, 0.05 to 0.09 in. (1.3 to 2.3 mm) in diameter, and demersal. Fry are light colored and drop into the gravel where they remain for 6 to 9 days. They then work their way back out of the gravel. At this time they are very black, and form in dense clouds over the nest for a time, then disperse. The male guards the nest and young during this time (Pflieger 1975). A female may leave one nest to spawn with another male. Hatching period ranges from 9.5 days at 55°F (12.8°C) to 2.25 days at 75°F (23.9°C) (Becker 1983).

HABITAT

Adult smallmouth bass are coolwater fish preferring temperatures of 68° to 79°F (20° to 26.1°C). At about 30°F (-1°C), they seek shelter and become inactive. They prosper in rocky or sandy, silt-free areas of medium to large lakes and streams. In hot weather, they retreat to deeper and cooler water. Although smallmouth bass seek areas with abundant cover such as rocks, shoals, or submerged logs, they do not associate with dense growths of aquatic vegetation to the same extent that the largemouth does. In summer they seek temperatures near 80°F (26.7°C) but may do well at lower temperatures. They apparently require at least 1,000 degree-days (days x degrees above freezing) with temperatures over 50°F (10°C) for population stability. They begin to feed in the spring when water temperatures reach 47°F (8.3°C). The smallmouth bass is more gregarious and wanders less than the largemouth (Scott and Crossman 1973; Coutant 1975; Edwards, Gebhart, and Maughan 1983; Shuter et al. 1985).

MANAGEMENT

Stable water level during spawning and fry rearing are important for strong year classes. This stability tends to reduce the hazards of fluctuating temperatures and high winds. An abundance of food is critical for smallmouth for their first few months. Smallmouth are competitive with largemouth bass in ideal smallmouth habitat, but not otherwise. Creel limits are generally in order; size limits are governed by local situations.

largemouth bass,
Micropterus salmoides
(Lacépède)
Plate 45

Etymology: *Micropterus* = small fin (apparently the type specimen for this genus was deformed); *salmoides,* from *Salmo,* meaning troutlike

Nomenclature: *Labrus salmoides* Lacépède 1802, *Micropterus salmoides* Jordan and Copeland 1878

IMPORTANCE

Over all of their range, largemouth bass are highly prized by anglers. Largemouth prosper over a wide variety of habitats from large, cool reservoirs to warm farm ponds. They are arguably the most important warmwater (58° to 82°F [14.4 to 27.8°C]) game fish in the United States. They provide a quality fishery in many Utah warm waters, particularly Lake Powell.

DESCRIPTION

Original

"SUPPLEMENT" Au Tableau et à la Synonymie "Du Genre des Labres" PREMIER SOUS-GENRE

La nageoire de la queue, fourchue, ou échancrée en croissant

Espèces. Le labre Salmoide (*Labrus salmoides*)

Caractères.

Neuf rayons aiguillonnés et treize rayons articulés à la nageoire du dos; treize rayons à la nageoire de l'anus; l'opercule composé de quatre lames, et terminé par une prolongation anguleuse; deux orifices à chaque narine; la couleur générale d'un brun noirâtre.

On devra au citoyen Bosc la connoissance du labre salmoïde et du labre iris, qui tous les deux habitent dans les eaux de la Caroline.

Le salmoïde a une petite élévation sur le nez; l'ouverture de la bouche fort large; la mâchoire inférieure un peu plus longue que la supérieure; l'une et l'autre garnies d'une grande quantité de dents très-menues; la langue charnue; le palais hérissé de petites dents que l'on voit disposées sur deux rangées et sur une plaque triangulaire; le gosier situé au-dessus et au-dessous de deux autres plaques également hérissées; l'oeil grand; les côtés de la tête, revêtus de petites écailles; la ligne latérale parallèle au dos; une fossette propre à recevoir la partie antérieure de la dorsale; les deux thoracines réunies par une membrane; l'iris jaune, et le ventre blanc.

On trouve un très-grand nombre d'individus de cette espèce dans toutes les rivières de la Caroline; on leur donne le nom de *traut* ou *truite*. On les prend à l'hameçon; on les attire par le moyen de morceaux de *cyprin*. Ils parviennent à la longueur de six ou sept décimètres; leur chair est ferme, et d'un goût très-agréable.

Translation

Addition to the description and synonymy of the genus of the wrasses. First sub genus.

The tail fins are forked, or increasingly deeply indented. Labrus salmoide (Labrus salmoïdes) Large-Mouth Bass.

Characteristics

Nine spiny rays and 13 articulated rays in the back fin; 13 rays in the anal fin, the opercle made up of four plates and terminated by an angular prolongation; two orifices at each nostril; general color a blackish brown.

One owes to citizen Bosc knowledge of the labrus salmoide and the labrus iris, both of which inhabit the waters of Carolina.

The salmoide has a slightly upturned snout; a very large mouth; the lower jaw somewhat longer than the upper; both lined with a large number of very small teeth; a fleshy tongue; the palate bristles with small teeth set in two rows on a triangular pad; above and below the throat are two other pads with brush-like teeth; the eye is large; the sides of the head are covered with small scales; the lateral line is parallel to the back; there is a depression into which the anterior section of the dorsal fin fits; the two thoracic fins joined by a membrane; the iris is yellow and the belly is white.

A very large number of individuals of this species can be found in all of the rivers of Carolina; they are given the name of *traut* or *trout*. They are taken with a hook; they can be attracted with pieces of minnow. They reach a length of 6 or 7 decimeters; their flesh is firm and has a very pleasant taste.

Contemporary

Largemouth bass are large, robust sunfish with an ovate body that is less compressed and deeper than the smallmouth bass. The head is large and long; its length is 26.6 to 31.7 percent of total body length (Scott and Crossman 1973). There is a long, deep notch over the eyes. The opercle is bony to the edge and pointed. The mouth is large and terminal with the lower jaw reaching past the center of the eye in adults. There are brushlike teeth on both jaws, palatines, vomers, and sometimes the tongue.

The first dorsal has 10 spines and is deeply separated from the soft ray portion. Thoracic pelvic fins have 1 spine; they originate under the origin of the first dorsal fin. The short, broad pectoral fins, with 13 to 15 rays, have rounded tips. There are 3 spines in the anal fin. The caudal fin is barely forked, blunt, and broad with rounded tips. The complete lateral line is high and only slightly arched. There are 55 to 69 ctenoid scales in the lateral series. The peritoneum is silvery and the intestine well differentiated (La Rivers 1962; Sigler and Miller 1963; Scott and Crossman 1973).

The upper parts of the body and head are greenish with a silvery or brassy luster. Sides are almost always dark in large fish. The belly is white to yellow (Pflieger 1975). In young fish there is a wide black lateral band that may extend from snout to the posterior edge of the opercle. It is broken or dull in adults. The sides of the head are olive to golden green with scattered black pigment. The inside of the mouth is milk white. Eyes are brown. Both dorsal and caudal fins are opaque and green to olive; anal and pelvic fins are greenish, fading to olive with some white, the pectoral fins are amber and clear (Sigler and Miller 1963; Scott and Crossman 1973; Simpson and Wallace 1978).

Young largemouth are pale green after yolk sac absorption, as compared to young smallmouth bass, which are black. The caudal fin of the young is like that of the adults but dull colored (Scott and Crossman 1973).

RANGE

Native range of the largemouth bass is most of the eastern half of the United States and north to southern Quebec and Ontario on the Atlantic slope. It includes the lower Great Lakes states and the central part of the Mississippi River system south to the Gulf of Mexico (MacCrimmon and Robbins 1975; Stuber, Gebhart, and Maughan 1982). They are also native to Florida. Their range now extends over the 48 contiguous states, to some extent into Canada, and south through much of Central America. Introductions have been made in England, Scotland, Germany, France, South Africa, Hong Kong, the Philippines, and Brazil (Lee et al. 1980). They have been stocked in most of Utah's lowland warm waters. The largest number are in Lake Powell. The original stocking in Utah was in 1890 in the Weber River and Utah Lake (Popov and Low 1950).

SIZE AND LONGEVITY

Largemouth bass are both fast growing and long lived. They are the largest member of the sunfish family. Carlander (1977) listed the Wisconsin State average length for fish ages 1 to 15 years old as follows: in inches, 3.3, 7.4, 10.5, 12.5, 14.0, 15.1, 16.3, 17.4, 18.1, 18.7, 19.5, 19.9, 20.2, 20.6, and 21.0; in mm, 84, 188, 227, 318, 356, 384, 414, 442, 460, 475, 495, 505, 513, 523, 533.

In the southern edge of their range, they may grow year round. Individuals in colder climates grow slower and live longer than individuals in a warm climate. The length at the end of each year for fish ages 1 to 15 in Lake Simcoe, Ontario, was: in inches, 4.0, 8.0, 10.0, 12.0, 13.5, 14.5, 16.0, 17.0, 17.5, 18.0, 19.0, 19.8, 20.4, 21.0, 21.4; in mm, 102, 203, 254, 305, 343, 368, 406, 432, 445, 457, 483, 503, 518, 533, 544 (MacCrimmon and Skobe 1970). Bennett et al. (1983) found that largemouth bass ages 1 to 7 in lower Snake River reservoirs had mean total lengths of: in inches, 3.3, 5.8, 9.1, 11.5, 14.1, 16.5, and 17.4; in mm, 84, 140, 231, 292, 358, 419, 442. La Rivers (1962) measured fish age 3, 4, 5, and 6 years from Ruby Marsh, Nevada; their lengths were: in inches, 7.0, 8.8, 12.8, and 15.8; in mm, 178, 224, 325, 401. In Cache Valley, Utah, the length of fish ages 1 to 8 at the end of each year was: in inches, 3.0, 5.6, 7.6, 10.4, 13.4, 15.5, 16.9, 18.6; in mm, 76, 142, 193, 264, 340, 394, 429, 472 (Sigler and Miller 1963). The world all-tackle, hook-and-line record largemouth bass weighed 22 lb, 4 oz (10.1 kg) (Fishing Hall of Fame 1993). The Utah record is 10 lb, 2 oz (4.6 kg).

FOOD AND FEEDING

Young largemouth bass feed on zooplankton, insects, and small fishes. The progression of food items as they grow is from small zooplankton (crustaceans), to large zooplankton, from small to large insects, then to fishes. Largemouth bass smaller than 0.3 in. (7.6 mm) do not feed; up to 1.5 in. (38 mm), the food is 90 percent crustaceans; as the young increase in length to 2.3 in. (58 mm), the percent of insects (mainly chironomids) increases (Miller and Kramer 1971). Wilde and Paulson (1988) found fishes were most common in the diet after young reached a length of 2.0 in. (51 mm). Their data on young fish were in general agreement with Keast and Webb (1966), Miller and Kramer (1971), and Carlander (1977).

Adult largemouth bass are primarily fish-eating predators, but they will readily take small mammals and ducklings. Feeding occurs at the surface morning and evening, but during midday it is in the water column or near the bottom. They are sight feeders, often moving in schools near shore and close to vegetation. At water temperatures below 50°F (10°C) feeding is curtailed except for maintenance feeding and decreases just before and during spawning. In Wisconsin they feed little between October to May (Carlander 1977). Largemouth bass eat almost any available fishes. They commonly take catfish, minnows, sunfish, shad, perch, and young largemouth. The size of the food taken increases as the predator grows. Reservoir drawdowns may temporarily make large amounts of feed more vulnerable. Low oxygen levels (2 ppm [mg/l]) may depress or halt feeding.

Limiting Factors

Largemouth bass embryos and fry are preyed on by other fishes, herons, bitterns, kingfishers, crayfishes, dragonfly nymphs, and predaceous diving beetles. In Ridge Lake, Illinois, bluegill were the primary decimating factor of young largemouth. In alternate years, the bluegill were removed and bass spawning was successful; in other years, it was not (Bennett 1954). Dropping water temperatures at spawning time, heavy wave action, nest desertion, fluctuating water levels, parasite-caused sterility, and food availability are strong decimating factors for young (Scott and Crossman 1973). The availability of invertebrate food of appropriate size, and at the right time and water temperature, governs the size of young during early August and determines their size and overwinter survival rate. This availability creates strong and weak year classes that are eventually reflected in the harvest (that is, year class strength is established by young-of-the-year class strength, which is impacted by overwintering capacity) (Summerfelt 1975). Overfishing generally is not a serious mortality factor except in the northern edges of their range where growth rates are slow. Bennett (1954) found that in no year of the 9-year study on Ridge Lake was there more than 6.3 percent of available poundage of largemouth bass taken on opening morning, which was the most successful time all season for anglers. On the other hand, Texas Parks and Wildlife Department officials thought that a 14-in. (356-mm) minimum size limit improved the largemouth bass fishing (Sport Fishing Institute 1990). Largemouth bass do not do well in areas of high turbidity, sparse cover, low oxygen concentrations, or high (more than 900 ppm [mg/l]) total alkalinities. To protect from overharvest (real or otherwise), nearly all states with largemouth populations have implemented some type of regulation. These regulations may take the form of minimum length limits, protected length ranges, slot limits, or others.

Breeding Habits

Largemouth bass in Lake Powell spawn from late April to mid-June (Miller and Kramer 1971). They commence when water temperatures reach 58° to 59°F (14.4° to 15°C). In California, Moyle (1976) observed that spawning activity begins in April when water temperatures reach 59°F (15°C); Sigler and Miller (1963) reported 62°F (16.6°C). Nest construction begins earlier at 53° to 57°F (11.7° to 13.9°C). They spawn for the first time in the second or third year of life, generally at 7 to 10 in. (178 to 254 mm) in length but earlier at higher elevations or in more northern populations. Nests are shallow depressions fanned out by the male in sand, gravel, or debris. They are generally in water 3 to 7 ft (0.9 to 2.1 m) deep, but it may vary considerably either way. Shallow nests are more likely to be destroyed by wind action. Nests are often built near cover. Spawning activity is similar to that of other black basses, but the male is less vigorous in his defense of the nest area. Abundant aquatic vegetation in quiet water may result in a pH increase to a point where bass become lethargic and temporarily stop spawning. Stable or rising water levels do not affect spawning success, dropping levels do. Each female lays eggs in one to several nests, the total eggs numbering from 2,000 to 90,000. Eggs are adhesive and attach to the substrate. They hatch within 5 to 6 days at 62° to 65°F (16.7° to 18.3°C). Sac fry spend 5 to 8 days in the nest or close to it. Broods formed by fry from one or more nests are protected by a male for about 2 weeks.

Habitat

Largemouth bass are warmwater fish and occupy a wide range of habitats, but they are primarily a lentic water fish. They are present in small, shallow lakes, ponds, shallow bays of large lakes, and often in large, slow rivers (for example, the Potomac). They tolerate high water temperatures and moderate turbidities. They have been stocked in reservoirs over most of their range. Largemouth are associated with soft bottoms, stumps or other cover, alkaline waters, and a heavy growth of emergent and submergent vegetation. They are rarely found in the rocky habitat preferred by smallmouth. Movement is not extensive, usually less than 5 mi (8 km), and summer territories are small. They often move to the bottom in winter but are active enough to provide an under-ice fishery. In the spring they return to previous spawning areas and summer territories. Largemouth bass seek higher water temperatures than smallmouth bass, preferring temperatures near 80°F (26.7°C) but tolerating 87° to 90°F (30.6° to 32.2°C). At temperatures in excess of 80°F (26.7°C) they become inactive, resting in shaded areas of aquatic or shore vegetation. They do not tolerate low oxygen concentrations well (Sigler and Miller 1963; Scott and Crossman 1973; Summerfelt 1975; Stuber, Gebhart, and Maughan 1982).

Recent behavioral studies indicate that this species may establish several "home territories" and move between them with a strong homing instinct. The movement between them is directional and swift. Winter habitat also seems to have critical importance (James Mayhew, personal communication, 1991).

Management

Stable water levels during spawning and adequate food for young largemouth are important in producing strong year classes. But a large population of bluegill can decimate or destroy a year class. It is generally agreed the largemouth can be overfished. Texas wildlife officials think a 14-in. (356-mm) minimum size limit has helped fishing there. On the other hand, Florida officials think a 12-in. (305-mm) size limit is unsound. The rate of growth of fish to these sizes is the critical factor. There are situations where a slot limit is in order. Overfishing is generally not a serious mortality factor in Illinois (Bennett 1954). However, in Idaho, overfishing is significant because growth rate is slower in the cold climes (Dave Bennett, personal communication, 1991). Knowledge of age class structure should help provide an answer to this less than simple management question.

Statement of Utah Division of Wildlife Resources

Largemouth bass have been present in Utah for a substantial length of time and have provided successful fisheries in a number of waters, particularly in the southern part of the state, most notably Lake Powell. Largemouth bass are undoubtedly the most desired sport fish in the United States. Bass anglers in Utah were a small minority for many years. In the 1970s, however, largely concurrent with the oil exploration boom, large numbers of people moved to Utah from the South, bringing with them a desire to fish for largemouth. This sudden demand for bass fishing led to a number of problems because bass are not ideally suited to most of Utah's environment. In the 1980s Utah's fisheries managers examined all of their waters, identified all of those that appeared to be suitable for largemouth bass, and started a number of new populations.

The extent of largemouth bass habitat, however, still remains limited. Utah's relatively short summers and cool evenings, even in the height of summer, lead to growth rates significantly below those achieved in most other parts of the country where bass are well adapted. As a result most largemouth bass populations, at least in northern Utah, are dominated by smaller, slow-growing young fish, and quite a few years are required to produce quality-sized bass. This delay has necessitated the imposition of size limits in some waters; and at this point, it is questionable how many waters will actually produce high-quality largemouth fishing. The best fisheries still occur in the southern part of the state, primarily at Quail Creek Reservoir and Lake Powell.

A second problem is that the average angler in Utah tends to favor trout and most of the bass fisheries are largely underutilized in terms of the number of anglers fishing per acre. As a predator, largemouth also exist at a higher trophic level than most trout fisheries. As a result, bass produce less harvestable biomass per year than would trout in the same body of water. These situations have led to some conflict between trout and bass anglers on what is desirable management on a given body of water. DWR has tried to balance demands and to provide quality bass fishing where it seems appropriate and also to satisfy the bulk of the state's anglers who still prefer rainbow trout. In a few cases, rainbow trout and bass are managed together with some degree of success. However, the cost of the trout program is raised significantly. In these waters rainbow are stocked at advanced fingerling size late in the fall when low temperatures have reduced bass metabolism sufficiently to allow survival of the stocked fingerlings. This plan worked well at Steinaker Reservoir until bluegill became abundant and outcompeted the rainbow trout fingerlings.

The desires of various elements of the fishing public will likely remain dynamic, and interest in warmwater species like largemouth bass will increase. Unfortunately, there are few waters left in Utah that are ideally suitable for bass and do not already contain them. As a result, increased bass angling opportunity may depend more on the smallmouth bass.

The growth in the smallmouth population in Flaming Gorge, coupled with the influx of anglers desiring bass in the 1970s, has led to a resurgence in interest in the smallmouth bass. The smallmouth seem better adapted to Utah's cooler climate than the largemouth and less of a threat to stocked trout fingerlings. As a result, beginning in the 1980s, experimentation with the use of smallmouth bass began around the state of Utah with a number of notable successes.

The smallmouth bass seem ideally suited to many of Utah's reservoirs and tend to prefer rocky substrate rather than vegetative substrate like the largemouth. They are able to feed effectively on the nonnative crayfish, which have spread throughout most of Utah and may be more suitable for mixed fisheries with trout than largemouth bass. Smallmouth seem also capable of feeding on the young of various nongame fish that compete with rainbow trout and thus may actually enhance trout fishing when managed together with trout in reservoirs containing abundant rough fish species. Smallmouth are presently abundant in a number of Utah reservoirs, including Flaming Gorge, Starvation, Deer Creek, Rockport, New Castle, and Lake Powell. Present studies concerning the interaction of smallmouth bass with rainbow trout in lower elevation reservoirs prove the success of the plan. If the angling public comes to place higher value on smallmouth bass populations, there may be a number of additional opportunities for using this fish.

---

white crappie, *Pomoxis annularis* Rafinesque

Etymology: *Pomoxis* = sharp opercle—the opercle ends in a point rather than a flap; *annularis* = having rings, vertical dark bars around the body

Nomenclature: *Pomoxis annularis* Rafinesque 1818b

IMPORTANCE

White crappie are an important game fish over much of their native range. In most areas, they are caught in greater numbers than largemouth bass and contribute greater weight to the creel than do the smaller sunfishes. They are not currently important in sportfishing in Utah because of limited distribution and numbers. Their flesh is white, flaky, and quite palatable (La Rivers 1962).

DESCRIPTION

Original

(Ring-tail *Pomoxis*.) Body silvery, scales ciliated, back and fins olivaceous, a gilt ring at the base of the tail, lateral line straight, lower jaw longer, tail forked; anal, dorsal, and caudal fins tipped with blackish, pectoral fins extended beyond the vent.

A curious small fish of the Ohio, rather scarce, length 2 or 3 in, vulgar name Silver Perch. The number of rays in the fins is as follow, dorsal fin 20 rays, where of 6 are spinescent; anal fin 22, whereof 6 are spinescent; thoracic fin 6, whereof 1 is spinescent; pectoral fin 15: caudal 28.

Contemporary

Crappie are larger than most other sunfishes. The white crappie is a slab-sided, deep-bodied fish, somewhat more elongate than the black crappie. The back is flattened, and the caudal peduncle is rather long and slightly narrower than that of the black crappie. The head length into total length is 3.2 to 4.0. The snout is short, sharply pointed, and not as deep as that of the black crappie. The mouth is large, terminal, and oblique. The lower jaw is large and protrudes beyond the upper jaw. Both jaws and the palatines have fine teeth. The close-set gill rakers are long and slender. There are 22 to 24 on the lower limb and 6 to 8 on the upper limb. Branchiostegal rays are 7.

The 2 dorsal fins are heavily joined. The first usually has 6 (4 to 7) spines of graduated length; the black crappie usually has 7 or 8. The second dorsal fin is longer and higher with 12 to 16 soft rays. White crappie have a moderately long and slightly forked caudal fin with rounded tips. The anal fin has a long base with 6 graduated spines and 17 to 18 soft rays. The edge is squarish to round. Origin of the pelvic fins is under the pectoral fins and far in advance of the dorsal with 1 spine and 5 rays. The pectoral fins are high and rounded with 13 rays; they are not long.

The ctenoid scales are rather large but are smaller and crowded on the anterior dorsal surface. The lateral line is complete and shallowly arched over the pectoral fin. There are 39 to 46 scales in the lateral series. There are no nuptial tubercles (Becker 1983).

The back and top of the head is dark green to olive brown. It may have a blue green or silver cast. The upper sides are a lighter and more iridescent green and may shade to silver. There are generally 5 to 10 vague, vertical blotches of black, sometimes extending down to the anal fin but becoming indistinct on the lower back and upper sides. Black crappie lack this pattern. The belly is silvery to milky white. The eye is yellow to green. The opercular bone may be iridescent pink or green. The dorsal, caudal, and anal fins are heavily vermiculated, contrasting with light-colored spots and opaque pelvic fins. The paired fins are lightly colored or unpigmented. The dark pigment and iridescent colors on head, chin, and breast are intensified on breeding males, which may be as heavily spotted as the male black crappie. The young have much less black pigment. The length of the dorsal fin is less than the distance from the front of the fin to the eye, which means the fin is further back than on the black crappie.

Range

The native range of the white crappie is restricted to the fresh waters of east-central North America: from southern Ontario to southwestern New York, west of the Appalachian Mountains to the Gulf Coast area of Alabama, then west to eastern Texas, north to South Dakota and southern Minnesota (Lee et al. 1980). They have been widely introduced in several other states. Early stockings were labeled crappies and may have been either or both white and black crappies (La Rivers 1962; Scott and Crossman 1973). In Utah they have been stocked in Gunnison Bend Reservoir and discussed for stocking in Lake Powell.

Size and Longevity

In northern waters, the white crappie reach lengths each year for ages 1 to 9 as follows: in inches, 2.6, 5.4, 7.6, 9.4, 10.6, 11.3, 12.3, 12.5, 14.3; in mm, 66, 137, 193, 239, 269, 287, 312, 318, 363. They grow at about the same rate in western waters, but usually live only 7 years (Carlander 1977).

White crappie in lower Snake River reservoirs have the following mean total lengths for fish ages 1 to 6: in inches, 2.7, 6.0, 8.6, 9.6, 10.2, and 10.6; in mm, 68.6, 150, 218, 244, 259, 269 (Bennett et al. 1983). Sexes grow at about the same rate. The world all-tackle record is 5 lb, 3 oz (2.35 kg) (Fishing Hall of Fame 1993).

Food and Feeding

White crappie are omnivorous and opportunistic in their feeding habits. They feed where forage is most abundant, in shallow water where insects are emerging or deeper waters where there are fishes (La Rivers 1962). Hansen (1951) gave the following percentage of volume for white crappies' food in Illinois: fishes 57.8, aquatic insects 34.9, unidentified animal matter 5.06, other aquatic invertebrates 1.17.

White crappie in lower Snake River reservoirs eat cladocerans, fishes, and aquatic insects. Cladocerans are 43.2 percent of the total and are eaten by 83 percent of the fish. Fishes represent 46.2 percent of total food volume and 13 percent of the identifiable species are suckers (Bennett et al. 1983). Young crappie feed on rotifers, copepods, and other zooplankton. Young feed mostly in the daytime, the adults mostly at night. The feeding mechanism is unusual in that it has long, fine gill rakers, suitable for straining small zooplankters from the water, combined with a large protrusible mouth capable of ingesting large prey, including fish.

Limiting Factors

Males die much earlier than females after the third year (Hansen 1951). White crappie are parasitized by protozoans, trematodes, cestodes, and leeches over much of their range. They are also attacked by the virus disease lymphocystis. They hybridize with black crappie. In some areas, removal of large crappies by anglers is a minor factor. Strong year classes may not appear when there is a strong age class of one-year-old largemouth bass. Recent evidence suggests that white crappie year-class abundance is influenced by abundance of age 1 crappie, due mostly to competition for zooplankton, primarily cladocerans and copepods. The age 0 and age 1 crappie apparently compete for the same food items into their second year.

Breeding Habits

Sexual maturity is usually in the second or third year. It may rarely be at age 1 or 4 years. Fish on nests are usually 6 to 8 in. (152 to 203 mm) long. White crappie spawning takes place for approximately 1 month in late spring to early summer at water temperatures of 57° to 73°F (13.9° to 22.8°C), but they are most active reproductively at temperatures of 61° to 68°F (16.1° to 20°C). The somewhat territorial males arrive at the spawning grounds first and clean out nests. These nests are not well defined but are approximately 5 to 12 in. (13 to 31 cm) in diameter with only a slight depression and are constructed in 8 in. to 5 ft (20 to 152 cm) of water. Hansen (1951) found a large disparity between sexes, females being more abundant. Nests are constructed near rooted plants or algae and close to undercut banks. White crappie generally nest in colonies of 35 to 50 with nests 2 to 4 ft (0.61 to 1.21 m) apart. Spawning takes place in the mornings with little of the active, circular swimming characteristic of some other sunfishes. Each spawning act is from 2 to 5 seconds, with the same pair spawning as many as 50 times, usually with 1 to 50 minutes between them. Only a small portion of the eggs is released at one time, and the same females may spawn in the nests of several males. Egg numbers vary; one 6-in. (152-mm) female had 1,908 eggs, one 13-in. (330-mm) female had 325,677 eggs (Morgan 1954). Some eggs may be resorbed. The eggs are 0.03 in. (0.7 mm) in diameter, colorless, adhesive, and demersal. They adhere to the substrate and plants. The male guards the nest and fans the eggs. Eggs hatch in 17.5 to 24 hours at a temperature of 70° to 74°F (21.1° to 23.3°C) (Morgan 1954). The transparent young remain on the nest only a short time and may leave as early as 4 days after hatching (Scott and Crossman 1973; Becker 1983). Breeding colors of males may be lost as early as the end of June.

Habitat

White crappie tend to be most abundant in warm, somewhat turbid lakes, reservoirs, and stream backwaters. They are also present in rather silted streams, lakes, and ponds and in muddy, slow-moving rivers. In the Great Lakes they are present in the mouths of tributary streams and in warm, weedy, sheltered bays. White crappie have greater tolerance than black crappie for high turbidities, alkaline waters, current, high temperatures, and lack of aquatic vegetation or other cover. They tend to school loosely and are often locally distributed. Individuals may move considerable distances but most are sedentary. Optimum temperatures appear to be 80° to 84°F (26.7° to 28.9°C). During the day they tend to congregate near cover in quiet water 6 to 13 ft (1.9 to 4.0 m) deep. White crappie may move out into open water to feed during evening and early morning; they are more nocturnal than diurnal (Becker 1983).

Management

Once a breeding stock is established in acceptable habitat, no stocking should be necessary. According to Carlander (1977) the California populations today probably are the progeny of 16 fish planted near Morena Reservoir in 1917. Stocking of other sunfishes in waters with established populations of white crappie should be avoided in lakes of less than 200 acres (81 ha). In Iowa, there are many lakes with populations of up to four species of sunfishes, and all do well (James Mayhew, personal communication, 1991).

Size limits may or may not be effective as a management tool. Texas Parks and Wildlife Department officials think a 10-in. (254-mm) minimum length limit has benefitted crappie fishing there. Age class size and composition are the determining factors.

black crappie, *Pomoxis nigromaculatus* (Lesueur)
Plate 46

Etymology: *Pomoxis* = sharp opercle—the opercle ends in a point rather than a flap; *nigromaculatus* = black spotted
Nomenclature: *Cantharus nigro-maculatus* Lesueur 1829 in Cuvier and Valenciennes 1828–1849, *Pomoxis nigromaculatus* (Lesueur) Bailey 1951

IMPORTANCE

Black crappie are popular because they are a medium-sized, easy-to-catch pan fish. Catch rates may be as high as several fish per hour. In Canada they are fished both for sport and commercially. The flesh is white, flaky, and very palatable (Sigler and Miller 1963; Scott and Crossman 1973).

DESCRIPTION

Original

Notre troisième *centrarchus* est celui qui a été gravé dans M. de Lacépède (tome III, pl 24, fig 2), d'après un dessin de M. Bosc, sous le nom de *labre sparoïde*. Il nous a été envoyé récemment par M. Lesueur, qui l'avait pris dans la rivière d'Ouabache, et qui le nommait *cantharus nigro-maculatus*. Il a bien, en effet, comme tous les *centrarchus*, quelque apparence de canthère; mais ses dents au palais et sur la langue, et les deux pointes de son opercule, ne permettent pas de le rapporter à la famille des spares.

Il se distingue du centrarchus bronzé par la forme de sa dorsale, qui est plus basse en avant, plus élevée en arrière, et qui n'a que huit rayons épineux. Son anale est aussi bien plus haute et plus longue. L'angle et le bord inférieur de son préopercule ont quelques dentelures irrégulières.

D. 8/16; A. 6/18; C. 17: P. 12; V. 1/5.

Tout son corps est irrégulièrement marbré et tacheté de noirâtre sur un fond qui paraît avoir été argenté. Les points noirâtres d'entre les rayons sont irréguliers comme les taches du corps.

Nos individus sont longs de près d'un pied.

M. Bosc dit que ces poissons abondent dans les eaux douces de la Caroline, et qu'on les recherche principalement au printemps.

Translation

Our third *centrarchus* is the one pictured in Lacépède (vol. III, pl 24, fig 2), after a drawing by Bosc, under the name *labre nigro-maculatus* [*Labrus sparoides*]. It was recently sent to us by Lesueur, who took it from the Wabash River, and who names it *cantharus nigro-maculatus*.

It definitely has, indeed, like all the *centrarchus*, some appearance of cantharus; but the teeth on the palate and tongue, and the two points of its opercule, don't permit it to belong to the spares family.

It is distinguished from the tan centrarchus by the shape of its dorsal, which is lower in front, higher in the rear, and has only 8 spiny rays. Its anal is also much higher and longer. The angle of the lower edge of its preopercule has some irregular indentations.

D. 8/16; A. 6/18; C. 17; P. 12; V. 1/5

The entire body is irregularly marbled and speckled with a blackish color over a silvery-appearing background. The blackish spots between the rays are irregular, as are the spots on the body.

Our individuals are almost a foot long.

Bosc says that these fish abound in the fresh waters of the Carolinas, and that one finds them principally in the spring.

Contemporary

The black crappie has 2 closely joined dorsal fins. The first dorsal has 7 or 8 spines of graduated length. White crappie usually have 6. The second dorsal is higher than the first; it has 14 to 16 soft rays and a rounded edge. The caudal fin is long, broad, and slightly forked with rounded tips. The anal fin has 5 or more spines and 16 to 18 rays. The thoracic pelvic fins have 5 rays and 1 spine; the tips are rounded. The base of the dorsal fin is about the same length as the base of the anal fin. The dorsal fin is further forward than it is in the white crappie. The pectoral fins, with 13 to 15 rays, are high on the body, long, broad, and rounded. Ctenoid scales are large but crowded anteriorly on the dorsal surface and breast. The lateral line is complete, high, and shallowly arched over the pectorals. There are 36 to 41 scales in the lateral series. Nuptial tubercles are not present (Sigler and Miller 1963; Simpson and Wallace 1978).

Black crappie are silver olive with numerous black or dark green splotches on the sides. Vertical bars, prominent in the young, are absent in adults. Sides are light, iridescent green to silvery. The head and sides have an irregular mosaic of black blotches. The belly is silvery to white. The dorsal, caudal, and anal fins are strikingly vermiculated with black, forming round or oblong yellow to pale green spots in the center of the vermiculations. The pelvic fins are opaque with some black on the tips of the membranes. The pectoral fins are dusky and transparent. When the fish are in clear, vegetated water they are dark with a contrasting color pattern; individuals from turbid water have a bleached look. In breeding males the black pattern, particularly on the head, becomes darker, more intense and velvety in color (Sigler and Miller 1963; Simpson and Wallace 1978). The young have less pigment and pattern.

The black crappie is deep bodied and less elongate than the white crappie. The head is long, almost one-third the body length with a narrow depression over the eyes. The back is rounded, and the snout is upturned, producing an S-shaped profile. The short snout is deeper than that of the white crappie. The terminal mouth is large and oblique, the large lower jaw extends beyond the upper jaw. The maxillary reaches to the posterior edge of the pupil. They have fine teeth on jaws and palatines. There are seven branchiostegal rays. Siefert (1969) discussed how to separate larval black and white crappie.

Range

Black crappie originally ranged in fresh waters of eastern and central North America from Quebec south through western New York (west of the mountains), south from Virginia to Florida, along the Gulf Coast to central Texas, then north to North Dakota and eastern Montana (Lee et al. 1980). They have been introduced widely. They are fairly abundant in Utah lowland warm waters from Cache Valley to Lake Powell.

Size and Longevity

In northern waters, black crappie ages 1 to 9 years had total lengths as follows: in inches, 2.5, 5.5, 7.4, 8.5, 9.8, 10.4, 11.6, 11.9, 12.2; in mm, 64, 140, 188, 216, 249, 264, 295, 302, 310. In Florida and Texas waters, age groups are somewhat larger. Growth varies tremendously with size of the population and habitat productivity. Mantua and Willard reservoirs in northern Utah, in the late 1970s, had vast populations of 7- to 8-in. (178- to 203-mm) black crappie but few large ones. In Wisconsin, fish ages 2 to 8 years had the following lengths: in inches, 5.9, 8.0, 9.0, 9.9, 10.7, 11.3, 11.6; in mm, 150, 203, 229, 251, 272, 287, 295 (Beckman 1949). Bennett et al. (1983) reported that fish ages 1 to 4 from lower Snake River, Washington, reservoirs have mean total lengths of: in inches, 2.9, 5.7, 7.7, and 8.6; in mm, 74, 145, 196, 218. Dominant year classes may appear following a period of high mortality or in new impoundments. The world all-tackle hook-and-line record is 6 lb (2.7 kg) (Fishing Hall of Fame 1993). The Utah record is 3 lb, 2 oz (1.4 kg).

Food and Feeding

Feeding mechanisms and food of black crappie are almost identical to those of white crappie. They are primarily midwater feeders; the young eat zooplankton and small Diptera larvae predominantly, and larger ones eat fishes and aquatic insects (Keast and Webb 1966). They need at least a partial diet of fishes to reach their maximum growth potential. Black crappie will feed at temperatures as low as 44°F (6.7°C) and therefore may feed year round. They feed anytime, day or night, but feeding generally peaks at noon, midnight, and early morning (Keast 1968). Cladocerans are the single most important food item for black crappie in lower Snake River reservoirs, 65.8 percent of total food eaten. Aquatic insects constitute 16 percent of total volume (Bennett et al. 1983).

LIMITING FACTORS

Turbidity and lack of forage fish slow growth rates and may produce stunted populations. Growth rates are better where there is an abundance of insects rather than copepods or other small invertebrates. Mortality may be high in the 2- to 4-year age groups, especially the males. Carlander (1977) stated that 93°F (33.9°C) temperatures are lethal. A lack of adequate breeding sites will reduce reproduction. Black crappie are parasitized by protozoans, trematodes, cestodes, and nematodes over most of their range. Black and white crappie hybridize.

BREEDING HABITS

Black crappie mature in the second or third year at about 6 to 8 in. (152 to 203 mm). Spawning habits are similar to those of the white crappie. Spawning is initiated in early spring as temperatures approach 58° to 64°F (14.4° to 17.8°C) and may continue until July. Males build nests, which are shallow depressions on bottoms ranging from mud to gravel to debris. Nests are usually built in water from 6 in. to 20 ft (0.15 to 6.1 m) deep near or in beds of aquatic vegetation. Males may construct a new nest close to neighboring nests. A female spawns with several males and releases only a small portion of her eggs at any one time. Females lay between 10,000 and 200,000 eggs, the number being roughly related to size and age. Eggs are slightly less than 0.04 inches (1.0 mm) in diameter, whitish, demersal, and adhesive. Hatching is in 3 to 5 days at 62°F. Eggs are generally guarded by the male for a short time. Fry then rise from the nest and spend the next few weeks drifting in open water, feeding on zooplankton (Sigler and Miller 1963).

HABITAT

Black crappie prosper in slightly alkaline, eutrophic waters with limits of 900 ppm (mg/l) total alkalinity, 250 ppm carbonates, and 200 ppm potassium and sodium (Carlander 1977). They do well in large, warm, clear lakes or in reservoirs that have an abundance of aquatic vegetation. They are also present in clear, quiet, warm waters of large ponds, small lakes, bays, and shallow areas of larger lakes. They are almost always near cover such as abundant aquatic vegetation and over sandy to muddy bottoms. Larval crappies were found in shallow water in Lake Ruthven, Iowa, until they reached a length of about 0.04 in. (1.0 mm); larger larval specimens are subsequently found in the limnetic (deepwater) zone in June and July, where temperatures may range from 55° to 72°F (12.8° to 22.2°C). Black crappie are less tolerant of turbidity than the white crappie. They grow and prosper at water temperatures of 75° to 87°F (23.9° to 30.6°C). They spend their days around shore cover, then move offshore to feed in open waters in the evenings and early mornings, or if food is limited, in all hours of the day.

MANAGEMENT

Generally, fishing regulations for black crappie can be liberal on established populations (see management section under white crappie).

Crappie are rarely if ever managed as a monoculture. The usual associates are bluegill, green sunfish, and perhaps other *Lepomis* spp., and largemouth bass. Limiting factors may be unknown or difficult to impossible to address or correct. A large age class every 3 to 4 years may produce adequate fishing. Large, acceptable-size populations of three to four species of fish in any given year are unlikely. A fish-forage base is the required common denominator. Neither species of crappie is recommended for stocking ponds of less than 10 acres (4 ha) as stunting occurs routinely in small bodies of water.

Perches (Family Percidae)

This family consists of two subfamilies, the perches (Percinae) and the darters (Etheostominae). The darters have 4 genera and 139 species. In Utah the perches have 2 genera and 2 species; nationally there are 3 species. The darters have 1 species (Robins et al. 1991).

Members of this family are usually elongate, terete, and somewhat laterally compressed. Mouth size and location varies between species; it may be large or small, terminal or inferior. Villiform teeth are present on the jaws, vomer, and palatines in bands; the lower pharyngeals bear sharp teeth.

The 2 dorsal fins are well separated, as contrasted to the sunfishes. The first dorsal has 6 to 15 spines. The pectoral fins are moderately long, and the pelvic fins are thoracic with 1 spine and 5 rays. The anal fin is small with 1 or 2 spines and the caudal fin lunate, truncate, or rounded. This family is circumpolar in distribution but most species are restricted to North America. The family inhabits waters that range from warm-temperate to cold-subarctic. Percinae are important to both sport and commercial fishing (Sigler and Sigler 1987).

---

yellow perch,
Perca flavescens
(Mitchill)
Plate 47

Etymology: *Perca* = dark colored; *flavescens* = yellow
Nomenclature: *Morone flavescens* Mitchill 1814b, *Perca flavescens* (Cuvier) Richardson 1836

IMPORTANCE

Yellow perch utilize a great variety of habitat types. They occur in schools and congregate near shore in the spring. These factors all tend to make them an important pan fish in Utah. In some areas of the United States and Canada, they are fished commercially. They feed actively and can be caught year round, taking most lures readily and providing a good sportfishery. Yellow perch rate high in palatability.

Underfished (exploited/harvested) populations may produce numerous small fish unappealing to anglers.

DESCRIPTION

Original

3—*Morone flavescens*

Lives in fresh water, both stagnant and running.

Head rather small, and tapering toward the snout; body deep and thick, but becoming slender towards the tail; colours brown or olive on the back, turning to yellow on the sides, and white on the belly; faint brown zones, to the number of 4 or more, diversifying the sides from back to belly; dorsal and pectoral fins brown; ventral & anal scarlet; gill-covers tripartite; lower and after edges of the foremost acutely serrated; middle one serrated at the lower edge, and striated radially on the broad side; there is one serrated bone on the thorax, immediately above the pectoral fin, at the posterior margin of the branchia opening, and 2 other bones with serrated edges above the first, near the upper part of the branchial opening; vent near the tail; lateral line almost straight; tail rather concave; scales rather hard & rough; eyes large; iris yellowish; both jaws roughened with very small teeth. The first ventral ray is spinous; so are the 2 first anal rays, all the rays of the foremost dorsal fin; and the foremost of the second dorsal. Is a beautiful fish. Length 10 in, depth 2 1/2 in length.

Rays, P. 14: V. 5: D. 12–14: A. 10: C. 10.

Contemporary

The two dorsal fins of the yellow perch are distinctly separated. The first is high and slightly rounded with 12 to 14 spines; the second is smaller with 12 to 13 soft rays. The pelvic fins are thoracic; the pectoral fins are broad and rounded with 13 to 15 rays. The caudal fin is slightly forked; the anal fin is square to rounded with 2 spines and 6 to 8 rays. There are 51 to 67 ctenoid scales in the lateral series. The lateral line is complete and slightly arched. Yellow perch have no nuptial tubercles (Sigler and Miller 1963).

Yellow perch are dark olive green on the back. The sides are yellow to brassy (the species name). The belly is whitish. The fish are distinguished by 6 to 8 dark vertical bars extending across the back and down the sides.

The body is elongate and oval rather than cylindrical; it is slightly compressed laterally. The moderately large mouth is terminal. The maxillary extends at least to the midpoint of the eye. Small teeth are present in brushlike bands on the jaws, palatines, and vomer.

RANGE

The native range of yellow perch in North America is from Nova Scotia to the Santee River drainage, South Carolina, west of the

Appalachian Mountains from Pennsylvania to upper Missouri and from eastern Kansas northwest to Montana, then north to Great Slave Lake, Alberta, Canada, and southeast to James Bay, Quebec, Canada, and New Brunswick, Canada (Lee et al. 1980). It has been introduced into most states including Utah. It occurs in Utah Lake, Bear Lake, Deer Creek, Sevier Bridge, Newton, and Hyrum reservoirs, and Provo and Cub rivers as well as other Utah waters.

Size and Longevity

Rate of growth of individual yellow perch varies with habitat, size of the fish, and numbers of competitors. Northern populations grow slower and live longer than southern ones. Where stunting occurs, adults may not exceed 7 in. (178 mm) in length. The yearly size for Klamath River, California, yellow perch ages 1 to 5 is: in inches, 3.5, 5.9, 7.9, 9.1, 10.6; in mm, 89, 150, 201, 231, 269 (Coots 1956). In Green Bay, Wisconsin, the yearly size for fish ages 1 to 7 is: in inches, 2.8, 4.5, 6.1, 7.4, 8.7, 9.9, 10.8; in mm, 71, 114, 155, 188, 221, 246, 274 (Herman et al. 1959). Yellow perch rarely live more than 9 years. Females grow faster than males and achieve a larger size. The world all-tackle record fish weighed 4 lb, 3 oz (1.9 kg) (Fishing Hall of Fame 1993). The Utah record is 2 lb, 11 oz (1.2 kg).

Food and Feeding

Principal food of the yellow perch is small, live animals, which are effectively strained out of the water by the comblike gill rakers. They feed largely on *Daphnia* spp., immature insects, large invertebrates, and fish. They feed in open water, near the surface or off the bottom. Adults may browse among patches of aquatic vegetation, eating crayfish, dragonfly larvae, and snails. Most adult feeding takes place during the day, with peaks of activity in the morning and at dusk when they move close inshore, then travel parallel to it. Large perch prefer fishes but readily shift to invertebrates. Young yellow perch feed on zooplankton near vegetation in shallow water (Herman et al. 1959).

Limiting Factors

Spawning may be reduced or eliminated if there is a sharp and protracted temperature drop just before the time spawning is normally initiated. Yellow perch decline in areas where aquatic vegetation is greatly reduced or lost.

They are preyed upon by almost all warm- to coolwater predatory fishes, especially basses and walleye. They are the most important prey species for largemouth bass in Idaho (Dave Bennett, personal communication, 1991). Many parasites afflict them. They also suffer from a number of fish diseases and pathological conditions such as tumors.

Breeding Habits

Males are generally mature at age 2 to 3 or, rarely, at age 1, females at age 2 to 3, rarely at age 4. Yellow perch spawn in early spring, usually at night. Spawning takes place on sand, gravel, or rubble bottoms or over submerged beds of aquatic vegetation at temperatures ranging from 44° to 52°F (6.7° to 11.1°C). Males move into the spawning area first. When ready to spawn, females make a series of rapid turns or other quick movements to attract males. The female then swims rapidly, releasing a long string of eggs encased in a gelatinous sheath that may be from 2 to 7 ft (0.6 to 2.1 m) long and 1.5 to 2 in. (3.8 to 5.1 cm) wide. Total number of eggs deposited may be as high as 76,000, but generally it is 4,000 to 40,000 and related to size and age of the female. Males follow the female and release sperm, which envelop the eggs. These sticky bands of eggs are draped across vegetation or over the bottom. The eggs hatch in 10 to 20 days at 50° to 62°F (10° to 16.7°C) and the larvae, which are 0.02 in. (0.5 mm) long, begin feeding on zooplankton in shallow water soon after hatching. Some reserve food is available in the yolk sac (Herman et al. 1959; Sigler and Miller 1963; Scott and Crossman 1973).

HABITAT

Yellow perch are very adaptable, thriving in cold, infertile Bear Lake and warm, productive Hyrum Reservoir. They also live in other large lakes and reservoirs or quiet rivers. Young yellow perch inhabit shallower water than adults. In Green Bay, Wisconsin, adults hug the bottom, but in Lake Mendota, Wisconsin, they may be 25 ft (7.6 m) off the bottom (Herman et al. 1959). They prefer lakes with moderate beds of vegetation and clear water over bottoms that range from muck to sand and gravel. Yellow perch are tolerant of low oxygen levels. Schools of 50 to 200 are typical, and aggressive actions toward other schools are rare.

MANAGEMENT

Stunting is more likely to occur in cold, infertile waters than in warm, eutrophic waters. Large lakes are most likely to produce predators that prey on, and therefore produce, desirable-size yellow perch. In Spirit Lake, Iowa, white bass, walleye, and northern pike reduced young perch populations by a magnitude of 99 percent in 6 weeks. Yellow perch are intensely competitive and populations tend to stunt, so they are of somewhat questionable value as either forage or sport fish in some waters. Stable habitat, especially at spawning time, is an important requirement of this species. Vegetation is also important.

---

logperch,
Percina caprodes
(Rafinesque)

Etymology: *Percina* = a diminutive of *Perca caprodes* (piglike), in reference to the snout

Nomenclature: *Sciena caprodes* Rafinesque 1818b (type locality Ohio

River), *Etheostoma caprodes* Rafinesque 1820a, *Pileoma semifasciatum* DeKay 1842, *Pileoma zebra* Agassiz 1850, *Pileoma fasciatum* Small 1865, *Percina caprodes* Jordan and Evermann 1896–1900 (Scott and Crossman 1973)

IMPORTANCE

The logperch supplies limited forage for game fishes. It is an interesting natural history entity.

DESCRIPTION

Original

Sciena caprodes Body cylindrical whitish, with 20 transverse brownish stripes, alternately smaller, a black dot at the base of the tail, tail forked, upper jaw longer, operculum acute, a single spine on it, first dorsal fin 15 spiny rays, second 12 rays, anal fin 12 rays, whereof 2 are spiny.

Contemporary

The color pattern of the logperch consists of a series of more or less alternating long and short, narrow vertical bars on both sides of the body. The body is a pale straw color, shading to pale olive on the back, and white on the belly. The long conical nose overhangs the mouth. The body is elongate and almost terete. The dorsal fins are close together. The lateral line is complete and straight. There is a small distinct spot on the caudal (Smith 1985).

RANGE

The range of this darter is much of the eastern United States, the upper Mississippi, and the central Atlantic slope, the Great Lakes, and Hudson Bay drainages. In Utah it is present in Willard Bay Reservoir.

SIZE AND LONGEVITY

Logperch from central Wisconsin grew as follows for 4 years: in inches, 2.5, 3.7, 4.6, 4.9; in mm, 64, 94, 117, 125 (Lutterbie 1976). The largest observed fish was 8 in. (203 mm). Few live longer than 5 years.

FOOD AND FEEDING

Adult logperch feed on insects, amphipods, entomostracans, leeches, and fish eggs. Young eat primarily copepods and cladocerans (Becker 1983).

LIMITING FACTORS

Reproductive success is hampered by siltation, flooding, and heavy egg predation by supernumerary males. Fish of all sizes are preyed upon by fishes and birds.

BREEDING HABITS

Logperch spawn in the spring from April to July, when water temperatures reach 72° to 79°F (22.2° to 26.1°C). Spawning is over sand and gravel riffles in water 4 to 8 in. (10 to 20 cm) deep. Eggs are adhesive, colorless, and demersal; no nest is prepared, and neither eggs nor young are guarded. Logperch mature at age 2, rarely 1 (Lutterbie 1976).

HABITAT

Logperch apparently prefer medium-size to large lakes and rivers. They may be found in such diverse habitats as swift water, quiet water, or in open water of large lakes, at depths of 30 to 75 ft (9 to 22.9 m). Schools feed in daytime, but break up and take cover at night. On sunny days in clear water they may seek cover or burrow into the bottom. After the breeding season they seek deep water (Lutterbie 1976).

MANAGEMENT

As with many fishes, high-quality water and stable water levels during breeding season are prime requisites.

---

walleye,
Stizostedion vitreum
(Mitchill)
Plate 48

Etymology: *Stizostedion* = pungent throat; *vitreum* = glassy, referring to the large silvery eyes

Nomenclature: *Perca vitrea* Mitchill 1818, *Stizostedion vitreum* (Mitchill) Jordan and Evermann 1896–1900, *Stizostedion vitreum vitreum* (Mitchill) Hubbs and Lagler 1941, *Stizostedion vitreum* Robins et al. 1991

IMPORTANCE

Walleye are valuable sport fish. They are also important in Canada as a commercial species. Walleye take a hook cautiously, are not spectacular fighters, and they are difficult for novices to hook. Fishing is best at night. Walleye rate very high in palatability and can be caught in all seasons. In spring spawning runs, walleye provide good sportfishing in Utah Lake, Willard Bay Reservoir, and elsewhere.

DESCRIPTION

Original

Glass eye—*Perca vitrea*, with the pupils of the eyes appearing like the semi-globes of glass in the decks of vessels, when illuminated on the opposite side, and with a yellow iris. Found in the Cayuga Lake, of a roundish (teres) figure; the middling magnitude about 18 in long, by 3 and quarter deep.

Colour of the body dark-yellowish, like that of the common pike; belly white, back darker than the sides. Scales stout, lateral line proceeds straight from the upper part of the gill-opening to the middle of the tail, and is of a deeper brown than the adjoining and surrounding skin. Ventral and anal fins light yellow. Two dorsal fins, the foremost of which is spinous, and consists of thirteen rays, and the hindmost filamentous and composed of twenty rays. Lower jaw rather longer than the upper; tail sinuated towards the middle, and rendering the caudal rays of that part shorter than those above and below. This character and description were taken

> from the drawing and notes of Simeon De Witt, Esq. made by him at Ithaca, in October 1816; was pronounced by that gentleman to be tolerably good eating.

Contemporary
The first and second dorsal fins are separated; the high, rounded first dorsal has 12 to 16 spines. The nearly square second dorsal is as high as the first with 1 fine spine and 18 to 22 rays. The broadly forked caudal is long with rounded tips. The anal fin has 2 spines and 11 to 14 rays. The thoracic pelvic fins have 1 spine and 5 rays; the pectoral fins have 13 to 16 rays and rounded tips. There are 86 to 92 ctenoid scales in the lateral series. The cheeks are scaleless. There is no nuptial tubercle. External differentiation of the sexes is difficult.

The body is elongate and subcylindrical in young but adults are laterally compressed. The snout is long and blunt; the large, terminal mouth is almost horizontal; the maxillary is long, extending to the posterior edge of the eye. Walleye have strong teeth on the premaxillaries, jaws, and head of the vomer and palatines. Canine teeth on the head of the vomer are large, sharp, and recurved. This serves to distinguish them from yellow perch.

Walleye color varies with both habitat and fish size. In turbid water, color is paler with the less obvious black pattern. In clear water, colors are more vivid. Background color is usually olive brown to golden brown or yellow. Some adults are dark silver to dark olive brown mottled with brassy spots. This may shade into yellow or milky white on the belly. In 4- to 14-in. (102- to 357-mm) fish, there are 6 to 7 vague to obvious dark, vertical bands on the back and sides. These bars are usually absent in adults. The fins are randomly spotted.

Range

Fresh waters, and rarely brackish waters, of North America are the principal range of the walleye. Native range is from Quebec, Canada, south to New Hampshire, and southwest to Pennsylvania; they occur west of the Appalachian Mountains to Alabama, northwest to eastern Oklahoma, north through the eastern half of the states from Kansas to North Dakota then north to near the Arctic coast in the McKenzie River, Canada, and finally southeast across James Bay to Quebec (Lee et al. 1980). They have been widely introduced outside their native range. They were introduced into Utah in 1951. They are now present in Willard Bay, Gunnison Bend, Dmad, and Starvation reservoirs, Utah Lake, Weber River, and Lake Powell. They are rare in the upper Colorado River drainage.

Size and Longevity

Walleye are relatively fast growing and moderately long lived. Growth is more rapid in the southern part of their range than in northern locations. One Minnesota female was judged to be 18 to 20 years old although few live longer than 12 years (Niemuth et al. 1959). Females grow faster and live longer than males. The difference in size is approximately 6 percent, resulting in females being 2 to 4 in. (51 to 102 mm) longer than males at a given age. Young walleye grow rapidly in length, older ones increase rapidly in weight. A 5-in. (127-mm) fish weighs 0.7 oz (20 g), a 10-in. (254-mm) fish 5.4 oz (153 g), a 15-in. (381- mm) fish 1.28 lb (0.5 kg), a 20-in. (508-mm) fish 2.9 lb (1.32 kg), and a 26-in. (666-mm) fish weighs 6 lb (2.72 kg) (Niemuth). In Utah Lake, walleye size is: in inches, 6.7, 11.6, 13.4, 15.2, 16.6, 17.0; in mm, 170, 295, 340, 386, 422, 432, for ages 1 to 6 (Arnold 1960). A Canadian population of fish ages 1 to 12 years reached the following approximate total lengths: in inches, 8.7, 13.2, 16.4, 19.0, 21.2, 22.8, 23.9, 25.2, 26.0, 26.6, 28.0, 28.9; in mm, 221, 335, 417, 483, 539, 579, 607, 640, 660, 676, 734 (Payne 1964).

Walleye may weigh less than 3.5 oz (99 g) the first year. Average adult size in most populations is 5 to 6 lb (2.3 to 2.7 kg). The world all-tackle hook-and-line record walleye weighed 25 lb (11.3 kg) (Fishing Hall of Fame 1993). The record for Utah is 12 lb, 5 oz (5.6 kg).

Food and Feeding

Young walleye first eat plankton, crustaceans, then insect larvae, primarily chironomids. Fishes appear in the diet when the young are 3 in. (76 mm) long. At 6 in. (152 mm), plankton is unimportant as a food item. Food items shift very quickly from invertebrates to fishes with increases in predator size. Adults are mainly piscivorous but also consume large invertebrates. Fish prey is whatever is available and vulnerable. Walleye are strong swimmers and can catch most prey species. Where there is a large diversity of food they appear to select yellow perch and freshwater drum (Niemuth et al. 1959). They also take crayfish, snails, frogs, and occasionally small mammals. In northern Iowa, feeding in shallow waters occurred at night.

Limiting Factors

Large populations of northern pike are one of the most effective predators of walleye. Walleye are also preyed on by other predatory fishes and to a lesser extent by fish-eating birds and mammals. Water temperature, stream flow, and wind at spawning time are important factors in controlling population levels (Schneider and Leach 1977). High winds may wash eggs ashore. Fry mortality, including natural death and cannibalism, may be as high as 99 percent in some populations. In East Okoboji Lake, Iowa, angling mortality is at least 32 percent and may be higher in some other Iowa populations. Annual natural mortality may be 10 to 15 percent for adults. A wide variety of parasites, including protozoans, trematodes, cestodes, nematodes, and others affect them over most of their range.

Breeding Habits

Walleye spawning occurs in spring shortly after the ice goes out in water temperatures of 38° to 44°F (3.3° to 6.7°C). Spawning in lakes is over boulders or coarse gravel on windswept shores in water 2 to 4 ft (0.6 to 1.2 m) deep. Stream-spawning fish move upstream immediately after ice breakup when lakes are still ice-covered. Walleye may travel as much as 100 mi (161 km) upstream to spawn. There is evidence of homing on the same spawning stream year after year.

Males move into spawning grounds ahead of females but are not territorial. No nest is built. Much prespawning activity occurs, including pursuit, pushing, circular swimming, and fin erection. Prespawning activity may occur at water temperatures as low as 34°F (1.1°C). One large female and one or two generally smaller males participate in this activity and then rush to the spawning area, which is frequently over boulders or coarse gravel shoals in lakes or streams. The female rolls on her side near the males and eggs and sperm are deposited; the eggs fall into crevices in the substrate and are sticky until water-hardened.

Males mature at 2 to 3 years of age and 12 to 13 in. (305 to 330 mm); females at age 3 to 4 and 15 to 17 in. (381 to 432 mm). One 12-lb (5.4-kg) female produced 388,000 eggs, and the number of eggs may be as high as 612,000 in very large females. Average egg production is about 50,000. Eggs are 0.05 in. (1.2 mm) in diameter and hatch in 26 days at water temperatures of 40°F (4.4°C), 21 days at 50° to 55°F (10° to 12.8°C), and 7 days when it is 57°F (13.9°C) (Niemuth et al. 1959). Newly hatched fry are 0.3 to 0.5 in. (8 to 13 mm) long and disperse into the upper levels of open water in 10 to 15 days after hatching (Sigler and Miller 1963; Scott and Crossman 1973).

Habitat

Walleye thrive in moderately fertile habitat. They tolerate a wide range of environmental conditions from acid bog lakes, to oligotrophic lakes, to eutrophic hardwater lakes. The most favorable conditions appear to exist in large, fertile, shallow, turbid lakes such as Spirit Lake, Iowa, or large streams or rivers, provided they are deep or turbid enough to afford cover.

Walleye do not have home ranges. They use boulders, shoals, and weed beds for cover. They move up and down in depth in response to light intensity, and seasonally or daily in response to temperatures and food availability. They live mainly on or near the bottom and are largely nocturnal. They may move inshore at twilight into or near incoming streams to feed. One individual in northern Utah migrated from Hyrum Reservoir to the mouth of the Bear River, a distance of 50 mi (81 km).

Management

Walleye are extremely voracious predators and may, therefore, be used as effective predators for pan-fish control. There is evidence that angling does not harm the population; there is also evidence that it does. This conflicting data makes management more of a lake-by-lake problem. Conditions at spawning-rearing time usually govern the strength of year classes. A strong year class may be heavily exploited. Some biologists believe that the walleye is so temperamental a biter that overfishing them is unlikely, but if they are fished year round by experienced walleye anglers, this may not be true. The most effective closed season is during spawning; they are more concentrated and less wary. Where there is heavy fishing or limited brood stock, stocking of subyearlings may be in order. In clearwater lakes with minimum cover, reefs concentrate forage fishes and walleye (Niemuth et al. 1959).

Minimum size limits are necessary when there is: (1) low reproduction, (2) good growth of small fish, (3) low natural mortality, and (4) high angling mortality. Slot size limits are appropriate when: (1) there is good natural reproduction, (2) small fish are growing slowly, (3) small fish have a high natural mortality rate, and (4) there is high angling effort. Maximum size limits are not widely used, more for social than for biological reasons. They may be used when: (1) it is necessary to protect brood stock, and (2) where recruitment is low. A third reason might be where anglers accept it. Or, for example, the limit might be one or two fish over 22 or 24 in. (559 to 610 mm) (Brousseau and Armstrong 1987). High flow-through, run-of-the-river reservoirs such as exist on the Columbia River, limit recruitment.

PART III

Fisheries, Fishing, and Recreation Areas

The Fisherman

John Jerry went fishing with a pin on a string.
His freckled face glowed 'till it made your heart sing.
He trolled, and he cast 'till the fish on the bank
Piled higher each time that his line gave a yank.
He caught sunfish, and swordfish, and squawfish and whales.
And one, when they weighed it, almost broke the scales.
The fishermen stared, quite amazed at his skill,
And he gave free advice as most all anglers will.
He opened the season with great ease and aplomb,
'Till the warden escorted John Jerry home.
And John Jerry strutted and whistled off key,
It was opening day, and John Jerry was three.

Rodello Hunter

CHAPTER 12

Bruce Schmidt

Management of Utah's Fishes: Agency Perspective for the Year 2000

The primary consideration for managing fishes in Utah relates to aquatic habitats: their quantity, quality, and suitability for various species, both native and introduced. Utah is second only to Nevada in the paucity of its precipitation, resulting in water being a scarce and highly valuable commodity for other than fisheries. When European settlers first arrived in what is now Utah, they encountered a desert region with most water resources concentrated in the higher mountain ranges. In order for settlers to succeed in establishing viable communities, it was necessary to capture what water resources were available and use them to support people. In fact, history records that City Creek was diverted onto agriculture fields the day immediately following the founding of Salt Lake City. Today, very few streams and lakes remain in original condition. Instead, they suffer from slight to overwhelming modifications from efforts to put them to beneficial use as defined by state water law. Unfortunately, state law does not recognize the in-stream use of water for sustaining fisheries as "beneficial."

Although the second lowest state in average precipitation, Utah is fortunate that most of the precipitation it receives falls in the form of snow. Because winter snowfall is much more reliable and predictable than summer thundershowers, pioneers in Utah found it relatively easy to tap the aquatic resource at higher elevations by constructing a series of reservoirs throughout various drainages. This damming and diverting of waters for human uses had the detrimental effect on fish of grossly altering natural stream flow patterns and causing major disruption in spawning. Waters were also polluted and silted, significantly affecting water quality. Some of the nonnative fish species introduced to utilize these altered waters placed further burdens on native populations through predation, disease, and competition.

Human alteration of Utah's aquatic systems was not all negative, however. The reservoirs created throughout Utah greatly increased the surface acreage of water available for fisheries statewide. Today, the majority of sportfishing in Utah exists in the artificially created environments of reservoirs and their tailwaters. In many cases water quality for sportfisheries in these waters is exceptional to excellent for several species of fishes, including trout, coolwater, and warmwater species. Where poor water quality or fluctuations in the irrigation demand are too great, however, managing sportfisheries in the artificially created environments presents significant challenges.

In order to simplify management, a number of separate programs for dealing with specific fisheries have been established within the Utah Division of Wildlife Resources Comprehensive Management Plan. This plan allows for more specific planning and marshalling of human and financial resources to each of the programs. In addition, two distinct organizations exist within the Division of Wildlife Resources (DWR) to deal with fisheries management programs. Nongame native fishes are managed largely through the Nongame Management Section of DWR; sport fishes, native and introduced, are managed by the Fisheries Management Section.

Management of native fishes is conducted under several programs within the Comprehensive Management Plan. These programs are defined as Colorado River fishes (Colorado squawfish, humpback chub, bonytail chub, and razorback sucker), June sucker, Virgin River fishes (woundfin, Virgin River chub), and other nongame fishes. Several activities are established within these programs. Initially, these little-understood fishes were systematically inventoried to determine abundance and distribution as well as to establish some of the basic life history parameters. Management activities now center around the protection of remaining habitat, and, where possible, restoration and re-creation of lost or degraded habitat. Other activities are focused on actions leading to recovery of the listed species. Significant coordination is needed to assure that sport fish management does not pose threats to native fish populations.

For sport fish management, there are three specific programs outlined in the Comprehensive Management Plan:

(1) The Sport Fishes program is primarily focused on producing quality fishing opportunity within the biological parameters of the resource.

(2) The Special Species program deals specifically with native sport fishes, particularly the cutthroat trout, and is geared toward protecting and perpetuating native fishes and bringing them into greater prominence in Utah's overall sport fish program. The primary objectives for the Special Species program relate to habitat protection and conservation of the species, with sport fish management objectives secondary.

(3) The Commercial Fishes program is largely regulatory and deals with the commercial harvest of some abundant aquatic species and with regulation of public aquaculture, and private fish ponds.

The Sport Fishes program is the largest and most complex fisheries program in the Comprehensive Management Plan. It is divided into four functional areas that address the varied needs of Utah's extensive sportfishery resource to accomplish the goals contained in the plan.

Sport fish management deals with regulations, population assessment, habitat classification and inventory, angler use, and stocking quotas.

Special Projects, formerly called Research, oversees management and surveys on the four large, difficult-to-manage waters (Bear Lake, Lake Powell, Flaming Gorge, Strawberry Reservoir) as well as conducting special surveys and studies to identify and solve specific problems statewide.

Fish Culture raises trout to meet management objectives and annually produces approximately 800,000 lb (360,000 kg) of trout, or up to 12 million fish of various sizes. In addition, warmwater species are acquired from out-of-state sources and a small number of smallmouth bass and tiger musky are produced at one small warmwater facility.

The Fisheries Experiment Station researches fish health management for wild populations.

Projects and activities conducted by all four functional areas must be coordinated. None of the functions operates independently, and coordination and decision making take place in a participative management framework.

Even though Utah is a dry state, there are several thousand reservoirs, high mountain lakes, and streams that constitute a valuable fishery resource. Although management biologists strive to tailor management programs to each body of water, they have found it helpful to categorize basic kinds of fisheries and set management objectives within these categories. The Sport Fishes program in the DWR Comprehensive Plan lists four management concepts and management targets for each. As management plans are written, each unit is assigned to one of the management concepts and standards are listed. Then, specific management objectives unique to each body of water are developed.

Of the four management concepts, the Basic Yield concept involves the largest number of waters in the state. This concept has the objective of producing reasonably fast fishing for moderate-sized fish, either coldwater, coolwater, or warmwater. Where natural reproduction will not sustain the fishery, stocking is on a put-grow-and-take basis. Creel limits are generally statewide or restricted in winter if ice fishing pressure is heavy or if special regulations are needed to protect spawning fish or to achieve specific size objectives. A key habitat activity for the fishery program is acquisition of conservation pools in fluctuating reservoirs. Purchase of these storage rights allows sufficient water to remain in the reservoir each winter for overwinter survival. Without conservation pools, many of these reservoirs would be nearly drained and large scale winterkill would occur.

The Trophy management concept is designed for waters that have the capacity to produce larger-than-average-size fish. Some waters, because of the diversity of species, are managed under both Trophy and Basic Yield concepts, based on each species. Management activities on trophy waters include special regulations to produce larger-than-average-size fish but prevent overcropping. The fisheries may be naturally reproducing or supported by stocking, depending on the capability of the water.

The Intensive Yield concept is directed at catchable-trout fisheries, although it could expand in the future to include catchable-size catfish. Intensive-yield waters are designated where heavy fishing pressure occurs due to proximity to a major city or major recreation area. Generally speaking, the target catch rates are relatively fast with a target size of approximately 9 in. (22.5 cm) for catchable-size rainbow trout. Because catchable-size trout are expensive to produce, targets for return of stocked fish call for a pound harvested for each pound stocked or a return of at least 70 percent of the number stocked. Where these catchable fisheries are not meeting the return targets, the waters are reclassified away from the intensive yield concept, and the catchables are reallocated to other waters where the return targets can be met.

The Wild Fish management concept sets the specific objective that the fishery be supported by natural reproduction. This program deals primarily with the high-quality trout streams that have adequate spawning and rearing habitat and that sustain a viable fishery. Regulations for these waters frequently include closures to protect spawning trout and slot or size limits to protect certain sizes. This program makes both biological and economic sense in habitats that are suitable, but the conversion of stocked waters to the Wild Trout concept has sometimes been controversial. Various segments of the angling public have differing views as to the value of stocked versus wild populations, and conversion of Basic Yield waters to the Wild concept takes place only after extensive public review and consensus among anglers. In some cases, conversion of waters to the Wild concept has been coupled with fishing improvement projects in nearby Basic Yield waters. This plan is intended to provide quality fishing, of several different kinds, in a given vicinity, satisfying the needs of different angling publics.

Responsibility for designating waters within various management concepts and recommending the appropriate management strategies is the responsibility of the five Regional Aquatic Program Managers. The Regional Aquatic Program Manager is also a key public contact point. Regional Managers are most knowledgeable about specific waters and are able to answer questions. They are also contacts for someone suggesting ideas for improvements to the fisheries management program. All recommendations for changes in fisheries management, whether generated from within the DWR or from outside interests, are submitted to the Regional Aquatic Program Managers for evaluation and recommendation. A favorable recommendation by the manager gives the strongest likelihood of a proposal being accepted. Part of the manager's job is to interact with the public. Individuals or groups may learn more about local fisheries resources or request specific management changes.

The second major sportfisheries program in the Comprehensive Plan is the Special Fishes program. This program is designed primarily for the Bonneville and Colorado River subspecies of cutthroat trout, but it also includes Lahontan cutthroat trout and native fishes. Objectives are to maintain existing populations of native species and expand distribution and abundance to prevent any decline that would warrant listing under the Endangered Species Act. Because these are high-quality sport fishes in their own right, additional objectives are to develop increased numbers for these species and bring them into more prominence within the overall management program. Management activities in this program include surveying and counting remnant populations of native cutthroat and the designation of suitable transplant waters where they can be reestablished.

Under the Special Species program, the primary objectives are geared toward conserving and expanding the populations, and sportfisheries objectives are secondary. Where harvest is acceptable, populations are open to fishing, but if problems develop regarding abundance, sportfishing will be foregone in favor of conservation. In addition, these populations are largely managed under the Wild Fish concept rather than utilizing stocking to support them. If populations decline or don't meet objectives, special regulations will be implemented and stocking will not be initiated.

Although both the Bonneville and Colorado River subspecies of cutthroat have been proposed for listing under the Endangered Species Act, recent management efforts have increased their abundance and distribution. Several wild brood populations are under development. They will produce eggs for reintroducing these natives on a much more widespread basis. Although their continued existence once appeared precarious, recent successes lead us to believe the native cutthroats are secure and destined to play a greater role in Utah's sport fish management program in the future.

The last program, the Commercial Fishes program, is largely regulatory and is designed to produce an orderly harvest of overabundant fishery resources, primarily carp and white bass. At present, this fishery exists primarily in Utah Lake, although permits have been issued for a few other waters. Harvest of these species yields relatively low profits, and, therefore, they have not generated much interest. Private commercial harvest of brine shrimp from Great Salt Lake is regulated under this program. Brine shrimp are valuable in the aquarium trade and in the shrimp and prawn culturing industries. Brine shrimp also provide a significant food resource for migratory waterfowl and wading birds around Great Salt Lake. Some avian species are almost completely dependent upon food reserves acquired through feeding at Great Salt Lake to fuel major migratory flights south for the winter.

Over 500 private ponds are actively stocked with fish each year. A major activity in this program is the review of species stocking requests to make sure that species stocked in a given area are compatible with the public resource in that area.

Successfully conducting all of these programs on the thousands of waters scattered around the state is presently performed by a staff of approximately 75 people and a budget of approximately 6.5 million dollars. The vast majority of the funding comes directly from anglers through fishing licenses and excise taxes on fishing tackle and motorboat fuels through the Federal Sport Fish Restoration Program, frequently referred to as the Dingell-Johnson or Wallop-Breaux programs. Nongame fish management programs additionally receive funds from the U.S. Fish and Wildlife Service through Section 6 of the Endangered Species Act for work to recover listed threatened or endangered species, a small amount of funds received from the voluntary Nongame Income Tax checkoff, and a small amount of the funding appropriated from the State General Fund.

As human pressures on aquatic habitats increase, however, efforts to protect and improve aquatic resources will become more difficult and require increasing support from the public.

The Wail of the Fisherman's Wife

I baked a cake and packed the lunch
(Sure takes a lot to feed that bunch!)
I nearly wore off both my legs
Scouting this town for salmon eggs.
I bought licenses and found Bill's creel,
And fixed the line on Tommy's reel,
Got ointment for John's ivy rash,
And looked for crawlers with the flash.
I pulled Bill's boots from a pile of junk
He'd stacked away in an attic trunk.
I brushed out all the sleeping bags,
And stitched the place where our old tent sags.
I packed the car; let them sleep a while,
Maybe I'd get a "thank you" smile.
I called "breakfast" and they arose,
Then I helped them find their fishing clothes.
And then they left! I felt so flat,
'Cause in my place, the neighbor sat.
"Poor Ed," Bill said, "never fished a bit!"
So poor Ed went, and here I sit.
I've saved a year to buy this rod.
And I'm going to use it if it does look odd.
I wonder what old Bill will think,
When he finds me fishing the kitchen sink!

Rodello Hunter

CHAPTER 13

Fishing Tips for Hook-and-Line Gear

Fishing Utah

There are three questions that anglers ask themselves before going fishing; these are "Where?" "When?" and "How?" "Where" to fish involves not only which lake or stream, but the precise spot. "When" may be time of day or month. "How" is a bit more complicated. Choices include type of boat or floatation device, clothes, and fishing gear (that is, rod, reel, line, and a multitude of lures and baits).

Fishing is both an art and a science. However, the relative importance of the art outweighs the science. The science once learned is retained, but the art is lessened or lost if it is not practiced. Confidence in yourself when fishing is of the utmost importance. You must believe you are going to catch a fish on every cast. The fact that you did not catch one on the last cast, or several casts, should have no bearing on your attitude. Of course you may want to move to another location and/or change baits or techniques, but all with confidence. This confidence should extend to lures and baits. Use ones that have caught fish before, but do not hesitate to try new ones. Be sure there is no debris or vegetation on the lure or lower line.

The lighter the rod and line, the more sensitive it is to strikes. However, the lighter the outfit, the more susceptible it is to breaking. Although the size of the fish sought obviously governs the size of the outfit, such factors as weeds or brushy obstacles are also important.

Fishhooks come in a multitude of sizes and shapes designed to meet all needs and desires. This variety would seem to call for a straightforward descriptive system. But, according to Klaus K. Kjelstrup, president, O. Mustad & Son, "The simple fact is that there is no set numbering standard for fishhook sizes. The fishhook is one of the oldest tools of mankind, and the numbering system, or lack of a numbering system, is something that developed over a long period of time, long before any theories of standardization were developed" (personal communication, 25 April 1989). In most instances hooks are numbered by size in one of two ways; no./0 (for example, 10/0) and number only (for example, 10.) In the no./0 series, the larger the number the larger the hook. In the number-only system, the larger the number the smaller the hook. The best way to handle this is to understand a given system or simply pick a hook that appears to be right.

A lure may be defined as any device designed to capture a fish by hooking it in the mouth. This may range from a single hook to a plug that holds two or more gang (three-prong) hooks. Hooks should be sharpened carefully with a handstone or an automatic sharpener. Vigorous action may damage the temper of the point. When sharp enough it will stick to a fingernail when dragged across it.

When to set the hook on a presumed strike is always a question. The set is accomplished by a sharp, but not violent, jerk on the line. The general answer is, if in doubt, do it. You may lose some but you will win more. Strikes are detected by a sense of feel and by watching the line. If you believe you have not set the hook securely the first time, reset it. A northern pike striking a moving lure leaves no doubt of a strike, but the soft bite of a walleye may go undetected. Hook size should be no larger than necessary to catch and hold the fish. Some people prefer treble hooks when trolling with earthworms.

A few general observations are in order. Fish are much deeper on clear days than on cloudy days. They are deeper in the middle of the day than at morning and evening. They are deeper where there is no cover than where there is cover. And the bigger the fish, the more wary and perhaps the deeper it is. Fish are less wary and more easily caught when spawning than other times of the year. At this time they strike lures in part out of irritation as well as a protective measure. The characteristics in a lure or bait that trigger positive or negative responses in fish are scent, sound, size, shape, color, texture, and action. Most or all of these features should be considered when selecting lures or baits. For example, catfishes rely heavily on scent, northern pike on sight (color, shape, action).

Fishing Gear

One does not have to have modern rod-and-reel-type gear to catch fish, but it helps. It helps a great deal. There are four types from which to choose: baitcasting, spinning, spincasting, and flycasting. Each is designed to present a lure in a way that entices a fish.

The advantage of modern gear over a cane pole and line, or other simple device, is the ability to reach out considerable distances to where fish are and to be able to play out and retrieve line without giving the fish a chance to have a dead pull. The outfit chosen depends on the angler's preference and the situation. Each type has its strong and weak points.

Freshwater baitcasting outfits are composed of a short (generally 4.5 to 6.5 ft [1.4 to 1.9 m]) rod, a reel mounted on top of the rod in a well, a line, and lure. The reel is made up of a free-spinning spool that pays out line, a drag to put tension on the line, a level wind, a brake, and a crank to retrieve the line. Light baitcasting outfits are quite accurate. Heavy gear is used almost exclusively for deep-water trolling and trophy fishing. Until recently no other type of gear was designed for this method of fishing. Now heavy spinning outfits are also used. The cast is made with the master hand; the rod is then shifted to the off hand and the line cranked in by the master hand. Baitcasting uses a fine monofilament line.

The greatest difference between baitcasting and spinning is that, in spinning, the spool is fixed and the line pays off the end of the spool in loops. The rod, usually somewhat longer and more limber than baitcasting rods, is straight, and the reel is mounted on the underside. The rod remains in the same hand during the cast and retrieve. Light spinning rods, using very light monofilament line, will handle very light lures. Medium to heavy outfits can be cast considerable distances, but accuracy is generally not as good as with baitcasting gear. Medium-weight to heavy outfits will handle a wide size range of lures and baits. They do not backlash, but the line can be fouled. With the addition of a bubble float, both live bait and artificial flies can be fished well away from the angler and at any desired depth. Spinning became popular in the United States after World War II and is probably the most widely used fishing gear today. However, baitcasting has made a tremendous comeback in recent years, due largely to the increased interest in bass fishing.

Spincasting attempts to combine the best features of baitcasting and spinning. It succeeds only within somewhat narrow limits. The rod is the same as the baitcasting rod, the reel has a fixed spool, as in a spinning reel, but the face is enclosed by a cone-shaped cover with a hole in the center for the line to pay through, or it may pay out around a center cover. During a cast the line is released by pushing the button on the back of the reel and releasing it. The payout is stopped by turning the crank. The cast is made with the master hand, then shifted to the off hand for retrieval. Spincasting reels hold much less line than spinning reels. Many have less spool power than is desirable when retrieving, and the line under the cover may snarl badly. Spincasting is easier to learn than any of the other systems. Therefore, for a beginner who wants to learn quickly, or for a very occasional angler, it may fulfill the need. And most spincasting outfits are relatively inexpensive.

In baitcasting, spinning, and spincasting, the weight of the lure propels it through the air, pulling the line behind it. In fly-fishing the opposite is true; the weight of the line propels itself through the air pulling the near weightless artificial fly and leader after it.

Fly rods are the longest of the fishing rods, up to 8.5 ft (2.6 m) in length. The fly rod reel is much less important than it is on the other types of fishing gear. It is essentially a line-storing device. There are two styles of reels, single action and automatic. The single action reel is simply a spool with a crank on it; the automatic reel is spring-loaded, which enables it to retrieve the line when a lever is pressed. Neither has a level wind device. The fly line is rugged, somewhat complicated, and always has a fine monofilament leader of 6 to 15 ft (1.8 to 4.6 m). The fly line generally has a braided nylon core with a plastic coating. It may be a uniform thickness throughout, or weighted (tapered) forward, or double tapered. It may float, sink, or part of it may float while the balance sinks. Each fly line has a descriptive label to match its weight to the rod. To fish, the rod is held in the master hand, while line is stripped off the reel and held in the off hand. The fly is propelled forward after a series of back and forth whiplike actions. This is repeated until the fly is placed in the desired spot. Fly fishing is to some a sport of the elite. Its use carries with it special prestige, real or imagined. It is also the most expensive of fishing outfits; and since it is highly specialized, one outfit generally will not suffice for all desired types of fishing. Its disadvantages are the need of more room, both front and back, than other outfits; greater difficulty to learn; and increased effects of the wind. But it presents a very realistic lure to the fish on a leader that is virtually invisible, and the accuracy is great.

Ice-fishing gear ranges all the way from a paddle to wrap a line around to a fancy short rod and reel. Many fishermen make their outfits from broken casting or spinning gear.

Some boat fishermen use live fish baskets—ones that float are preferable. Other anglers prefer killing the fish and putting them on ice. The use of dip nets reduces landing losses. Releasing fish should be done gently, immediately, and with wet hands. When fish are to be released, the playing time should be as brief as possible. As a general rule, boat fishermen are somewhat more successful than shore fishermen on large lakes and large streams. The boat used should be large enough to handle the water embarked upon under adverse weather conditions.

Fishing Tips

brook trout

Small to medium-size brook trout feed on aquatic invertebrates; the large ones feed on fish. This species inhabits high, cold streams, beaver ponds, and cold lakes. Most brook trout are caught on worms or small spinners. Large ones, which are extremely wary, are caught on a variety of artificial lures. Here are a few suggestions about where to fish for brook trout: Browne Lake, Antimony Lake, Blind Lake, Spirit Lake, and Whiterocks River. A check with the local Division of Wildlife Resources personnel in your favorite part of the state may reveal other locations.

cutthroat trout

Cutthroat trout, the only trout native to Utah, were once present in most of the cold and cool streams and lakes of the state, except certain waters in the high Uinta Mountains. Today, their range is restricted in lowland waters, but they are in many mountain lakes and streams. Cutthroat feed mostly on invertebrates until they reach 1.5 to 2.0 lb (0.7 to 0.9 kg), then they turn to whatever fish are available. The smaller cutthroats (12 in. [305 mm] or less) are more likely to be inshore than are the larger ones. In streams, adults are in deep holes or close to cover during the day; at twilight they move into the riffles to feed. Natural baits include worms, insects, crayfish, fish eggs, cheese, marshmallows, and waxworms. A large variety of artificial flies and lures such as flatfish, Rappalas, and spoons catch cutthroat. Here are a few suggestions about where to fish for them: Bear Lake, Strawberry Reservoir, Johnson Valley Reservoir, Weber River, Colorado River, and Gooseberry Reservoir. Local tackle or bait shop personnel can probably suggest additional sites in a particular area of the state.

lake trout

Lake trout are present in Bear Lake, Fish Lake, and first and foremost in abundance in Flaming Gorge Lake. In late fall just before freeze-up, these fish move out of the deeper, colder waters, where they have been most of the year, into shallow water. This movement is reversed in the early spring after the ice goes out. Relatively few fish are taken from shore or under the ice. These are slow-moving, soft-biting fish that do not leap or fight hard. Their value is in their trophy size. Boat fishermen troll or use jigs. All types of fishing gear are fished by bouncing the lure along or just off the bottom. Trollers use downriggers, steel or leadcore lines, or diving devices to keep the lure near the bottom. Lures include flatfish, daredevils, Rappalas, and Luhr Jensen spoons. Jigging is a jerky, up-and-down (2 to 3 ft) (0.6 to 0.9 m) movement just off the bottom while the boat is stationary or drifting slowly. Leadheaded jigs tipped with an artificial minnow, a Castmaster, or a spoon are used frequently. June and July are the best months of the year to fish in Flaming Gorge Lake, and probably this is true of the other two lake trout haunts.

rainbow trout

Rainbow trout are the most abundant and wide-ranging trout in Utah, primarily because they are stocked so heavily. They are present and at home in coolwater and large coldwater lakes, small farm ponds, and both large and small streams. In many medium to small streams, stocked fish may not move more than a few hundred yards in a lifetime. Wild or semiwild populations behave somewhat differently. Some lake populations are pelagic (living in open water), whereas others are more often inshore. Rainbow may feed more openly in daytime than do cutthroat or brown trout. Stream fish use deep water, overhanging banks, bankside vegetation, and obstructions for cover.

Rainbow are caught on about any natural bait from worms to marshmallows. Some anglers use artificial flies that emulate insects occurring naturally in the water, others use outlandish patterns. Both catch fish. Artificial lures such as red and white spoons, silver or gold spoons, and plugs that do or do not imitate small fish, all catch fish, sometimes. Small lures should be used for small or medium-sized fish. If one lure does not work, try another, then still another. Do not stick with a lure that is not working. When changing lures fails, move to another place and start over. Here are a few suggestions about where to fish for rainbow trout: Strawberry Reservoir, Fish Lake, Flaming Gorge Lake, Logan River, Colorado River, and Aspen–Mirror Lake. Local tackle or bait shop personnel can probably suggest additional sites in a particular area of the state.

Bonneville cisco

Bonneville cisco, fish that are rarely more than 8.5 in. (216 mm) long, have a very small mouth, and feed on small invertebrates. They are unique to Bear Lake, Utah-Idaho, where they live in the coldwater zone in warm weather. When cold weather comes they move inshore to feed. They also move inshore to spawn annually, on about January 16, plus or minus five days, where they may be dip-netted. A very few are caught on hook and line. Try the east side of Bear Lake, between North and South Eden canyons about January 25.

Bonneville whitefish

Bonneville whitefish, like the Bonneville cisco, are unique to Bear Lake, Utah-Idaho. They feed mainly on invertebrates but may take small fish. In warm weather they live in deep, cold water, but from late fall to early spring may be inshore. In shallow water they are caught mostly on small to medium-size spoons or red and white daredevils fished along the bottom. Try the east side of Bear Lake about dawn.

mountain whitefish

Mountain whitefish feed on aquatic invertebrates and occasional terrestrial insects that fall into the water. They are present in many of the medium to large coldwater streams in the state. They are caught with a small (12–18) hook baited with worms, or on artificial flies. Best success is at twilight at the head of riffles. Here are a few suggestions about where to fish for mountain whitefish: Bear River, Weber River, Duchesne River, and Blacksmith Fork River. Local tackle or bait shop personnel can probably mention additional sites in a particular area of the state.

northern pike

Northern pike are present in only a few waters in Utah; Redmond Lake generally has the best population. They feed both day and night, but more often in daytime, on fish, frogs, and other vertebrates that are unfortunate enough to get close. They inhabit inshore weedy areas or anywhere there is a population of fish. They are taken on a large variety of lures such as red and white spoons, surface plugs, or silver spoons. They are most effectively fished by casting from a boat. They strike hard and fight vigorously. Considering their rather formidable teeth, a dip net is in order. Although northern pike do not school, where there is one there may be more nearby. In addition to Redmond Lake, try Sevier Bridge Reservoir. There are some in the Green River and Lake Powell.

black bullhead

Black bullhead are present in most lowland, warmwater lakes, sluggish streams, and even barrow pits. The fact that they are easy to catch and taste good make them a favorite of young fishermen. They feed day and night on the bottom and are omnivorous. These habits mean that a number of natural baits such as worms, dead fish, chicken guts, and other meats—the smellier the better—are effective. Weights 2 to 3 ft (60 to 90 cm) away from the lure work well. A free-sliding weight held away from the lure by a split shot makes it more effective. Bullheads bite slowly and lazily; do not hurry them. A single hook is adequate and is easier to remove than multiple hooks, although they may hold some baits better. The practice is always still fishing from a boat, dock, or levee. Bullhead are not active in cold water (55°F [12.8°C] or less). Try Utah Lake, Pineview Reservoir, lower Bear and Logan rivers, or Cutler Reservoir.

channel catfish

Channel catfish are omnivorous. That is, they eat about anything, alive or dead, including such things as elm tree seeds. They have an acute sense of smell that helps them respond to odiferous food including bait. Baits include worms, dead fish, chicken livers and guts, cheese, prepared material, and occasionally artificial lures. In shallow lakes they may be anywhere there is food and cover; in deep lakes they are more likely to be inshore. In streams channel catfish congregate in deep pools to rest but move into riffle areas just above the pools to feed. They may also be near any cover such as snags, logs, bank cover, and cutbanks. Channel catfish may be still fished either from a boat or shore. The bait is placed on or just off the bottom. Very slow trolling may help locate fish. They are soft, slow biters so patience is in order. The size of fish sought dictates the size of the hook used. For 12- to 16-in. (305- to 406-mm) fish, use a 1/0 or a 2/0 hook. Here are a few suggestions about where to fish for channel catfish: Utah Lake, lower Bear River, Price River, Willard Bay Reservoir, and the Colorado River. They are locally abundant in Lake Powell.

striped bass

Striped bass in Utah are present only in Lake Powell, where they are relatively abundant, and in the river just above the lake. Except for juveniles, striped bass feed primarily on threadfin shad and other fish. In spring when the water warms to the low 60s°F (15.6°C), mature stripers move inshore just off points. This is generally from early April to mid-June. After spawning, fish move to deep water. By mid-August young threadfin shad migrate from the coves and backwater areas into the main body of the lake, then young striped bass (11–17 in. [280–432 mm]) move to the surface to feed on the shad. When water temperatures drop in the fall, late September to early October, the larger striped bass move to the surface to feed. When the lake temperature drops below 60°F (15.6°C), generally in mid- to late November, striped bass move to deep water. Stripers can be caught from shore when they are spawning, but most are caught from boats by trolling, jigging, or casting. Most of them are caught on artificial lures; dead fish are also effective. White Marabou, Zara Spook, white bucktail, or Cordell Red Fin are used in the spring. In summer when the small bass are feeding, small lures are in order. As with white bass, a striper feeding frenzy may drive little fish to the surface or out on shore, where they are fed on by gulls and other birds. Winter fishing by deep-water trolling is perhaps the slowest sport, but it may produce large fish.

white bass

White bass prefer to feed on small fish, but when none is available they readily turn to midwater and surface invertebrates. Their frenzied feeding in large schools of small fish sometimes sends the small fish skipping along the surface or even out on shore in an all-out effort to escape. This activity may cause gulls and terns to congregate and feed on the small fish, and fishermen in turn to prey on the white bass. Schools of white bass move inshore and then parallel to shore just at twilight. Otherwise they feed in open water and near the surface. Adults are often present near the windward shore, while the young feed near the lee shore. White bass prosper best in large, shallow, cool to warmwater lakes. They are present less often in large, slow streams but do not fare as well there as in lakes. Most white bass are caught on artificial lures. They swim fast and strike at about anything that moves and appears to be food. A white bucktail with a willow leaf spinner is a favorite. Other spinners or spoons, sometimes with a worm or fish, also catch this fish. White bass are common in Utah Lake.

black crappie

Black crappie are present in many large warmwater lakes and ponds in Utah. They are invariably close to cover; brush piles, overhanging banks, and docks seem to be preferred. As a schooling fish they strike readily, especially just before or during the spawning season (58° to 68°F (14.4° to 20°C). They spawn in shallow, sandy bottom areas. Crappies feed all day but more actively at twilight. They are also caught under the ice. Lights attract them at night. They are caught from shore, but boat fishing is generally more effective. Drifting may help locate schools. They take live bait readily, especially worms. Leadhead jigs, with or without a float, brightly colored plastic-coated hooks, and small spoons as well as a number of artificial flies are all effective at times. They have a soft mouth, so hooking and landing should be gentle. In eastern Ontario black crappies are caught on hooks baited with small (2 in. [51 mm]) minnow, light line, no leads—bait skipped on surface behind a slowly moving boat. Here are a few suggestions about where to fish for black crappie: Willard Bay Reservoir, Lake Powell, Pineview Reservoir, and Holmes Creek Reservoir. Local tackle or bait shop personnel can probably provide additional sites in a particular area of the state.

bluegill

Bluegill are present in many lowland warmwater lakes in Utah including Lake Powell. They are often stocked in ponds along with largemouth bass. They are caught mostly during the day, even on bright days. They move into shallow, sandy bottom areas to spawn when temperatures reach about 75°F (23.9°C). They are easier to catch then, although not difficult to catch anytime, except for a few large ones. They may also be caught under the ice. They can be caught by wading, although using a boat is more effective. When not spawning they are in or near weed beds or near the mouth of streams. They will be deeper when the water becomes quite warm (85°F [29.4°C] or more). They are always in schools. Bluegill readily take worms, artificial flies, leadhead jigs, and brightly colored plastic-coated lures. Very small hooks are a must. With Polaroid[R] glasses a fisherman may be able to see the target fish. Bluegill do not pursue a lure or strike hard, but with an ultralight outfit they are fun to catch and are good to eat. In addition to Lake Powell, try Gunnison Reservoir and Holmes Creek Reservoir. Local tackle or bait shop personnel can probably suggest additional sites in a particular area of the state.

largemouth bass

Largemouth bass are one of the most, if not the most, sought-after game fish in America. The number of professionals dedicated to catching this fish has exploded in recent years, but they were pursued ardently by many people long before there were professionals per se. The main foods of this aggressive predator are fish, frogs, crayfish, large insects, and just about anything they can catch including mice, snakes, and ducklings. They rarely scavenge dead food. These warmwater fish are equally at home in large weedy lakes and small ponds. They are also present in sluggish rivers. Largemouth have a strong affinity for weed beds and hidden structures that afford cover and harbor small fish. Preferred cover types include abrupt changes in bottom contour-reefs, artificial or natural riprap, and boat docks.

From ice-out until the water warms to about 55°F (12.8°C) the bass are apt to be in deep water, often near the bottom, and close to cover. As spawning temperatures approach (about 62°F [16.7°C]) males, then females, move into shallow water that has a sand or gravel bottom.

Following spawning, female bass are quite inactive for 1.5 to 3.0 weeks. Other than to attack anything that invades the nest he is guarding, the male is inactive until the eggs hatch. He then guards the young until they are 2 to 3 weeks old.

Largemouth are most active at twilight and to a slightly less extent at night in summer. They are caught on such live bait as worms, frogs, salamanders, crayfish, crickets, grasshoppers, and an astonishing array of artificial lures. Live bait may be cast, trolled, or still fished. Dead-fish bait is cast or trolled. Artificial lures may be fished near the surface, midwater, or occasionally deep. In or near weed beds, weedless hooks are needed. Many lures such as spinners or spoons often include added items such as nightcrawlers or porkrind to enhance the lure. Of all the lures offered to the largemouth, red or red and white ones are probably the first choice. Plastic worms are widely used as largemouth bait, so a discussion of size and color (this applies within limits to other lures) is in order. Use large worms for large fish and vice versa. Large worms are for cloudy days, nighttime, and murky water. For bright days and clear water use light colors; for cloudy days, for murky water, or at night use dark colors. Here are a few suggestions about where to fish for largemouth bass: Lake Powell, Pelican Lake, Pineview Reservoir, Gunnison Reservoir, Bullock Reservoir, and Gunlock Reservoir.

smallmouth bass

Smallmouth bass, widely sought in many areas, are not especially popular in Utah primarily because there are only scattered populations. They are present in Lake Powell, Flaming Gorge Lake, and a few streams in eastern Utah. They are also present in Starvation Reservoir and Brough Reservoir. In lakes, soon after the ice is gone, the smallmouth move from deep water inshore to rocky areas, undercut ledges, and in general near any cover. They feed ravenously from then until spawning. During this time they will take a variety of lures: blue, white, or purple hair-dressed jigs, small yellow or red-and-white plugs, or spoons. In summer they move to deep water, but are back in the shallows in the fall. In their native range they are more of a stream than a lake fish. In small streams they are fished from shore, in large streams, with waders, floats, or by boat. They frequent deep holes or areas near cover in the daytime but move into the shallows at twilight. They bite most freely in early spring until spawning and caring for young is complete. The same lures that work inshore on lakes are equally effective on streams.

yellow perch

Yellow perch are present in many of the warm and some of the cool lakes of Utah. They are rarely in streams. They feed off and on throughout the day, but feeding is more pronounced in the morning and evening, generally ceasing at night. They are readily caught through the ice. They often live in the vicinity of weed beds and other cover and often move close to stream inlets at or just before twilight. Yellow perch readily take live bait, especially worms, and artificial lures such as leadhead jigs, spoons, brightly colored plastic-coated hooks, and a variety of flies. Flies may be fished with a fly rod or by spinning or spincasting, using a bobber 3 to 5 ft (90 to 150 cm) ahead of the fly. All lures should be small. When fish are located the boat should be more or less stationary and, as with all schooling fishes, when a fish is hooked it should be landed quickly so that another can be caught before the school moves away.

walleye

Walleye are largely piscivorous but also feed on crayfish, frogs, and other vertebrates. Only quite young fish or adults in desperation feed on small invertebrates. They feed during the day in deep water, and at night or sometimes twilight may move inshore, especially to the mouth of a stream carrying food. Walleye are cold- to coolwater, big-lake fish. They live close to the bottom, often in the vicinity of rock areas, brush piles, drop offs, or islands. If this cover is in shallow water, the fish frequently stay in the vicinity of deep water. Walleye are also large, slow, river fish, most active in early spring as spawning time approaches. They are not a schooling fish in the true sense but may be concentrated in the vicinity of food or cover.

Walleye are soft biters, so soft that many strikes are missed or not even detected. The answer, in part, is to keep a taut line and set the hook even if there is only a hint of a strike. Line should be taken up as the tip of the rod is lowered; this is especially effective when jigging. Leadheads are often used as lures for jigging. June bug spinners, baited with live worms, are a favorite trolling or drifting lure in both lakes and streams. Even large walleye tend to feed on small (2- to 3-in. [51- to 76-mm]) fish, so a small lure is in order. Rappala shad, number three bucktail, Mepps, small spoons, and much more elaborate rigs all catch walleye at times. No lure is surefire. Early spring fishing for walleye is best. Try feeder streams running into lakes. In summer, Willard Bay Reservoir, Utah Lake, Lake Powell, American Fork Creek, and Jordan River are good locations.

Where the Fish Are

After the gear has been assembled and the decision has been made to go fishing, then the question of "where" arises. When the questions of how much time there is and boat availability are answered, then the specific location can be chosen. Each body of water has a unique ecosystem that favors certain fish.

Lake Powell is known for largemouth and striped bass. Other large game fish include walleye, channel catfish, rainbow trout, and smallmouth bass. It also has populations of black crappie and bluegill.

Flaming Gorge Lake, on the Green River, is best known for producing large lake trout and brown trout. It also has rainbow trout, smallmouth bass, and kokanee.

The high Uinta waters have three trout: cutthroat, rainbow, and brook. Utah Lake has walleye, channel catfish, black bullhead, and white bass.

Bear Lake has cutthroat and lake trout, Bonneville whitefish, and Bonneville cisco. Fish Lake is noted for lake trout, rainbow trout, and some brook trout.

Mountain whitefish are present in many moderate-size, cool to cold streams. Lowland lakes and streams may have temperate to warmwater fishes or only warmwater fishes.

CHAPTER 14

Visiting Utah

Utah is a land of natural variety and contrast. But many areas have also been modified by human activities and changed to fit human requirements. Below we present cursory information on some of the more notable natural and man-made features in Utah. Most have aquatic features of some type. All are interesting and reflect the character of the state. In all cases, direction is provided for obtaining additional information. Information included was accurate when published. Names, addresses, and telephone numbers may have been changed.

Utah State Parks

Utah parks include 45 sites classified into water recreation, scenic, and heritage park areas. Only a few are listed here. Additional information regarding Utah State Parks can be obtained from Utah Division of Parks and Recreation, 1636 West North Temple, Salt Lake City, UT 84116, phone (801) 538–7220.

Bear Lake State Park

General Location: The Rocky Mountains on the Utah-Idaho border
Features: Waterskiing, fishing, swimming, camping, and sailing; Annual January Cisco run
Facilities: Marina, beach, and a visitor center
Information: P.O. Box 184, Garden City, UT 84028–0184, phone (801)946–3343

Fremont Indian State Park

General Location: Clear Creek Canyon, Sevier
Features: Rock art and archaeological sites
Facilities: Interpretive trails (one wheelchair-accessible), camping, fishing, and picnicking
Information: P.O. Box 93, Green River, UT 84525–0093, phone (801) 564–3633

Goblin Valley State Park

General Location: Green River
Features: Eroded rock formations that resemble goblinlike creatures
Facilities: Campground with modern facilities, visitor observation shelter

Information: P.O. Box 93, Green River, UT 84525–0093, phone (801) 564–3633

Willard Bay State Park

General Location: North of Great Salt Lake flood plain, near Willard
Features: Freshwater lake, boating, waterskiing, and year-round fishing
Facilities: Marinas and modern campsites
Information: 650 North 900 West #A, Willard, UT 84340–9999, phone (801) 734–9494

National Parks, Recreation Areas, and Monuments in Utah

Arches National Park

General Location: Southern Utah, near Moab
Features: World's largest concentration of natural stone arches
Facilities: Hiking, year-round visitor center, campsites
Information: Box 907, Moab, UT 84532, phone (801) 259–8161

Bryce Canyon National Park

General Location: Southern Utah
Features: Colorful columns, spires, and windows sculpted by erosion
Facilities: Hiking, overlooks, year-round visitor center
Information: Bryce Canyon National Park, Bryce Canyon, UT 84717, phone (801) 834–5322

Canyonlands National Park

General Location: Junction of Colorado and Green rivers, near Moab
Features: Hiking, rafting, biking, jeeping
Facilities: Improved camping
Information: Canyonlands National Park, Moab, UT 84532, phone (801) 259–7164

Capitol Reef National Park

General Location: South Central Utah, near Torrey
Features: Artifacts from pre-Columbian Native Americans
Facilities: Year-round visitor center, camping
Information: Capitol Reef National Park, Torrey, UT 84775, phone (801) 425–3791

Flaming Gorge National Recreation Area

General Location: Northeast corner of Utah into Wyoming
Features: Trophy trout fishing, boating
Facilities: Camping, marinas, beach
Information: Box 157, Dutch John, UT 84023, phone (801) 885–3315 or 785–3445 (Manila)

Rainbow Bridge National Monument

General Location: On Lake Powell, southern Utah
Features: One of the seven natural wonders of the world and the largest known natural bridge
Facilities: Fishing, boating, hiking trails

Information: Glen Canyon National Recreation Area, Box 1507, Page AZ 86040, phone (602) 645–2471

Zion National Park

General Location: Southern Utah, near Springdale
Features: Colorful, sheer-walled canyons and unique formations
Facilities: Visitor center open year-round. Annual Southern Utah Folklife Festival in September
Information: Zion National Park, Springdale, UT 84767, phone (801) 772–3256

National Forests in Utah

Ashley National Forest

General Location: Northeastern Utah encompassing the Uinta Mountains
Features: Flaming Gorge Dam, Green River
Facilities: Camping (improved and primitive)
Information: Forest Supervisor, 355 North Vernal Avenue, Vernal, UT 84078, phone (801) 789–1181

Dixie National Forest

General Location: Southern Utah, around Cedar City
Features: Largest national forest in Utah, includes divide between Great Basin and Colorado Plateau country, Navajo and Panguitch lakes, Pine Valley, and other wilderness areas
Facilities: Campgrounds, nature trails, fishing access
Information: Forest Supervisor, 82 North 100 East, Cedar City, UT 84720, phone (801) 865–3700

Fishlake National Forest

General Location: South Central Utah, Richfield
Features: Forest, mountains, plateaus, streams, ponds, and reservoirs
Facilities: Campgrounds, picnic areas, a boating site, and three year-round resorts
Information: Forest Supervisor, 115 East 900 North, Richfield, UT 84701, phone (801) 896–9233

CHAPTER 15

Water and the Law

Steven E. Clyde

The prior appropriation doctrine originated from custom and usage in the early mining camps and irrigated farms of the West. Its basic tenet—first in time is first in right—rewarded those who were simply first, with little regard to the efficiency of their use or whether more beneficial uses of water were being precluded.[1] Beneficial use established the measure and the limit of the water right,[2] and was generally equated with the application of water to the economic benefit of humans.[3] Irrigation, industrial, mining, power generation, and municipal purposes were all recognized beneficial uses.[4] An appropriation under state law generally required an actual diversion of water from the natural water course and the application of the water so diverted to some recognized beneficial use.[5]

Once perfected,[6] a water right becomes a vested, perpetual property interest, subject only to prior rights, the public interest, and dominant federal interests. The perfected water right is entitled to full legal protection, including due process.[7]

The federal government's acquiescence in the settlement of its western lands and the appropriation of its water under state law promoted western migration and the expansion of our national economy. The doctrine of "first in time, first in right" assured the early settlers of a relatively stable water supply and protected them against unreasonable interference by junior appropriators. Water rights remained subject to the assertion of dominant federal interests that have the potential to curtail and even displace state-created appropriated rights. These water rights take two forms: reserved rights and rights created through the imposition of federal regulatory controls.

The federal government has a dual interest in western water. Its first interest is that of the sovereign exercising the specific powers granted it by the United States Constitution. Its second interest is that of a proprietary owner of the western lands and the water arising thereon.[8]

The federal government's sovereign powers are conferred by the Constitution and cannot be delegated away.[9] These powers include the authority to make treaties, to regulate commerce, and to control navigation. Federal enterprises are essentially free of state control.[10]

The federal government holds title to much of the western lands as a proprietary owner.[11] Under the Property Clause of the Constitution,[12] the federal government can dispose of its property, including its land and its water, like any other proprietary owner. Congress, in the Act of 1866,[13] released its land to settlement.

In the Desert Land Act of 1877,[14] Congress severed the unappropriated and nonnavigable water from the federal land. Patents issued thereafter conveyed no interest in the appurtenant water. The appropriation of water was therefore left subject to state control.[15]

Congress can release its proprietary interest in land and water and allow the states to control the appropriation and use of the water. However, the relinquishment of its proprietary interest does not also relinquish the sovereign powers of the United States. Congress still has the power to regulate commerce and to control navigation. Its failure to exercise that power to its fullest in the past will not preclude it from doing so in the future.[16] All state-created rights in the source are clearly subordinate to these dominant federal interests. Consequently, no compensation need be paid if these state-created water rights are impaired by the assertion of the government's dominant servitude.[17]

The federal government may exercise its proprietary powers by withdrawing some of its land from use and its water from state-controlled appropriation. The reservation of land may also entail the reservation of unappropriated, appurtenant water necessary for the purposes of the specific reservation. These federal reserved water rights have been a source of concern and conflict in the West.[18]

The reserved rights doctrine was first established in connection with Indian water rights in *Winters v. United States*.[19] There the Court held that the government, in withdrawing lands for the establishment of an Indian reservation, had also, by implication, reserved sufficient water for Indian use with a date of priority equal to the date of the withdrawal or the establishment of the reservation.[20] The Supreme Court in *Arizona v. California*[21] clearly indicated that although the reserved rights may be used for purposes other than irrigation, the total quantity of water reserved for Indian use was to be determined by the needs of their irrigable lands.[22] The reserved rights doctrine has been extended to other federal reservations as well.[23]

Water rights appropriated under state law prior to the date of the federal reservation are vested and fully protected under law.[24] Any stated-created right appropriated after Congress withdraws its land from settlement and reserves the unappropriated, appurtenant water for federal use is clearly subordinate to this federal water right.[25]

The quantity of water reserved is limited to that quantity necessary to accomplish the purpose or purposes of the federal reservation.[26] Where the stream is fully appropriated, the doctrine must be applied with sensitivity to its impact upon those who have vested rights under state law.[27]

The full extent of the federal reserved rights (including those claimed by the various Indian tribes) is presently unknown. These quantities may prove to be quite small. However, agencies of the federal government continue to assert novel theories, which if validated, may have the effect of considerably increasing the quantity of water so reserved. These new claims have been hotly contested in litigation in Colorado.[28]

The United States Supreme Court rocked the western water world by holding that water and water rights were commodities capable of being bought and sold in the marketplace.[29] The Court further held that state-created water rights were subject to federal regulatory control in interstate commerce. The *Sporhase*[30] decision heightened the awareness of those who wish to buy and sell water rights of water's inherent marketability as well as its subordinate position to national interests.

The sale and purchase of water rights is not new. Water rights have been freely traded in the appropriation doctrine states from the doctrine's inception. The most typical transaction involved the purchase and sale of irrigated farmland where the water rights simply transferred with title to the land as an appurtenance.

The last ten years have seen a marked difference in the type of water-sale transactions and also in the nature of the interests being asserted and protected in water resources. Existing water rights are being reallocated to new, higher economic uses through changes of use. For example, industrial water users have purchased substantial blocks of water, stripped them from the land where they had been historically used, and applied them to industrial use. Municipalities in the desert southwest have purchased "water ranches" to acquire the groundwater underlying the land to meet the ever-increasing demands of their growing populations.

Noneconomic interests in water rights have also received considerable attention in recent years. Water rights may now be acquired for the sole purpose of leaving the water in the stream for maintenance of fisheries, protection of our national forests and other federal reservations, and for other similar "public trust" uses.[31] To date, only governmental agencies have been given the power to appropriate or reallocate water to in-stream uses. Private groups have tried unsuccessfully to obtain that authority, but state legislatures have been reluctant to grant them that power. Nevertheless, recognition of the aesthetic value of water in the stream has received both judicial and legislative sanction. In-stream appropriations are a radical departure from the long-standing rule that an appropriation must be accompanied by the artificial diversion of water from the stream and its application to some recognized beneficial use.[32]

The recognition of in-stream uses demonstrates the shift in societal values. It also involves the interplay between the states and the dominant federal interest in the water supply of the western United States. Some of the more pressing issues in water law today are: the reallocation of water through marketplace transactions and the reduction and/or curtailment of use caused by the exercise of federal regulatory controls over the diversion and use of vested water rights under the federal authority to regulate commerce.[33]

There are three major regulatory programs that give the federal government the authority to disrupt if not displace vested water rights. They are Section 404 of the Clean Water Act, the Federal Power Act, and the Endangered Species Act. These programs have in effect created a new class of federal water rights that differs from other federal reserve rights or state-created rights. The principal difference is that they lack any definitive date of priority, which makes their integration into the state system of water rights administration almost impossible in those appropriation doctrine states where water rights administration is based largely on priority of appropriation. Further, there is no requirement that these regulatory rights be beneficially used.[34]

Although these regulatory rights have the potential to "take" state-created rights, that is not generally the case. All water rights are appropriated subject to the public interest,[35] and therefore are subject to adjustment to meet the changing demands caused by competing interests for our water resources. Generally, vested rights should not be curtailed but merely reduced to protect other public interest values in the water resources. Reductions of use, as distinguished from outright curtailments, are not generally considered to be takings.[36]

Section 404 of the Clean Water Act[37] requires the issuance of a permit by the Corps of Army Engineers for the dredging or filling of the waters of the United States. It also provides protection for wetlands. The diversion of water under a state-created water right may require the issuance of a Section 404 permit. If that permit is not issued by the Corps or if its issuance is vetoed by the Environmental Protection Agency (EPA) under its cojurisdiction, the denial may render it impossible to enjoy the water right.[38]

The Clean Water Act contains some exceptions that protect existing farming and timber-harvesting activities, but the exceptions are clearly limited to existing activities.[39] A farmer seeking to drain a swamp to create new irrigable farmland would be required to obtain a 404 permit.[40] Similarly, an attempt to characterize a dike that would have blocked the flow of water to a wetlands area as an exempt irrigation facility has failed in the federal courts.[41]

If a state water-right holder cannot fall within one of the limited exceptions to Section 404, he or she may be prevented from exercising the water right to its fullest potential. The act contains impressive language that arguably was intended to protect state-created water rights.[42] Notwithstanding this broad policy statement, the federal courts have not hesitated to subordinate state water rights to the effect of the act.[43]

Section 401 of the Clean Water Act also incorporates state water-quality issues and policies into federal permits. The section requires all federal permittees to obtain a state certification that the proposed activity will comply with any applicable state water-quality standards and any other appropriate requirement of state law.[44] This requires compliance with both the effluent limitations and water-quality limitations. Federal permittees are prohibited from altering Section 401 conditions.[45] There is an ongoing dispute among federal permittees and the states over the reach of Section 401. Permittees argue that it should be limited to pollution discharges (effluent limitations) and has no application to maintaining minimum stream flows for fishery protection or antidegradation provisions to maintain a designated use of a stream. Some states have taken a broader view.[46]

An applicant for a Federal Energy Regulatory Commission (FERC) license under the Federal Power Act[47] is required to obtain a state water-right permit for its hydropower project.[48] Inconsistent state laws are deemed preempted by this federal law.[49] FERC may require its licensee to release water from reservoirs at times that are detrimental to downstream water users' interests in order to protect fish and other wildlife resources. These conditions may be mandatory. FERC's right to impose license conditions that may impair state-created vested rights have been upheld as a valid assertion of the federal government's authority to regulate commerce and navigation.[50] Arguably, where this situation occurs the states should have the power to protect the vested water rights of its citizens by conditioning a FERC license condition on noninterference of vested water rights.[51]

The Endangered Species Act[52] imposes an absolute duty on federal agencies to take all required steps to protect threatened and endangered species. This mandatory compliance may well require the subordination of state-created water rights to this federal interest.[53] Section 7 is the teeth of the act.[54] It requires an agency or a federal licensee or permittee to consult with the Secretary of Interior before undertaking any action that may jeopardize an endangered or threatened species.[55] If the Secretary concludes, after consultation, that the proposed project will jeopardize the endangered or threatened species, the Secretary is to suggest reasonable and prudent alternatives that would not harm the species in question and therefore would not violate the mandate of Section 7 to not jeopardize the species. The act has been amended to create some general flexibility into the protection process.[56] The burden is not on the agency or the private applicant to demonstrate that the value of the project or activity outweighs the protection of the threatened or endangered species. If, after consultation, it is concluded that the conflict cannot be resolved, the exemption application is sent to a cabinet-level committee for review.[57]

The alternative of not diverting water or not constructing an impoundment facility is one that may be suggested and/or a required condition as part of the Section 404 permitting process. Restricting diversions or mandating the maintenance of minimum stream flows to sustain a downstream ecosystem under the act may seriously reduce the water right and may even make it impossible to use it.

This is clearly what happened in the case of the proposed Grayrocks Dam on the North Platte River. The Court set aside a Section 404 permit for construction of the dam because of the concern that the additional impoundment of water would harm the habitat of the whooping crane.[58] The Endangered Species Act may well require a federal agency to operate a federal reservoir to maximize the protection of the protected species, which may, in turn, force the subordination of state-created vested water rights.[59]

Other recent federal laws have taken bold steps toward protection of fish habitat and have required the sponsors of federal reclamation projects to maintain minimum stream flows, to acquire water rights and dedicate them to that purpose, and to perform additional environmental mitigation to offset damage caused during construction.[60]

Water law in the West is ever changing in response to our shifting social values. That is the beauty of the common law—its ability to adjust to accommodate the changing needs of the society that it serves. Professor Frank Trelease has written:

> In all of the western states, a water right is a property right, defensible and protected, firm enough to give security to investments and enterprises, flexible enough to allow changes to new and more productive uses, subject to governmental controls that insure beneficial use and protect other public interest including the environment. That is what water law is all about.[61]

The existing appropriation doctrine is inherently flexible and can and will adapt to meet the competing needs of our multifaceted society.

Notes

1. R. Dewsnup & D. Jensen, *A Summary Digest of State Water Laws*, 475, 719 (1973).
2. Utah Code Ann. 73-1-3 (1980).
3. Utah Code Ann. 73-1-3 (1953).
4. *See generally* Trelease, *The Concept of Reasonable Beneficial Use in the Law of Surface Streams*, 12 Wyo. L. J. 1 (1957). The Supreme Court of Utah once held that the appropriation of water for water fowl propagation was not a beneficial use.

5. Bountiful City v. De Luca, 77 Utah 107, 292 P. 194 (1930); Sowards v. Meagher, 37 Utah 212, 108 P. 1112 (1910). *See generally* Trelease, *The Concept of Reasonable Beneficial Use in the Law of Surface Streams*, 12 Wyo. L. J. 1 (1957).

6. Perfection means that water has been placed into use. Once an application is approved, the applicant is given a specific amount of time within which to complete the construction of his diversion works and to place the water to beneficial use. An applicant may be granted additional time within which to complete the appropriation upon a showing of diligence or reasonable cause for delay. Diligence requires the applicant to make a reasonable effort to accomplish his undertaking with the dispatch expected of men engaged in a like enterprise, who desire a speedy accomplishment of their designs. Carbon Canal Co. v. Sanpete Water Users Ass'n., 10 Utah 2d 376, 353 P.2d 916 (1960).

7. *See e.g.* Hunter v. United States, 388 F.2d 148, 153 (9th Cir. 1967); Hughes v. Lincoln Land Co., 27 F. Supp. 972 (D.C. Wyo. 1939); Town of Sterling v. Pawnee Ditch Ext. Co., 42 Colo. 421, 94 p. 339 (1908).

8. *See* S. E. Clyde, *State Prohibitions on the Interstate Exportation of Scarce Water Resources*, 53 U. Colo. L. R. 557, Spring, Number 3 (1982).

9. Cooley v. Board of Wardens, 53 U.S. (12 How.) 299 (1851).

10. California v. FERC, 110 S. Ct. 2024, 495 U.S. 490, (1990), California v. United States, 438 U.S. 645 (1978); Arizona v. California, 373 U.S. 546 (1963); Dugan v. Rank, 372 U.S. 609 (1963); Ivanhoe Irr. Dist. v. McCracken, 357 U.S. 275 (1958), and First Iowa Hydro-Electric Cooperative v. Federal Power Commission, 328 U.S. 152 (1946).

11. The United States owns its reserved water rights and can sell, lease, quit claim, release, encumber or convey its own rights like any other proprietary owner. Greely v. Confederated Salish and Kootenai Tribes of the Flathead Reservation, 219 Mont. 76, 712 P.2d 754 (1985).

12. U. S . Const., Art. IV, 3, cl. 2; Alabama v. Texas, 347 U.S. 272 (1954).

13. Act of July 26, 1866, ch. 262, 14 Stat. 251.

14. Desert Land Act of 1877, Act of March 3, 1877, ch. 107, 19 Stat. 377.

15. California-Oregon Power Co., v. Beaver Portland Power Co., 295 U.S. 142 (1935).

16. *E.g.* United States v. Twin City Power Co., 350 U.S. 222 (1956); Federal Power Commission v. Niagara Mohawk Power Co., 347 U.S. 239 (1954).

17. United States v. Rands, 389 U.S. 121 (1967), U.S. v. Rio Grande Dam and Irr. Co., 174 U.S. 690 (1899).

18. *See generally*, S. E. Clyde, *Legal and Institutional Barriers to Market Transfers and Reallocation of Water Resources*, 29 S. D. L. R. 233,252, Spring (1984).

19. 207 U.S. 564 (1908).

20. *Id.* at 576-77.

21. 73 U.S. 546 (1963).

22. *See also*, In Re. General Adjudication of All Water Rights in the Big Horn River System, 753 P.2d 76 (Wyo. 1989).

23. United States v. Cappaert, 426 U.S. 128 (1976)(a National Monument); and United States v. New Mexico, 438 U.S. 696 (1978)(a National Forest).

24. Hunter v. United States, 388 F.2d 148 (9th Cir. 1967).

25. *See* S. E. Clyde, note 18, *infra.*, p. 252, and Tarlock, *Law of Water Rights and Resources,* 9–43, Clark Boardman Company, Ltd., N.Y. N.Y. (1994).

26. United States v. Cappaert, 426 U.S. 128 (1976).

27. United States v. New Mexico, 438 U.S. 696 (1978); In Re. General Adjudication of All Water Rights in the Big Horn River System, 753 P.2d 76 (Wyo. 1989).

28. Sierra Club v. Yeutter, 911 F.2d 1405 (10th Cir. 1990), Aurora v. Bell, 799 P.2d 33 (Colo. 1990), United States v. Jessee, 744 P.2d 491 (Colo. 1987); United States v. City and County of Denver, 656 P.2d 1 (Colo. 1982).

29. 458 U.S. 941 (1982).

30. *Id.* note 27.

31. *E.g.* National Audubon Society v. Superior Court, 33 Cal 3d 419, 658 P.2d 709, 189 Cal. Rptr. 346, *cert. denied* 464 U.S. 977 (1983)(wherein the court held that perfected water rights may be reconsidered where their exercise threatens certain public values in water resources); *see also* United States v. State Water Resources Control Board, 182 Cal. App.3d 82, 227 Cal Rptr. 161 (1986); Kootenai Envtl. Alliance, Inc. v. Panhandle Yacht Club, Inc., 105 Idaho 622, 671 P.2d 1085 (1983); Galt v. State, 44 Mont. 103, 731 P.2d 912 (1987); Montana Coalition for Stream Access, Inc. v. Hildreth, 211 Mont. 29, 684 P.2d 1088 (1984) and Montana Coalition for Stream Access, Inc. v. Curran, 210 Mont. 38, 682 P.2d 163 (1984); Ritter v. Standal, 98 Idaho 446, 566 P.2d 769 (1977); Southern Idaho Fish & Game Ass'n. v. Picabo Livestock, Inc., 96 Idaho 360, 528 P.2d 1295 (1974); State Department of Parks v. Idaho Depart of Water Administration, 96 Idaho 440, 520 P.2d 924 (1974); Deseret Livestock Co. v. State, 110 Utah 239, 171 P.2d 401 (1946); Utah Code Ann.§73-3-3 (1988).

32. *E.g.* National Audubon Society v. Superior Court, 33 Cal 3d 419, 658 P.2d 709, 189 Cal. Rptr. 346, *cert. denied* 464 U.S. 977 (1983)(wherein the court held that perfected water rights may be reconsidered where their exercise threatens certain public values in water resources); *see also* United States v. State Water Resources Control Board, 182 Cal. App.3d 82, 227 Cal Rptr. 161 (1986); Kootenai Envtl. Alliance, Inc. v. Panhandle Yacht Club, Inc., 105 Idaho 622, 671 P.2d 1085 (1983); Galt v. State, 44 Mont. 103, 731 P.2d 912 (1987); Montana Coalition for Stream Access, Inc. v. Hildreth, 211 Mont. 29, 684 P.2d 1088 (1984) and Montana Coalition for Stream Access Inc. v. Curran, 210 Mont. 38, 682 P.2d 163 (1984); Ritter v. Standal, 98 Idaho 446, 566 P.2d 769 (1977); Southern Idaho Fish & Game Ass'n. v. Picabo Livestock, Inc., 96 Idaho 360, 528 P.2d 1295 (1974); State Department of Parks v. Idaho Depart of Water Administration, 96 Idaho 440, 520 P.2d 924 (1974); Deseret Livestock Co. v. State, 110 Utah 239, 171 P.2d 401 (1946); Utah Code Ann. §73-3-3 (1988).

33. *See generally* S. E. Clyde, *Adapting to the Changing Demand for Water Use Through Continued Refinement of the Prior Appropriation Doctrine: An Alternate Approach to Wholesale Reallocation*, Vol. 29 Natural Resources Journal, 435, No. 2 (Spring 1989).

34. *See* Tarlock, pp. 9–28, *Law of Water Rights and Water Resources*, Clark Boardman (1994).

35. *See* Sporhase v. Nebraska, 458 U.S. 941 (1982); Hughes v. Oklahoma, 441 U.S. 322 (1979). *See* S. E. Clyde, *Legal and Institutional Barriers to Market Transfers and Reallocation of Water Resources*, 29 S.D.L.R. 232, 243, Spring (1984).

36. National Audubon Society v. Superior Court, 33 Cal. 3d 419, 189 Cal. Rptr. 346, 658 P.2d 709, *cert. denied* Los Angeles Dep't of Water & Power v. National Audubon Society, 464 U.S. 977 (1983); *see* Tarlock, pp. 9–28, note 34, *infra.*, wherein he states: "All water rights are subject to adjustment to meet the changing demands of competing users. In most cases regulatory water rights will not curtail an existing use but will merely reduce the margin of safety built into the right. These reductions are not per se takings."

37. §404, 33 U.S.C. §1344.

38. Wyoming v. Hoffman, 23 F. Supp. 450 (D. Wyo. 1976).

39. U.S.A. v. Huebner, 752 F.2d 1235 (7th Cir.), *cert. denied* 474 U.S. 817 (1985); U.S. v. Zanger, 767 F. Supp. 1030 (N.D. Cal. 1991); U.S. v. Sinclair Oil Co.,

767 F. Supp. 200 (D. Mont. 1990), channel modification to ease flood erosion without benefit of permit violated Section 404.

40. Avoyelles Sportsman's League, Inc. v. Marsh, 715 F.2d 897 (5th Cir. 1983).

41. United States v. Akers, 785 F.2d 814 (9th Cir. 1986).

42. 33 U.S.C. § 1251(g). Critical to water users and especially the Western States is the stated policy in the 1970 Wallop Amendment to the Act that provides:

> [T]he authority of each State to allocate quantities of water within its jurisdiction shall not be superseded, abrogated or otherwise impaired by this chapter. It is further the policy of Congress that nothing in this chapter shall be construed to supersede or abrogate rights to quantities of water which have been established by any State. Federal agencies shall co-operate with State and local agencies to develop comprehensive solutions to prevent, reduce and eliminate pollution in concert with programs for managing water resources.

43. U.S. v. Akers, 785 F.2d 814 (9th Cir.) *cert. denied* Riverside Irr. Dist. v. Andrews, 758 F.2d 508 (10th Cir. 1985), held that even if a denial of a nationwide dredge and fill permit under §404 of the Act impaired the state's authority to allocate water, the Corps of Army Engineers was within its authority in denying the permit where the proposed project would have resulted in the depletion of stream flows from increased consumptive use of water that would in turn have adversely affected the critical habitat of the whooping crane. The Court held in National Wildlife Federation v. Gorsuch, 693 F.2d 156, 224 U.S. App. D.C. 272 (1980), that the statement of policy is not intended to take precedence over legitimate and necessary water quality considerations.

44. 33 U.S.C. § 1341.

45. U.S. Dep't of Interior v. Federal Energy Regulatory Comm'n, 952 F.2d 538 (D.C. Cir. 1992).

46. Arnold Irr. Dist. v. Dept. of Envtl. Quality, 717 P.2d 1274 (Or. Ct. App. 1986), *reviewed denied*, 726 P.2d 377 (1986); Dep't of Ecology v. Public Utility Dist. No. 1, 849 P.2d 646 (1993) *aff'd*, ___ U.S. ___, 114 S. Ct. 1900 (1994), where the Supreme Court upheld the state's imposition of minimum stream flow requirements as a part of a §401 Certification, holding that §401 requires permit applicants to comply with both use designations as part of the anti-degradation provisions of the Clean Water Act, as well as the water quality criteria of the state's standards. *But see* Niagara Mohawk Power v. New York Dep't of Envtl. Conservation, 592 N.Y.S.2d 141 (A.D. 3Dept. 1993), that confined the state's §401 certifications to the state's water quality standards. *See generally,* Tarlock, 9-32.1.

47. 16 U.S.C. §791 *et. seq.*, Winnebago Tribe of Neb. v. Ray, 621 F.2d 269 (8th Cir.), *cert. denied*, 449 U.S. 836 (1980).

48. Escondido Mutual Water Dist. v. La Jolla Band of Mission Indians, 446 U.S. 765, *reh'g denied*, 467 U.S. 1267 (1984).

49. California v. FERC, 495 U.S. 490, 506 S. Ct. 2024, 2034 (1990); First Iowa Hydroelectric Co. v. FPC, 328 U.S. 152, *reh'g denied*, 378 U.S. 879 (1946); *but see* PG&E Co. v. State Energy Resources Conservation and Development Comm'n, 461 U.S. 190 (1983); California Coastal Comm'n v. Granite Rock Co., 480 U.S. 572 (1987), which has limited the preemption argument in connection with Section 8 of the Reclamation Act of 1902.

50. California v. Federal Power Commission, 345 F.2d 917 (9th Cir.), *cert. denied*, 382 U.S. 941 (1965). FERC denies that the states have any regulatory controls over federal power projects such as the imposition of minimum stream flow releases due to federal pre-emption in this area. California v. FERC, 877 F.2d 743 (9th Cir. 1989), *aff'd*. Calif. v. FERC, 110 S. CT. 2024, 495 U.S. 490, (1990).

51. *See* Tarlock, 9-26 through 9-27, *infra.* note 34.

52. 16 U.S.C. §1531 *et. seq.*

53. *See generally* Tarlock, *Law of Water Rights and Resources*, 9-30, Clark Boardman Company, N.Y. N.Y. (1990).

54. 16 U.S.C. §1536.

55. 16 U.S.C. §1536(a)(2).

56. P. L. 97-304, 96 STAT. 1417 (1982).

57. 16 U.S.C. §1536(c)(p).

58. Neb. v. REA, 12 Env't Rep. Cas. 1150 (D. Neb. 1978), *appeal vacated and dismissed*, 594 F.2d 879 (8th Cir. 1979). *See also,* Riverside Irrigation Dist. v. Stipo, 658 F.2d 762 (10th Cir. 1981); *on remand*, Riverside Irrigation Dist. v. Andrews, 568 F. Supp. 583 (D. Colo. 1983). The Corps' authority to impose downstream protection conditions on a section 404 permit was upheld by the Tenth Circuit in Riverside Irrigation Dist. v. Andrews, 758 F.2d 508 (10th Cir. 1985). *See generally* Tarlock, *The Recognition of In-stream Flow Rights: New Public Western Water Rights*, 25 Rocky Mnt. Min. L. Inst. 24-31 (1979).

59. Carlson-Truckee Water Conservancy District v. Clark, 549 F. Supp. 704 (D. Nev. 1982), *aff'd in part & rev's in part*, 741 F.2d 257 (9th Cir. 1984), *cert. denied sub nom.,* Nevada v. Hodel, 470 U.S. 1083 (1985); and the Orr ditch litigation, Carlson-Truckee Water Conservancy District v. Watt, 54 F. SUPP. 704, 7708 (D. Nev. 1982), where all parties agreed that the Secretary of Interior had the duty in operating the Stampede Reservoir to prefer fish to municipal and industrial uses in the allocation of water.

60. Reclamation Projects Authorization and Adjustment Act of 1992, P. L. 102-575, October 30, 1992, and particularly Titles II through IV, the Central Utah Project Completion Act provisions relating to maintenance of minimum stream flows in the Provo River to protect and maintain the blue ribbon trout fishery in the Provo River.

61. Trelease, *Back to Basics—Taking the Politics Out of Water Law*, (1979), (unpublished manuscript).

APPENDIX A

Federal Statutes Affecting Management of Water Resources in Utah (partial listing)

1. *Clean Water Act and Amendments*, P.L.92–500; 33 U.S.C. 1251. Congressional Declaration of Goals and Policy

(a) The objective of this chapter is to restore and maintain the chemical, physical, and biological integrity of the Nation's waters. In order to achieve this objective it is hereby declared that, consistent with the provisions of this chapter—

(1) it is the national goal that the discharge of pollutants into the navigable waters be eliminated by 1985;

(2) it is the national goal that wherever attainable, an interim goal of water quality which provides for the procreation and propagation of fish, shellfish, and wildlife and provides for recreation in and on the water be achieved by July 1, 1983;

(3) it is the national policy that the discharge of toxic pollutants in toxic amounts be prohibited;

(4) it is the national policy that federal financial assistance be provided to construct publicly owned waste treatment works;

(5) it is the national policy that area-wide waste treatment planning processes be developed and implemented to assure adequate control of sources of pollutants in each state, and

(6) it is the national policy that a major research and demonstration effort be made to develop technology necessary to eliminate the discharge of pollutants into the navigable waters, waters of the contiguous zone, and the oceans.

(b) Congressional recognition, preservation, and protection of primary responsibilities and rights of states

2. *Clean Air Act and Amendments* P.L. 91–604. 42 U.S.C. 7401. Congressional Findings of Declaration of Purpose

(b) The purposes of this subchapter are—

(1) to protect and enhance the quality of the Nation's air resources so as to promote the public health and welfare and the productive capacity of its population;

(2) to initiate and accelerate a national research and development program to achieve the prevention and control of air pollution;

(3) to provide technical and financial assistance to State and local

governments in connection with the development and execution of their air prevention pollution programs; and

(4) to encourage and assist the development and operation of air pollution control programs.

3. *Endangered Species Act* (*as amended*) P.L. 93–205 16 U.S.C. 1531 (1991). Congressional Findings and Declaration of Purposes and Policy

(a) Findings—The Congress finds and declares that—

(1) various species of fish, wildlife, and plants in the United States have been rendered extinct as a consequence of economic growth and development untempered by adequate concern and conservation;

(2) other species of fish, wildlife, and plants have been so depleted in numbers that they are in danger of or threatened with extinction;

(3) these species of fish, wildlife, and plants are of esthetic, ecological, educational, historical, recreational, and scientific value to the Nation and its people;

(4) The United States has pledged itself as a sovereign state in the international community to conserve to the extent practicable the various species of fish or wildlife and plants facing extinction, pursuant to—

(A) migratory bird treaties with Canada and Mexico;
(B) the Migratory and Endangered Bird Treaty with Japan;
(C) the Convention of Nature Protection and Wildlife Preservation in the Western Hemisphere;
(D) The International Convention for the Northwest Atlantic Fisheries;
(E) The International Convention for the High Seas Fisheries of the North Pacific Ocean;
(F) the Convention on International Trade in Endangered Species of Wild Fauna and Flora; and
(G) other international agreements.

(5) Encouraging the States and other interested parties, through federal financial assistance and a system of incentives, to develop and maintain conservation programs which meet national and international standards is a key to meeting the Nation's international commitments and to better safeguarding, for the benefit of all citizens, the Nation's heritage in fish, wildlife, and plants.

(b) Purposes

The purposes of this chapter are to provide a means whereby the ecosystems upon which endangered species and threatened species depend may be conserved, to provide a program for the conservation of such endangered species and threatened species, and to take such steps as may be appropriate to achieve the purposes of the treaties and conventions set forth in subsection (a) of this section.

4. *Safe Drinking Water Act (as amended)* P.L. 95–190 42 U.S.C. 300g.
Coverage
Subject to sections 300g–4 and 300g–5 of this title, national primary drinking water regulations under this part shall apply to each public water system in each state; except that such regulations shall not apply to a public water system—

(1) which consists only of distribution and storage facilities (and does not have any treatment or collection facilities);

(2) which obtains all of its water from, but is not owned or operated by, a public water system to which such regulations apply;

(3) which does not sell water to any person; and

(4) which is not a carrier which conveys passengers in interstate commerce.

42 U.S.C. 300g–1. National drinking water regulations

(a) National primary drinking water regulations; maximum contaminant level goals; simultaneous publication of regulations and goals.

5. Executive Order 11644 Use of Off-Road Vehicles on Public Lands 42 U.S.C. 4321

Section 1. Purpose.

It is the purpose of this order to establish policies and provide for procedures that will ensure that the use of off-road vehicles on public lands will be controlled and directed so as to protect the resources of those lands, to promote the safety of all users of those lands, and to minimize all conflicts among the various uses of those lands.

6. *National Environmental Policy Act of 1969* P.L. 91–190 42 U.S.C. 4321–4370c

4331. Congressional Declaration of national environmental policy

The Congress declares that it is the continuing policy of the Federal government in cooperation with State and local governments and other interested organizations to use all practicable means and measures, including technical and financial assistance, to create and maintain conditions under which man and nature can exist in productive harmony and fulfill the social, economic, and other requirements of present and future generations of Americans.

APPENDIX B Utah Fishes, Past and Present

Key: **Bold** highlights species with statutory protection. E = endangered (U.S. Endangered Species Act); P = protected; N = native to Utah. Utah status not repeated where species is protected under federal statute. O = Exotic or native fishes no longer found in Utah. X = Considered extinct. See Miller and Smith 1981.

Order Anguilliformes

Family Anguillidae—freshwater eels

O	American eel	*Anguilla rostrata* (Lesueur, 1817)

Order Clupeiformes

Family Clupeidae—herrings

O	American shad	*Alosa sapidissima* (Wilson, 1811)
P	**gizzard shad**	*Dorosoma cepedianum* (Lesueur, 1818)
	threadfin shad	*Dorosoma petenense* (Günther, 1867)

Order Cypriniformes

Family Cyprinidae—carps and minnows

	goldfish	*Carassius auratus* (Linnaeus, 1758)
O	grass carp	*Ctenopharyngodon idella* (Valenciennes, 1844)
	red shiner	*Cyprinella lutrensis* (Baird and Girard, 1853a)
	common carp	*Cyprinus carpio* Linnaeus, 1758
N	Utah chub	*Gila atraria* (Girard, 1856)
N	leatherside chub	*Gila copei* (Jordan and Gilbert, 1881)
N,E	**humpback chub**	*Gila cypha* Miller, 1945a
N,E	**bonytail**	*Gila elegans* Baird and Girard, 1853b
N,E	**roundtail chub**	*Gila robusta* Baird and Girard, 1853b
N,P	**Colorado roundtail chub**	*Gila robusta robusta* Miller, 1945c
N,P	**Virgin roundtail chub**	*Gila robusta seminuda* Cope and Yarrow, 1875
	brassy minnow	*Hybognathus hankinsoni* Hubbs, 1929 (in Jordan 1929)
N,P	**least chub**	*Iotichthys phlegethontis* (Cope, 1874)
N,P	**Virgin spinedace**	*Lepidomeda mollispinis mollispinis* Miller and Hubbs, 1960

O	common shiner	*Luxilus cornutus* (Mitchill, 1817)
O	hornyhead chub	*Nocomis biguttatus* (Kirtland, 1840)
	golden shiner	*Notemigonus crysoleucas* (Mitchill, 1814)
	emerald shiner	*Notropis atherinoides* Rafinesque, 1818
	spottail shiner	*Notropis hudsonius* (Clinton, 1824)
	sand shiner	*Notropis stramineus* (Cope, 1865)
O	bluntnose minnow	*Pimephales notatus* (Rafinesque, 1820)
	fathead minnow	*Pimephales promelas* Rafinesque, 1820
O	bullhead minnow	*Pimephales vigilax* (Baird and Girard, 1853)
N,E	**woundfin**	*Plagopterus argentissimus* Cope, 1874
N,E	**Colorado squawfish**	*Ptychocheilus lucius* Girard, 1856
N	longnose dace	*Rhinichthys cataractae* (Valenciennes, 1842 in Cuvier and Valenciennes 1842)
N	speckled dace	*Rhinichthys osculus* (Girard, 1856)
N	Sevier River speckled dace	*Rhinichthys osculus adobe* (Jordan and Evermann, 1891)
N	Bonneville speckled dace	*Rhinichthys osculus carringtoni* (Cope, 1871a)
O	blacknose dace	*Rhinichthys atratulus*(Hermann, 1804)
N	redside shiner	*Richardsonius balteatus* (Richardson, 1836)
N	Columbia redside shiner	*Richardsonius balteatus balteatus* (Richardson, 1836)
N	Bonneville redside shiner	*Richardsonius balteatus hydrophlox* Cope, 1871b
	creek chub	*Semotilus omaculatus* (Mitchill, 1818)
	Family Catostomidae—suckers	
N	Utah sucker	*Catostomus ardens* Jordan and Gilbert, 1881
N	desert sucker	*Catostomus clarki* Baird and Girard, 1854
	white sucker	*Catostomus commersoni* (Lacépède, 1803)
N	bluehead sucker	*Catostomus discobolus* Cope, 1872
N	flannelmouth sucker	*Catostomus latipinnis* Baird and Girard, 1853a
N	mountain sucker	*Catostomus platyrhynchus* (Cope, 1874)
N,O,X	June sucker	*Chamistes liorus liorus* Jordan, 1878
N,E	**June sucker**	*Chasmistes liorus mictus* Miller and Smith, 1981
N,P	**razorback sucker**	*Xyrauchen texanus* (Abbott, 1861)
	Order Siluriformes	
	Family Ictaluridae—bullhead catfishes	
	black bullhead	*Ameiurus melas* (Rafinesque, 1820)[1]
	yellow bullhead	*Ameiurus natalis* (Lesueur, 1819)
	channel catfish	*Ictalurus punctatus* (Rafinesque, 1818)

1. See Robins et al. 1991 for explanation of *Ameiurus* taxonomic status.

	Order Salmoniformes	
	Family Esocidae—pikes	
	northern pike	*Esox lucius* Linnaeus, 1758
	Family Osmeridae—smelts	
O	delta smelt	*Hypomesus transpacificus* McAllister, 1963
	Family Salmonidae—trouts	
O	lake whitefish	*Coregonus clupeaformis* (Mitchill, 1818)
	golden trout	*Oncorhynchus aguabonita* (Jordan, 1893a)
N	cutthroat trout	*Oncorhynchus clarki* (Richardson, 1836)
N	Yellowstone cutthroat trout	*O. c. bouvieri* (Bendire, 1882)
	Lahontan cutthroat trout	*O. c. henshawi* (Gill and Jordan in D. S. Jordan, 1878)
N	Colorado cutthroat trout	*O. c. pleuriticus* (Cope, 1872)
N,P	**Bonneville cutthroat trout**	*O. c. utah* (Suckley, 1874)
O	chum salmon	*Oncorhynchus keta* (Walbaum, 1792)
O	coho salmon	*Oncorhynchus kisutch* (Walbaum, 1792)
	rainbow trout	*Oncorhynchus mykiss* (Walbaum, 1792)
O	steelhead trout	(not differentiated from rainbow trout)
O	Kamloops trout	(not differentiated from rainbow trout)
	sockeye salmon (kokanee)	*Oncorhynchus nerka* (Walbaum, 1792)
O	chinook salmon	*Oncorhynchus tshawytscha* (Walbaum, 1792)
N	Bear Lake whitefish	*Prosopium abyssicola* (Snyder, 1919)
N	Bonneville cisco	*Prosopium gemmifer* (Snyder, 1919)[2]
N	Bonneville whitefish	*Prosopium spilonotus* (Snyder, 1919)
N	mountain whitefish	*Prosopium williamsoni* (Girard, 1856)
O	Atlantic salmon	*Salmo salar* Linnaeus, 1758
	brown trout	*Salmo trutta* Linnaeus, 1758
	brook trout	*Salvelinus fontinalis* (Mitchill, 1814)
	lake trout	*Salvelinus namaycush* (Walbaum, 1792)
	Arctic grayling	*Thymallus arcticus* (Pallas, 1776)
	Order Percopsiformes	
	Family Percopsidae—trout-perches	
	trout-perch	*Percopsis omiscomaycus* (Walbaum, 1792)
	Order Atheriniformes	
	Family Cyprinodontidae—killifishes	
	plains killifish	*Fundulus zebrinus* Jordan and Gilbert, 1883
	rainwater killifish	*Lucania parva* (Baird and Girard, 1855)

2. Name change accomplished in Bailey et al. 1960 AFS special publication 2.

Family Poeciliidae—livebearers

	western mosquitofish	*Gambusia affinis* (Baird and Girard, 1853)

Order Gasterosteiformes

Family Gasterosteidae—sticklebacks

	brook stickleback	*Culaea inconstans* (Kirtland, 1841)

Order Scorpaeniformes

Family Cottidae—sculpins

N,O,X	Utah Lake sculpin	*Cottus echinatus* Bailey and Bond, 1963
N	mottled sculpin	*Cottus bairdi* Girard, 1850
N	Paiute sculpin	*Cottus beldingi* Eigenmann and Eigenmann, 1891
N	Bear Lake sculpin	*Cottus extensus* Bailey and Bond, 1963

Order Perciformes

Family Percichthyidae—temperate basses

	white bass	*Morone chrysops* (Rafinesque, 1820)
	striped bass	*Morone saxatilis* (Walbaum, 1792)

Family Centrarchidae—sunfishes

	Sacramento perch	*Archoplites interruptus* (Girard, 1854)
O	rock bass	*Ambloplites rupestris* (Rafinesque, 1817)
	green sunfish	*Lepomis cyanellus* Rafinesque, 1819
	bluegill	*Lepomis macrochirus* Rafinesque, 1819
O	redear sunfish	*Lepomis microlophus* (Günther, 1859)
	smallmouth bass	*Micropterus dolomieu* Lacépède, 1802
	largemouth bass	*Micropterus salmoides* (Lacépède, 1802)
	white crappie	*Pomoxis annularis* Rafinesque, 1818b
	black crappie	*Pomoxis nigromaculatus* (Lesueur, 1829)

Family Percidae—perches

	yellow perch	*Perca flavescens* (Mitchill, 1814)
	logperch	*Percina caprodes* (Rafinesque 1818)
	walleye	*Stizostedion vitreum* (Mitchill, 1818)

Glossary

abdominal On the belly. When fins are located on the belly behind the pectoral fins, they are termed *abdominal.*

acre-foot A volume of water equal to an acre covered with one foot of water—43,560 cubic feet of water.

adipose fin A small fin that occurs between the dorsal fin and caudal fin of some families of fish (salmonids and catfishes).

alevin Yolk sac fish emerged from gravel.

alluvial A deposit of sand, mud, or other material left when flowing water receded.

anadromous Characteristic trait of some fishes (for example, salmonids) whereby they migrate from fresh to salt water, grow for a period of time, and return to fresh water to spawn.

anal fin Fin located behind the anus on the ventral median line.

anterior Preceding or in front of, opposite of posterior.

autochthonous Produced within the system under discussion.

axils The region under or behind the base of pelvic or pectoral fins.

barbels Fleshy, thin projections, usually on the head, on some fishes (for example, catfishes).

basibranchials Three median bones on the floor of the gill chamber in certain fish species.

benthic On or near the bottom, as benthic feeders.

binomial nomenclature Taxonomic names of all species are composed of two names, one for genus and one for species.

bony fishes Species of fishes that have hard, calcified skeletons as opposed to cartilaginous ones.

branchiostegals Bony rays supporting the branchiostegal membrane under the head of fishes. Below the opercular bones, behind the lower jaw, and attached to the hyoid arch.

breast An area of indefinite extent between the pectoral fins and the isthmus, sometimes called chest.

buccal Of the mouth.

caecum (pl. caeca) Blind sac or cavity connected to the alimentary canal.

canine teeth Long, sharp, slender teeth.

cardiform teeth Arranged like a series of combs.

carnivorous Eaters of meat, feeding or preying on live animals.

cartilaginous Noncalcified, referring to skeleton.

caudal fin Tail fin.

caudal peduncle Slender, tapering portion of the body of a fish behind the last ray of the anal fin and forward of the flare of the tail or caudal fin.

charr Old name for fishes belonging to the genus *Salvelinus*.

cheek The area of a fish's face between the eye and the preopercular bone.

chironomid Midge (member of a family [Chironomidae] of true flies [Diptera]).

circumpolar Occurring around one of the earth's poles.

cloaca A chamber in the lower part of the gut into which the ducts from the kidney and reproductive organs empty, with one external opening instead of separate vent and urogenital openings.

compressed Flattened from side to side.

convoluted Coiled or twisted.

copepods Small organisms in the Class Crustacea.

cranium Portion of the skull that encloses the brain.

ctenoid scales Scales possessing comblike margins of tiny prickles or ctenii on posterior surface (for example, in sunfishes).

cycloid scales Scales possessing a smooth, evenly curved posterior margin (for example, in suckers)

decimate Destroy, literally reduce by 10 percent.

decurved Downward curving.

decurved lateral line A lateral line that dips deeply toward the belly, as in the golden shiner.

degree-day Measure of time/temperature with reference to egg incubation. One degree-day is a 24-hour period in which the temperature is 1 degree above freezing (33°F, 0.56°C).

demersal Characteristic of eggs and plankton material that is heavier than water and therefore sinks.

desiccation Drying out, as in large lakes.

detritus Generally plant debris deposited on the bottom of an aquatic habitat or suspended in the water column.

diploid Two similar complements of genetic material.

dorsal Of the back.

dorsal fin Fin or fins attached on the midline of the back (upper) surface of a fish. May consist of soft rays only, or of both soft rays and spiny rays.

effluent Outflow.

elasmobranch Taxonomic group of cartilaginous fishes that includes sharks and rays.

emarginate More weakly forked, crescent-shaped, as in a fin outline.

endemic Occurring only at a given location (for example, Bonneville cisco is a Bear Lake endemic species).

epilimnion Uppermost layer of circulating water in a lake, separated from the hypolimnion by the thermocline.

eutrophic Nutrient rich, polluted, opposite of oligotrophic.

exoskeleton Hard outer shell.

extirpate Destroy completely.

eyed eggs Stage of fish egg development in which eye spots are visible.

faunal Animal.

fecundity Measure of potential reproductive capacity using production of mature eggs.

filamentous Threadlike.

fin ray Flexible and usually branched strut of small rectangular bones supporting the membrane of a fin. The number of rays in a fin is usually counted from the first fully elongated ray to the last one, which is branched to its base and counted as one.

fin spine Unbranched, sharp, bony struts supporting fins; usually sharp and inflexible, except, for example, in sculpins, which have soft, unbranched spines in the dorsal and anal fins.

fish Vertebrate animal adapted for aquatic existence by means of gills that remove oxygen from the water and pass waste materials out of the system. When used in the plural form (fishes) it indicates two or more species.

forage Seek food.

fork length Length of a fish as measured from the anteriormost margin of the head to the tip of the middle ray (or fork) of the caudal fin. Contrasted with total length.

form A division of subspecies with no taxonomic status.

fry Fish that are newly hatched but beyond alevin stage.

ganoid scales Platelike (for example, in gars).

gastropod Taxonomic group of mollusks to which all snails belong.

gill Type of fish tissue that is highly vascular and used in respiration and waste metabolism in an aquatic medium.

gill arch Curved supports for gill filaments and gill rakers, extending from the neurocranium to the throat, behind the eye and jaws.

gill cover Paired plates made up of opercle, preopercle, interopercle, subopercle, and branchiostegal rays, covering the gills.

gill filaments The vascularized, posterior projections from gill arches, for exchange of oxygen, carbon dioxide, and ions.

gill rakers The anterior, fingerlike projections from gill arches, usually toothed, for catching and sorting food items.

gonopodium Literally, sexual foot. An organ adapted for sexual use (for example, in mosquito fish)

gradient Change from one level or type to another over time, space, or other medium.

gravid Female fish swollen with eggs or embryos.

herbivorous Plant eating.

heterocercal Descriptor for tail or caudal fin that has an upper lobe larger than the lower lobe.

Holarctic Palaearctic and Nearctic, two biogeographical regions of the Arctic.

homocercal Descriptor for tail or caudal fin that has more or less equal upper and lower lobes.

hybrid Product of sexual union between two genera or two species.

hypocercal Descriptor for tail or caudal fin that has dissimilar lobes; the lower lobe is longer.

hypolimnion The layer of water below the thermocline in lakes; may stagnate during summer heat.

inferior Refers to the lower jaw of a fish when it is shorter than the snout.

insertion of fin The point of attachment of the trailing edge of a fin to the body.

interspecific Between two species.

landlocked Describes the condition of fish that do not migrate to the ocean in any part of their life cycle because of barriers to migration (for example, kokanee).

lateral On the side, as in lateral line.

lateral line The series of sense organ pores located along each side of a fish.

lateral line scales The row(s) of scales, from the shoulder to the base of the tail, each with a tube housing sensory structures.

lateral series of scales Diagonal rows of scales along the fish's sides, from the gill cover to the caudal base. The number of rows, usually about the same as the number of scales in the lateral line (if present), is counted to help identify many fish.

length Standard length is a measurement of fish length from the tip of the snout to the last vertebra; fork length is a measurement of fish length from the tip of the snout to the fork in the tail; total length is a measurement of fish length from the tip of the snout to the end of the tail.

lentic Water that is standing, as in a lake; opposite of lotic.

live bearer Fishes in which development through the larval stage occurs within the mother, following internal fertilization.

maxillae Paired bones forming the back part of the upper jaw edge. It is usually toothed in soft-rayed fishes, usually not toothed in spiny-rayed fishes.

membranes, fin Skin webbing between fin rays or spines.

mesotrophy A nutrient state of water between eutrophy and oligotrophy.

metalimnion Layer of very steep thermal gradient (high rate of change of temperature) (see Thermocline)

molar teeth Broad, flattened teeth, as on the pharyngeal bones of carp, for example.

nuchal The anteriormost part of the back, just behind the head. Enlarged with massive muscles in some Colorado River *Gila* or a bony keel in *Xyrauchen* of the Colorado River.

oligotrophic Said of waters, generally lakes, that are nutrient poor, contrasted with eutrophic, nutrient rich.

opercle The bone that is the main gill cover. Surrounded by the preopercle (in front) and the interopercle and subopercle (below).

opercular flap Extension of the gill cover, usually bearing a spot used in social displays.

origin of fin The point of attachment of the leading edge of a fin to the fish's body.

palatine Paired bones, often bearing teeth, on the sides of the roof of the mouth internal to (mesial to) the maxillae and lateral to the vomer.

papillae Small, raised clusters of taste buds in fish mouths and on sucker lips.

pectoral fins Paired fins attached to shoulder bones, directly behind the head.

peduncle, caudal Body section between the anal and caudal fins. Unusually slender in some large, Colorado River *Gila* and *Catostomus*.

pelagic Of or relating to deep water, open water away from shore.

pelvic fins Paired ventral fins behind or below the pectoral fins (in spiny-rayed fishes, for example) or below the dorsal fin or midbody (in soft-rayed fishes, for example).

pharyngeal teeth Teeth on the posterior gill arches in the pharynx, below or beside the esophagus and between the shoulder bones. These are readily dissected with a scalpel or dental tool, for examination. Each species has unique pharyngeal teeth.

physoclistic Fish having a swim bladder that is isolated from the esophagus (fish cannot swallow air).

physostomous Fish having a swim bladder connected to the esophagus by a duct (these fish can swallow air).

posterior Toward the tail.

premaxillae Paired bones forming the front of the upper jaw.

preopercle Half-moon–shaped cheekbone below and behind the eye and in front of the opercle; the site of insertion of jaw muscles. The posterior edge may be serrated or spiny in cottids and some percoids.

prickles Small bony spines in the skin of sculpins, especially in Bear Lake and Utah Lake sculpins, for example.

principal rays The fin rays counted from the upper leading edge of the fin to the last, excluding the small rays anterior to the long one reaching the outer edge of the fin.

pseudobranch False gill arch with gill filaments located on the inside surface of the gill cover.

rosette of lower lip papillae Half-moon–shaped pattern of anterior sensory papillae on the lower lip of *Catostomus platyrhynchus*.

sawtooth belly scales Hard, sharp-edged, and pointed scales on the belly of herring and shad.

scales Overlapping bony plates within the skin of fishes. Usually cycloid, without teeth, in soft-rayed fishes, and ctenoid, with an exposed tooth patch, in spiny-rayed fishes.

serrated spine The pectoral spines of catfishes and dorsal and anal spines of carp and goldfish, bearing bony hooks or posterior sawteeth, respectively.

slot limits Definition of fish lengths (for example, 12 to 14 inches) for which all fish in that size range are legally defined as "keep" or "return."

standard length Body length measured from the anterior tip of the head to the base of the caudal fin, excluding tail length.

subterminal mouth Mouth position slightly below the tip of the head, so that the lower jaw is well below the snout and extends slightly less anteriorly than the upper jaw. A close look at the size and position of the mouth is crucial for the identification of fish, especially minnows.

swim-up fry Also referred to as "yolk-sac fry." An indeterminate stage of life for fishes with egg yolk sacs. Fry are "swim-up" when they emerge from the gravel (redds) and enter the water column and begin to feed just prior to complete absorption of the yolk.

terminal mouth Mouth position at the end of the head, so that upper and lower jaws both reach the leading point of the fish.

thermocline Zone of rapidly changing water temperature separating the epilimnion (uppermost) from the hypolimnion (lower) layers of water in a lake water circulation event.

ventral Away from the neurocranium or axial skeleton toward the throat or belly position.

ventral fins Equal to pelvic fins in fish.

ventral mouth Mouth position well below snout, on ventral profile of the head and body, as in some suckers.

vermiculate Marked with irregular lines or blotches.

villiform Having fingerlike projections, said of teeth that are slender and close together.

viviparous Bearing live young.

vomer Anterior bone on the roof of the mouth.

water column A section of water from the surface to the bottom or some other definable depth.

water year The period from 1 October to 30 September during which precipitation is measured and calculated in many western states.

zooplankton Small aquatic invertebrates.

Literature Cited

Abbott, C. C. 1861. Description of Our New Species of North American Cyprinidae. Proceedings of the Academy of Natural Sciences of Philadelphia 12:437–474.

Agassiz, J.L.R. 1850. Lake Superior. Its Physical Character, Vegetation, and Animals, Compared with Those of Other and Similiar Regions. Gould, Kendall, and Lincoln, Boston, Mass.

Allendorf, F. W., and R. F. Leary. 1988. Conservation and Distribution of Genetic Variation in a Polytypic Species, the Cutthroat Trout. Conservation Biology 2:170–184.

Appleget, J., and L. L. Smith. 1951. The Determination and Rate of Growth from Vertebrae of the Channel Catfish, *Ictalurus lacustris punctatus*. Transactions of the American Fisheries Society 80(1950):119–139.

Archer, D. L., L. R. Keating, B. D. Burdick, and C. W. McAda. 1985. A Study of the Endangered Fishes of the Upper Colorado River. U.S. Fish and Wildlife Service, Colorado River Fishery Project 529 25 1/2 Road, Grand Junction, Colorado.

Arnold, B. B. 1960. Life History Notes on the Walleye, *Stizostedion vitreum vitreum* (Mitchill) in a Turbid Water, Utah Lake, Utah. MS Thesis, Utah State University, Logan, Utah.

Arnow, T. 1980. Water Budget and Water Surface Fluctuations of Great Salt Lake. Pages 255–262 *in* J. Wallace Gwynn, ed. Great Salt Lake, a Scientific, Historical and Economic Overview. Utah Geological and Mineralogical Survey Bulletin 116. Salt Lake City, Utah.

Arnow, T., and D. Stephens. 1990. Hydraulic Characteristics of the Great Salt Lake, Utah: 1837–1986. United States Geological Survey Water-Supply Paper 2332.

Austin, L. H. 1980. Lake Level Predictions of the Great Salt Lake. Pages 273–277 *in* J. Wallace Gwynn, ed. Great Salt Lake, a Scientific, Historical and Economic Overview. Utah Geological and Mineralogical Survey Bulletin 116. Salt Lake City, Utah.

Bailey, J. E. 1952. Life History and Ecology of the Sculpin, *Cottus bairdi punctulatus* in Southwestern Montana. Copeia 1952(4):243–255.

Bailey, R. M. 1951. A Check-list of the Fishes of Iowa, with Keys for Identification. Pages 185–237 *in* J. R. Harlan and E. B. Speaker. Iowa Fish and Fishing. Iowa State Conservation Commission, Des Moines, Iowa.

Bailey, R. M., and C. E. Bond. 1963. Four New Species of Freshwater Sculpins, Genus *Cottus*, from Western North America. Occasional Papers, Museum of Zoology, University of Michigan, No. 634:1–27.

Bailey, R. M., and C. R. Robins. 1988. Changes in North America Fish Names,

Especially as Related to the International Code of Zoological Nomenclature, 1988. Bulletin of Zoological Nomenclature 45(2).

Bailey, R. M., E. A. Lachner, C. C. Lindsey, C. R. Robins, R. M. Roedel, W. B. Scott, and L. P. Woods. 1960. A List of Common and Scientific Names of Fishes from the United States and Canada, 2nd ed. American Fisheries Society Special Publication No. 2.

Baird, S. F., and C. Girard. 1853a. Descriptions of New Species of Fishes Collected by Mr. John H. Clark, on the U.S. and Mexican Boundary Survey, Under Lt. Col. Jas. D. Graham. Proceedings of the Academy Natural Science of Philadelphia 6:387–390.

——. 1853b. Descriptions of Some New Fishes from the River Zuni. Proceedings of the Academy of Natural Sciences of Philadelphia 6:369.

——. 1854. Descriptions of New Species of Fishes Collected in Texas, New Mexico, and Sonora, by Mr. John Clark, on the U.S. and Mexican Border Survey and in Texas by Capt. Stevant van Vliet, USA. Proceedings of the Academy of Natural Sciences of Philadelphia, 7:24–29.

——. 1855. Report on the Fishes Observed on the Coasts of New Jersey and Long Island During the Summer of 1854, by Spencer F. Baird, Assistant Secretary of the Smithsonian. Ninth Annual Report, Board of Regents, Smithsonian Institution.

Barlow, G. W. 1961. Causes and Significance of Morphological Variation in Fishes. Systematic Zoology 10:105–117.

Baskin, J. A. 1978. *Bensonomys, Calomys,* and the Origin of the Phyllotine Group of Neotropical Cricetines (Rodentia: Cricetidae). Journal of Mammalogy 59:125–135.

Baugh, T. M. 1980. Spawning of the Least Chub (*Iotichthys phlegethontis*). Great Basin Naturalist 40(2):139–140.

Baxter, G. T., and J. R. Simon. 1970. Wyoming Fishes. Wyoming Game and Fish Department, Bulletin 4, Cheyenne, Wyo.

Becker, G. C. 1983. Fishes of Wisconsin. University of Wisconsin Press, Madison, Wis.

Beckman, W. C. 1949. The Rate of Growth and Sex Ratio for Seven Michigan Fishes. Transactions of the American Fisheries Society 76(1946):63–81.

Behnke, R. J. 1979. Monograph of the Native Trout of the Genus *Salmo* of Western North America. U.S. Forest Service, U.S. Fish and Wildlife Service, U.S. Bureau of Land Management, Washington, D.C.

——. 1981. Systematic and Zoogeographical Interpretation of Great Basin Trouts. Pages 95–124 *in* R. J. Naiman and D. L. Soltz, eds. Fishes in North American Deserts. John Wiley and Sons, New York, N.Y.

——. 1992. Native Trout of Western North America. American Fisheries Society Monograph 6.

Behnke, R. J., and D. E. Benson. 1980. Endangered and Threatened Fishes of the Upper Colorado River Basin. Colorado State Univ., Extension Service Bulletin 503A:1–34.

Behrens, P. 1980. Industrial Processing of Great Salt Lake Brines by Great Salt Lake Minerals & Chemicals Corporation. Pages 223–229 *in* J. Wallace Gwynn, ed. Great Salt Lake, a Scientific, Historical and Economic Overview. Utah Geological and Mineralogical Survey Bulletin 116. Salt Lake City, Utah.

Bendire, C. E. 1882. Notes of Salmonidae of the Upper Columbia. Proceedings of the U.S. National Museum 4:81–87.

Bennett, D. H., P. M. Bratovich, W. Knox, D. Palmer, and H. Hansel. 1983. Status of the Warmwater Fishery and the Potential of Improving Warmwater Fish Habitat in Lower Snake Reservoirs. Completion Report, U.S. Army Corps of Engineers, Contract No. DACW68–79–0057, Walla Walla, Wash.

Bennett, G. W. 1954. Largemouth Bass in Ridge Lake, Coles County, Illinois. Illinois Natural History Survey Bulletin 26(2):217–275.

Benson, L. V., D. R. Currey, R. I. Dorn, K. R. Lajoie, C. G. Oviatt, S. W. Robinson, G. I. Smith, and S. Stine. 1990. Chronology of Expansion and Contraction of Four Great Lake Systems During the Past 35,000 Years. Palaeogeography, Palaeoclimatology, Palaeoecology 78:241–286.

Berry, C. R. 1986. Effects of Cold Shock on Colorado Squawfish Larvae. Final Report. Contract 14-16-009-1501-WOS. Utah Cooperative Fish and Wildlife Research Unit, Utah State University, Logan, Utah.

Berry, F. H., M. T. Huishy, and H. Moody. 1956. Spawning Mortality of the Threadfin Shad, *Dorosoma petenense* (Günther), in Florida. Copeia 1956(3):192.

Black, E. C. 1953. Upper Lethal Temperatures of Some British Columbia Freshwater Fishes. Journal of Fisheries Research Board of Canada 10(4):196–210.

Bond, C. E. 1979. Biology of Fishes. Holt, Rinehart and Winston, CBS College Publishing, New York.

Booke, H. E. 1974. A Cytotaxonomic Study of the Round Whitefishes, Genus *Prosopium*. Copeia 1974 (1):115–119.

Bradford, G. P., and W. A. Hubert. 1988. Reproductive Characteristics of Two Kokanee Stocks in Tributaries to Flaming Gorge Reservoir, Utah and Wyoming. Great Basin Naturalist 4(1):46–50.

Bradley, C., S. de la Plain, S. Garrett, S. L. Mayer, J. MacLennan, T. A. Siefring, and R. Swink. 1980. Rand McNally Encyclopedia of World Rivers. Bison Books, Chicago, Ill.

Breder, C. M., and D. E. Rosen. 1966. Modes of Reproduction in Fishes. Natural History Press, New York.

Bright, R. C. 1963. Pleistocene Lakes Thatcher and Bonneville, Southeastern Idaho. PhD Diss., University of Minnesota, Minneapolis, Minn.

——— . 1967. Late-Pleistocene Stratigraphy in Thatcher Basin, Southeastern Idaho. Teviwa, Journal of the Idaho State University Museum 10:1–7.

Broecker, W. S., and A. Kaufman. 1965. Radiocarbon Chronology of Lake Lahontan and Lake Bonneville II, Great Basin. Geological Society of America Bulletin 76:537–566.

Brousseau, C. S., and E. R. Armstrong. 1987. The Role of Size Limits in Walleye Management. Fisheries 12(1):2–5.

Brown, C.J.D. 1971. Fishes of Montana. Agricultural Experiment Station, Montana State University, Bozeman, Mont.

Brown, L. G. 1972. Early Life History of the Mountain Whitefish *Prosopium williamsoni* (Girard) in the Logan River, Utah. MS Thesis, Wildlife Resource Department, Utah State University, Logan, Utah.

Brynildson, O. N., V. A. Hacker, and T. A. Klick. 1963. Brown Trout: Its Life History, Ecology and Management. Wisconsin Conservation Department Publication 234, Madison, Wis.

Bulkley, R. V. 1960. Use of Branchiostegal Rays to Determine the Age of Lake Trout, *Salvelinus namaycush* (Walbaum). Transactions of the American Fisheries Society 89(4):344–350.

Burdick, B. D. 1979. Biology, Reproductive Potential and the Impact of Fishing Pressure on the Bluegill Fishery of Pelican Lake, Uintah County, Utah. MS Thesis, Utah State University, Logan, Utah.

Busack, C. A., and G. A. E. Gall. 1981. Introgressive Hybridization in Populations of Paiute Cutthroat Trout (*Salmo clarki seleniris*). Canadian Journal of Fisheries and Aquatic Science 38:939–951.

Busack, C. A., G. H. Thorgaard, M. P. Bannon, and G.A.E. Gall. 1980. An Electrophoretic, Karyotypic and Meristic Characterization of the Eagle Lake Trout, *Salmo gairdneri aquilarum*. Copeia (3):418–424.

Bush, G. L. 1975. Modes of Animal Speciation. Annual Review of Ecology and Systematics 6:339–364.

Butts, D. S. 1980. Factors Affecting the Concentration of Great Salt Lake Brines. Pages 163–168 *in* J. Wallace Gwynn, ed. Great Salt Lake, a Scientific, Historical and Economic Overview. Utah Geological and Mineral Survey Bulletin 116. Salt Lake City, Utah.

Cannamela, D. A., J. D. Brader, and D. W. Johnson. 1979. Feeding Habits of Catfish in Barkley and Kentucky Lakes. Proceedings of the Annual Conference of the Southeastern Association of Fish and Wildlife Resource Agencies 32:686–691.

Carbine, W. 1936. The Life History of the Chub *Tigoma atraria* Girard, of the Great Basin Area of Utah. MS Thesis, University of Utah, Salt Lake City, Utah.

Carlander, K. D. 1953. First Supplement to Handbook of Freshwater Fishery Biology. William C. Brown Company, Dubuque, Iowa.

——— . 1969. Handbook of Freshwater Fishery Biology, Vol. 1. Iowa State University Press, Ames, Iowa.

——— . 1977. Handbook of Freshwater Fishery Biology, Vol. 2. Iowa State University Press, Ames, Iowa.

Carlson, C. A., and E. M. Carlson. 1982. Review of Selected Literature on the Upper Colorado River System. Pages 1–8 in W. H. Miller, H. M. Tyus, and C. A. Carlson, eds. Fishes of the Upper Colorado River System, Present and Future. Proceedings of a Symposium, Annual Meeting of the American Fisheries Society, Albuquerque, New Mexico, September 18, 1981. American Fisheries Society, Bethesda, Md.

Carney, D. A., and L. M. Page. 1990. Meristic Characteristics and Zoogeography of the Genus *Ptychocheilus* (Teleostei: Cyprinidae). Copeia 1990:171–181.

Carter, D. R. 1969. A History of Commercial Fishing on Utah Lake. MS Thesis, Brigham Young University, Provo, Utah.

Chronic, H. 1990. Roadside Geology of Utah. Mountain Press Publishing Co., Missoula, Mont.

Clady, M. D. 1981. Cool-Weather Growth of Channel Catfish Held in Pens Alone and with Other Species. Progressive Fish Culturist 43(2):92–95.

Clinton, D. 1824. Description of a New Species of Fish from the Hudson River (*Clupea hudsonia*). Annals of the Lyceum of Natural History of New York 1:49–50.

Constantz, G. D. 1981. Life History Patterns of Desert Fishes. Pages 237–290 in

R J. Naiman and D. L. Soltz, eds. Fishes of the North American Deserts. John Wiley and Sons, New York.

Cooper, E. L., ed. 1987. Carp in North America. American Fisheries Society, Bethesda, Md.

Cooper, S. D., and C. R. Goldman. 1980. Opossum Shrimp (*Mysis relicta*) Predation on Zooplankton. Canadian Journal of Fisheries and Aquatic Sciences 37(6):909–919.

Coots, M. 1956. The Yellow Perch, *Perca flavescens* (Mitchill), in the Klamath River. California Fish and Game 42(7):219–228.

Cope, E. D. 1865. Partial Catalogue of the Cold-blooded Vertebrata of Michigan, Pt. 1. Proceedings of the Academy of Natural Sciences of Philadelphia 16:276–285.

——. 1871a. Report on the Recent Reptiles and Fishes Obtained by the Naturalists on the Expedition. Preliminary Report of the U.S. Geological Survey of Wyoming and Portions of Contiguous Territories. Pages 432–442 *in* F. V. Hayden, Part 4, Chapter 8, Special Reports. U.S. Govt. Printing Office, Washington, D. C.

——. 1871b. Report on the Recent Reptiles and Fishes of the Survey, Collected by Campbell Carrington and C. M. Dawes. Part 4, Chapter 6, pages 467–476 *in* F. V. Hayden, ed. Fifth Annual Report, United States Geological Survey of Montana and Portions of Adjacent Territories. U.S. Govt. Printing Office, Washington, D. C.

——. 1872a. Report on the Recent Reptiles and Fishes of the Survey, Collected by Campbell Carrington and C. M. Dawes. Pages 467–476 *in* F. V. Hayden, ed. Fifth Annual Report, United States Geological Survey of Montana and Portions of Adjacent Territories. U.S. Govt. Printing Office, Washington, D.C.

——. 1872b. Recent Reptiles and Fishes, Report on the Reptiles and Fishes Obtained by the Naturalists of the Expedition. Part 4, Chapter 6, *in* F. V. Hayden, ed. Special Reports of Preliminary Report of the U.S. Geological Survey of Wyoming and Portions of Contiguous Territories. U.S. Govt. Printing Office, Washington, D.C.

——. 1874. On the Plagopterinnae and the Ichthyology of Utah. Proceedings of the American Philosophical Society 14:122–139.

Cope, E. D., and H. C. Yarrow. 1874. On the Plagopterinae and the Ichthyology of Utah. Read Before the American Philosophical Society, March 20, 1874, by Edward D. Cope, A. M. Proceedings of the American Philosophical Society 14:129–139.

——. 1875. Reports Upon the Collections of Fishes Made in Portions of Nevada, Utah, California, Colorado, New Mexico, and Arizona, During 1871, 1872, 1873, and 1874. Volume 5, Chapter 6, pages 635–703 *in* United States Army Engineer Department Report on the Geography and Geology of the Explorations and Surveys West of the 100th Meridian, in Charge of George M. Wheeler.

Copes, F. 1975. Ecology of the Brassy Minnow, *Hybognathus hankonsoni* Hubbs. Report No. 10, Part 3, pages 46–72, *in* G. C. Becker, H. E. Booke, and C. A. Long, eds. Fauna and Flora of Wisconsin. University of Wisconsin, Museum of Natural History, Stevens Point, Wis.

——. 1978. Ecology of the Creek Chub, *Semotilus atromaculatus* (Mitchill), in Northern Waters. Report No. 12, pages 1–21, *in* G. C. Becker, H. E. Booke, and

C. A. Long, eds. Fauna and Flora of Wisconsin. University of Wisconsin, Museum of Natural History, Stevens Point, Wis.

Cordone, A., S. Nicola, P. Baker, and T. Frantz. 1971. The Kokanee Salmon in Lake Tahoe. California Fish and Game 57(1):28–43.

Courtenay, W. R., Jr., and J. R. Stauffer, Jr., eds. 1984. Distribution, Biology, and Management of Exotic Fishes. Johns Hopkins University Press, Baltimore, Md.

Coutant, C. C. 1975. Responses of Bass to Natural and Artificial Temperature Regimes. Pages 272–285 *in* R. H. Stroud and H. Clepper, eds. Black Bass Biology and Management. Sport Fishing Institute, Washington, D.C.

Crawford, M. 1979. Reproductive Modes of the Least Chub (*Iotichthys phlegethontis* Cope). MS Thesis, Utah State University, Logan, Utah.

Crist, L. 1990. A Study/Monitoring Plan for Least Chub (*Iotichthys phlegethontis*) in Snake Valley, Utah. BIO/WEST, Inc. Report Prepared for Utah Division of Wildlife Resources, Salt Lake City, Utah.

Cross, J. N. 1975. Ecological Distribution of the Fishes of the Virgin River (Utah, Arizona, Nevada). MS Thesis, University of Nevada, Las Vegas, Nev.

——. 1978. Status and Ecology of the Virgin River Roundtail Chub, *Gila robusta seminuda* (Osteichthyes: Cyprinidae). Southwestern Naturalist 23:519–528.

Currey, D. R. 1980. Coastal Geomorphology of Great Salt Lake and Vicinity. Pages 69–82 *in* J. Wallace Gwynn, ed. Great Salt Lake, a Scientific, Historical and Economic Overview. Utah Geological and Mineralogical Survey Bulletin 116. Salt Lake City, Utah.

——. 1990. Quarternary Paleolakes in the Evolution of Semidesert Basins, with Special Emphasis on Lake Bonneville and the Great Basin, U.S.A. Palaeogeography, Palaeoclimatology, and Palaeoecology 76:241–286.

Currey, D. R., G. Atwood, and D. R. Mabey. 1984. Major Levels of Great Salt Lake and Lake Bonneville. Utah Geological and Mineralogical Survey. Map 73. Salt Lake City, Utah.

Currey, D. R., C. G. Oviatt, and G. B. Plyler. 1983. Lake Bonneville Stratigraphy, Geomorphology, and Isostatic Deformation in West-Central Utah. Utah Geological and Mineralogical Survey Special Studies 62:63–82.

Cuvier, G. A., and M. A. Valenciennes. 1828–1849. Histoire naturalle des poissons. Levrault, Strasbourg. 22 volumes. Paris.

Dall, W. H. 1870. Alaska and Its Resources. Boston, Lee, and Sheperd, Boston, Mass.

Dalton, R. A., T. H. Lee, J. L. Hesse, and W. T. Helm. 1965. Distribution of Sculpin, *Cottus extensus*, in Bear Lake, Utah-Idaho. Proceedings of the Utah Academy of Arts and Sciences 42(1):70–73.

Deacon, J. E. 1977. Habitat Requirements of the Woundfin in the Virgin River in Relation to the Proposed Warner Valley Project. *In* Vaughn Hansen Associates, eds. Impact of Warner Valley Project on Endangered Fish of the Virgin River. Prepared for the City of St. George, Utah.

DeKay, J. E. 1842. Natural History of New York. Part 1. Zoology. Reptiles and Fishes. Part 4. Fishes. Appleton and Co., and Wilby and Putman, Albany, N.Y.

Devries, D. R., and R. A. Stein. 1990. Manipulating Shad to Enhance Sport Fisheries in North America: An Assessment. North American Journal of Fisheries Management 10:209–223.

Duff, D. A. 1988. Bonneville Cutthroat Trout: Current Status and Management.

Pages 121–127 *in* R. E. Gresswell, ed. Status and Management of Interior Stocks of Cutthroat Trout. American Fisheries Society Symposium 4, Bethesda, Md.

Dymond, J. R. 1943. The Coregonine Fishes of Northwestern Canada. Transactions of the Royal Canadian Institute 24(2):171–231.

——. 1947. A List of the Freshwater Fishes of Canada East of the Rocky Mountains, with Keys. Royal Ontario Museum. Zoological Miscellaneous Publication 1.

Ebert, V. W., and R. C. Summerfelt. 1969. Contributions to the Life History of the Paiute Sculpin, *Cottus beldingii* Eigenmann and Eigenmann, in Lake Tahoe. California Fish and Game 55(2):100–120.

Edwards, E. A., G. Gebhart, and O. E. Maughan. 1983. Habitat Suitability Information: Smallmouth Bass. U.S. Department of the Interior, Fish and Wildlife Service. FWS/OBS–82/10.36.

Eigenmann, C. H. 1895. Results of Explorations in Western Canada and the Northwestern United States. U.S. Fish Commission Bull. (1894)14:101–132.

Eigenmann, C. H., and R. S. Eigenmann. 1891. *Cottus beldingi* Species. Nov. American Naturalist 25:1132.

Eschmeyer, P. H., and T. G. Scott. eds. 1983. Fisheries and Wildlife Research 1982. U.S. Fish and Wildlife Service. U.S. Govt. Printing Office, Washington, D.C.

Felsenstein, J. 1988. Phylogenies from Molecular Sequences. Inference and Reliability. Annual Review of Genetics 22:321–365.

Fishing Hall of Fame. 1993. Official World and USA State Fresh Water Angling Records. National Fresh Water Fishing Hall of Fame, Hayard, Wis.

Fleming, I. A., and M. R. Gross. 1990. Latitudinal Clines: A Trade-off Between Egg Number and Size in Pacific Salmon. Ecology 7(1):1–11.

Flittner, G. A. 1964. Morphology and Life History of the Emerald Shiner, *N. atherinoides*. PhD Diss., University of Michigan, Ann Arbor, Mich.

Foerster, R. E. 1968. The Sockeye Salmon *Oncorhynchus nerka*. Fisheries Research Board of Canada Bulletin 162.

Forbes, S. A. 1884. A Catalogue of the Native Fishes of Illinois. Report of the Illinois State Fish Commissioner for 1884:60–89.

Forbes, S. A., and R. E. Richardson. 1920. The Fishes of Illinois, 2nd ed. Illinois Department of Registration and Education, Division of the Natural History Survey.

Foster, N. R. 1967. Comparative Studies on the Biology of Killifishes (Pisces: Cyprinodontidae). PhD Diss., Cornell University, Ithaca, N.Y.

Gerald, J. W. 1971. Sound Production During Courtship in Six Species of Sunfishes (Centrarchidae). Evolution 25(1):75–87.

Gerdes, J. H., and W. J. McConnell. 1963. Food Habits and Spawning of the Threadfin Shad in a Small, Desert Impoundment. Journal of the Arizona Academy of Sciences 2(3):113–116.

Gibbons, W. P. 1855. Description of a New Trout. Proceedings of the California Academy of Natural Sciences 1 (1854).

Gilbert, G. K. 1890. Lake Bonneville. U.S. Geological Survey, Monograph 1. U.S. Govt. Printing Office, Washington, D.C.

Girard, C. F. 1850. A Monograph of the Freshwater *Cottus* of North America. American Association for the Advancement of Science (1849) 2:409–411.

——. 1854. Descriptions of New Fishes Collected by A. L. Hermann, Naturalist Attached to the Survey of the Pacific Railroad, and Lt. R. S. Williamson, U.S.A.

Proceedings of the Academy of Natural Sciences of Philadelphia (1856)8:136.
——. 1856a. Contributions to the Ichthyology of the Western Coast of the United States, Museum of the Smithsonian Institution. Proceedings of the Academy of Natural Sciences of Philadelphia 8:131–137.
——. 1856b. Researches Upon the Cyprinoid Fishes Inhabiting the Fresh Waters of the United States of America, West of the Mississippi Valley, from Specimens in the Museum of the Smithsonian Institution. Proceedings of the Academy Natural Science of Philadelphia 8:165–213.
——. 1857. Notice Upon the Species of the Genus *Salmo* of Authors, Observed Chiefly in Oregon and California. Proceedings of the Academy of Natural Sciences of Philadelphia (1856) 8:217–220.
Graham, R. J. 1961. Biology of the Utah Chub in Hebgen Lake, Montana. Transactions of the American Fisheries Society 90(3):269–276.
Grant, J.W.A., and D.L.G. Noakes. 1988. Aggressiveness and Foraging Mode of Young-of-the-year Brook Charr, *Salvelinus fontinalis* (Pisces, Salmonidae). Behavioral Ecology and Sociobiology 22:435–445.
Greeley, J. R. 1939. The Fresh-water Fishes of Long Island and Staten Island with Annotated List. Pages 29–44 *in* A Biological Survey of the Freshwaters of Long Island. Supplement. Twenty-eighth Annual Report, New York State Conservation Dept. (12938).
Greer, D. C., K. D. Gurgel, W. L. Wahlquist, H. A. Christy, and G. B. Peterson, eds. 1981. Atlas of Utah. Weber State College, Brigham Young University Press, Provo, Utah.
Greger, P. D., and J. E. Deacon. 1988. Food Partitioning Among Fishes of the Virgin River. Copeia 1988(2):314–323.
Grove, J. M. 1988. The Little Ice Age. Methuen, New York, N.Y.
Günther, A. 1864. Catalogue of Fishes of the British Museum. Vol. 5.
——. 1866. Catalogue of Fishes in the British Museum. Volume 6:368 pp.
——. 1868. Catalogue of the Fishes in the British Museum. Volume 7:512 pp.
Gustaveson, W. A., T. D. Pettengill, J. E. Johnson, and J. R. Wahl. 1984. Evidence of In-Reservoir Spawning of Striped Bass in Lake Powell, Utah-Arizona. North American Journal of Fish Management 4:540–546.
Hamill, J. F. 1993. Endangered Colorado River Fishes (Upper Basin). Chapter 5 *in* D. A. Henderickson, ed. Proceedings of the Desert Fishes Council 24.
Hamman, R. L. 1981. Spawning and Culture of Colorado Squawfish in Raceways. Progressive Fish Culturist 43(4):173–177.
——. 1982a. Induced Spawning and Culture of Bonytail Chub. Progressive Fish Culturist 44(4):201–203.
——. 1982b. Spawning and Culture of Humpback Chub. Progressive Fish Culturist 44(4):213–216.
——. 1985. Induced Spawning and Culture of Hatchery-reared Bonytail. Progressive Fish Culturist 47(3):239–241.
Hansen, D. F. 1951. Biology of the White Crappie in Illinois. Illinois State Natural History Survey Bulletin 25(4):211–265.
Harlan, J. R., and E. B. Speaker. 1956. Iowa's Fish and Fishing. Iowa State Conservation Commission, Des Moines, Iowa.
Harlan, J. R., and E. B. Speaker, with J. Mayhew. 1987. Iowa Fish and Fishing. Iowa Department of Natural Resources, Des Moines, Iowa. 115 pp.
Harrington, C. D. 1985. A Revision in the Glacial History of Jackson Hole,

Wyoming. Mountain Geologist 22:28–32.
Harrington, R. W., and E. S. Harrington. 1961. Food Selection Among Fishes Invading a High Subtropical Salt Marsh from Onset of Flooding through the Progress of a Mosquito Brood. Ecology 42(4):646–656.
Hauptman, C. 1988. Basic Freshwater Fishing. Stackpole Books, Harrisburg, Pa. 223 pp.
Hauser, W. J. 1969. Life History of the Mountain Sucker, *Catostomus platyrhynchus* in Montana. Transactions of the American Fisheries Society 98(2):209–224.
Hawkins, J. A. 1992. Age and Growth of Colorado Squawfish from the Upper Colorado River Basin, 1978–1990. Prepared for Colorado Division of Wildlife, Fort Collins, Colo. MS thesis, Colorado State University, Fort Collins. 75 pp.
Hayes, S. P. 1935. A Taxonomical, Morphological, and Distributional Study of the Utah Cyprinidae. MS Thesis, Brigham Young University, Provo, Utah.
Heckmann, R. A., Study of the Utah Cyprinidae. MS Thesis, Brigham Young University, Provo, Utah.
Heckmann, R. A., A. K. Kimball, and J. A. Short. 1987. Parasites of the Mottled Sculpin *Cottus bairdi* Girard, from Five Locations in Utah and Wasatch Counties, Utah. Great Basin Naturalist 47(1):13–21.
Heckmann, R. A., C. W. Thompson, and D. A. White. 1981a. Fishes of Utah Lake. Pages 107–127 *in* S.L. Wood, ed. Great Basin Naturalist Memoirs. Utah Lake Monograph, Brigham Young University, Provo, Utah.
——. 1981b. Fishes of Jackson Hole, Wyoming. Mountain Geologist 22:28–32.
Herman, E. W. Wisby, L. Wiegert, and M. Burdick. 1959. The Yellow Perch, Its Life History, Ecology and Management. Wisconsin Conservation Department Publication 228.
Hessel, R. 1878. Carp and Its Culture in Rivers and Lakes: and Its Introduction in America. United States Commission of Fish and Fisheries, Report for 1875–1876, Part 7:865–900. U.S. Govt. Printing Office, Washington, D.C.
Hickman, T. J. 1984. Establishing Low Flow Requirement for the Fishes of the Virgin River. Abstract. Page 38 *in* E. P. Pister, ed. 1987 Proceedings of the Desert Fishes Council, Bishop, Calif.
Hickman, T. J., and D. A. Duff. 1978. Current Status of the Cutthroat Trout Subspecies in the Western Bonneville Basin. Great Basin Naturalist 38:193–202.
Hickman, T. J., and R. F. Raleigh. 1982. Habitat Suitability Index, Provo, Utah. Models: Cutthroat Trout. U.S. Department of the Interior, Fish and Wildlife Service, FWS/OBS–82/10.5.
Holden, P. B. 1978. A Study of Habitat Use and Movement of the Rare Fishes in the Green River, Utah. Transactions of the Bonneville Chapter of the American Fisheries Society 1978:64–69.
——. 1980. *Ptychocheilus lucius* Girard, Colorado Squawfish. Page 348 *in* D. S. Lee, C. R. Gilbert, C. H. Hocutt, R. E. Jenkins, D. E. McAllister, and J. R. Stauffer, Jr., eds. Atlas of North American Freshwater Fishes. North Carolina State Museum of Natural History, Raleigh, N.C.
Holden, P. B., and C. B. Stalnaker. 1970. Systematic Studies of the Cyprinid Genus *Gila* in the Upper Colorado River Basin. Copeia 1970:409–420.
Holden, P. B., and E. J. Wick. 1982. Life History and Prospects for Recovery of Colorado Squawfish. Pages 98–108 in W. H. Miller, H. M. Tyus, and C. A. Carlson, eds. Fishes of the Upper Colorado River System: Present and Future. Western Division, American Fisheries Society, Washington, D.C.

Holt, G. D. 1955. Comparative Morphometry of the Rocky Mountain Whitefish (*Prosopium williamsoni*). MS Thesis, Montana State College, Bozeman, Mont.

Houghton, S. G. 1976. A Trace of Desert Waters: The Great Basin History. Arthur H. Clark Co., Glendale, Calif.

Hubbs, C. L. 1926. A Checklist of the Fishes of the Great Lakes and Tributary Waters, with Nomenclatural Notes and Analytical Keys. University of Michigan, Museum of Zoology Miscellaneous Publication 15.

Hubbs, C. L., and G. P. Cooper. 1935. Age and Growth of the Long-eared and Green Sunfishes in Michigan. Papers of the Michigan Academy of Science, Arts, and Letters 20:669–696.

Hubbs, C. L., and G. W. Greene. 1928. Further Notes on the Fishes of the Great Lakes and Tributary Waters. Papers of the Michigan Academy of Science, Arts, and Letters (1927) 8:371–392.

Hubbs, C. L., and K. F. Lagler. 1941. Guide to the Fishes of the Great Lakes and Tributary Waters. Cranbook Institute of Science. Bulletin 18.

Hubbs, C. L., and R. R. Miller. 1948. Correlation Between Fish Distribution and Hydrographic History in Desert Basins of the Western United States. Pages 17–144 *in* The Great Basin, with Emphasis on Glacial and Postglacial Times. University of Utah 38, Biol. Ser. Bull. 10(7).

——. 1965. Studies of Cyprinodont Fishes. XXII. Variation in *Lucania parva:* Its Establishment in Western United States and Description of a New Species from an Interior Basin in Coahuila, Mexico. University of Michigan, Museum of Zoology, Miscellaneous Publication 127.

Hubbs, C. L., R. R. Miller, and L. C. Hubbs. 1974. Hydrographic History and Relict Fishes of the North-Central Great Basin. California Academy of Sciences Memoir 7:1–259.

IGFA (International Game and Fish Association). 1993. World Record Game Fishes: Freshwater, Saltwater, and Fly Fishing. Pompano Beach, Fla.

Inhat, J. M. 1981. Seasonal Temperature Preference of Adult Mountain Whitefish, *Prosopium williamsoni*. MS Thesis, Utah State University, Logan, Utah.

Inskip, P. D. 1982. Habitat Suitability Index Models: Northern Pike. U.S. Dept. of the Interior, Fish and Wildlife Service, FWS/OBS–82/10.17.

Itzkowitz, M. 1971. Preliminary Study of the Social Behavior of Male *Gambusia affinis* (Baird and Girard) (Pisces: Poeciliidae) in Aquaria. Chesapeake Science 12(4):219–224.

Jacobson, L., and W. Wurtsbaugh. 1989. Seasonal and Size-related Shifts in the Diet of Bear Lake Cutthroat Trout (*Oncorhynchus clarki*). Transactions of the Bonneville Chapter, American Fisheries Society, Utah.

Janssen, P. J. 1983. Investigation of Selected Aspects of Kokanee (*Oncorhynchus nerka*) Ecology in Porcupine Reservoir, Utah, with Management Implications. MS Thesis, Utah State University, Logan, Utah.

Jensen, B. L. 1983. Culture Techniques for Selected Colorado River Imperiled Fishes. Thirty-Fourth Annual Northwest Fish Culture Workshop, Moscow, Ida.

Johnson, J. E. 1970. Age, Growth and Population Dynamics of the Threadfin Shad, *Dorosoma petenense* (Günther), in Central Arizona Reservoirs. Transactions of the American Fisheries Society 99(4):739–753.

——. 1971. Maturity and Fecundity of Threadfin Shad, *Dorosoma petenense* (Günther) in Central Arizona Reservoirs. Transactions of the American Fisheries Society 100(1):74–85.

Johnson, J. E., and B. L. Jensen. 1991. Hatcheries for Endangered Freshwater Fishes. Pages 199–217 in W. L. Minckley and James E. Deacon, eds. Battle Against Extinction: Native Fish Management in the American West. University of Arizona Press, Tucson, Ariz.

Jones, W. R., and J. Janssen. 1992. Lateral line development and feeding behavior in the mottled sculpin, *Cottus bairdi* (Scorpaeniformes: Cottidae). Copeia 2:485–492.

Jordan, D. S. 1878a. A Catalogue of the Fishes of Illinois. Illinois State Laboratory of Natural History Bulletin 1(2):37–70.

———. 1878b. A Synopsis of the Family Catostomidae. U.S. National Museum Bulletin 12:97–237.

———. 1878c. Manual of the Vertebrates of the Northern United States, Including the District East of the Mississippi River and North of North Carolina and Tennessee, Exclusive of Marine Species, 2nd ed. Jansen, McClury, and Company, Chicago, Ill.

———. 1893a. Description of the Golden Trout of Kern County, California (*Salmo mykiss aqua-bonita*). Proceedings of the U.S. National Museum 15:481–483.

———. 1893b. Description of a New Species of Salmon. Forest Stream 39:405–406.

———. 1929. A Manual of the Vertebrate Animals of the Northeastern United States, 13th ed. World Book Company, Yonkers-on-Hudson, N. Y.

Jordan, D. S., and H. E. Copeland. 1878. A Catalogue of the Fishes of the Fresh Waters of North America. United States Geological and Geographical Survey of the Territories (Hayden) Bulletin 4:407–442.

Jordan, D. S., and B. M. Evermann. 1891. Pages 1–40 *in* D. S. Jordan. Report of Explorations in Colorado and Utah During the Summer of 1889, with an Account of the Fishes Found in Each of the River Basins Examined. U.S. Fish Commission Bulletin 9 (1889).

———. 1896–1900. The Fishes of North and Middle America. A Descriptive Catalogue of the Species of Fish-like Vertebrates Found in the Waters of North America, North of the Isthmus of Panama. Bulletin of the U.S. National Museum 47 (1–4).

———. 1904. American Food and Game Fishes: A Popular Account of All the Species Found in America North of the Equator, with Keys for Ready Identification, Life Histories and Methods of Capture. Doubleday, Page and Co., New York.

Jordan, D. S., and C. H. Gilbert. 1881. Notes on a Collection of Fishes from Utah Lake. Proceedings of the United States National Museum 3 (175):459–464 (1880).

———. 1883. Synopsis of the Fishes of North America. U.S. National Museum Bulletin 16:1–1018.

Jordan, D. S., B. W. Evermann, and H. W. Clark. 1930. Check List of the Fishes and Fishlike Vertebrates of North and Middle America North of the Northern Boundary of Venezuela and Colombia. A reprint of Appendix X to the Report of the United States Commissioner of Fisheries for the Fiscal Year 1928. U.S. Government Printing Office. Washington, D.C.

Kaeding, L. R., and M. A. Zimmerman. 1983. Life History and Ecology of the Humpback Chub in the Little Colorado Rivers of the Grand Canyon. Transactions of the American Fisheries Society 112:577–594.

Kaeding, L. R., B. D. Burdick, P. A. Schrader, and C. W. McAda. 1990. Temporal and Spatial Relations Between the Spawning of Humpback Chub and Roundtail Chub in the Upper Colorado River. Transactions of the American Fisheries Society 119:135–144.

Karp, C. A., and H. M. Tyus. 1990. Humpback Chub (*Gila cypha*) on the Yampa and Green Rivers, Dinosaur National Monument, with Observations on the Roundtail Chub (*G. robusta*) and Other Sympatric Fishes. Great Basin Naturalist 50(3):257–264.

Keast, A. 1968. Feeding Biology of the Black Crappie, *Pomoxis nigromaculatus*. Journal of the Fisheries Research Board of Canada 24(1):285–297.

Keast, A., and D. Webb. 1966. Mouth and Body Form Relative to Feeding Ecology in the Fish Fauna of a Small Lake, Lake Opinicon, Ontario. Journal of the Fisheries Research Board of Canada 23(12):1845–1867.

Kessler, L. G., and J. C. Avise. 1985. Microgeographic Lineage Analysis by Mitochondrial Genotype. Variation in the Cotton Rat (*Sigmodon hispidus*). Evolution 39:831–837.

Koehn, R. K., and W. F. Eanes. 1978. Molecular Structure and Protein Variation Within and Among Populations. Pages 39–100 *in* M. K. Hecht, W. C. Steere, and B. Wallace, eds. Evolutionary Biology. Vol. 11. Plenum Press, New York.

Krumholtz, L. A. 1948. Reproduction in the Western Mosquitofish *Gambusia affinis affinis* (Baird and Girard) and Its Use in Mosquito Control. Ecological Monographs 18:1–43.

Lacépède, B. G. 1802. Histoire naturelle des poissons. Volume 4. Plassan, Paris.

——. 1803. Histoire naturelle des poissons. Volume 5. Plassan, Paris.

Lamarra, V. A., M. C. Lamarra, and J. G. Carter. 1985. Ecological Investigations of a Suspected Spawning Site of Colorado Squawfish in the Yampa River, Utah. Great Basin Naturalist 45(1):127–140.

Lannigan, S. H., and H. M. Tyus. 1989. Population Size and Status of the Razorback Sucker in the Green River Basin, Utah and Colorado. North American Journal of Fisheries Management 9:68–73.

Large, T. 1903. A List of the Native Fishes of Illinois, with Keys. Appendix to Report of the State Board of Fish Commissioners for September 30, 1900, to October 30, 1902.

La Rivers, I. 1962. Fishes and Fisheries of Nevada. Nevada State Fish and Game Commission, Reno, Nev.

Lawler, R. E. 1960. Observations on the Life History of Channel Catfish *Ictalurus punctatus* (Rafinesque), in Utah Lake. MS Thesis, Utah State University, Logan, Utah.

Leary, R. F., F. W. Allendorf, and K. L. Knudsen. 1983. Consistently High Meristic Counts in Natural Hybrids between Brook Trout and Bull Trout. Systematic Zoology 32:369–376.

Leary, R. F., F. W. Allendorf, S. R. Phelps, and K. L. Knudsen. 1987. Genetic Divergence and Identification of Seven Cutthroat Trout Subspecies and Rainbow Trout. Transactions of the American Fisheries Society 116:580–587.

Lee, D. S., C. R. Gilbert, C. H. Hocutt, R. E. Jenkins, D. E. McCallister, and J. R. Stauffer, Jr. 1980. Atlas of North American Freshwater Fishes. North Carolina State Museum of Natural History, Raleigh, N.C.

Leitritz, E., and R. C. Lewis. 1980. Trout and Salmon Culture. Department of Fish and Game Bulletin 164, Sacramento, Calif.

LeSueur, C. A. 1818. Description of Several New Species of North American Fishes. Academy of Natural Sciences of Philadelphia Journal 1:222–235, 359–368.

——. 1819. Notice sur quelques poissons découverts dans les lacs du haut Canada, durant l'été de 1816. Mémoires du Musée d' Histoire Naturelle de Paris (1819) 5:154–156.

Linnaeus, C. 1758. Systema Naturae per Regna Tria Naturae, Secundum Classes, Ordines, Genera, Species, Cum Characteribus, Differentiis, Synonymis, Locis. Laurentii Salvii, Holmiae. 12th ed. Vol. 1.

Lundberg, J. G. 1989. (Untitled). American Society of Ichthyology and Herpetology. Annual Meeting Abstracts, p. 113.

Lutterbie, G. W. 1976. The Darters (Pisces: Percidae: Ethestominae) of Wisconsin. MS Thesis, University of Wisconsin, Stevens Point, Wis.

MacCrimmon, H. R., and W. H. Robbins. 1975. Distribution of the Black Basses in North America. Pages 56–66 *in* R. H. Stroud and H. Clepper, eds. Black Bass Biology and Management. Sport Fishing Institute, Washington, D.C.

MacCrimmon, H. R., and E. Skobe. 1970. The Fisheries of Lake Simcoe. Ontario Department of Lands and Forests, Toronto.

Maddux, H. R., and W. G. Kepner. 1988. Spawning of Bluehead Sucker in Kanab Creek, Arizona (Pisces: Catastomidae). Southwestern Naturalist 33:364–365.

Madsen, D. B. 1980. The Human Prehistory of the Great Salt Lake Region. Pages 19–31 *in* J. Wallace Gwynn, ed. Great Salt Lake, a Scientific, Historical and Economic Overview. Utah Geological and Mineralogical Survey Bulletin 116. Salt Lake City, Utah.

Madsen, D. B., and D. R. Currey. 1979. Late Quarternary Glacial and Vegetation Changes, Little Cottonwood Canyon Area, Wasatch Mountains, Utah. Quarternary Research 12:254–270.

Malde, H. E. 1965. The Snake River Plain. Pages 255–264 *in* H. E. Wright, Jr. and D. J. Frey, eds. The Quaternary of the United States. Princeton University Press, Princeton, N.J.

——. 1968. The Catastrophic Late Pleistocene Bonneville Flood in the Snake River Plain, Idaho. U.S. Geological Survey Professional Paper, No. 596:1–52.

Marsh, P. C., and D. R. Langhorst. 1988. Feeding and Fate of Wild Larval Razorback Sucker. Environmental Biology of Fishes 21(1):59–67.

Marsh, P. C., and W. L. Minckley. 1989. Observations on Recruitment and Ecology of Razorback Sucker: Lower Colorado River, Arizona-California-Nevada. Great Basin Naturalist 49:171–178.

Martinez, A. M. 1988. Identification and Status of Colorado River Cutthroat Trout in Colorado. Pages 81–89 *in* R. E. Gresswell, ed. Status and Management of Interior Stocks of Cutthroat Trout. American Fisheries Society Symposium, Bethesda, Md.

Mayden, R. L. 1988. Vicariance Biogeography, Parsimony, and Evolution in North American Freshwater Fishes. Systematic Zoology 37:329–355.

——. 1989. Phylogenetic Studies of North American Minnows, with Emphasis on the Genus *Cyprinella* (Eleostei: Cypriniformes). University of Kansas, Museum of Natural History, Miscellaneous Publication No. 80.

Mayden, R. L., W. J. Rainboth, and D. G. Buth. 1991. Phylogenetic Systematics of the Cyprinid Genera *Mylopharodon* and *Ptychocheilus*: Comparative Morphometry. Copeia 1991:819–834.

McAda, C. W. 1977. Aspects of the Life History of Three Catostomids Native to the Upper Colorado River Basin. MS Thesis, Utah State University, Logan, Utah.

McAda, C. W., and R. S. Wydoski. 1980. The Razorback Sucker *Xyrauchen texanus,* in the Upper Colorado River Basin, 1974–76. U.S. Fish and Wildlife Service, Technical Paper 99. Washington, D.C.

McAllister, D. E., S. P. Plantania, F. W. Schueler, M. E. Baldwin, and D. S. Lee. 1986. Ichthyological Patterns on a Geographic Grid. Pages 17–52 *in* C. H. Hocutt and E. O. Wiley, eds. The Zoogeography of North American Freshwater Fishes. John Wiley & Sons, New York, N.Y.

McConnell, W. J., W. J. Clark, and W. F. Sigler. 1957. Bear Lake, Its Fish and Fishing. Utah State Department of Fish and Game, Idaho Department of Fish and Game, Wildlife Management Department of Utah State Agricultural College, Logan, Utah.

McCoy, W. D. 1987. Quaternary Aminostratigraphy of the Bonneville Basin, Western United States. Bulletin of the Geological Society of America 98:99–112.

McHugh, J. L. 1940. Food of the Rocky Mountain Whitefish *Prosopium williamsoni* (Girard). Journal of the Fisheries Research Board of Canada 5(2):131–137.

———. 1941. Growth of the Rocky Mountain Whitefish. Journal of the Fisheries Research Board of Canada 5(4):337–343.

McPhail, J. D., and C. C. Lindsey. 1986. Zoogeography of the Freshwater Fishes of Cascadia (the Columbia System and Rivers North to the Stikine). Pages 615–638 *in* C. H. Hocutt and E. O. Wiley, eds. The Zoogeography of North American Freshwater Fishes. John Wiley & Sons, New York, N.Y.

Meffe, Gary K. 1992. Plasticity of Life-History Characters of Eastern Mosquitofish (*Gambusia holbrooki*: Poecillidae) in response to thermal stress. Copeia 1:94–102.

Miller, D. E. 1980. Great Salt Lake: A Historical Sketch. Pages 1–14 *in* J. Wallace Gwynn, ed. Great Salt Lake, a Scientific, Historical and Economic Overview. Utah Geological and Mineralogical Survey Bulletin 116. Salt Lake City, Utah.

Miller, K. D., and R. H. Kramer. 1971. Spawning and Early Life History of Largemouth Bass (*Micropterus salmoides*) in Lake Powell. Pages 73–83 *in* Reservoir Fisheries and Limnology. American Fisheries Society Special Publication No. 8.

Miller, R. B., and W. A. Kennedy. 1948. Pike (*Esox lucius*) from Four Northern Canadian Lakes. Journal of the Fishery Research Board of Canada 7(4):190–199.

Miller, R. G. 1951. The Natural History of Lake Tahoe Fishes. PhD Diss., Stanford University, Stanford, Calif.

Miller, R. R. 1945a. *Gila cypha,* a Remarkable New Species of Cyprinid Fish from the Colorado River in Grand Canyon, Arizona. Journal of the Washington Academy of Sciences 36(12):409–415.

———. 1945b. *Snyderichthys*, a New Generic Name for the Leatherside Chub of the Bonneville and Upper Snake Drainages in Western United States. Washington Academy of Science Journal 35:28.

———. 1945c. A New Cyprinid Fish from Southern Arizona and Sonora, Mexico, with the Description of a New Subgenus of *Gila* and a Review of Related Species. Copeia 1945:104–110.

——. 1958. Origin and Affinities of the Freshwater Fish Fauna of Western North America. Pages 187–222 *in* C. L. Hubbs, ed. Zoogeography, a Symposium of the American Association for the Advancement of Science, Publication 51, Washington, D.C.

——. 1963. Genus *Dorosoma* Rafinesque 1820, Gizzard Shad, Threadfin Shad. Memoir Sears Foundation for Marine Research, 1(3):443–451.

——. 1965. Quaternary Freshwater Fishes of North America. Pages 569–81 *in* H. E. Wright, Jr. and D. G. Frye, eds. The *Quaternary of the United States.* Princeton University Press, Princeton, N.J.

——. 1984. *Rhinichthys deaconi*, a New Species of Dace (Pisces: Cyprinidae) from Southern Nevada. Occasional Papers of the Museum of Zoology, University of Michigan 707:1–21.

Miller, R. R., and C. L. Hubbs. 1960. The Spiny-rayed Cyprinid Fishes (Plagopterini) of the Colorado River System. Miscellaneous Publications of the Museum of Zoology, University of Michigan 115:1–39.

Miller, R. R., and G. R. Smith. 1981. Distribution and Evolution of *Chasmistes* (Pisces: Catostomidae) in Western North America. Occasional Papers of the Museum of Zoology, University of Michigan 696:1–46.

Minckley, W. L. 1973. Fishes of Arizona. Arizona Game and Fish Department, Phoenix, Ariz.

Minckley, W. L., D. A. Hendrickson, and C. E. Bond. 1986. Geography of Western North American Fishes: Description and Relationships to Intracontinental Tectonism. Chapter 15 *in* E. O. Wiley and C. H. Hocutt, eds. Zoogeography of North American Freshwater Fishes. Wiley Interscience.

Minckley, W. L., G. K. Meffe, and D. L. Soltz. 1991. Conservation and Management of Short-Lived Fishes: The Cyprinodontoids. Chapter 15, pages 247–282 *in* W. L. Minckley and J. E. Deacon, eds. Battle Against Extinction: Native Fish Management in the American West. University of Arizona Press, Tuscon, Ariz.

Mitchill, S. L. 1814a. The Fisheries of New York, Described and Arranged. Transactions of the Literary Philosophical Society (New York) 1:355–492.

——. 1814b. Report in Part of Samuel L. Mitchill, M.D., on the Fishes of New York. D. Carlisle, New York, N.Y.

——. 1818. Memoirs on Ichthyology. The Fishes of New York Described and Arranged. American Monthly Magazine of Critical Review, 1817–-1818, 2:241–248, 321–328.

Modde, T., and E. Wick. 1993. Status Review of the Razorback Sucker, *Syrauchen texanus,* in the Upper Green River. Volume 24, page 59 *in* D. A. Hendrickson, ed. Proceedings of the Desert Fishes Council.

Morain, S. A. 1984. Systematic and Regional Biogeography. Van Nostrand and Reinhold, New York.

Morgan, D. L. 1947. The Great Salt Lake. University of Nebraska Press, Lincoln and London.

Morgan, G. D. 1954. The Life History of the White Crappie *Pomoxis annularis*, of Buckeye Lake, Ohio. Denison Univ. Science Laboratory Journal 43(618): 113–114.

Morrison, R. B. 1965. New Evidence on Lake Bonneville Stratigraphy from Southern Promontory Point, Utah. Pages 110–119 *in* U.S. Geological Survey Professional Paper 525C.

Morrow, J. E. 1980. The Freshwater Fishes of Alaska. Alaska Northwest Publishing Company, Anchorage, Alaska.

Moyle, P. B. 1976. Inland Fishes of California. University of California Press, Berkeley, Calif.

Mueller, G. 1989. Observations of Spawning Razorback (*Xyrauchen texanus*) Utilizing Riverine Habitat in the Lower Colorado River, Arizona-Nevada. The Southwestern Naturalist 34(1):147–149.

Murphy, D. R. 1981. Drainage. Page 49 *in* D. C. Greer, K. D. Gurgel, W. L. Wahlquist, H. A. Christy, and G. B. Peterson, eds. Atlas of Utah. Weber State College, Brigham Young University Press, Provo, Utah.

Murphy, G. I. 1948. A Contribution to the Life History of the Sacramento Perch (*Archoplites interruptus*) in Clear Lake, Lake County, California. California Fish and Game 34(3):93–100.

Nelson, E. W. 1876. A Partial Catalogue of the Fishes of Illinois. Illinois Museum of Natural History Bulletin l(l):33–52.

Nelson, J. S. 1968. Distribution and Nomenclature of North American Kokanee, *Oncorhynchus nerka*. Journal of the Fisheries Research Board of Canada 25(2):409–414.

——. 1984. Fishes of the World, 2nd ed. John Wiley and Sons, New York.

Nelson, M. E., and J. H. Madsen, Jr. 1980. A Summary of Pleistocene Fossil Vertebrate Localities in the Northern Bonneville Basin of Utah. Pages 97–113 *in* J. Wallace Gwynn, ed. Great Salt Lake, a Scientific, Historical and Economic Overview. Utah Geological and Mineralogical Survey Bulletin 116. Salt Lake City, Utah.

Nelson, P. H. 1954. The American Grayling in Montana. Journal of Wildlife Management 18(3):324–342.

Neuhold, J. M. 1957. Age and Growth of the Utah Chub, *Gila atraria* (Girard). Transactions of the American Fisheries Society 85(1955):217–233.

Newby, J. E. 1980. Great Salt Lake Railroad Crossing. Pages 393–400 *in* J. Wallace Gwynn, ed. Great Salt Lake, a Scientific, Historical and Economic Overview. Utah Geological and Mineralogical Survey Bulletin 116. Salt Lake City, Utah.

Nichols, P. R. 1966. The Striped Bass. U.S. Department of the Interior, Fish and Wildlife Service, Bureau of Commercial Fisheries, Fishery Leaflet 592.

Nielson, B., and L. Lentsch. 1988. Bonneville Cutthroat Trout in Bear Lake: Status and Management. Pages 128–133 *in* R. E. Gresswell, ed. Status and Management of Interior Stocks of Cutthroat Trout. American Fisheries Society Symposium 4, Bethesda, Md.

Niemuth, W., W. Churchill, and T. Wirth. 1959. The Walleye Life History, Ecology and Management. Wisconsin Conservation Department Publication No. 227.

Norden, C. R. 1970. Evolution and Distribution of the Genus *Prosopium*. Pages 67–80 *in* C. C. Lindsey and C. S. Woods, eds. Biology of Coregonid Fishes. University of Manitoba Press, Winnipeg.

Nyquist, D. 1967. Eutrophication Trends of Bear Lake, Utah-Idaho, and Their Effect on the Distribution and Biological Productivity of Zooplankton. PhD Diss., Utah State University, Logan, Utah.

O'Donnell, D. J. 1935. Annotated List of the Fishes of Illinois. Illinois Natural History Survey Bulletin 20(5):473–500.

Olson, H. 1959. The Biology of the Utah Chub, *Gila atraria* (Girard), of Scofield Reservoir, Utah. MS Thesis, Utah State University, Logan, Utah.

Ono, R. D., J. D. Williams, and A. Wagner. 1983. Vanishing Fishes of North America. Stone Wall Press, Washington, D.C.

Osmundson, D. B. 1985. 1985 Status Survey of the Least Chub (*Iotichthys phlegethontis*) in Desert Springs of Western Utah. Utah State Division of Wildlife Resources, Salt Lake City, Utah.

Osmundson, D. B., and L. R. Kaeding. 1989. Studies of the Colorado Squawfish and Razorback Sucker Use of the 15-Mile Reach of the Upper Colorado River as Part of the Conservation Measures for the Green Mountain and Ruedi Reservoir Sites. U.S. Fish and Wildlife Service, Grand Junction, Colo.

Oviatt, C. F. 1984. Lake Bonneville Stratigraphy at the Old River Bed and Leamington, Utah. PhD Diss., University of Utah, Salt Lake City, Utah.

Pallas, P. S. 1776. Reise durch verschiedene Provinzen des Russischen Reichs (1768–1774). Vol. 3. St. Petersburg.

Payne, N. R. 1964. The Life History of the Walleye, *Stizostedion vitreum vitreum* (Mitchill), in the Bay of Quinte. MA Thesis, University of Toronto, Toronto, Ontario.

Peale, A. C. 1879. Report of A. C. Peale, M.D., Geologists of the Green River Division. Annual Report U.S. Geological and Geographical Survey of the Territories (Hayden Survey) 11 (1877): 509–646.

Pearson, J. C. 1938. The Life History of the Striped Bass, or Rockfish, *Roccus saxatillis* (Walbaum). U.S. Department of Commerce, Bureau of Fisheries Bulletin, No. 28: 825–851.

Penlington, B. P. 1983. Lake-shore Spawning of Rainbow Trout at Lake Rotoma, New Zealand. New Zealand Journal of Marine and Freshwater Research 17:349–355.

Pflieger, W. L. 1975. The Fishes of Missouri. Missouri Department of Conservation, Jefferson City, Mo.

Pimentel, R., and R. V. Bulkley. 1983. Concentrations of Total Dissolved Solids Preferred or Avoided by Endangered Colorado River Fishes. Transactions of the American Fisheries Society 112:595–600.

Platts, W. S. 1958. Age and Growth of the Cutthroat Trout in Strawberry Reservoir, Utah. Proceedings of the Utah Academy of Science, Arts, and Letters 35:101–103.

Popov, B. H., and J. B. Low. 1950. Game, Fur Animals and Fish: Introductions into Utah. Utah Department of Fish and Game Miscellaneous Publication 4, Salt Lake City, Utah.

Purkett, C. A. 1958. Growth of Fishes in the Salt River, Missouri. Transactions of the American Fisheries Society 87(1957):116–131.

Radant, R. D., and T. J. Hickman. 1983. Status of the June Sucker (*Chasmistes liorus*). Pages 277–282 *in* E. P. Pister, ed. Proceedings of the Desert Fishes Council, Volumes 13–15-B, the Thirteenth-Fifteenth Annual Symposia. Desert Fishes Council, Bishop, Calif.

Rafinesque, C. S., 1818a. Description of Two New Genera of North American Fishes, *Fohsanus* and *Notropis.* American Monthly Magazine Critical Review 2(3):203–204.

——. 1818b. Discoveries in Natural History Made During a Journey through the

Western Region of the United States. American Monthly Magazine Critical Review 3 (5):354–356.

——. 1818c. Further Account of Discoveries in Natural History Made During a Journey Through the Western Region of the United States. American Monthly Magazine Critical Review 4(1):39–42.

——. 1819. Prodome de 70 nouveaux genres d'animaux découverts dans l'intérieur des Etats Unis d'Amérique, durant l'année 1818. Journal de Physique, Paris.

——. 1820a. Ichthyologia Ohiensis, or Natural History of the Fishes Inhabiting the River Ohio and Its Tributary Streams, Preceded by a Physical Description of the Ohio and Its Branches. Lexington, Ky.

——. 1820b. Description of the Silures or Catfishes of the Ohio River. Quarterly Journal of Science, Literature, and Arts, Royal Institute, London, 9:48–52.

Raleigh, R. F. 1982. Habitat Suitability Index Models: Brook Trout. U.S. Dept. of the Interior, Fish and Wildlife Service. FWS/OBS–82/10.24.

Raleigh, R. F., L. D. Zuckerman, and P. C. Nelson. 1986. Habitat Suitability Index Models and Instream Flow Suitability Curves: Brown Trout, Revised. U.S. Dept. of the Interior, Fish and Wildlife Service. Biological Report 82(10.124).

Raleigh, R. F., T. Hickman, R. C. Solomon, and P. C. Nelson. 1984. Habitat Suitability Information: Rainbow Trout. U.S. Dept. of the Interior, Fish and Wildlife Service. FWS/OBS–82–10.60.

Rawley, E. V. 1980. Wildlife of the Great Salt Lake. Pages 287–303 *in* J. Wallace Gwynn, ed. Great Salt Lake, a Scientific, Historical and Economic Overview. Utah Geological and Mineralogical Survey Bulletin 116. Salt Lake City, Utah.

Reiber, R. W. 1983. Reproduction of Arctic Grayling, *Thymallus arcticus*, in Lobdell Lake System, California. California Fish and Game 69(3):191–192.

Reimers, M. 1979. A History of a Stunted Brook Trout Population in an Alpine Lake: a Lifespan of 24 Years. California Fish and Game 65(4):196–215.

Reiser, D. W., and T. A. Wesche. 1977. Determination of Physical and Hydraulic Preferences of Brown and Brook Trout in the Selection of Spawning Locations. Wyoming Water Resources Institute Serial No. 64, Laramie, Wyo.

Richardson, J. 1836. Fauna Boreali-Americana: On the Zoology of the Northern Parts of British America, Containing Descriptions of the Objects of Natural History. Collected on the Late Northern Land Expeditions under Command of Sir John Franklin, R.N. Part 3. The Fish: 327 pp. Richard Bentley, London.

Rick, E. J., and J. A. Hawkins. 1991. Colorado Squawfish Winter Habitat Study, Yampa River: A Desert Fish Under Ice. Pages 85–86 *in* E. P. Pister, ed. Proceedings of the Desert Fishes Council, Volumes 20 and 21, Bishop, Calif.

Rinne, W. E. 1971. The Life History of *Lepidomeda mollispinis mollispinis* (the Virgin River Spinedace), a Unique Western Cyprinid. MS Thesis, University of Nevada, Las Vegas, Nev.

Robertson, G. C. 1978. Surficial Deposits and Geologic History, Northern Bear Lake Valley, Idaho. MS Thesis, Utah State University, Logan, Utah.

Robins, C. R., R. M. Bailey, C. E. Bond, J. R. Brooker, E. A. Lachner, R. N. Lea, and W. B. Scott. 1991. Common and Scientific Names of Fishes from the United States and Canada, 5th ed. American Fisheries Society Special Publication 20, Bethesda, Md.

Roselund, B. C. 1975. Letters to Wendel Minckley, Arizona State University. U.S. Fish and Wildlife Service. Alchesay-Williams Creek National Fish Hatchery.

Rosenfeld, M. J. 1990. Systematic Studies of Members of the Genus *Gila* (Pisces:

Cyprinidae) from the Great Basin and Colorado River: Protein Electrophoretic and Cytogenetic Variation. PhD Diss., University of Utah, Salt Lake City, Utah.

Rosenfeld, M. J., and J. A. Wilkinson. 1989. Biochemical Genetics of the Colorado River *Gila* complex (Pisces: Cyprinidae). Southwestern Naturalist 34:232–244.

Schneider, J., and J. H. Leach. 1977. Walleye (*Stizostedion vitreum vitreum*) Fluctuations in the Great Lakes and Possible Causes, 1800–1975. Journal of the Fisheries Research Board of Canada 34(10):1878–1889.

Schneidervin, R. W., and W. A. Hubert. 1987. Diet Overlap Among Zooplanktonphagous Fishes in Flaming Gorge Reservoir, Wyoming-Utah. North American Journal of Fisheries Management 7:379–385.

Schoenherr, A. A. 1981. The Role of Competition in the Replacement of Native Fishes by Introduced Species. Pages 173–204 *in* R. J. Naiman and D. L. Soltz, eds. Fishes in North American Deserts. John Wiley & Sons, New York, N.Y.

Schreck, C. B., and R. J. Behnke. 1971. Trouts of the Upper Kern River Basin, California, with Reference to Systematics and Evolution of Western North American *Salmo*. Journal of the Fisheries Research Board of Canada 28(7):987–998.

Scott, W. B. 1958. A Checklist of the Freshwater Fishes of Canada and Alaska. Royal Ontario Museum of Paleontology, Toronto.

Scott, W. B., and E. J. Crossman. 1973. Freshwater Fishes of Canada. Fisheries Research Board of Canada Bulletin 184.

Seethaler, K. 1978. Life History and Ecology of the Colorado Squawfish (*Ptychocheilus lucius*) in the Upper Colorado Basin. MS Thesis, Utah State University, Logan, Utah.

Shapovalov, L., W. A. Dill, and S. J. Cordone. 1959. A Revised Checklist of the Freshwater and Anadromous Fishes of California. California Fish and Game 45(3):159–180.

Shirley, D. J. 1983. Spawning Ecology and Larval Development of the June Sucker. Transactions of the Bonneville Chapter of the American Fisheries Society: 18–36.

Shuter, B. J., J. A. McLean, F. E. J. Fry, and H. A. Regier. 1980. Stochastic Simulation of Temperature Effects on First-Year Survival of Smallmouth Bass. Transactions of the American Fisheries Society, Bethesda, Md. 109:1–34.

Siefert, R. E. 1969. Characteristics for Separation of White and Black Crappie Larvae. Transactions of the American Fisheries Society 98(2):326–328.

Sigler, J. W. 1972. Investigations of the Algal Productivity of Selected and Limited Sites Along the Western Shore of Bear Lake, Utah-Idaho. MS Thesis, Utah State University, Logan, Utah.

Sigler, J. W. and W. F. Sigler. 1994. Fishes of the Great Basin and the Colorado Plateau: Past and Present Forms. Chapter 9, pages 163–2210 *in* K. T. Harper, L. L. St. Clair, K. H. Thorne, and W. M. Hess, eds. Natural History of the Colorado Plateau and Great Basin. University Press of Colorado, Niwot.

Sigler, W. F. 1949. Life History of the White Bass, *Lepibema chrysops* (Rafinesque) of Spirit Lake, Iowa. Iowa Agricultural Experiment Station Bulletin 366.

——— . 1951. The Life History and Management of the Mountain Whitefish *Prosopium williamsoni* (Girard) in Logan River, Logan, Utah. Utah State Agricultural College Bulletin 347, Logan, Utah.

———. 1952. Age and Growth of the Brown Trout, *Salmo trutta fario* Linnaeus, in Logan River, Utah. Transactions of the American Fisheries Society 81(1951):171–178.

———. 1953. The Rainbow Trout in Relation to Other Fish in Fish Lake. Utah Agricultural Experiment Station Bulletin 358, Logan, Utah.

———. 1958a. The Ecology and Use of Carp in Utah. Utah Agricultural Experiment Station Bulletin 405. Logan, Utah.

———. 1958b. Fish Life History Series: The Whitefishes of Bear Lake. Utah Fish and Game Magazine 14(12):20–21.

———. 1962. Bear Lake and Its Future. Twenty-sixth Honor Lecture. The Faculty Association, Utah State University, Logan, Utah.

Sigler, W. F., and J. B. Low. 1950. Age Composition and Growth of Fish and Fishermen Success in Utah's High Uintah Lakes. Utah Academy of Science, Arts, and Letters 27:32–36.

Sigler, W. F., and R. R. Miller. 1963. Fishes of Utah. Utah Department of Fish and Game, Salt Lake City, Utah.

Sigler, W. F., and J. W. Sigler. 1987. Fishes of the Great Basin–A Natural History. University of Nevada Press, Reno, Nev.

Sigler, W. F., and G. W. Workman. 1975. Studies on the Least Chub, *Iotichthys phlegethontis* (Cope), in Geothermal Activities Area of Snake and Tule Valleys, Utah. *In* Studies for Wildlife on Energy Areas. U.S. Department of the Interior, Bureau of Land Management, Washington, D.C.

———. 1978. The Bonneville Cisco of Bear Lake, Utah-Idaho. Utah Agricultural Experiment Station Research Report 33, Logan, Utah.

Sigler, W. F., W. T. Helm, P. A. Kucera, S. Vigg, and G. W. Workman. 1983. Life History of the Lahontan Cutthroat Trout, *Salmo clarki henshawi* in Pyramid Lake, Nevada. Great Basin Naturalist 3(1):1–29.

Simon, J. R. 1946. Wyoming Fishes. Wyoming Game and Fish Department Bulletin 4:1–173.

Simpson, J. C., and R. L. Wallace. 1978. Fishes of Idaho, 1st ed. University of Idaho Press, Moscow, Ida.

Simpson, J. C., and R. L. Wallace. 1982. Fishes of Idaho, 2nd ed. University Press, Moscow, Ida.

Small, H. B. 1865. The Animals of North America. Ser. 2. Fresh-water Fish. M. Longmoore & Co., Montreal, Quebec.

Smart, E. W. 1958. An Ecological Study of the Bottom Fauna of Bear Lake, Utah and Idaho. PhD Diss., Utah State University, Logan, Utah.

Smith, C. L. 1985. The Inland Fishes of New York State, New York. The New York State Department of Environmental Conservation.

Smith, G. R. 1966. Distribution and Evolution of the North American Catostomid Fishes of the Subgenus *Pantosteus*, Genus *Catostomus*. University of Michigan, Museum of Zoology, Miscellaneous Publications 129:1–33.

———. 1975. Fishes of the Pliocene Glenns Ferry Formation, Southwest Idaho. University of Michigan Papers in Paleontology 14:1–68.

———. 1978. Biogeography of Intermountain Fishes. Pages 17–42 *in* K. T. Harper and J. L. Reveal, eds. Intermountain Biogeography: A Symposium. Great Basin Naturalist Memoirs 2.

———. 1981a. Effects of Habitat Size on Species Richness and Adult Body Sizes of Desert Fishes. Pages 125–171 *in* R. J. Naiman and D. L. Soltz, eds. Fishes in North American Deserts. John Wiley & Sons, New York.

——. 1981b. Late Cenozoic Freshwater Fishes of North America. Annual Review of Ecological Systematics 12:163–193.

Smith, G. R., and R. F. Stearley. 1989. The Classification and Scientific Names of Rainbow Trout and Cutthroat Trouts. Fisheries 14(1):4–10.

Smith, G. R., and T. N. Todd. 1984. Evolution of Species Flocks of Fishes in Northern Temperature Lakes. Pages 45–68 *in* A. Echelle and I. Kernfield, eds. Species Flocks of Species. Oklahoma State University Press.

Smith, G. R., R. R. Miller, and W. D. Sable. 1979. Species Relationships among Fishes of the Genus *Gila* in the Upper Colorado River Drainage. Pages 613–623 *in* R. M. Linn, ed. Proceedings of the First Conference on Scientific Research in the National Parks. U.S. Department of the Interior, National Park Service, Washington, D.C.

Smith, G. R., W. L. Stokes, and K. F. Horn. 1968. Some Late Pleistocene Fishes of Lake Bonneville. Copeia 1968:807–816.

Smith, M. L. 1981. Late Cenozoic Fishes in the Warm Deserts of North America: A Reinterpretation of Desert Adaptations. Pages 11–38 *in* R. J. Naiman and D. L. Soltz, eds. Fishes in North American Deserts. John Wiley & Sons, New York.

Smith, P. W. 1979. The Fishes of Illinois. Published for the Illinois State Natural History Survey. University of Illinois Press, Urbana, Ill.

Snow, H., A. Ensign, and J. Klingbiel. 1960. The Bluegill: Its Life History, Ecology and Management. Wisconsin Conservation Department Publication 230, Madison, Wis.

Snyder, D. E., and R. T. Muth. 1990. Descriptions and Identification of Razorback, Flannelmouth, White, Utah, Bluehead, and Mountain Sucker Larvae and Early Juveniles. Colorado Division of Wildlife Technical Publication No. 38.

Snyder, J. O. 1915. Notes on a Collection of Fishes Made by Dr. Edgar A. Mearns from Rivers Tributary to the Gulf of California. U.S. National Museum Proceedings 49:573–586.

——. 1919. Three New Whitefishes from Bear Lake, Idaho and Utah. Bulletin of the United States Bureau of Fisheries. Volume 36, 1917–1918. Department of Commerce. U.S. Government Printing Office, Washington, D.C.

Spencer, R. J., M. J. Baedecker, H. P. Eugster, R. M. Forester, M. B. Goldhaber, B. F. Jones, K. Kelts, J. McKenzie, D. B. Madsen, S. L. Rettig, M. Rubin, and C. J. Bowser. 1984. Great Salt Lake and Precursors, Utah: The Last 30,000 Years. Contributions to Mineralogy and Petrology 86:321–334.

Sport Fishing Institute. 1990. Crappie Limits Benefit Fishery. Sport Fishing Institute Bulletin No. 414 (May):4–5.

Sprugel, G., Jr. 1955. The Growth of the Green Sunfish (*Lepomis cyanellus*) in Little Wall Lake, Iowa. Ames, Iowa State College Journal of Science 29(4):707–719.

Stevens, R. E. 1984. Historical Overview of Striped Bass Culture and Management. Pages 1–15 *in* J. P. McCraren, ed. The Aquaculture of Striped Bass: A Proceedings. University of Maryland Sea Grant Publication UM-SG-MAP 84–01. University of Maryland, College Park, Md.

Stokes, W. L. 1980. Geological Setting of Great Salt Lake. Pages 55–67 *in* J. Wallace Gwynn, ed. Great Salt Lake, a Scientific, Historical and Economic Overview. Utah Geological and Mineralogical Survey Bulletin 116. Salt Lake City, Utah.

——. 1986. Geology of Utah. Utah Museum of Natural History and Utah Geological and Mineralogical Survey.

Stokes, W. L., G. R. Smith, and K. F. Horn. 1964. Fossil Fishes from the

Stansbury Level of Lake Bonneville, Utah. Proceedings of the Utah Academy of Science 41:87–88.

Stroud, R. H., and H. Clepper (chairman and editor, respectively). 1975. Black Bass Biology and Management. Sport Fishing Institute, Washington, D.C.

Stuber, R. J., G. Gebhart, and O. E. Maughan. 1982. Habitat Suitability Index Models: Largemouth Bass. U.S. Department of the Interior, Fish and Wildlife Service FWS/OBS–82/10.16.

Sturm, P. A. 1980. The Great Salt Lake Brine System. Pages 147–162 *in* J. Wallace Gwynn, ed. Great Salt Lake, a Scientific, Historical and Economic Overview. Utah Geological and Mineralogical Survey Bulletin 116. Salt Lake City, Utah.

Suckley, G. 1874. On the North American Species of Salmon and Trout. Report of the U.S. Fish Commissioner 1872–73. Part 2.

Summerfelt, R. C. 1975. Relationship Between Weather and Year-Class Strength of Largemouth Bass. Page 166–175 *in* R. H. Stroud and H. Clepper, eds. Black Bass Biology and Management. Sport Fishing Institute, Washington, D.C.

Tanner, V. M. 1936. A Study of the Fishes of Utah. Proceedings of the Utah Academy of Sciences, Arts, and Letters 13:155–184.

Taylor, W. R. 1954. Records of Fishes in the John N. Lowe Collection from the Upper Peninsula of Michigan. Museum of Zoology, University of Michigan, Miscellaneous Publications 87.

Tomelleri, J. R., and M. E. Eberle. 1990. Fishes of the Central United States. University of Kansas Press, Lawrence, Kansas.

Trautman, M. B. 1981. The Fishes of Ohio, 2nd ed. Ohio State University Press, Columbus, Ohio, in collaboration with the Ohio Sea Grant Program Center for Lake Erie Research.

Trotter, P. C. 1987. Cutthroat: Native Trout of the West. Colorado Associated University Press, Boulder, Colo.

Tyus, H. M. 1987. Distribution, Reproduction, and Habitat Use of the Razorback Sucker in the Green River, Utah, 1979–1986. Transactions of the American Fisheries Society 116:111–116.

——. 1990. Potamodromy and Reproduction of Colorado Squawfish in the Green River Basin, Colorado and Utah. Transactions of the American Fisheries Society 119:1035–1047.

——. 1991. Management for Recovery of Colorado Squawfish. Page 51 *in* E. P. Pister, ed. Proceedings of the Desert Fishes Council 20.

Tyus, H. M., and J. M. Beard. 1990. *Esox lucius* (Esocidae) and *Stizostedion vitreum* (Percidae) in the Green River Basin, Colorado and Utah. Great Basin Naturalist 50(1):33–39.

Tyus, H. M., and W. L. Minckley. 1988. Migrating Mormon Crickets, *Anabrus simplex* (Orthoptera: Tettigoniidae), as Food for Stream Fishes. Great Basin Naturalist 48:25–30.

Tyus, H. M., R. L. Jones, and L. A. Trinca. 1987. Colorado River Fishes Monitoring Project. 1982–1985. Final Report. U.S. Department of the Interior, Fish and Wildlife Service, Vernal, Utah.

Tyus, H. M., B. D. Burdick, R. A. Valdez, C. M. Haynes, T. A. Lytle, and C. M. Berry. 1982. Fishes of the Upper Colorado River Basin. Distribution, Abundance, and Status. Pages 12–70 *in* W. H. Miller, H. M. Tyus, and C. A. Carlson, eds. Fishes of the Upper Colorado River System, Present and Future. Proceedings of a Symposium, Annual Meeting of the American Fisheries Society, Albuquerque, N. M., September 18, 1981. American Fisheries Society, Bethesda, Md.

Ulmer, L., ed. 1983. Endangered Colorado River Fishes Newsletter. California Department of Fish and Game, Blythe, Calif.

USGS (United States Geological Survey) 1985. Water Resources Data for Utah, Water Year 1984. U.S. Geological Survey. Prepared in cooperation with other agencies.

USGS (United States Geological Survey). 1987. Water Resources Data for Utah, Water Year 1986. U.S. Geological Survey. Prepared in cooperation with other agencies.

Utah Division of Wildlife Resources. 1981. Lakes of the High Uintas: Ashley Creek Drainage. Publication 81–6. Salt Lake City, Utah.

———. 1982. Lakes of the High Uintas: Dry Gulch and Uinta River Drainages. Publication 82–7. Salt Lake City, Utah.

———. 1983. Lakes of the High Uintas: Yellowstone, Lake Fork, and Swift Creek Drainages. Publication 83–5. Salt Lake City, Utah.

———. 1983. Lakes of the High Uintas: Duchesne Drainage; Provo and Weber River Drainages. Publication 83–6. Salt Lake City, Utah.

———. 1985. Lakes of the High Uintas: Bear River and Blacks Forks Drainages. Publication 85–7. Salt Lake City, Utah.

———. 1986. Lakes of the High Uintas: Sheep Creek, Carter Creek, and Burnt Fork Creek. Publication 86–9. Salt Lake City, Utah.

———. 1986. Lakes of the High Uintas: Smiths Fork, Henrys Fork, and Beaver Creek Drainages. Publication 86–10. Salt Lake City, Utah.

———. 1987. Lakes of the High Uintas: Whiterocks River Drainage. Publication 87–6. Salt Lake City, Utah.

Uyeno, T. 1960. Osteology and Phylogeny of American Cyprinid Fishes Allied to the Genus *Gila*. PhD Diss., University of Michigan, Ann Arbor, Mich.

Uyeno, T., and R. R. Miller. 1965. Middle Pliocene Cyprinid Fishes from the Bidahochi Formation, Arizona. Copeia 1965:28–41.

Valdez, R. A. 1985. Cataract Canyon Fish Study. Final Report: Contract No. 5-CS-40-02820. U.S. Department of the Interior, Bureau of Reclamation, Salt Lake City, Utah.

———. 1990. The Endangered Fish of Cataract Canyon. Final Report Prepared for the United States Department of Interior, Bureau of Reclamation, Salt Lake City, Utah. Contract 6-CS-40-03980, Fisheries Biology and Rafting. Bio/West Report No. 134-3.

Valdez, R. A., and G. L. Clemmer. 1982. Life History and Prospects for Recovery of the Humpback Chub and Bonytail Chub. Pages 109–119 *in* W. F. Hiller, H. M. Tyus, and C. H. Carlson, eds. Fishes of the Upper Colorado River System, Present and Future. Western Division of the American Fisheries Society, Bethesda, Md.

Valdez, R. A., and W. J. Masslich. 1991. Wintertime Movement and Habitat of Adult Colorado Squawfish and Razorback Suckers in the Green River. Pages 27–46 in E. P. Pister, ed. Proceedings of the Desert Fishes Council, Volumes 20 and 21. Desert Fishes Council, Bishop, Calif.

Valdez, R. A., and R. D. Williams. 1991. Endangered Fishes of Cataract Canyon. Pages 25–26 in E. P. Pister, ed. Proceedings of the Desert Fishes Council, Volumes 20 and 21. Desert Fishes Council, Bishop, Calif.

———. 1993. Ichthyofauna of the Colorado and Green Rivers in Canyonlands National Park, Utah. First Conference Proceedings on Research in Colorado Plateau National Parks. National Park Service, Denver, Colo.

Valdez, R. A., J. G. Carter, and R. J. Ryel. 1985. Drift of Larval Fishes in the Upper Colorado River. Proceedings of the Western Association of Fish and Wildlife Agencies 1985:519–536.

Valdez, R. A., P. B. Holden, and T. B. Hardy. 1990. Habitat Suitability Index Curves for Humpback Chub in the Upper Colorado River Basin. Rivers 1:31–42.

Valdez, R. A., W. J. Masslich, R. Radant, and D. Knight. 1991. Status of the Virgin Spinedace (*Lepidomeda mollispinis mollispinis*) in the Virgin River Drainage, Utah. Southwestern Naturalist.

Van Dan Argyle, M. J., and J. W. Evans. 1990. Temperature Selection by Striped Bass in a Gulf of Mexico Coastal River System. North American Journal of Fisheries Management 10:58–66.

Vanicek, C. D., and R. H. Kramer. 1969. Life History of the Colorado Chub (*Gila robusta*) in the Green River in Dinosaur National Monument 1964–1966. Transactions of the American Fisheries Society 98:193–208.

Varley, J. D., and P. Schullery. 1983. Freshwater Wilderness: Yellowstone Fishes and Their World. Yellowstone Library and Museum Association, Yellowstone National Park, Wyo.

Vigg, S., and P. A. Kucera. 1981. Contributions to the Life History of the Sacramento Perch, *Archoplites interruptus* (Girard), in Pyramid Lake Nevada. Great Basin Naturalist 41(3):278–289.

Walbaum, J. J. 1792. Petri Artedi renovati, i.e. bibliotheca et philosophia ichthyologica. Ichthyologiae pars III. Grypeswaldiae. Ant. Ferdin, Roese.

Wales, J. H. 1946. Castle Lake Trout Investigation. First Phase: Interrelationships of Four Species. California Fish and Game 32(3):109–143.

Walters, V. 1955. Fishes of Western Arctic America and Alaska. American Museum of Natural History Bulletin 106:259–368.

Westenfelder, C., F. M. Birch, R. L. Baranowski, M. J. Rosenfeld, D. K. Shiozawa, and C. Kablitz. 1988. Atrial Natriuretic Factor and Salt Adaptation in the Teleost Fish *Gila atraria*. American Journal of Physiology 256:F1281–1286.

Wetzel, R. G. 1983. Limnology, 2nd ed. Saunders, Philadelphia, Pa.

Wheeler, H. E., and E. F. Cook. 1954. Structural and Stratigraphic Significance of the Snake River Capture, Idaho-Oregon. Journal of Geology 62:525–536.

White, M.J.D. 1978. Modes of Speciation. Freeman, San Francisco, Calif.

White, R. G. 1974. Endemic Whitefishes of Bear Lake, Utah-Idaho: A Problem in Systematics. PhD Diss., Utah State University, Logan, Utah.

Whitehead, P.J.P., and A. C. Wheeler. 1967. The Generic Names Used for the Sea Basses of Europe and North America (Pisces, Serranidae). Annali del Museo Civico di Storia Naturale "Giacomo Doria," Genova, 1966–1967, 76:23–41.

Wilde, G. R., and L. J. Paulson. 1988. Food Habits of the Young-of-the-year Largemouth in Lake Mead and Lake Mohave, Arizona–Nevada. Great Basin Naturalist 48(4):485–488.

Williams, J. E., and C. E. Bond. 1980. *Gila boraxobius*, a New Species of Cyprinid Fish from Southeastern Oregon, with a Comparison to *G. alvordensis* Hubbs and Miller. Proceedings of the Biological Society of Washington 93:291–298.

Williams, J. E., D. B. Bowman, J. E. Brooks, A. A. Echelle, R. J. Edwards, D. A. Hendrickson, and J. J. Landye. 1985. Endangered Aquatic Ecosystems in North American Deserts with a List of Vanishing Fishes of the Region. Journal of the Arizona-Nevada Academy of Science 20:1–62.

Workman, G. W. 1963. An Ecological Study of the Bear Lake Littoral Zone, Utah-Idaho. PhD Diss., Utah State University, Logan, Utah.

Workman, G. W., and W. F. Sigler. 1965. The Physical and Chemical Factors of Bear Lake and Its Tributaries, Utah-Idaho. Utah Academy of Sciences, Arts, and Letters 41:34–48, Part 1.

Workman, G. W., W. F. Sigler, and W. G. Workman. 1976. The Least Chub, *Iotichthys phlegethontis* (Cope), in Juab County, Utah. Proceedings of the Utah Academy of Sciences, Arts, and Letters 53(2):16–22.

Wurtsbaugh, W. A., and T. S. Berry. 1990. Cascading Effects of Decreased Salinity on the Plankton, Chemistry, and Physics of the Great Salt Lake (Utah). Canadian Journal of Fisheries and Aquatic Sciences 47:100–109.

Wurtsbaugh, W. A., and D. Nevermann. 1988. Post-feeding Thermotaxis and Daily Vertical Migration in a Larval Fish. Nature 333(6176):846–848.

Wurtsbaugh, W., C. Hawkins, and E. Moreno. 1989. Invertebrate Prey Abundance and the Diets of Fishes in Bear Lake (Utah-Idaho). Transactions of the Bonneville Chapter, Utah, American Fisheries Society.

Wydoski, R. S., and R. R. Whitney. 1979. Inland Fishes of Washington. University of Washington Press, Seattle, Wash.

Wynne-Edwards, V. C. 1952. Fishes of the Arctic and Subarctic. Pages 5–24 *in* Freshwater Vertebrates of the Arctic and Subarctic. Fisheries Research Board of Canada 94.

Zarbock, W. M. 1952. Life History of the Utah Sculpin, *Cottus bairdi semiscaber* (Cope), in Logan River, Utah. Transactions of the American Fisheries Society 81(1951):249–259.

About the Authors and Contributors

STEVEN CLYDE is managing director of Clyde, Snow, and Swenson, P.C. He specializes in natural resources law.

RODELLO HUNTER is a Utah author and poet who has published over 200 poems and several books. She is the former associate editor of *Utah Fish and Game*.

SHARON OHLHORST (Ph.D. Yale 1981) has been on the faculty of the College of Natural Resources at Utah State University since 1982. She has conducted research on the endemic fishes of Bear Lake, the Utah cutthroat, and the Nevada tui chub.

MARK J. ROSENFELD is a former professor of geography in the Department of Geography and former curator at the Utah Museum of Natural History, University of Utah.

BRUCE SCHMIDT is former chief of fisheries, Utah Division of Wildlife Resources.

JOHN W. SIGLER is an aquatic biology and natural resources management specialist. He currently works in the regulatory compliance arena for a consulting company. He is coauthor of *Fishes of the Great Basin* (1988) and *Recreational Fisheries Management: Theory and Practice* (1990) with William F. Sigler.

GERALD R. SMITH is professor of biology and curator of fishes at the University of Michigan.

JOSEPH R. TOMELLERI is a freelance artist and biologist whose illustrations have been widely published in magazines and as posters and fine arts prints.

TOM WHARTON has been an outdoor writer for the *Salt Lake Tribune* since 1976.

IN MEMORIAM

William F. Sigler
1909–1995

William F. Sigler, long-time fisheries biologist, author, and outdoorsman, died June 25, 1995 in Logan, Utah, his home for almost fifty years. At the time of his death, he had authored over a hundred scientific and lay publications on fisheries, wildlife, the outdoors, and natural resource management. This second edition of *Fishes of Utah* was initiated in 1990 with his son John as junior author.

Dr. Sigler began his association with Utah State University in the Department of Wildlife in 1947, assuming the position of department head in 1950 and continuing in that position until his retirement in 1974. He was honored by his peers as a Distinguished Graduate of Iowa State University, USU Faculty Honor Lecturer, and Wildlife Conservationist of the Year for Utah. He was elected a Fellow of the Institute of Fisheries Research Biologists in 1960 and a Fellow of the American Association for the Advancement of Science in the same year.

His contribution to wildlife management in the western United States will long be remembered through the hundreds of students he taught and with whom he interacted. As a scientist, educator, sportsman, and friend, he will be missed by many.

Index